Contemporary Sociological Theory

BLACKWELL READERS IN SOCIOLOGY

Each volume in this authoritative series aims to provide students and scholars with comprehensive collections of classic and contemporary readings for all the major sub-fields of sociology. They are designed to complement single-authored works, or to be used as stand-alone textbooks for courses. The selected readings sample the most important works that students should read and are framed by informed editorial introductions. The series aims to reflect the state of the discipline by providing collections not only on standard topics but also on cutting-edge subjects in sociology to provide future directions in teaching and research.

Contemporary Sociological Theory

Edited by

Craig Calhoun, Joseph Gerteis,
James Moody, Steven Pfaff,
and Indermohan Virk

BLACKWELL PUBLISHING
350 Main Street, Malden, MA 02148-5020, USA
9600 Garsington Road, Oxford OX4 2DQ, UK
550 Swanston Street, Carlton, Victoria 3053, Australia

First published 2002 by Blackwell Publishing Ltd

7   2006

Library of Congress Cataloging-in-Publication Data has been applied for.

ISBN-13: 978-0-631-21349-9 (hardback)
ISBN-10: 0-631-21349-X (hardback)
ISBN-13: 978-0-631-21350-5 (paperback)
ISBN-10: 0-631-21350-3 (paperback)

A catalogue record for this title is available from the British Library.

Set in 10 on 12 pt Sabon Roman
by Kolam Information Services Pvt. Ltd, Pondicherry
Printed and bound in the United Kingdom
by TJ International Ltd, Padstow, Cornwall

The publisher's policy is to use permanent paper from mills that operate a sustainable forestry
policy, and which has been manufactured from pulp processed using acid-free and elementary
chlorine-free practices. Furthermore, the publisher ensures that the text paper and cover board
used have met acceptable environmental accreditation standards.

For further information on
Blackwell Publishing, visit our website:
www.blackwellpublishing.com

Contents

Contributors

Craig Calhoun is Professor of Sociology and History at New York University and since 1999 has been President of the Social Science Research Council. He was previously editor of *Sociological Theory*. His books include *Neither Gods Nor Emperors: Students and the Struggle for Democracy in China* (1995), *Critical Social Theory: Culture, History, and the Challenge of Difference* (1995), and *Nationalism* (1997). He is also editor-in-chief of the Oxford Dictionary of the Social Sciences.

Joseph Gerteis is Assistant Professor of Sociology at the University of Minnesota, Twin Cities. His work explores the link between categorical identities and social action in politics and social movements. His recent work examines southern labor movements of the late nineteenth century.

James Moody is Assistant Professor of Sociology at Ohio State University. He studies informal social organization through social networks, including the distribution of sexually transmitted diseases, adolescent friendship structure, and relations through the Internet.

Steven Pfaff is Assistant Professor of Sociology at the University of Washington. His scholarly interests include sociological theory, comparative and historical sociology, and research on collective action and social movements. His current research focuses on popular protest in the East German revolution of 1989–90.

Indermohan Virk is a Ph.D. candidate in the Department of Sociology at the University of North Carolina and a Visiting Lecturer at Indiana University. Her current research addresses the transformation of public space and its impact on the public sphere in the late twentieth-century United States.

Acknowledgments

The authors and publishers gratefully acknowledge the following for permission to reproduce copyright material:

1 Alfred Schutz, "The Phenomenology of the Social World." From Alfred Schutz, *The Phenomenology of the Social World*. Translated by George Walsh and Frederick Lehnert, with an Introduction by George Walsh. Copyright © 1967, Northwestern University Press, pp. 107, 113–16, 126–36;

2 Peter L. Berger and Thomas Luckmann, "The Social Construction of Reality." From Peter L. Berger and Thomas Luckmann, *The Social Construction of Reality: A Treatise in the Sociology of Knowledge*. Copyright © 1966 by Peter L. Berger and Thomas Luckmann. Used by permission of Doubleday, a division of Random House, Inc., pp. 50–62;

3 Erving Goffman, "The Presentation of Self in Everyday Life." From Erving Goffman, *The Presentation of Self in Everyday Life*. Copyright © 1959 by Erving Goffman. Reprinted by permission of The Overlook Press, pp. 17–25, 30–6, 56–61, 65–6, 70–7;

4 Herbert Blumer, "Symbolic Interactionism." From Herbert Blumer, *Symbolic Interactionism*. Copyright © 1998. Reprinted by permission of Prentice-Hall, Inc., Upper Saddle River, NJ, pp. 1, 46–8, 50–52, 78–89;

5 George C. Homans, "Social Behavior as Exchange." *American Journal of Sociology* 63, 6. Copyright © 1958 by the University of Chicago Press. Reprinted by permission of the University of Chicago Press, pp. 598–606;

6 Peter M. Blau, "Exchange and Power in Social Life." From Peter M. Blau, *Exchange and Power in Social Life*. Copyright © 1964 by John Wiley and Sons, Inc. Reprinted by permission of Transaction Publishers, pp. 19–31, 91–5;

7 James S. Coleman, "Social Capital in the Creation of Human Capital." *American Journal of Sociology* 94. Copyright © 1988 by the University of Chicago Press. Reprinted by permission of the University of Chicago Press, pp. S97–S98, S100–S108;

8 James S. Coleman, "Foundations for a Theory of Collective Decisions." *American Journal of Sociology* 71, 6. Copyright © 1966 by the University of Chicago Press. Reprinted by permission of the University of Chicago Press, pp. 615–23;

9 Mancur Olson, "The Logic of Collective Action." Reprinted by permission of the publisher from Mancur Olson, *The Logic of Collective Action: Public Goods and the Theory of Groups*. Cambridge, MA: Harvard University Press. Copyright © 1965, 1971 by the President and Fellows of Harvard College, pp. 9–16;

10 Niklas Luhmann, "Limits of Steering." *Theory, Culture and Society* 14, 1. Copyright © 1997 by Sage Publications Ltd. Reprinted by permission of Sage Publications Ltd., pp. 41–57;

11   Charles Tilly, "Coercion, Capital, and European States." From Charles Tilly, *Coercion, Capital, and European States, AD 990–1992*. Copyright © 1990, 1992 by Charles Tilly. Reprinted by permission of Blackwell Publishers, pp. 17–32;

12   Paul J. DiMaggio and Walter W. Powell, "The Iron Cage Revisited: Institutional Isomorphism and Collective Rationality in Organizational Fields." *American Sociological Review* 48. Copyright © 1983 by the American Sociological Association. Reprinted by permission of the American Sociological Association, pp. 147–60;

13   Michel Foucault, "The Birth of the Clinic." From Michel Foucault, *The Birth of the Clinic: An Archaeology of Medical Perception*. Translated by A. M. Sheridan-Smith. Translation copyright © 1973 by Tavistock Publications, Ltd. Reprinted by permission of Pantheon Books, a division of Random House, Inc., and by Taylor & Francis Books, Ltd., pp. 22–36;

14   Michel Foucault, "Truth and Power." From Michel Foucault, *Power/Knowledge: Selected Interviews and Other Writings 1972–1977*. Edited by Colin Gordon. Copyright © 1972, 1975, 1976, 1977 by Michel Foucault. Reprinted by permission of Pantheon Books, a division of Random House, Inc., pp. 113, 115–17, 118–26, 131–3;

15   Michel Foucault, "Discipline and Punish." From Michel Foucault, *Discipline and Punish: The Birth of the Prison*. Originally published in French as *Surveiller et Punir: Naissance de la Prison*. Translated by Alan Sheridan. Copyright © 1975 by Les Éditions Gallimard. Reprinted by permission of Georges Borchardt, Inc., and by Penguin Books, Ltd., pp. 200–2, 215–16, 218–24;

16   Anthony Giddens, "Some New Rules of Sociological Method." From Anthony Giddens, *New Rules of Sociological Method: A Positive Critique of Interpretive Sociologies*. Copyright © 1976 by Anthony Giddens. Reprinted by permission of Anthony Giddens, pp. 155–62;

17   Anthony Giddens, "Agency, Structure." From Anthony Giddens, *Central Problems in Social Theory: Action, Structure and Contradiction in Social Analysis*. Copyright © 1979 by Anthony Giddens. Reprinted by permission of the University of California Press, and by Macmillan Publishers Ltd., pp. 49, 53–9, 62, 64–6, 68–73, 82–4, 94–5;

18   Anthony Giddens, "The Consequences of Modernity." From Anthony Giddens, *The Consequences of Modernity*. Copyright © 1990 by the Board of Trustees of the Leland Standford Junior University. Reprinted by permission of Stanford University Press and Blackwell Publishers, pp. 112–14, 120–5, 131–4, 137–50;

19   Pierre Bourdieu, "Social Space and Symbolic Space." From Pierre Bourdieu, "Social Space and Symbolic Space: Toward a Japanese Reading of Distinction." *Poetics Today* 12, 4. Copyright © 1991, Porter Institute for Poetics and Semiotics. All rights reserved. Reprinted by permission of Duke University Press, pp. 627–38;

20   Pierre Bourdieu, "Structures, *Habitus*, Practices." From Pierre Bourdieu, *The Logic of Practice*. Translated by Richard Nice. Originally published in French as *Le Sens Pratique*. Copyright © 1980, Les Éditions de Minuit. Translation copyright © 1990, Polity Press in association with Blackwell Publishers.

Reprinted by permission of Stanford University Press, and by Blackwell Publishers;

21 Pierre Bourdieu, "The Field of Cultural Production, or: The Economic World Reversed." *Poetics* 12. Copyright © 1983, Elsevier Science Publishers, B.V. Reprinted by permission of Elsevier Science, Ltd., and by Pierre Bourdieu, pp. 312–13, 315–16, 319–26, 341–6, 349–50, 353–6;

22 Dorothy E. Smith, "The Conceptual Practices of Power." From Dorothy E. Smith, *The Conceptual Practices of Power: A Feminist Sociology of Knowledge*. Copyright © 1990 by Dorothy E. Smith. Reprinted with the permission of Northeastern University Press, pp. 12–19, 21–7;

23 Patricia Hill Collins, "Black Feminist Epistemology." From Patricia Hill Collins, *Black Feminist Thought: Knowledge, Consciousness, and the Politics of Empowerment*. Second Edition. Copyright © 2000 by Patricia Hill Collins. Reproduced by permission of Taylor & Francis, Inc., *http://www.routledge-ny.com*, pp. 251–6, 266–71;

24 Frantz Fanon, "Black Skin, White Masks." From Frantz Fanon, *Black Skin, White Masks*. Translated by Charles Lam Markham. Copyright © 1967 by Grove Press, Inc. Reprinted by permission of Grove Press, Inc., and by Éditions du Seuil, pp. 17–18, 109–16, 216–22;

25 Orlando Patterson, "The Paradoxes of Integration." From Orlando Patterson, *The Ordeal of Integration: Progress and Resentment in America's "Racial" Crisis*. Copyright © 1997 by Orlando Patterson. Reprinted by permission of Counterpoint Press, a division of Perseus Books, L.L.C., pp. 15–16, 64–6, 68–74, 76–7;

26 Jürgen Habermas, "Civil Society and the Political Public Sphere." From Jürgen Habermas, *Between Facts and Norms: Contributions to a Discourse Theory of Law and Democracy*. Translated by William Rehg. Copyright © 1996 by The MIT Press. Reprinted by permission of The MIT Press, pp. 359–87;

27 Jürgen Habermas, "The Tasks of a Critical Theory of Society." From Jürgen Habermas, *The Theory of Communicative Action, Volume 2: Lifeworld and System: A Critique of Functionalist Reason*. Translated by Thomas McCarthy. Originally published as *Theorie des kommunikativen Handelns, Band 2: Zur Kritik der funktionalistischen Vernuft*, copyright © 1981 by Suhrkamp Verlag, Frankfurt am Main. Translator's preface and translation copyright © 1987 by Beacon Press. Reprinted by permission of Beacon Press, pp. 374–403;

28 Jürgen Habermas, "Theory and Practice." From Jürgen Habermas, *Theory and Practice*. Translated by John Viertel. English translation copyright © 1973 by Beacon Press. Reprinted by permission of Beacon Press, pp. 7–16, 19–24.

29 Norbert Elias, "The Social Constraint toward Self-Constraint." From Norbert Elias, *The Civilizing Process: The History of Manners and State Formation and Civilization*. Translated by Edmund Jephcott. Copyright © 1939, 1968 by Norbert Elias. Translation copyright © 1978 by Basil Blackwell Ltd. Reprinted by permission of Blackwell Publishers, Ltd., pp. 443–8, 450–6;

30 Zygmunt Bauman, "A Sociological Theory of Postmodernity." From Zygmunt Bauman, *Intimations of Postmodernity*. Copyright © 1992 by Zygmunt Bauman. Reprinted by permission of Taylor & Francis Books, Ltd., pp. 187–203;

31   Niklas Luhmann, "Describing the Future." From Niklas Luhmann, *Observations on Modernity*. Translated by William Whobrey. Originally published in German as *Beobachtungen der Moderne*, copyright © 1992 Westdeutcher Verlag GmbH. Reprinted with the permission of the publishers, Stanford University Press. This translation copyright © 1998 by the Board of Trustees of the Leland Stanford Junior University. Stanford University Press, 1998, pp. 63, 64–74.

The publishers apologize for any errors or omissions in the above list and would be grateful to be notified of any corrections that should be incorporated in the next edition or reprint of this book.

Introduction

Contemporary Sociological Theory is the sister volume to *Classical Sociological Theory*. It is common to distinguish between "classical" and "contemporary" work, but the demarcation is vague. The dividing line continually shifts, in large part because of the dynamic nature of the relationship between "classical" and "contemporary" work. In the 1930s, for example, the great American sociological theorist Talcott Parsons set out to synthesize what he regarded as crucial in the "classical" tradition. In his view, Max Weber and Emile Durkheim were among the most important classics. Each wrote during the late nineteenth and early twentieth centuries. Parsons saw himself as continuing work they had started. Part of what made them classical was precisely this continuing importance their work had for later analyses. But Parsons also saw himself as the new kid on the block, an innovator in his contemporary scene. He continued to produce influential original work through the 1960s and remained active until his death in 1979. Today, however, *his* work seems "classical." This has four meanings:

First, calling work "classical" means partly just that it has stood the test of time and we are still interested in it. It is the opposite of "best forgotten." In this sense, Parsons surely aspired to have his work become classical.

Second, work we call classical tends to define broad orientations in the field of sociology that resonate for contemporary work. Reference to classical sociological theory is used to signal analytic approaches; it offers signposts to guide readers in seeing the intellectual heritage on which new theorists are drawing. In this way, not every old work gets called "classical," since a classic is something that still orients contemporary work. Reference to Parsons signals, for example, a concern for "functionalist" approaches to questions of social integration, that is for understanding different social institutions and practices in terms of how they contribute to the successful workings of the whole. Moreover, some work falls from the classical canon when it no longer speaks to us.

Third, we term work "classical" when we acknowledge that there have been major new developments since it was written. This doesn't mean that the "classical" work has been superseded. What it means is that new perspectives and debates have been introduced to which the classical social theorist has not been able to respond. In Parsons' case, a variety of innovations began to come to the fore in the 1960s. Some of these were direct criticisms of or challenges to Parsons' functionalism. He did respond to many, defending his perspective most of the time but also modifying it where he saw potential for improvement. Other parts of the new work, however, represented approaches that Parsons didn't consider. Jürgen Habermas, for example, combined some of Parsons' concerns with Marxism and critical theory in a way that

Parsons had never anticipated.[1] Jeffrey Alexander led the way in developing a "neofunctionalism" that not only built on Parsons and Durkheim, but shifted the emphases of their theories in much more cultural directions, away from the sides of their work that emphasized economic organization and social institutions, and away from strong presumptions of value consensus.[2] Thus, classical theory still matters, but we see it in new ways based on new ideas and interests. This is also the reason why new theorists are occasionally added to the "classics."

Fourth, in order to understand classical social theory we make a special effort to understand its distinctive historical context. In fact all theory needs to be understood in historical context, but part of what we mean when we identify certain theories as "contemporary" is that we share the same broad historical situation with their authors. For this reason, it is important to examine the historical context that has shaped contemporary work as well.

Mid-Twentieth-Century Transformations in Sociological Theory's Historical Context

When Parsons started writing his great synthetic work, *The Structure of Social Action*, in the 1930s, the First World War was the biggest historical watershed separating the classical theories from the contemporary. Soon, though, the Great Depression of the 1930s – which was contemporary to Parsons – loomed larger as a divide. This was not just because of its historical importance but because of its theoretical importance. It led to work like that of the economist John Maynard Keynes and the sociologist Thomas Marshall. Keynes' theory played a central role in changing the way both social scientists and policy-makers thought about the relationship of the state to the economy. Keynes held that states could use their financial clout as major purchasers of goods and services to help to stimulate the economy and smooth out the tendency Marx had noted for capitalism to suffer recurrent crises of overproduction.[3] His theories influenced the New Deal in the United States and the rise of the welfare state in Europe – both projects that shaped social life and changed the issues with which social theory had to deal. Marshall's theory of citizenship also responded to the Great Depression (and to the new sorts of state responses), suggesting that citizenship needed to be reconceptualized as referring not merely to political rights, but to social and economic rights as well.[4]

In addition to the Great Depression – and recovery from it – the rise of fascism, the Second World War, and the Cold War between the Communist East and the Capitalist West were shaping influences on social theory during the course of Talcott Parsons' career. There is debate about how they influenced his writing – for example, about the extent to which he was an advocate for what he saw as American values in a specifically Cold War framework – but there is no doubt that the historical context shaped his work.

These factors also shaped the work of most social theorists writing between the 1930s and 1960s. They posed big questions – like, what enabled some societies to develop democratic institutions while others were prone to dictatorship? As the American sociologist Barrington Moore famously argued, this was a matter of different paths to modernization and of some very old historical conditions – like whether the premodern agriculture of a country involved serfs who were tied to the land in near slavery, or was based on more or less independent peasants.[5] The Cold War influenced the ways in which American sociologists looked at other societies in the world. This was a matter not just of theoretical orientation but of financial support. Much new research was made possible by the fact that the US government gave grants for "foreign area studies," including help to social scientists to learn non-Western languages and engage in detailed studies of other ways of life. The government was concerned that in order to compete effectively with the Soviet Union in the Cold War, America needed experts on other societies. This provided the basis for great expansion in social knowledge. At the same time, this knowledge was often guided by theories that asked whether other societies were likely to become "modern" in the European and American way – that is, as capitalist democracies – or in the problematic communist way. It took some time before people began to consider that there might be other ways of becoming modern that didn't fit either of those models – or that the economic and political power of the US and Europe might stand in the way of development in other countries as often as it helped it.

Especially from the 1960s forward, the historical context started to change in important ways. Not least of all, young sociologists began their careers who had been born after the Second World War and never experienced the Great Depression. This doesn't mean that there was a sharp break. Many of the sociologists who became important leaders of the field in the 1960s and '70s were old enough to remember the war (if not very much the Depression). New historical perspectives were important, though, both in leading to new theoretical ideas and in encouraging different uses of resources offered by classical theory. Immanuel Wallerstein, for example, emerged as one of the most important revitalizers of the Marxist tradition, and moved it forward in new and distinctive ways with his "world systems theory."[6] One of Wallerstein's central points was that in a world dominated by capitalist trade, poorer countries could not grow wealthy simply by following the example of those that had done so earlier. Because European and American countries already dominated the core of the capitalist world economy, the fate of other countries was not simply based on how "modern" they were, but on whether and how they could compete in capitalist trade. Countries with less advanced technology and industry were always at a disadvantage in this. The likelihood that they would suffer under dictatorships rather than democracies was also explicable not just by internal factors, but by the influence of more powerful countries – including the US and the USSR.

To draw a dividing line in the 1960s is partly symbolic but not arbitrary. It reflects the importance of the baby boom generation born after the Second World War, the renewed attention to internationalism and globalization that flourished in that decade after relative isolationism in the 1950s, the emergence of important new voices from the global South or Third World, the beginnings of the greatest phase so far of the modern women's movement, a variety of other social movements from environment to gay rights, and the impact of the American war in Vietnam. The events of the 1960s reshaped what social theorists saw as most significant in the social world – even if they did not always see these things in the same way. The 1960s pushed sociological theorists to focus more on processes of social change (and resistance to change), on social inequality and on processes of marginalization and exploitation that shape it, on power relations and social movements that contest them, and on cultural and other differences among individuals and groups. These themes animate the work of many of the authors included in this volume.

Individual and Society

Among the themes that came to the fore, none was more important than the relationship between the individual and society. This was obviously not all new, but it became newly unsettled and demanded attention. Erving Goffman, an American sociologist who changed forever the way in which people understood interpersonal relations, was only a few years younger than Parsons and began to publish important work in the 1950s, but his analyses did not become widely influential until the 1960s. By then they were pivotal, however, in calling attention to the way that ritual and strategy intertwined in everyday phenomena like dating.[7] A date is like theater, in that each person has a role to play, and can play it better or worse. To some extent everyone knows that they are playing roles, not simply expressing themselves openly. At the same time, a date – like all social interaction – calls for improvisation. Participants seek to manage the impressions others form of them. But in order to do this successfully, they have to accept the social roles at least to some extent. Among other things, the popularity of Goffman's work reflected a new critical perspective on the social conformity of the 1950s.

One feature in the changed context was a widespread sense that people had more choice about their lives and the social roles they would assume. This reflected the new opportunities opening up in a society that was rapidly growing wealthier. The percentage of the population going to college more than tripled, for example, reflecting not only growing wealth but the growing shift from an industrial to an information society. As the American sociologist Daniel Bell wrote in one of the first books to analyze this change, to an ever-greater extent society was being organized around the production of knowledge, not only material goods.[8] Renewed attention to individuals and how they might fit into society was also shaped by what another American social theorist, Philip Rieff, called "the triumph of the therapeutic."[9] By this, Rieff meant the prominent place that both introspection and attempts at reformation of the self had assumed in modern culture. People not only went to therapists, they expected therapeutic work from ministers, teachers, and even television. This encouraged sociologists not only to analyze therapy, but to ask what was behind the change in culture.

The critical theorist Herbert Marcuse noted that capitalism had long seemed to require a certain repression of impulses. In *The Protestant Ethic and the Spirit of Capitalism*, for example, Weber had described the importance of saving and re-investment, both dependent on resisting impulses to enjoy luxuries. Equally, it was important for workers and managers alike to be committed to hard work, disciplined, and rationalistic. This extended from strictly economic realms, Marcuse suggested, to sexuality and artistic creativity. (This is one reason why the Bohemian artist had long seemed such an affront to capitalism and to businessmen's understanding of rationalism.) The more consumer-oriented capitalism of the late 1950s and 1960s, however, brought with it a loosening of repression.[10] Not least, Marcuse argued, disciplining workers was no longer the main issue for capitalists; it was increasingly supplanted by motivating consumers. This could be a matter of ir- rational eroticism, for example selling cars by showing them with sexy models draped over the hood. Tolerance for new levels of aesthetic and erotic expression not only encouraged consumption, it muted tendencies to challenge the established order. In the era of the Keynesian welfare state, the established system of power and wealth was better able to manage the resistance and rebellions of ordinary people. This very idea is an indication of why we see this period as "contemporary" in regard to society and social theory, even though there have obviously been significant changes.

There were many different ways in which sociologists explored the relationship between individual and society. These drew on different roots in earlier, "classical" social theory. What the new theorists shared was a sense that there was a tension in this relationship. Although most agreed that there was no such thing as "pure individuality" outside of society, and that human beings developed personhood only as parties to social relationships, they did not take this to mean that the relationship between individuals and actually existing forms of society was always harmonious or fulfilling. On the contrary, in various ways these theorists pointed to how people found themselves limited by their social conditions. This was a matter not just of blockages, of course, but often also of the absence of support systems. At the same time, people's aspirations did not simply come from within them; they were socially produced. Whether it was a matter of wanting faster cars, bigger TVs, or more fashionable clothes, this could not be understood simply from looking inside individuals, it had to be understood at a sociological level. Likewise, the means people chose to pursue their goals were not automatic. Some would drop out of school to enjoy consumer goods immediately, even though this hurt their long-term prospects. Others would study hard in order to get into competitive colleges and graduate schools. Some would stick completely to legal means, while others would turn to crime. Who did what was based on an interaction between personal charac- teristics and social organization.

One important approach to these questions focused on the ways in which people developed identities for themselves and for others. "Labeling theory" was rooted in the symbolic interactionism of George Herbert Mead and his followers.[11] It started with the commonplace observation that many children steal but few become professional thieves (and conversely, most do homework but few become real scholars). Labeling theorists acknowledged that differences in talent and opportun- ity were and are important. For example, having parents wealthy enough to be able to send their children to college is a big predictor of whether those children become well-educated. But they added that what happens is also shaped by the labels that others come to apply (and individuals sometimes accept for themselves). Thus a youth who is caught and punished repeatedly for theft may come to be known as a thief (while one who gets away does not). Having the identity "thief" may close some doors, making it harder for example to get an honest job. Accepting the label for oneself may reduce inhibitions against stealing in the future. In short, the identity of the person and the social role ("thief," in this example) are both socially constructed. They do not exist "objectively," separate from social life and culture.

The Social and Cultural Construction of Knowledge

Many of the new explorations of the individual/society relationship were guided by attention to the capacities that individuals have for constructing the social world in new ways. For example, as Alfred Schutz emphasized, the process of people sharing understanding of their social world – what he called intersubjectivity – helps to shape both the social world itself and people's identities as individuals within it.[12] Peter Berger and Thomas Luckmann drew on Schutz's work to explore the ways in which the very construction of social knowledge was itself analyzable not simply as a matter of externally verifiable discovery but as a reflection of social relations and everyday life concerns.[13] These theorists drew on phenomenology, a theoretical approach that had developed largely outside of sociology as a form of attention to individual consciousness, to develop a new sociology of knowledge and intersubjective understanding. Durkheim had been interested in phenomenology and some sociologists – like Goffman and Garfinkel – combined Durkheimian attention to social structure with phenomenological concern for the ways in which individuals construct their social lives and their knowledge of the everday social world.

The classical social theory of George Herbert Mead addressed similar questions and provided an alternative approach for many of the new generation of thinkers. Mead's theory was rooted in pragmatism, an American approach to philosophy that emphasized the extent to which all knowledge was grounded in practical experience and communication – not based simply on holding up a mirror to objective reality.[14] There are many different ways to understand any specific object in the world, the pragmatists suggested; which ones become important to people will depend on the tasks they are engaged in and the ways others they care about grasp the same objects. What this implied is that there is no way that anyone simply and directly gets reality right. Different cultures and even different scientific theories can with equal validity understand similar phenomena differently.

Questions about the social construction of knowledge – whether everday or scientific – have become one of the major themes of the post-1960s period. Here the work of theorists reflects both struggles to come to terms with history and new awareness of cross-cultural diversity. For example, a number of social theorists have addressed the transformations in Western culture. Some of their work was shaped by a concern to understand how what had seemed in the nineteenth century to be a straightforward march of reason and progress could issue in the twentieth century in Nazism – or for that matter Stalinism. Their explorations involved not just research on fascism or communism as special cases, but inquired into how there might be potential for such disasters built into Western culture more generally.[15]

Michel Foucault, for example, sought to uncover the different characteristic approaches to knowledge of different epochs and emphasized the dramatic differences between them.[16] He saw the modern period as shaped by the rise of the individual, both as the basis of epistemology – the source of knowledge understood as empirical observation and philosophical reflection – and as a basic value – the independent actor. But instead of presenting this simply as progress, looking at it from within an individualistic point of view, he presented this as opening up a new set of problems. Individualism was a way of seeing the world and living in it,

Foucault argued, and as such it was not a starting point for analysis but an effect to be explained. What produced this effect, he suggested, was more than anything else a set of disciplinary practices. The modern individual was ideologically understood as the fount of freedom – a self craving free expression – but in fact was produced by demanding of people that they take on the task of self-discipline. The new individual was a person constantly aware of the gaze of others, including especially the gaze of authority. This was produced by the development of medical examinations, of schooling, of government statistics. It was reflected in an approach to law and morality that emphasized not just what people did – the external manifestations of wrongdoing – but also their inner intentions. Even sexuality, Foucault suggested, was not simply a natural self-expression but a social phenomenon. It was shaped by ideas about "normality" and "performance" that were reflected not just in hostility towards homosexuals or other "deviants" but in anxieties to conform to expectations, the proliferation of "self-help" and "how-to" books and comparisons of each individual's own experience to that in movies or literature.[17]

Foucault was one of the most important social theorists to emerge in an initially French intellectual movement commonly called "structuralism" and later "post-structuralism."[18] Structuralism shared some of its classical roots with the sociology of Emile Durkheim, especially in its examination of the social sources of knowledge and intellectual categories.[19] Influenced by the linguist Ferdinand de Saussure, structuralism stressed the extent to which systems of meaning (language or culture) were based on the reference of terms to each other. Thus words get their meaning from relations to other words, not simply by pointing to things, nor from historical origins. The Austrian philosopher Ludwig Wittgenstein developed similar notions in his later work.[20] Both structuralism and Wittgenstein influenced social theory in and after the 1960s. They challenged not only ideas about language but underlying theories of knowledge that approached it as a more or less transparent mental representation of external reality. Some structuralists, like the French anthropologist Claude Lévi-Strauss, endeavored to decode universal patterns of meaning, possibly rooted in the brain itself.[21] Others, including Foucault, focused increasingly on the ways power and historical change shaped knowledge; this was what led to the label of "post-structuralism." Post-structuralists emphasized the difficulties of transcending specific cultures or systems of meaning without the dominance of one over another. They also urged attention to the ways in which each system of knowledge blocked attention to some kinds of understanding, imposing silences as well as enabling speech. Together these influences led to a new concern with culture not as a source of values that unite a society (as Parsons had thought of it), but as an arena of contestation and difference.

Another post-structuralist sociologist, Pierre Bourdieu emphasized "symbolic violence" and the "struggle over classification."[22] Even within one society, he argued, culture was used not only to unite but to dominate. Widespread ideology claimed that culture was simply a matter of meaning, thought, or aesthetic taste. This suggested that it was somehow the opposite of power and economic determination. But clearly, claims to have highly cultivated taste could be used to exclude those with "baser" tastes. Moreover, ideas like "art for art's sake" might seem to represent the reversal of the economic world but in fact they revealed economies of their own in which participants struggled over "cultural capital" rather than material, monetary capital. The logic of the competition was different, but it was still a competition. Indeed, to gain prestige as an artist, for example, it was necessary to demonstrate that one put creativity ahead of material gain, to show individual "genius" required not producing art that found too easy and widespread a popular acceptance. To be seen as a literary artist and not just a writer, thus, a novelist had to differentiate himself from a journalist.[23] Outside the specialized field of art, the state and other powerful actors used cultural goods – like diplomas and public honors – to supplement the direct workings of the monetary economy. The operation of schemes of classification by race, gender, class, sexual orientation, artistic taste or other criteria offered a way to uphold social hierarchies that granted privilege to those on top.

Inequality, Power, and Difference

One of the big issues that changed sociological theory in and after the 1960s was a new level of attention to class, race, ethnicity, gender, and sexual orientation. Of course these had been noticed by earlier generations. Class was a central theme for both Marx and Weber. The Chicago School that helped to pioneer American sociology had studied ethnicity both as a feature of urban life and as one of the issues resulting from immigration to the United States.[24] Chicago sociologists had also addressed race, though the most important classic work was that of America's first great Black sociologist, W. E. B. Du Bois.[25] Despite the fact that sociologists had always been attentive to issues of social inequality and difference, though, during the period of functionalist dominance after the Second World War the theoretical emphasis had fallen overwhelmingly on social integration, consensus, and factors that held society together. The development of new social movements and conflicts during the 1960s and '70s brought inequality, difference, and struggle to center stage.

One symptom of this was that when Talcott Parsons produced his account of classical social theory, Marx was not an important figure. Each new generation has the opportunity to redefine what it finds useful in the classics, however, and during the 1960s and '70s Marx was reclaimed, as were the later Marxists like the Italian Antonio Gramsci, and the German critical theorists. They had always been better known in Europe than in the US (and indeed, functionalism was more dominant in the US). Younger sociologists were looking for different classics largely in order to analyze better the inequalities and conflicts they saw in contemporary society. Influenced by Marx and by actual social conflicts, they presented a model of society in which tensions and struggles were basic and unity was largely maintained by power. Parsons, by contrast, had paid little attention to the ways in which some people wielded power over others and controlled aspects of social organization. When he used the word "power" his emphasis was on the overall capacity of a society, not on the dominance of some members by others.[26]

Parsons and other functionalists emphasized the "systemic" character of social life, the extent to which social organization fitted together so that every feature was necessary to the whole. The new generation of theorists criticized the implicit conservatism in this. They asked more frequently how society could change, how individuals could have an impact on the whole, and whether the functionalist model of the system masked real differences among members of a society. When functionalists said that the social system "worked," the critics asked, "for whom?" In both Europe and America, younger sociologists pointed out that society might successfully educate workers to have the skills needed for its industry but that didn't mean it educated students in all social classes equally, or gave them equal opportunities for creativity. They argued that if generating wealth was one indicator of a society "working" then how equally or fairly that wealth was distributed should be another. Leading functionalists had argued that differences in wages and salaries mainly reflected a necessary incentive system.[27] The critics charged that it had more to do with power, with what class someone happened to be born into, with privileges based unfairly on sex, race, ethnicity, and similar characteristics, and with the needs of capitalism rather than of society as such.

Starting with the premise that social inequalities were not always necessary or fair, theorists set out to understand what form they took, why they existed, how they could change and what power structures resisted change. This applied both domestically and internationally. Rather than assuming that "modernization" would bring about a convergence of all societies in which these would necessarily develop on a European–American model, researchers analyzed the structures of global inequality, who benefited from them, and how they were produced and maintained. Central to the new theoretical orientations were attention to power and to historical change and variability. These encouraged more critical perspectives because they shared the ideas that society could be different, that choices could be made.[28] It was necessary, in other words, to avoid equating the actually existing with the necessary or normal.

For example, many sociologists had long assumed that assimilation and integration were the necessary end results of migration – including the forced migration that brought Africans to America as slaves. Sociologists, like anthropologists, had long questioned the scientific status of racial distinctions. They argued that using skin color to classify human populations was arbitrary and a result of historical circumstance and was therefore pseudo-science (a view that genetic research has more recently supported). But during the 1960s, influenced by the Black Power movement, many sociologists began to go beyond this, questioning the goals of assimilation and racial integration. The basic question was, how much of their own culture, identity, and claims to respect did African-Americans have to surrender in order to assimilate? It appeared to many that ending forced segregation (a main goal of the civil rights movement) only addressed half the issue. This goal questioned keeping Blacks out of white neighborhoods and other preserves, but didn't question whiteness as such, or the extent to which integration was only offered on the condition that Blacks act like whites. It appeared, in other words, as if greater economic and political equality for Blacks was offered at the expense of recognition of the cultural achievements and self-understanding of Blacks themselves.

As a variety of theorists and researchers argued, the history of American society had produced a distinctive racial formation.[29] This was reproduced generation after generation, and old categories were extended to new groups (as for example in the case of Asian immigrants). This process involved not merely the recognition of objective differences, but the "racialization" of social groups – the use of race to construct them in specific ways. Although this was most obvious in the case of minority groups against which there was discrimination it was true also of whites. Whiteness was treated as a kind of normal characteristic, as simply American. It needed to be recognized that it was in fact one particular – racialized – category, and that it was being given hierarchical privilege.

Similar concerns were raised in relation to gender, sexual orientation, ethnicity and other lines of difference. Rather than seeing differences between male and female as simply natural, for example, sociologists increasingly focused on the processes by which such differences were culturally constructed.[30] They did not treat this as a neutral feature of cultural difference, but went on to examine the ways in which the subordination of women was reproduced and maintained. The question was both one of cultural differentiation (women were more likely to become nurses, men more likely to drive trucks) and one of economic hierarchy (truck drivers were paid more than nurses).

The issue of difference was not just a matter of groups defined by a specific identity like race or gender. It applied to a whole variety of social practices. Consider family. The term "nuclear family" was coined in 1949 by the anthropologist George Peter Murdoch. Murdoch described it as a basic building block of larger structures – lineages, clans, and "extended families." He acknowledged, though, that America was unusual because Americans commonly expected the nuclear family to stand alone. Over time, this expectation became normalized. Television shows like "Ozzie and Harriett" and "Leave it to Beaver" presented this as simply the way families were. But as the sociologist Stephanie Coontz pointed out, this is not how most families ever really were.[31] And in fact, starting in the 1960s, nuclear families began to account for a smaller and smaller percentage of American households. From 45 percent in 1960 the proportion fell to 23.5 percent by 2000.[32] Even as this happened, the nuclear family continued to be treated by many as morally right and normal, and as stable and supportive, even if it was at variance with actual conditions. From a functionalist point of view, the large proportion of families that did not fit this model sometimes appeared as a breakdown in the normal pattern of social organization – even though historically the "normal" pattern was the exception rather than the rule. To others, it didn't signify anything good or bad in itself; the questions were whether the other living arrangements brought people satisfaction, support, or other desirable results. Many pointed out that part of the rise of other living arrangements was in fact made possible by new levels of affluence and freedom of choice.

The most important of the new theoretical orientations emphasizing difference was feminism. Women's struggles for social equality entered a new phase of growth in the 1960s and theory was closely linked to the practical movement. This reflected in part the need to explain why gender inequality was as pervasive as it was, and why it was not inevitable (as functionalist theory suggested) but open to change. Feminist theory simultaneously addressed two crucial themes: the material inequality between men and women, and the implications of the conceptual construction of gender categories. Sociologists studying class had often compared the incomes or wealth of men without attention to that of women; many reasoned that this was necessary because men were the main breadwinners in families. Especially in and after the 1960s, research focused on questions like what men and women earned when they had similar jobs or levels of education, and what explained the substantial inequalities that were found. As in the case of race and ethnicity, many of the newer sociological theories emphasized the role of power. This was often physical power, sometimes backed up by law. But it was also often the power of dominant culture – power that people were socialized to accept. This raised the second major theme. The Canadian sociologist Dorothy Smith, for example, drew on both ethnomethodology and Marxism to construct a theory of the "conceptual practices of power."[33] Work like this drew attention to the ways in which seemingly neutral classifications like those of law courts and welfare agencies, censuses and even sociological surveys reproduced and helped to enforce certain normative understandings of how the world *should* work. These normative understandings commonly benefited men at the expense of women – for example by associating housework "naturally" with childbearing.

Feminist theory generally argued that material equality would be hard to achieve so long as cultural categories remained biased against women. This left open a major question, though. Did the elimination of bias necessarily mean seeing men and women as essentially the same? Or could it mean recognizing gender differences but valuing men and women equally? The issue was similar to that of whether the elimination of ethnic and racial discrimination necessarily depended on the assimilation of immigrants into host cultures – or, in the case of US race relations, on making Blacks more like whites. An influential strand of theory in both racial and gender studies argued that such assimilationist thinking was a further reflection of inequality and power, not a way around it. Why should women need to become more like men in order to gain equivalent political or economic rights? While much of the empirical research in sociology continued to focus on material dimensions of gender inequality – in workplaces, political institutions, and families – a major strand of feminist theory focused more on questions of the cultural construction of difference. This was influenced both by the critical theory tradition and by French post-structuralist theory. Feminist theory of this sort also influenced the development of critical theories of sexuality. Linking these theories was concern to avoid assuming that there was one correct model for human identity or social life. Rather, theorists suggested, theory needed to address the ways in which differences could be recognized without unjust discrimination.

On an international scale, paying attention to power, inequality, and cultural difference meant rethinking the ideas of progress and development. Much earlier work was based on evolutionary assumptions about social change which (unlike most biological theories of evolution) suggested that historical change moved "forwards," that societies "advanced," and therefore that the conditions of the "leading" societies of any one period would reveal the future of others.[34] It was this sort of thinking that led Alexis de Tocqueville to travel to America to see Europe's future, and Friedrich Engels to go to England during the industrial revolution to see what lay in store for Germany, even though neither Tocqueville nor Engels was strictly an evolutionary theorist. Many other theorists, however, placed a greater emphasis on the "natural" ways in which they thought society would develop. The most influential of these in the twentieth century were "modernization" theorists.

Modernization theory drew on the actual social conditions of the richer Western European countries and the United States to construct a model of modernity. Then followers analyzed the paths by which other countries and parts of the world could become more modern, emphasizing the lessons offered by past "successful modernizers" like Britain and the United States. A common concern was for how poor countries (conceived as "traditional") could achieve the developmental momentum to "take off" into a process of self-sustaining economic growth and modernization.[35] Modernization theory guided a range of important research projects, which did indeed produce useful knowledge. However, especially in and after the 1960s, it was challenged on several fronts. Among the most important was the unilinear concept of social change widespread within it. Modernization was understood as a process moving in one predetermined direction. Closely related was the criticism that modernization theory neglected power, including the power by which some societies dominated others and also the power by which elites within societies shaped the course of their growth and change. Third was the argument that modernization theory lumped all manner of very different cultural and social formations together into the category of "traditional" or pre-modernity.

As we noted above, more recent thinkers often argued that it was difficult for newly developing countries to follow the paths of those that industrialized in the nineteenth century precisely because they had to compete with these already technologically and economically advanced countries. Some have also questioned whether "modern" is a sufficiently precise concept. If one means "capitalism" or "democracy," these theorists suggest, it is best to say so clearly and study when and how they are linked rather than assuming that they automatically combine in "modernity." In the same vein, many hold that it is important to ask whether there might be multiple versions of modernity, different projects of modernization rather than a single path. For example, is socialism an alternative form of modern economy to capitalism? Is it right to see religious conservatives as always antimodern? Or, are some Islamists, Hindu fundamentalists, and many Catholics and Protestants seeking to shape versions of modernity that accord with their values? These questions have come to the fore recently in response to the renewed pace of globalization of the 1990s and early 2000s. What it means to be a part of the modern world system has become an even more important question with the expansion of market relations, globalization of media, and far-flung migrations. But fights over the World Trade Organization, exploitation of the environment, human rights, and other questions all suggest that there are diverse visions of modernity. Power and struggle, not just a natural course of development, shape which ones are realized. One of the advantages of recent sociological theory is the opportunity to learn from the history of the twentieth century.

Empirical Research

When Karl Marx and Friedrich Engels began to develop their sociological theory in the 1840s, empirical research was also in its infancy. Marx relied heavily on government reports and investigations into industrial conditions undertaken by British Parliamentary Commissions. These were not products of scientific research but rather interviews undertaken by officials, physicians, and others concerned about public welfare. Engels actually conducted one of the first sociological investigations into urban life. He walked several routes through Manchester and its environs and systematically recorded what he saw, and what he learned from those he talked to. Along with other data garnered mainly from businesses, this became a crucial basis for his book, *The Condition of the Working Class in England in 1844.*

At roughly the same time, a few other social scientists were pioneering empirical research methods. Economics was in the lead, but sociology second and close behind. Frédéric Le Play, for example, set out to examine the conditions of family life, systematically comparing different communities and economic conditions to see how they affected the organization of households.[36] Though he himself did not conduct significant empirical research, Auguste Comte heralded the significance of empirical evidence in his designation of a new "positivist" epoch in the organization of human affairs, in which science could truly guide practical organization.[37] Herbert Spencer relied on systematic examination of the reports of missionaries, colonial administrators and occasionally scientists to describe the social organization of different peoples around the world and construct his evolutionary theory.[38] His contemporary Charles Darwin had the advantage of personal participation in documenting biological diversity, but also relied on similar analyses of the reports of others, including, substantially, lay observers.[39]

The situation was only modestly better at the end of the nineteenth century and beginning of the twentieth, when Max Weber and Emile Durkheim produced their pioneering sociological analyses. Governments had begun to collect information about the population of most European countries on regular intervals – the modern census was basically created during the nineteenth century. Censuses were supplemented by labor statistics, mortality statistics, and a host of other indicators of the social experience of populations. Economic data on trade, business organizations, taxes and the like led the way, but widespread concern for the possible effects of industrialization and other social changes pressed the collection of other sorts of social data to the fore as well. When Durkheim set out in the 1890s to examine the social causes of suicide, he was able to rely on data about deaths collected by government agencies in several countries.[40] This improved the record-keeping that had long been undertaken by churches as they recorded births, marriages, deaths, and similar information in different parishes. It was not yet fully scientific data insofar as there was relatively little research underpinning techniques of data collection, but it was increasingly systematic data. Indeed, the growth of the state – and especially of a variety of government agencies charged with specific administrative tasks from education to defense to regulating the quality of food – was basic to the development of systematic data collection. The data gathered, in turn, were basic to helping sociology (and other social sciences) become more scientific.

At the same time, sociological theorists began to see the need to collect their own data. Max Weber was not satisfied with the information publicly available when he set out to analyze property relations and economic conditions in Germany's East Elbian district; he organized the collection of new data on "Junker capitalism" and the proletarianization of German peasants.[41] George Herbert Mead conducted systematic observations of children and ran rudimentary experiments.[42] In each case, the developments of their theories led these pioneering sociologists to ask questions that previously available data couldn't answer.

From the seventeenth century on, but especially in the twentieth century, the simple availability of more reliable data was supplemented by improvements in statistics – quantitative techniques for the analysis of data.[43] Indeed, in many cases the development of statistical techniques outstripped the availability of rigorous data. It was especially hard to gather certain sorts of data because they were controversial. Early sociologists wanted to know, for example, how employers treated their workers, how many hours child laborers worked, and what occupational injuries workers in different crafts suffered. They were not able to go directly to factories and survey employees; they relied instead on those who came forward as voluntary witnesses. Early social scientists also pioneered ways of collecting data systematically even when it could not be rendered in quantitative form. Anthropologists carefully documented kinship systems, for example, while at the same time sociologists set out to describe the forms of life in Europe's and America's rapidly growing cities or to record how immigrants adjusted.

What is most important to see here is the extent to which the growth of social theory was intertwined with the development of new approaches to empirical social research. If this was a factor in the nineteenth century, it became ever more vitally important in the twentieth. The development of sociological theory was more clearly separated from the normative concerns of political philosophy; explanation became increasingly its goal. Theory also became part of a shared sociological enterprise with empirical research. Attention centered increasingly on the way the two came together in analyzing specific phenomena, and answering specific questions. Not only, how did society work in general, but also, how did cities grow, and why did they grow in the particular patterns that they did? Why did people migrate from one country to another, and what determined their success or integration into new settings? What kinds of social groups stuck together under pressure, which ones tended to split up, and why? How sociologists posed these questions, which ones they thought were important, and how they went about answering them were all shaped by theory. But at the same time, the theories offered predictions and explanations that either fitted with available data or didn't – and contradictory data could drive the theorists back to the drawing board.

New data didn't change overall perspectives on society, but it changed the ways in which theorists explained specific aspects of social life within each perspective. For example, there was no datum that could prove it right to follow Weber in a more individualistic approach to social action or Durkheim in a more holistic approach to society as a separate level of analysis. But from both perspectives, theorists struggled to explain new information about how society worked. This included both the results of empirical research into the relationship between specific variables, and empirical observations of new events and historical developments. For example, the rise of fascism in the 1930s involved something new in history; it had not existed before and it challenged theories based on previous experience. But Weber's and Durkheim's theories were able to contribute to the analysis of fascism because they grasped important features. Weber's account of charismatic leadership could help explain Hitler's or Mussolini's roles in German and Italian mass movements. Durkheim's account of how large-scale rituals bind people together could help to explain why the grand spectacles staged by fascists were effective not just in spreading ideology or offering entertainment but in leading individuals to accept that the social whole was more important than any of its parts. But new research also added new dimensions that neither theoretical perspective completely anticipated. In their research on "the authoritarian personality," for example, Adorno and his colleagues showed that how individually rational people would be, and how they would respond to charismatic leadership depended on their upbringing and experience of work and other relationships. This new research didn't overturn either Weber's or Durkheim's theory, but it pushed followers of each to add new dimensions, and to make general arguments about the nature of human beings and social life more attentive to variations in historical circumstances and culture. It also pressed for better integration between sociological and psychological analysis.

It was mainly in the 1950s and '60s that quantitative empirical research in sociology took on its modern form and became a large-scale enterprise. The Depression and the Second World War played decisive roles as social science research was mobilized to aid first the New Deal and similar projects of social reconstruction elsewhere and then the war effort. On topics from social stratification and mobility to formal organizations, demography, and group dynamics, this produced important new knowledge and more precise tests of hypotheses. At the same time, the advances in research contributed to a differentiation between two senses of theory. On the one hand, some theory was very close to empirical research projects; it consisted largely of relatively formalized structures of hypotheses. On the other hand, much of the classical tradition of sociological theory tried to offer large-scale perspectives on social life in general. Writing in the late 1950s, the American sociologist C. Wright Mills contrasted what he called "grand theory" and "abstracted empiricism."[44] The "grand theory" to which he referred was the attempt to build an all-encompassing theory of society, exemplified by Talcott Parsons' functionalism. The "abstracted empiricism" was the practice of social research more and more concerned with technique, especially statistical technique. Mills was unhappy about both. While they took opposite paths, they complemented each other because neither encouraged the kind of critical awareness of social life that Mills thought important. Moreover, neither engaged adequately with the challenge of understanding specific patterns of historical change. They didn't help as much as the classical traditions of Marx, Weber, and Durkheim to connect the social issues people experienced in their everyday lives to an analysis of large-scale social patterns. Unemployment, divorce, and military service, for example, were biographical experiences of millions of individuals. The job of sociology, Mills contended, was to help people see how these were also organized on a society-wide scale: who was most likely to experience each? How did this reflect the class structure or the nature of political power?

Mills' Columbia University colleague Robert Merton was also concerned about the gap between the broadest theoretical perspectives that illuminated social life in general and the specific hypotheses and tests of empirical research. His suggestion was to emphasize what he called "theories of the middle range."[45] By these he meant theories that attempted to explain social phenomena which occurred in many different situations. They were thus more general than specific empirical findings about particular cases, and at the same time more specific than broad theoretical perspectives like functionalism, Marxism, or symbolic interactionism. Merton thought these broad perspectives were valuable as orientations, aids to thinking through more specific analyses. But he thought it crucial for a relatively young science like sociology to seek rigorous explanations of phenomena that were concrete but generalizable. His examples included theories of social roles, deviance, and reference groups. The last, for example, refers to analysis of the ways in which people compare themselves to others. Everyone derives a sense of his or her particular identity, level of success in life, and other characteristics largely through comparisons with other people. But no one compares himself with everyone; a key sociological question is how people determine who are the relevant comparisons. In the army, for example, sergeants are apt to compare themselves with lieutenants and corporals but not with generals. In high schools, football players are likely to compare themselves with other athletes more than with students in general, and with other students more than with drop-outs or adults. This and other examples yield the generalizable finding that the most meaningful comparisons are those with fairly similar and local others. There is more to reference group theory, but this illustrates the idea of identifying a generalizable phenomenon – comparison within specific groups – that is neither a general theory of society nor a research finding specific to one case, merely a single tested hypothesis. Reference groups are influential in dating behavior (as people judge who is likely to go out with them or how others view their partners), in job satisfaction (as people judge whether their salaries and their treatment by peers and superiors are fair), and even in job performance (as people look at others to see whether they are working hard enough, or harder than they have to).

The connection between empirical research and sociological theory is often strongest and most balanced at the level of theories of the middle range. These may focus on a wide variety of phenomena from revolutions to consumer behavior. Two of the most important lines of development of middle-range theories address structures of social relations (networks) and the way social actors make decisions (exchange and rational choice theories). In the work of the most ambitious advocates for each theory, these may look like grand theoretical perspectives in the manner of Parsons' functionalism – i.e., a few passionate theorists claiming that *everything* is a matter of either network structures or rational choice. But although these theories and others are shaped by broad perspectives and orientations, they are at their most productive in abstracting certain generalizable features of social life and concentrating on how they operate in different kinds of social circumstances. Rational choice theorists know that no one is perfectly rational and network theorists know that structural patterns are only part of what makes social relationships meaningful. But each of these theories makes it possible to abstract from particular cases and compare aspects of social life across diverse contexts.

The central idea in network approaches to social structure, for example, is to abstract the *form* of social relationships from their *content* and then to compare formal structures and analyze the effects of variation. For example, within any collection of people, we could start by asking what is the "density" of their inter-relationships (i.e., how many of any specific type of possible connections between them actually exist). How many of the brothers in a fraternity are actually close friends, for example? Then one can go on to ask what factors explain where the connections exist and where they are absent (is it, for example, a matter of which year in school the men are, or what they study, or where their rooms in a shared house are located?). Finally, one could compare many fraternities and ask what are the differences in the patterns of relationships found. The same sort of analysis has been applied not only to friendship groups but to network structures linking corporations through their boards of directors; those linking banks or law firms to particular clients; those shaping organizations and the recruitment of participants to protest movements; and those determining the spread of sexually transmitted diseases. In developing such analyses it is as important to see where relationships are absent as where they are present. For example, in groups of equivalent density, there are usually some members closely tied into the group and others who are relatively isolated. Analysts ask whether there are consistent, predictable patterns to the behavior of these social isolates or to those more strongly integrated into networks.

While the phenomenological and symbolic interactionist (or pragmatist) approaches to relations of individual and society emphasized the construction of meaningful relationships, others emphasized pursuit of strategic advantage. People did not simply adapt to social norms or follow cultural rules, theorists suggested. Rather, social actors chose strategies for trying to present themselves in the most favorable light, trying to get the best possible response from other people, trying to come out ahead in interpersonal relationships even while preserving the illusion of equality or reciprocity. Drawing on economics and on behavioral psychology, theorists like Peter Blau and George Homans approached social interactions as exchanges.[46] Later theorists expanded these approaches into "rational choice theory," continuing to draw on interdisciplinary collaboration with psychology and especially economics.[47] They stressed Weberian methodological individualism, but for the most part abandoned Weber's interpretative search for the meaning actors attach to their social actions. Instead, rational choice theorists tried to develop models that predicted what rational, self-interested actors would do to pursue their advantage in any situation. When would it be rational to cooperate, for example, and when not? The answer would depend, of course, not just on the characteristics of the actors, but also on the structure of opportunities and constraints open to them. These models could then be used to explain actual behavior – or to identify deviations from rational action in order to seek explanations for these.

Examining the relationship between individual and society is one of the sources of intellectual excitement in modern sociology, and also one of the reasons why it always remains controversial. This is partly simply because sociology challenges a widespread but often unstated acceptance of individualism in contemporary society – an individualism that is particularly extreme in the US. Sociology reminds people who like to think they are in complete control of their own lives that they are not; it reminds people who say they are completely independent that they in fact depend on others and on a whole social system. It even reveals that when we make our own choices they do not simply express our individual distinctiveness, they also tend to reproduce predictable sociological patterns. Much in our contemporary world is set up to encourage people to think in terms of the uniqueness of individual identity and the complete freedom of choice. People sometimes resist recognizing limits to these.

Controversy and Resistance

Another reason that sociology has often been controversial is the tendency of sociologists to make explicit and accessible the social phenomena that many people have strong interests in keeping implicit and inaccessible. Certainly this includes issues like who benefits from social inequality and injustice. Call them the "big issues"; there are certainly big interests behind keeping them obscure. But the resistance to clear sociological understanding comes not only from the rich and the powerful. It comes from all of us.

We all invest ourselves in social misunderstandings, and some of these actually help to make social relationships work. We say, for example, that we give gifts out of a pure spirit of love or generosity. In fact, most people modulate their giving to match gifts they receive from others. The American sociological theorist Alvin Gouldner attributed this to the "norm of reciprocity," the idea that social relationships depend on exchanges that people judge to be appropriate.[48] This applies even in conversation itself. If I say "hello," the norm of reciprocity requires you to respond in kind. But, as the French sociological theorist Pierre Bourdieu points out, this is a more complex game than it appears. It depends not only on a good sense of what is appropriate (how to play the game) but on shared and socially reproduced "misrecognitions."[49] We say the gift requires no response, and we believe it. However, at some level we expect one, either a matching gift in a kind of exchange, or appropriate thanks and deference. But we resent having this pointed out. We prefer to think of ourselves simply as being generous, and the gift only does its work in cementing relationships if the norm of reciprocity does not become too obvious. If it is seen as too transparent an attempt to curry favor, then it is less valuable.

From the relatively humble example of gifts, we can see some of the sources of resistance to sociological analysis, to attempts to expose the real interests behind accepted social practices and arrangements. And this extends through the building of personal relationships (e.g., dating and marriage), the building of complex organizations (like businesses or political parties), to the creation of states, governments, and whole societies. People getting married say that it is "until death do us part" even though they know that nearly half of marriages end in divorce. They often really mean it, and meaning it may help nurture commitment and make marriages last. A variety of social factors influence whether marriages actually last – financial circumstances, career pressures, children, support groups. Love and commitment between two individuals are important, but not the whole story. Yet, we tend to resist the message that something so personal could be explained by generalizable social factors – or at least, we resist applying those generalizations to ourselves.

Take a different example: is rap music an expression of individual artistic creativity, Black culture, or corporate capitalism? Rappers have an investment in the first and they and their listeners often have an investment in both the first and the second. But rappers, audiences, and music companies all have an interest in the last not being too apparent. As the West Indian-born sociologist Paul Gilroy observes, rappers may appear as sexual rebels and as Black men challenging authority, but the organization of the music industry channels this for profit and the organization of actual politics makes this form of challenge – unlike some other forms of Black Power movements – largely impotent. Gilroy worries that a musical tradition that was genuinely creative and politically challenging is being reduced to "marketing hollow defiance."[50] But listeners who want to hear a deeper politics, or fit into a fashion, or simply have a good time, all have an interest in not considering the question – as do rappers who want to stay popular and music companies that want to make money.

This is not simply a matter of deceit. Rappers and record companies may both be honest about being in the business for the money. It is a matter of how people construct meaning in social life and resist disruptions to it. This works on a larger scale too. Many people believe that their ethnic, racial, or national identities are clear-cut and natural. They resist sociological analyses showing how blurred the boundaries are, how much the categories are invented, and how often they are manipulated. Within each group, people may have an ideology that stresses community and sharing a common fate, and which also obscures how some members of the group take advantage of others. They resist sociological analyses demonstrating how deeply social class divides members of the same race or nation or how appeals to upholding traditional ethnicity may carry a gender bias.

Conclusion

Contemporary sociological theory is enormously diverse and multifaceted. It includes macroscopic studies of the structures of power, production, and trade that link and separate countries. It includes studies of interpersonal relations that emphasize both the process of communication and the formal structure of networks. And it includes a variety of levels of analysis in between.

No single theory or perspective is dominant. Contemporary sociological theory includes a variety of contending but also often complementary perspectives and is informed by work in various neighboring disciplines and interdisciplinary fields. While any particular sociologist may make more use of feminist theory or rational choice theory or some other specific approach in his or her analyses, almost all draw on several theoretical traditions. These include both classical and more recent theoretical writings. Indeed, all contemporary theories draw on some combination of classical influences, though some of today's theorists follow more in the line of Marx, others Weber, and still others Durkheim or Mead.

That different theories can complement each other doesn't mean that they always fit neatly together. On the contrary, theories often start with different assumptions about human nature, or about the nature of knowledge (epistemology); they frequently focus on different levels of social reality. These differences mean that fitting them together in any specific analysis always requires creative work and decisions. Theory is something to do, not simply to read. The theoretical resources available to today's sociologists are enormous, but this doesn't mean that theoretical work can stop.

Notes

1   Jürgen Habermas, *The Theory of Communicative Action* (Boston: Beacon, 1984, 1988; 2 vols.).
2   Jeffrey Alexander, *Neofunctionalism and After* (Cambridge, MA: Blackwell, 1998).
3   John Maynard Keynes, *General Theory of Employment, Interest, and Money* (New York: Harvest, orig. 1935).
4   T. H. Marshall, *Citizenship and Social Class* (London: Pluto, 1970; orig. 1950).
5   Barrington Moore, *Social Origins of Dictatorship and Democracy* (Boston: Beacon, 1966).

6   Immanuel Wallerstein, *The Modern World System*, vol. 1 (New York: Academic Press, 1974).

7   Erving Goffman, *The Presentation of Self in Everyday Life* (New York: Doubleday, 1961).

8   Daniel Bell, *The Coming of Post-Industrial Society* (New York: Basic Books, 1974).

9   Philip Rieff, *The Triumph of the Therapeutic* (Chicago: University of Chicago Press, 1987).

10   Herbert Marcuse, *One-Dimensional Man* (Boston: Beacon, 1964).

11   Howard Becker, *Outsiders: Studies in the Sociology of Deviance* (New York: Free Press, 1963); Edwin Lemert, *Social Pathology* (New York: McGraw-Hill, 1951).

12   Alfred Schutz, *Phenomenology of the Social World* (Evanston, IL: Northwestern University Press, 1960).

13   Peter Berger and Thomas Luckmann, *The Social Construction of Knowledge* (New York: New American Library, 1967).

14   Richard Rorty clarifies the difference between pragmatism and more conventional philosophical epistemology in *Philosophy and the Mirror of Nature* (Princeton: Princeton University Press, 1977).

15   As we considered in *Classical Sociological Theory*, the sister volume to this reader, this was an important theme for the critical theory of Max Horkheimer and Theodor Adorno, e.g., *Dialectic of Enlightenment* (New York: Herder and Herder, 1972; orig. 1946). This enjoyed a surge of popularity in the 1960s and '70s.

16   Michel Foucault, *Discipline and Punish* (New York: Pantheon, 1977) and *The Order of Things* (New York: Random House, 1966) among many other works.

17   Michel Foucault, *The History of Sexuality* (New York: Pantheon, 1976–88, 3 vols.).

18   See François Dosse, *History of Structuralism* (Minneapolis: University of Minnesota Press, 1997). Though related, this is distinct from the structural approach to the study of social relationships and networks prominent among American sociologists (see below).

19   Emile Durkheim, *The Elementary Forms of Religious Life* (Glencoe, IL: Free Press, 1976; orig. 1912).

20   Ludwig Wittgenstein, *Philosophical Investigations* (Englewood Cliffs, NJ: Prentice-Hall, 1999).

21   Claude Lévi-Strauss, *Structural Anthropology* (New York: Basic Books, 1970); *The Raw and the Cooked* (Chicago: University of Chicago Press, 1967).

22   Pierre Bourdieu, *Outline of a Theory of Practice* (Cambridge: Cambridge University Press, 1976); *Practical Reason* (Stanford: Stanford University Press, 1998).

23   Pierre Bourdieu, *Distinction* (Cambridge, MA: Harvard University Press, 1984); *The Rules of Art* (Stanford: Stanford University Press, 1996).

24   W. I. Thomas and Florian Znaniecki, *The Polish Peasant in Europe and America* (Urbana: University of Illinois Press, 1995).

25   See especially W. E. B. Du Bois, *The Souls of Black Folk* (New York: Dover, 1989; orig. 1903).

26   Talcott Parsons, *The Social System* (Glencoe, IL: Free Press, 1951); Anthony Giddens, "The Concept of 'Power' in the Writings of Talcott Parsons," in *Studies in Social and Political Theory* (New York: Basic Books, orig. 1967).

27   In the words of Kingsley Davis and W. E. Moore, "Social inequality is … an unconsciously evolved device by which societies ensure that the most important positions are conscientiously filled by the most qualified persons," "Some Principles of Stratification," *American Sociological Review* 10(2) (1945): 242–9, p. 48.

28   This is the basic premise of critical theory in contrast to what is often called "positivism." See Craig Calhoun, "The Critical Dimension in Social Theory," in Jonathan Turner, ed., *Sociological Theory Today* (Beverly Hills: Sage).

29 See, for an influential theoretical synthesis of this line of analysis, Michael Omi and Howard Winant, *Racial Formation in the United States* (New York: Routledge, 1994, 2nd edn.).

30 This focus had its own classics to draw on, of course, including not least of all Margaret Mead's *Sex and Temperament in Three Primitive Societies* (New York: Morrow, 1988; orig. 1935).

31 Stephanie Coontz, *The Way We Never Were* (New York, 1992).

32 US Bureau of the Census, preliminary reports on the US Census for 2000; *Statistical Abstract of the United States, 2000*. Note that these statistics involve a fairly strict definition of the nuclear family – two parents living together with children. While this arrangement has become less common it still reflects a social ideal. Moreover, alternatives are not simply "non-families" but different arrangements: single parents with children; married couples who live with one or more of their parents, etc.

33 Dorothy E. Smith, *The Conceptual Practices of Power* (Boston: Northeastern University Press, 1990).

34 For a critique of the confusion of development with evolution, see Robert Nisbet, *Social Change and History* (New York: Oxford University Press, 1969).

35 See notably W. W. Rostow, *The Stages of Economic Growth* (Cambridge: Cambridge University Press, 1960).

36 Frédéric Le Play, *L'Organisation de la famille selon le vrai modèle signalé par l'histoire de toutes les races et de tous les temps* (Tours: Mame, 1870).

37 Auguste Comte, *The Positive Philosophy* (New York: AMS Press, 1987).

38 Herbert Spencer, *The Principles of Sociology* (New Brunswick, NJ: Transaction Publishers, 2001).

39 Charles Darwin, *The Origin of Species* (New York: Viking, 1982).

40 Emile Durkheim, *Suicide* (New York: Free Press, 1951; orig. 1897).

41 Max Weber, "Die ländliche Arbeitsverfassung," in *Gesammelte Aufsätze zur Sozial- und Wirtschaftsgeschichte* (Tubingen: J. C. B. Mohr, 1924).

42 George Herbert Mead, "The Child and His Environment," *Transactions of the Illinois Society for Child-Study* 3 (1898): 1–11.

43 See Stephen M. Stigler, *The History of Statistics: The Measurement of Uncertainty before 1900* (Cambridge, MA: Harvard University Press, 1990).

44 C. Wright Mills, *The Sociological Imagination* (Harmondsworth: Penguin, 1959).

45 Robert M. Merton, *Social Theory and Social Structure* (Glencoe, IL: Free Press, third edn., 1968).

46 Peter M. Blau, *Exchange and Power in Social Life* (New York: Wiley, 1964); George C. Homans, *Social Behavior: Its Elementary Forms* (New York: Harcourt, Brace, and World, 1961).

47 The single most influential and broadly developed sociological contribution to rational choice theory is James Coleman's *Foundations of Social Theory* (Cambridge, MA: Harvard University Press, 1990).

48 Alvin Gouldner, "The Norm of Reciprocity," *American Sociological Review* 25 (1960): 161–78.

49 Pierre Bourdieu, *The Logic of Practice* (Stanford: Stanford University Press, 1988; orig. 1980).

50 Paul Gilroy, *Against Race: Imagining Political Culture beyond the Color Line* (Cambridge, MA: Harvard University Press, 2000), p. 206.

Part I

Micro-Sociological Analysis

INTRODUCTION TO PART I

Social life is part of every individual and every interaction, not only of the large-scale affairs of governments, economies, and complex organizations. Sociology that focuses primarily on persons and interpersonal relations is called "micro-sociology." This can be relevant on a large scale. How members of a corporation's board of directors interact, for example, can determine whether 10,000 people lose their jobs or an entire country experiences economic crisis. Micro-decisions, each small in itself, can also be aggregated to have huge effects. For example, individuals or families make decisions to have children or to migrate and these create population explosions or brain drain. Even without attention to their large-scale effects, though, micro-sociological phenomena matter to each of us because we can see their effects on the people involved. Indeed, it is often easiest for us to see ourselves in the "micro" part of sociology.

There are many different approaches to micro-sociological analysis. Perhaps the most prominent is symbolic interactionism, developed on the basis of work by George Herbert Mead in the early twentieth century. Herbert Blumer was its most important pioneer. This approach emphasizes the ways in which people develop their own identities and their senses of how society works and what constitutes fair play in the course of people's interaction with each other. It is linked theoretically to the pragmatist school of American philosophy, which emphasizes the ways in which not only social order but all knowledge is achieved in practically situated action.

A second major line of micro-sociological analysis is rooted in the European philosophical tradition called phenomenology. This emphasizes close observation of human experience and especially the ways in which the basic categories of understanding are formed. This has been developed directly in the social phenomenology of Alfred Schutz and followers like Peter Berger and Thomas Luckmann, and has been a major influence on "ethnomethodology," an approach developed especially by Harold Garfinkel and colleagues in California. Ethnomethodology refers to the methods ordinary people use to construct their own everyday understandings of social life, confronting practical challenges and shaping reality through the ways in which they conceptualize it. In this sense, it is a bottom-up rather than top-down approach to the study of culture (*ethnos*).

Still a third approach reveals some similarities to each of the others but is also distinct. This is the idiosyncratic but highly influential sociology of Erving Goffman. Goffman built his approach to micro-analysis on the basis of Durkheim's social theory, trying to show the ways in which the sort of large-scale phenomena Durkheim analyzed were produced and reproduced in interpersonal interaction. Much interaction is ritualized, he suggested, in ways that make it reinforce the social order and prevent it from becoming highly disruptive. Goffman also developed theoretical approaches to aspects of communication, institutional analysis, and perhaps most famously the presentation of self in everyday life – the ways in which we show ourselves to others (and simultaneously determine which aspects are visible and which hidden).

Challenges of Micro-Sociological Analysis

Micro-sociological theory grew, in large part, as a counterpoint to the dominance of structural functionalism in the mid-twentieth century, although its antecedents had been present in sociological theory, and in philosophy, far earlier. Structural functionalism, and the Durkheimian tradition in sociology more generally, focused on the social system as a whole, its functional requirements, and the ways that these requirements are met (see Part VI of *Classical Sociological Theory*, the sister volume to this reader). In doing so, it tended to treat human agents as cogs in the machine of social forces. Even the early work of Talcott Parsons, which was greatly concerned with social action, was more clearly about action *systems* than about *actors* and their subjective orientation to the action at hand and to the other actors it involved.

Micro-sociologists, by contrast, emphasized the other side of social existence. Just as humans are shaped by the social system in which they act, the micro-sociologists emphasized that the social system was also a human creation. Rather than order being imposed on individuals by the system, micro-sociologists see social order as produced from below – either as an emergent phenomenon produced through human interaction or as the result of discrete, self-interested action and exchange. It is created and maintained, they claim, by the institutions that we actively produce, even when we are not aware of them. Because of this, society itself rests on the ability of human agents to communicate with one another through the use of symbols to signify particular meanings. This highly evolved capacity for communication based on complex, abstract symbolic systems, is, in fact, one of the features that distinguish humans from other species. Although there are different theoretical traditions in micro-sociology, some of which will be discussed more fully below, in a general sense it can be said that micro-sociology is characterized by at least three common elements.

First, micro-sociologists place emphasis on the face-to-face social interaction of human agents rather than on the workings of the social system as an abstract entity. It is not quite correct to say that they focus on individuals, since it is really the creation and maintenance of stable systems of meaning *between* individuals that micro-sociologists find fascinating. But it is correct to say that micro-sociologists generally focus on the interactions of concrete human agents or sets of agents rather than abstract social units such as classes.

Second, micro-sociologists place emphasis on meanings rather than functions. Here the influences of Max Weber and George Herbert Mead are evident in later micro-sociology. For Weber, sociology was the study of social action. Because it is individuals that carry on social action, Weber stressed that sociology had to be an interpretive science. That is, we should strive to provide *objective* accounts of the *subjective* motivations of the actions of individuals. Doing this necessarily involved taking into account the meanings that people assigned to their actions. Weber's own empirical analyses tended to examine highly routine forms of social action however. Later micro-sociologists began to examine the way that even everyday interactions are supported by the meanings produced and maintained in social interaction. Here Mead's emphasis on the role of verbal and non-verbal symbols in the creation of meaning became central to micro-sociology. Although we are all born with the capacity to interpret symbols, it is only through the use of such symbols in inter-action that humans acquire a "self" – a sense of who we are in the world. In this way, the micro-sociologists stress the *intersubjective* aspects of human existence.

Third, micro-sociologists emphasize lived experience rather than an abstracted (or reified) concept of "society." The authors in this section generally grant that social institutions, once produced, confront us as external and "objective" realities. Never-theless, they focus on the way that human agents experience regularized patterns of social interaction (or "institutions") and how they support them in both big and small ways. The exchange of symbols allows us to form solidarity with others by allowing us to come to common definitions of the world. Even seemingly banal social institutions such as greeting rituals have important symbolic meanings. As the sociologist Harold Garfinkel showed, we rarely recognize the importance of such institutions until they break down.[1] When we cannot take such minor routines for granted in our interactions, we have to do a great deal of interpretive work to figure out how to understand each interaction we face. Additionally, as the readings below will argue, our past experiences matter in how we interpret the world. This is why people who meet for the first time, especially when they come from very different backgrounds, have to spend so much more energy to understand one another than the people who see each other every day.

The Development of Micro-Sociological Analysis

Micro-sociology did not develop all at once, and it did not all develop in the same way. While the core concerns of the authors presented below are common enough to warrant including them in one section, we must take some care to note some of the different traditions of micro-sociological analysis as well. Loosely speaking, the authors in this section may be grouped under three headings – phenomenology, symbolic interactionism, and the "dramaturgical" approach of Erving Goffman.

Phenomenology is the oldest of the traditions. Originally a branch of social philosophy, its modern form was related to the existentialist thought of Kierkegaard, Heidegger, and later Sartre. It became a more properly sociological tradition with the work of Alfred Schutz (1899–1959) and others. Sociological versions of phe-nomenology were influenced by several sources, including Marx and the Frankfurt School critical theorists (see Parts I and V of *Classical Sociological Theory*). Schutz's version, unquestionably the most prominent, was deeply influenced by Weber's conception of a sociology based on interpretive understanding, as will become clear in the reading included here.

In all its forms, phenomenology was concerned with an old question – what makes things knowable? Phenomenologists were strongly concerned with the idea of "situatedness" in the world, claiming that the possibility for knowledge was based in empirical sensory perception, rather than in abstract categories of knowledge such as general conceptions of "Man" (in the case of some versions of philosophy) or "society" (in the case of some sociological traditions).

Schutz emphasized the everyday world of lived experience, which is predicated first on our physical being and therefore our sensory knowledge of the world, but secondly on the socially constructed concepts that we use to organize and interpret our experiences. The reading provided here, from his key work *The Phenomenology of the Social World* (1967 [1932]), is most centrally concerned with the concept of "intersubjective understanding." Schutz argues that subjectivity is not just something that is isolated in individuals; rather it grows in social relationships. To illustrate the problem of how we understand another person, Schutz revisits a famous example from Weber of a man cutting wood. To know what the woodcutter is doing, we have to make an interpretive leap – to put ourselves in his place, as it were, by drawing on our past experience. This process is much facilitated by the use of language and other meaningful signs. Such signs are conventions that act as a sort of bridge between minds, allowing people to connect their own experiences to those of others. Once created and put into use, they act as data that allow us to interpret others' meaning and motives. Schutz notes that such communication is also crucial to our reflective understanding of ourselves – we are not consciously aware of our own motives until we try to interpret them as we would interpret those of another person.

The work of Peter Berger (b. 1929) and Thomas Luckmann (b. 1927) also stemmed from the phenomenological tradition, and extended some of Schutz's ideas in a manner intended to engage an English-speaking sociological audience of the 1960s, more familiar with Parsonian functionalism than with Husserl. The reading included in this section is from their book *The Social Construction of Reality: A Treatise in the Sociology of Knowledge* (1966). The key term in this reading is "institutionalization," which the authors distinguish from "habitualization," a more properly individual process. Habitualization happens when an individual actor develops a set process for dealing with a situation that he or she faces many times. Institutionalization, they claim, occurs with reciprocal habituation among many actors. Thus, institutions are produced and maintained by human agents. As social creations, institutions always have a history, and are always bound up with social control, the authors claim.

This claim is particularly important when contrasted with functionalist work, which treated institutions as properties of an abstract social-system level, which met equally abstract social needs. Rather than proposing an equally one-sided "subjective" account to counter this "objective" vision, they attempt to show how micro-processes can lead to macro-level order. Berger and Luckmann argue that institutions may grow to possess a reality of their own, at which point social actors experience them as objective realities. But they are nevertheless human products. As they put it, "*Society is a human product. Society is an objective reality. Man is a social product.*"

The second major tradition of micro-sociology represented in this section is known as symbolic interactionism, a term coined by Herbert Blumer (1900–87). For much of his career a professor at the University of Chicago, Blumer's work was deeply indebted to Mead, as well as to his colleagues Robert E. Park and W. I. Thomas. Particularly important for Blumer was Mead's emphasis on the role of symbols in the maintenance of social interaction and the constitution of the self as a social process. In the same manner as Schutz's phenomenology, symbolic interactionists placed a strong emphasis on empiricism rather than the social realism typified by Durkheimian and functionalist sociology.

The reading included here is from Blumer's best-known work, *Symbolic Interactionism* (1969). Blumer begins by defining symbolic interaction as an approach that studies the "natural world of human group life and human conduct." The reading uses this concept of "naturalistic" studies of social life to issue an extremely sharp critique of functionalist methods. Nestled within this critique is Blumer's statement about how social analysis ought to be done. Blumer lays out four central claims: people act in relation to things and other people on the basis of the meanings attached to them; human interaction ("association") is necessary for the making of meaning; social acts are necessarily embedded therefore in an interpretive process; and because of this, social networks and institutions are inherently fluid, and are always being renegotiated to some extent.

The work of Erving Goffman (1922–82) is often considered to be part of the tradition of symbolic interactionism (and indeed, "symbolic interactionism" is often used misleadingly as a term for almost all micro-sociological analysis). Goffman's graduate work at Chicago overlapped with the last part of Blumer's stay there, and Goffman later joined Blumer as a colleague at Berkeley.[2] Nevertheless, Goffman built a body of work distinct from that of Blumer, and indeed distinct from just about everything else in the discipline. His work emphasized how people used symbols in the performance of their social roles. This is often called the "dramaturgical approach" because it suggests that people are always staging their performances for others, and analyzes how such performances play out to others. A central concern of Goffman's work is the tactical repertoire that actors develop in order to manage their social identities and to defend themselves from unwanted scrutiny and the negative appraisal of others. Sometimes this leads them to act together, as when members of a group put on a team performance to gain what they want from others or when those sharing a common "stigma" (or a marker of an undesirable social identity) frame themselves in less damaging terms.

Like the other authors in this section, Goffman focused on the way that human social interaction makes the social possible. But in contrast to the other authors in this section, Goffman had a certain affinity with the work of Durkheim. He saw himself as a sort of Durkheimian working on the "micro" side of the social equation. More than any of the other authors in this section, Goffman emphasized the importance of integration in the social process. To be an actor on the social stage requires not only that one claim a role, but that others recognize the claim, grant it, and act accordingly. Goffman also emphasized the fact that social performances serve broader functional needs. Our performances are done in such a way as to keep social life going smoothly. For example, even when we fail, others are likely to overlook our mistakes so as not to disrupt everyone's performances.

The reading included here is from *The Presentation of Self in Everyday Life* (1959). One of the central concepts in the reading is that of "front" – the part of a person's performance that serves to define a relevant context for the "audience." It therefore includes the props that go along with the physical setting, as well as the clothes, manners, and other symbols that can be used to corroborate the impression that one wishes to convey. The concept is important for pointing out not only the way that performances are realized, but also the degree to which they are situational. For example, it is easy for a person to put on a convincing performance as a serious professor or a diligent student in the context of a classroom – but it is difficult and awkward to maintain the same relation when the professor and the student notice each other in a supermarket or in a tavern.

Legacy of micro-sociological analysis

All the different approaches to micro-sociological analysis presented here remain active in contemporary sociology. They are sometimes joined with each other, or with various macro-sociological theories. For example, in developing Marx's theory of alienation, several sociologists have drawn on social phenomenology. Jürgen Habermas relies significantly on symbolic interactionism in his theory of communicative action and how it shapes modern law and politics (see Part VIII of this volume). Pierre Bourdieu has drawn on ethnomethodology and especially the work of Erving Goffman in his theory of social practice (Part VI). Ethnomethodology also informs Anthony Giddens' analyses of reflexive modernization with its new consciousness of risk and new kinds of individualism (Part V). The various micro-analytic approaches have also influenced theories that are not specifically either macro or micro. Feminism and gender studies, for example, have benefited from symbolic interactionism and especially the analysis of "otherness" developed in that tradition (Part VII). Another example is the importance of Blumer's work for exchange theory (Part II).

The micro-sociological theories are especially influential in the tradition of qualitative sociology. This refers mainly to methodological approaches that emphasize direct communication with social actors and observation of everyday social life. Ethnography, participant observation, interviews and other methodological strategies are all examples. A key link to the micro-sociological theories presented in this section is that these methods are used most often when sociologists want to develop analyses that make sense of the ways in which ordinary people understand their lives and the social world. This need not mean claiming that everyone already understands social interaction adequately, or that everyday concepts can serve without modification as scientific ones. But it does mean trying to grasp how everyday understanding and concepts work and how actors help to shape the reality in which they act.

Notes

1   Garfinkel (1967).
2   Ritzer (1996: 74).

Select Bibliography

Berger, Peter and Thomas Luckmann. 1966. *The Social Construction of Reality: A Treatise in the Sociology of Knowledge.* New York: Doubleday Anchor. (Applies the methods of Schutz's phenomenology to problems in the sociology of knowledge. This has been one of the most important introductions to social phenomenology for English-language readers.)
Blumer, Herbert. 1969. *Symbolic Interactionism: Perspective and Method.* Englewood Cliffs, NJ: Prentice-Hall. (Blumer's own introductory overview to the approach he helped to create.)

Collins, Randall. 1981. "On the Micro-foundations of Macro-sociology," *American Journal of Sociology* 80: 984–1014. (A classic article on the ways in which micro-sociological analysis can support larger scale theory-building.)

Coulter, Jeff. 1989. *Mind in Action.* (Provides a useful link between ethnomethodology and cognitive approaches to sociological analysis.)

Fine, Gary Alan, James B. House, and Karen Cook. 1995. *Sociological Perspectives on Social Psychology.* Boston: Allyn and Bacon. (Includes chapters on each of the theories presented here, and on different themes in which they are important.)

Garfinkel, Harold. 1967. *Studies in Ethnomethodology.* Englewood Cliffs, NJ: Prentice-Hall. (The classic foundation of ethnomethodology, based on several case studies of disruptions in the established order of mutual understanding. Some of these were produced by Garfinkel's famous "breeching method" of introducing clashes of categories.)

Goffman, Erving. 1959. *The Presentation of Self in Everyday Life.* New York: Anchor. (Probably Goffman's most famous book, a fascinating account of the ways in which people seek – consciously – to control the ways in which other people see them.)

Goffman, Erving. 1982. *Interaction Ritual: Essays on Face-to-Face Behavior.* New York: Pantheon. (Contains several of Goffman's most famous studies in the ways interpersonal interaction is socially organized.)

Goffman, Erving. 1988. *Frame Analysis: An Essay on the Organization of Experience.* (One of Goffman's last major books, finished with the help of Bennett Berger, this provides an approach to studying the ways in which experience is structured by the frames – social or "natural" – through which we grasp it.)

Joas, Hans. 1997. *G. H. Mead: A Contemporary Re-Examination of His Thought.* Cambridge, MA: MIT Press. (The most substantial reinterpretation and representation of Mead's thought and the theoretical foundations of symbolic interactionism for modern readers.)

Manning, Philip. 1993. *Erving Goffman and Modern Sociology.* Stanford: Stanford University Press. (A brief but clear introductory overview of Goffman's thought and legacy.)

Ritzer, George. 1996. *Modern Sociological Theory*, 4th edn. New York: McGraw Hill.

Schutz, Alfred. 1967. *The Phenomenology of the Social World.* Evanston, IL: Northwestern University Press. (The major synthetic statement of Schutz's approach to the basic categories through which we gain consciousness of the social world.)

Schutz, Alfred and Thomas Luckmann. 1989. *The Structures of the Lifeworld.* (Schutz and his most important student collaborate to present a phenomenological approach to the world of direct experience in everyday life.)

Stryker, Sheldon. 1980. *Symbolic Interactionism: A Social Structural Version.* Menlo Park, CA: Benjamin Cummings. (An attempt to connect micro- and macro-order based on symbolic interactions.)

1 The Phenomenology of the Social World

Alfred Schutz

The Ambiguities in the Ordinary Notion of Understanding the Other Person

Before we proceed further, it would be well to note that there are ambiguities in the ordinary notion of understanding another person. Sometimes what is meant is intentional Acts directed toward the other self; in other words, my lived experiences of you. At other times what is in question is *your* subjective experiences. Then, the arrangements of all such experiences into meaning-contexts (Weber's comprehension of intended meaning) is sometimes called "understanding of the other self," as is the classification of others' behavior into motivation contexts. The number of ambiguities associated with the notion of "understanding another person" becomes even greater when we bring in the question of understanding the signs he is using. On the one hand, what is understood is the sign itself, then again *what* the other person means by using this sign, and finally the significance of the fact *that* he is using the sign, here, now, and in this particular context. . . .

The Nature of Genuine Intersubjective Understanding

Having established that all genuine understanding of the other person must start out from Acts of explication performed by the observer on his own lived experience, we must now proceed to a precise analysis of this genuine understanding itself. From the examples we have already given, it is clear that our inquiry must take two different directions. First we must study the genuine understanding of actions which are performed *without any communicative intent*. The action of the woodcutter would be a good example. Second we would examine cases where such communicative intent was present. The latter type of action involves a whole new dimension, the using and interpreting of signs.

Let us first take actions performed without any communicative intent. We are watching a man in the act of cutting wood and wondering what is going on in his mind. Questioning him is ruled out, because that would require entering into a social relationship with him, which in turn would involve the use of signs.

Let us further suppose that we know nothing about our woodcutter except what we see before our eyes. By subjecting our own perceptions to interpretation, we know that we are in the presence of a fellow human being and that his bodily movements indicate he is engaged in an action which we recognize as that of cutting wood.

Originally translated by George Walsh and Frederick Lehnert.

Now how do we know what is going on in the woodcutter's mind? Taking this interpretation of our own perceptual data as a starting point, we can plot out in our mind's eye exactly how *we* would carry out the action in question. Then we can actually imagine ourselves doing so. In cases like this, then, we project the other person's goal as if it were our own and fancy ourselves carrying it out. Observe also that we here project the action in the future perfect tense as completed and that our imagined execution of the action is accompanied by the usual retentions and reproductions of the project, although, of course, only in fancy. Further, let us note that the imagined execution may fulfill or fail to fulfill the imagined project.

Or, instead of imagining for ourselves an action wherein we carry out the other person's goal, we may recall in concrete detail how we once carried out a similar action ourselves. Such a procedure would be merely a variation on the same principle.

In both these cases, we put ourselves in the place of the actor and identify our lived experiences with his. It might seem that we are here repeating the error of the well-known "projective" theory of empathy. For here we are reading our own lived experiences into the other person's mind and are therefore only discovering our own experiences. But, if we look more closely, we will see that our theory has nothing in common with the empathy theory except for one point. This is the general thesis of the Thou as the "other I," the one whose experiences are constituted in the same fashion as mine. But even this similarity is only apparent, for we start out from the general thesis of the other person's flow of duration, while the projective theory of empathy jumps from the mere fact of empathy to the belief in other minds by an act of blind faith. Our theory only brings out the implications of what is already present in the self-explicative judgment "I am experiencing a fellow human being." We know with certainty that the other person's subjective experience of his own action is in principle different from our own imagined picture of what we would do in the same situation. The reason, as we have already pointed out, is that the intended meaning of an action is always in principle subjective and accessible only to the actor. The error in the empathy theory is twofold. First, it naïvely tries to trace back the constitution of the other self within the ego's consciousness to empathy, so that the latter becomes the direct source of knowledge of the other. Actually, such a task of discovering the constitution of the other self can only be carried out in a transcendentally phenomenological manner. Second, it pretends to a knowledge of the other person's mind that goes far beyond the establishment of a structural parallelism between that mind and my own. In fact, however, when we are dealing with actions having no communicative intent, all that we can assert about their meaning is already contained in the general thesis of the alter ego.

It is clear, then, that we imaginatively project the in-order-to motive of the other person as if it were our own and then use the fancied carrying-out of such an action as a scheme in which to interpret his lived experiences. However, to prevent misunderstanding, it should be added that what is involved here is only a reflective analysis of another person's completed act. It is an interpretation carried out after the fact. When an observer is directly watching someone else to whom he is attuned in simultaneity, the situation is different. Then the observer's living intentionality carries him along without having to make constant playbacks of his own past or imaginary experiences. The other person's action unfolds step by step before his eyes. In such a situation, the identification of the observer with the observed person is not carried out by starting with the goal of the act as already given and then proceeding to reconstruct the lived experiences which must have accompanied it. Instead, the observer keeps pace, as it were, with each step of the observed person's action, identifying himself with the latter's experiences within a common "we-relationship." We shall have much more to say about this later.

So far we have assumed the other person's bodily movement as the only datum given to the observer. It must be emphasized that, if the bodily movement is taken by itself in this way, it is necessarily isolated from its place within the stream of the observed person's living experience. And this context is important not only to the observed person but to the observer as well. He can, of course, if he lacks other data, take a mental snapshot of the observed bodily movement and then try to fit it into a phantasied filmstrip in accordance with the way he thinks he would act and feel in a similar situation. However, the observer can draw much more reliable conclusions about his subject if he knows something about his past and something about the over-all plan into which this action fits. To come back to Max Weber's example, it would be important for the observer to know whether the woodcutter was at his regular job or just chopping wood for physical exercise. An adequate model of the observed person's subjective experiences calls for just this wider context. We have already seen, indeed, that the unity of the action is a function of the project's span. From the observed bodily movement, all the observer can infer is the single course of action which has directly led to it. If, however, I as the observer wish to avoid an inadequate interpretation of what I see another person doing, I must "make my own" all those meaning-contexts which make sense of this action on the basis of my past knowledge of this particular person. We shall come back later on to this concept of "inadequacy" and show its significance for the theory of the understanding of the other person.

Meaning-Establishment and Meaning-Interpretation

We have now seen that the sign has two different functions. First it has a *significative function*. By this we mean that it can be ordered by an interpreter within a previously learned sign system of his own. What he is doing here is interpreting the sign as an item of his own experience. His act is just another example of what we call self-interpretation. But there is a second kind of interpretation in which he can engage. He can inquire into the subjective and occasional meaning of the sign, in short, the *expressive* function which it acquires within the context of discourse. This subjective meaning can be his own, in which case he must go back in memory to the experiences he had at the moment of using the sign and establishing its meaning. Or it can be someone else's, in which case he must try to find out about the other person's subjective experiences when *he* used the sign. But in any case, when interpreting signs used by others, we will find two components involved, the objective and the subjective. Objective meaning is the meaning of the sign as such, the kernel, so to speak; whereas subjective meaning is the fringe or aura emanating from the subjective context in the mind of the sign-user.

Let us take a conversation between two people as an example. As one person speaks, thoughts are building up in his mind, and his listener is following him every step of the way just as the thoughts occur. In other words, none of the thoughts come out as prefabricated unities. They are constructed gradually, and they are interpreted gradually. Both speaker and listener live through the conversation in such a manner that on each side Acts of meaning-establishment or meaning-interpretation are filled in and shaded with memories of what has been said and anticipations of what is yet to be said. Each of these Acts can in turn be focused upon introspectively and analyzed as a unit in itself. The meaning of the speaker's discourse consists for him *and* for his listener in his individual sentences and these, in turn, in their component words as they come, one after another. The sentences for both of them serve as the meaning-contexts of the words, and the whole discourse as the meaning-context of the separate sentences.

Understanding the conscious Acts of another person who is communicating by means of signs does not differ in principle from understanding his other Acts. Like the latter, it occurs in the mode of simultaneity or quasi-simultaneity. The interpreter puts himself in the place of the other person and imagines that he himself is selecting and using the signs. He interprets the other person's subjective meaning as if it were his own. In the process he draws upon his whole personal knowledge of the speaker, especially the latter's ways and habits of expressing himself. Such personal knowledge continues to build itself up in the course of a conversation.

The same process goes on in the mind of the speaker. His words will be selected with a view to being understood by his listener. And the meaning he seeks to get across will not only be objective meaning, for he will seek to communicate his personal attitude as well. He will sketch out his communicative aim in the future perfect tense, just as he does the project of any other act. His choice of words will depend on the habits he has built up in interpreting the words of others, but it will, of course, also be influenced by his knowledge of his listener.

However, if the speaker is focused on what is going on in the mind of his listener, his knowledge of the latter is still quite uncertain. He can only estimate how much he is actually getting across. Any such estimate is necessarily vague, especially considering the fact that the listener's interpretation is always subsequent to the choice of words and fulfills or fails to fulfill the speaker's project in making that choice.

The listener is in a different position. For him the actual establishment of the meaning of the words has already occurred. He can start out with the objective meaning of the words he has heard and from there try to discover the subjective meaning of the speaker. In order to arrive at that subjective meaning, he imagines the project which the speaker must have had in mind. However, this picturing of the project starts out from the speaker's already spoken words. Contrary to the case of the speaker who is picturing something future on the basis of something present, the listener is picturing something pluperfect on the basis of something past. Another difference is that he is starting from words which have either succeeded or failed in fulfilling the speaker's project, and he is trying to uncover that project. The speaker, on the other hand, starts out with his own project as datum and tries to estimate whether it is going to be fulfilled by the listener's future interpretation.

Now since the words chosen by the speaker may or may not express his meaning, the listener can always doubt whether he is understanding the speaker adequately.

The project of the speaker is always a matter of imaginative reconstruction for his interpreter and so is attended by a certain vagueness and uncertainty.

To illustrate what we mean, consider the fact that, in a conversation, thoughts like the following may run through the heads of the participants. The person about to speak will say to himself, "Assuming that this fellow speaks my kind of language, I must use such and such words." A moment later his listener will be saying to himself, "If this other fellow is using words the way I understand them, then he must be telling me such and such." The first statement shows how the speaker always chooses his words with the listener's interpretation in mind. The second statement shows how the listener always interprets with the speaker's subjective meaning in mind. In either case an intentional reference to the other person's scheme is involved, regardless of whether the scheme is interpretive or expressive.

As the speaker chooses his words, he uses, of course, his own interpretive scheme. This depends partly upon the way he himself usually interprets words and partly upon his knowledge of his listener's interpretive habits. When I read over a letter I have written to someone, I tend to interpret it just as if I were the receiver and not the sender. Now, my purpose in writing the letter was not merely to communicate an objective meaning to the reader but my subjective meaning as well. To put it in another way, I want him to rethink my thoughts. It may very well be, therefore, that when I read over my letter I shall decide that it falls short of this purpose. Knowing the person to whom I am writing and knowing his customary reactions to certain words and phrases, I may decide that this or that expression is open to misinterpretation or that he will not really be in a position to understand this or that thought of mine. Or I may fear that he will, as he reads, miss the point I am trying to make due to some subjective bias or some failure of attention on his part.

On the other hand, the recipient of the letter can carry out the opposite process. He can take a sentence and imagine that he himself wrote it. He can try to reconstruct the intention of the writer by guessing at some possible intentions and then comparing them with the actual propositional content of the sentence. He may conclude, "I see what he was trying to say, but he really missed his mark and said something else. If I had been he, I should have put it in such and such a way." Or the reader may say to himself instead, "My friend always uses that term in an odd way, but I see what he means, since I know the way he thinks. It's lucky that I am the one reading the letter. A third party would have been thrown off the track entirely at this point." In the last case, the reader really carries out a threefold interpretation. First, he interprets the sentence objectively on the basis of his ordinary habits of interpretation. Second, from his knowledge of the writer, he reconstructs what must be the latter's real meaning. Third, he imagines how the ordinary reader would understand the sentence in question.

These considerations hold true quite generally for all cases in which signs are either used or interpreted. This being the case, it ought to be clear that in interpreting the subjective meaning of the signs used by someone else, or in anticipating someone else's interpretation of the subjective meaning of our own signs, we must be guided by our knowledge of that person. Naturally, therefore, the degree of intimacy or anonymity in which the person stands to us will have a great deal to do with the matter. The examples we have just used were all cases where knowledge of the other person was derived from direct contact; they belong to what we call the domain of directly experienced social reality. However, the use and interpretation of signs are to be found in the other areas of social life as well, such as the worlds of contemporaries and of predecessors, where direct knowledge of the people with whom we are dealing is minimal or even absent. Our theory of the establishment and interpretation of the meaning of signs will naturally undergo various modifications as it is applied to these areas. Even in the direct social relations we have used as examples, it was obviously impossible for the participants to "carry out the postulate of grasping each other's intended meaning," a point that we discussed earlier. The subjective meaning that the interpreter *does* grasp is at best an approximation to the sign-user's intended meaning, but never that meaning itself, for one's knowledge of another person's perspective is always necessarily limited. For exactly the same reason, the person who expresses himself in signs is never quite sure of how he is being understood.

What we have been discussing is the content of communication. But we must remember that the actual *communicating* is itself a meaningful act and that we must interpret that act and the way it is done as things in their own right.

The Meaning-Context of Communication. Recapitulation

Once the interpreter has determined both the objective and subjective meanings of the content of any communication, he may proceed to ask why the communication was made in the first place. He is then seeking the in-order-to motive of the person communicating. For it is essential to every act of communication that it have an extrinsic goal. When I say something to you, I do so for a reason, whether to evoke a particular attitude on your part or simply to explain something to you. Every act of communication has, therefore, as its in-order-to motive the aim that the person being addressed take cognizance of it in one way or another.

The person who is the object or recipient of the communication is frequently the one who makes this kind of interpretation. Having settled what are the objective and subjective meanings of the content of the communication by finding the corresponding interpretive or expressive schemes, he proceeds to inquire into the reason why the other person said this in the first place. In short, he seeks the "plan" behind the communication.

However, the seeker of the in-order-to motive need not be the person addressed at all. A nonparticipant observer may proceed to the same kind of interpretation. I can, indeed I must, seek the in-order-to motive of the communication if I am ever to know the goal toward which the communication is leading. Furthermore, it is self-evident that one can seek the in-order-to motives even of those acts of other people which have no communicative intent. What an actor's subjective experience actually is we can only grasp if we find his in-order-to motive. We must first light upon his project and then engage in a play-by-play phantasy of the action which would fulfill it. In the case of action without communicative intent, the completed act itself is properly interpreted as the fulfillment of the in-order-to motive. However, if I happen to know that the completed act is only a link in a chain of means leading to a further end, then what I must do is interpret the subjective experiences the other person has of that further goal itself.

Now, we have already seen that we can go beyond the in-order-to motive and seek out the because-motive. Of course, knowledge of the latter presupposes in every case knowledge of the former. The subjective meaning-context which is the in-order-to motive must first be seen and taken for granted as an already constituted object in itself before any venture into deeper levels is undertaken. To speak of such deeper levels *as existing* by no means implies that the actor actually experiences them subjectively as meaning-contexts of his action. Nor does it mean that he can become aware even retrospectively of those polythetic Acts which, according to my interpretation, have constituted the in-order-to motive. On the contrary, there is every evidence against the view that the actor ever has any awareness of the because-motive of his action. This applies to one who is establishing a meaning as well as to any other actor. To be sure, he lives through the subjective experiences and intentional Acts which I have interpreted as his because-motive. However, he is not as a rule aware of them, and, when he is, it is no longer as actor. Such awareness, when it occurs, is a separate intentional Act independent of and detached from the action it is interpreting. It is then that a man can be said to understand himself. Such self-understanding is essentially the same as understanding others, with this difference – that usually, but not always, we have at our disposal a much richer array of information about ourselves and our past than others do.

Later on we shall describe the relation of the in-order-to motive to the because-motives in the various regions of the social world. At this point we shall merely try to recapitulate the complex structures involved in understanding another person insofar as these bear on communication and the use of signs. For to say, as we do, that for the user of the sign the sign stands in a meaning-context involves a number of separate facts which must be disentangled.

First of all, whenever I make use of a sign, those lived experiences signified by that sign stand for me in a meaning-context. For they have already been constituted into a synthesis, and I look upon them as a unit.

In the second place, for me the sign must already be part of a sign system. Otherwise I would not be able to use it. A sign must already have been interpreted before it can be used. But the understanding of a sign is a complicated synthesis of lived experiences resulting in a special kind of meaning-context. This meaning-context is a configuration involving two elements: the sign as object in itself and the *signatum*, each of which, of course, involves separate meaning-contexts in its own right. The total new meaning-context embracing them both we have called the "coordinating scheme" of the sign.

Third, the Act of selecting and using the sign is a special meaning-context for the sign-user to the extent that each use of a sign is an expressive action. Since every action comprises a meaning-context by virtue of the fact that the actor visualizes all the successive lived experiences of that action as one unified act, it follows that every expressive action is therefore a meaning-context. This does not mean that every case of sign-using is *ipso facto* a case of communication. A person may, talking to himself for instance, use a sign purely as an act of self-expression without any intention of communication.

Fourth, the meaning-context "sign-using as act" can serve as the basis for a superimposed meaning-context "sign-using as communicative act" without in any way taking into account the particular person addressed.

Fifth, however, this superimposed meaning-context can enter into a still higher and wider meaning-context in which the addressee *is* taken into account. In this case the communicating act has as its goal not merely that someone take cognizance of it but that its message should motivate the person cognizing to a particular attitude or piece of behavior.

Sixth, the fact that this particular addressee is communicated with *here, now,* and *in this way* can be placed within a still broader context of meaning by finding the in-order-to motive of that communicative act.

All these meaning-contexts are in principle open to the interpreter and can be uncovered systematically by him. Just which ones he does seek to inquire into will depend upon the kind of interest he has in the sign.

However, the statement that all these meaning-contexts in principle lie open to interpretation requires some modification. As we have said repeatedly, the structure of the social world is by no means homogeneous. Our fellow men and the signs they use can be given to us in different ways. There are different approaches to the sign and to the subjective experience it expresses. Indeed, we do not even need a sign in order to gain access to another person's mind; a mere indication can offer us the opening. This is what happens, for instance, when we draw inferences from artifacts concerning the experiences of people who lived in the past.

Subjective and Objective Meaning. Product and Evidence

We have now seen the different approaches to the genuine understanding of the other self. The interpreter starts with his own experience of the animate body of the other person or of the artifacts which the latter has produced. In either case he is interpreting Objectivations in which the other's subjective experiences manifest themselves. If it is the body of the other that is in question, he concerns himself with act-objectifications, i.e., movements, gestures, or the results of action. If it is artifacts that are in question, these may be either signs in the narrower sense or manufactured external objects such as tools, monuments, etc. All that these Objectivations have in common is that they exist only as the result of the action of rational beings. Because they are products of action, they are *ipso facto* evidence of what went on in the minds of the actors who made them. It should be noted that *not all evidences are signs*, but all signs are evidences. For an evidence to be a sign, it must be capable of becoming an element in a sign system with the status of coordinating scheme. This qualification is lacking in some evidence. A tool, for instance, although it is an evidence of what went on in the mind of its maker, is surely no sign. However, under "evidences" we mean to include not only equipment that has been produced by a manufacturing process, but judgment that has been produced by thought, or the message content which has been produced by an act of communication.

The problematic of subjective and objective meaning includes evidences of all sorts. That is to say, anyone who encounters a given product can proceed to interpret it in two different ways. First, he can focus his attention on its status as an object, either real or ideal, but at any rate independent of its maker. Second, he can look upon it as evidence for what went on in the mind of its makers at the moment it was being made. In the former case the interpreter is subsuming his own experiences (*erfahrende Akte*) of the object under the interpretive schemes which he has at hand. In the latter case, however, his attention directs itself to the constituting Acts of consciousness of the producer (these might be his own as well as those of another person).

This relation between objective and subjective meaning will be examined in a more detailed way at a later point. *We speak, then, of the subjective meaning of the product if we have in view the meaning-context within which the product stands or stood in the mind of the producer. To know the subjective meaning of the product means that we are able to run over in our own minds in simultaneity or quasi-simultaneity the polythetic Acts which constituted the experience of the producer.*

We keep in view, then, the other person's lived experiences as they are occurring; we observe them being constituted step by step. For us, the other person's products are indications of those lived experiences. The lived experiences stand for him, in turn, within a meaning context. We know this by means of a particular evidence, and we can in an act of genuine understanding be aware of the constituting process in his mind.

Objective meaning, on the contrary, we can predicate only of the product as such, that is, of the already constituted meaning-context of the thing produced, whose actual production we meanwhile disregard. The product is, then, in the fullest sense the end result of the process of production, something that is finished and complete. It is no longer part of the process but merely points back to it as an event in the past. The product itself is, however, not an event but an entity (*ein Seiendes*) which is the sediment of past events within the mind of the producer. To be sure, even the interpretation of the objective meaning of the product occurs in step-by-step polythetic Acts. Nevertheless, it is exhausted in the ordering of the interpreter's experiences of the product within the total meaning-context of the interpretive act. And, as we have said, the interpreter leaves the original step-by-step creation of the product quite out of account. It is not that he is unaware that it has occurred; it is just that he pays no attention to it. Objective meaning therefore consists only in a meaning-context within the mind of the interpreter, whereas subjective meaning refers beyond it to a meaning-context in the mind of the producer.

A subjective meaning-context, then, is present if what is given in an objective meaning-context was created as a meaning-context by a Thou on its own part. Nothing, however, is thereby implied either about the particular kind of meaning-context into which the Thou orders its lived experiences or about the quality of those experiences themselves.

We have already noted that the interpreter grasps the other person's conscious experiences in the mode of simultaneity or quasi-simultaneity. Genuine simultaneity is the more frequent, even though it is a special case of the process. It is tied to the world of directly experienced social reality and presupposes that the interpreter witnesses the actual bringing-forth of the product. An example would be a conversation, where the listener is actually present as the speaker performs Acts that bring forth meaningful discourse and where the listener performs these Acts with and after the speaker. A case of quasi-simultaneous interpretation would be the reading of a book. Here the reader relives the author's choice of words as if the choice were made before his very eyes. The same would hold for a person inspecting some artifacts, such as tools, and imagining to himself how they were made. However, in saying that we can observe such subjective experiences on the part of the producer, we only meant that we can grasp the fact *that* they occur. We have said nothing about how we understand *what* experiences occur, nor how we understand *the way* in which they are formed. We shall deal with these problems when we analyze the world of contemporaries, the world of direct social experience, and the world of the genuine We-relationship. Still, it can be said even at this point that what is essential to this further knowledge is a knowledge of the person being interpreted. When we ask what the subjective meaning of a product is, and therefore what conscious experiences another person has, we are asking what particular polythetically constructed lived experiences are occurring or have occurred in a particular other person. This other person, this Thou, has his own unique experiences and meaning-contexts. No other person, not even he himself at another moment, can stand in his shoes at this moment.

The objective meaning of a product that we have before us is, on the other hand, by no means interpreted as evidence for the particular lived experience of a particular Thou. Rather, it is interpreted as already constituted and established, abstracted from every subjective flow of experience and every subjective meaning-context that could exist in such a flow. It is grasped as an objectification endowed with "universal meaning." Even though we implicitly refer to its author when we call it a "product," still we leave this author and everything personal about him out of account when we are interpreting objective meaning. He is hidden behind the impersonal "one" (someone, someone or other). This anonymous "one" is merely the linguistic term for the fact that a Thou exists, or has once existed, of whose particularity we take no account. I myself or you or some ideal type or Everyman could step into its shoes without in any way altering the subjective meaning of the product. We can say nothing about the subjective processes of this anonymous "one," for the latter has no duration, and the temporal dimension we ascribe to it, being a logical fiction, is in principle incapable of being experienced. But precisely for this reason the objective meaning remains, from the point of view of the interpreter, invariant for all possible creators of the meaningful object. Insofar as that object contains within its very meaning the ideality of the "and so forth" and of the "I can do it again," to that extent is that meaning independent of its maker and the circumstances of its origination. The product is abstracted from every individual consciousness and indeed from every consciousness as such. Objective meaning is merely the interpreter's ordering of his experiences of a product into the total context of his experience.

It follows from all we have said that every interpretation of subjective meaning involves a reference to a particular person. Furthermore, it must be a person of whom the interpreter has some kind of experience (*Erfahrung*) and whose subjective states he can run through in simultaneity or quasi-simultaneity, whereas objective meaning is abstracted from and independent of particular persons. Later we shall study this antithesis in greater detail, treating it as a case of polar opposition. Between the understanding of subjective meaning and the understanding of pure objective meaning there is a whole series of intermediate steps based on the fact that the social world has its own unique structure derived, as it is, from the worlds of direct social experience, of contemporaries, of predecessors, and of successors.

2 The Social Construction of Reality

Peter L. Berger and Thomas Luckmann

Origins of Institutionalization

All human activity is subject to habitualization. Any action that is repeated frequently becomes cast into a pattern, which can then be reproduced with an economy of effort and which, *ipso facto*, is apprehended by its performer *as* that pattern. Habitualization further implies that the action in question may be performed again in the future in the same manner and with the same economical effort. This is true of non-social as well as of social activity. Even the solitary individual on the proverbial desert island habitualizes his activity. When he wakes up in the morning and resumes his attempts to construct a canoe out of matchsticks, he may mumble to himself, "There I go again," as he starts on step one of an operating procedure consisting of, say, ten steps. In other words, even solitary man has at least the company of his operating procedures.

Habitualized actions, of course, retain their meaningful character for the individual although the meanings involved become embedded as routines in his general stock of knowledge, taken for granted by him and at hand for his projects into the future....

Institutionalization occurs whenever there is a reciprocal typification of habitualized actions by types of actors. Put differently, any such typification is an institution. What must be stressed is the reciprocity of institutional typifications and the typicality of not only the actions but also the actors in institutions. The typifications of habitualized actions that constitute institutions are always shared ones. They are *available* to all the members of the particular social group in question, and the institution itself typifies individual actors as well as individual actions. The institution posits that actions of type X will be performed by actors of type X. For example, the institution of the law posits that heads shall be chopped off in specific ways under specific circumstances, and that specific types of individuals shall do the chopping (executioners, say, or members of an impure caste, or virgins under a certain age, or those who have been designated by an oracle).

Institutions further imply historicity and control. Reciprocal typifications of actions are built up in the course of a shared history. They cannot be created instantaneously. Institutions always have a history, of which they are the products. It is impossible to understand an institution adequately without an understanding of the historical process in which it was produced. Institutions also, by the very fact of their existence, control human conduct by setting up predefined patterns of conduct, which channel it in one direction as against the many other directions that would theoretically be possible. It is important to stress that this controlling character is inherent in institutionalization as such, prior to or apart from any mechanisms of sanctions specifically set up to support an institution. These mechanisms (the sum of which constitute what is generally called a system of social control) do, of course, exist in many institutions and in all the agglomerations of institutions that we call societies. Their controlling efficacy, however, is of a secondary or supplementary kind. As we shall see again later, the primary social control is given in the existence of an institution as such. To say that a segment of human activity has been institutionalized is already to say that this segment of human activity has been subsumed under social control. Additional control mechanisms are required only insofar as the processes of institutionalization are less than completely successful. Thus, for instance, the law may provide that anyone who breaks the incest taboo will have his head chopped off. This provision may be necessary because there have been cases when individuals offended against the taboo. It is unlikely that this sanction will have to be invoked continually (unless the institution delineated by the incest taboo is itself in the course of disintegration, a special case that we need not elaborate here). It makes little sense, therefore, to say that human sexuality is socially controlled by beheading certain individuals. Rather, human sexuality is socially controlled by its institutionalization in the course of the particular history in question. One may add, of course, that the incest taboo itself is nothing but the negative side of an assemblage of typifications, which define in the first place which sexual conduct is incestuous and which is not.

In actual experience institutions generally manifest themselves in collectivities containing considerable numbers of people. It is theoretically important, however, to emphasize that the institutionalizing process of reciprocal typification would occur even if two individuals began to interact *de novo*. Institutionalization is incipient in every social situation continuing in time. Let us assume that two persons from entirely different social worlds begin to interact. By saying "persons" we presuppose that the two individuals have formed selves, something that could, of course, have occurred only in a social process. We are thus for the moment excluding the cases of Adam and Eve, or of two "feral" children meeting in a clearing of a primeval jungle. But we are assuming that the two individuals arrive at their meeting place from social worlds that have been historically produced in segregation from each other, and that the interaction therefore takes place in a situation that has not been institutionally defined for either of the participants. It may be possible to imagine a Man Friday joining our matchstick-canoe builder on his desert island, and to imagine the former as a Papuan and the latter as an American. In that case, however, it is likely that the American will have read or at least have heard about the story of Robinson Crusoe, which will introduce a measure of predefinition of the situation at least for him. Let us, then, simply call our two persons A and B.

As A and B interact, in whatever manner, typifications will be produced quite quickly. A watches B perform. He attributes motives to B's actions and, seeing the actions recur, typifies the motives as recurrent. As B goes on performing, A is soon able to say to himself, "Aha, there he goes again." At the same time, A may assume that B is doing the same thing with regard to him. From the beginning, both A and B assume this reciprocity of typification. In the course of their interaction these typifications will be expressed in specific patterns of conduct. That is, A and B will begin to play roles *vis-à-vis* each other. This will occur even if each continues to perform actions different from those of the other. The possibility of taking the role of the other will appear with regard to the same actions performed by both. That is, *A* will inwardly appropriate *B*'s reiterated roles and make them the models for his own role-playing. For example, *B*'s role in the activity of preparing food is not only typified as such by *A*, but enters as a constitutive element into *A*'s own food-preparation role. Thus a collection of reciprocally typified actions will emerge, habitualized for each in roles, some of which will be performed separately and some in common. While this reciprocal typification is not yet institutionalization (since, there only being two individuals, there is no possibility of a typology of actors), it is clear that institutionalization is already present *in nucleo*.

At this stage one may ask what gains accrue to the two individuals from this development. The most important gain is that each will be able to predict the other's actions. Concomitantly, the interaction of both becomes predictable. The "There he goes again" becomes a "There *we* go again." This relieves both individuals of a considerable amount of tension. They save time and effort, not only in whatever external tasks they might be engaged in separately or jointly, but in terms of their respective psychological economies. Their life together is now defined by a widening sphere of taken-for-granted routines. Many actions are possible on a low level of attention. Each action of one is no longer a source of astonishment and potential danger to the other. Instead, much of what goes on takes on the triviality of what, to both, will be everyday life. This means that the two individuals are constructing a background, in the sense discussed before, which will serve to stabilize both their separate actions and their interaction. The construction of this background of routine in turn makes possible a division of labor between them, opening the way for innovations, which demand a higher level of attention. The division of labor and the innovations will lead to new habitualizations, further widening the background common to both individuals. In other words, a social world will be in process of construction, containing within it the roots of an expanding institutional order.

Generally, all actions repeated once or more tend to be habitualized to some degree, just as all actions observed by another necessarily involve some typification on his part. However, for the kind of reciprocal typification just described to occur there must be a continuing social situation in which the habitualized actions of two or more individuals interlock. Which actions are likely to be reciprocally typified in this manner?

The general answer is, those actions that are relevant to both *A* and *B* within their common situation. The areas likely to be relevant in this way will, of course, vary in different situations. Some will be those facing *A* and *B* in terms of their previous biographies, others may be the result of the natural, presocial circumstances of the situation. What will in all cases have to be habitualized is the communication process between *A* and *B*. Labor, sexuality and territoriality are other likely foci of typification and habitualization. In these various areas the situation of *A* and *B* is paradigmatic of the institutionalization occurring in larger societies.

Let us push our paradigm one step further and imagine that *A* and *B* have children. At this point the situation changes qualitatively. The appearance of a third party changes the character of the ongoing social interaction between *A* and *B*, and it will change even further as additional individuals continue to be added. The institutional world, which existed *in statu nascendi* in the original situation of *A* and *B*, is now passed on to others. In this process institutionalization perfects itself. The habitualizations and typifications undertaken in the common life of A and B, formations that until this point still had the quality of *ad hoc* conceptions of two individuals, now become historical institutions. With the acquisition of historicity, these formations also acquire another crucial quality, or, more accurately, perfect a quality that was incipient as soon as A and B began the reciprocal typification of their conduct: this quality is objectivity. This means that the institutions that have now been crystallized (for instance, the institution of paternity as it is encountered by the children) are experienced as existing over and beyond the individuals who "happen to" embody them at the moment. In other words, the institutions are now experienced as possessing a reality of their own, a reality that confronts the individual as an external and coercive fact.

As long as the nascent institutions are constructed and maintained only in the interaction of A and B, their objectivity remains tenuous, easily changeable, almost playful, even while they attain a measure of objectivity by the mere fact of their formation. To put this a little differently, the routinized background of A's and B's activity remains fairly accessible to deliberate intervention by A and B. Although the routines, once established, carry within them a tendency to persist, the possibility of changing them or even abolishing them remains at hand in consciousness. A and B alone are responsible for having constructed this world. A and B remain capable of changing or abolishing it. What is more, since they themselves have shaped this world in the course of a shared biography which they can remember, the world thus shaped appears fully transparent to them. They understand the world that they themselves have made. All this changes in the process of transmission to the new generation. The objectivity of the institutional world "thickens" and "hardens," not only for the children, but (by a mirror effect) for the parents as well. The "There we go again" now becomes "This is how these things are done." A world so regarded attains a firmness in consciousness; it becomes real in an ever more massive way and it can no longer be changed so readily. For the children, especially in the early phase of their socialization into it, it becomes *the* world. For the parents, it loses its playful quality and becomes "serious." For the children, the parentally transmitted world is not fully transparent. Since they had no part in shaping it, it confronts them as a given reality that, like nature, is opaque in places at least.

Only at this point does it become possible to speak of a social world at all, in the sense of a comprehensive and given reality confronting the individual in a manner analogous to the reality of the natural world. Only in this way, *as an objective world*, can the social formations be transmitted to a new generation. In the early phases of socialization the child is quite incapable of distinguishing between the objectivity of natural phenomena and the objectivity of the social formations. To take the most important item of socialization, language appears to the child as inherent in the nature of things, and he cannot grasp the notion of its conventionality. A thing *is* what it is called, and it could not be called anything else. All institutions appear in the same way, as given, unalterable and self-evident. Even in our empirically unlikely example of parents having constructed an institutional world *de novo*, the objectivity of this world would be increased for them by the socialization of their children, because the objectivity experienced by the children would reflect back upon their own experience of this world. Empirically, of course, the institutional world transmitted by most parents already has the character of historical and objective reality.

The process of transmission simply strengthens the parents' sense of reality, if only because, to put it crudely, if one says, "This is how these things are done," often enough one believes it oneself.

An institutional world, then, is experienced as an objective reality. It has a history that antedates the individual's birth and is not accessible to his biographical recollection. It was there before he was born, and it will be there after his death. This history itself, as the tradition of the existing institutions, has the character of objectivity. The individual's biography is apprehended as an episode located within the objective history of the society. The institutions, as historical and objective facticities, confront the individual as undeniable facts. The institutions are *there*, external to him, persistent in their reality, whether he likes it or not. He cannot wish them away. They resist his attempts to change or evade them. They have coercive power over him, both in themselves, by the sheer force of their facticity, and through the control mechanisms that are usually attached to the most important of them. The objective reality of institutions is not diminished if the individual does not understand their purpose or their mode of operation. He may experience large sectors of the social world as incomprehensible, perhaps oppressive in their opaqueness, but real nonetheless. Since institutions exist as external reality, the individual cannot understand them by introspection. He must "go out" and learn about them, just as he must to learn about nature. This remains true even though the social world, as a humanly produced reality, is potentially understandable in a way not possible in the case of the natural world.

It is important to keep in mind that the objectivity of the institutional world, however massive it may appear to the individual, is a humanly produced, constructed objectivity. The process by which the externalized products of human activity attain the character of objectivity is objectivation. The institutional world is objectivated human activity, and so is every single institution. In other words, despite the objectivity that marks the social world in human experience, it does not thereby acquire an ontological status apart from the human activity that produced it. The paradox that man is capable of producing a world that he then experiences as something other than a human product will concern us later on. At the moment, it is important to emphasize that the relationship between man, the producer, and the social world, his product, is and remains a dialectical one. That is, man (not, of course, in isolation but in his collectivities) and his social world interact with each other. The product acts back upon the producer. Externalization and objectivation are moments in a continuing dialectical process. The third moment in this process, which is internalization (by which the objectivated social world is retrojected into consciousness in the course of socialization), will occupy us in considerable detail later on. It is already possible, however, to see the fundamental relationship of these three dialectical moments in social reality. Each of them corresponds to an essential characterization of the social world. *Society is a human product. Society is an objective reality. Man is a social product.* It may also already be evident that an analysis of the social world that leaves out any one of these three moments will be distortive. One may further add that only with the transmission of the social world to a new generation (that is, internalization as effectuated in socialization) does the fundamental social dialectic appear in its totality. To repeat, only with the appearance of a new generation can one properly speak of a social world.

At the same point, the institutional world requires legitimation, that is, ways by which it can be "explained" and justified. This is not because it appears less real. As we have seen, the reality of the social world gains in massivity in the course of its transmission. This reality, however, is a historical one, which comes to the new generation as a tradition rather than as a biographical memory. In our paradigmatic example, A and B, the original creators of the social world, can always reconstruct the circumstances under which their world and any part of it was established. That is, they can arrive at the meaning of an institution by exercising their powers of recollection. A's and B's children are in an altogether different situation. Their knowledge of the institutional history is by way of "hearsay." The original meaning of the institutions is inaccessible to them in terms of memory. It, therefore, becomes necessary to interpret this meaning to them in various legitimating formulas. These will have to be consistent and comprehensive in terms of the institutional order, if they are to carry conviction to the new generation. The same story, so to speak, must be told to all the children. It follows that the expanding institutional order develops a corresponding canopy of legitimations, stretching over it a protective cover of both cognitive and normative interpretation. These legitimations are learned by the new generation during the same process that socializes them into the institutional order. This, again, will occupy us in greater detail further on.

The development of specific mechanisms of social controls also becomes necessary with the historicization and objectivation of institutions. Deviance from the institutionally "programmed" courses of action becomes likely once the institutions have become realities divorced from their original relevance in the concrete social processes from which they arose. To put this more simply, it is more likely that one will deviate from programs set up for one by others than from programs that one has helped establish oneself. The new generation posits a problem of compliance, and its socialization into the institutional order requires the establishment of sanctions. The institutions must and do claim authority over the individual, independently of the subjective meanings he may attach to any particular situation. The priority of the institutional definitions of situations must be consistently maintained over individual temptations at redefinition. The children must be "taught to behave" and, once taught, must be "kept in line." So, of course, must the adults. The more conduct is institutionalized, the more predictable and thus the more controlled it becomes. If socialization into the institutions has been effective, outright coercive measures can be applied economically and selectively. Most of the time, conduct will occur "spontaneously" within the institutionally set channels. The more, on the level of meaning, conduct is taken for granted, the more possible alternatives to the institutional "programs" will recede, and the more predictable and controlled conduct will be.

In principle, institutionalization may take place in any area of collectively relevant conduct. In actual fact, sets of institutionalization processes take place concurrently. There is no a priori reason for assuming that these processes will necessarily "hang together" functionally, let alone as a logically consistent system. To return once more to our paradigmatic example, slightly changing the fictitious situation, let us assume this time, not a budding family of parents and children, but a piquant triangle of a male A, a bisexual female B, and a Lesbian C. We need not belabor the point that the sexual relevances of these three individuals will not coincide. Relevance A-B is not shared by C. The habitualizations engendered as a result of relevance A-B need bear no relationship to those engendered by relevances B-C and C-A. There is, after all, no reason why two processes of erotic habitualization, one heterosexual and one Lesbian, cannot take place side by side without functionally integrating with each other or with a third habitualization based on a shared interest in, say, the growing of flowers (or whatever other enterprise might be jointly relevant to an active heterosexual male and an active Lesbian). In other words, three processes of habitualization or incipient institutionalization may occur without their being functionally or logically integrated as social phenomena. The same reasoning holds if A, B and C are posited as collectivities rather than individuals, regardless of what content their relevances might have. Also, functional or logical integration cannot be assumed *a priori* when habitualization or institutionalization processes are limited to the same individuals or collectivities, rather than to the discrete ones assumed in our example.

Nevertheless, the empirical fact remains that institutions do tend to "hang together." If this phenomenon is not to be taken for granted, it must be explained. How can this be done? First, one may argue that *some* relevances will be common to all members of a collectivity. On the other hand, many areas of conduct will be relevant only to certain types. The latter involves an incipient differentiation, at least in the way in which these types are assigned some relatively stable meaning. This assignment may be based on presocial differences, such as sex, or on differences brought about in the course of social interaction, such as those engendered by the division of labor. For example, only women may be concerned with fertility magic and only hunters may engage in cave painting. Or, only the old men may perform the rain ceremonial and only weapon makers may sleep with their maternal cousins. In terms of their external social functionality, these several areas of conduct need not be integrated into *one* cohesive system. They can continue to coexist on the basis of segregated performances. But while performances can be segregated, meanings tend toward at least minimal consistency. As the individual reflects about the successive moments of his experience, he tries to fit their meanings into a consistent biographical framework. This tendency increases as the individual shares with others his meanings and their biographical integration. It is possible that this tendency to integrate meanings is based on a psychological need, which may in turn be physiologically grounded (that is, that there may be a built-in "need" for cohesion in the psycho-physiological constitution of man). Our argument, however, does not rest on such anthropological assumptions, but rather on the analysis of meaningful reciprocity in processes of institutionalization.

It follows that great care is required in any statements one makes about the "logic" of institutions. The logic does not reside in the institutions and their external functionalities, but in the way these are treated in reflection about them. Put differently, reflective consciousness superimposes the quality of logic on the institutional order.

Language provides the fundamental superimposition of logic on the objectivated social world. The edifice of legitimations is built upon language and uses language as its principal instrumentality. The "logic" thus attributed to the institutional order is part of the socially available stock of knowledge and taken for granted as such. Since the well-socialized individual "knows" that his social world is a consistent whole, he will be constrained to explain both its functioning and malfunctioning in terms of this "knowledge." It is very easy, as a result, for the observer of any society to assume that its institutions do indeed function and integrate as they are "supposed to."

De facto, then, institutions *are* integrated. But their integration is not a functional imperative for the social processes that produce them; it is rather brought about in a derivative fashion. Individuals perform discrete institutionalized actions within the context of their biography. This biography is a reflected-upon whole in which the discrete actions are thought of not as isolated events, but as related parts in a subjectively meaningful universe whose meanings are not specific to the individual, but socially articulated and shared. Only by way of this detour of socially shared universes of meaning do we arrive at the need for institutional integration.

This has far-reaching implications for any analysis of social phenomena. If the integration of an institutional order can be understood only in terms of the "knowledge" that its members have of it, it follows that the analysis of such "knowledge" will be essential for an analysis of the institutional order in question. It is important to stress that this does not exclusively or even primarily involve a pre-occupation with complex theoretical systems serving as legitimations for the institutional order. Theories also have to be taken into account, of course. But theoretical knowledge is only a small and by no means the most important part of what passes for knowledge in a society. Theoretically sophisticated legitimations appear at particular moments of an institutional history. The primary knowledge about the institutional order is knowledge on the pretheoretical level. It is the sum total of "what everybody knows" about a social world, an assemblage of maxims, morals, proverbial nuggets of wisdom, values and beliefs, myths, and so forth, the theoretical integration of which requires considerable intellectual fortitude in itself, as the long line of heroic integrators from Homer to the latest sociological system-builders testifies. On the pretheoretical level, however, every institution has a body of transmitted recipe knowledge, that is, knowledge that supplies the institutionally appropriate rules of conduct.

Such knowledge constitutes the motivating dynamics of institutionalized conduct. It defines the institutionalized areas of conduct and designates all situations falling within them. It defines and constructs the roles to be played in the context of the institutions in question. *Ipso facto*, it controls and predicts all such conduct. Since this knowledge is socially objectivated *as* knowledge, that is, as a body of generally valid truths about reality, any radical deviance from the institutional order appears as a departure from reality. Such deviance may be designated as moral depravity, mental disease, or just plain ignorance. While these fine distinctions will have obvious consequences for the treatment of the deviant, they all share an inferior cognitive status within the particular social world. In this way, the particular social world becomes the world *tout court*. What is taken for granted as knowledge in the society comes to be coextensive with the knowable, or at any rate provides the framework within which anything not yet known will come to be known in the future. This is the knowledge that is learned in the course of socialization and that mediates the internalization within individual consciousness of the objectivated structures of the social world. Knowledge, in this sense, is at the heart of the fundamental dialectic of society. It "programs" the channels in which externalization produces an objective world. It objectifies this world through language and the cognitive apparatus based on language, that is, it orders it into objects to be apprehended as reality. It is internalized again *as* objectively valid truth in the course of socialization. Knowledge about society is thus a *realization* in the double sense of the word, in the sense of apprehending the objectivated social reality, and in the sense of ongoingly producing this reality.

3 The Presentation of Self in Everyday Life

Erving Goffman

Masks are arrested expressions and admirable echoes of feeling, at once faithful, discreet, and superlative. Living things in contact with the air must acquire a cuticle, and it is not urged against cuticles that they are not hearts; yet some philosophers seem to be angry with images for not being things, and with words for not being feelings. Words and images are like shells, no less integral parts of nature than are the substances they cover, but better addressed to the eye and more open to observation. I would not say that substance exists for the sake of appearance, or faces for the sake of masks, or the passions for the sake of poetry and virtue. Nothing arises in nature for the sake of anything else; all these phases and products are involved equally in the round of existence....

George Santayana, *Soliloquies in England and Later Soliloquies* (New York: Scribner's, 1922), pp. 131–2.

Belief in the Part One is Playing

When an individual plays a part he implicitly requests his observers to take seriously the impression that is fostered before them. They are asked to believe that the character they see actually possesses the attributes he appears to possess, that the task he performs will have the consequences that are implicitly claimed for it, and that, in general, matters are what they appear to be. In line with this, there is the popular view that the individual offers his performance and puts on his show "for the benefit of other people." It will be convenient to begin a consideration of performances by turning the question around and looking at the individual's own belief in the impression of reality that he attempts to engender in those among whom he finds himself.

At one extreme, one finds that the performer can be fully taken in by his own act; he can be sincerely convinced that the impression of reality which he stages is the real reality. When his audience is also convinced in this way about the show he puts on – and this seems to be the typical case – then for the moment at least, only the sociologist or the socially disgruntled will have any doubts about the "realness" of what is presented.

At the other extreme, we find that the performer may not be taken in at all by his own routine. This possibility is understandable, since no one is in quite as good an observational position to see through the act as the person who puts it on. Coupled with this, the performer may be moved to guide the conviction of his audience only as a means to other ends, having no ultimate concern in the conception that they have of him or of the situation. When the individual has no belief in his own act and no ultimate concern with the beliefs of his audience, we may call him cynical, reserving the term "sincere" for individuals who believe in the impression fostered by their own performance. It should be understood that the cynic, with all his professional disinvolvement, may obtain unprofessional pleasures from his masquerade, experiencing a kind of gleeful spiritual aggression from the fact that he can toy at will with something his audience must take seriously.

It is not assumed, of course, that all cynical performers are interested in deluding their audiences for purposes of what is called "self-interest" or private gain. A cynical individual may delude his audience for what he considers to be their own good, or for the good of the community, etc. For illustrations of this we need not appeal to sadly enlightened showmen such as Marcus Aurelius or Hsun Tzǔ. We know that in service occupations practitioners who may otherwise be sincere are sometimes forced to delude their customers because their customers show such a heartfelt demand for it. Doctors who are led into giving placebos, filling station attendants who resignedly check and recheck tire pressures for anxious women motorists, shoe clerks who sell a shoe that fits but tell the customer it is the size she wants to hear – these are cynical performers whose audiences will not allow them to be sincere. Similarly, it seems that sympathetic patients in mental wards will sometimes feign bizarre symptoms so that student nurses will not be subjected to a disappointingly sane performance. So also, when inferiors extend their most lavish reception for visiting superiors, the selfish desire to win favor may not be the chief motive; the inferior may be tactfully attempting to put the superior at ease by simulating the kind of world the superior is thought to take for granted.

I have suggested two extremes: an individual may be taken in by his own act or be cynical about it. These extremes are something a little more than just the ends of a continuum. Each provides the individual with a position which has its own particular securities and defenses, so there will be a tendency for those who have traveled close to one of these poles to complete the voyage. Starting with lack of inward belief in one's role, the individual may follow the natural movement described by Park:

> It is probably no mere historical accident that the word person, in its first meaning, is a mask. It is rather a recognition of the fact that everyone is always and everywhere, more or less consciously, playing a role ... It is in these roles that we know each other; it is in these roles that we know ourselves.[1]

In a sense, and in so far as this mask represents the conception we have formed of ourselves – the role we are striving to live up to – this mask is our truer self, the self we would like to be. In the end, our conception of our role becomes second nature and an integral part of our personality. We come into the world as individuals, achieve character, and become persons.[2]

This may be illustrated from the community life of Shetland. For the last four or five years the island's tourist hotel has been owned and operated by a married couple of crofter origins. From the beginning, the owners were forced to set aside their own conceptions as to how life ought to be led, displaying in the hotel a full round of middle-class services and amenities. Lately, however, it appears that the managers have become less cynical about the performance that they stage; they themselves are becoming middle class and more and more enamored of the selves their clients impute to them.

Another illustration may be found in the raw recruit who initially follows army etiquette in order to avoid physical punishment and eventually comes to follow the rules so that his organization will not be shamed and his officers and fellow soldiers will respect him.

As suggested, the cycle of disbelief-to-belief can be followed in the other direction, starting with conviction or insecure aspiration and ending in cynicism. Professions which the public holds in religious awe often allow their recruits to follow the cycle in this direction, and often recruits follow it in this direction not because of a slow realization that they are deluding their audience – for by ordinary social standards the claims they make may be quite valid – but because they can use this cynicism as a means of insulating their inner selves from contact with the audience. And we may even expect to find typical careers of faith, with the individual starting out with one kind of involvement in the performance he is required to give, then moving back and forth several times between sincerity and cynicism before completing all the phases and turning-points of self-belief for a person of his station. Thus, students of medical schools suggest that idealistically oriented beginners in medical school typically lay aside their holy aspirations for a period of time. During the first two years the students find that their interest in medicine must be dropped that they may give all their time to the task of learning how to get through examinations. During the next two years they are too busy learning about diseases to show much concern for the persons who are diseased. It is only after their medical schooling has ended that their original ideals about medical service may be reasserted.

While we can expect to find natural movement back and forth between cynicism and sincerity, still we must not rule out the kind of transitional point that can be sustained on the strength of a little self-illusion. We find that the individual may attempt to induce the audience to judge him and the situation in a particular way, and he may seek this judgment as an ultimate end in itself, and yet he may not completely believe that he deserves the valuation of self which he asks for or that the impression of reality which he fosters is valid. . . .

Front

I have been using the term "performance" to refer to all the activity of an individual which occurs during a period marked by his continuous presence before a particular set of observers and which has some influence on the observers. It will be convenient to label as "front" that part of the individual's performance which regularly functions in a general and fixed fashion to define the situation for those who observe the performance. Front, then, is the expressive equipment of a standard kind intentionally or unwittingly employed by the individual during his performance. For preliminary purposes, it will be convenient to distinguish and label what seem to be the standard parts of front.

First, there is the "setting," involving furniture, décor, physical layout, and other background items which supply the scenery and stage props for the spate of human action played out before, within, or upon it. A setting tends to stay put, geographically speaking, so that those who would use a particular setting as part of their performance cannot begin their act until they have brought themselves to the appropriate place and must terminate their performance when they leave it. It is only in exceptional circumstances that the setting follows along with the performers; we see this in the funeral cortège, the civic parade, and the dream-like processions that kings and queens are made of. In the main, these exceptions seem to offer some kind of extra protection for performers who are, or who have momentarily become, highly sacred. These worthies are to be distinguished, of course, from quite profane performers of the peddler class who move their place of work between performances, often being forced to do so. In the matter of having one fixed place for one's setting, a ruler may be too sacred, a peddler too profane.

In thinking about the scenic aspects of front, we tend to think of the living room in a particular house and the small number of performers who can thoroughly identify themselves with it. We have given insufficient attention to assemblages of sign-equipment which large numbers of performers can call their own for short periods of time. It is characteristic of Western European countries, and no doubt a source of stability for them, that a large number of luxurious settings are available for hire to anyone of the right kind who can afford them. . . .

If we take the term "setting" to refer to the scenic parts of expressive equipment, one may take the term "personal front" to refer to the other items of expressive equipment, the items that we most intimately identify with the performer himself and that we naturally expect will follow the performer wherever he goes. As part of personal front we may include: insignia of office or rank; clothing; sex, age, and racial characteristics; size and looks; posture; speech patterns; facial expressions; bodily gestures; and the like. Some of these vehicles for conveying signs, such as racial characteristics, are relatively fixed and over a span of time do not vary for the individual from one situation to another. On the other hand, some of these sign vehicles are relatively mobile or transitory, such as facial expression, and can vary during a performance from one moment to the next.

It is sometimes convenient to divide the stimuli which make up personal front into "appearance" and "manner," according to the function performed by the information that these stimuli convey. "Appearance" may be taken to refer to those stimuli which function at the time to tell us of the performer's social statuses. These stimuli also tell us of the individual's temporary ritual state, that is, whether he is engaging in formal social activity, work, or informal recreation, whether or not he is celebrating a new phase in the season cycle or in his life-cycle. "Manner" may be taken to refer to those stimuli which function at the time to warn us of the interaction role the performer will expect to play in the oncoming situation. Thus a haughty, aggressive manner may give the impression that the performer expects to be the one who will initiate the verbal interaction and direct its course. A meek, apologetic manner may give the impression that the performer expects to follow the lead of others, or at least that he can be led to do so.

We often expect, of course, a confirming consistency between appearance and manner; we expect that the differences in social statuses among the interactants will be expressed in some way by congruent differences in the indications that are made of an expected interaction role. . . . But, of course, appearance and manner may tend to contradict each other, as when a performer who appears to be of higher estate than his audience acts in a manner that is unexpectedly equalitarian, or intimate, or apologetic, or when a performer dressed in the garments of a high position presents himself to an individual of even higher status.

In addition to the expected consistency between appearance and manner, we expect, of course, some coherence among setting, appearance, and manner. Such coherence represents an ideal type that provides us with a means of stimulating our attention to and interest in exceptions....

Dramatic Realization

While in the presence of others, the individual typically infuses his activity with signs which dramatically highlight and portray confirmatory facts that might otherwise remain unapparent or obscure. For if the individual's activity is to become significant to others, he must mobilize his activity so that it will express *during the interaction* what he wishes to convey. In fact, the performer may be required not only to express his claimed capacities during the interaction but also to do so during a split second in the interaction. Thus, if a baseball umpire is to give the impression that he is sure of his judgment, he must forgo the moment of thought which might make him sure of his judgment; he must give an instantaneous decision so that the audience will be sure that he is sure of his judgment.

It may be noted that in the case of some statuses dramatization presents no problem, since some of the acts which are instrumentally essential for the completion of the core task of the status are at the same time wonderfully adapted, from the point of view of communication, as means of vividly conveying the qualities and attributes claimed by the performer. The roles of prizefighters, surgeons, violinists, and policemen are cases in point. These activities allow for so much dramatic self-expression that exemplary practitioners – whether real or fictional – become famous and are given a special place in the commercially organized fantasies of the nation.

In many cases, however, dramatization of one's work does constitute a problem. An illustration of this may be cited from a hospital study where the medical nursing staff is shown to have a problem that the surgical nursing staff does not have:

> The things which a nurse does for post-operative patients on the surgical floor are frequently of recognizable importance, even to patients who are strangers to hospital activities. For example, the patient sees his nurse changing bandages, swinging orthopedic frames into place, and can realize that these are purposeful activities. Even if she cannot be at his side, he can respect her purposeful activities.
>
> Medical nursing is also highly skilled work.... The physician's diagnosis must rest upon careful observation of symptoms over time where the surgeon's are in larger part dependent on visible things. The lack of visibility creates problems on the medical. A patient will see his nurse stop at the next bed and chat for a moment or two with the patient there. He doesn't know that she is observing the shallowness of the breathing and color and tone of the skin. He thinks she is just visiting. So, alas, does his family who may thereupon decide that these nurses aren't very impressive. If the nurse spends more time at the next bed than at his own, the patient may feel slighted.... The nurses are "wasting time" unless they are darting about doing some visible thing such as administering hypodermics.[3]

Similarly, the proprietor of a service establishment may find it difficult to dramatize what is actually being done for clients because the clients cannot "see" the overhead costs of the service rendered them. Undertakers must therefore charge a great deal for their highly visible product – a coffin that has been transformed into a casket – because many of the other costs of conducting a funeral are ones that cannot be readily dramatized. Merchants, too, find that they must charge high prices for things that look intrinsically expensive in order to compensate the establishment for expensive things like insurance, slack periods, etc., that never appear before the customers' eyes.

The problem of dramatizing one's work involves more than merely making invisible costs visible. The work that must be done by those who fill certain statuses is often so poorly designed as an expression of a desired meaning, that if the incumbent would dramatize the character of his role, he must divert an appreciable amount of his energy to do so. And this activity diverted to communication will often require different attributes from the ones which are being dramatized. Thus to furnish a house so that it will express simple, quiet dignity, the householder may have to race to auction sales, haggle with antique dealers, and doggedly canvass all the local shops for proper wallpaper and curtain materials. To give a radio talk that will sound genuinely informal, spontaneous, and relaxed, the speaker may have to design his script with painstaking care, testing one phrase after another, in order to follow the content, language, rhythm, and pace of everyday talk. Similarly, a *Vogue* model, by her clothing, stance, and facial expression, is able expressively to portray a cultivated understanding of the book she poses in her hand; but those who trouble to express themselves so appropriately will have very little time left over for reading. As Sartre suggested: "The attentive pupil who wishes to *be* attentive, his eyes riveted on the teacher, his ears open wide, so exhausts himself in playing the attentive role that he ends up by no longer hearing anything."[4] And so individuals often find themselves with the dilemma of expression *versus* action. Those who have the time and talent to perform a task well may not, because of this, have the time or talent to make it apparent that they are performing well. It may be said that some organizations resolve this dilemma by officially delegating the dramatic function to a specialist who will spend his time expressing the meaning of the task and spend no time actually doing it.

If we alter our frame of reference for a moment and turn from a particular performance to the individuals who present it, we can consider an interesting fact about the round of different routines which any group or class of individuals helps to perform. When a group or class is examined, one finds that the members of it tend to invest their egos primarily in certain routines, giving less stress to the other ones which they perform. Thus a professional man may be willing to take a very modest role in the street, in a shop, or in his home, but, in the social sphere which encompasses his display of professional competency, he will be much concerned to make an effective showing. In mobilizing his behavior to make a showing, he will be concerned not so much with the full round of the different routines he performs but only with the one from which his occupational reputation derives. It is upon this issue that some writers have chosen to distinguish groups with aristocratic habits (whatever their social status) from those of middle-class character. The aristocratic habit, it has been said, is one that mobilizes all the minor activities of life which fall outside the serious specialities of other classes and injects into these activities an expression of character, power, and high rank. . . .

Idealization

It was suggested earlier that a performance of a routine presents through its front some rather abstract claims upon the audience, claims that are likely to be presented to them during the performance of other routines. This constitutes one way in which a performance is "socialized," molded, and modified to fit into the understanding and expectations of the society in which it is presented. I want to consider here another important aspect of this socialization process – the tendency for performers to offer their observers an impression that is idealized in several different ways.

The notion that a performance presents an idealized view of the situation is, of course, quite common. Cooley's view may be taken as an illustration:

> If we never tried to seem a little better than we are, how could we improve or "train ourselves from the outside inward?" And the same impulse to show the world a better or idealized aspect of ourselves finds an organized expression in the various professions and classes, each of which has to some extent a cant or pose, which its members assume unconsciously, for the most part, but which has the effect of a conspiracy to work upon the credulity of the rest of the world. There is a cant not only of theology and of philanthropy, but also of law, medicine, teaching, even of science – perhaps especially of science, just now, since the more a particular kind of merit is recognized and admired, the more it is likely to be assumed by the unworthy.[5]

Thus, when the individual presents himself before others, his performance will tend to incorporate and exemplify the officially accredited values of the society, more so, in fact, than does his behavior as a whole.

To the degree that a performance highlights the common official values of the society in which it occurs, we may look upon it, in the manner of Durkheim and Radcliffe-Brown, as a ceremony – as an expressive rejuvenation and reaffirmation of the moral values of the community. Furthermore, in so far as the expressive bias of performances comes to be accepted as reality, then that which is accepted at the moment as reality will have some of the characteristics of a celebration. To stay in one's room away from the place where the party is given, or away from where the practitioner attends his client, is to stay away from where reality is being performed. The world, in truth, is a wedding. . . .

The expressive coherence that is required in performances points out a crucial discrepancy between our all-too-human selves and our socialized selves. As human beings we are presumably creatures of variable impulse with moods and energies that change from one moment to the next. As characters put on for an audience, however, we must not be subject to ups and downs. As Durkheim suggested, we do not allow our higher social activity "to follow in the trail of our bodily states, as our sensations and our general bodily consciousness do."[6] A certain bureaucratization of the spirit is expected so that we can be relied upon to give a perfectly homogeneous performance at every appointed time. As Santayana suggests, the socialization process not only transfigures, it fixes:

> But whether the visage we assume be a joyful or a sad one, in adopting and emphasizing it we define our sovereign temper. Henceforth, so long as we continue under the spell of this self-knowledge, we do not merely live but act; we compose and play our chosen character, we wear the buskin of deliberation, we defend and idealize our passions, we encourage ourselves eloquently to be what we are, devoted or scornful or careless or austere; we soliloquize (before an imaginary audience) and we wrap ourselves grace-fully in the mantle of our inalienable part. So draped, we solicit applause and expect to die amid a universal hush. We profess to live up to the fine sentiments we have uttered, as we try to believe in the religion we profess. The greater our difficulties the greater our zeal. Under our published principles and plighted language we must assiduously hide all the inequalities of our moods and conduct, and this without hypocrisy, since our deliberate character is more truly ourself than is the flux of our involuntary dreams. The portrait we paint in this way and exhibit as our true person may well be in the grand manner, with column and curtain and distant landscape and finger pointing to the terrestrial globe or to the Yorick-skull of philosophy; but if this style is native to us and our art is vital, the more it transmutes its model the deeper and truer art it will be. The severe bust of an archaic sculpture, scarcely humanizing the block, will express a spirit far more justly than the man's dull morning looks or casual grimaces. Everyone who is sure of his mind, or proud of his office, or anxious about his duty assumes a tragic mask. He deputes it to be himself and transfers to it almost all his vanity. While still alive and subject, like all existing things, to the undermining flux of his own substance, he has crystallized his soul into an idea, and more in pride than in sorrow he has offered up his life on the altar of the Muses. Self-knowledge, like any art or science, renders its subject-matter in a new medium, the medium of ideas, in which it loses its old dimensions and its old place. Our animal habits are transmuted by conscience into loyalties and duties, and we become "persons" or masks.[7]

Through social discipline, then, a mask of manner can be held in place from within. But, as Simone de Beauvoir suggests, we are helped in keeping this pose by clamps that are tightened directly on the body, some hidden, some showing:

> Even if each woman dresses in conformity with her status, a game is still being played: artifice, like art, belongs to the realm of the imaginary. It is not only that girdle, brassiere, hair-dye, make-up disguise body and face; but that the least sophisticated of women, once she is "dressed," does not present *herself* to observation; she is, like the picture or the statue, or the actor on the stage, an agent through whom is suggested someone not there – that is, the character she represents, but is not. It is this identifica-tion with something unreal, fixed, perfect as the hero of a novel, as a portrait or a bust, that gratifies her; she strives to identify herself with this figure and thus to seem to herself to be stabilized, justified in her splendor.[8]

Misrepresentation

It was suggested earlier that an audience is able to orient itself in a situation by accepting performed cues on faith, treating these signs as evidence of something greater than or different from the sign-vehicles themselves. If this tendency of the audience to accept signs places the performer in a position to be misunderstood and makes it necessary for him to exercise expressive care regarding everything he does when before the audience, so also this sign-accepting tendency puts the audience in a position to be duped and misled, for there are few signs that cannot be used to attest to the presence of something that is not really there. And it is plain that many performers have ample capacity and motive to misrepresent the facts; only shame, guilt, or fear prevent them from doing so.

As members of an audience it is natural for us to feel that the impression the performer seeks to give may be true or false, genuine or spurious, valid or "phony." So common is this doubt that, as suggested, we often give special attention to features of the performance that cannot be readily manipulated, thus enabling ourselves to judge the reliability of the more misrepresentable cues in the perform-ance. (Scientific police work and projective testing are extreme examples of the application of this tendency.) And if we grudgingly allow certain symbols of status to establish a performer's right to a given treatment, we are always ready to pounce on chinks in his symbolic armor in order to discredit his pretensions.

When we think of those who present a false front or "only" a front, of those who dissemble, deceive, and defraud, we think of a discrepancy between fostered appear-ances and reality. We also think of the precarious position in which these performers place themselves, for at any moment in their performance an event may occur to catch them out and baldly contradict what they have openly avowed, bringing them immediate humiliation and sometimes permanent loss of reputation. We often feel that it is just these terrible eventualities, which arise from being caught out *flagrante delicto* in a patent act of misrepresentation, that an honest performer is able to avoid. This common-sense view has limited analytical utility.

Sometimes when we ask whether a fostered impression is true or false we really mean to ask whether or not the performer is authorized to give the performance in question, and are not primarily concerned with the actual performance itself. When we discover that someone with whom we have dealings is an impostor and out-and-out fraud, we are discovering that he did not have the right to play the part he played, that he was not an accredited incumbent of the relevant status. We assume that the impostor's performance, in addition to the fact that it misrepresents him, will be at fault in other ways, but often his masquerade is discovered before we can detect any other difference between the false performance and the legitimate one which it simulates. Paradoxically, the more closely the impostor's performance approximates to the real thing, the more intensely we may be threatened, for a competent performance by someone who proves to be an impostor may weaken in our minds the moral connection between legitimate authorization to play a part and the capacity to play it. (Skilled mimics, who admit all along that their intentions are unserious, seem to provide one way in which we can "work through" some of these anxieties.)

The social definition of impersonation, however, is not itself a very consistent thing. For example, while it is felt to be an inexcusable crime against communication to impersonate someone of sacred status, such as a doctor or a priest, we are often less concerned when someone impersonates a member of a disesteemed, non-crucial, profane status, such as that of a hobo or unskilled worker. When a disclosure shows that we have been participating with a performer who has a higher status than he led us to believe, there is good Christian precedent for our reacting with wonderment and chagrin rather than with hostility. Mythology and our popular magazines, in fact, are full of romantic stories in which the villain and the hero both make fraudulent claims that are discredited in the last chapter, the villain proving not to have a high status, the hero proving not to have a low one.

Further, while we may take a harsh view of performers such as confidence men who knowingly misrepresent every fact about their lives, we may have some sympathy for those who have but one fatal flaw and who attempt to conceal the fact that they are, for example, ex-convicts, deflowered, epileptic, or racially impure, instead of admitting their fault and making an honorable attempt to live it down. Also, we distinguish between impersonation of a specific, concrete individual, which we usually feel is quite inexcusable, and impersonation of category membership, which we may feel less strongly about. So, too, we often feel differently about those who misrepresent themselves to forward what they feel are the just claims of a collectivity, or those who misrepresent themselves accidentally or for a lark, than about those who misrepresent themselves for private psychological or material gain.

Finally, since there are senses in which the concept of "a status" is not clear-cut, so there are senses in which the concept of impersonation is not clear either. For example, there are many statuses in which membership obviously is not subject to formal ratification. Claims to be a law graduate can be established as valid or invalid, but claims to be a friend, a true believer, or a music-lover can be confirmed or disconfirmed only more or less. Where standards of competence are not objective, and where *bona fide* practitioners are not collectively organized to protect their mandate, an individual may style himself an expert and be penalized by nothing stronger than sniggers....

In previous sections of this chapter some general characteristics of performance were suggested: activity oriented towards work-tasks tends to be converted into activity oriented towards communication; the front behind which the routine is presented is also likely to be suitable for other, somewhat different routines and so is likely not to fit completely any particular routine; sufficient self-control is exerted so as to maintain a working consensus; an idealized impression is offered by accentuating certain facts and concealing others; expressive coherence is maintained by the performer taking more care to guard against minor disharmonies than the stated purpose of the performance might lead the audience to think was warranted. All of these general characteristics of performances can be seen as interaction constraints which play upon the individual and transform his activities into performances. Instead of merely doing his task and giving vent to his feelings, he will express the doing of his task and acceptably convey his feelings. In general, then, the representation of an activity will vary in some degree from the activity itself and therefore inevitably misrepresent it. And since the individual will be required to rely on signs in order to construct a representation of his activity, the image he constructs, however faithful to the facts, will be subject to all the disruptions that impressions are subject to.

While we could retain the common-sense notion that fostered appearances can be discredited by a discrepant reality, there is often no reason for claiming that the facts discrepant with the fostered impression are any more the real reality than is the fostered reality they embarrass. A cynical view of everyday performances can be as one-sided as the one that is sponsored by the performer. For many sociological issues it may not even be necessary to decide which is the more real, the fostered impression or the one the performer attempts to prevent the audience from receiving. The crucial sociological consideration, for this report at least, is merely that impressions fostered in everyday performances are subject to disruption. We will want to know what kind of impression of reality can shatter the fostered impression of reality, and what reality really is can be left to other students. We will want to ask, "What are the ways in which a given impression can be discredited?" and this is not quite the same as asking, "What are the ways in which the given impression is false?"

We come back, then, to a realization that while the performance offered by impostors and liars is quite flagrantly false and differs in this respect from ordinary performances, both are similar in the care their performers must exert in order to maintain the impression that is fostered. Thus, for example, we know that the formal code of British civil servants and of American baseball umpires obliges them not only to desist from making improper "deals" but also to desist from innocent action which might possibly give the (wrong) impression that they are making deals. Whether an honest performer wishes to convey the truth or whether a dishonest performer wishes to convey a falsehood, both must take care to enliven their performances with appropriate expressions, exclude from their performances expressions that might discredit the impression being fostered, and take care lest the audience impute unintended meanings. Because of these shared dramatic contingencies, we can profitably study performances that are quite false in order to learn about ones that are quite honest. . . .

Reality and Contrivance

In our own Anglo-American culture there seems to be two common-sense models according to which we formulate our conceptions of behavior: the real, sincere, or honest performance; and the false one that thorough fabricators assemble for us, whether meant to be taken unseriously, as in the work of stage actors, or seriously, as in the work of confidence men. We tend to see real performances as something not purposely put together at all, being an unintentional product of the individual's unselfconscious response to the facts in his situation. And contrived performances we tend to see as something painstakingly pasted together, one false item on another, since there is no reality to which the items of behavior could be a direct response. It will be necessary to see now that these dichotomous conceptions are by way of being the ideology of honest performers, providing strength to the show they put on, but a poor analysis of it.

First, let it be said that there are many individuals who sincerely believe that the definition of the situation they habitually project is the real reality. In this report I do not mean to question their proportion in the population but rather the structural relation of their sincerity to the performances they offer. If a performance is to come off, the witnesses by and large must be able to believe that the performers are sincere. This is the structural place of sincerity in the drama of events. Performers may be sincere – or be insincere but sincerely convinced of their own sincerity – but this kind of affection for one's part is not necessary for its convincing performance.

There are not many French cooks who are really Russian spies, and perhaps there are not many women who play the part of wife to one man and mistress to another; but these duplicities do occur, often being sustained successfully for long periods of time. This suggests that while persons usually are what they appear to be, such appearances could still have been managed. There is, then, a statistical relation between appearances and reality, not an intrinsic or necessary one. In fact, given the unanticipated threats that play upon a performance, and given the need (later to be discussed) to maintain solidarity with one's fellow performers and some distance from the witnesses, we find that a rigid incapacity to depart from one's inward view of reality may at times endanger one's performance. Some performances are carried off successfully with complete dishonesty, others with complete honesty; but for performances in general neither of these extremes is essential and neither, perhaps, is dramaturgically advisable.

The implication here is that an honest, sincere, serious performance is less firmly connected with the solid world than one might first assume. And this implication will be strengthened if we look again at the distance usually placed between quite honest performances and quite contrived ones. In this connection take, for example, the remarkable phenomenon of stage acting. It does take deep skill, long training, and psychological capacity to become a good stage actor. But this fact should not blind us to another one: that almost anyone can quickly learn a script well enough to give a charitable audience some sense of realness in what is being contrived before them. And it seems this is so because ordinary social intercourse is itself put together as a scene is put together, by the exchange of dramatically inflated actions, counter-actions, and terminating replies. Scripts even in the hands of unpracticed players can come to life because life itself is a dramatically enacted thing. All the world is not, of course, a stage, but the crucial ways in which it isn't are not easy to specify.

The recent use of "psychodrama" as a therapeutic technique illustrates a further point in this regard. In these psychiatrically staged scenes patients not only act out parts with some effectiveness, but employ no script in doing so. Their own past is available to them in a form which allows them to stage a recapitulation of it. Apparently a part once played honestly and in earnest leaves the performer in a position to contrive a showing of it later. Further, the parts that significant others played to him in the past also seem to be available, allowing him to switch from being the person that he was to being the persons that others were for him. This capacity to switch enacted roles when obliged to do so could have been predicted; everyone apparently can do it. For in learning to perform our parts in real life we guide our own productions by not too consciously maintaining an incipient familiarity with the routine of those to whom we will address ourselves. And when we come to be able properly to manage a real routine we are able to do this in part because of "anticipatory socialization,"[9] having already been schooled in the reality that is just coming to be real for us.

When the individual does move into a new position in society and obtains a new part to perform, he is not likely to be told in full detail how to conduct himself, nor will the facts of his new situation press sufficiently on him from the start to determine his conduct without his further giving thought to it. Ordinarily he will be given only a few cues, hints, and stage directions, and it will be assumed that he already has in his repertoire a large number of bits and pieces of performances that will be required in the new setting. The individual will already have a fair idea of what modesty, deference, or righteous indignation looks like, and can make a pass at playing these bits when necessary. He may even be able to play out the part of a hypnotic subject or commit a "compulsive" crime on the basis of models for these activities that he is already familiar with.

A theatrical performance or a staged confidence game requires a thorough scripting of the spoken content of the routine; but the vast part involving "expression given off" is often determined by meager stage directions. It is expected that the performer of illusions will already know a good deal about how to manage his voice, his face, and his body, although he – as well as any person who directs him – may find it difficult indeed to provide a detailed verbal statement of this kind of knowledge. And in this, of course, we approach the situation of the straightforward man in the street. Socialization may not so much involve a learning of the many specific details of a single concrete part – often there could not be enough time or energy for this. What does seem to be required of the individual is that he learn enough pieces of expression to be able to "fill in" and manage, more or less, any part that he is likely to be given. The legitimate performances of everyday life are not "acted" or "put on" in the sense that the performer knows in advance just what he is going to do, and does this solely because of the effect it is likely to have. The expressions it is felt he is giving off will be especially "inaccessible" to him. But as in the case of less legitimate performers, the incapacity of the ordinary individual to formulate in advance the movements of his eyes and body does not mean that he will not express himself through these devices in a way that is dramatized and pre-formed in his repertoire of actions. In short, we all act better than we know how.

When we watch a television wrestler gouge, foul, and snarl at his opponent we are quite ready to see that, in spite of the dust, he is, and knows he is, merely playing at being the "heavy," and that in another match he may be given the other role, that of clean-cut wrestler, and perform this with equal verve and proficiency. We seem less ready to see, however, that while such details as the number and character of the falls may be fixed beforehand, the details of the expressions and movements used do not come from a script but from command of an idiom, a command that is exercised from moment to moment with little calculation or forethought.

In reading of persons in the West Indies who become the "horse" or the one possessed of a voodoo spirit, it is enlightening to learn that the person possessed will be able to provide a correct portrayal of the god that has entered him because of "the knowledge and memories accumulated in a life spent visiting congregations of the cult"; that the person possessed will be in just the right social relation to those who are watching; that possession occurs at just the right moment in the ceremonial undertakings, the possessed one carrying out his ritual obligations to the point of participating in a kind of skit with persons possessed at the time with other spirits. But in learning this, it is important to see that this contextual structuring of the horse's role still allows participants in the cult to believe that possession is a real thing and that persons are possessed at random by gods whom they cannot select.

And when we observe a young American middle-class girl playing dumb for the benefit of her boy friend, we are ready to point to items of guile and contrivance in her behavior. But like herself and her boy friend, we accept as an unperformed fact that this performer *is* a young American middle-class girl. But surely here we neglect the greater part of the performance. It is commonplace to say that different social groupings express in different ways such attributes as age, sex, territory, and class status, and that in each case these bare attributes are elaborated by means of a distinctive complex cultural configuration of proper ways of conducting oneself. To *be* a given kind of person, then, is not merely to possess the required attributes, but also to sustain the standards of conduct and appearance that one's social grouping attaches thereto. The unthinking ease with which performers consistently carry off such standard-maintaining routines does not deny that a performance has occurred, merely that the participants have been aware of it.

A status, a position, a social place is not a material thing, to be possessed and then displayed; it is a pattern of appropriate conduct, coherent, embellished, and well articulated. Performed with ease or clumsiness, awareness or not, guile or good faith, it is none the less something that must be enacted and portrayed, something that must be realized. Sartre, here, provides a good illustration:

> Let us consider this waiter in the café. His movement is quick and forward, a little too precise, a little too rapid. He comes toward the patrons with a step a little too quick. He bends forward a little too eagerly; his voice, his eyes express an interest a little too solicitous for the order of the customer. Finally there he returns, trying to imitate in his walk the inflexible stiffness of some kind of automaton while carrying his tray with the recklessness of a tightrope-walker by putting it in a perpetually unstable, perpetually broken equilibrium which he perpetually re-establishes by a light movement of the arm and hand. All his behavior seems to us a game. He applies himself to chaining his movements as if they were mechanisms, the one regulating the other; his gestures and even his voice seem to be mechanisms; he gives himself the quickness and pitiless rapidity of things. He is playing, he is amusing himself. But what is he playing? We need not watch long before we can explain it: he is playing at being a waiter in a café. There is nothing there to surprise us. The game is a kind of marking out and investigation. The child plays with his body in order to explore it, to take inventory of it; the waiter in the café plays with his condition in order to *realize* it. This obligation is not different from that which is imposed on all tradesmen. Their condition is wholly one of ceremony. The public demands of them that they realize it as a ceremony; there is the dance of the grocer, of the tailor, of the auctioneer, by which they endeavor to persuade their clientele that they are nothing but a grocer, an auctioneer, a tailor. A grocer who dreams is offensive to the buyer, because such a grocer is not wholly a grocer. Society demands that he limit himself to his function as a grocer, just as the soldier at attention makes himself into a soldier-thing with a direct regard which does not see at all, which is no longer meant to see, since it is the rule and not the interest of the moment which determines the point he must fix his eyes on (the sight "fixed at ten paces"). There are indeed many precautions to imprison a man in what he is, as if we lived in perpetual fear that he might escape from it, that he might break away and suddenly elude his condition.[10]

Notes

1   Robert Ezra Park, *Race and Culture* (Glencoe, Ill.: The Free Press, 1950), p. 249.
2   Ibid., p. 250.
3   Edith Lentz, "A Comparison of Medical and Surgical Floors" (Mimeo: New York State School of Industrial and Labor Relations, Cornell University, 1954), pp. 2–3.

4 Jean-Paul Sartre, *Being and Nothingness*, trans. by Hazel E. Barnes (New York: Philosophical Library, 1956), p. 60.

5 Charles H. Cooley, *Human Nature and the Social Order* (New York: Scribner's, 1922), pp. 352–3.

6 Emile Durkheim, *The Elementary Forms of the Religious Life*, trans. J. W. Swain (London: Allen & Unwin, 1926), p. 272.

7 George Santayana, *Soliloquies in England and Later Soliloquies* (New York: Scribner's, 1922), pp. 133–4.

8 Simone de Beauvoir, *The Second Sex*, trans. H. M. Parshley (New York: Knopf, 1953), p. 533.

9 See R. K. Merton, *Social Theory and Social Structure* (Glencoe: The Free Press, revised and enlarged edition, 1957), p. 265 ff.

10 Sartre, *Being and Nothingness*, p. 59.

4 Symbolic Interactionism

Herbert Blumer

The Methodological Position of Symbolic Interactionism

Exploration and inspection, representing respectively depiction and analysis, constitute the necessary procedure in direct examination of the empirical social world. They comprise what is sometimes spoken of as "naturalistic" investigation – investigation that is directed to a given empirical world in its natural, ongoing character instead of to a simulation of such a world, or to an abstraction from it (as in the case of laboratory experimentation), or to a substitute for the world in the form of a preset image of it. The merit of naturalistic study is that it respects and stays close to the empirical domain. This respect and closeness is particularly important in the social sciences because of the formation of different worlds and spheres of life by human beings in their group existence. Such worlds both represent and shape the social life of people, their activities, their relations, and their institutions. Such a world or sphere of life is almost always remote and unknown to the research scholar; this is a major reason why he wants to study it. To come to know it he should get close to it in its actual empirical character. Without doing this he has no assurance that his guiding imagery of the sphere or world, or the problem he sets forth for it, or the leads he lays down, or the data he selects, or the kinds of relations that he prefigures between them, or the theoretical views that guide his interpretations are empirically valid. Naturalistic inquiry, embracing the dual procedures of exploration and inspection, is clearly necessary in the scientific study of human group life. It qualifies as being "scientific" in the best meaning of that term.

My presentation has set forth rather sharply the opposition between naturalistic inquiry, in the form of exploration and inspection, and the formalized type of inquiry so vigorously espoused in current methodology. This opposition needs to be stressed in the hope of releasing social scientists from unwitting captivity to a format of inquiry that is taken for granted as the naturally proper way in which to conduct scientific study. The spokesmen for naturalistic inquiry in the social and psychological sciences today are indeed very few despite the fact that many note-worthy studies in the social sciences are products of naturalistic study. The consideration of naturalistic inquiry scarcely enters into the content of present-day methodology. Further, as far as I can observe, training in naturalistic inquiry is soft-pedaled or not given at all in our major graduate departments. There is a widespread ignorance of it and an accompanying blindness to its necessity. This is unfortunate for the social and psychological sciences since, as empirical sciences, their mission is to come to grips with their empirical world.

Methodological orientation

Symbolic interactionism is a down-to-earth approach to the scientific study of human group life and human conduct. Its empirical world is the natural world of such group life and conduct. It lodges its problems in this natural world, conducts its studies in it, and derives its interpretations from such naturalistic studies. If it wishes to study religious cult behavior it will go to actual religious cults and observe them carefully as they carry on their lives. If it wishes to study social movements it will trace carefully the career, the history, and the life experiences of actual movements. If it wishes to study drug use among adolescents it will go to the actual life of such adolescents to observe and analyze such use. And similarly with respect to other matters that engage its attention. Its methodological stance, accordingly, is that of direct examination of the empirical social world – the methodological approach that I have discussed above. It recognizes that such direct examination permits the scholar to meet all of the basic requirements of an empirical science: to confront an empirical world that is available for observation and analysis; to raise abstract problems with regard to that world; to gather necessary data through careful and disciplined examination of that world; to unearth relations between categories of such data; to formulate propositions with regard to such relations; to weave such propositions into a theoretical scheme; and to test the problems, the data, the relations, the propositions, and the theory by renewed examination of the empirical world. Symbolic interactionism is not misled by the mythical belief that to be scientific it is necessary to shape one's study to fit a pre-established protocol of empirical inquiry, such as adopting the working procedure of advanced physical science, or devising in advance a fixed logical or mathematical model, or forcing the study into the mould of laboratory experimentation, or imposing a statistical or mathematical framework on the study, or organizing it in terms of preset variables, or restricting it to a particular standardized procedure such as survey research. Symbolic interactionism recognizes that the genuine mark of an empirical science is to respect the nature of its empirical world – to fit its problems, its guiding conceptions, its procedures of inquiry, its techniques of study, its concepts, and its theories to that world. It believes that this determination of problems, concepts, research techniques, and theoretical schemes should be done by the *direct* examination of the actual empirical social world rather than by working with a simulation of that world, or with a preset model of that world, or with a picture of that world derived from a few scattered observations of it, or with a picture of that world fashioned in advance to meet the dictates of some imported theoretical scheme or of some scheme of "scientific" procedure, or with a picture of the world built up from partial and untested accounts of that world. For symbolic interactionism the nature of the empirical social world is to be discovered, to be dug out by a direct, careful, and probing examination of that world. . . .

Granted that human group life has the character that is stated by the premises of symbolic interactionism, the general topic I wish to consider is how does one study human group life and social action. I do not have in mind an identification and analysis of the numerous separate procedures that may be employed at one or another point in carrying on exploration and inspection. There is a sizeable literature, very uneven to be true, on a fair number of such separate procedures, such as direct observation, field study, participant observation, case study, interviewing, use of life histories, use of letters and diaries, use of public documents, panel discussions, and use of conversations. There is great need, I may add, of careful circumspective study of such procedures, not to bring them inside a standardized format but to improve their capacity as instruments for discovering what is taking place in actual group life. My current concern, however, lies in a different direction, namely, to point out several of the more important methodological implications of the symbolic interactionist's view of human group life and social action. I want to consider such implications in the case of each of four central conceptions in symbolic interactionism. These four central conceptions are: (1) people, individually and collectively, are prepared to act on the basis of the meanings of the objects that comprise their world; (2) the association of people is necessarily in the form of a process in which they are making indications to one another and interpreting each other's indications; (3) social acts, whether individual or collective, are constructed through a process in which the actors note, interpret, and assess the situations confronting them; and (4) the complex interlinkages of acts that comprise organization, institutions, division of labor, and networks of interdependency are moving and not static affairs. I wish to discuss each of these in turn.

(1) The contention that people act on the basis of the meaning of their objects has profound methodological implications. It signifies immediately that if the scholar wishes to understand the action of people it is necessary for him to see their objects as they see them. Failure to see their objects as they see them, or a substitution of his meanings of the objects for their meanings, is the gravest kind of error that the social scientist can commit. It leads to the setting up of a fictitious world. Simply put, people act toward things on the basis of the meaning that these things have for them, not on the basis of the meaning that these things have for the outside scholar. Yet we are confronted right and left with studies of human group life and of the behavior of people in which the scholar has made no attempt to find out how the people see what they are acting toward. This neglect is officially fostered by two pernicious tendencies in current methodology: (1) the belief that mere expertise in the use of scientific techniques plus facility in some given theory are sufficient equipment to study an unfamiliar area; and (2) the stress that is placed on being objective, which all too frequently merely means seeing things from the position of the detached outside observer. We have multitudes of studies of groups such as delinquents, police, military elites, restless students, racial minorities, and labor unions in which the scholar is unfamiliar with the life of the groups and makes little, if any, effort to get inside their worlds of meanings. We are compelled, I believe, to recognize that this is a widespread practice in the social sciences.

To try to identify the objects that comprise the world of an individual or a collectivity is not simple or easy for the scholar who is not familiar with that world. It requires, first of all, ability to place oneself in the position of the individual or collectivity. This ability to take the roles of others, like any other potential skill, requires cultivation to be effective. By and large, the training of scholars in the social sciences today is not concerned with the cultivation of this ability nor do their usual practices in research study foster its development. Second, to identify the objects of central concern one must have a body of relevant observations. These necessary observations are rarely those that are yielded by standard research procedure such as questionnaires, polls, scales, use of survey research items, or the setting of predesignated variables. Instead, they are in the form of descriptive accounts from the actors of how they see the objects, how they have acted toward the objects in a variety of different situations, and how they refer to the objects in their conversations with members of their own group. The depiction of key objects that emerge from such accounts should, in turn, be subject to probing and critical collective discussion by a group of well-informed participants in the given world. This latter procedure is a genuine "must" to guard against the admitted deficiencies of individual accounts. Third, as mentioned in earlier discussion, research scholars, like human beings in general, are slaves to their own pre-established images and thus are prone to assume that other people see the given objects as they, the scholars, see them. Scholars need to guard against this proneness and to give high priority to deliberate testing of their images.

All these observations make clear the need for a different methodological approach if one takes seriously the proposition that people act toward objects on the basis of the meaning of such objects for them. This proposition calls for kinds of inquiry significantly different from those generally sanctioned and encouraged today. Since people everywhere and in all of their groups live in worlds of objects and act in terms of the meaning of these objects to them, it is a matter of simple sense that one has to identify the objects and their meaning. The research position of symbolic interaction is predicated on this recognition. . . .

Society as Symbolic Interaction

The term "symbolic interaction" refers, of course, to the peculiar and distinctive character of interaction as it takes place between human beings. The peculiarity consists in the fact that human beings interpret or "define" each other's actions instead of merely reacting to each other's actions. Their "response" is not made directly to the actions of one another but instead is based on the meaning which they attach to such actions. Thus, human interaction is mediated by the use of symbols, by interpretation, or by ascertaining the meaning of one another's actions. This mediation is equivalent to inserting a process of interpretation between stimulus and response in the case of human behavior.

The simple recognition that human beings interpret each other's actions as the means of acting toward one another has permeated the thought and writings of many scholars of human conduct and of human group life. Yet few of them have endeavored to analyze what such interpretation implies about the nature of the human being or about the nature of human association. They are usually content with a mere recognition that "interpretation" should be caught by the student, or with a simple realization that symbols, such as cultural norms or values, must be introduced into their analyses. Only G. H. Mead, in my judgment, has sought to think through what the act of interpretation implies for an understanding of the human being, human action, and human association. The essentials of his analysis are so penetrating and profound and so important for an understanding of human group life that I wish to spell them out, even though briefly.

The key feature in Mead's analysis is that the human being has a self. This idea should not be cast aside as esoteric or glossed over as something that is obvious and hence not worthy of attention. In declaring that the human being has a self, Mead had in mind chiefly that the human being can be the object of his own actions. He can act toward himself as he might act toward others. Each of us is familiar with actions of this sort in which the human being gets angry with himself, rebuffs himself, takes pride in himself, argues with himself, tries to bolster his own courage, tells himself that he should "do this" or not "do that," sets goals for himself, makes compromises with himself, and plans what he is going to do. That the human being acts toward himself in these and countless other ways is a matter of easy empirical observation. To recognize that the human being can act toward himself is no mystical conjuration.

Mead regards this ability of the human being to act toward himself as the central mechanism with which the human being faces and deals with his world. This mechanism enables the human being to make indications to himself of things in his surroundings and thus to guide his actions by what he notes. Anything of which a human being is conscious is something which he is indicating to himself – the ticking of a clock, a knock at the door, the appearance of a friend, the remark made by a companion, a recognition that he has a task to perform, or the realization that he has a cold. Conversely, anything of which he is not conscious is, *ipso facto*, something which he is not indicating to himself. The conscious life of the human being, from the time that he awakens until he falls asleep, is a continual flow of self-indications – notations of the things with which he deals and takes into account. We are given, then, a picture of the human being as an organism which confronts its world with a mechanism for making indications to itself. This is the mechanism that is involved in interpreting the actions of others. To interpret the actions of another is to point out to oneself that the action has this or that meaning or character.

Now, according to Mead, the significance of making indications to oneself is of paramount importance. The importance lies along two lines. First, to indicate something is to extricate it from its setting, to hold it apart, to give it a meaning or, in Mead's language, to make it into an object. An object – that is to say, anything that an individual indicates to himself–is different from a stimulus; instead of having an intrinsic character which acts on the individual and which can be identified apart from the individual, its character or meaning is conferred on it by the individual. The object is a product of the individual's disposition to act instead of being an antecedent stimulus which evokes the act. Instead of the individual being surrounded by an environment of pre-existing objects which play upon him and call forth his behavior, the proper picture is that he constructs his objects on the basis of his on-going activity. In any of his countless acts – whether minor, like dressing himself, or major, like organizing himself for a professional career – the individual is designating different objects to himself, giving them meaning, judging their suitability to his action, and making decisions on the basis of the judgment. This is what is meant by interpretation or acting on the basis of symbols.

The second important implication of the fact that the human being makes indications to himself is that his action is constructed or built up instead of being a mere release. Whatever the action in which he is engaged, the human individual proceeds by pointing out to himself the divergent things which have to be taken into account in the course of his action. He has to note what he wants to do and how he is to do it; he has to point out to himself the various conditions which may be instrumental to his action and those which may obstruct his action; he has to take account of the demands, the expectations, the prohibitions, and the threats as they may arise in the situation in which he is acting. His action is built up step by step through a process of such self-indication. The human individual pieces together and guides his action by taking account of different things and interpreting their significance for his prospective action. There is no instance of conscious action of which this is not true.

The process of constructing action through making indications to oneself cannot be swallowed up in any of the conventional psychological categories. This process is distinct from and different from what is spoken of as the "ego" – just as it is different from any other conception which conceives of the self in terms of composition or organization. Self-indication is a moving communicative process in which the individual notes things, assesses them, gives them a meaning, and decides to act on the basis of the meaning. The human being stands over against the world, or against "alters," with such a process and not with a mere ego. Further, the process of self-indication cannot be subsumed under the forces, whether from the outside or inside, which are presumed to play upon the individual to produce his behavior. Environmental pressures, external stimuli, organic drives, wishes, attitudes, feelings, ideas, and their like do not cover or explain the process of self-indication. The process of self-indication stands over against them in that the individual points out to himself and interprets the appearance or expression of such things, noting a given social demand that is made on him, recognizing a command, observing that he is hungry, realizing that he wishes to buy something, aware that he has a given feeling, conscious that he dislikes eating with someone he despises, or aware that he is thinking of doing some given thing. By virtue of indicating such things to himself, he places himself over against them and is able to act back against them, accepting them, rejecting them, or transforming them in accordance with how he defines or interprets them. His behavior, accordingly, is not a result of such things as environmental pressures, stimuli, motives, attitudes, and ideas but arises instead from how he interprets and handles these things in the action which he is constructing. The process of self-indication by means of which human action is formed cannot be accounted for by factors which precede the act. The process of self-indication exists in its own right and must be accepted and studied as such. It is through this process that the human being constructs his conscious action.

Now Mead recognizes that the formation of action by the individual through a process of self-indication always takes place in a social context. Since this matter is so vital to an understanding of symbolic interaction it needs to be explained carefully. Fundamentally, group action takes the form of a fitting together of individual lines of action. Each individual aligns his action to the action of others by ascertaining what they are doing or what they intend to do – that is, by getting the meaning of their acts. For Mead, this is done by the individual "taking the role" of others – either the role of a specific person or the role of a group (Mead's "generalized other"). In taking such roles the individual seeks to ascertain the intention or direction of the acts of others. He forms and aligns his own action on the basis of such interpretation of the acts of others. This is the fundamental way in which group action takes place in human society.

The foregoing are the essential features, as I see them, in Mead's analysis of the bases of symbolic interaction. They presuppose the following: that human society is made up of individuals who have selves (that is, make indications to themselves); that individual action is a construction and not a release, being built up by the individual through noting and interpreting features of the situations in which he acts; that group or collective action consists of the aligning of individual actions, brought about by the individuals' interpreting or taking into account each other's actions. Since my purpose is to present and not to defend the position of symbolic interaction I shall not endeavor in this essay to advance support for the three premises which I have just indicated. I wish merely to say that the three premises can be easily verified empirically. I know of no instance of human group action to which the three premises do not apply. The reader is challenged to find or think of a single instance which they do not fit.

I wish now to point out that sociological views of human society are, in general, markedly at variance with the premises which I have indicated as underlying symbolic interaction. Indeed, the predominant number of such views, especially those in vogue at the present time, do not see or treat human society as symbolic interaction. Wedded, as they tend to be, to some form of sociological determinism, they adopt images of human society, of individuals in it, and of group action which do not square with the premises of symbolic interaction. I wish to say a few words about the major lines of variance.

Sociological thought rarely recognizes or treats human societies as composed of individuals who have selves. Instead, they assume human beings to be merely organisms with some kind of organization, responding to forces which play upon them. Generally, although not exclusively, these forces are lodged in the make-up of the society, as in the case of "social system," "social structure," "culture," "status position," "social role," "custom," "institution," "collective representation," "social situation," "social norm," and "values." The assumption is that the behavior of people as members *of a society* is an expression of the play on them of these kinds of factors or forces. This, of course, is the logical position which is necessarily taken when the scholar explains their behavior or phases of their behavior in terms of one or another of such social factors. The individuals who compose a human society are treated as the media through which such factors operate, and the social action of such individuals is regarded as an expression of such factors. This approach or point of view denies, or at least ignores, that human beings have selves – that they act by making indications to themselves. Incidentally, the "self" is not brought into the picture by introducing such items as organic drives, motives, attitudes, feelings, internalized social factors, or psychological components. Such psychological factors have the same status as the social factors mentioned: they are regarded as factors which play on the individual to produce his action. They do not constitute the process of self-indication. The process of self-indication stands over against them, just as it stands over against the social factors which play on the human being. Practically all sociological conceptions of human society fail to recognize that the individuals who compose it have selves in the sense spoken of.

Correspondingly, such sociological conceptions do not regard the social actions of individuals in human society as being constructed by them through a process of interpretation. Instead, action is treated as a product of factors which play on and through individuals. The social behavior of people is not seen as built up by them through an interpretation of objects, situations, or the actions of others. If a place is given to "interpretation," the interpretation is regarded as merely an expression of other factors (such as motives) which precede the act, and accordingly disappears as a factor in its own right. Hence, the social action of people is treated as an outward flow or expression of forces playing on them rather than as acts which are built up by people through their interpretation of the situations in which they are placed.

These remarks suggest another significant line of difference between general socio-logical views and the position of symbolic interaction. These two sets of views differ in where they lodge social action. Under the perspective of symbolic interaction, social action is lodged in acting individuals who fit their respective lines of action to one another through a process of interpretation; group action is the collective action of such individuals. As opposed to this view, sociological conceptions generally lodge social action in the action of society or in some unit of society. Examples of this are legion. Let me cite a few. Some conceptions, in treating societies or human groups as "social systems," regard group action as an expression of a system, either in a state of balance or seeking to achieve balance. Or group action is conceived as an expression of the "functions" of a society or of a group. Or group action is regarded as the outward expression of elements lodged in society or the group, such as cultural demands, societal purposes, social values, or institutional stresses. These typical conceptions ignore or blot out a view of group life or of group action as consisting of the collective or concerted actions of individuals seeking to meet their life situ-ations. If recognized at all, the efforts of people to develop collective acts to meet their situations are subsumed under the play of underlying or transcending forces which are lodged in society or its parts. The individuals composing the society or the group become "carriers," or media for the expression of such forces; and the interpretative behavior by means of which people form their actions is merely a coerced link in the play of such forces.

The indication of the foregoing lines of variance should help to put the position of symbolic interaction in better perspective. In the remaining discussion I wish to sketch somewhat more fully how human society appears in terms of symbolic interaction and to point out some methodological implications.

Human society is to be seen as consisting of acting people, and the life of the society is to be seen as consisting of their actions. The acting units may be separate individuals, collectivities whose members are acting together on a common quest, or organizations acting on behalf of a constituency. Respective examples are individual purchasers in a market, a play group or missionary band, and a business corporation or a national professional association. There is no empirically observable activity in a human society that does not spring from some acting unit. This banal statement needs to be stressed in light of the common practice of sociologists of reducing human society to social units that do not act – for example, social classes in modern society. Obviously, there are ways of viewing human society other than in terms of the acting units that compose it. I merely wish to point out that in respect to concrete or empirical activity human society must necessarily be seen in terms of the acting units that form it. I would add that any scheme of human society claiming to be a realistic analysis has to respect and be congruent with the empirical recognition that a human society consists of acting units.

Corresponding respect must be shown to the conditions under which such units act. One primary condition is that action takes place in and with regard to a situation. Whatever be the acting unit – an individual, a family, a school, a church, a business firm, a labor union, a legislature, and so on – any particular action is formed in the light of the situation in which it takes place. This leads to the recognition of a second major condition, namely, that the action is formed or constructed by interpreting the situation. The acting unit necessarily has to identify the things which it has to take into account – tasks, opportunities, obstacles, means, demands, discomforts, dangers, and the like; it has to assess them in some fashion and it has to make decisions on the basis of the assessment. Such interpretative behavior may take place in the individual guiding his own action, in a collectivity of individuals acting in concert, or in "agents" acting on behalf of a group or organization. Group life consists of acting units developing acts to meet the situations in which they are placed.

Usually, most of the situations encountered by people in a given society are defined or "structured" by them in the same way. Through previous interaction they develop and acquire common understandings or definitions of how to act in this or that situation. These common definitions enable people to act alike. The common repetitive behavior of people in such situations should not mislead the student into believing that no process of interpretation is in play; on the contrary, even though fixed, the actions of the participating people are constructed by them through a process of interpretation. Since ready-made and commonly accepted definitions are at hand, little strain is placed on people in guiding and organizing their acts. However, many other situations may not be defined in a single way by the participating people. In this event, their lines of action do not fit together readily and collective action is blocked. Interpretations have to be developed and effective accommodation of the participants to one another has to be worked out. In the case of such "undefined" situations, it is necessary to trace and study the emerging process of definition which is brought into play.

Insofar as sociologists or students of human society are concerned with the behavior of acting units, the position of symbolic interaction requires the student to catch the process of interpretation through which they construct their actions. This process is not to be caught merely by turning to conditions which are antecedent to the process. Such antecedent conditions are helpful in understanding the process insofar as they enter into it, but as mentioned previously they do not constitute the process. Nor can one catch the process merely by inferring its nature from the overt action which is its product. To catch the process, the student must take the role of the acting unit whose behavior he is studying. Since the interpretation is being made by the acting unit in terms of objects designated and appraised, meanings acquired, and decisions made, the process has to be seen from the standpoint of the acting unit. It is the recognition of this fact that makes the research work of such scholars as R. E. Park and W. I. Thomas so notable. To try to catch the interpretative process by remaining aloof as a so-called "objective" observer and refusing to take the role of the acting unit is to risk the worst kind of subjectivism –

the objective observer is likely to fill in the process of interpretation with his own surmises in place of catching the process as it occurs in the experience of the acting unit which uses it.

By and large, of course, sociologists do not study human society in terms of its acting units. Instead, they are disposed to view human society in terms of structure or organization and to treat social action as an expression of such structure or organization. Thus, reliance is placed on such structural categories as social system, culture, norms, values, social stratification, status positions, social roles and institutional organization. These are used both to analyze human society and to account for social action within it. Other major interests of sociological scholars center around this focal theme of organization. One line of interest is to view organization in terms of the functions it is supposed to perform. Another line of interest is to study societal organization as a system seeking equilibrium; here the scholar endeavors to detect mechanisms which are indigenous to the system. Another line of interest is to identify forces which play upon organization to bring about changes in it; here the scholar endeavors, especially through comparative study, to isolate a relation between causative factors and structural results. These various lines of sociological perspective and interest, which are so strongly entrenched today, leap over the acting units of a society and bypass the interpretative process by which such acting units build up their actions.

These respective concerns with organization on one hand and with acting units on the other hand set the essential difference between conventional views of human society and the view of it implied in symbolic interaction. The latter view recognizes the presence of organization to human society and respects its importance. However, it sees and treats organization differently. The difference is along two major lines. First, from the standpoint of symbolic interaction the organization of a human society is the framework inside of which social action takes place and is not the determinant of that action. Second, such organization and changes in it are the product of the activity of acting units and not of "forces" which leave such acting units out of account. Each of these two major lines of difference should be explained briefly in order to obtain a better understanding of how human society appears in terms of symbolic interaction.

From the standpoint of symbolic interaction, social organization is a framework inside of which acting units develop their actions. Structural features, such as "culture," "social systems," "social stratification," or "social roles," set conditions for their action but do not determine their action. People – that is, acting units – do not act toward culture, social structure or the like; they act toward situations. Social organization enters into action only to the extent to which it shapes situations in which people act, and to the extent to which it supplies fixed sets of symbols which people use in interpreting their situations. These two forms of influence of social organization are important. In the case of settled and stabilized societies, such as isolated primitive tribes and peasant communities, the influence is certain to be profound. In the case of human societies, particularly modern societies, in which streams of new situations arise and old situations become unstable, the influence of organization decreases. One should bear in mind that the most important element confronting an acting unit in situations is the actions of other acting units. In modern society, with its increasing criss-crossing of lines of action, it is common for situations to arise in which the actions of participants are not previously regularized and standardized. To this extent, existing social organization does not shape the situations. Correspondingly, the symbols or tools of interpretation used by acting units in such situations may vary and shift considerably. For these reasons, social action may go beyond, or depart from, existing organization in any of its structural dimensions. The organization of a human society is not to be identified with the process of interpretation used by its acting units; even though it affects that process, it does not embrace or cover the process.

Perhaps the most outstanding consequence of viewing human society as organization is to overlook the part played by acting units in social change. The conventional procedure of sociologists is (*a*) to identify human society (or some part of it) in terms of an established or organized form, (*b*) to identify some factor or condition of change playing upon the human society or the given part of it, and (*c*) to identify the new form assumed by the society following upon the play of the factor of change. Such observations permit the student to couch propositions to the effect that a given factor of change playing upon a given organized form results in a given new organized form. Examples ranging from crude to refined statements are legion, such as that an economic depression increases solidarity in the families of working-men or that industrialization replaces extended families by nuclear families. My concern here is not with the validity of such propositions but with the methodological position which they presuppose. Essentially, such propositions either ignore the role of the interpretative behavior of acting units in the given instance of change, or else regard the interpretative behavior as coerced by the factor of change. I wish to point out that any line of social change, since it involves change in human action, is necessarily mediated by interpretation on the part of the people caught up in the change – the change appears in the form of new situations in which people have to construct new forms of action. Also, in line with what has been said previously, interpretations of new situations are not predetermined by conditions antecedent to the situations but depend on what is taken into account and assessed in the actual situations in which behavior is formed. Variations in interpretation may readily occur as different acting units cut out different objects in the situation, or give different weight to the objects which they note, or piece objects together in different patterns. In formulating propositions of social change, it would be wise to recognize that any given line of such change is mediated by acting units interpreting the situations with which they are confronted.

Students of human society will have to face the question of whether their preoccupation with categories of structure and organization can be squared with the interpretative process by means of which human beings, individually and collectively, act in human society. It is the discrepancy between the two which plagues such students in their efforts to attain scientific propositions of the sort achieved in the physical and biological sciences. It is this discrepancy, further, which is chiefly responsible for their difficulty in fitting hypothetical propositions to new arrays of empirical data. Efforts are made, of course, to overcome these shortcomings by devising new structural categories, by formulating new structural hypotheses, by developing more refined techniques of research, and even by formulating new methodological schemes of a structural character. These efforts continue to ignore or to explain away the interpretative process by which people act, individually and collectively, in society. The question remains whether human society or social action can be successfully analyzed by schemes which refuse to recognize human beings as they are, namely, as persons constructing individual and collective action through an interpretation of the situations which confront them.

Part II

Exchange and Rationality

INTRODUCTION TO PART II

One way of analyzing social action is to ask what interests it serves. A researcher might start by asking who benefits from any system of interactions? Beyond this, more specific questions might involve which of their interests people are able to realize, and how interests are translated into action. Answering such questions involves analyzing the ways in which people's actions are guided by strategies – consciously or unconsciously – and the extent to which those strategies are rational. This need not be a psychological inquiry into how people think. For sociology, it starts crucially with examination of how efficiently particular courses of action achieve desired or desirable results. This is clearly a matter of whole social systems as well as individual actors. Making the assumption that people will act more or less rationally and on the bases of their interests enables sociologists to predict patterns of behavior on both small and large scales.

Social exchange theory starts mainly at the level of interpersonal interaction. In this section, we present work from two of its pioneers. George Homans (1910–89) draws on behavioral psychology to show the ways in which participants in inter-action are always learning – which sorts of actions are successful, which fail – and thus being conditioned by other actors. Peter M. Blau (b. 1918) follows a more economic approach, stressing that interactions in fact involve transactions – that is, participants give and receive. In all exchange theory, the emphasis falls not on explaining action by values or norms, but on explaining action by what works effectively for actors seeking to realize their interests. How they understand those interests, of course, may be shaped partly by their previous experience of social interaction.

Rational choice theory builds on similar foundations. Its authors generally place more emphasis, however, on identifying rational (that is, efficient) courses of action in the abstract and comparing actual behavior to them. Such comparisons frequently show that with an accurate understanding of the interests actors pursue and the mix of resources and constraints they face, one can predict or explain their actions. While exchange theory is rooted in interpersonal relations, rational choice theory is more often used to identify the effects of the interdependent action of individuals on the behavior of the social system as a whole. This section presents the work of James Coleman (1926–95), sociology's most influential rational choice theorist, and Mancur Olson (1932–88), an economist who shifted his attention to sociological explanation.

Both exchange and rational choice theories start with the actions and interactions of individuals – this is called "methodological individualism" – but seek explan-ations at the level of larger social systems. As James Coleman pointed out, social systems are rarely observed as wholes.[1] Instead, we observe the actions and inter-actions of actors within the system. From this we make inferences about the system as a whole, and on this basis rational choice and exchange theories seek to explain it. While "system" here could refer to an entire national or even global society, analyses are usually focused on smaller social systems: a particular organization, or social movement for example.

Work in this theoretical tradition generally does not seek to explain the behavior of particular individuals in terms of their personal feelings or motivations. Rather, it focuses on aggregate patterns of action in social systems. Toward this end, simplifying assumptions about behavior are often employed. The most basic is the postulate of rationality. This states that people are purposive actors who seek to *optimize*.[2] Given a set of potential actions, people choose the one that provides them the best outcome.

The postulate of rationality, seemingly banal when applied to individual decisions such as finding the fastest route home from work, becomes sociologically interesting when action becomes interdependent. Thus, the individually optimal route home transforms into a collective nightmare during rush hour, as each person's driving affects those around him or her. Moreover, when the goods one optimizes are *social* (such as praise, esteem, or honor) the quality of interaction changes. Since the value of social goods is hard to identify and can only be realized through interaction with others, the problem of optimization immediately becomes a problem of *social exchange*.

Social Exchange Theory

The strongest initial influence on George Homans' exchange theory came from the behaviorist ideas of B. F. Skinner. For behaviorists, the primary determinant of individual action is the *operant conditioning* relationship between an actor and his or her environment. Operant conditioning states that any behavior elicits a response from the environment (which could be composed of other people). If the response is positive, actors are more likely to repeat the behavior, and when the response is negative they will be less likely to repeat the behavior. For example, the behavior "touching a hot stove" results in pain, which lessens the likelihood that one will touch the stove again. The same holds true in the social environment. Based on the responses of others to past behavior, people modify their behavior in an attempt to maximize positive reactions and minimize negative reactions.

George Herbert Mead adopted behaviorism as a way to examine the effect of society on the self. Homans used the idea to examine the way society emerges from individual behavior. Like Mead, Homans posited that other people form the social environment to which each of us reacts. Because each of us is also part of the environment of others, there is a dual nature to interaction that can best be characterized as exchange. Simply put, "interaction between persons is an exchange of goods, material and non-material."[3] Homans' goal was to explain how this interaction could yield stable patterns of social order. For example, we sanction those who disappoint us, and we avoid disappointing others, and so norms are created. Once they are created, norms are upheld because we want to avoid the social punishments people enforce when a norm is violated. Homans later formalized his conception of social exchange theory into a set of basic propositions about individual behavior, which specified how people could be expected to act in the face of various types of rewards and punishments.

Homans' work was a direct response to the work of functionalists such as Talcott Parsons. Homans argued that the elaborate theoretical schemes proposed by functionalists were fictions that could not be observed and that were ineffective at explaining social behavior. Instead of grand structures, Homans wanted to explain more "elementary" forms of social life. From these elementary building blocks, one could construct a more complete – and grounded – theory of social life. Parsons and Homans engaged in an extended debate over which theoretical approach was most appropriate for sociology. At the heart of the debate was the question of what we can and cannot know about society. Parsons argued that certain fundamental features of social systems were entirely social and could not be reduced to the individual level. Homans, on the other hand, felt that any element of a social system must have its roots in the actions of individuals. While each actively engaged the other, no resolution between the two approaches emerged.

A second version of exchange theory was developed by Peter Blau. Blau's focus was on understanding collective outcomes, such as the distribution of power in a society. Instead of basing his work on operant conditioning, however, he worked more explicitly from an economic framework, arguing that social interaction has value to people. People become involved in social exchanges for the same reason that they become involved in economic exchanges – they need things from each other that they cannot provide for themselves. Moreover, Peter Blau attempted to develop exchange theory without giving up the non-reducible character of social interaction. In sharp contrast to Homans, Blau explicitly stated that some properties of social exchange are *emergent*. In other words, the sum of social interaction cannot be reduced to the psychological states of individuals. Building on Simmel's formal sociology, Blau argued that extended patterns of exchange give rise to organizational forms with qualities beyond those of the people in the organization.

For Blau, the basis of social exchange rests on the anticipated rewards of association. Rewards may be either intrinsic (the inner pleasure of being with someone), extrinsic (a tangible good or service that someone can provide), or both. Social exchange, like economic exchange, occurs when association provides both parties with a reward they could not get on their own. There are significant differences, however, between economic exchange and social exchange that hinge on the ambiguous nature of social exchange. First, because social goods (such as favors or advice) do not carry explicit values, one cannot be certain that an exchange is equal. Second, social exchanges usually occur over long periods. For example, gifts often cannot be repaid right away, and so become a kind of social debt. Because of this, there is no assurance that a "good" given will be returned.

These problems result in two special features of social exchange. First, the ambiguity associated with social exchange requires trust for the exchange to function, and trust is usually built slowly. Second, if the value of a good is ambiguous, and if people want to remain out of debt to others, then there is a tendency for social exchange to escalate. Social integration emerges from these processes, both motivated by individual desire for rewards. As Blau puts it, "An apparent 'altruism' pervades social life; people are anxious to benefit one another and to reciprocate for the benefits they receive. But beneath this seeming selflessness an underlying 'egoism' can be discovered; the tendency to help others is frequently motivated by the expectation that doing so will bring social rewards."[4]

Peter Blau's work also clearly incorporates issues of power and inequality. Power rests fundamentally on the ability to control access to a particular good. If actors have exclusive access to something that other actors want, then they can extract greater rewards from them. While this is clear with a simple material commodity such as water, Blau argued that the same principle works for intrinsic social rewards. He illustrates this clearly with the example of the "principle of least interest" and romantic love. When one person in a relationship loves the other more (finds higher intrinsic value in the relationship) he or she will give up more to remain in the relationship, giving power to the one who loves the least.

If power comes from having something others want, then powerful people can extract social value from less powerful people through exchange. However, the one social commodity that *everyone* has access to is his or her own ability. As such, Blau argues that *subordination* is the one universal good that all can use for exchange. Those without access to a desired good can exchange with those who do have the good by subordinating themselves to the powerful, so that an imbalance in exchange leads directly to inequalities of power.

Exchange and Rational Choice

One direction of continued development in exchange theory has been further study of the social psychology of interactions. Researchers pose questions about how action varies with different kinds of motivations, cultures, or groups. More influential within sociology has been a second direction of development, rational choice theory. This shifts the focus away from exchange itself and toward the outcomes of interdependent action when individual actors are assumed to be rational. The broad insight of this work is that what appears rational to an individual – even to every individual in a group – may not yield rationality for the entire group. For example, if three gas stations compete at an intersection, it may be rational for one to lower prices to attract customers away from the others. But if all three follow the same rational course of action this will drive prices down to an uncomfortably low level. The group would be better served by some agreement to charge the same higher prices (though of course, their customers have different interests). A key sociological question is when and how groups can organize cooperation to achieve such collective interests.

This distinction between group and individual rationality was made clearly by Mancur Olson in his famous work, *The Logic of Collective Action*. Analyzing situations just like that of the competing gas stations – but also social movements on a broad scale – Olson showed that the existence of common interests among a group of people is not sufficient to produce collective action that would realize those interests. When a good is indivisible – that is, when it is a "collective good" and everyone would benefit from it regardless of who contributed to producing it – rational individuals will not participate in helping to provide the good, all else being equal. This is because the costs of producing the good are borne only by those who participate. People will therefore prefer to let others produce the good. Of course, when everyone acts this way the good will not be produced at all. In our example, each gas station owner would like the others to keep the general prices up, while giving him the chance to undercut them with a slightly lower price. Having shown that simply sharing interests in some outcome would not lead a group to act collectively to achieve it, Olson focused analysts' attention on the conditions under which people would participate in the production of collective goods. For example, not surprisingly, it is easier to organize cooperation in smaller groups, where each person can see what the others contribute. More generally, interpersonal relations – or social exchanges of the type Blau identified – are important for producing collective actions.

James Coleman sought to show the usefulness of rational choice theory in explaining many different kinds of sociological phenomena. Most basically, he focused on identifying how norms arise from a collection of self-interested actors. Many other theorists treated norms as already established before action – for example as given by culture. They then used such norms to explain action. Coleman sought to explain the origins of norms themselves. Norms – and regulative behavior more generally – require that individuals subordinate their interests to collective interests. Given the problems identified by Olson, such behavior is often hard to produce, even when it is needed.

In line with the earlier exchange theorists, Coleman identified networks of trust as an essential element in modern society. In his now classic treatment of "social capital," Coleman described how the relations actors have with others provide them with a generalized capacity for action – in much the same way as economic capital allows investors to build factories and start companies. Defining exactly what counts as social capital has sparked something of a minor industry in sociology, but all agree that the informal interactions among people contribute to a generalized capacity to act. For example, knowing many people increases your odds of knowing someone who can help you find a job, which provides a clear example of how social capital can generate economic capital. At the aggregate level, theorists have argued that social capital is key to understanding political participation and the ability of communities to cooperate for common good.[5]

The Legacy of Exchange and Rationality

Critics of rational choice and exchange theory perspectives have leveled several important charges.[6] First, many people argue that the basic behavioral assumptions of rational choice theory are incorrect. People simply do not optimize for their own self-interest, but instead act habitually, normatively or simply irrationally. While some rational choice theorists respond by changing the focus of rationality (a seemingly irrational act – such as throwing oneself on a grenade – is made rational by referencing one's perceived reputation as a hero), such maneuvers quickly lead to tautology. That is, if people always behave rationally, then any course of action is rational by definition. Second, critics point out that the complex interdependence implicit in interaction makes predicting future outcomes impossible. As such, simple rational choice models that depend on people making judgments about the future are seen to be unrealistic. Finally, still other critics argue that sociology is best served by focusing on macro-level aspects of social organization directly, and that the search for a micro model of macro behavior is not productive. Indeed, Peter Blau himself moved away from social exchange theory in favor of a macro-level model of social interaction based on the distribution of types of people in the population.

However, exchange and rational choice theories remain prominent. They offer several advantages, including parsimony – the ability to explain a good deal by very simple theoretical assumptions. Largely for this reason, they lend themselves well to computer-modeling and mathematical sociology. Rational choice theory also helps to make clearer many of the assumptions about human behavior that have remained implicit in empirical work that considers large aggregates of decisions – for example, in demographic studies that need to establish links between parental decisions to have a certain number of children and overall fertility rates or population growth patterns. Exchange and rational choice theories have also provided a set of micro-foundations for such macrosociological theories as systems theory.[7]

Notes

1 Coleman (1990).
2 Coleman and Fararo (1992: xi).
3 Homans (1958: 597).
4 Blau (1964: 17).
5 Putnam (2000).
6 For a very clear review and clarification of many of these issues, see Hollis (1988).
7 Collins (1981).

Select Bibliography

Blau, Peter M. 1964. *Exchange and Power in Social Life*. New York: Wiley. (The major statement of Peter Blau's exchange theory. An excellent source for those seeking deeper understanding of his approach to social exchange theory.)
——. 1977. *Inequality and Heterogeneity: A Primitive Theory of Social Structure*. New York: Free Press. (The most complete presentation of Blau's macrosociological work, which interestingly argues for a foundation of sociology at the macro level, recanting his own earlier work.)
——. 1994. *Structural Contexts of Opportunities*. Chicago and London: University of Chicago Press. (A nice summary of all of Blau's work, that seeks to integrate the ideas of both *Exchange and Power* and *Inequality and Heterogeneity* by situating exchange within the macro level.)
Coleman, James S. 1988. "Social Capital in the Creation of Human Capital." *American Journal of Sociology* 94: s95–s120. (While not the first introduction of the concept of social capital in sociology, the one that has sparked most of the current works on social capital recently.)
——. 1990. *Foundations of Social Theory*. Cambridge, MA: Belknap Press. (Arguably Coleman's magnum opus. A work that seeks to develop a complete theory of social organization from an individualist methodological standpoint. A difficult, though rewarding, work.)
Coleman, James S. and Thomas J. Fararo. 1992. *Rational Choice Theory: Advocacy and Critique*. Newbury Park, CA: Sage Publications. (An edited volume that contains some very good papers, both pro and con, on the value of rational choice theory in sociology.)
Collins, Randall. 1981. "On the Micro-foundations of Macro-sociology," *American Journal of Sociology* 80: 984–1014. (A classic article on the ways in which microsociological analysis can support larger scale theory-building.)

Cook, Karen. 1991. "The Microfoundations of Social Structure: An Exchange Perspective," pp. 29–45 in Joan Huber, ed., *Macro–Micro Linkages in Sociology.* Beverly Hills, CA: Sage. (A clear review of the ways in which different kinds of exchange theory can provide the bases for macrosociological accounts of social structure.)

Hollis, Martin. 1988. *The Cunning of Reason.* Cambridge: Cambridge University Press. (A very clear examination of the conceptual and analytic issues involved in methodological individualism and rational choice analysis by a philosopher of social science.)

Homans, George C. 1958. "Social Behavior as Exchange." *American Journal of Sociology* 63: 597–606. (The first introduction of exchange from a behaviorist standpoint.)

——. 1961. *Social Behavior: Its Elementary Forms.* New York: Harcourt, Brace and World, Inc. (The full, expanded treatment of Homans' social exchange theory.)

Olson, Mancur. 1965. *The Logic of Collective Action: Public Goods and the Theory of Groups.* Cambridge, MA: Harvard University Press. (Olson's classic book provides a concise statement of why collective action among rational actors is rare.)

Putnam, Robert D. 2000. *Bowling Alone: The Collapse and Revival of American Community.* New York: Simon & Schuster. (Putnam describes trends and changes in the national distribution of social capital, conceived of as involvement in secondary associations.)

Willer, David, editor. 1999. *Network Exchange Theory.* Westport, Connecticut: Praeger. (A nice overview book that summarizes the basic tenets of Network Exchange Theory, the theoretical assumptions, and empirical findings of this field.)

5 Social Behavior as Exchange

George C. Homans

An Exchange Paradigm

I start with the link to behavioral psychology and the kind of statement it makes about the behavior of an experimental animal such as the pigeon.[1] As a pigeon explores its cage in the laboratory, it happens to peck a target, whereupon the psychologist feeds it corn. The evidence is that it will peck the target again; it has learned the behavior, or, as my friend Skinner says, the behavior has been reinforced, and the pigeon has undergone *operant conditioning*. This kind of psychologist is not interested in how the behavior was learned: "learning theory" is a poor name for his field. Instead, he is interested in what determines changes in the rate of emission of learned behavior, whether pecks at a target or something else.

The more hungry the pigeon, the less corn or other food it has gotten in the recent past, the more often it will peck. By the same token, if the behavior is often reinforced, if the pigeon is given much corn every time it pecks, the rate of emission will fall off as the pigeon gets *satiated*. If, on the other hand, the behavior is not reinforced at all, then, too, its rate of emission will tend to fall off, though a long time may pass before it stops altogether, before it is *extinguished*. In the emission of many kinds of behavior the pigeon incurs *aversive stimulation*, or what I shall call "cost" for short, and this, too, will lead in time to a decrease in the emission rate. Fatigue is an example of a "cost." Extinction, satiation, and cost, by decreasing the rate of emission of a particular kind of behavior, render more probable the emission of some other kind of behavior, including doing nothing. I shall only add that even a hard-boiled psychologist puts "emotional" behavior, as well as such things as pecking, among the unconditioned responses that may be reinforced in operant conditioning. As a statement of the propositions of behavioral psychology, the foregoing is, of course, inadequate for any purpose except my present one.

We may look on the pigeon as engaged in an exchange – pecks for corn – with the psychologist, but let us not dwell upon that, for the behavior of the pigeon hardly determines the behavior of the psychologist at all. Let us turn to a situation where the exchange is real, that is, where the determination is mutual. Suppose we are dealing with two men. Each is emitting behavior reinforced to some degree by the behavior of the other. How it was in the past that each learned the behavior he emits and how he learned to find the other's behavior reinforcing we are not concerned with. It is enough that each does find the other's behavior reinforcing, and I shall call the reinforcers – the equivalent of the pigeon's corn – *values*, for this, I think, is what we mean by this term. As he emits behavior, each man may incur costs, and each man has more than one course of behavior open to him.

This seems to me the paradigm of elementary social behavior, and the problem of the elementary sociologist is to state propositions relating the variations in the values and costs of each man to his frequency distribution of behavior among alternatives, where the values (in the mathematical sense) taken by these variables for one man determine in part their values for the other.[2]

I see no reason to believe that the propositions of behavioral psychology do not apply to this situation, though the complexity of their implications in the concrete case may be great indeed. In particular, we must suppose that, with men as with pigeons, an increase in extinction, satiation, or aversive stimulation of any one kind of behavior will increase the probability of emission of some other kind. The problem is not, as it is often stated, merely, what a man's values are, what he has learned in the past to find reinforcing, but how much of any one value his behavior is getting him now. The more he gets, the less valuable any further unit of that value is to him, and the less often he will emit behavior reinforced by it.

The Influence Process

We do not, I think, possess the kind of studies of two-person interaction that would either bear out these propositions or fail to do so. But we do have studies of larger numbers of persons that suggest that they may apply, notably the studies by Festinger, Schachter, Back, and their associates on the dynamics of influence. One of the variables they work with they call *cohesiveness*, defined as anything that attracts people to take part in a group. Cohesiveness is a value variable; it refers to the degree of reinforcement people find in the activities of the group. Festinger and his colleagues consider two kinds of reinforcing activity: the symbolic behavior we call "social approval" (sentiment) and activity valuable in other ways, such as doing something interesting.

The other variable they work with they call *communication* and others call *interaction*. This is a frequency variable; it is a measure of the frequency of emission of valuable and costly verbal behavior. We must bear in mind that, in general, the one kind of variable is a function of the other.

Festinger and his co-workers show that the more cohesive a group is, that is, the more valuable the sentiment or activity the members exchange with one another, the greater the average frequency of interaction of the members.[3] With men, as with pigeons, the greater the reinforcement, the more often is the reinforced behavior emitted. The more cohesive a group, too, the greater the change that members can produce in the behavior of other members in the direction of rendering these activities more valuable.[4] That is, the more valuable the activities that members get, the more valuable those that they must give. For if a person is emitting behavior of a certain kind, and other people do not find it particularly rewarding, these others will suffer their own production of sentiment and activity, in time, to fall off. But perhaps the first person has found their sentiment and activity rewarding, and, if he is to keep on getting them, he must make his own behavior more valuable to the others. In short, the propositions of behavioral psychology imply a tendency toward a certain proportionality between the value to others of the behavior a man gives them and the value to him of the behavior they give him.[5]

Schachter also studied the behavior of members of a group toward two kinds of other members, "conformers" and "deviates."[6] I assume that conformers are people whose activity the other members find valuable. For conformity is behavior that coincides to a degree with some group standard or norm, and the only meaning I can assign to *norm* is "a verbal description of behavior that many members find it valuable for the actual behavior of themselves and others to conform to." By the same token, a deviate is a member whose behavior is not particularly valuable. Now Schachter shows that, as the members of a group come to see another member as a deviate, their interaction with him – communication addressed to getting him to change his behavior – goes up, the faster the more cohesive the group. The members need not talk to the other conformers so much; they are relatively satiated by the conformers' behavior: they have gotten what they want out of them. But if the deviate, by failing to change his behavior, fails to reinforce the members, they start to withhold social approval from him: the deviate gets low sociometric choice at the end of the experiment. And in the most cohesive groups – those Schachter calls "high cohesive-relevant" – interaction with the deviate also falls off in the end and is lowest among those members that rejected him most strongly, as if they had given him up as a bad job. But how plonking can we get? These findings are utterly in line with everyday experience.

Practical Equilibrium

At the beginning of this paper I suggested that one of the tasks of small-group research was to show the relation between the results of experimental work done under laboratory conditions and the results of field research on real-life small groups. Now the latter often appear to be in practical equilibrium, and by this I mean nothing fancy. I do not mean that all real-life groups are in equilibrium. I certainly do not mean that all groups must tend to equilibrium. I do not mean that groups have built-in antidotes to change: there is no homeostasis here. I do not mean that we assume equilibrium. I mean only that we sometimes *observe* it, that for the time we are with a group – and it is often short – there is no great change in the values of the variables we choose to measure. If, for instance, person A is interacting with B more than with C both at the beginning and at the end of the study, then at least by this crude measure the group is in equilibrium.

Many of the Festinger–Schachter studies are experimental, and their propositions about the process of influence seem to me to imply the kind of proposition that empirically holds good of real-life groups in practical equilibrium. For instance, Festinger et al. find that, the more cohesive a group is, the greater the change that members can produce in the behavior of other members. If the influence is exerted in the direction of conformity to group norms, then, when the process of influence has accomplished all the change of which it is capable, the proposition should hold good that, the more cohesive a group is, the larger the number of members that conform to its norms. And it does hold good.[7]

Again, Schachter found, in the experiment I summarized above, that in the most cohesive groups and at the end, when the effort to influence the deviate had failed, members interacted little with the deviate and gave him little in the way of sociometric choice. Now two of the propositions that hold good most often of real-life groups in practical equilibrium are precisely that the more closely a member's activity conforms to the norms the more interaction he receives from other members and the more liking choices he gets from them too. From these main propositions a number of others may be derived that also hold good.[8]

Yet we must ever remember that the truth of the proposition linking conformity to liking may on occasion be masked by the truth of other propositions. If, for instance, the man that conforms to the norms most closely also exerts some authority over the group, this may render liking for him somewhat less than it might otherwise have been.[9]

Be that as it may, I suggest that the laboratory experiments on influence imply propositions about the behavior of members of small groups, when the process of influence has worked itself out, that are identical with propositions that hold good of real-life groups in equilibrium. This is hardly surprising if all we mean by equilibrium is that all the change of which the system is, under present conditions, capable has been effected, so that no further change occurs. Nor would this be the first time that statics has turned out to be a special case of dynamics.

Profit and Social Control

Though I have treated equilibrium as an observed fact, it is a fact that cries for explanation. I shall not, as structural-functional sociologists do, use an assumed equilibrium as a means of explaining, or trying to explain, why the other features of a social system should be what they are. Rather, I shall take practical equilibrium as something that is itself to be explained by the other features of the system.

If every member of a group emits at the end of, and during, a period of time much the same kinds of behavior and in much the same frequencies as he did at the beginning, the group is for that period in equilibrium. Let us then ask why any one member's behavior should persist. Suppose he is emitting behavior of value A_1. Why does he not let his behavior get worse (less valuable or reinforcing to the others) until it stands at $A_1 - \Delta A$? True, the sentiments expressed by others toward him are apt to decline in value (become less reinforcing to him), so that what he gets from them may be $S_1 - \Delta S$. But it is conceivable that, since most activity carries cost, a decline in the value of what he emits will mean a reduction in cost to him that more than offsets his losses in sentiment. Where, then, does he stabilize his behavior? This is the problem of social control.[10]

Mankind has always assumed that a person stabilizes his behavior, at least in the short run, at the point where he is doing the best he can for himself under the circumstances, though his best may not be a "rational" best, and what he can do may not be at all easy to specify, except that he is not apt to think like one of the theoretical antagonists in the *Theory of Games*. Before a sociologist rejects this answer out of hand for its horrid profit-seeking implications, he will do well to ask himself if he can offer any other answer to the question posed. I think he will find that he cannot. Yet experiments designed to test the truth of the answer are extraordinarily rare.

I shall review one that seems to me to provide a little support for the theory, though it was not meant to do so. The experiment is reported by H. B. Gerard, a member of the Festinger–Schachter team, under the title "The Anchorage of Opinions in Face-to-Face Groups."[11] The experimenter formed artificial groups whose members met to discuss a case in industrial relations and to express their opinions about its probable outcome. The groups were of two kinds: high-attraction groups, whose members were told that they would like one another very much, and low-attraction groups, whose members were told that they would not find one another particularly likable.

At a later time the experimenter called the members in separately, asked them again to express their opinions on the outcome of the case, and counted the number that had changed their opinions to bring them into accord with those of other members of their groups. At the same time, a paid participant entered into a further discussion of the case with each member, always taking, on the probable outcome of the case, a position opposed to that taken by the bulk of the other members of the group to which the person belonged. The experimenter counted the number of persons shifting toward the opinion of the paid participant.

The experiment had many interesting results, from which I choose only those summed up in tables 5.1 and 5.2. The three different agreement classes are made up of people who, at the original sessions, expressed different degrees of agreement with the opinions of other members of their groups. And the figure 44, for instance, means that, of all members of high-attraction groups whose initial opinions were strongly in disagreement with those of other members, 44 per cent shifted their opinion later toward that of others.

In these results the experimenter seems to have been interested only in the differences in the sums of the rows, which show that there is more shifting toward the group, and less shifting toward the paid participant, in the high-attraction than in the low-attraction condition. This is in line with a proposition suggested earlier. If you think that the members of a group can give you much – in this case, liking – you are apt to give them much – in this case, a change to an opinion in accordance with their views – or you will not get the liking. And, by the same token, if the group can give you little of value, you will not be ready to give it much of value. Indeed, you may change your opinion so as to depart from agreement even further, to move, that is, toward the view held by the paid participant.

Table 5.1 *Percentage of subjects changing toward someone in the group*

	Agreement	Mild Disagreement	Strong Disagreement
High attraction	0	12	44
Low attraction	0	15	9

Table 5.2 *Percentage of subjects changing toward the paid participant*

	Agreement	Mild Disagreement	Strong Disagreement
High attraction	7	13	25
Low attraction	20	38	8

So far so good, but, when I first scanned these tables, I was less struck by the difference between them than by their similarity. The same classes of people in both tables showed much the same relative propensities to change their opinions, no matter whether the change was toward the group or toward the paid participant. We see, for instance, that those who change least are the high-attraction, agreement people and the low-attraction, strong-disagreement ones. And those who change most are the high-attraction, strong-disagreement people and the low-attraction, mild-disagreement ones.

How am I to interpret these particular results? Since the experimenter did not discuss them, I am free to offer my own explanation. The behavior emitted by the subjects is opinion and changes in opinion. For this behavior they have learned to expect two possible kinds of reinforcement. Agreement with the group gets the subject favorable sentiment (acceptance) from it, and the experiment was designed to give this reinforcement a higher value in the high-attraction condition than in the low-attraction one. The second kind of possible reinforcement is what I shall call the "maintenance of one's personal integrity," which a subject gets by sticking to his own opinion in the face of disagreement with the group. The experimenter does not mention this reward, but I cannot make sense of the results without something much like it. In different degrees for different subjects, depending on their initial positions, these rewards are in competition with one another: they are alternatives. They are not absolutely scarce goods, but some persons cannot get both at once.

Since the rewards are alternatives, let me introduce a familiar assumption from economics – that the cost of a particular course of action is the equivalent of the forgone value of an alternative[12] – and then add the definition: Profit = Reward – Cost.

Now consider the persons in the corresponding cells of the two tables. The behavior of the high-attraction, agreement people gets them much in the way of acceptance by the group, and for it they must give up little in the way of personal integrity, for their views are from the start in accord with those of the group. Their profit is high, and they are not prone to change their behavior. The low-attraction, strong-disagreement people are getting much in integrity, and they are not giving up for it much in valuable acceptance, for they are members of low-attraction groups. Reward less cost is high for them, too, and they change little. The high-attraction, strong-disagreement people are getting much in the way of integrity, but their costs in doing so are high, too, for they are in high-attraction groups and thus forgoing much valuable acceptance by the group. Their profit is low, and they are very apt to change, either toward the group or toward the paid participant, from whom they think, perhaps, they will get some acceptance while maintaining some integrity. The low-attraction, mild-disagreement people do not get much in the way of integrity, for they are only in mild disagreement with the group, but neither are they giving up much in acceptance, for they are members of low-attraction groups. Their rewards are low; their costs are low too, and their profit – the difference between the two – is also low. In their low profit they resemble the high-attraction, strong-disagreement people, and, like them, they are prone to change their opinions, in this case, more toward the paid participant. The subjects in the other two cells, who have medium profits, display medium propensities to change.

If we define profit as reward less cost, and if cost is value forgone, I suggest that we have here some evidence for the proposition that change in behavior is greatest when perceived profit is least. This constitutes no direct demonstration that change in behavior is least when profit is greatest, but if, whenever a man's behavior brought him a balance of reward and cost, he changed his behavior away from what got him, under the circumstances, the less profit, there might well come a time when his behavior would not change further. That is, his behavior would be stabilized, at least for the time being. And, so far as this were true for every member of a group, the group would have a social organization in equilibrium.

I do not say that a member would stabilize his behavior at the point of greatest conceivable profit to himself, because his profit is partly at the mercy of the behavior of others. It is a commonplace that the short-run pursuit of profit by several persons often lands them in positions where all are worse off than they might conceivably be. I do not say that the paths of behavioral change in which a member pursues his profit under the condition that others are pursuing theirs too are easy to describe or predict; and we can readily conceive that in jockeying for position they might never arrive at any equilibrium at all.

Distributive Justice

Yet practical equilibrium is often observed, and thus some further condition may make its attainment, under some circumstance, more probable than would the individual pursuit of profit left to itself. I can offer evidence for this further condition only in the behavior of subgroups and not in that of individuals. Suppose that there are two subgroups, working close together in a factory, the job of one being somewhat different from that of the other. And suppose that the members of the first complain and say: "We are getting the same pay as they are. We ought to get just a couple of dollars a week more to show that our work is more responsible." When you ask them what they mean by "more responsible," they say that, if they do their work wrong, more damage can result, and so they are under more pressure to take care.[13] Something like this is a common feature of industrial behavior. It is at the heart of disputes not over absolute wages but over wage differentials – indeed, at the heart of disputes over rewards other than wages.

In what kind of propostion may we express observations like these? We may say that wages and responsibility give status in the group, in the sense that a man who takes high responsibility and gets high wages is admired, other things equal. Then, if the members of one group score higher on responsibility than do the members of another, there is a felt need on the part of the first to score higher on pay too. There is a pressure, which shows itself in complaints, to bring the *status factors*, as I have called them, into line with one another. If they are in line, a condition of *status congruence* is said to exist. In this condition the workers may find their jobs dull or irksome, but they will not complain about the relative position of groups.

But there may be a more illuminating way of looking at the matter. In my example I have considered only responsibility and pay, but these may be enough, for they represent the two kinds of thing that come into the problem. Pay is clearly a reward; responsibility may be looked on, less clearly, as a cost. It means constraint and worry

– or peace of mind forgone. Then the proposition about status congruence becomes this: If the costs of the members of one group are higher than those of another, distributive justice requires that their rewards should be higher too. But the thing works both ways: If the rewards are higher, the costs should be higher too. This last is the theory of *noblesse oblige*, which we all subscribe to, though we all laugh at it, perhaps because the *noblesse* often fails to *oblige*. To put the matter in terms of profit: though the rewards and costs of two persons or the members of two groups may be different, yet the profits of the two – the excess of reward over cost – should tend to equality. And more than "should." The less-advantaged group will at least try to attain greater equality, as, in the example I have used, the first group tried to increase its profit by increasing its pay.

I have talked of distributive justice. Clearly, this is not the only condition determining the actual distribution of rewards and costs. At the same time, never tell me that notions of justice are not a strong influence on behavior, though we sociologists often neglect them. Distributive justice may be one of the conditions of group equilibrium.

Exchange and Social Structure

I shall end by reviewing almost the only study I am aware of that begins to show in detail how a stable and differentiated social structure in a real-life group might arise out of a process of exchange between members. This is Peter Blau's description of the behavior of sixteen agents in a federal law-enforcement agency.[14]

The agents had the duty of investigating firms and preparing reports on the firms' compliance with the law. Since the reports might lead to legal action against the firms, the agents had to prepare them carefully, in the proper form, and take strict account of the many regulations that might apply. The agents were often in doubt what they should do, and then they were supposed to take the question to their supervisor. This they were reluctant to do, for they naturally believed that thus confessing to him their inability to solve a problem would reflect on their competence, affect the official ratings he made of their work, and so hurt their chances for promotion. So agents often asked other agents for help and advice, and, though this was nominally forbidden, the supervisor usually let it pass.

Blau ascertained the ratings the supervisor made of the agents, and he also asked the agents to rate one another. The two opinions agreed closely. Fewer agents were regarded as highly competent than were regarded as of middle or low competence; competence, or the ability to solve technical problems, was a fairly scarce good. One or two of the more competent agents would not give help and advice when asked, and so received few interactions and little liking. A man that will not exchange, that will not give you what he has when you need it, will not get from you the only thing you are, in this case, able to give him in return, your regard.

But most of the more competent agents were willing to give help, and of them Blau says:

A consultation can be considered an exchange of values: both participants gain something, and both have to pay a price. The questioning agent is enabled to perform better than he could otherwise have done, without exposing his difficulties to his supervisor. By asking for advice, he implicitly pays his respect to the superior proficiency of his colleague. This acknowledgment of inferiority is the cost of receiving assistance. The consultant gains prestige, in return for which he is willing to devote some time to the consultation and permit it to disrupt his own work. The following remark of an agent illustrates this: "I like giving advice. It's flattering, I suppose, if you feel that others come to you for advice."[15]

Blau goes on to say: "All agents liked being consulted, but the value of any one of very many consultations became deflated for experts, and the price they paid in frequent interruptions became inflated."[16] This implies that, the more prestige an agent received, the less was the increment of value of that prestige; the more advice an agent gave, the greater was the increment of cost of that advice, the cost lying precisely in the forgone value of time to do his own work. Blau suggests that something of the same sort was true of an agent who went to a more competent colleague for advice: the more often he went, the more costly to him, in feelings of inferiority, became any further request. "The repeated admission of his inability to solve his own problems... undermined the self-confidence of the worker and his standing in the group."[17]

The result was that the less competent agents went to the more competent ones for help less often than they might have done if the costs of repeated admissions of inferiority had been less high and that, while many agents sought out the few highly competent ones, no single agent sought out the latter much. Had they done so (to look at the exchange from the other side), the costs to the highly competent in interruptions to their own work would have become exorbitant. Yet the need of the less competent for help was still not fully satisfied. Under these circumstances they tended to turn for help to agents more nearly like themselves in competence. Though the help they got was not the most valuable, it was of a kind they could themselves return on occasion. With such agents they could exchange help and liking, without the exchange becoming on either side too great a confession of inferiority.

The highly competent agents tended to enter into exchanges, that is, to interact with many others. But, in the more equal exchanges I have just spoken of, less competent agents tended to pair off as partners. That is, they interacted with a smaller number of people, but interacted often with these few. I think I could show why pair relations in these more equal exchanges would be more economical for an agent than a wider distribution of favors. But perhaps I have gone far enough. The final pattern of this social structure was one in which a small number of highly competent agents exchanged advice for prestige with a large number of others less competent and in which the less competent agents exchanged, in pairs and in trios, both help and liking on more nearly equal terms.

Blau shows, then, that a social structure in equilibrium might be the result of a process of exchanging behavior rewarding and costly in different degrees, in which the increment of reward and cost varied with the frequency of the behavior, that is, with the frequency of interaction. Note that the behavior of the agents seems also to have satisfied my second condition of equilibrium: the more competent agents took more responsibility for the work, either their own or others', than did the less competent ones, but they also got more for it in the way of prestige. I suspect that the same kind of explanation could be given for the structure of many "informal" groups.

Summary

The current job of theory in small-group research is to make the connection between experimental and real-life studies, to consolidate the propositions that empirically hold good in the two fields, and to show how these propositions might be derived from a still more general set. One way of doing this job would be to revive and make more rigorous the oldest of theories of social behavior – social behavior as exchange.

Some of the statements of such a theory might be the following. Social behavior is an exchange of goods, material goods but also non-material ones, such as the symbols of approval or prestige. Persons that give much to others try to get much from them, and persons that get much from others are under pressure to give much to them. This process of influence tends to work out at equilibrium to a balance in the exchanges. For a person engaged in exchange, what he gives may be a cost to him, just as what he gets may be a reward, and his behavior changes less as profit, that is, reward less cost, tends to a maximum. Not only does he seek a maximum for himself, but he tries to see to it that no one in his group makes more profit than he does. The cost and the value of what he gives and of what he gets vary with the quantity of what he gives and gets. It is surprising how familiar these propositions are; it is surprising, too, how propositions about the dynamics of exchange can begin to generate the static thing we call "group structure" and, in so doing, generate also some of the propositions about group structure that students of real-life groups have stated.

In our unguarded moments we sociologists find words like "reward" and "cost" slipping into what we say. Human nature will break in upon even our most elaborate theories. But we seldom let it have its way with us and follow up systematically what these words imply.[18] Of all our many "approaches" to social behavior, the one that sees it as an economy is the most neglected, and yet it is the one we use every moment of our lives – except when we write sociology.

Note

1   B. F. Skinner, *Science and Human Behavior* (New York: Macmillan Co., 1953).
2   Ibid., pp. 297–329. The discussion of "double contingency" by T. Parsons and E. A. Shils could easily lead to a similar paradigm (see *Toward a General Theory of Action* [Cambridge, Mass.: Harvard University Press, 1951], pp. 14–16).
3   K. W. Back, "The Exertion of Influence through Social Communication," in L. Festinger, K. Back, S. Schachter, H. H. Kelley, and J. Thibaut (eds.), *Theory and Experiment in Social Communication* (Ann Arbor: Research Center for Dynamics, University of Michigan, 1950), pp. 21–36.
4   S. Schachter, N. Ellertson, D. McBride, and D. Gregory, "An Experimental Study of Cohesiveness and Productivity," *Human Relations*, IV (1951), 229–38.
5   Skinner, *Science and Human Behavior*, p. 100.

6   S. Schachter, "Deviation, Rejection, and Communication," *Journal of Abnormal and Social Psychology*, XLVI (1951), 190–207.

7   L. Festinger, S. Schachter, and K. Back, *Social Pressures in Informal Groups* (New York: Harper & Bros., 1950), pp. 72–100.

8   For propositions holding good of groups in practical equilibrium see G. C. Homans, *The Human Group* (New York: Harcourt, Brace & Co., 1950), and H. W. Riecken and G. C. Homans, "Psychological Aspects of Social Structure," in G. Lindzey (ed.), *Handbook of Social Psychology* (Cambridge, Mass.: Addison-Wesley Publishing Co., 1954), II, 786–832.

9   See Homans, *The Human Group.*, pp. 244–8, and R. F. Bales, "The Equilibrium Problem in Small Groups," in A. P. Hare, E. F. Borgatta, and R. F. Bales (eds.), *Small Groups* (New York: A. A. Knopf, 1953), pp. 450–6.

10 Homans, *The Human Group*, pp. 281–301.

11 *Human Relations*, VII (1954), 313–25.

12 G. J. Stigler, *The Theory of Price* (rev. ed.; New York: Macmillan Co., 1952), p. 99.

13 G. C. Homans, "Status among Clerical Workers," *Human Organization*, XII (1953), 5–10.

14 Peter M. Blau, *The Dynamics of Bureaucracy* (Chicago: University of Chicago Press, 1955), 99–116.

15 Ibid., p. 108.

16 Ibid., p. 108.

17 Ibid., p. 109.

18 *The White-Collar Job* (Ann Arbor: Survey Research Center, University of Michigan, 1953), pp. 115–27.

6   Exchange and Power in Social Life

Peter M. Blau

Basic Processes

The basic social processes that govern associations among men have their roots in primitive psychological processes, such as those underlying the feelings of attraction between individuals and their desires for various kinds of rewards. These psychological tendencies are primitive only in respect to our subject matter, that is, they are taken as given without further inquiry into the motivating forces that produce them, for our concern is with the social forces that emanate from them.

The simpler social processes that can be observed in interpersonal associations and that rest directly on psychological dispositions give rise to the more complex social processes that govern structures of interconnected social associations, such as the social organization of a factory or the political relations in a community. New social forces emerge in the increasingly complex social structures that develop in societies, and these dynamic forces are quite removed from the ultimate psychological base of all social life. Although complex social systems have their foundation in simpler ones, they have their own dynamics with emergent properties. In this section, the basic processes of social associations will be presented in broad strokes, to be analyzed subsequently in greater detail, with special attention to their wider implications.

Social attraction is the force that induces human beings to establish social associations on their own initiative and to expand the scope of their associations once they have been formed. Reference here is to social relations into which men enter of their own free will rather than to either those into which they are born (such as kinship groups) or those imposed on them by forces beyond their control (such as the combat teams to which soldiers are assigned), although even in these involuntary relations the extent and intensity of the association depend on the degree of mutual attraction. An individual is attracted to another if he expects associating with him to be in some way rewarding for himself, and his interest in the expected social rewards draws him to the other. The psychological needs and dispositions of individuals determine which rewards are particularly salient for them and thus to whom they will be attracted. Whatever the specific motives, there is an important difference between the expectation that the association will be an intrinsically rewarding experience and the expectation that it will furnish extrinsic benefits, for example, advice. This difference calls attention to two distinct meanings of the term "attraction" and its derivatives. In its narrower sense, social attraction refers to liking another person *intrinsically* and having positive feelings toward him; in the broader sense, in which the term is now used, social attraction refers to being drawn to another person for any reason whatsoever. The customer is attracted in this broader sense to the merchant who sells goods of a given quality at the lowest price, but he has no intrinsic feelings of attraction for him, unless they happen to be friends.

A person who is attracted to others is interested in proving himself attractive to them, for his ability to associate with them and reap the benefits expected from the association is contingent on their finding him an attractive associate and thus wanting to interact with him. Their attraction to him, just as his to them, depends on the anticipation that the association will be rewarding. To arouse this anticipation, a person tries to impress others. Attempts to appear impressive are pervasive in the early stages of acquaintance and group formation. Impressive qualities make a person attractive and promise that associating with him will be rewarding. Mutual attraction prompts people to establish an association, and the rewards they provide each other in the course of their social interaction, unless their expectations are disappointed, maintain their mutual attraction and the continuing association.

Processes of social attraction, therefore, lead to processes of social exchange. The nature of the exchange in an association experienced as intrinsically rewarding, such as a love relationship, differs from that between associates primarily concerned with extrinsic benefits, such as neighbors who help one another with various chores, but exchanges do occur in either case. A person who furnishes needed assistance to associates, often at some cost to himself, obligates them to reciprocate his kindness. Whether reference is to instrumental services or to such intangibles as social approval, the benefits each supplies to the others are rewards that serve as inducements to continue to supply benefits, and the integrative bonds created in the process fortify the social relationship.

A situation frequently arises, however, in which one person needs something another has to offer, for example, help from the other in his work, but has nothing the other needs to reciprocate for the help. While the other may be sufficiently rewarded by expressions of gratitude to help him a few times, he can hardly be expected regularly to devote time and effort to providing help without receiving any return to compensate him for his troubles. (In the case of intrinsic attraction, the only return expected is the willingness to continue the association.) The person in need of recurrent services from an associate to whom he has nothing to offer has several alternatives. First, he may force the other to give him help. Second, he may obtain the help he needs from another source. Third, he may find ways to get along without such help.[1] If he is unable or unwilling to choose any of these alternatives, however, there is only one other course of action left for him; he must subordinate himself to the other and comply with his wishes, thereby rewarding the other with power over himself as an inducement for furnishing the needed help. Willingness to comply with another's demands is a generic social reward, since the power it gives him is a generalized means, parallel to money, which can be used to attain a variety of ends. The power to command compliance is equivalent to credit, which a man can draw on in the future to obtain various benefits at the disposal of those obligated to him.[2] The unilateral supply of important services establishes this kind of credit and thus is a source of power.

Exchange processes, then, give rise to differentiation of power. A person who commands services others need, and who is independent of any at their command, attains power over others by making the satisfaction of their need contingent on their compliance. This principle is held to apply to the most intimate as well as the most distant social relations. The girl with whom a boy is in love has power over him, since his eagerness to spend much time with her prompts him to make their time together especially pleasant for her by acceding to her wishes. The employer can make workers comply with his directives because they are dependent on his wages. To be sure, the superior's power wanes if subordinates can resort to coercion, have equally good alternatives, or are able to do without the benefits at his disposal. But given these limiting conditions, unilateral services that meet basic needs are the penultimate source of power. Its ultimate source, of course, is physical coercion. While the power that rests on coercion is more absolute, however, it is also more limited in scope than the power that derives from met needs.

A person on whom others are dependent for vital benefits has the power to enforce his demands. He may make demands on them that they consider fair and just in relation to the benefits they receive for submitting to his power. On the other hand, he may lack such restraint and make demands that appear excessive to them, arousing feelings of exploitation for having to render more compliance than the rewards received justify. Social norms define the expectations of subordinates and their evaluations of the superior's demands. The fair exercise of power gives rise to approval of the superior, whereas unfair exploitation promotes disapproval. The greater the resources of a person on which his power rests, the easier it is for him to refrain from exploiting subordinates by making excessive demands, and consequently the better are the chances that subordinates will approve of the fairness of his rule rather than disapprove of its unfairness.

There are fundamental differences between the dynamics of power in a collective situation and the power of one individual over another. The weakness of the isolated subordinate limits the significance of his approval or disapproval of the superior. The agreement that emerges in a collectivity of subordinates concerning their judgment of the superior, on the other hand, has far-reaching implications for developments in the social structure.

Collective approval of power legitimates that power. People who consider that the advantages they gain from a superior's exercise of power outweigh the hardships that compliance with his demands imposes on them tend to communicate to each other their approval of the ruler and their feelings of obligation to him. The consensus that develops as the result of these communications finds expression in group pressures that promote compliance with the ruler's directives, thereby strengthening his power of control and legitimating his authority. "A feeling of obligation to obey the commands of the established public authority is found, varying in liveliness and effectiveness from one individual to another, among the members of any political society."[3] Legitimate authority is the basis of organization. It makes it possible to organize collective effort to further the achievement of various objectives, some of which could not be attained by individuals separately at all and others that can be attained more effectively by coordinating efforts. Although power that is not legitimated by the approval of subordinates can also be used to organize them, the stability of such an organization is highly precarious.

Collective disapproval of power engenders opposition. People who share the experience of being exploited by the unfair demands of those in positions of power, and by the insufficient rewards they receive for their contributions, are likely to communicate their feelings of anger, frustration, and aggression to each other.

There tends to arise a wish to retaliate by striking down the existing powers. "As every man doth, so shall it be done to him, and retaliation seems to be the great law that is dictated to us by nature."[4] The social support the oppressed give each other in the course of discussing their common grievances and feelings of hostility justifies and reinforces their aggressive opposition against those in power. It is out of such shared discontent that opposition ideologies and movements develop – that men organize a union against their employer or a revolutionary party against their government.

In brief, differentiation of power in a collective situation evokes contrasting dynamic forces: legitimating processes that foster the organization of individuals and groups in common endeavors; and countervailing forces that deny legitimacy to existing powers and promote opposition and cleavage. Under the influence of these forces, the scope of legitimate organization expands to include ever larger collectivities, but opposition and conflict recurrently redivide these collectivities and stimulate reorganization along different lines.

The distinctive characteristic of complex social structures is that their constituent elements are also social structures. We may call these structures of interrelated groups "macrostructures" and those composed of interacting individuals "microstructures." There are some parallels between the social processes in microstructures and macrostructures. Processes of social attraction create integrative bonds between associates, and integrative processes also unite various groups in a community. Exchange processes between individuals give rise to differentiation among them, and intergroup exchanges further differentiation among groups. Individuals become incorporated in legitimate organizations, and these in turn become part of broader bodies of legitimate authority. Opposition and conflict occur not only within collectivities but also between them. These parallels, however, must not conceal the fundamental differences between the processes that govern the interpersonal associations in microstructures and the forces characteristic of the wider and more complex social relations in macrostructures.

First, value consensus is of crucial significance for social processes that pervade complex social structures, because standards commonly agreed upon serve as mediating links for social transactions between individuals and groups without any direct contact. Sharing basic values creates integrative bonds and social solidarity among millions of people in a society, most of whom have never met, and serves as functional equivalent for the feelings of personal attraction that unite pairs of associates and small groups. Common standards of valuation produce media of exchange – money being the prototype but not the only one – which alone make it possible to transcend personal transactions and develop complex networks of indirect exchange. Legitimating values expand the scope of centralized control far beyond the reach of personal influence, as exemplified by the authority of a legitimate government. Opposition ideals serve as rallying points to draw together strangers from widely dispersed places and unite them in a common cause. The study of these problems requires an analysis of the significance of social values and norms that must complement the analysis of exchange transactions and power relations but must not become a substitute for it.

A second emergent property of macrostructures is the complex interplay between the internal forces within substructures and the forces that connect the diverse substructures, some of which may be microstructures composed of individuals while others may themselves be macrostructures composed of subgroups. The processes of integration, differentiation, organization, and opposition formation in the various substructures, which often vary greatly among the substructures, and the corresponding processes in the macrostructure all have repercussions for each other. A systematic analysis of these intricate patterns would have to constitute the core of a general theory of social structures.

Finally, enduring institutions typically develop in macrostructures. Established systems of legitimation raise the question of their perpetuation through time. The strong identification of men with the highest ideals and most sacred beliefs they share makes them desirous to preserve these basic values for succeeding generations. The investments made in establishing and expanding a legitimate organization create an interest in stabilizing it and assuring its survival in the face of opposition attacks. For this purpose, formalized procedures are instituted that make the organization independent of any individual member and permit it to persist beyond the life span or period of tenure of its members. Institutionalization refers to the emergence of social mechanisms through which social values and norms, organizing principles, and knowledge and skills are transmitted from generation to generation. A society's institutions constitute the social matrix in which individuals grow up and are socialized, with the result that some aspects of institutions are reflected in their own personalities, and others appear to them as the inevitable external conditions of human existence. Traditional institutions stabilize social life but also introduce rigidities that make adjustment to changing conditions difficult. Opposition movements may arise to promote such adjustment, yet these movements themselves tend to become institutionalized and rigid in the course of time, creating needs for fresh oppositions. . . .

There is a strain toward imbalance as well as toward reciprocity in social associations. The term "balance" itself is ambiguous inasmuch as we speak not only of balancing our books but also of a balance in our favor, which refers, of course, to a lack of equality between inputs and outputs. As a matter of fact, the balance of the accounting sheet merely rests, in the typical case, on an underlying imbalance between income and outlays, and so do apparent balances in social life. Individuals and groups are interested in, at least, maintaining a balance between inputs and outputs and staying out of debt in their social transactions; hence the strain toward reciprocity. Their aspirations, however, are to achieve a balance in their favor and accumulate credit that makes their status superior to that of others; hence the strain toward imbalance.

Arguments about equilibrium – that all scientific theories must be conceived in terms of equilibrium models or that any equilibrium model neglects the dynamics of real life – ignore the important point that the forces sustaining equilibrium on one level of social life constitute disequilibrating forces on other levels. For supply and demand to remain in equilibrium in a market, for example, forces must exist that continually disturb the established patterns of exchange. Similarly, the circulation of the elite, an equilibrium model, rests on the operation of forces that create imbalances and disturbances in the various segments of society. The principle suggested is that balanced social states depend on imbalances in other social states; forces that restore equilibrium in one respect do so by creating disequilibrium in others. The processes of association described illustrate this principle.

A person who is attracted to another will seek to prove himself attractive to the other. Thus a boy who is very much attracted to a girl, more so than she is to him, is anxious to make himself more attractive to her. To do so, he will try to impress her and, particularly, go out of his way to make associating with him an especially rewarding experience for her. He may devote a lot of thought to finding ways to please her, spend much money on her, and do the things she likes on their dates rather than those he would prefer. Let us assume that he is successful and she becomes as attracted to him as he is to her, that is, she finds associating with him as rewarding as he finds associating with her, as indicated by the fact that both are equally eager to spend time together.

Attraction is now reciprocal, but the reciprocity has been established by an imbalance in the exchange. To be sure, both obtain satisfactory rewards from the association at this stage, the boy as the result of her willingness to spend as much time with him as he wants, and the girl as the result of his readiness to make their dates enjoyable for her. These reciprocal rewards are the sources of their mutual attraction. The contributions made, however, are in imbalance. Both devote time to the association, which involves giving up alternative opportunities, but the boy contributes in addition special efforts to please her. Her company is sufficient reward by itself, while his is not, which makes her "the more useful or otherwise superior" in terms of their own evaluations, and he must furnish supplementary rewards to produce "equality in a sense between the parties." Although two lovers may, of course, be equally anxious to spend time together and to please one another, it is rare for a perfect balance of mutual affection to develop spontaneously. The reciprocal attraction in most intimate relations – marriages and lasting friendships as well as more temporary attachments – is the result of some imbalance of contributions that compensates for inequalities in spontaneous affection, notably in the form of one partner's greater willingness to defer to the other's wishes. . . .

The theoretical principle that has been advanced is that a given balance in social associations is produced by imbalances in the same associations in other respects. This principle, which has been illustrated with the imbalances that underlie reciprocal attraction, also applies to the process of social differentiation. A person who supplies services in demand to others obligates them to reciprocate. If some fail to reciprocate, he has strong inducements to withhold the needed assistance from them in order to supply it to others who do repay him for his troubles in some form. Those who have nothing else to offer him that would be a satisfactory return for his services, therefore, are under pressure to defer to his wishes and comply with his requests in repayment for his assistance. Their compliance with his demands gives him the power to utilize their resources at his discretion to further his own ends. By providing unilateral benefits to others, a person accumulates a capital of willing compliance on which he can draw whenever it is to his interest to impose his will upon others, within the limits of the significance the continuing supply of his benefits has for them. The general advantages of power enable men who cannot otherwise repay for services they need to obtain them in return for their compliance; although in the extreme case of the person who has much power and whose benefits are in great demand, even an offer of compliance may not suffice to obtain them.

Here, an imbalance of power establishes reciprocity in the exchange. Unilateral services give rise to a differentiation of power that equilibrates the exchange. The exchange balance, in fact, rests on two imbalances: unilateral services and unilateral power. Although these two imbalances make up a balance or equilibrium in terms of one perspective, in terms of another, which is equally valid, the exchange equilibrium reinforces and perpetuates the imbalances of dependence and power that sustain it. Power differences not only are an imbalance by definition but also are actually experienced as such, as indicated by the tendency of men to escape from domination if they can. Indeed, a major impetus for the eagerness of individuals to discharge their obligations and reciprocate for services they receive, by providing services in return, is the threat of becoming otherwise subject to the power of the supplier of the services. While reciprocal services create an interdependence that balances power, unilateral dependence on services maintains an imbalance of power.

Differentiation of power evidently constitutes an imbalance in the sense of an inequality of power; but the question must be raised whether differentiation of power also necessarily constitutes an imbalance in the sense of a strain toward change in the structure of social relations. Power differences as such, analytically conceived and abstracted from other considerations, create such a pressure toward change, because it can be assumed that men experience having to submit to power as a hardship from which they would prefer to escape. The advantages men derive from their ruler or government, however, may outweigh the hardships entailed in submitting to his or its power, with the result that the analytical imbalance or disturbance introduced by power differences is neutralized. The significance of power imbalances for social change depends, therefore, on the reactions of the governed to the exercise of power.

Social reactions to the exercise of power reflect once more the principle of reciprocity and imbalance, although in a new form. Power over others makes it possible to direct and organize their activities. Sufficient resources to command power over large numbers enable a person or group to establish a large organization. The members recruited to the organization receive benefits, such as financial remuneration, in exchange for complying with the directives of superiors and making various contributions to the organization. The leadership exercises power within the organization, and it derives power from the organization for use in relation with other organizations or groups. The clearest illustration of this double power of organizational leadership is the army commander's power over his own soldiers and, through the force of their arms, over the enemy. Another example is the power business management exercises over its own employees and, through the strength of the concern, in the market. The greater the external power of an organization, the greater are its chances of accumulating resources that put rewards at the disposal of the leadership for possible distribution among the members.

The normative expectations of those subject to the exercise of power, which are rooted in their social experience, govern their reactions to it. In terms of these standards, the benefits derived from being part of an organization or political society may outweigh the investments required to obtain them, or the demands made on members may exceed the returns they receive for fulfilling these demands. The exercise of power, therefore, may produce two different kinds of imbalance, a positive imbalance of benefits for subordinates or a negative imbalance of exploitation and oppression.

If the members of an organization, or generally those subject to a governing leadership, commonly agree that the demands made on them are only fair and just in view of the ample rewards the leadership delivers, joint feelings of obligation and loyalty to superiors will arise and bestow legitimating approval on their authority. A positive imbalance of benefits generates legitimate authority for the leadership and thereby strengthens and extends its controlling influence. By expressing legitimating approval of, and loyalty to, those who govern them subordinates reciprocate for the benefits their leadership provides, but they simultaneously fortify the imbalance of power in the social structure.

If the demands of the men who exercise power are experienced by those subject to it as exploitative and oppressive, and particularly if these subordinates have been unsuccessful in obtaining redress for their grievances, their frustrations tend to promote disapproval of existing powers and antagonism toward them. As the oppressed communicate their anger and aggression to each other, provided there are opportunities for doing so, their mutual support and approval socially justify and reinforce the negative orientation toward the oppressors, and their collective hostility may inspire them to organize an opposition. The exploitative use of coercive power that arouses active opposition is more prevalent in the relations between organizations and groups than within organizations. Two reasons for this are that the advantages of legitimating approval restrain organizational superiors and that the effectiveness of legitimate authority, once established, obviates the need for coercive measures. But the exploitative use of power also occurs within organizations, as unions organized in opposition to exploitative employers show. A negative imbalance for the subjects of power stimulates opposition. The opposition negatively reciprocates, or retaliates, for excessive demands in an attempt to even the score, but it simultaneously creates conflict, disequilibrium, and imbalance in the social structure.[5]

Even in the relatively simple structures of social association considered here, balances in one respect entail imbalances in others. The interplay between equilibrating and disequilibrating forces is still more evident, if less easy to unravel, in complex macrostructures with their cross-cutting substructures, where forces that sustain reciprocity and balance have disequilibrating and imbalancing repercussions not only on other levels of the same substructure but also on other substructures. As we shall see, disequilibrating and re-equilibrating forces generate a dialectical pattern of change in social structures.

Unspecified Obligations and Trust

The concept of exchange can be circumscribed by indicating two limiting cases. An individual may give another money because the other stands in front of him with a gun in a holdup. While this could be conceptualized as an exchange of his money for his life, it seems preferable to exclude the result of physical coercion from the range of social conduct encompassed by the term "exchange." An individual may also give away money because his conscience demands that he help support the underprivileged and without expecting any form of gratitude from them. While this could be conceptualized as an exchange of his money for the internal approval of his superego, here again it seems preferable to exclude conformity with internalized norms from the purview of the concept of social exchange. A social exchange is involved if an individual gives money to a poor man because he wants to receive the man's expressions of gratitude and deference and if he ceases to give alms to beggars who withhold such expressions.

"Social exchange," as the term is used here, refers to voluntary actions of individuals that are motivated by the returns they are expected to bring and typically do in fact bring from others. Action compelled by physical coercion is not voluntary, although compliance with other forms of power can be considered a voluntary service rendered in exchange for the benefits such compliance produces, as already indicated. Whereas conformity with internalized standards does not fall under the definition of exchange presented, conformity to social pressures tends to entail indirect exchanges. Men make charitable donations, not to earn the gratitude of the recipients, whom they never see, but to earn the approval of their peers who participate in the philanthropic campaign. Donations are exchanged for social approval, though the recipients of the donations and the suppliers of the approval are not identical, and the clarification of the connection between the two requires an analysis of the complex structures of indirect exchange. Our concern now is with the simpler direct exchanges.

The need to reciprocate for benefits received in order to continue receiving them serves as a "starting mechanism" of social interaction and group structure, as Gouldner has pointed out.[6] When people are thrown together, and before common norms or goals or role expectations have crystallized among them, the advantages to be gained from entering into exchange relations furnish incentives for social interaction, and the exchange processes serve as mechanisms for regulating social interaction, thus fostering the development of a network of social relations and a rudimentary group structure. Eventually, group norms to regulate and limit the exchange transactions emerge, including the fundamental and ubiquitous norm of reciprocity, which makes failure to discharge obligations subject to group sanctions. In contrast to Gouldner, however, it is held here that the norm of reciprocity merely reinforces and stabilizes tendencies inherent in the character of social exchange itself and that the fundamental starting mechanism of patterned social intercourse is found in the existential conditions of exchange, not in the norm of reciprocity. It is a necessary condition of exchange that individuals, in the interest of continuing to receive needed services, discharge their obligations for having received them in the past. Exchange processes utilize, as it were, the self-interests of individuals to produce a differentiated social structure within which norms tend to develop that require individuals to set aside some of their personal interests for the sake of those of the collectivity. Not all social constraints are normative constraints, and those imposed by the nature of social exchange are not, at least, not originally.

Social exchange differs in important ways from strictly economic exchange. The basic and most crucial distinction is that social exchange entails *unspecified* obligations. The prototype of an economic transaction rests on a formal contract that stipulates the exact quantities to be exchanged. The buyer pays $30,000 for a specific house, or he signs a contract to pay that sum plus interest over a period of years. Whether the entire transaction is consummated at a given time, in which case the contract may never be written, or not, all the transfers to be made now or in the future are agreed upon at the time of sale. Social exchange, in contrast, involves the principle that one person does another a favor, and while there is a general expectation of some future return, its exact nature is definitely *not* stipulated in advance. The distinctive implications of such unspecified obligations are brought into high relief by the institutionalized form they assume in the Kula discussed by Malinowski:

> The main principle underlying the regulations of actual exchange is that the Kula consists in the bestowing of a ceremonial gift, which has to be repaid by an equivalent counter-gift after a lapse of time....But it can never be exchanged from hand to hand, with the equivalence between the two objects being discussed, bargained about and computed....The second very important principle is that the equivalence of the counter-gift is left to the giver, and it cannot be enforced by any kind of coercion....
> If the article given as a counter-gift is not equivalent, the recipient will be disappointed and angry, but he has no direct means of redress, no means of coercing his partner....[7]

Social exchange, whether it is in this ceremonial form or not, involves favors that create diffuse future obligations, not precisely specified ones, and the nature of the return cannot be bargained about but must be left to the discretion of the one who makes it. Thus, if a person gives a dinner party, he expects his guests to reciprocate at some future date. But he can hardly bargain with them about the kind of party to which they should invite him, although he expects them not simply to ask him for a quick lunch if he had invited them to a formal dinner. Similarly, if a person goes to some trouble in behalf of an acquaintance, he expects *some* expression of gratitude, but he can neither bargain with the other over how to reciprocate nor force him to reciprocate at all.

Since there is no way to assure an appropriate return for a favor, social exchange requires trusting others to discharge their obligations. While the banker who makes a loan to a man who buys a house does not have to trust him, although he hopes he will not have to foreclose the mortgage, the individual who gives another an expensive gift must trust him to reciprocate in proper fashion. Typically, however, exchange relations evolve in a slow process, starting with minor transactions in which little trust is required because little risk is involved. A worker may help a colleague a few times. If the colleague fails to reciprocate, the worker has lost little and can easily protect himself against further loss by ceasing to furnish assistance. If the colleague does reciprocate, perhaps excessively so out of gratitude for the volunteered help and in the hope of receiving more, he proves himself trustworthy of continued and extended favors. (Excessive reciprocation may be embarrassing, because it is a bid for a more extensive exchange relation than one may be willing to enter.) By discharging their obligations for services rendered, if only to provide inducements for the supply of more assistance, individuals demonstrate their trustworthiness, and the gradual expansion of mutual service is accompanied by a parallel growth of mutual trust. Hence, processes of social exchange, which may originate in pure self-interest, generate trust in social relations through their recurrent and gradually expanding character.

Only social exchange tends to engender feelings of personal obligation, gratitude, and trust; purely economic exchange as such does not. An individual is obligated to the banker who gives him a mortgage on his house merely in the technical sense of owing him money, but he does not feel personally obligated in the sense of experiencing a debt of gratitude to the banker, because all the banker's services, all costs and risks, are duly taken into account in and fully repaid by the interest on the loan he receives. A banker who grants a loan without adequate collateral, however, does make the recipient personally obligated for this favorable treatment, precisely because this act of trust entails a social exchange that is superimposed upon the strictly economic transaction.

In contrast to economic commodities, the benefits involved in social exchange do not have an exact price in terms of a single quantitative medium of exchange, which is another reason why social obligations are unspecific. It is essential to realize that this is a substantive fact, not simply a methodological problem. It is not just the social scientist who cannot exactly measure how much approval a given helpful action is worth; the actors themselves cannot precisely specify the worth of approval or of help in the absence of a money price. The obligations individuals incur in social exchange, therefore, are defined only in general, somewhat diffuse terms. Furthermore, the specific benefits exchanged are sometimes primarily valued as symbols of the supportiveness and friendliness they express, and it is the exchange of the underlying mutual support that is the main concern of the participants. Occasionally, a time-consuming service of great material benefit to the recipient might be properly repaid by mere verbal expressions of deep appreciation, since these are taken to signify as much supportiveness as the material benefits.[8] In the long run, however, the explicit efforts the associates in a peer relation make in one another's behalf tend to be in balance, if only because a persistent imbalance in these manifestations of good would raise questions about the reciprocity in the underlying orientations of support and congeniality.

Notes

1   The last two of these alternatives are noted by Talcott Parsons (*The Structure of Social Action* (New York: McGraw-Hill, 1937), p. 252) in his discussion of a person's reactions to having his expectations frustrated by another.
2   See Talcott Parsons, "On the Concept of Influence," *Public Opinion Quarterly*, 27 (1963), 37–62, esp. pp. 59–60.
3   Bertrand de Jouvenel, *Sovereignty* (University of Chicago Press, 1957), p. 87.
4   Adam Smith, *The Theory of Moral Sentiments*, 2nd edn. (London: A. Millar, 1761), p. 139.
5   Organized opposition gives expression to latent conflicts and makes them manifest.
6   Alvin W. Gouldner, "The Norm of Reciprocity," *American Sociological Review*, 25 (1960), 161–78, esp. p. 176.
7   Bronislaw Malinowski, *Argonauts of the Western Pacific* (New York: Dutton, 1961), pp. 95–6.
8   See Erving Goffman, *Asylums* (Chicago: Aldine, 1962), pp. 274–86.

7   Social Capital in the Creation of Human Capital

James S. Coleman

Social Capital

I see two major deficiencies in earlier work that introduced "exchange theory" into sociology, despite the pathbreaking character of this work. One was the limitation to microsocial relations, which abandons the principal virtue of economic theory, its ability to make the micro–macro transition from pair relations to system. This was evident both in Homans's (1961) work and in Blau's (1964) work. The other was the attempt to introduce principles in an ad hoc fashion, such as "distributive justice" (Homans, 1964, p. 241) or the "norm of reciprocity" (Gouldner, 1960). The former deficiency limits the theory's usefulness, and the latter creates a pastiche.

If we begin with a theory of rational action, in which each actor has control over certain resources and interests in certain resources and events, then social capital constitutes a particular kind of resource available to an actor.

Social capital is defined by its function. It is not a single entity but a variety of different entities, with two elements in common: they all consist of some aspect of social structures, and they facilitate certain actions of actors – whether persons or corporate actors – within the structure. Like other forms of capital, social capital is productive, making possible the achievement of certain ends that in its absence would not be possible. Like physical capital and human capital, social capital is not completely fungible but may be specific to certain activities. A given form of social capital that is valuable in facilitating certain actions may be useless or even harmful for others.

Unlike other forms of capital, social capital inheres in the structure of relations between actors and among actors. It is not lodged either in the actors themselves or in physical implements of production. Because purposive organizations can be actors ("corporate actors") just as persons can, relations among corporate actors can constitute social capital for them as well (with perhaps the best-known example being the sharing of information that allows price-fixing in an industry). However, in the present paper, the examples and area of application to which I will direct attention concern social capital as a resource for persons....

Human Capital and Social Capital

Probably the most important and most original development in the economics of education in the past 30 years has been the idea that the concept of physical capital as embodied in tools, machines, and other productive equipment can be extended to include human capital as well (see Schultz, 1961; Becker, 1964). Just as physical capital is created by changes in materials to form tools that facilitate production, human capital is created by changes in persons that bring about skills and capabilities that make them able to act in new ways.

Social capital, however, comes about through changes in the relations among persons that facilitate action. If physical capital is wholly tangible, being embodied in observable material form, and human capital is less tangible, being embodied in the skills and knowledge acquired by an individual, social capital is less tangible yet, for it exists in the *relations* among persons. Just as physical capital and human capital facilitate productive activity, social capital does as well. For example, a group within which there is extensive trustworthiness and extensive trust is able to accomplish much more than a comparable group without that trustworthiness and trust.

Forms of Social Capital

The value of the concept of social capital lies first in the fact that it identifies certain aspects of social structure by their functions, just as the concept "chair" identifies certain physical objects by their function, despite differences in form, appearance, and construction. The function identified by the concept of "social capital" is the value of these aspects of social structure to actors as resources that they can use to achieve their interests.

By identifying this function of certain aspects of social structure, the concept of social capital constitutes both an aid in accounting for different outcomes at the level of individual actors and an aid toward making the micro-to-macro transitions without elaborating the social structural details through which this occurs. For example, in characterizing the clandestine study circles of South Korean radical students as constituting social capital that these students can use in their revolutionary activities, we assert that the groups constitute a resource that aids in moving from individual protest to organized revolt. If, in a theory of revolt, a resource that accomplishes this task is held to be necessary, then these study circles are grouped together with those organizational structures, having very different origins, that have fulfilled the same function for individuals with revolutionary goals in other contexts, such as the *Comités d'action lycéen* of the French student revolt of 1968 or the workers' cells in tsarist Russia described and advocated by Lenin ([1902] 1973). . . .

Obligations, expectations, and trustworthiness of structures

If A does something for B and trusts B to reciprocate in the future, this establishes an expectation in A and an obligation on the part of B. This obligation can be conceived as a credit slip held by A for performance by B. If A holds a large number of these credit slips, for a number of persons with whom A has relations, then the analogy to financial capital is direct. These credit slips constitute a large body of credit that A can call in if necessary – unless, of course, the placement of trust has been unwise, and these are bad debts that will not be repaid.

In some social structures, it is said that "people are always doing things for each other." There are a large number of these credit slips outstanding, often on both sides of a relation (for these credit slips appear often not to be completely fungible across areas of activity, so that credit slips of B held by A and those of A held by B are not fully used to cancel each other out). The El Khalili market in Cairo constitutes an extreme case of such a social structure. In other social structures where individuals are more self-sufficient and depend on each other less, there are fewer of these credit slips outstanding at any time.

This form of social capital depends on two elements: trustworthiness of the social environment, which means that obligations will be repaid, and the actual extent of obligations held. Social structures differ in both these dimensions, and actors within the same structure differ in the second. A case that illustrates the value of the trustworthiness of the environment is that of the rotating-credit associations of Southeast Asia and elsewhere. These associations are groups of friends and neighbors who typically meet monthly, each person contributing to a central fund that is then given to one of the members (through bidding or by lot), until, after a number of months, each of the n persons has made n contributions and received one payout. As Geertz (1962) points out, these associations serve as efficient institutions for amassing savings for small capital expenditures, an important aid to economic development.

But without a high degree of trustworthiness among the members of the group, the institution could not exist – for a person who receives a payout early in the sequence of meetings could abscond and leave the others with a loss. For example, one could not imagine a rotating-credit association operating successfully in urban areas marked by a high degree of social disorganization – or, in other words, by a lack of social capital.

Differences in social structures in both dimensions may arise for a variety of reasons. There are differences in the actual needs that persons have for help, in the existence of other sources of aid (such as government welfare services), in the degree of affluence (which reduces aid needed from others), in cultural differences in the tendency to lend aid and ask for aid (see Banfield, 1967), in the closure of social networks, in the logistics of social contacts (see Festinger, Schachter, and Back, 1963), and other factors. Whatever the source, however, individuals in social structures with high levels of obligations outstanding at any time have more social capital on which they can draw. The density of outstanding obligations means, in effect, that the overall usefulness of the tangible resources of that social structure is amplified by their availability to others when needed.

Individual actors in a social system also differ in the number of credit slips outstanding on which they can draw at any time. The most extreme examples are in hierarchically structured extended family settings, in which a patriarch (or "godfather") holds an extraordinarily large set of obligations that he can call in at any time to get what he wants done. Near this extreme are villages in traditional settings that are highly stratified, with certain wealthy families who, because of their wealth, have built up extensive credits that they can call in at any time.

Similarly, in political settings such as a legislature, a legislator in a position with extra resources (such as the Speaker of the House of Representatives or the Majority Leader of the Senate in the U.S. Congress) can, by effective use of resources, build up a set of obligations from other legislators that makes it possible to get legislation passed that would otherwise be stymied. This concentration of obligations constitutes social capital that is useful not only for this powerful legislator but also in getting an increased level of action on the part of a legislature. Thus, those members of legislatures among whom such credits are extensive should be more powerful than those without extensive credits and debits because they can use the credits to produce bloc voting on many issues. It is well recognized, for example, that in the U. S. Senate, some senators are members of what is called "the Senate Club," while others are not. This in effect means that some senators are embedded in the system of credits and debits, while others, outside the "Club," are not. It is also well recognized that those in the Club are more powerful than those outside it.

Information channels

An important form of social capital is the potential for information that inheres in social relations. Information is important in providing a basis for action. But acquisition of information is costly. At a minimum, it requires attention, which is always in scarce supply. One means by which information can be acquired is by use of social relations that are maintained for other purposes. Katz and Lazarsfeld (1955) showed how this operated for women in several areas of life in a midwestern city around 1950. They showed that a woman with an interest in being in fashion, but no interest in being on the leading edge of fashion, used friends who she knew kept up with fashion as sources of information. Similarly, a person who is not greatly interested in current events but who is interested in being informed about important developments can save the time of reading a newspaper by depending on spouse or friends who pay attention to such matters. A social scientist who is interested in being up-to-date on research in related fields can make use of everyday interactions with colleagues to do so, but only in a university in which most colleagues keep up-to-date.

All these are examples of social relations that constitute a form of social capital that provides information that facilitates action. The relations in this case are not valuable for the "credit slips" they provide in the form of obligations that one holds for others' performances or for the trustworthiness of the other party but merely for the information they provide.

Norms and effective sanctions

When a norm exists and is effective, it constitutes a powerful, though sometimes fragile, form of social capital. Effective norms that inhibit crime make it possible to walk freely outside at night in a city and enable old persons to leave their houses without fear for their safety. Norms in a community that support and provide effective rewards for high achievement in school greatly facilitate the school's task.

A prescriptive norm within a collectivity that constitutes an especially important form of social capital is the norm that one should forgo self-interest and act in the interests of the collectivity. A norm of this sort, reinforced by social support, status, honor, and other rewards, is the social capital that builds young nations (and then dissipates as they grow older), strengthens families by leading family members to act selflessly in "the family's" interest, facilitates the development of nascent social movements through a small group of dedicated, inward-looking, and mutually rewarding members, and in general leads persons to work for the public good. In some of these cases, the norms are internalized; in others, they are largely supported through external rewards for selfless actions and disapproval for selfish actions. But, whether supported by internal or external sanctions, norms of this sort are important in overcoming the public goods problem that exists in collectivities.

As all these examples suggest, effective norms can constitute a powerful form of social capital. This social capital, however, like the forms described earlier, not only facilitates certain actions; it constrains others. A community with strong and effective norms about young persons' behavior can keep them from "having a good time." Norms that make it possible to walk alone at night also constrain the activities of criminals (and in some cases of noncriminals as well). Even prescriptive norms that reward certain actions, like the norm in a community that says that a boy who is a good athlete should go out for football, are in effect directing energy away from other activities. Effective norms in an area can reduce innovativeness in an area, not only deviant actions that harm others but also deviant actions that can benefit everyone. (See Merton [1968, pp. 195–203] for a discussion of how this can come about.)

Social Structure that Facilitates Social Capital

All social relations and social structures facilitate some forms of social capital; actors establish relations purposefully and continue them when they continue to provide benefits. Certain kinds of social structure, however, are especially important in facilitating some forms of social capital.

Closure of social networks

One property of social relations on which effective norms depend is what I will call closure. In general, one can say that a necessary but not sufficient condition for the emergence of effective norms is action that imposes external effects on others (see Ullmann-Margalit, 1977; Coleman, 1987). Norms arise as attempts to limit negative external effects or encourage positive ones. But, in many social structures where these conditions exist, norms do not come into existence. The reason is, what can be described as lack of closure of the social structure. Figure 7.1 illustrates why. In an open structure like that of figure 7.1a, actor A, having relations with actors B and C, can carry out actions that impose negative externalities on B or C or both. Since they have no relations with one another, but with others instead (D and E), then they cannot combine forces to sanction A in order to constrain the actions. Unless either B or C alone is sufficiently harmed and sufficiently powerful vis-à-vis A to sanction alone, A's actions can continue unabated. In a structure with closure, like that of figure 7.1b, B and C can combine to provide a collective sanction, or either can reward the other for sanctioning A. (See Merry [1984] for examples of the way gossip, which depends on closure of the social structure, is used as a collective sanction.)

In the case of norms imposed by parents on children, closure of the structure requires a slightly more complex structure, which I will call intergenerational closure.

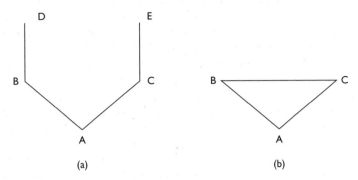

Figure 7.1   *Network without (a) and with (b) closure*

Intergenerational closure may be described by a simple diagram that represents relations between parent and child and relations outside the family. Consider the structure of two communities, represented by figure 7.2. The vertical lines represent relations across generations, between parent and child, while the horizontal lines represent relations within a generation. The point labeled *A* in both figure 7.2*a* and figure 7.2*b* represents the parent of child *B*, and the point labeled *D* represents the parent of child *C*. The lines between *B* and *C* represent the relations among children that exist within any school. Although the other relations among children within the school are not shown here, there exists a high degree of closure among peers, who see each other daily, have expectations toward each other, and develop norms about each other's behavior.

The two communities differ, however, in the presence or absence of links among the parents of children in the school. For the school represented by figure 7.2*b*, there is intergenerational closure; for that represented by figure 7.2*a*, there is not. To put it colloquially, in the lower community represented by 7.2*b*, the parents' friends are the parents of their children's friends. In the other, they are not.

The consequence of this closure is, as in the case of the wholesale diamond market or in other similar communities, a set of effective sanctions that can monitor and guide behavior. In the community in figure 7.2*b*, parents *A* and *D* can discuss their children's activities and come to some consensus about standards and about sanctions. Parent *A* is reinforced by parent *D* in sanctioning his child's actions; beyond that, parent *D* constitutes a monitor not only for his own child, *C*, but also for the other child, *B*. Thus, the existence of intergenerational closure provides a quantity of social capital available to each parent in raising his children – not only in matters related to school but in other matters as well.

Closure of the social structure is important not only for the existence of effective norms but also for another form of social capital: the trustworthiness of social structures that allows the proliferation of obligations and expectations. Defection from an obligation is a form of imposing a negative externality or another. Yet, in a structure without closure, it can be effectively sanctioned, if at all, only by the person to whom the obligation is owed. Reputation cannot arise in an open structure, and collective sanctions that would ensure trustworthiness cannot be applied. Thus, we may say that closure creates trustworthiness in a social structure.

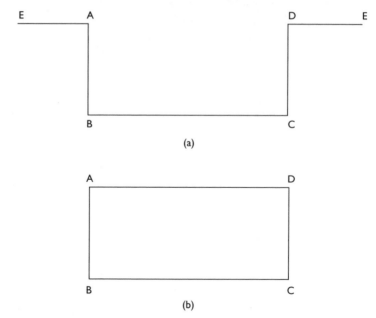

Figure 7.2 *Network involving parents (A, D) and children (B, C) without (a) and with (b) intergenerational closure*

References

Banfield, Edward. 1967. *The Moral Basis of a Backward Society*. New York: Free Press.
Becker, Gary. 1964. *Human Capital*. New York: National Bureau of Economic Research.
Blau, Peter. 1964. *Exchange and Power in Social Life*. New York: Wiley.
Coleman, James S. 1987. "Norms as Social Capital." Pp. 133–55 in *Economic Imperialism*, edited by Gerard Radnitzky and Peter Bernholz. New York: Paragon.
Festinger, Leon, Stanley Schachter, and Kurt Back. 1963. *Social Pressures in Informal Groups*. Stanford, Calif.: Stanford University Press.
Geertz, Clifford. 1962. "The Rotating Credit Association: A 'Middle Rung' in Development." *Economic Development and Cultural Change* 10: 240–63.
Gouldner, Alvin. 1960. "The Norm of Reciprocity: A Preliminary Statement." *American Sociological Review* 25: 161–78.
Katz, E., and P. Lazarsfeld. 1955. *Personal Influence*. New York: Free Press.
Lenin, V. I. (1902) 1973. *What Is To Be Done*. Peking: Foreign Language Press.
Merry, Sally E. 1984. "Rethinking Gossip and Scandal." Pp. 271–302 in *Toward a General Theory of Social Control*. Vol. 1, *Fundamentals*, edited by Donald Black. New York: Academic.
Merton, Robert K. 1968. *Social Theory and Social Structure*, 2nd ed. New York: Free Press.
Schultz, Theodore. 1961. "Investment in Human Capital." *American Economic Review* 51 (March): 1–17.
Ullmann-Margalit, Edna. 1977. *The Emergence of Norms*. Oxford: Clarendon.

8 Foundations for a Theory of Collective Decisions

James S. Coleman

The Problem of Collective Action

From the point of view of purposive action theory, an *action* by an actor is easily explained. The one governing principle of the theory serves to explain it: the actor is striving to maximize his utility.

There is no such principle, however, to explain joint or collective action. For the principle is posed at the level of the individual actor and not at the level of a pair or collectivity. The utility of the collectivity is a meaningless quantity. Is it to be the sum of the utilities of the individual actors? If so, what weights are to be applied to the individual actors' utilities?

The lack of such a principle of behavior for "collective actors" does not prevent explanation of many types of social interaction by use of the individual calculus of purposive behavior. Recent books by Homans, Thibaut and Kelley, and Blau use that calculus to explain many types of behavior in social situations.[1] Even more broadly, economic theory uses this calculus as the basis for explaining the functioning of economic systems, and economic systems involve much interaction between actors. The calculus of individual purposive behavior explains the functioning of economic systems in a way illustrated by Adam Smith's famous statement in *The Wealth of Nations*. "It is not by the benevolence of the butcher, the brewer, or the baker that we expect our dinner, but from their regard to their own interest."[2]

Yet there is a whole set of social phenomena that this calculus will not explain. It is best illustrated by examining somewhat more fundamentally the economic interactions to which it is so well suited. Why is it that an economic exchange involving two actors is carried out? Clearly, in terms of this theoretical approach, it will be carried out only if both actors find it to their individual advantage to do so. It involves the voluntary action of two actors, A and B, and, consequently, four possibilities exist: neither A nor B finds the action beneficial; A finds it beneficial, but B does not; B finds it beneficial, but A does not; or both A and B find it beneficial.

An economic exchange occurs, or a social interaction occurs, when the last of these conditions holds. This is spontaneous action, for it is willed by both actors involved. But does this means that no action will take place except when the last condition holds? If such were the case, almost any action on the part of a large collectivity would be impossible, because as the actors increase to A, B, C, then A,B,C,D, A,B,C,D,E, and so on, the number of no-action conditions increases to 7, 15, 31, and so on, in powers of 2, while there remains only one condition for action: the condition in which the same action alternative is preferred by all.

This is one of the two fundamental problems of collective action. Only under the most extreme condition of consensus does action spring spontaneously from the actors' individual goals. Under any other condition, there is no spontaneous action, for at least one actor prefers a different course of action.

The second fundamental problem of collective action may be called the problem of "contingency." The action may be beneficial to all parties but only if other parties participate in it (and thus pay the cost of participation). That is, there may be complete consensus on the action, contingent on the participation of others. (Even in an exchange, the problem of contingency arises. The exchange is to the mutual advantage of both actors only if both carry out their half of the exchange.) But it is even more to the advantage of each not to participate, if all others do. This problem arises in the economics of public finance, and is known as the "free-rider" problem. Recently, Mancur Olson has treated such action problems more generally, in the context of voluntary associations such as trade unions. He has developed from it a theory of interest-group formation and strength at some variance with existing interest-group theory.[3]

This problem of contingency ordinarily arises only for those collective actions that are implemented by acts of members of the collectivity, such as payment of taxes, and even more for those actions that involve no collective decision at all, but only individual decisions, such as contributions to a voluntary fire association. For other collective actions, such as declaration of war or the decision to build a new court-house, the decision is truly collective, and the action is implemented by an agency of the collectivity. Even for those collective actions that entail actions of members of the collectivity, it is often the case that a collective decision includes a provision for enforcement designed to remove the problem of contingency. Though the problem is never fully solved, it will not be treated in this paper. It will be assumed that any collective decision includes some provision for enforcement or is implemented by an agency of the collectivity.

Returning to the problem of consensus, societies and organizations have evolved numerous devices by which the problem may be partly circumvented and collective action carried out. One of the most fully formalized of these is the institution of voting, together with the voting rule. A majority rule is a simple and pervasive rule, but one in which nearly half the actors may prefer another action. A plurality rule (when there are several alternatives) is even weaker, for a majority may prefer actions other than the one selected by the rule. Other rules are more stringent than a majority rule, for example, a two-thirds majority. And in some instances one finds, even in a large and diverse society, the most stringent rule; a requirement that the action be unanimous.

These are the rules made in a society that partially solve the practical problem of collective action. But they neither wholly solve the practical problem nor in any way solve the theoretical problem. For what is to prevent those who disagree from simply withdrawing from the collectivity or refusing to accept the action and rebelling against it? There are many examples of small but violently opposed minorities that refuse to accept a collective action. Civil rights activity has been the scene of many such examples, both by certain segregationists and by certain integrationists who refuse to obey laws they disagree with. This in fact is a curious case, for minorities on each side have refused to accept the collective actions of the society as a whole.

There are many other examples of refusal to accept the collective action under a given set of decision rules in an organization or a society. The physical barriers to exodus from Iron Curtain countries stand as reminders that many persons would withdraw from these societies rather than accept the collective actions if they were not physically constrained. The splitting of sects from a parent church exemplifies the same unwillingness to accept the actions of the collectivity as a whole. The revolutions and *coups d'état* in many developing countries and the extreme instability of governments throughout the world are sufficient indication that mere construction of a decision rule does not begin to solve the problem.

Another way of putting the issue is that the construction of a constitution is nothing more than putting words on paper and can be done by a dolt, but the construction of a constitution that will allow collective action to proceed without splitting the society apart is nearly equivalent to devising a complete theory of collective action....

Approaches to the Problem of Collective Action

Sociologists have not been numerous among those who have made attempts to solve this fundamental problem. I do not know the reason for sociologists' neglect, except for the relative absence throughout sociology of systematic theory and the tendency in sociological theory to take social structures as given and thus to accept coercion, authority, and constitutions without raising theoretical questions about why the actors themselves accept them or refuse to accept them.

Political scientists and economists have shown the greatest concern over this problem of consensus in collective action. The classical political philosophers, such as Thomas Hobbes, John Locke, and John Stuart Mill, took this as a central problem. Among economists, those concerned with public finance and, in general, welfare economists have had to face it. This is most obvious in taxation, for one is forced to ask such questions as what is a "just" distribution of taxes and public services? Or less normatively, what is a distribution of taxes and services that the society will accept?

One of the best known contributions to this theory is a negative one, by an economist, Kenneth Arrow, who showed that no voting decision rule could give a socially "reasonable" outcome under all distributions of individual preferences.[4] But this does not help much, for several reasons. First, the correct task is not to find socially reasonable outcomes but, rather, to link together individual preferences and collective action in the way they are in fact linked in social organization. Second, the theory, to be at all useful, should indicate the conditions under which collective action can be taken by a social organization and the conditions under which it will lead to withdrawal, revolt, or disobedience.

It should first be recognized that there are many kinds of social organizations and many kinds of collective actions. The religious rites of a sect or a primitive tribe are collective actions apparently spontaneously entered into by all members, directed toward a common goal desired by all members. At the other extreme, the actions of a bureaucracy are directed toward a goal held only by a very few at the top of the bureaucracy, and there is no expectation that the goal will be shared by all members of the organization. The collective actions of a feudal estate, a medieval household, or a slave-holding plantation are designed to benefit the actor at the top of the authority pyramid, yet many contribute to these actions.

The actions of a trade union and other mass-based collectivities are not always toward goals collectively held, but the very existence of the collectivity is based upon action toward collective goals. The government of a large, diverse nation carries out many collective actions as the acting agency of the nation as a whole, yet it is obvious that none of these is directed toward goals held by every member of the nation.

As a consequence of this diversity of kinds of social organizations, the theory of collective action must be a diverse one indeed. It is clear that in some of these organizations the principal process is a stable pattern of exchange and can perhaps be treated as a branch of the general theory of exchange. For example, in a rational bureaucracy the employee explicitly exchanges autonomy over his actions in return for money or similar resources that make the exchange a profitable one for him. In this way an entrepreneur who begins with enough such resources can organize a collective action involving the interdependence of many individual actors. In such a circumstance no confrontation of diverse preferences is necessary, since the entrepreneur has "bought" the action of his employees and can so organize it to carry out his own goals. It thus appears, at least on the surface, that the explanation of collective action in such organizations requires no new theoretical principles.

It is quite different, however, for social organizations in which the power over collective action is distributed over more than one person. It is in such organizations that some device such as a voting rule is established for bringing this dispersed power to bear on questions of collective action. And it is clear that such procedures exist at some point in most social organizations, so that the problem of collective action arises somewhere in the organization.

I will take as the focus of inquiry, then, social organizations in which there is a genuine collective decision, where power over the outcome is distributed over more than one person. This means also that I will not ask how that distribution of power arose. I will not examine the question of a "constitution," either informal or formal, but will take the constitution, which establishes the decision-making procedure, as given.

Perhaps the best way to see the difficulties that arise in moving from individual rationality to collective decisions is to study the contradictions that arise in voting rules. Consider a simple decision involving a collectivity of these actors with a choice among three alternatives. Each actor has a preference ordering for the three alternatives; a possible preference ordering is shown in table 8.1.

The situation shown in table 8.1 produces curious results. For suppose the alternatives are presented to the voters in a pairwise fashion, first A and B, and then the winner versus C. In the A versus B vote, A wins with two votes. In the A versus C vote, C wins with two votes. But now suppose we start with a different pair in the

Table 8.1 *Preferences of Actors X, Y, and Z for Alternatives A, B, and C*

Rank	X	Y	Z
1	A	B	C
2	B	C	A
3	C	A	B

first vote, say B versus C. In the B versus C vote, B wins; and then in the B versus A vote, A wins. Thus merely by shifting the order of voting, the over-all outcome shifts from C to A. If the third order were used, starting with A versus C, this would result in still a different winner, B.

This decision rule appears to violate one's sense of what is a reasonable outcome, for the outcome should not change merely by changing the order of voting. This is the general direction of the argument Kenneth Arrow made. He laid down several conditions that any decision rule should meet if it were to give "reasonable" social outcomes, and then showed that such a decision rule was logically impossible.

Such a result, however, flies in the face of reality. Social organizations do establish decision rules, decisions are made, and the organizations persist. Are we reduced to saying that their actions are as grossly unreasonable as the example above suggests?

As numerous students of this problem have pointed out, there would be no difficulty if we had some measure of intensity of feeling. For example, in table 8.1, suppose there were a number expressing the amount of utility that X, Y, and Z each associate with alternatives A, B, and C, as indicated in table 8.2. In this example, alternative A clearly has the highest total amount of utility. A decision rule that merely determined the outcome by the highest aggregate utility would always give the decision to alternative A, independent of the order of comparison, and no "unreasonable" outcomes would result.

The fatal flaw in this solution is that there is no meaning to the notion of "amount of utility" or "intensity of feeling" unless it is expressible in the behavior under consideration. Voting certainly allows no such expression, but only registering a preference. Looking at the matter naïvely, we might then say that we could merely ask each actor to write down the amount of utility each alternative held for him. Then we would have the data for table 8.2 and could merely aggregate the amounts and arrive at a winner.

But, in truth, this is merely chasing after a chimera. The matter is not solved so easily, for such a procedure invites strategic behavior, writing down whatever utilities will be most likely to give the outcome one wants. For example, Z has merely to inflate the quantity he writes down for C, and C will win – unless, of course, X and Y do the same for their favorites. In effect, asking an actor to write down utilities for each alternative, subject to an over-all maximum, say, of thirty, is nothing other than asking him to cast thirty votes rather than one. Since his goal is to maximize his expected utility, he will cast these votes in a way he hopes will do that, rather than to express the "relative utility" each has for him. However, if there were some way, in the decision process itself, for each actor in his behavior to express his intensity of preference, then this would give a start toward the solution.

Table 8.2 *Amounts of Utility of Alternatives A, B, and C for Actors X, Y, and Z*

	X	Y	Z	Total
u_a	10	8	9	27
u_b	5	10	8	23
u_c	1	9	10	20

Behavior in a System of Collective Decisions

An examination of empirical voting systems immediately yields a wealth of such behavior. First, suppose we put back this single decision into the context from which it was abstracted – taking for simplicity a legislature as the context, with a whole sequence of collective decisions on which to act. In such a situation, is it possible to express intensity of preference? The answer is that legislators do so by using the resources at their disposal. These resources consist of a number things, depending on their positions within the legislature. But the most simple case, and a relatively frequent one, is an exchange of resources: legislator X agrees to vote as Y wishes on one action in return for Y's agreement to vote as X wishes on another action. They do so because each sees a gain. Each loses his vote on an action where the outcome makes little difference to him but gains a vote on an action where the outcome matters more. Each has in that exchange expressed something about his intensity of preference. Each has given up a vote on an issue in which the utility difference between alternatives is *less* than the utility difference between alternatives on the vote he has gained. This can be stated more precisely by means of algebra, but the substantive point is most important. By this action, there has been introduced into the system the first step in transforming ordinal preferences into cardinal utility differences that can be aggregated to arrive at a collective decision.

It is not true, however, that any procedure for arriving at cardinal utility differences will be sufficient for use in collective decisions. It would not be correct, for example, merely to use a von Neumann-Morgenstern lottery ticket procedure for arriving at cardinal utility differences and then aggregate them to arrive at a collective decision.[5] It is crucial to the establishment of a measure of utility that the behavior carried out by the actors involve resources they control within the system under consideration. The reasons for this are evident below.

It does not require much stretch of the imagination to see how this first step can be followed by others, so that each actor, through the vote exchanges or agreements he makes, expresses in minute gradation the interest he has in a given outcome, that is, the difference in utilities that the different possible outcomes would have for him. However, for each step toward a fine expression of intensity of interest in an action, another action is needed. Each actor needs a large set of votes on actions of varying interest to him to be able to express precisely his interest in any one. Each of these votes has the same function as goods in an economic system with barter exchange: it has certain direct utility for him if he uses it to satisfy his own interests; but it also has a certain value to others, so that its use in exchange might bring him resources more relevant to his interests....

The necessity for replacing the single action back in its context of a whole set of collective actions should now be obvious. Without these other actions, each actor has no resources he can use to express how strongly he feels about this one. With only the single action, it is of supreme importance to all, for there is nothing to measure it against. The only measuring instruments are provided by the costs of the alternatives to accepting an unfavorable collective decision. Withdrawal, rebellion, and disobedience, together with their many variations, are the alternatives; and some measure of the intensity of his interest in the outcome is given by his willingness to resort to one of these alternatives.

Power in the System

[The case of refusal to accept the decision will be examined later at somewhat more length.] However, it is useful first to consider more carefully the question of power and the comparison between utilities of different persons. We can approach the matter very heuristically by reflecting on what does in fact constitute power in such a system. Quite simply, we think of power of an actor in a system of collective decisions as the ability to obtain the outcomes that will give him highest utility. He is given by the constitution or rules a certain amount of direct control over various collective decisions – for example, in a legislature, each member ordinarily has one vote on each action. In the general case, he will have differing amounts of control over different actions. He may have a large amount of control over a number of actions. Does this mean he has a great amount of power in the system? It is easy to see that it does not, for it could be that no one is interested in the outcomes of the actions over which he has a great amount of control.

It is clear, then, that his power, or ability to get what he wants in the system, depends both upon his formal control of various collective actions and on the interest of others in those actions. If he has a large amount of control over only one action, but that action has much interest to many other actors, then this is a very valuable resource for him, and he can use it to get his way on those actions of interest to him.

For an ideal system, comparable to a market with pure competition, there are a great many collective actions of widely varying interest to the actors. For such a system, in which exchanges can be carried out to express minute differences in interest, the precise expression for the power of an actor can be given. In words, it can be stated this way:

The value of control over an action is equal to the sum of the interests of each actor in that action times the total power of that actor. In turn, the total power of an actor is equal to his constitutional control over each action times the value of that action, summed over all actions in the system.

The basis for this definition of the value of control over an event can be seen as follows: Suppose an actor has some interest in an action. The effect of this interest is to make him willing to employ a portion of his resources, that is, his partial control of other actions. But his resources depend on the value of the actions that he has some control over, that is, on the amount of interest that those with power have in the actions he has control over.

On the other hand, suppose another actor has some control over this action which interests the first actor. He will want to exact the highest price he can get for giving up this control. He will hold out for the most power he can get, either in control of actions of interest to him or control of actions that he can further exchange for control that interests him.

Thus the definition of value is one in which there is a simultaneous calibration of the value of different actions and the power of different actors. Actions are valuable when powerful actors have a great deal of interest in them. Actors are powerful when the actions they control have high value. A consequence of this definition is that the value of an action is the cost of obtaining complete control over it (in this perfect market). Thus, with a probabilistic decision rule, an actor can fully control an action only if he has total power greater than the value of the action and is willing to employ all his resources toward gaining control of it.[6]

There are numerous examples which illustrate the way this principle operates in a social system. The classical example is that of the king who has control over nearly all actions but suddenly becomes entranced with a poor but beautiful girl who has nothing but her own autonomy. His interests are now focused on the actions he does not have control over, the actions of this girl. Thus, her power in the society jumps from near zero to the greatest of all, for she has control over the only actions that interest the king, who controls everything that interests anyone else. Obviously, for such a system to work, the girl must be in no way beholden to the king, a matter which in such tales is usually contrived by her being the daughter of a poor but independent woodchopper living off the forest at the edge of the kingdom.

Interpersonal Comparison of Utility

This examination of power allows us to return to the question of interpersonal comparison of utility. As an earlier point in the paper, it was evident that one could not naïvely ask people to give their intensity of feeling, and then merely add up these utilities to arrive at a collective decision that "maximized utility." But now, with somewhat more sophistication, we can come back to the question of interpersonal comparison of utility, having defined the value of an action and the power of an actor, as indicated above. The exchanges themselves provide a comparison of different actors' utilities or interests.

As a result of the exchanges, each actor has a certain power. Thus, just as the value of an action is the sum over all actors of their power times their interest in that action, the value of one actor's interest in an action is his power times his interest in it. That is, if two actors have identical interests in an action (i.e., action occupies the same proportion of their total interests), then actor A's interests are more valuable than B's if his total power is greater than B's. This difference in power results, of course, from the fact that A has control over more valuable resources than does B and thus has more power to see his interests realized.

Thus an interpersonal comparison of utility automatically occurs in exchange, weighting an actor's interests by his total power. But such a comparison raises questions about interpersonal comparison in the usual sense. Are we not assuming that individuals communicate with others the precise size of their interests in arriving at a value? The answer to this is "No." The only communication assumed here is that assumed in any market: what exchanges an actor will make and what ones he will not. The perfect functioning of the market assumes that he has complete knowledge of what exchanges others will make and can thus assess the value-in-exchange of any power he gains in an exchange. It does not assume, however, that he makes his interests known in any way beyond stating which exchanges he will agree to and which ones he will refuse. It is worthwhile to note the sense in which the actor's power provides a scale by which his utilities may be compared to others. His wants are exactly as important as is his ability to realize them. If A has twice the power of B, his wants or interests are worth twice B's. This is no value judgment of ours as analysts but a description of the value judgment implicit in the distribution of control over actions in the system.

A question can be raised in this context concerning the maximization of social welfare. In a perfect exchange system, as described above, do the exchanges result in a maximization of social welfare? This is a reasonable question because each exchange will benefit at least both parties to it; and in a perfect exchange system, when the state has been reached in which no other exchanges are possible, is this not a maximization of social welfare?

It becomes clear that this question can only be answered relative to a given framework of constitutional control. The situation is exactly analogous to a perfect market of private goods. Utility for each trader is maximized, but relative to the goods he brought to the market, that is, the resources he began with. Similarly in collective actions. The perfect exchange system maximizes social welfare, but only when each person's welfare is weighted according to his power that derives from his constitutional control of actions. The scientific question becomes: Given the distribution among actors of constitutional control over collective actions, what procedures will insure that each actor's interests will be realized to the extent provided by his power? The answer lies in making the system most closely approximate a perfect market in which resources may be exchanged. But the ultimate question of what degree of constitutional control each actor should have is outside the system and becomes truly an ethical question or else one that is answered in terms of the ultimate recourse, the physical force that can be used by each actor in fixing his constitutional control.

Notes

1   George C. Homans, *Social Behavior: Its Elementary Forms* (New York: Harcourt, Brace, & World, 1961); John W. Thibaut and Harold H. Kelley, *The Social Psychology of Groups* (New York: John Wiley & Sons, 1959); Peter M. Blau, *Exchange and Power in Social Life* (New York: John Wiley & Sons, 1964).
2   Adam Smith, *The Wealth of Nations* (New York: Modern Library, 1937), p. liv.
3   Mancur Olson, *The Logic of Collective Action* (Cambridge: Harvard University Press, 1965); also see Richard Musgrave, *The Theory of Public Finance* (New York: McGraw-Hill Book Co., 1959), for the general problem in economic theory.
4   Kenneth J. Arrow, *Social Choice and Individual Values* (New York: John Wiley & Sons, 1951).
5   Patrick Suppes and Muriel Winet, "An Axiomatization of Utility Based on the Notion of Utility Differences," *Management Science*, I (1955), 259, describes such a procedure.
6   A probabilistic decision rule, in which the probability of a positive outcome is proportional to the proportion of positive votes, is the only one in which the actual control of an actor over an action is equal to his constitutional control and not contingent on the particular coalition.

9 The Logic of Collective Action

Mancur Olson

The combination of individual interests and common interests in an organization suggests an analogy with a competitive market. The firms in a perfectly competitive industry, for example, have a common interest in a higher price for the industry's product. Since a uniform price must prevail in such a market, a firm cannot expect a higher price for itself unless all of the other firms in the industry also have this higher price. But a firm in a competitive market also has an interest in selling as much as it can, until the cost of producing another unit exceeds the price of that unit. In this there is no common interest; each firm's interest is directly opposed to that of every other firm, for the more other firms sell, the lower the price and income for any given firm. In short, while all firms have a common interest in a higher price, they have antagonistic interests where output is concerned. This can be illustrated with a simple supply-and-demand model. For the sake of a simple argument, assume that a perfectly competitive industry is momentarily in a disequilibrium position, with price exceeding marginal cost for all firms at their present output. Suppose, too, that all of the adjustments will be made by the firms already in the industry rather than by new entrants, and that the industry is on an inelastic portion of its demand curve. Since price exceeds marginal cost for all firms, output will increase. But as all firms increase production, the price falls; indeed, since the industry demand curve is by assumption inelastic, the total revenue of the industry will decline. Apparently each firm finds that with price exceeding marginal cost, it pays to increase its output, but the result is that each firm gets a smaller profit. Some economists in an earlier day may have questioned this result,[1] but the fact that profit-maximizing firms in a perfectly competitive industry can act contrary to their interests as a group is now widely understood and accepted.[2] A group of profit-maximizing firms can act to reduce their aggregate profits because in perfect competition each firm is, by definition, so small that it can ignore the effect of its output on price. Each firm finds it to its advantage to increase output to the point where marginal cost equals price and to ignore the effects of its extra output on the position of the industry. It is true that the net result is that all firms are worse off, but this does not mean that every firm has not maximized its profits. If a firm, foreseeing the fall in price resulting from the increase in industry output, were to restrict its own output; it would lose more than ever, for its price would fall quite as much in any case and it would have a smaller output as well. A firm in a perfectly competitive market gets only a small part of the benefit (or a small share of the industry's extra revenue) resulting from a reduction in that firm's output.

Originally translated by Martin Hohlweck and edited by John Paterson.

For these reasons it is now generally understood that if the firms in an industry are maximizing profits, the profits for the industry as a whole will be less than they might otherwise be. And almost everyone would agree that this theoretical conclusion fits the facts for markets characterized by pure competition. The important point is that this is true because, though all the firms have a common interest in a higher price for the industry's product, it is in the interest of each firm that the other firms pay the cost – in terms of the necessary reduction in output – needed to obtain a higher price.

About the only thing that keeps prices from falling in accordance with the process just described in perfectly competitive markets is outside intervention. Government price supports, tariffs, cartel agreements, and the like may keep the firms in a competitive market from acting contrary to their interests. Such aid or intervention is quite common. It is then important to ask how it comes about. How does a competitive industry obtain government assistance in maintaining the price of its product?

Consider a hypothetical, competitive industry, and suppose that most of the producers in that industry desire a tariff, a price-support program, or some other government intervention to increase the price for their product. To obtain any such assistance from the government, the producers in this industry will presumably have to organize a lobbying organization; they will have to become an active pressure group. This lobbying organization may have to conduct a considerable campaign. If significant resistance is encountered, a great amount of money will be required. Public relations experts will be needed to influence the newspapers, and some advertising may be necessary. Professional organizers will probably be needed to organize "spontaneous grass roots" meetings among the distressed producers in the industry, and to get those in the industry to write letters to their congressmen. The campaign for the government assistance will take the time of some of the producers in the industry, as well as their money.

There is a striking parallel between the problem the perfectly competitive industry faces as it strives to obtain government assistance, and the problem it faces in the marketplace when the firms increase output and bring about a fall in price. *Just as it was not rational for a particular producer to restrict his output in order that there might be a higher price for the product of his industry, so it would not be rational for him to sacrifice his time and money to support a lobbying organization to obtain government assistance for the industry. In neither case would it be in the interest of the individual producer to assume any of the costs himself. A lobbying organization, or indeed a labor union or any other organization, working in the interest of a large group of firms or workers in some industry, would get no assistance from the rational, self-interested individuals in that industry.* This would be true even if everyone in the industry were absolutely convinced that the proposed program was in their interest (though in fact some might think otherwise and make the organization's task yet more difficult).

Although the lobbying organization is only one example of the logical analogy between the organization and the market, it is of some practical importance. There are many powerful and well-financed lobbies with mass support in existence now, but these lobbying organizations do not get that support because of their legislative achievements. The most powerful lobbying organizations now obtain their funds and their following for other reasons, as later parts of this study will show.

Some critics may argue that the rational person will, indeed, support a large organization, like a lobbying organization, that works in his interest, because he knows that if he does not, others will not do so either, and then the organization will fail, and he will be without the benefit that the organization could have provided. This argument shows the need for the analogy with the perfectly competitive market. For it would be quite as reasonable to argue that prices will never fall below the levels a monopoly would have charged in a perfectly competitive market, because if one firm increased its output, other firms would also, and the price would fall; but each firm could foresee this, so it would not start a chain of price-destroying increases in output. In fact, it does not work out this way in a competitive market; nor in a large organization. When the number of firms involved is large, no one will notice the effect on price if one firm increases its output, and so no one will change his plans because of it. Similarly, in a large organization, the loss of one dues payer will not noticeably increase the burden for any other one dues payer, and so a rational person would not believe that if he were to withdraw from an organization he would drive others to do so.

The foregoing argument must at the least have some relevance to economic organizations that are mainly means through which individuals attempt to obtain the same things they obtain through their activities in the market. Labor unions, for example, are organizations through which workers strive to get the same things they get with their individual efforts in the market – higher wages, better working conditions, and the like. It would be strange indeed if the workers did not confront some of the same problems in the union that they meet in the market, since their efforts in both places have some of the same purposes.

However similar the purposes may be, critics may object that attitudes in organizations are not at all like those in markets. In organizations, an emotional or ideological element is often also involved. Does this make the argument offered here practically irrelevant?

A most important type of organization – the national state – will serve to test this objection. Patriotism is probably the strongest non-economic motive for organizational allegiance in modern times. This age is sometimes called the age of nationalism. Many nations draw additional strength and unity from some powerful ideology, such as democracy or communism, as well as from a common religion, language, or cultural inheritance. The state not only has many such powerful sources of support; it also is very important economically. Almost any government is economically beneficial to its citizens, in that the law and order it provides is a prerequisite of all civilized economic activity. But despite the force of patriotism, the appeal of the national ideology, the bond of a common culture, and the indispensability of the system of law and order, no major state in modern history has been able to support itself through voluntary dues or contributions. Philanthropic contributions are not even a significant source of revenue for most countries. Taxes, *compulsory* payments by definition, are needed. Indeed, as the old saying indicates, their necessity is as certain as death itself.

If the state, with all of the emotional resources at its command, cannot finance its most basic and vital activities without resort to compulsion, it would seem that large private organizations might also have difficulty in getting the individuals in the groups whose interests they attempt to advance to make the necessary contributions voluntarily.

The reason the state cannot survive on voluntary dues or payments, but must rely on taxation, is that the most fundamental services a nation-state provides are, in one important respect, like the higher price in a competitive market: they must be available to everyone if they are available to anyone. The basic and most elementary goods or services provided by government, like defense and police protection, and the system of law and order generally, are such that they go to everyone or practically everyone in the nation. It would obviously not be feasible, if indeed it were possible, to deny the protection provided by the military services, the police, and the courts to those who did not voluntarily pay their share of the costs of government, and taxation is accordingly necessary. The common or collective benefits provided by governments are usually called "public goods" by economists, and the concept of public goods is one of the oldest and most important ideas in the study of public finance. A common, collective, or public good is here defined as any good such that, if any person X_i in a group $X_1, \ldots, X_i, \ldots, X_n$ consumes it, it cannot feasibly be withheld from the others in that group. In other words, those who do not purchase or pay for any of the public or collective good cannot be excluded or kept from sharing in the consumption of the good, as they can where noncollective goods are concerned.

Students of public finance have, however, neglected the fact that *the achievement of any common goal or the satisfaction of any common interest means that a public or collective good has been provided for that group.* The very fact that a goal or purpose is *common* to a group means that no one in the group is excluded from the benefit or satisfaction brought about by its achievement. As the opening paragraphs of this chapter indicated, almost all groups and organizations have the purpose of serving the common interests of their members. As R. M. MacIver puts it, "Persons ... have common interests in the degree to which they participate in a cause ... which indivisibly embraces them all."[3] It is of the essence of an organization that it provides an inseparable, generalized benefit. It follows that the provision of public or collective goods is the fundamental function of organizations generally. A state is first of all an organization that provides public goods for its members, the citizens; and other types of organizations similarly provide collective goods for their members.

And just as a state cannot support itself by voluntary contributions, or by selling its basic services on the market, neither can other large organizations support themselves without providing some sanction, or some attraction distinct from the public good itself, that will lead individuals to help bear the burdens of maintaining the organization. The individual member of the typical large organization is in a position analogous to that of the firm in a perfectly competitive market, or the taxpayer in the state: his own efforts will not have a noticeable effect on the situation of his organization, and he can enjoy any improvements brought about by others whether or not he has worked in support of his organization.

There is no suggestion here that states or other organizations provide *only* public or collective goods. Governments often provide noncollective goods like electric power, for example, and they usually sell such goods on the market much as private firms would do. Moreover, as later parts of this study will argue, large organizations that are not able to make membership compulsory *must also* provide some noncollective goods in order to give potential members an incentive to join. Still, collective goods are the characteristic organizational goods, for ordinary noncollective goods can always be provided by individual action, and only where common purposes or collective goods are concerned is organization or group action ever indispensable.[4]

Notes

1 See J. M. Clark, *The Economics of Overhead Costs* (Chicago: University of Chicago Press, 1923), p. 417, and Frank H. Knight, *Risk, Uncertainty and Profit* (Boston: Houghton Mifflin, 1921), p. 193.
2 Edward H. Chamberlin, *Monopolistic Competition*, 6th ed. (Cambridge, Mass.: Harvard University Press, 1950), p. 4.
3 R. M. MacIver in *Encyclopaedia of the Social Sciences*, VII (New York: Macmillan, 1932), 147.
4 It does not, however, follow that organized or coordinated group action is *always* necessary to obtain a collective good.

Part III

Institutional Analysis

INTRODUCTION TO PART III

The concept of the "institution" is one of the most enduring concepts in sociology. Unfortunately, it is also one of the most poorly defined. This theoretical ambiguity has led some theorists such as Homans (b. 1951) to avoid the term altogether, but the concept is one that sociologists do not seem to be able to do without. In this section, we examine the concept broadly, using work from three very different sociological domains. The work of Paul J. DiMaggio (b. 1951) and Walter Powell (b. 1951) on institutional isomorphism shows why certain organizational features dominate, even when they are not economically rational. Charles Tilly (b. 1929) identifies the historical processes that led to the development of the nation-state, showing that the resulting institutional arrangements look nothing like what would have been expected a thousand years ago. Finally, the work of Niklas Luhmann (1927–98) on steering builds on notions of institutions as complex interdependent systems and identifies the difficulty of controlling such systems.

The Collective Nature of Institutions

Most theories of social institutions are rooted in Durkheim's treatment of social facts (see Part II of *Classical Sociological Theory*). Although they are socially created and maintained, we experience them as external forces that have some power over us. But what are they? Talcott Parsons gave us one answer to this question. Parsons argued that an institution could be defined as "a set of regulatory norms that give rise to social structure or organization."[1] Two elements of this definition should be emphasized. First, institutions are *collective* in nature. Because they exist as sets of norms, they can be said to exist only to the degree that a social group recognizes them and acts on the basis of them. Second, institutions for Parsons are *sets* of norms that go together, they are "a complex of institutionalized role integrates"[2] and are thus broader than particular norms.

As we would expect, Parsons argued that institutions are functional, contributing to the social order by ensuring that individual behavior conforms to societal interests. But they have two additional functions as well. First, they channel social action into acceptable patterns – ones that are "in conformity with ultimate values." In so doing, they provide a second function by giving people incentives to live up to collective expectations. For an institution to continue to exist, people must view it as legitimate. People tend to do so because they have internalized the ultimate values implicit in the norm, but also because "once really established, a system of institutional norms creates an interlocking of interests" that help keep it in place, even if individual devotion to the underlying values starts to fade.[3]

Parsons' definition established the basis for much of the contemporary thinking about institutions, with one exception. According to Coleman, Parsons' emphasis on the functional aspects of institutions from an *individual's* point of view was a fundamental mistake. By focusing on how individuals experience institutions, it is impossible to identify how institutions form, because the creation of norms rests on *interdependent* action. That is, showing that an institution is in an actor's long-term interest is not sufficient to explain the formation of the institution, since it might be in his or her short-term interest to violate the norm. Thus, "What [Parsons] failed to recognize was that the path from action to system lies in the relation between different actors' actions – it is there that the complexities arise and generate different kinds of systems of action."[4] Modern institutional analysis seeks to understand the interdependent patterns of action that create and maintain collective institutions.

Institutional Analysis

Identifying the role of institutions in social life has had something of a renaissance recently, especially within economic sociology. Much of this work has been a reaction to treatments of social life based on rational actor models, and is often "united by little but a common skepticism toward atomistic accounts of social processes and a common conviction that institutional arrangements and social processes matter," according to Powell and DiMaggio.[5] This attack on individualism is made apparent in work by Williamson,[6] which identifies weaknesses with standard microeconomic assumptions. In Williamson's model, actors have limited cognitive capacity, poor information, often cannot monitor agreements and act opportunistically. Under these conditions, economic institutions develop to solve some very deep problems. Institutions reduce uncertainty and lower transaction costs, providing an efficient solution to bounded individual action.

How institutions come to exist, how they evolve, and the extent to which they are economically efficient are all hotly debated topics within institutional theories of economic sociology. Work on organizational behavior often starts with a process of rationalization based on Weber's famous prediction that organizations, through the dual engines of competition and rationalization, should become ever more bureaucratically rational (see Part III of *Classical Sociological Theory*). Empirical researchers, however, have had difficulty describing organizational behavior in such terms. Instead, organizations seem to accept a great deal of inefficiency in adopting almost ritual responses to new problems. For example, while organizations face many different challenges, DiMaggio and Powell find that the range of organizational responses is remarkably small. Why?

Their answer rests on understanding organizational behavior through an institutional lens. They argue that rational competition alone cannot explain organizational similarity, or "isomorphism." Organizations tend to conform to each other by adopting one of three sets of norms. Conformity can come from the legal and political rules of an organization's milieu ("coercive isomorphism"), from the responses of other organizations to an uncertain environment ("mimetic isomorphism"), or from the internalized norms of the people that make up the organization ("normative isomorphism"). This approach to understanding organizational behavior rests on a multi-level model of organizations; pressures at the organizational level (a search for legitimacy, standard conventions to control uncertainty) are combined with the socialization process of firm managers (professionalization). DiMaggio and Powell challenge theories that rest on elite control or simple population dynamics, arguing "that a theory of institutional isomorphism may help explain the observation that organizations are becoming more homogeneous, and that elites often get their way, while at the same time enabling us to understand the irrationality, the frustration of power, and the lack of innovation that are so commonplace in organizational life."[7]

Moving from economic to political institutions, Tilly examines the formation of the nation-state. Tilly argues that the modern nation-state developed over the last 1,000 years through the organization of capital and coercive practices. Capital consists of "any tangible mobile resources, and enforceable claims on such resources," according to Tilly. Coercion "includes all concerted application, threatened or actual, of action that commonly causes loss or damage to the person or possessions of individuals or groups who are aware of both the action and the potential damage." National states develop when both capital and armed force develop simultaneously, which depends on how war-making practices unfold in combination with city capital structure. Warfare, the primary activity of states in this period, always entails two linked dilemmas. First, domination entails administration since conquering an area requires extracting resources and controlling the new territory. Second, preparing for war requires extracting capital to fund the fighting. In both cases, an administrative apparatus must be developed. Various solutions to these dilemmas resulted in three types of states in Europe. First, tribute-taking empires maximized warfare and extractive capacity, while letting locals maintain control of administrative duties. Second, systems of city-states developed that used temporary federations and coalitions to wage war and defend themselves. Third, national states developed that incorporated military, extraction, and administration functions within one governmental apparatus. To do so required a coalition with capitalists, resulting in a state formation process that intimately connects city development to the means of armed conflict.

Tilly carefully highlights the fact that the process of institutional formation is situated in a particular time and place. Properly identifying how institutions such as states develop and change requires understanding the historical specificity of each case. Still, while keeping a careful eye on the historical details he is able to identify the general features of early European social organization that gave rise to the modern nation-state system. This trade-off between generality and specificity is an important point for any analysis of institutions.

If institutional analysis starts from the premise of interdependent social action, Luhmann takes this position to its most radical conclusion by examining the institutional nature of human interaction itself. To understand Luhmann's argument, it helps to begin with an examination of the classic "other minds" problem. One cannot know another *consciousness*, but instead can only know what another person *communicates*, and understanding communication always implies selecting and filtering meaning through the categories of one's own mind. Interaction is thus nothing more than systems of communication attempts and observations. Luhmann follows Durkheim in suggesting that society is differentiated into various subsystems (such as the legal system, science, religion, economics, etc.). "Autopoiesis," or the fact that subsystems are self-referentially closed, implies that each subsystem is faced with the exact analog of the "other minds" problem: one system observes behavior in another system, but can only interpret (i.e., construct) such actions in terms of the binary oppositions unique to that system. For example, the legal system must interpret everything in terms of the legal–illegal distinction, the religious in terms of sacred or profane, the scientific in terms of truth or falsity. There is never any *direct* transfer from one system to another. Each system observes and reacts to the others (based on its own specific construction of the world), who then observe and react in turn.

The assumption that each subsystem in society is completely self-referential has dramatic implications for how one system can affect another. Luhmann uses the term "steering" to describe attempts at social planning in a system. However, the self-referential nature of social systems implies a "double contingency" that hampers planning. Each subsystem selects and interprets information from the environment, including its perception of other systems, in a manner that is invisible to other systems. Each system cannot view the selection criteria used by the other subsystems, and thus cannot ever be certain of how its own actions are understood from the standpoint of the other. Since planning consists of attempting to change the conditions within one system (economics affecting politics, church affecting state, etc.) and since one system cannot change another directly, steering always reduces to self-steering. Systems may make changes within their own realm (changing what is legal, for example), but cannot know how such changes will be interpreted by the other systems. As such, planning is always a difficult and unsure business. Luhmann's approach is thus radically constructivist, but applied to social institutions instead of individuals. The results of his theory are not optimistic for those seeking public policy levers. It does, however, provide keen insights into why attempts at manipulating such levers have so often met with unexpected results.

Institutionalism in Modern Sociology

The ubiquitous nature of social institutions – almost every aspect of human interaction is imbued with normative and cultural significance – suggests that institutional theory affects most subfields in sociology. Some of the most concerted theoretical energy has been devoted to accounting for the emergence of social institutions. Interestingly, it is rational choice theorists who are doing much of this work, in order to defend against the strong critiques made by institutional thinkers. Others, such as Tilly, take a more contextual view, and use careful comparative analyses to explain differences in institutions ranging from family organization to religious practice. A second dimension to the general problem of institutions involves understanding how norms and culture are internalized and transmitted. Simple socialization theories are challenged both for failing to account for widespread social disorganization and, in their extreme, for being unfalsifiable. This problem is particularly acute in cases where corporate actors (firms, nations) are the 'agents' being socialized. The remarkable diversity of social institutions, combined with a general distrust within the field for grand theoretical approaches such as functionalism, virtually assures that this aspect of social theory will remain diverse, lively, and contentious.

Notes

1   Coleman (1990: 334). This is also echeed in Parsons' own language thus: "This system of regulatory norms, of rules governing actions in pursuit of immediate ends in terms of their conformity with the ultimate common value-system of community, is what I call its institutions approached from the subjective point of view" (Parsons [1934] 1990: 324).
2   Parsons (1951: 39).
3   Parsons ([1934] 1990: 325–6).
4   Coleman (1990: 338).
5   Powell and DiMaggio (1991: 3).
6   Williamson (1975, 1985).
7   Powell and DiMaggio (1991: 3).

Select Bibliography

Coleman, James S. 1990. "Commentary: Social Institutions and Social Theory." *American Sociological Review* 55: 333–9. (A discussion of Parsons' paper, that includes Coleman's own understanding of what an institution is and how theory should approach the study of institutions.)

Form, William. 1990. "Institutional Analysis: An Organizational Approach." Pp. 257–71 in *Change in Societal Institutions*, Maureen T. Hallinan, David M. Klein, and Jennifer Glass, eds. New York: Plenum Publishing Corporation. (A nice review of the concept of institution, providing a new approach based on inter-organizational connections.)

King, M. and A. Schütz. 1994. "The Ambitions Modesty of Niklas Luhmann." *Journal of Law and Society* 21: 261–87. (A very detailed and coherent introduction to Luhmann's work. The best first place to start reading on Luhmann.)

Luhmann, Niklas. 1995. *Social Systems*. Trans. J. Bednarz. Stanford, California: Stanford University Press. (Luhmann's major statement of his total social theory, but very difficult to read; described by Luhmann himself as a "labyrinth.")

——. 1997. "Limits of Steering." *Theory, Culture & Society* 14: 41–57.

Meyer, John W., John Boli, George M. Thomas, Francisco O. Ramirez. 1997. "World Society and the Nation-State." *American Journal of Sociology* 103, 1: 144–81. (This article exemplifies some of the new work treating nation-states and national alliances as institutions.)

Parsons, Talcott. 1951. *The Social System*. Glencoe, IL: The Free Press. (A classic in the structural functionalist tradition.)

Parsons, Talcott. 1990 [1934]. "Prolegomena to a Theory of Social Institutions." *American Sociological Review* 55: 319–33. (A recently re-discovered piece that outlines Parsons's early thinking on institutions.)

Powell, Walter W. and Paul J. DiMaggio. 1991. *The New Institutionalism in Organizational Analysis*. Chicago: University of Chicago Press. (The first chapter of this book provides a nice treatment of institutions as they relate to modern organizational theory.)

Sewell, William H., Jr. 1992. "A Theory of Structure: Duality, Agency, and Transformation." *American Journal of Sociology* 98: 1–29. (A good discussion of the meaning of "structure" in social theory. Insights here can readily be linked to the problems of various meanings of "institution.")

Tilly, C. 1992. *Coercion, Capital and European States, AD 1900–1992*. Cambridge, MA: Blackwell. (Tilly's major work on state formation.)

Williamson, Oliver E. 1975. *Markets and Hierarchies*. New York: Free Press. (A key work in the application of institutional ideas to economic sociology, along with the later *The Economic Institutions of Capitalism* [1985. New York: The Free Press].)

Williamson, Oliver E. 1985. *The Economic Institutions of Capitalism*. New York: Free Press. (This work is now a classic in the application of institutional ideas to economic sociology.)

Winship, Christopher and Sherwin Rosen. 1988. "Introduction: Sociological and Economic Approaches to the Analysis of Social Structure." *American Journal of Sociology* 94: s1–s16. (Contains a nice discussion of how sociological ideas of institutions contribute to understanding economic problems.)

10 Limits of Steering

Niklas Luhmann

I

In the politics of society the term 'steering' is still much discussed. Uncertainty about the capability to influence the future leads to appeals for something to be done (see, for example, Evers and Nowotny, 1987). From a scientific point of view, something like Nature no longer exists and precisely therefore it seems that one has to try to maintain Nature or restore the state of nature, for example by reintroducing old-fashioned methods in agriculture or by counter-interventions in planned interventions. The subject world of the risk society and of normal catastrophes does not render the discussion about the possibility of planning society futile but rather it is all the more important in which sense this 'planning of society' could be used. Critique and crisis are only meaningful if one trusts that there is a possibility that things could be different. Only this allows the Green political movement to speak about alternatives. On the other hand, the theory of planning is in a desolate state. It has for decades had to deal with the problem of complexity but could at first hope to find better solutions using an approximate method of building models or simulations, by a slow adaptation of society to planning, this means by getting used to being planned and by the due concentration of attention. In the meantime, this problem of being able to shape society has taken on a new dimension with the appearance of a consciousness of ecological problems. It is difficult, almost impossible, to abandon the notion of steering and to let the future come as it comes. The semantics of time of modern society, the accentuation of the differences between past and future seem to prohibit this. And, on the other hand, it is not easy to see if and how at least some of the expectations related to steering could be saved.

Systems theory analyses that start from the idea of self-referential systems and with it use conceptions of autopoiesis, self-organization, etc., are primarily interested in the self-steering of the system, in the context of our analysis the self-steering of the economy. The hopes of social policy are looking for an addressee who could even control the self-steering systems and think that it is politics. This leads to discrepancies of theoretical, but also of highly practical and, last but not least, of political importance, burdens the discourse between politics and the economy, and revives the idea of the 19th century that what the economy cannot achieve (or cannot achieve satisfactorily) by self-steering must be performed by politics. But this idea collides hard with the fact of functional differentiation which excludes the replacement of systems by each other. No policy can renew the economy, parts of the economy or even single firms because for this one needs money and thus the economy.

No scientific analysis (because this is already a third functional system) can abruptly change these expectations by its own achievements (even if these achievements should be proven truths or untruths). But perhaps it is nevertheless useful to think at the end of the study of economy which idea of steering is at the base of these expectations; and accordingly: with which manipulations of the idea one could irritate these expectations.

Abstractly expressed steering always means *the reduction of a difference*. In everyday life, for example when steering a car, one thinks of the reduction of a difference in the direction of movement. The steering refers then to the spatial relationship of a movement. One supposes that in an extreme situation the difference between another direction appearing and the desired direction can be reduced almost to zero with the consequence, however, that there might appear further differences – be they caused by external influences, be they because of an increasing inaccuracy of the steering – and the further differences require a further steering even if one only wants to keep on course. The metaphor also allows the image of a change of course. One has forgotten something and has to turn back. This can be effected by steering only, and in this case by the construction of *another* difference.

And where does the difference come from? At the first attempt, one might say either from the environment, from the holes in the road, from the gentle pressure of the winds; or from the inaccuracy of the steering. Thus either from the environment or from the system. If one needs *both* of them, *system and environment*, one has to go back to the *world* if one wants to explain the reasons for the problems of steering. With this the problem is given to religion. From a scientific point of view this answer is not satisfying. Thus again: where does the difference come from?

From the theory of subjects one can answer with Fichte: it is set by the subject. From the theory of language it is, since Saussure, language itself. From systems theory, it is the system. How meaningful these theoretical differences are depends on what one can do with them. Does this mean: how one can steer the development of theories with them? Anyway, if these distinctions mark differences this leads back to the question: who causes these differences, who distinguishes here, who steers here? A super subject that knows what it knows? A metalanguage? A world system? Or perhaps an interest in the 'subtle distinctions' in the system of science? In any case, the problem is repeated in the answer if one does not want to see the answer as the final metaphor (and this would mean perhaps to philosophize) (see, for example, Blumenberg, 1960).

Alexander had, as is well known, another answer ready in front of such a knot knotted on itself. And also George Spencer Brown. The calculation of the theory of differences described by Spencer Brown (1970) starts with the instruction: 'Draw a distinction!' Divide the 'unmarked space'! This means that one has to distinguish the distinction one uses from other distinctions (thus one has already to get started when starting) (see also Glanville and Varela, 1981), which is ignored in a sovereign manner (and one can be sure in the intention to construct a theory). This means also that the question 'Who or what distinguishes?' is not asked. One can keep it open, but this presupposes an observer who can distinguish who distinguishes. The arbitrariness of the beginning is arbitrariness only for him who observes the beginning; and for him this leads to the question of what observer he is observing (see also the Saussure interpretation of Glanville, 1984). Distinctions function in a recursive network of the observation of observations as the conditions of the reproduction of this very network. One can state that this is true – but only by observing the observing, thus by the operative taking part in this very network (see von Foerster, 1981 on second-order cybernetics). In the theory of observing observations the presupposition of recursive closure replaces the traditional questions of reasons.

But steering is not only observation, not only the use of a distinction to mark the one and not the other side. Steering designates a very specific use of distinctions, namely the attempt to *reduce the difference*. With regard to the distinction of men and women, the problem of steering is not the description or classification of the specimen and also it is not the description of the one side, the woman, as a bad version of the other (*masculus occasionatus, homme manqué*), but the reduction of their difference. Steering is thus distinguished from other uses of distinctions, and it lies not far away, and one can suppose that the distinctions steering is using to distinguish itself from other uses of distinctions are accordingly chosen if and in what interest reduction of differences is appropriate or could be appropriate. Steering then presupposes these recursive observing relations; otherwise it could not distinguish itself. But steering uses them also in a specific sense. This causes a theory of steering the problem of observing and describing these facts.

II

The fact that we describe steering as an operation that uses a distinction to minimize the difference this distinction marks already suggests first of all an approach based on a theory of action. One will immediately hit the question, who is steering and the answer: nobody, or the answer: the person you are distinguishing as observer, will not at first sight satisfy. The theory of action offers in this situation the advantage of referring to the subject one can point to, one can observe and question or that one can use in another manner for purposes of empirical research. Everything else then becomes a question of aggregation of data that can be gathered in this manner.

Renate Mayntz (1987: 93ff) proposes this line clearly and consistently to define the notion of steering as the action of steering. This requires one, when using the notion, to state a subject, an object and an intention (i.e. a goal of steering). In this way the area of the phenomenon is in a typical manner split; there are added experiences of 'the limits of steering' which are external to the helmsman and to the theory which observes him. External to the notion these are then the centre of the discussion. They can be (1) unexpected and/or undesired side-effects or (2) the so-called 'deficits of execution' and finally (3) the so-called 'self-fulfilling' or in this case rather 'self-defeating prophecies'. For example, there are very social value-laden union supported programmes to improve the working conditions of women. But if introduced they cause the exclusion of women from the labour market and therefore women are fighting against these programmes.

That even the best intentions can backfire is not an entirely new experience. In principle these are old and well-known problems; but in the time of decreasing steering optimism in the 1970s they could be called back anew and effectively (see, for example, Boudon, 1977). If one puts a purpose in the world one has to play with this purpose against the world and this can go wrong or at least not work as expected.

These effects of steering action (without steering action they would not exist) occur unsteered; and further, if one leaves aside the possibility of making mistakes, these effects cannot be steered. If they could be included in the steering and if they were included in the steering they would disappear. Also every notion of rationality referring to action must, if one thinks exactly, shut them out. Consequently action theory grasps only a part of the whole problem, only the cause of the problems with which the theoretician of action, who is himself without steering, necessarily has to deal if he wants to stay at the helm. The theory is in any case responsible for the manner in which it uses distinctions and one may ask: 'why so exactly and why so exactly under exclusion of these important problems?'

Systems theory is in this respect in a better position. It builds in the problem of limits with the help of the distinction between system and environment. This distinction says that it is not a theory of objects but a theory of the world because everything that can exist is for every system seen either as system or environment. All important innovations of systems theory in the last decades start here and reformulate the difference between system and environment. This is especially true for the concept of the self-referential closure of autopoietic systems.

To what extent this changes the form of the treatment of the three problems of 'side-effects', 'execution deficits' and 'self-defeating prophecies' is very unclear. At least for the last-mentioned case, for 'self-defeating prophecies', there is a large body of literature searching for forms of stability which can be established 'nevertheless' (see, Simon, 1957a). It is possible that they are based on a misunderstanding of mathematical notions like the 'fixed point theorem' (see Øfsti and Østerberg, 1982; Simon, 1957b) or the concept of 'Eigen values'; but at least it may be fruitful to keep in sight the further developments both in mathematics and in sociology.

Regarding side-effects and deficits of execution, a theory of self-referentially closed systems presupposes that the systems are structure-determined, meaning that the systems can change their own structures only by their own operations. All steering is, therefore, always an operation (or a sub-system of operations) among many others in the system, which is reproduced this way independent from the further question whether the steering is concerned with the system itself or with its environment. In both cases something else also always happens simultaneously with the steering operations (and this means also that this cannot be influenced by the steering operations). Moreover, one has to distinguish the operation of steering, which produces its own effects, from the operation of observing this operation, which produces for its own part its own effects. The observation of steering can, and typically will, use other distinctions than the steering itself, for instance will carry out the imputation of successes and failures in a different manner than he to whom the steering is imputed as action. Seen like this, it is no wonder that social steering and social criticism provoke with dialectical synthesis a common resignation. In the same way one starts to wonder within management theories, what is caused by the fact that managing (but not, to speak exactly, managers) takes place within the system that manages itself in this way. Also this question can be reduced to the problems of the conditions of stability of recursive observing relations, that is in systems where it is observed that it is observed. Everything that happens can then be described in the language of this self-including second-order cybernetics. All steering uses distinctions, admittedly with the specific intention of reducing differences, that are themselves distinguished. There is no *external co*operation, no external advice (see Willke, 1984), but there is the possibility of including temporary foreign advice systems in the system. That means above all that omissions are also observed in the system as variations of action and that by observation structures and negatives also become causal.

In this respect systems theory can at least offer reformulated questions and save the problems mentioned from the shadowy existence where the notion of action has banished them. This is similar for progress which emerges within cybernetics. The decisive discovery was the feedback mechanism that steers the system by a comparison of inputs with principal goals. This meant always the minimization of a difference and the perpetual control of the self-renewing difference. The difference served as its own correction, to put it with Watzlawick (1985: 372). In spite of the existence of this concept of a self-referential circle, the old-cybernetics literature with its paradigm of a thermostat presupposed a mechanism which influences the environment of the steering installation and which changes this environment (relatively directly!) in a way that can be seen from the continuously measured input values. Therefore, one could only speak of cybernetics in cases of reliably functioning causal relationships of output and input, thus only for a very low complexity of the system/ environment relation and/or a very specific choice of this complexity. This presupposes limitation to only a few variables and systems in systems. Thermostats control room temperature not world temperature.

By the transition to a theory of self-referential closed systems and the consequent transition to second-order cybernetics, this limitation is, so to speak, on the quiet, abolished. For this systems theory there are no cross-border inputs and outputs as conditions determining the structure of autopoiesis; there are at most observers who observe other systems with their own distinctions but who are not dependent on inputs and outputs but only on this very self-constructed distinction. What is seen in the steering process as input is only information constructed in the system itself and this construction is nothing else than a component of the distinction of which difference the system tries to minimize. In the external world there are neither inputs nor outputs, neither information nor areas of possibilities from which information can be chosen. The external world is as it is: stubborn, without possibilities and unknown.

The steering of the system is thus always self-steering, regardless of whether the steering refers to the system itself by an internally constructed distinction of self-reference and outside reference or whether the steering refers to the environment of the system. The political system is in this respect no exception; politics too can only steer itself, and if the steering refers to the environment then it is only to *its* environment. An observer may see this differently but he cannot do it differently. Therefore, steering is also not dependent on an adequately structured area of causal relations as it were provided by the external world. With this insight, the steering mechanism is detached from the very strongly restricting presuppositions about the external world and can be recognized in its universality. In the external world there are no temperatures – although I do not want to deny that one is irritated, starts to feel cold and finally checks why the heating is not working in winter.

Finally, systems theory allows one to reconstruct what action theory postulates as purposes. A difference-minimizing programme still needs within the distinction it deals with an asymmetry as an indication of direction. Purposes render distinctions asymmetrical. The equalization of educational chances, says the purpose, shall not be reached by decreasing but by increasing the education of all; and the programme of Bentham was as much happiness for as many as possible and not participation of as many as possible in the common suffering. In practice the effect will often be a new distribution with a smaller view, thus a loss of excellence. But the reduction to a middle level is not the goal of steering but is its (perhaps inevitable) fate. Its intention is the equalization upwards and this guarantees the Sisyphus-like duration of its function.

III

The action theory approach forces the raising of the question about the steering of social systems (or even of any system) as 'who' questions. Almost immediately this leads to the assumption that it is the task of politics to steer society and almost as immediately this inevitably leads to the realization of its failure. Just as the theory of action suffers from perverse effects, so the theory of political steering suffers in an exact parallel and for the same reasons from 'state failure'. In any case, problem experiences and problem formulations are caused by the approach of the theory and in the meantime one could wonder if this section, this division of the world into these two halves is at all fruitful. In other words, does one see everything that is to be seen if one observes with a scheme of action and resistance?

The political theory starting point for questions of the theory of steering is at first sight not without plausibility. On the one hand it comes close to the old European reminiscences, but above all the starting point is supported by the high degree of organization of collective capabilities to act in the context of the function to allow collective binding decisions. In fact the differentiation of a political system depended in the beginning on the differentiation of regional centres of domination and from the late middle ages it depended on the formation of a sovereign territorial organization which is since called 'state'. But this success of organization which allows, supports, maintains and reproduces the differentiation of the political system must not lead to the illusion that politics can represent or even steer society. Already the fact that society is differentiated into functional systems which are not only distinct objects each with its own will and difficult to control but also different ways to realize the whole society as a distinction of sub-system and sub-system environment is difficult to reconcile with the concept of central steering. The political system is only one system among others that is working with its own difference-minimizing programmes. Attempts to minimize differences take place everywhere, they are everywhere the making of society, and at the same time society produces differences by allowing difference-minimizing programmes to start and operate under functionally specific aspects. This also occurs of course in the political system by using the function to make possible collectively binding decision-taking. But also in marriages and families there are such attempts, also in the economic system, in the educational system, in the system of medical treatment. Like every system, politics cannot transcend itself and act on higher orders. There is no instance that could condition such orders and could supervise their execution. In functionally differentiated societies there is not even one unrivalled representation of the society in the society (cf. Luhmann, 1986). The political system is thus only able to steer itself by a specific political construction of the difference between system and environment. That this happens and how it happens has without doubt tremendous effects on the society because the other functional systems must orient themselves along the differences thus produced. *But this effect is certainly not steering and it is not possible to steer it* because it depends on the construction of differences in the context of other systems and because it falls under the steering programmes operating in these systems.

Often the limit of the possibility to steer society politically is described as a problem of complexity. This is not entirely wrong but it does not get to the heart of the matter. Even relatively simple systems like families pose insurmountable problems to politics if their self-steering is not working. If the family is not able to minimize its differences sufficiently (whatever this may mean from the point of view of sociological systems theory) politics is even less able to do so. It can only provide the administrative implementation of its own programmes, finance women's refuges, make divorce more or less difficult to obtain, distribute the financial burdens of divorce and by this create deterrents to divorce or ill-considered marriages – in short: do politics. The families themselves cannot be steered in this way.

One may uphold a different opinion on this point. One may certainly duplicate the ambitions of modern welfare states and/or ecological programmes and work them out as a political programme. One should only refrain from calling this social steering. It is, as so many things, steering in the society; here: self-steering of politics in the society. But this does not exhaust all the possibilities of investigating steering problems in modern society.

IV

On the level of terminology and of theory we can summarize after this the considerations of competing theories:

1   Steering is always self-steering of systems and only in this framework action-guiding distinguishing. In other words: one has to look for the unit that steers itself (instead of hastily making this unit invisible by differentiating intention and perverse effect) and this unit is not an action but a system.
2   Steering is the decreasing of differences within a distinction and is distinguished by this from other forms of using distinctions.
3   Programmes to decrease differences in practical steering are understood not as programmes of shrinking towards a middle level (in the sense of the old European concept of measure, middle, justice) but as adjustment in a certain direction. Steering, therefore, presupposes the asymmetricalization of the difference and nevertheless still the reduction, if not elimination, of the difference.

Even from this summary it becomes clear how many improbabilities are built in if one universalizes such a concept and applies it to the entire society. In any case it cannot be meant that steering must achieve intended successes and all the more not that order could be understood as a result of steering and that failure of steering causes disorder. At the same time, the manner of using distinctions by steering shows exactly the specificity of this use of distinctions and this leads to the first limiting considerations.

Guiding differences are often, and especially in the organization of functional systems, established as binary codes that are not suited for steering but obstruct it. It is rather impossible to try to minimize the difference between legal and illegal or that between to have and have not, or that between truth and untruth or between immanence and transcendence. To be sure, the codes that serve the differentiation of functional systems establish a distinction. They formulate also a preferential value, namely the positive value, which allows the connecting up of the operations in the autopoietic system. The negative value (illegality, not to have, untrue, transcendence) marks the reflection of the conditions (or if one wants: the non-self-evidence) of the possibility to connect up; therefore it marks nothing which should be diminished by steering efforts towards the other value. Even politics would collapse if it would use its possibilities of self-steering to minimize the difference between superiority of power and inferiority of power, or the difference between government programme and opposition programme. Perhaps one would doubt if this is also the same for morals or if morals is in reality a steering programme of society with the implication that evil should be diminished as fast as possible towards the good. But then one will fairly soon discover that (is exactly why?) it was not possible to differentiate a functional system of morals.

Not all distinctions are, therefore, steering distinctions and in particular not those serving to differentiate functional systems by coding. It follows that steering intentions always have to fight against structures which were not created by them and which regenerate themselves because of the character of autopoietic systems. All steering works against externally generated material – even if all structures are exclusively laid down by the system which is steering itself. On the same line there is a second limitation. Distinctions serve observing and description. When observing, the distinctions that are used by the observed observations themselves may be used but this is not necessary. If this happens it is called 'evaluation'. But not all observation of steering is evaluation. One can also observe with moral distinctions; or with the scheme latent/manifest, thus for instance critique of ideology; or simply from the point of view of an interest that only checks if it is supported sufficiently by the steering or how it has to protect and defend itself against the steering. The steering achieves its goal of diminishing a difference or it does not. But in any case, steering always creates an additional effect by being observed and by the reactions of the observer in the one or the other way. This can be included in the planning of steering as the forecast of reactions. But this forecast is subject to the same rule as soon as it can be observed.

These remarks lead us back to a previous viewpoint. In modern society, functional systems, above all, have the possibility of self-steering. Society itself has delegated all the problems and therefore does not possess any agencies that could, as a super-function of perception, perceive all the functions. Although all steering takes place within society and therefore always executes the autopoiesis of society (i.e. communicates) there is, in the strict sense of the word, no self-steering of society on the level of the entire system.

Nevertheless society brings itself to bear because it doesn't leave it to arbitrariness, and above all not to the helmsman or woman themselves, how to observe steering. Since the bourgeois movement, since the ideological abolition of the distinctions of former social formations, the principle of equality at least is forced upon steering as a rule of observation insofar as society as a whole stands in view. The difference-minimizing programmes are directed towards the diminishing of inequalities. Inequalities are no longer seen as a description of the perfection of the world (as *multitudio et distinctio* in the sense of medieval cosmology) but as a reason for counter-steering. And like the steering of ships or cars in space, the steering which is oriented towards society has a task which is regenerating itself. By steering, all functional systems always also create differences and in effect inequalities; because their respective rationalities distinguish better solutions from the worse. Moreover, from the ground of the desired equality flourish meritocratic distinctions or, to put it with Hermann Lübbe, users of equality who are favoured by equality of opportunity. It will always be profitable to distinguish oneself from what is set or what is aspired to as standard expectations. Steering finds new food in the winners who profit from steering. It creates in its self-perpetuation very specific structures – for example, those of career and opposition against career, those of indirect ways and those which leave behind seekers after sense. What happens is in the end the result of the observation of the observer, of a recursive network of observations, and in this connection a readiness emerges to recognize inequalities as a problem or to accept them as a base for operations.

The postulate of equality explains, notwithstanding the peculiarities of single functional systems, the steering impulses, indeed the from time to time exaggerated steering mania, of modern society. The distinction equal/unequal offers a particularly favourable scheme for difference-minimizing programmes of all kinds and this is a particular challenge for politics. The scheme equal/unequal offers finally a particular opportunity to make oneself understood with steering intentions in modern society and to expose oneself to observations. But naturally it does not offer a chance that steering may actually eliminate the difference of equal/unequal towards equality and then leave it in this position. The scheme of equality has only the function to give steering a kind of 'legitimacy' – i.e. security against unspecified observers.

V

If one looks at the extremely complex system of society as a whole, it should be clear that the mechanism that was presupposed by old cybernetic steering theories is missing, namely a relatively direct causality that made it possible that the output of system mechanisms reappeared almost immediately as a change of input, as in the paradigm: the heating starts and it becomes warmer. Instead everything happens in the big black box of the system – black box seen from the outside but also from the inside. Nevertheless steering is possible because it presupposes only the choice of distinctions with regard to the differences one wants to minimize. As long as observers observe this unexcitedly it may function and, if acceptance is transferred from one distinction to another, steering may follow – e.g. to proceed from rather socialistic to rather welfare state oriented to rather ecological difference-minimizing programmes. But in any case the mechanisms presupposed by the old cybernetics do not exist.

The question is whether this changes if one changes the system reference and studies the self-steering possibilities of sub-systems of society. This is one of the famous wide fields. We can by way of a trial once consider in what sense one can speak of the self-steering of economy or, more narrowly, of the self-steering of the firms and households participating in the economy.

If one understands economy as the autopoiesis of paying, then it is clear that all economic steering deals with *differences of money supply*. Further, if one understands steering cybernetically as the minimization of differences, the problem is always the minimization of differences expressed in sums of money. This does not implicitly recommend a monetary central bank policy, but says only that there is no other possibility. A steering that orients its programme not towards the difference of money supply is not self-steering of the economic system. It may, for example, always still be politically reasonable to pursue the decrease of the number of jobless. But if one wants to examine why somebody gets this idea and what he will do to steer in this sense, one has to observe the political and not the economic system; and one will have to observe how the political system observes the economic system and what (perhaps 'perverse') effects it produces when it acts according to its own observations.[1]

Steering programmes may be planned thoroughly idealistically, e.g. under the maxim as much profit as possible. Operationalization would then presuppose precise steps, e.g. the fixing of expectations with regard to sums and units of time. Firms and households are distinguished by the fact that the former use balances, the latter budgets for operationalization and control. Depending on which of these forms is given to the specification of the sub-programmes and depending on the scheme used as the basis for the subdivision (i.e. depending on the distinction of the distinction of sums of money) there are very different steering effects and very different occasions for counter-steering. One has only to think of the well-known tendency for budget-ized systems to spend the disposable money, i.e. to minimize the money supply (and not to maximize it). These types of programmes also reflect already for a long time their structural effects and consequential problems. Firms organized according to division of labour need budgets for organizational reasons and large households have to pay particular attention to income-efficient expenditure. All of this can no longer preoccupy us here. In our context, it is sufficient to show how the cybernetics of the system of economy specifies itself towards finally controllable causalities.

Regardless of how the system structures its complexity, the original sin of differentiation cannot be taken back. One cannot return to paradise. The system, in spite of all self-steering, always remains a historical system which can only include its own reactions to its own situations in these very situations. To put it differently, the system-differentiating difference between system and environment never becomes a steering distinction, never becomes a difference-minimizing programme. It is impossible to set the goal to realize as much system as possible and as little environment as possible and equally vice versa. This means also that the system cannot become its own purpose with regard to which differences were to be minimized. So understood, self-steering would be impossible. What remains possible, however, is: to develop in connection to the money code difference-minimizing programmes to orient observations with these programmes up to a degree of specification which would remain unobtainable without these restricting presuppositions.

It is self-evident that a central bank will always observe how politics observes the economy. It can understand itself with an appropriate auxiliary construction as an instance of political steering of the economy, and given high political dependency it may be used in this way. But this does not change the fact that system references of politics and economics remain separated, nor that the self-steering of economics can only specify itself by distinctions of money supply. If one sees oneself as an intervening actor, one may ignore this fact. But then one is enticed to decompose reality by the distinction of action and resistance or of purpose and perverse effects. And then one sees only what one can see if one observes exactly with this distinction. In principle, there is nothing to be said against this. But an observer who observes this will also see that also with this distinction a blind spot is chosen which is exactly this distinction. And if second-order cybernetics, the theory of circular observation of observers, teaches anything then it is: that it is also possible to observe this.

VI

Finally we return to the relationship of politics and economics from the point of view of steering theory. Under the condition of the social structure of functional differentiation the immovable starting point is the self-referential autonomy of functional sub-systems, besides which there is not a society in society and thus also no representation of the entire society. This means: every functional system orients itself by its own distinctions, thus by its own construction of reality and thus also by its own code. No steering attempt can eliminate these distinctions or bridge them. But every system includes programmes in its own operational context and these can be planned as difference-minimization programmes, i.e. it can mark either disturbances or goals with regard to which a state of the system can be approximated, which difference shall thus be minimized. It is now this distinction of code and programme we can use for our problem.

Codes are invariant for the system which identifies itself by them. The economic system will never doubt that there is a distinction between payment and non-payment. Programmes, on the other hand, can be varied, on condition that the code remains unchanged. This characteristic of the difference between coding and programming can be used by external interventions (here of politics in the economy). Under the condition that the system difference is preserved, and under the further condition that in politics only political and in the economy only economical programmes can be realized, politics can very well see it as its task to influence the difference-minimization programmes according to which the economy acts. Such intentions remain political programmes. If they will influence the economy it is not sufficient just to observe simply politically relevant numbers (e.g. average income or the spread of income differentials, unemployment numbers, regional differences in these numbers, etc.). Politics has no cybernetic mechanism (heating, cooling) that could influence these numbers. They are the result of the complex cooperation of self-steering institutions (difference-minimization programmes) of the economy.

Politics can therefore only create conditions that influence the programme and in this way the self-steering of the economy. It can prohibit something, it can create costs, it can create conditions for utilities, etc.

When closely examining these possibilities one will probably establish that in most cases the point is to interfere in the relative attraction of the programmes although this steering effect is no goal of politics nor could it be named a political success. It is possible, for example, that environmental controls drive certain firms into bankruptcy because they cannot be financed or only with unobtainable credits. The relevant difference becomes greater instead of smaller. But politics will show its success with measures of environmental pollution, will practice its difference-minimization programmes with regard to this and will not show the number of bankruptcies as a programme. If politics notices what havoc it causes it may try to start a bankruptcy prevention programme and, starting from empirical numbers, try to reduce the number of bankruptcies per year or try to increase the number of firms saved from bankruptcy. But these are political programmes and it remains to be seen what deformations of economic programmes they will cause in their turn. If help is available, bankruptcy may become attractive.

Another problem became visible with the failure of politically induced development projects in underdeveloped countries. Politics tried to create profit opportunities and so to stimulate activities; but the real economy does not try to minimize the difference to a possible profit, but the difference to a possible risk (cf. Boudon, 1984: 123, based on Bhaduri, 1973; see also Roumasset, 1976). This is also a sign that politics can achieve with political programmes political successes or political failures and can steer itself in this way but that it can intervene in the self-steering of economics only if and insofar as it may hit the direction and the conditions of economic difference minimization. Probably this same discrepancy exists also in industrially highly-developed regions to a higher degree than is assumed by the prevailing political (but also market-theoretical, i.e. economical) steering concepts. In any case, one must first be able to observe how the other system works before one can influence its self-steering; and it is a consequence of the theory represented here that even this observation is only possible with its own reality constructions and only with the help of self-constructed information, thus not with the help of information that (e.g. as market data) can be obtained ready-made from the observed system.

Seen as a whole, steering is probably always difference-minimization and difference-increasing at the same time. Moreover, it is always an enterprise specified by distinctions that cannot distinguish itself sufficiently but that differentiates itself operationally. Especially in political theory one has reacted to the observation of the situation with claims for participation – a grandiose mistake that is based on a wrong diagnosis of the system. A rather sceptical 'postmodern' version runs that those who are not participating in the discourse by speaking or by keeping silent become victims (see Lyotard, 1988: esp. ch. 1). But the fact of perpetual reproduction of differences, for which there is no meta-regulation, does not yet mean that the excluded become victims. They become observers who use their own distinctions and who can eventually employ their own difference-minimization programmes. There may, however, also be cases where the steerings of different functional systems converge towards an exclusive effect where observers are silenced, who cannot express themselves in the language of law (by raising claims) nor in the language of the economy (by payment or non-payment) nor in the language of politics (by force).

If it is true that every observation, every description and in a very specific sense every steering as operation marks differences and by this causes system-building (exclusive) effects, then it is not to be expected that this problem can ever be solved by a kind of dialectical synthesis. However, one can see it as a task of scientific analysis and sociological enlightenment to include it in the self-description of modern society.

Note

1 It is not disputed that within organizations of the economic system programmes can be developed and executed which do not follow this type of economic steering. A programme to diminish alcoholism in a firm or even the therapy of employees with alcohol problems need not (and cannot) be planned with regard to economic effects. There is only the vague supposition that the result will have effects on the performance of the firm and this argument is only needed for legitimation and to distinguish it from programmes of religious mission of which no one will believe that they influence the employees' motivation.

References

Bhaduri, Amit (1973) 'A Study of Agricultural Backwardness under Semi-Feudalism', *Economic Journal* 83: 120–37.
Blumenberg, Hans (1960) *Paradigmen zu einer Metaphorologie*. Bonn: Bouvier.
Boudon, Raymond (1977) *Effets pervers et ordre social*. Paris: Presses Universitaires de France.
Boudon, Raymond (1984) *La place du désordre: critique des théories du changement social*. Paris: Quadrige/Presses Universitaires de France.
Evers, Adalbert and Helga Nowotny (1987) *Über Umgang mit Unsicherheit: Die Entdeckung der Gestaltbarkeit von Gesellschaft*. Frankfurt: Suhrkamp.
Foerster, Heinz von (1981) *Observing Systems*. Seaside, CA: Intersystems Publications.
Glagow, Manfred and Helmut Willke (eds) (1987) *Dezentrale Gesellschaftssteuerung: Probleme der Integration polyzentrischer Gesellschaft*. Pfaffenweiler: Centaurus.
Glanville, Ranulph (1984) 'Distinguished and Exact Lies', pp. 655–62 in Robert Trappl (ed.) *Cybernetics and Systems Research 2*. New York.
Glanville, Ranulph and Francisco Varela (1981) '"Your Inside is Out and Your Outside is In" (Beatles 1968)', pp. 638–41 in George E. Lasker (ed.) *Applied Systems and Cybernetics*. New York.
Luhmann, Niklas (1986) 'La rappresentazione della società nella società', pp. 127–37 in Roberto Cipriani (ed.) *Legittimazione e società*. Rome: Armando; English translation in *Current Sociology* 35 (1987): 101–8.
Lyotard, Jean-François (1988) *The Differend: Phrases in Dispute*, translated by Georges van den Abbeele. Manchester: Manchester University Press.
Mayntz, Renate (1987) 'Politische Steuerung und gesellschaftliche Steuereungs-probleme – Anmerkungen zu einem theoretischen Paradigma', *Jahrbuch zur Staats- und Verwaltungswissenschaft* 1: 89–110.

Øfsti, Audun and Dag Østerberg (1982) 'Self-Defeating Predictions and the Fixed Point Theorem: A Refutation', *Inquiry* 25: 331–52.

Roumasset, James A. (1976) *Rice and Risk: Decision-Making Among Low-Income Farmers*. Amsterdam: North-Holland.

Simon, Herbert A. (1957a) 'Bandwagon and Underdog Effects of Election Prediction', in *Models of Man: Social and Rational: Mathematical Essays on Rational Human Behavior in a Social Setting*. New York: Wiley.

Simon, Herbert A. (1957b) 'Elections Predictions: A Reply', pp. 361–4 in *Models of Man: Social and Rational: Mathematical Essays on Rational Human Behavior in a Social Setting*. New York: Wiley.

Spencer Brown, George (1970) *Laws of Form*. London: Allen & Unwin.

Watzlawick, Paul (1985) 'Management oder – Konstruktion von Wirklichkeiten', pp. 365–76 in Gilbert J. B. Probst and Hans Siegwart (eds) *Integriertes Management: Bausteine des systemorientierten Managements, Festschrift Hans Ulrich*. Bern: Haupt.

Willke, Helmut (1984) 'Zum Probleme der Intervention in selbstreferentielle Systeme', *Zeitschrift für systemische Therapie* 2: 191–200.

11 Coercion, Capital, and European States

Charles Tilly

Logics of Capital and Coercion

Capital – cities – exploitation

Let us think of *capital* generously, including any tangible mobile resources, and enforceable claims on such resources. Capitalists, then, are people who specialize in the accumulation, purchase, and sale of capital. They occupy the realm of *exploitation*, where the relations of production and exchange themselves yield surpluses, and capitalists capture them. Capitalists have often existed in the absence of capitalism, the system in which wage-workers produce goods by means of materials owned by capitalists. Through most of history, indeed, capitalists have worked chiefly as merchants, entrepreneurs, and financiers, rather than as the direct organizers of production. The system of capitalism itself arrived late in the history of capital. It grew up in Europe after 1500, as capitalists seized control of production. It reached its apex – or, depending on your perspective, its nadir – after 1750, when capital-concentrated manufacturing became the basis of prosperity in many countries. For millennia before then, capitalists had flourished without much intervening in production.

The processes that accumulate and concentrate capital also produce cities. Cities figure prominently in this book's analyses, both as favored sites of capitalists and as organizational forces in their own right. To the extent that the survival of households depends on the presence of capital through employment, investment, redistribution or any other strong link, the distribution of population follows that of capital. (Capital, however, sometimes follows cheap labor; the relationship is reciprocal.) Trade, warehousing, banking, and production that depends closely on any of them all benefit from proximity to each other. Within limits set by the productivity of agriculture, that proximity promotes the formation of dense, differentiated populations having extensive outside connections – cities. When capital both accumulates and concentrates within a territory, urban growth tends to occur throughout the same territory – more intensely at the greatest point of concentration, and secondarily elsewhere (see figure 11.1). The form of urban growth, however, depends on the balance between concentration and accumulation. Where capital accumulation occurs quite generally, but concentration remains relatively low, many smaller centers develop. Where a single concentration of capital emerges, urban population concentrates around that center.

Properly speaking, then, cities represent regional economies; around every city or urban cluster lies a zone of agriculture and trade (and sometimes of manufacturing as well) that interacts closely with it. Where accumulation and concentration occur in tandem, a hierarchy from small centers to large tends to take shape (see figure 11.2). These tendencies have always operated within important limits. City people normally depend on others to raise most or all of their food and fuel; the transportation and preservation of these requisites for large cities consumes a great deal of energy. Until very recently, most of the world's agricultural areas, including those of Europe, were too unproductive to permit much more than a tenth of the nearby population to live off the land. Cities that could not reach agricultural areas conveniently by means of low-cost water transportation, furthermore, faced prohibitively high food costs. Berlin and Madrid provide good examples: except as their rulers force-fed them, they did not grow.

Health mattered as well. Through almost all of the last thousand years, despite their disproportionate recruitment of vigorous migrants of working age, cities have had significantly higher death rates than their hinterlands. Only after 1850, with improvements in urban sanitation and nutrition, did the balance shift in favor of city-dwellers. As a result, cities have only grown rapidly when agriculture and transportation were becoming relatively efficient or when powerful pressures were driving people off the land.

The sheer growth of cities, however, produced a spiral of change in all these regards. In the vicinity of active cities, people farmed more intensively and devoted a higher proportion of their farming to cash crops; in Europe of the sixteenth century, for example, highly productive agriculture concentrated in the two most urbanized regions, northern Italy and Flanders. Similarly, urban growth stimulated the creation and improvement of transportation by water and land; the Netherlands' superb system of canals and navigable streams brought down the cost, and brought up the speed, of communication among its swarm of cities, thus serving as both cause and effect of urbanization (de Vries, 1978). The pressures that drove people off the land, furthermore, often resulted in part from urbanization, as when urban landlords drove smallholders from the hinterland or urban demand fostered the

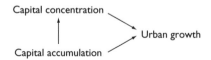

Figure 11.1   *How capital generates urban growth*

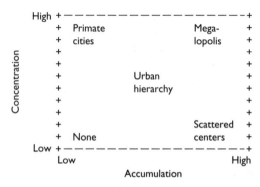

Figure 11.2   *Alternative forms of urban growth as functions of capital accumulation and concentration*

capitalization of the hinterland's agriculture. Accumulation and concentration of capital fostered urban growth, while transforming the regions surrounding new clusters of cities.

Coercion – states – domination

What of coercion? Coercion includes all concerted application, threatened or actual, of action that commonly causes loss or damage to the persons or possessions of individuals or groups who are aware of both the action and the potential damage. (The cumbersome definition excludes inadvertent, indirect, and secret damage.) Where capital defines a realm of exploitation, coercion defines a realm of domination. The means of coercion center on armed force, but extend to facilities for incarceration, expropriation, humiliation, and publication of threats. Europe created two major overlapping groups of specialists in coercion: soldiers and great landlords; where they merged and received ratification from states in the form of titles and privileges they crystallized into nobilities, who in turn supplied the principal European rulers for many centuries. Coercive means, like capital, can both accumulate and concentrate: some groups (such as monastic orders) have few coercive means, but those few are concentrated in a small number of hands; others (such as armed frontiersmen) have many coercive means that are widely dispersed. Coercive means and capital merge where the same objects (e.g. workhouses) serve exploitation and domination. For the most part, however, they remain sufficiently distinct to allow us to analyze them separately.

When the accumulation and concentration of coercive means grow together, they produce states; they produce distinct organizations that control the chief concentrated means of coercion within well-defined territories, and exercise priority in some respects over all other organizations operating within those territories (see figure 11.3). Efforts to subordinate neighbors and fight off more distant rivals create state structures in the form not only of armies but also of civilian staffs that gather the means to sustain armies and that organize the ruler's day-to-day control over the rest of the civilian population.

War drives State Formation and Transformation

The deployment of coercive means in war and domestic control presents warriors with two dilemmas. First, to the extent that they are successful in subduing their rivals outside or inside the territory they claim, the wielders of coercion find themselves obliged to administer the lands, goods, and people they acquire; they become involved in extraction of resources, distribution of goods, services, and income, and adjudication of disputes. But administration diverts them from war, and

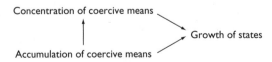

Figure 11.3   *How coercion generates the growth of states*

creates interests that sometimes tell against war. We can see the dilemma in the five-century conquest of Muslim Spain by Christian warriors. Starting with the taking of Coimbra in 1064, standard siege practice ran like this:

> Residents of a town under siege who surrendered promptly could remain with full freedoms after the conquest. If the Muslims surrendered after having been under siege for some time, they could leave with only those goods they could carry. If they waited for the town to fall by force, they faced death or enslavement. (Powers, 1988: 18)

Any of the three responses set a problem for conquerors. The first imposed the obligation – at least temporarily – to establish a system of parallel rule. The second called for a redistribution of property as well as the settlement and administration of a depopulated town. The third left slaves in the hands of the victors, and posed even more sharply the challenge of reestablishing production and population. In one way or another, conquest entailed administration. On a larger scale, these problems dogged the whole reconquest of Iberia. In different forms, they marked the history of conquest throughout Europe.

The second dilemma parallels the first. Preparation for war, especially on a large scale, involves rulers ineluctably in extraction. It builds up an infrastructure of taxation, supply, and administration that requires maintenance of itself and often grows faster than the armies and navies that it serves; those who run the infrastructure acquire power and interests of their own; their interests and power limit significantly the character and intensity of warfare any particular state can carry on. Europe's Mongol and Tatar states resolved the dilemmas by raiding and looting without building much durable administration, but their strategy put inherent limits on their power, and eventually made them vulnerable to well-financed mass armies. In contrast highly commercial states such as Genoa resolved the dilemmas by borrowing or contracting out the structure necessary to extract the means of war. Between the two extremes, European states found a number of other ways of reconciling the demands of warmaking, extraction, and other major activities.

European states differed significantly, indeed, with respect to their salient activities and organizations. Three different types of state have all proliferated in various parts of Europe during major segments of the period since 990: tribute-taking empires; systems of fragmented sovereignty such as city-states and urban federations, and national states. The first built a large military and extractive apparatus, but left most local administration to regional powerholders who retained great autonomy. In systems of fragmented sovereignty, temporary coalitions and consultative institutions played significant parts in war and extraction, but little durable state apparatus emerged on a national scale. National states unite substantial military, extractive, administrative, and sometimes even distributive and productive organizations in a relatively coordinated central structure. The long survival and coexistence of all three types tells against any notion of European state formation as a single, unilinear process, or of the national state – which did, indeed, eventually prevail – as an inherently superior form of government.

Over the centuries, tribute-taking empires have dominated the world history of states. Empires appeared mainly under conditions of relatively low accumulation of coercive means with high concentration of the available means. When anyone other than the emperor accumulated important coercive means, or the emperor lost the ability to deploy massive coercion, empires often disintegrated. For all its appearance of massive durability, the Chinese Empire suffered incessantly from rebellions, invasions, and movements for autonomy, and long spent a major part of its budget on tribute to Mongols and other nomadic predators. Nor did Europe's empires enjoy greater stability. Napoleon's 1808 invasion of the Iberian peninsula, for instance, shattered much of the Spanish overseas empire. Within months, movements for independence formed in most of Spanish Latin America, and within ten years practically all of the region had broken into independent states.

Federations, city-states, and other arrangements of fragmented sovereignty differed from empires in almost every respect. They depended on relatively high accumulations, and relatively low concentrations, of coercion; the widespread urban militias of fourteenth-century western Europe typify that combination. In such states, a relatively small coalition of nominal subjects could equal the ruler's forces, while individuals, groups, and whole populations had abundant opportunities for defection to competing jurisdictions.

Fourteenth-century Prussia and Pomerania offer a telling contrast: in Prussia, then dominated by the Teutonic Knights, no great princes rivalled the Knights' Grand Master, and towns wielded little power. But the landlords installed by the Knights had wide discretion within their own extensive domains, just so long as revenues flowed to the Knights. In nearby Pomerania, a duchy established simultaneously by smaller-scale German conquests and alliances, many armed rivals to the duke arose, and smaller lords took to outright banditry, as towns dominated the duchy's Estates and provided major military forces in time of war.

During the 1326–8 war between the dukes of Pomerania and Mecklenburg, Pomerania's towns generally sided with their duke while nobles aligned themselves with Mecklenburg. When the Pomeranian house won, the Estates, in which the cities had much say, "were granted far-reaching privileges: the guardianship over minor dukes, the decision whether new ducal castles should be built or pulled down, the right to choose a new master if ever the duke broke his promises or wronged his subjects" (Carsten, 1954: 90). The cities' ability to give or withhold support afforded them great bargaining power.

In between tribute-taking empires and city-states stand national states – built around war, statemaking, and extraction like other states, but compelled by bargaining over the subject population's cessation of coercive means to invest heavily in protection, adjudication, and sometimes even production and distribution. The later history of Prussia illustrates the process by which national states formed. During the fourteenth century, as we have seen, the Teutonic Knights established a centralized empire there. During the fifteenth century, the Knights, shaken by plague, out-migration of peasants, and military defeat, began to disintegrate, and the regional magnates they had previously controlled became Prussian political powers in their own right. They used their power to impose greater and greater restrictions on the peasants who remained on their estates; with coerced labor the increasingly powerful landlords shifted toward demesne farming and the export of grain to western Europe.

At the same time, the rulers of Brandenburg and Pomerania, previously weakened by alliances of their dukes with prosperous burghers, began to win their incessant struggles with the towns, as the towns' position in international trade declined and the ability of the Hanseatic League to intercede on their behalf weakened. The rulers then had to bargain with noble-dominated Estates, which acquired the fundamental power to grant – or deny – royal revenues for war and dynastic aggrandizement. Over the next few centuries the Hohenzollern margraves of Brandenburg fought their way to pre-eminence in what became Brandenburg-Prussia, absorbing much of old Pomerania in the process; they contracted marriage and diplomatic alliances that eventually expanded their domains into adjacent areas and into the capital-rich areas of the lower Rhine; and they negotiated agreements with their nobility that ceded privileges and powers to the lords within their own regions, but gave the monarch access to regular revenues.

Out of battles, negotiations, treaties, and inheritances emerged a national state in which the great landlords of Prussia, Brandenburg, and Pomerania had great power within domains the crown had never wrested from them. During the eighteenth century, such monarchs as Frederick the Great locked the last pieces of the structure into place by incorporating peasants and lords alike into the army, the one under the command of the other. Prussia's army mimicked the countryside, with nobles serving as officers, free peasants as sergeants, and serfs as ordinary soldiers. Peasants and serfs paid the price: many peasants fell into serfdom, and "In war and peace Old Prussia's military obligations weakened the social position, the legal rights, and the property holding of serfs vis à vis the noble estate" (Busch, 1962: 68). In this respect, Prussia followed a different path from Great Britain (where peasants became rural wage-workers) and France (where peasants survived with a fair amount of property into the nineteenth century). But Prussia, Great Britain, and France all trembled with struggles between monarch and major classes over the means of war, and felt the consequent creation of durable state structure.

As military allies and rivals, Prussia, Great Britain, and France also shaped each other's destinies. In the nature of the case, national states always appear in competition with each other, and gain their identities by contrast with rival states; they belong to *systems* of states. The broad differences among major types of state structure are schematized in figure 11.4. Well developed examples of all four kinds of state existed in different parts of Europe well after AD 990. Full-fledged empires flourished into the seventeenth century, and the last major zones of fragmented sovereignty only consolidated into national states late in the nineteenth.

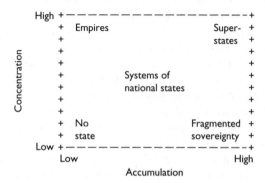

Figure 11.4 *Alternative conditions of state growth as functions of accumulation and concentration of coercion*

Rulers of the three types faced some common problems, but faced them differently. Of necessity, they distributed means of coercion unevenly through the territories they sought to control. Most often they concentrated force at the center and at the frontiers, attempting to maintain their authority in between by means of secondary coercive clusters, loyal local wielders of coercion, roving patrols, and widespread collection of intelligence. The Ottoman Empire, for example, created two overlapping systems, one consisting of the *kazas* and other units of civil administration, governed by kadis, the other composed of *sancaks* and other districts of the feudal cavalry, governed by a military commander; in time of conquest, the military system tended to absorb the civilian, at the cost of losses in revenue (Pitcher, 1972: 124).

The larger the state and the greater the discrepancy between the distribution of coercion and that of capital, however, the stronger the incentives to resist central control, and for alliances to form among different enemies of the state, whether inside or outside its territory. In the *sancak* of Belgrade, part of nineteenth-century Ottoman Serbia, the empire-serving notables (*avan*)

> logically concluded that they could enrich themselves more easily by creating their own redistributive system than by serving simply as the stewards of redistribution. They seized a share in the production of the peasantry, levied illegal tolls on the passage of livestock, and retained a portion of the fees collected at the customs stations of the Sava and Danube entrepôts, especially Belgrade, through which passed the cotton exports of Serres and Salonika destined for Vienna and Germany. In particular, they asserted their right to the *deveto*, ostensibly an illegal tribute of one-ninth of a peasant's harvest after the collection by the timariot (in return for cavalry service to the state) of the *deseto* or tenth. By this action and other acts of violence against person or property, the dues in kind exacted from many Serbian peasants were suddenly doubled, sometimes tripled. (Stoianovitch, 1989: 262–3)

This sort of devolution of power occurred widely in the disintegrating Ottoman Empire of the nineteenth century. But in one version or another, agents of indirect rule everywhere in Europe faced temptations to emulate their Serbian cousins. Given the costs of communication and the advantages regional agents of the crown could gain by evading demands from the center or by using delegated national means for local or individual ends, all rulers faced repeated challenges to their hegemony.

Rulers of empires generally sought to co-opt local and regional powerholders without utterly transforming their bases of power and to create a distinctive corps of royal servants – often present or former comrades in arms – whose fate depended on that of the crown. Mamluk sultans, to take an extreme case, maintained a whole caste of enslaved foreigners who became warriors and administrators; except for fiefs directly supporting officials, however, the Mamluks left local magnates in place within their domains. With such a system, slaves actually ruled Egypt and adjacent areas of the Middle East from 1260 to 1517 (Garcin, 1988). Rulers of national states usually tried harder to create a complete administrative hierarchy and to eliminate autonomous bases of power. The Electors and kings of Brandenburg-Prussia, for example, ceded great power to the landholding Junkers, but tied them closely to the crown by means of offices, tax exemptions, and military service.

Those who ruled, or claimed to rule, in city-states, federations, and other states of fragmented sovereignty often managed to exercise tight control over a single city and its immediate hinterland. Beyond that scale, however, they had no choice but to bargain with the authorities of competing centers. The local control usually depended not only on the city's coercive forces, but also on extensive rural land-holding by the urban ruling class. Once Florence began its aggressive expansion beyond the municipal level during the fourteenth century, its tyrants replaced the rulers of conquered cities with their own men as much as possible, but selected the replacements from among the local patricians.

All these arrangements left considerable power and discretion in the hands of local potentates, just so long as they contained the monarch's enemies and kept the revenues flowing to the national capital. On a national scale, in fact, no European state (except, perhaps, Sweden) made a serious attempt to institute direct rule from top to bottom until the era of the French Revolution. Before then all but the smallest states relied on some version of indirect rule, and thus ran serious risks of disloyalty, dissimulation, corruption, and rebellion. But indirect rule made it possible to govern without erecting, financing, and feeding a bulky administrative apparatus.

The transition to direct rule gave rulers access to citizens and the resources they controlled through household taxation, mass conscription, censuses, police systems, and many other invasions of small-scale social life. But it did so at the cost of widespread resistance, extensive bargaining, and the creation of rights and perquisites for citizens. Both the penetration and the bargaining laid down new state structures, inflating the government's budgets, personnel, and organizational diagrams. The omnivorous state of our own time took shape.

It is all too easy to treat the formation of states as a type of engineering, with kings and their ministers as the designing engineers. Four facts compromise the image of confident planning.

1 Rarely did Europe's princes have in mind a precise model of the sort of state they were producing, and even more rarely did they act efficiently to produce such a model state. As the Norman Roger de Hauteville wrested Sicily from Arab control between 1060 and 1075, for example, he improvised a government by incorporating segments of the existing Muslim administration, drew Muslim soldiers into his own army, and maintained Muslim, Jewish, and Greek Christian churches, but took over large tracts of land as his own domain and parceled out other lands to his followers. Calabria, which belonged to Sicily, remained very Greek in culture and political style, with Byzantine offices and rituals brought wholesale into Norman government. But Arab institutions also had their place: Roger's chief minister bore the wonderful title Emir of Emirs and Archonte of Archontes. The resulting state was certainly distinctive and new, but it did not emanate from a coherent plan. Roger de Hauteville and his followers created a mosaic of adaptations and improvisations (Mack Smith, 1968: 15–25).

2 No one designed the principal components of national states – treasuries, courts, central administrations, and so on. They usually formed as more or less inadvertent by-products of efforts to carry out more immediate tasks, especially the creation and support of armed force. When the French crown, greatly expanding its involvement in European wars during the 1630s, stretched its credit to the point of bankruptcy, the local authorities and officeholders on whom the king's ministers ordinarily relied for the collection of revenues ceased cooperating. At that point

chief minister Richelieu, in desperation, began sending out his own agents to coerce or bypass local authorities (Collins, 1988). Those emissaries were the royal intendants, who became the mainstays of state authority in French regions under Colbert and Louis XIV. Only in faulty retrospect do we imagine the intendants as deliberately designed instruments of Absolutism.

3 Other states – and eventually the entire system of states – strongly affected the path of change followed by any particular state. From 1066 to 1815, great wars with French monarchs formed the English state, French intervention complicated England's attempts to subdue Scotland and Ireland, and French competition stimulated England's adoption of Dutch fiscal innovations. From the sixteenth century onward, settlements of major wars regularly realigned the boundaries and the rulers of European states, right up to World War II; the division of Germany, the incorporation of Estonia, Latvia, and Lithuania into the Soviet Union, and the dismantling of most European overseas empires all stemmed more or less directly from the settlements of World War II. In none of these cases can we reasonably think of a self-guided state acting on its own.

4 Struggle and bargaining with different classes in the subject population significantly shaped the states that emerged in Europe. Popular rebellions, for example, usually lost, but each major one left marks on the state in the form of repressive policies, realignments of classes for or against the state, and explicit settlements specifying the rights of the affected parties. During the fierce revolt of the Florentine workers (the Ciompi) in 1378, two of the three new woolworkers' guilds formed during the rebellion defected to the government and thereby destroyed a front that had seized effective power in the city; in the settlement, the still-insurrectionary (and more proletarian) guild lost its right to exist, but the two collaborators joined the guilds that paraded and deliberated as part of the official municipal government (Schevill, 1963: 279; Cohn, 1980: 129–54).

On a smaller scale, both the resistance and the cooperation of knights, financiers, municipal officers, landlords, peasants, artisans, and other actors created and recreated state structure over the long run. Thus the class structure of the population that fell under the jurisdiction of a particular state significantly affected the organization of that state, and variations in class structure from one part of Europe to another produced systematic geographic differences in the character of states. Not only the ruling classes, but all classes whose resources and activities affected preparation for war, left their imprint on European states.

Twin facts, for example, strongly affected the path of Swedish state formation: first, the overwhelming presence of a peasantry that held plenty of land well into the eighteenth century; second, the relative inability of landlords either to form great estates or to coerce peasant labor on their lands. That exceptional rural class structure prevented the royal strategy of granting nobles fiscal and judicial privileges and assistance in bending peasants to their will in return for collaboration in extracting revenues and military service from the peasantry – even though such a strategy prevailed in nearby areas such as Prussia and Russia. It also helps explain the survival of a separate peasant Estate which actually had some power over governmental action, and the fact that in its period of imperial expansion Sweden turned rapidly from the hiring of mercenaries on the European market to the creation of militias whose members received land, or the income from land, in return for their service. In Sweden as elsewhere, the ambient class structure constrained rulers' attempts to create armed force, and therefore left its impact on the very organization of the state.

A more general and schematic statement of the essential relationships is given in figure 11.5. The diagram takes this shape for the reasons we surveyed earlier: war and preparation for war involved rulers in extracting the means of war from others who held the essential resources – men, arms, supplies, or money to buy them – and were reluctant to surrender them without strong pressure or compensation. The organization of major social classes within a state's territory, and their relations to the state, significantly affected the strategies rulers employed to extract resources, the resistance they met, the struggle that resulted, the sorts of durable organization extraction and struggle laid down, and therefore the efficiency of resource extraction. Within limits set by the demands and rewards of other states, extraction and struggle over the means of war created the central organizational structures of states. The organization of major social classes, and their relations to the state, varied significantly from Europe's coercion-intensive regions (areas of few cities and agricultural predominance, where direct coercion played a major part in production) to its capital-intensive regions (areas of many cities and commercial predominance, where markets, exchange, and market-oriented production prevailed). Demands major classes made on the state, and the influence of those classes over the state, varied correspondingly. The relative success of different extractive strategies, and the strategies rulers actually applied, therefore varied significantly from coercion-intensive to capital-intensive regions. As a consequence, the organizational forms of states followed distinctly different trajectories in these different parts of Europe. Such circumstances belie any idea that European monarchs simply adopted a visible model of state formation and did their best to follow it.

Long Trends and Interactions

Another illusion must also disappear. So far I have presented the relationships as though capital and coercion always moved toward greater accumulation and concentration. For the thousand years that concern us here, those have been the main trends. Yet even within the European experience many states have undergone deflation in both regards; Poland endured many reversals in capital and coercion, successive Burgundian and Habsburg empires collapsed, and the sixteenth-century religious

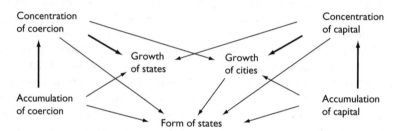

Figure 11.5 *Relations among coercion, capital, states, and cities*

wars seriously depleted Europe's stocks of capital and coercive means. The history of European state formation runs generally upward toward greater accumulation and concentration, but it runs across jagged peaks and profound valleys.

Accumulation probably made the larger long-term difference to the history of the European economy. But concentration, deconcentration, and reconcentration of coercion mark off major chapters in the story of state formation; the concentration came to depend in important degree on the availability of concentrated capital. Exactly why and how that was so will preoccupy this book's later sections and take us into complicated questions of fiscal policy. Yet the central link is simple: over the long run, far more than other activities, war and preparation for war produced the major components of European states. States that lost wars commonly contracted, and often ceased to exist. Regardless of their size, states having the largest coercive means tended to win wars; efficiency (the ratio of output to input) came second to effectiveness (total output).

Through the interplay of competition, technological change, and the sheer scale of the largest belligerent states, war and the creation of coercive means became immensely more expensive over time. As that happened, fewer and fewer rulers could create military means from their own routine resources; more and more they turned to short-term borrowing and long-term taxation. Both activities went more easily where concentrations of capital already existed. But everywhere they produced changes in governmental organization.

How did changes in warfare and state organization relate to each other? As a first approximation, we can divide the years since AD 990 into four segments, with varying temporal limits from one part of Europe to another:

1   *patrimonialism*: a time (up to the fifteenth century in much of Europe) when tribes, feudal levies, urban militias, and similar customary forces played the major part in warfare, and monarchs generally extracted what capital they needed as tribute or rent from lands and populations that lay under their immediate control;
2   *brokerage*: an era (roughly 1400 to 1700 in important parts of Europe) when mercenary forces recruited by contractors predominated in military activity, and rulers relied heavily on formally independent capitalists for loans, for management of revenue-producing enterprises, and for installation and collection of taxes;
3   *nationalization*: a period (especially 1700 to 1850 or so in much of Europe) when states created mass armies and navies drawn increasingly from their own national populations, while sovereigns absorbed armed forces directly into the state's administrative structure, and similarly took over the direct operation of the fiscal apparatus, drastically curtailing the involvement of independent contractors;
4   *specialization*: an age (from approximately the mid-nineteenth century to the recent past) in which military force grew as a powerful specialized branch of national government, the organizational separation of fiscal from military activity increased, the division of labor between armies and police sharpened, representative institutions came to have a significant influence over military expenditures, and states took on a greatly expanded range of distributive, regulatory, compensatory, and adjudicative activities.

Clearly the relations between capital and coercion changed significantly from one period to the next.

The transformation of states by war, in its turn, altered the stakes of war. Through the period of patrimonialism, conquerors sought tribute much more than they sought the stable control of the population and resources within the territories they overran; whole empires grew up on the principle of extracting rents and gifts from the rulers of multiple regions without penetrating significantly into their systems of rule. In the move to brokerage and then to nationalization, a closely administered territory became an asset worth fighting for, since only such a territory provided the revenues to sustain armed force. But in the age of specialization, states accumulated claimants to their services so rapidly that war became, even more than before, a means of satisfying the economic interests of the ruling coalition by gaining access to the resources of other states. Since World War II, with the extension of the European state system to the entire world and the accompanying rigidification of national boundaries, that has increasingly meant exercising influence over other states without actually incorporating their territory into that of the more powerful state.

Those were the broad trends. Yet more than one combination of capital and coercion appeared at each stage in the growth of European states. We might distinguish a coercion-intensive, a capital-intensive, and a capitalized coercion path to state formation. They do not represent alternative "strategies" so much as contrasting conditions of life. Rulers pursuing similar ends – especially successful preparation for war – in very different environments responded to those environments by fashioning distinctive relations to the major social classes within them. The reshaping of relations between ruler and ruled produced new, contrasting forms of government, each more or less adapted to its social setting.

In the *coercion-intensive* mode, rulers squeezed the means of war from their own populations and others they conquered, building massive structures of extraction in the process. Brandenburg and Russia – especially in their phases as tribute-taking empires – illustrate the coercion-intensive mode. At the very extreme of the mode, however, armed landlords wielded so much power that no one of them could establish durable control over the rest; for several centuries, the Polish and Hungarian nobilities actually elected their own kings, and struck them down when they strove too hard for supreme power.

In the *capital-intensive* mode, rulers relied on compacts with capitalists – whose interests they served with care – to rent or purchase military force, and thereby warred without building vast permanent state structures. City-states, city-empires, urban federations, and other forms of fragmented sovereignty commonly fall into this path of change. Genoa, Dubrovnik, the Dutch Republic, and, for a time, Catalonia, exemplify the capital-intensive mode. As the history of the Dutch Republic illustrates, at the extreme this mode produced federations of largely autonomous city-states, and constant negotiation among them over state policy.

In the intermediate *capitalized coercion* mode, rulers did some of each, but spent more of their effort than did their capital-intensive neighbors on incorporating capitalists and sources of capital directly into the structures of their states. Holders of capital and coercion interacted on terms of relative equality. France and England eventually followed the capitalized coercion mode, which produced full-fledged national states earlier than the coercion-intensive and capital-intensive modes did.

Driven by the pressures of international competition (especially by war and preparation for war) all three paths eventually converged on concentrations of capital and of coercion out of all proportion to those that prevailed in AD 990. From the seventeenth century onward the capitalized coercion form proved more effective in war, and therefore provided a compelling model for states that had originated in other combinations of coercion and capital. From the nineteenth century to the recent past, furthermore, all European states involved themselves much more heavily than before in building social infrastructure, in providing services, in regulating economic activity, in controlling population movements, and in assuring citizens' welfare; all these activities began as by-products of rulers' efforts to acquire revenues and compliance from their subject populations, but took on lives and rationales of their own. Contemporary socialist states differ from capitalist states, on the average, in exerting more direct, self-conscious control over production and distribution. As compared with the range of states that have existed in Europe over the last thousand years, nevertheless, they belong recognizably to the same type as their capitalist neighbors. They, too, are national states.

Before their recent convergence, the coercion-intensive, capital-intensive and capitalized coercion paths led to very different kinds of states. Even after convergence, states retained some features – for example, the character of their representative institutions – that clearly reflected their earlier historical experiences. All three types of state were quite viable under certain conditions that actually prevailed in Europe at various times before the present. Indeed, at the abdication of Charles V in 1555, the major part of Europe lay under imperial hegemony, rather than under the control of national states in any strong sense of the term.

At that point, Suleyman the Magnificent's Ottoman Empire (in addition to dominating Anatolia and much of the Middle East) occupied most of the Balkans and held in vassalage states from the Volga to the Adriatic. Charles V, as Holy Roman Emperor, Emperor of Spain, and Elder of the Habsburgs, then claimed rule over Spain, the Netherlands, Milan, Naples, Sicily, Sardinia, Austria, Bohemia, Burgundy, Franche-Comté and (more contestably) the swarm of states in the territory we now call Germany. Further east, Poland, Lithuania, Muscovy, and the Don Cossacks also organized in imperial style. In 1555, northern Italy, Switzerland, and significant parts of the Holy Roman Empire remained areas of intensely fragmented sovereignty, while only France and England resembled our conventional models of national states. By that time, city-states and other small-scale organizations were losing ground relative to other forms of state. Yet the Dutch Republic was soon to prove that federations of cities and adjacent territories could still hold their own as world powers. Empires, furthermore, were advancing. Nothing then assured the ultimate victory of the national state.

The lesson is clear. To use twentieth-century strength as the main criterion of effective state formation (as many analysts do) means succumbing to the temptations of teleology, misconceiving the relations among cities, states, capital, and coercion in the European past. We can avoid these pitfalls by following the choices of statemakers, and the consequences of those choices, forward from an early date – here set arbitrarily at AD 990 – to the present.

References

Busch, Otto, 1962 *Militarsystem und Sozialleben im alten Preussen 1713–1807: Die Anfänge der sozialen Militarisierung der preussisch-deutschen Gesellschaft*. Berlin: de Gruyter.

Carsten, F. L., 1954 *The Origins of Prussia*. Oxford: Clarendon Press.

Cohn, Jr, Samuel Kline, 1980 *The Laboring Classes in Renaissance Florence*. New York: Academic Press.

Collins, James B., 1988 *Fiscal Limits of Absolutism. Direct Taxation in Early Seventeenth-Century France*. Berkeley, California: University of California Press.

Garcin, Jean-Claude, 1988 "The Mamluk Military System and the Blocking of Medieval Moslem Society," in Jean Baechler, John A. Hall and Michael Mann, eds, *Europe and the Rise of Capitalism*. Oxford: Basil Blackwell.

Mack Smith, Dennis, 1968 *A History of Sicily. Medieval Sicily, 800–1713*. London: Chatto & Windus.

Pitcher, Donald Edgar, 1972 *An Historical Geography of the Ottoman Empire from Earliest Times to the End of the Sixteenth Century*. Leiden: Brill.

Powers, James F., 1988 *A Society Organized for War. The Iberian Municipal Militias in the Central Middle Ages, 1000–1284*. Berkeley, California: University of California Press.

Schevill, Ferdinand, 1963 *Medieval and Renaissance Florence*. New York: Harper Torchbooks, 2 vols. First published in 1936.

Stoianovich, Traian, 1989 "The Segmentary State and *La Grande Nation*," In Eugene D. Genovese and Leonard Hochberg, eds, *Geographic Perspectives in History*. Oxford: Basil Blackwell.

Vries, Jan de, 1973 "On the Modernity of the Dutch Republic," *Journal of Economic History* 33: 191-202.

12 The Iron Cage Revisited: Institutional Isomorphism and Collective Rationality in Organizational Fields

Paul J. DiMaggio and Walter W. Powell

In *The Protestant Ethic and the Spirit of Capitalism*, Max Weber warned that the rationalist spirit ushered in by asceticism had achieved a momentum of its own and that, under capitalism, the rationalist order had become an iron cage in which humanity was, save for the possibility of prophetic revival, imprisoned "perhaps until the last ton of fossilized coal is burnt" (Weber, 1952: 181–2). In his essay on bureaucracy, Weber returned to this theme, contending that bureaucracy, the rational spirit's organizational manifestation, was so efficient and powerful a means of controlling men and women that, once established, the momentum of bureaucratization was irreversible (Weber, 1968).

The imagery of the iron cage has haunted students of society as the tempo of bureaucratization has quickened. But while bureaucracy has spread continuously in the eighty years since Weber wrote, we suggest that the engine of organizational rationalization has shifted. For Weber, bureaucratization resulted from three related causes: competition among capitalist firms in the marketplace; competition among states, increasing rulers' need to control their staff and citizenry; and bourgeois demands for equal protection under the law. Of these three, the most important was the competitive marketplace. "Today," Weber (1968: 974) wrote:

> it is primarily the capitalist market economy which demands that the official business of administration be discharged precisely, unambiguously, continuously, and with as much speed as possible. Normally, the very large, modern capitalist enterprises are themselves unequalled models of strict bureaucratic organization.

We argue that the causes of bureaucratization and rationalization have changed. The bureaucratization of the corporation and the state have been achieved. Organizations are still becoming more homogeneous, and bureaucracy remains the common organizational form. Today, however, structural change in organizations seems less and less driven by competition or by the need for efficiency. Instead, we will contend, bureaucratization and other forms of organizational change occur as the result of processes that make organizations more similar without necessarily making them more efficient. Bureaucratization and other forms of homogenization emerge, we argue, out of the structuration (Giddens, 1979) of organizational fields. This process, in turn, is effected largely by the state and the professions, which have become the great rationalizers of the second half of the twentieth century. For reasons that we will explain, highly structured organizational fields provide a context in which individual efforts to deal rationally with uncertainty and constraint often lead, in the aggregate, to homogeneity in structure, culture, and output.

Organizational Theory and Organizational Diversity

Much of modern organizational theory posits a diverse and differentiated world of organizations and seeks to explain variation among organizations in structure and behavior (e.g., Woodward, 1965; Child and Kieser, 1981). Hannan and Freeman begin a major theoretical paper (1977) with the question, "Why are there so many kinds of organizations?" Even our investigatory technologies (for example, those based on least-squares techniques) are geared towards explaining variation rather than its absence.

We ask, instead, why there is such startling homogeneity of organizational forms and practices; and we seek to explain homogeneity, not variation. In the initial stages of their life cycle, organizational fields display considerable diversity in approach and form. Once a field becomes well established, however, there is an inexorable push towards homogenization.

Coser, Kadushin, and Powell (1982) describe the evolution of American college textbook publishing from a period of initial diversity to the current hegemony of only two models, the large bureaucratic generalist and the small specialist. Rothman (1980) describes the winnowing of several competing models of legal education into two dominant approaches. Starr (1980) provides evidence of mimicry in the development of the hospital field; Tyack (1974) and Katz (1975) show a similar process in public schools; Barnouw (1966–8) describes the development of dominant forms in the radio industry; and DiMaggio (1981) depicts the emergence of dominant organizational models for the provision of high culture in the late nineteenth century.

What we see in each of these cases is the emergence and structuration of an organizational field as a result of the activities of a diverse set of organizations; and, second, the homogenization of these organizations, and of new entrants as well, once the field is established.

By organizational field, we mean those organizations that, in the aggregate, constitute a recognized area of institutional life: key suppliers, resource and product consumers, regulatory agencies, and other organizations that produce similar services or products. The virtue of this unit of analysis is that it directs our attention not simply to competing firms, as does the population approach of Hannan and Freeman (1977), or to networks of organizations that actually interact, as does the interorganizational network approach of Laumann et al. (1978), but to the totality of relevant actors. In doing this, the field idea comprehends the importance of both *connectedness* (see Laumann et al., 1978) and *structural equivalence* (White et al., 1976).[1]

The structure of an organizational field cannot be determined a priori but must be defined on the basis of empirical investigation. Fields only exist to the extent that they are institutionally defined. The process of institutional definition, or "structuration," consists of four parts: an increase in the extent of interaction among organizations in the field; the emergence of sharply defined interorganizational structures of domination and patterns of coalition; an increase in the information load with which organizations in a field must contend; and the development of a mutual awareness among participants in a set of organizations that they are involved in a common enterprise (DiMaggio, 1982).

Once disparate organizations in the same line of business are structured into an actual field (as we shall argue, by competition, the state, or the professions), powerful forces emerge that lead them to become more similar to one another. Organizations may change their goals or develop new practices, and new organizations enter the field. But, in the long run, organizational actors making rational decisions construct around themselves an environment that constrains their ability to change further in later years. Early adopters of organizational innovations are commonly driven by a desire to improve performance. But new practices can become, in Selznick's words (1957: 17), "infused with value beyond the technical requirements of the task at hand." As an innovation spreads, a threshold is reached beyond which adoption provides legitimacy rather than improves performance (Meyer and Rowan, 1977). Strategies that are rational for individual organizations may not be rational if adopted by large numbers. Yet the very fact that they are normatively sanctioned increases the likelihood of their adoption. Thus organizations may try to change constantly; but, after a certain point in the structuration of an organizational field, the aggregate effect of individual change is to lessen the extent of diversity within the field.[2] Organizations in a structured field, to paraphrase Schelling (1978: 14), respond to an environment that consists of other organizations responding to their environment, which consists of organizations responding to an environment of organizations' responses.

Zucker and Tolbert's (1981) work on the adoption of civil-service reform in the United States illustrates this process. Early adoption of civil-service reforms was related to internal governmental needs, and strongly predicted by such city characteristics as the size of immigrant population, political reform movements, socio-economic composition, and city size. Later adoption, however, is not predicted by city characteristics, but is related to institutional definitions of the legitimate structural form for municipal administration. Marshall Meyer's (1981) study of the bureaucratization of urban fiscal agencies has yielded similar findings: strong relationships between city characteristics and organizational attributes at the turn of the century, null relationships in recent years. Carroll and Delacroix's (1982) findings on the birth and death rates of newspapers support the view that selection acts with great force only in the early years of an industry's existence. Freeman (1982: 14) suggests that older, larger organizations reach a point where they can dominate their environments rather than adjust to them.

The concept that best captures the process of homogenization is *isomorphism*. In Hawley's (1968) description, isomorphism is a constraining process that forces one unit in a population to resemble other units that face the same set of environmental conditions. At the population level, such an approach suggests that organizational characteristics are modified in the direction of increasing compatibility with environmental characteristics; the number of organizations in a population is a function of environmental carrying capacity; and the diversity of organizational forms is isomorphic to environmental diversity. Hannan and Freeman (1977) have significantly extended Hawley's ideas. They argue that isomorphism can result because nonoptimal forms are selected out of a population of organizations *or* because organizational decision makers learn appropriate responses and adjust their behavior accordingly. Hannan and Freeman's focus is almost solely on the first process: selection.

Following Meyer (1979) and Fennell (1980), we maintain that there are two types of isomorphism: competitive and institutional. Hannan and Freeman's classic paper (1977), and much of their recent work, deals with competitive isomorphism, assuming a system rationality that emphasizes market competition, niche change, and fitness measures. Such a view, we suggest, is most relevant for those fields in which free and open competition exists. It explains parts of the process of bureaucratization that Weber observed, and may apply to early adoption of innovation, but it does not present a fully adequate picture of the modern world of organizations. For this purpose it must be supplemented by an institutional view of isomorphism of the sort introduced by Kanter (1972: 152–4) in her discussion of the forces pressing communes toward accommodation with the outside world. As Aldrich (1979: 265) has argued, "the major factors that organizations must take into account are other organizations." Organizations compete not just for resources and customers, but for political power and institutional legitimacy, for social as well as economic fitness. The concept of institutional isomorphism is a useful tool for understanding the politics and ceremony that pervade much modern organizational life.

Three mechanisms of institutional isomorphic change

We identify three mechanisms through which institutional isomorphic change occurs, each with its own antecedents: 1) *coercive* isomorphism that stems from political influence and the problem of legitimacy; 2) *mimetic* isomorphism resulting from standard responses to uncertainty; and 3) *normative* isomorphism, associated with professionalization. This typology is an analytic one: the types are not always empirically distinct. For example, external actors may induce an organization to conform to its peers by requiring it to perform a particular task and specifying the profession responsible for its performance. Or mimetic change may reflect environmentally constructed uncertainties.[3] Yet, while the three types intermingle in empirical setting, they tend to derive from different conditions and may lead to different outcomes.

Coercive isomorphism. Coercive isomorphism results from both formal and informal pressures exerted on organizations by other organizations upon which they are dependent and by cultural expectations in the society within which organizations function. Such pressures may be felt as force, as persuasion, or as invitations to join in collusion. In some circumstances, organizational change is a direct response to government mandate: manufacturers adopt new pollution control technologies to conform to environmental regulations; nonprofits maintain accounts, and hire accountants, in order to meet tax law requirements; and organizations employ affirmative-action officers to fend off allegations of discrimination. Schools mainstream special students and hire special education teachers, cultivate PTAs and administrators who get along with them, and promulgate curricula that conform with state standards (Meyer et al., 1981). The fact that these changes may be largely ceremonial does not mean that they are inconsequential. As Ritti and Goldner (1979) have argued, staff become involved in advocacy for their functions that can alter power relations within organizations over the long run.

The existence of a common legal environment affects many aspects of an organization's behavior and structure. Weber pointed out the profound impact of a complex, rationalized system of contract law that requires the necessary organizational controls to honor legal commitments. Other legal and technical requirements of the state – the vicissitudes of the budget cycle, the ubiquity of certain fiscal years, annual reports, and financial reporting requirements that ensure eligibility for the receipt of federal contracts or funds – also shape organizations in similar ways. Pfeffer and Salancik (1978: 188–224) have discussed how organizations faced with unmanageable interdependence seek to use the greater power of the larger social system and its government to eliminate difficulties or provide for needs. They observe that politically constructed environments have two characteristic features: political decisionmakers often do not experience directly the consequences of their actions; and political decisions are applied across the board to entire classes of organizations, thus making such decisions less adaptive and less flexible.

Meyer and Rowan (1977) have argued persuasively that as rationalized states and other large rational organizations expand their dominance over more arenas of social life, organizational structures increasingly come to reflect rules institutionalized and legitimated by and within the state (also see Meyer and Hannan, 1979). As a result, organizations are increasingly homogeneous within given domains and increasingly organized around rituals of conformity to wider institutions. At the same time, organizations are decreasingly structurally determined by the constraints posed by technical activities, and decreasingly held together by output controls. Under such circumstances, organizations employ ritualized controls of credentials and group solidarity.

Direct imposition of standard operating procedures and legitimated rules and structures also occurs outside the governmental arena. Michael Sedlak (1981) has documented the ways that United Charities in the 1930s altered and homogenized the structures, methods, and philosophies of the social service agencies that depended upon them for support. As conglomerate corporations increase in size and scope, standard performance criteria are not necessarily imposed on subsidiaries, but it is common for subsidiaries to be subject to standardized reporting mechanisms (Coser et al., 1982). Subsidiaries must adopt accounting practices, performance evaluations, and budgetary plans that are compatible with the policies of the parent corporation. A variety of service infrastructures, often provided by monopolistic firms – for example, telecommunications and transportation – exert common pressures over the organizations that use them. Thus, the expansion of the central state, the centralization of capital, and the coordination of philanthropy all support the homogenization of organizational models through direct authority relationships.

We have so far referred only to the direct and explicit imposition of organizational models on dependent organizations. Coercive isomorphism, however, may be more subtle and less explicit than these examples suggest. Milofsky (1981) has described the ways in which neighborhood organizations in urban communities, many of which are committed to participatory democracy, are driven to developing organizational hierarchies in order to gain support from more hierarchically organized donor organizations. Similarly, Swidler (1979) describes the tensions created in the free schools she studied by the need to have a "principal" to negotiate with the district superintendent and to represent the school to outside agencies. In general, the need to lodge responsibility and managerial authority at least ceremonially in a formally defined role in order to interact with hierarchical organizations is a constant obstacle to the maintenance of egalitarian or collectivist organizational forms (Kanter, 1972; Rothschild-Whitt, 1979).

Mimetic processes. Not all institutional isomorphism, however, derives from coercive authority. Uncertainty is also a powerful force that encourages imitation. When organizational technologies are poorly understood (March and Olsen, 1976), when goals are ambiguous, or when the environment creates symbolic uncertainty, organizations may model themselves on other organizations. The advantages of mimetic behavior in the economy of human action are considerable; when an organization faces a problem with ambiguous causes or unclear solutions, problemistic search may yield a viable solution with little expense (Cyert and March, 1963).

Modeling, as we use the term, is a response to uncertainty. The modeled organization may be unaware of the modeling or may have no desire to be copied; it merely serves as a convenient source of practices that the borrowing organization may use. Models may be diffused unintentionally, indirectly through employee transfer or turnover, or explicitly by organizations such as consulting firms or industry trade associations. Even innovation can be accounted for by organizational modeling. As Alchian (1950) has observed:

> While there certainly are those who consciously innovate, there are those who, in their imperfect attempts to imitate others, unconsciously innovate by unwittingly acquiring some unexpected or unsought unique attributes which under the prevailing circumstances prove partly responsible for the success. Others, in turn, will attempt to copy the uniqueness, and the innovation-imitation process continues.

One of the most dramatic instances of modeling was the effort of Japan's modernizers in the late nineteenth century to model new governmental initiatives on apparently successful western prototypes. Thus, the imperial government sent its officers to study the courts, Army, and police in France, the Navy and postal system in Great Britain, and banking and art education in the United States (see Westney, forthcoming). American corporations are now returning the compliment by implementing (their perceptions of) Japanese models to cope with thorny productivity and personnel problems in their own firms. The rapid proliferation of quality circles and quality-of-work-life issues in American firms is, at least in part, an attempt to model Japanese and European successes. These developments also have a ritual aspect; companies adopt these "innovations" to enhance their legitimacy, to demonstrate they are at least trying to improve working conditions. More generally, the wider the population of personnel employed by, or customers served by, an organization, the stronger the pressure felt by the organization to provide the programs and services offered by other organizations. Thus, either a skilled labor force or a broad customer base may encourage mimetic isomorphism.

Much homogeneity in organizational structures stems from the fact that despite considerable search for diversity there is relatively little variation to be selected from. New organizations are modeled upon old ones throughout the economy, and managers actively seek models upon which to build (Kimberly, 1980). Thus, in the arts one can find textbooks on how to organize a community arts council or how to start a symphony women's guild. Large organizations choose from a relatively small set of major consulting firms, which, like Johnny Appleseeds, spread a few organizational models throughout the land. Such models are powerful because structural changes are observable, whereas changes in policy and strategy are less easily noticed. With the advice of a major consulting firm, a large metropolitan public television station switched from a functional design to a multidivisional structure. The stations' executives were skeptical that the new structure was more efficient; in fact, some services were now duplicated across divisions. But they were convinced that the new design would carry a powerful message to the for-profit firms with whom the station regularly dealt. These firms, whether in the role of corporate underwriters or as potential partners in joint ventures, would view the reorganization as a sign that "the sleepy nonprofit station was becoming more business-minded" (Powell, forthcoming). The history of management reform in American government agencies, which are noted for their goal ambiguity, is almost a textbook case of isomorphic modeling, from the PPPB of the McNamara era to the zero-based budgeting of the Carter administration.

Organizations tend to model themselves after similar organizations in their field that they perceive to be more legitimate or successful. The ubiquity of certain kinds of structural arrangements can more likely be credited to the universality of mimetic processes than to any concrete evidence that the adopted models enhance efficiency. John Meyer (1981) contends that it is easy to predict the organization of a newly emerging nation's administration without knowing anything about the nation itself, since "peripheral nations are far more isomorphic – in administrative form and economic pattern – than any theory of the world system of economic division of labor would lead one to expect."

Normative pressures. A third source of isomorphic organizational change is normative and stems primarily from professionalization. Following Larson (1977) and Collins (1979), we interpret professionalization as the collective struggle of members of an occupation to define the conditions and methods of their work, to control "the production of producers" (Larson, 1977: 49–52), and to establish a cognitive base and legitimation for their occupational autonomy. As Larson points out, the professional project is rarely achieved with complete success. Professionals must compromise with nonprofessional clients, bosses, or regulators. The major recent growth in the professions has been among organizational professionals, particularly managers and specialized staff of large organizations. The increased professionalization of workers whose futures are inextricably bound up with the fortunes of the organizations that employ them has rendered obsolescent (if not obsolete) the dichotomy between organizational commitment and professional allegiance that characterized traditional professionals in earlier organizations (Hall, 1968). Professions are subject to the same coercive and mimetic pressures as are organizations. Moreover, while various kinds of professionals within an organization may differ from one another, they exhibit much similarity to their professional counterparts in other organizations. In addition, in many cases, professional power is as much assigned by the state as it is created by the activities of the professions.

Two aspects of professionalization are important sources of isomorphism. One is the resting of formal education and of legitimation in a cognitive base produced by university specialists; the second is the growth and elaboration of professional networks that span organizations and across which new models diffuse rapidly. Universities and professional training institutions are important centers for the development of organizational norms among professional managers and their staff. Professional and trace associations are another vehicle for the definition and promulgation of normative rules about organizational and professional behavior. Such mechanisms create a pool of almost interchangeable individuals who occupy similar positions across a range of organizations and possess a similarity of orientation and disposition that may override variations in tradition and control that might otherwise shape organizational behavior (Perrow, 1974).

One important mechanism for encouraging normative isomorphism is the filtering of personnel. Within many organizational fields filtering occurs through the hiring of individuals from firms within the same industry; through the recruitment of fast-track staff from a narrow range of training institutions; through common promotion practices, such as always hiring top executives from financial or legal departments; and from skill-level requirements for particular jobs. Many professional career tracks are so closely guarded, both at the entry level and throughout the career progression, that individuals who make it to the top are virtually indistinguishable. March and March (1977) found that individuals who attained the position of school superintendent in Wisconsin were so alike in background and orientation as to make further career advancement random and unpredictable. Hirsch and Whisler (1982) find a similar absence of variation among *Fortune* 500 board members. In addition, individuals in an organizational field undergo anticipatory socialization to common expectations about their personal behavior, appropriate style of dress, organizational vocabularies (Cicourel, 1970; Williamson, 1975) and standard methods of speaking, joking, or addressing others (Ouchi, 1980). Particularly in industries with a service or financial orientation (Collins, 1979, argues that the importance of credentials is strongest in these areas), the filtering of personnel approaches what Kanter (1977) refers to as the "homosexual reproduction of management." To the extent managers and key staff are drawn from the same universities and filtered on a common set of attributes, they will tend to view problems in a similar fashion, see the same policies, procedures and structures as normatively sanctioned and legitimated, and approach decisions in much the same way.

Entrants to professional career tracks who somehow escape the filtering process – for example, Jewish naval officers, woman stockbrokers, or Black insurance executives – are likely to be subjected to pervasive on-the-job socialization. To the extent that organizations in a field differ and primary socialization occurs on the job, socialization could reinforce, not erode, differences among organizations. But when organizations in a field are similar and occupational socialization is carried out in trade association workshops, in-service educational programs, consultant arrangements, employer–professional school networks, and in the pages of trade magazines, socialization acts as an isomorphic force.

The professionalization of management tends to proceed in tandem with the structuration of organizational fields. The exchange of information among professionals helps contribute to a commonly recognized hierarchy of status, of center and periphery, that becomes a matrix for information flows and personnel movement across organizations. This status ordering occurs through both formal and informal means. The designation of a few large firms in an industry as key bargaining agents in union–management negotiations may make these central firms pivotal in other respects as well. Government recognition of key firms or organizations through the grant or contract process may give these organizations legitimacy and visibility and lead competing firms to copy aspects of their structure or operating procedures in hope of obtaining similar rewards. Professional and trade associations provide other arenas in which center organizations are recognized and their personnel given positions of substantive or ceremonial influence. Managers in highly visible organizations may in turn have their stature reinforced by representation on the boards of other organizations, participation in industry-wide or inter-industry councils, and consultation by agencies of government (Useem, 1979). In the nonprofit sector, where legal barriers to collusion do not exist, structuration may proceed even more rapidly. Thus executive producers or artistic directors of leading theatres head trade or professional association committees, sit on government and foundation grant-award panels, or consult as government- or foundation-financed management advisors to smaller theatres, or sit on smaller organizations' boards, even as their stature is reinforced and enlarged by the grants their theatres receive from government, corporate, and foundation funding sources (DiMaggio, 1982).

Such central organizations serve as both active and passive models; their policies and structures will be copied throughout their fields. Their centrality is reinforced as upwardly mobile managers and staff seek to secure positions in these central organizations in order to further their own careers. Aspiring managers may undergo anticipatory socialization into the norms and mores of the organizations they hope to join. Career paths may also involve movement from entry positions in the center organizations to middle-management positions in peripheral organizations. Personnel flows within an organizational field are further encouraged by structural homogenization, for example the existence of common career titles and paths (such as assistant, associate, and full professor) with meanings that are commonly understood.

It is important to note that each of the institutional isomorphic processes can be expected to proceed in the absence of evidence that they increase internal organizational efficiency. To the extent that organizational effectiveness is enhanced, the reason will often be that organizations are rewarded for being similar to other organizations in their fields. This similarity can make it easier for organizations to transact with other organizations, to attract career-minded staff, to be acknowledged as legitimate and reputable, and to fit into administrative categories that define eligibility for public and private grants and contracts. None of this, however, insures that conformist organizations do what they do more efficiently than do their more deviant peers.

Pressures for competitive efficiency are also mitigated in many fields because the number of organizations is limited and there are strong fiscal and legal barriers to entry and exit. Lee (1971: 51) maintains this is why hospital administrators are less concerned with the efficient use of resources and more concerned with status competition and parity in prestige. Fennell (1980) notes that hospitals are a poor market system because patients lack the needed knowledge of potential exchange partners and prices. She argues that physicians and hospital administrators are the actual consumers. Competition among hospitals is based on "attracting physicians, who, in turn, bring their patients to the hospital." Fennell (p. 505) concludes that:

> Hospitals operate according to a norm of social legitimation that frequently conflicts with market considerations of efficiency and system rationality. Apparently, hospitals can increase their range of services not because there is an actual need for a particular service or facility within the patient population, but because they will be defined as fit only if they can offer everything other hospitals in the area offer.

These results suggest a more general pattern. Organizational fields that include a large professionally trained labor force will be driven primarily by status competition. Organizational prestige and resources are key elements in attracting professionals. This process encourages homogenization as organizations seek to ensure that they can provide the same benefits and services as their competitors.

Predictors of Isomorphic Change

It follows from our discussion of the mechanism by which isomorphic change occurs that we should be able to predict empirically which organizational fields will be most homogeneous in structure, process, and behavior. While an empirical test of such predictions is beyond the scope of this paper, the ultimate value of our perspective will lie in its predictive utility. The hypotheses discussed below are not meant to exhaust the universe of predictors, but merely to suggest several hypotheses that may be pursued using data on the characteristics of organizations in a field, either cross-sectionally or, preferably, over time. The hypotheses are implicitly governed by *ceteris paribus* assumptions, particularly with regard to size, technology, and centralization of external resources.

A. *Organizational-level predictors.* There is variability in the extent to and rate at which organizations in a field change to become more like their peers. Some organizations respond to external pressures quickly; others change only after a long period of resistance. The first two hypotheses derive from our discussion of coercive isomorphism and constraint.

Hypothesis A-1: *The greater the dependence of an organization on another organization, the more similar it will become to that organization in structure, climate, and behavioral focus.* Following Thompson (1957) and Pfeffer and Salancik (1978), this proposition recognizes the greater ability of organizations to resist the demands of organizations on whom they are not dependent. A position of dependence leads to isomorphic change. Coercive pressures are built into exchange relationships. As Williamson (1979) has shown, exchanges are characterized by transaction-specific investments in both knowledge and equipment. Once an organization chooses a specific supplier or distributor for particular parts or services, the supplier or distributor develops expertise in the performance of the task as well as idiosyncratic knowledge about the exchange relationship. The organization comes to rely on the supplier or distributor and such transaction-specific investments give the supplier or distributor considerable advantages in any subsequent competition with other suppliers or distributors.

Hypothesis A-2: *The greater the centralization of organization A's resource supply, the greater the extent to which organization A will change isomorphically to resemble the organizations on which it depends for resources.* As Thompson (1967) notes, organizations that depend on the same sources for funding, personnel, and legitimacy will be more subject to the whims of resource suppliers than will organizations that can play one source of support off against another. In cases where alternative sources are either not readily available or require effort to locate, the stronger party to the transaction can coerce the weaker party to adopt its practices in order to accommodate the stronger party's needs (see Powell, 1983).

The third and fourth hypotheses derive from our discussion of mimetic isomorphism, modeling, and uncertainty.

Hypothesis A-3: *The more uncertain the relationship between means and ends the greater the extent to which an organization will model itself after organizations it perceives to be successful.* The mimetic thought process involved in the search for models is characteristic of change in organizations in which key technologies are only poorly understood (March and Cohen, 1974). Here our prediction diverges somewhat from Meyer and Rowan (1977) who argue, as we do, that organizations which lack well-defined technologies will import institutionalized rules and practices. Meyer and Rowan posit a loose coupling between legitimated external practices and internal organizational behavior. From an ecologist's point of view, loosely coupled organizations are more likely to vary internally. In contrast, we expect substantive internal changes in tandem with more ceremonial practices, thus greater homogeneity and less variation and change. Internal consistency of this sort is an important means of interorganizational coordination. It also increases organizational stability.

Hypothesis A-4: *The more ambiguous the goals of an organization, the greater the extent to which the organization will model itself after organizations that it perceives to be successful.* There are two reasons for this. First, organizations with ambiguous or disputed goals are likely to be highly dependent upon appearances for legitimacy. Such organizations may find it to their advantage to meet the expectations of important constituencies about how they should be designed and run. In contrast to our view, ecologists would argue that organizations that copy other organizations usually have no competitive advantage. We contend that, in most situations, reliance on established, legitimated procedures enhances organizational legitimacy and survival characteristics. A second reason for modeling behavior is found in situations where conflict over organizational goals is repressed in the interest of harmony; thus participants find it easier to mimic other organizations than to make decisions on the basis of systematic analyses of goals since such analyses would prove painful or disruptive.

The fifth and sixth hypotheses are based on our discussion of normative processes found in professional organizations.

Hypothesis A-5: *The greater the reliance on academic credentials in choosing managerial and staff personnel, the greater the extent to which an organization will become like other organizations in its field.* Applicants with academic creden-tials have already undergone a socialization process in university programs, and are thus more likely than others to have internalized reigning norms and dominant organizational models.

Hypothesis A-6: *The greater the participation of organizational managers in trade and professional associations, the more likely the organization will be, or will become, like other organizations in its field.* This hypothesis is parallel to the insti-tutional view that the more elaborate the relational networks among organizations and their members, the greater the collective organization of the environment (Meyer and Rowan, 1977).

B. *Field-level predictors.* The following six hypotheses describe the expected effects of several characteristics of organizational fields on the extent of isomorph-ism in a particular field. Since the effect of institutional isomorphism is homogeniza-tion, the best indicator of isomorphic change is a decrease in variation and diversity, which could be measured by lower standard deviations of the values of selected indicators in a set of organizations. The key indicators would vary with the nature of the field and the interests of the investigator. In all cases, however, field-level measures are expected to affect organizations in a field regardless of each organiza-tion's scores on related organizational-level measures.

Hypothesis B-1: *The greater the extent to which an organizational field is depend-ent upon a single (or several similar) source of support for vital resources, the higher the level of isomorphism.* The centralization of resources within a field both directly causes homogenization by placing organizations under similar pressures from re-source suppliers, and interacts with uncertainty and goal ambiguity to increase their impact. This hypothesis is congruent with the ecologists' argument that the number of organizational forms is determined by the distribution of resources in the environ-ment and the terms on which resources are available.

Hypothesis B-2: *The greater the extent to which the organizations in a field transact with agencies of the state, the greater the extent of isomorphism in the field as a whole.* This follows not just from the previous hypothesis, but from two elements of state/private-sector transactions: their rule-boundedness and formal rationality, and the emphasis of government actors on institutional rules. Moreover, the federal government routinely designates industry standards for an entire field which require adoption by all competing firms. John Meyer (1979) argues convincingly that the aspects of an organization which are affected by state transactions differ to the extent that state participation is unitary or fragmented among several public agencies.

The third and fourth hypotheses follow from our discussion of isomorphic change resulting from uncertainty and modeling.

Hypothesis B-3: *The fewer the number of visible alternative organizational models in a field, the faster the rate of isomorphism in that field.* The predictions of this hypothesis are less specific than those of others and require further refine-ment; but our argument is that for any relevant dimension of organizational strat-egies or structures in an organizational field there will be a threshold level, or a tipping point, beyond which adoption of the dominant form will proceed with increasing speed (Granovetter, 1978; Boorman and Leavitt, 1979).

Hypothesis B-4: *The greater the extent to which technologies are uncertain or goals are ambiguous within a field, the greater the rate of isomorphic change.*

Somewhat counterintuitively, abrupt increases in uncertainty and ambiguity should, after brief periods of ideologically motivated experimentation, lead to rapid isomorphic change. As in the case of A-4, ambiguity and uncertainty may be a function of environmental definition, and, in any case, interact both with centralization of resources (A-1, A-2, B-1, B-2) and with professionalization and structuration (A-5, A-6, B-5, B-6). Moreover, in fields characterized by a high degree of uncertainty, new entrants, which could serve as sources of innovation and variation, will seek to overcome the liability of newness by imitating established practices within the field.

The two final hypotheses in this section follow from our discussion of professional filtering, socialization, and structuration.

Hypothesis B-5: *The greater the extent of professionalization in a field, the greater the amount of institutional isomorphic change.* Professionalization may be measured by the universality of credential requirements, the robustness of graduate training programs, or the vitality of professional and trade associations.

Hypothesis B-6: *The greater the extent of structuration of a field, the greater the degree of isomorphics.* Fields that have stable and broadly acknowledged centers, peripheries, and status orders will be more homogeneous both because the diffusion structure for new models and norms is more routine and because the level of interaction among organizations in the field is higher. While structuration may not lend itself to easy measurement, it might be tapped crudely with the use of such familiar measures as concentration ratios, reputational interview studies, or data on network characteristics.

This rather schematic exposition of a dozen hypotheses relating the extent of isomorphism to selected attributes of organizations and of organizational fields does not constitute a complete agenda for empirical assessment of our perspective. We have not discussed the expected nonlinearities and ceiling effects in the relationships that we have posited. Nor have we addressed the issue of the indicators that one must use to measure homogeneity. Organizations in a field may be highly diverse on some dimensions, yet extremely homogeneous on others. While we suspect, in general, that the rate at which the standard deviations of structural or behavioral indicators approach zero will vary with the nature of an organizational field's technology and environment, we will not develop these ideas here. The point of this section is to suggest that the theoretical discussion is susceptible to empirical test, and to lay out a few testable propositions that may guide future analyses.

Notes

1   By *connectedness* we mean the existence of transactions tying organizations to one another: A set of organizations that are strongly connected to one another and only weakly connected to other organizations constitutes a *clique*. By *structural equivalence* we refer to similarity of position in a network structure.

2   By organizational change, we refer to change in formal structure, organizational culture, and goals, program, or mission.

3   This point was suggested by John Meyer.

References

Alchian, Armen (1950) "Uncertainty, evolution, and economic theory." *Journal of Political Economy* 58:211–21.

Aldrich, Howard (1979) *Organizations and Environments*. Englewood Cliffs, NJ: Prentice-Hall.

Althusser, Louis (1969) *For Marx*. London: Allan Lane.

Barnouw, Erik (1966–8) *A History of Broadcasting in the United States*, 3 volumes. New York: Oxford University Press.

Boorman, Scott A. and Paul R. Levitt (1979) "The cascade principle for general disequilibrium dynamics." Cambridge/New Haven: Harvard-Yale Preprints in Mathematical Sociology. Number 15.

Carroll, Glenn R. and Jacques Delacroix (1982) "Organizational mortality in the newspaper industries of Argentina and Ireland: an ecological approach." *Administrative Science Quarterly* 27:169–98.

Child, John and Alfred Kieser (1981) "Development of organizations over time." Pp. 28–64 in Paul C. Nystrom and William H. Starbuck (eds.), *Handbook of Organizational Design*. New York: Oxford University Press.

Cicourel, Aaron (1970) "The acquisition of social structure: toward a developmental sociology of language." Pp. 136–68 in Jack D. Douglas (ed.), *Understanding Everyday Life*. Chicago: Aldine.

Collins, Randall (1979) *The Credential Society*. New York: Academic Press.

Coser, Lewis, Charles Kadushin and Walter W. Powell (1982) *Books: The Culture and Commerce of Book Publishing*. New York: Basic Books.

Cyert, Richard M. and James G. March (1963) *A Behavioral Theory of the Firm*. Englewood Cliffs, NJ: Prentice-Hall.

DiMaggio, Paul (1982) "The structure of organizational fields: an analytical approach and policy implications." Paper prepared for SUNY-Albany Conference on Organizational Theory and Public Policy. April 1 and 2.

Fennell, Mary L. (1980) "The effects of environmental characteristics on the structure of hospital clusters." *Administrative Science Quarterly* 25:484–510.

Freeman, John H. (1982) "Organizational life cycles and natural selection processes." Pp. 1–32 in Barry Staw and Larry Cummings (eds.), *Research in Organizational Behavior*. Vol. 4. Greenwich, CT: JAI Press.

Giddens, Anthony (1979) *Central Problems in Social Theory: Action, Structure, and Contradiction in Social Analysis*. Berkeley: University of California Press.

Granovetter, Mark (1978) "Threshold models of collective behavior." *American Journal of Sociology* 83:1420–43.

Hall, Richard (1968) "Professionalization and bureaucratization." *American Sociological Review* 33:92–104.

Hannan, Michael T. and John H. Freeman (1977) "The population ecology of organizations." *American Journal of Sociology* 82:929–64.

Hawley, Amos (1968) "Human ecology." Pp. 328–37 in David L. Sills (ed.), *International Encyclopedia of the Social Sciences*. New York: Macmillan.

Hirsch, Paul and Thomas Whisler (1982) "The view from the boardroom." Paper presented at Academy of Management Meetings, New York, NY.

Kanter, Rosabeth Moss (1972) *Commitment and Community*. Cambridge, MA: Harvard University Press.

——(1977) *Men and Women of the Corporation*. New York: Basic Books.

Katz, Michael B. (1975) *Class, Bureaucracy, and Schools: The Illusion of Educational Change in America*. New York: Praeger.

Kimberley, John (1980) "Initiation, Innovation, and Institutionalization in the Creation Process." Pp. 18–43 in John Kimberley and Robert B. Miles (eds.), *The Organizational Life Cycle*. San Francisco: Jossey-Bass.

Larson, Magali Sarfatti (1977) *The Rise of Professionalism: A Sociological Analysis*. Berkeley: University of California Press.

Laumann, Edward O., Joseph Galaskiewicz and Peter Marsden (1978) "Community structure as interorganizational linkage." *Annual Review of Sociology* 4:455–84.

Lee, M. L. (1971) "A conspicuous production theory of hospital behavior." *Southern Economic Journal* 38:48–58.

March, James G. and Michael Cohen (1974) *Leadership and Ambiguity: The American College President*. New York: McGraw-Hill.

March, James C. and James G. March (1977) "Almost random careers: the Wisconsin school superintendency, 1940–72." *Administrative Science Quarterly* 22:378–409.

March, James G. and Johan P. Olsen (1976) *Ambiguity and Choice in Organizations*. Bergen, Norway: Universitetsforlaget.

Meyer, John W. (1979) "The impact of the centralization of educational funding and control on state and local organizational governance." Stanford, CA: Institute for Research on Educational Finance and Governance, Stanford University, Program Report No. 79–B20.

Meyer, John W. and Michael Hannan (1979) *National Development and the World System: Educational, Economic, and Political Change*. Chicago: University of Chicago Press.

Meyer, John W. and Brian Rowan (1977) "Institutionalized organizations: formal structure as myth and ceremony." *American Journal of Sociology* 83:340–63.

Meyer, John W., W. Richard Scott and Terence C. Deal (1981) "Institutional and technical sources of organizational structure explaining the structure of educational organizations." In Herman Stein (ed.), *Organizations and the Human Services: Cross-Disciplinary Reflections*. Philadelphia, PA: Temple University Press.

Meyer, Marshall (1981) "Persistence and change in bureaucratic structures." Paper presented at the annual meeting of the American Sociological Association, Toronto, Canada.

Milofsky, Carl (1981) "Structure and process in community self-help organizations." New Haven: Yale Program on Non-Profit Organizations, Working Paper No. 17.

Ouchi, William G. (1980) "Markets, bureaucracies, and clans." *Administrative Science Quarterly* 25:129–41.

Perrow, Charles (1974) "Is business really changing?" *Organizational Dynamics* Summer: 31–44.

Pfeffer, Jeffrey and Gerald Salancik (1978) *The External Control of Organizations: A Resource Dependence Perspective*. New York: Harper & Row.

Powell, Walter W. (Forthcoming) "The Political Economy of Public Television." New Haven: Program on Non-Profit Organizations.

——(1983) "New solutions to perennial problems of bookselling: whither the local bookstore?" *Daedalus*: Winter.

Ritti, R. R. and Fred H. Goldner (1979) "Professional pluralism in an industrial organization." *Management Science* 16:233–46.

Rothman, Mitchell (1980) "The evolution of forms of legal education." Unpublished manuscript. Department of Sociology, Yale University, New Haven, CT.

Rothschild-Whitt, Joyce (1979) "The collectivist organization: an alternative to rational bureaucratic models." *American Sociological Review* 44:509–27.

Schelling, Thomas (1978) *Micromotives and Macrobehavior*. New York: W. W. Norton.

Sedlak, Michael W. (1981) "Youth policy and young women, 1950–1972: the impact of private-sector programs for pregnant and wayward girls on public policy." Paper presented at National Institute for Education Youth Policy Research Conference, Washington, D.C.

Selznick, Philip (1957) *Leadership in Administration*. New York: Harper & Row.

Starr, Paul (1980) "Medical care and the boundaries of capitalist organization." Unpublished manuscript. Program on Non-Profit Organizations, Yale University, New Haven, CT.

Swidler, Ann (1979) *Organization Without Authority: Dilemmas of Social Control of Free Schools*. Cambridge: Harvard University Press.

Thompson, James (1967) *Organizations in Action*. New York: McGraw-Hill.

Tyack, David (1974) *The One Best System: A History of American Urban Education*. Cambridge, MA: Harvard University Press.

Useem, Michael (1979) "The social organization of the American business elite and participation of corporation directors in the governance of American institutions." *American Sociological Review* 44:553–72.

Weber, Max (1952) *The Protestant Ethic and the Spirit of Capitalism*. New York: Scribner.

——(1968) *Economy and Society: An Outline of Interpretive Sociology*. Three volumes. New York: Bedminster.

Westney, D. Eleanor (Forthcoming) *Organizational Development and Social Change in Meiji, Japan*.

White, Harrison C., Scott A. Boorman and Ronald L. Breiger (1976) "Social structure from multiple networks. I. Blockmodels of roles and positions." *American Journal of Sociology* 81:730–80.

Williamson, Oliver E. (1975) *Markets and Hierarchies, Analysis and Antitrust Implications: A Study of the Economics of Internal Organization*. New York: Free Press.

——(1979) "Transaction-cost economics: the governance of contractual relations." *Journal of Law and Economics* 22:233–61.

Woodward, John (1965) *Industrial Organization, Theory and Practice*. London: Oxford University Press.

Zucker, Lynne G. and Pamela S. Tolbert (1981) "Institutional sources of change in the formal structure of organizations: the diffusion of civil service reform, 1880–1935." Paper presented at American Sociological Association annual meeting, Toronto, Canada.

Part IV

The Sociological Theory of Michel Foucault

INTRODUCTION TO PART IV

The work of Michel Foucault (1926–84) has had a tremendous impact on a number of disciplines. Although not a sociologist by training, his work addresses deeply sociological issues and it has had significant influence on the work of other sociologists. Foucault did not attempt to construct a systematic theory. Rather, as Cousins and Hussain put it, one encounters certain "habitual features of Foucault's analyses."[1] These features are both substantive and methodological in nature. Substantively, Foucault explores issues of power through his historical examination of different "discourses" such as madness, medicine, prisons, and sexuality. Methodologically, Foucault creatively employs archaeology and genealogy as analytical tools. While some scholars consider Foucault to be a neo-structuralist,[2] he has been most closely associated with the intellectual movement known as "post-structuralism." Others (most notably, Dreyfus and Rabinow, 1983) oppose such categorizations of Foucault's work. They suggest that he employs a unique interpretation of different intellectual traditions.

Foucault's Life and Intellectual Context

Foucault was born in Poitiers, France. He received his early education at local state schools, and then transferred to a Catholic school where he attained his *baccalauréat* with distinction. Foucault went on to study philosophy and psychology at the prestigious École Normale Supérieure, and also obtained a diploma in psychopathology. At the École, Foucault became acquainted with Louis Althusser, who introduced him to Marxist structuralism. Foucault later also acknowledged an intellectual debt to Jean Hyppolite, whose work focused on Hegel's philosophy; to Georges Canguilhem, an historian of ideas; and to Georges Dumezil, whose interests included the history of myth, art, and religion. After receiving his diploma, Foucault worked as an intern at a mental hospital in Paris and taught courses in psychopathology at the Sorbonne. In 1954, Foucault left France to teach French at Uppsala University in Sweden, then at the University of Warsaw and the University of Hamburg. During this period, Foucault began a study of the history of psychiatry. This resulted in the *Histoire de la folie à l'âge classique* (later translated in abridged form as *Madness and Civilization*), which was accepted as his doctoral thesis in the history of science in 1960.

Foucault returned to France the same year to head the philosophy department at the University of Clermont-Ferrand. While the *Histoire de la folie à l'âge classique* and his next book, *The Birth of the Clinic*, did not initially receive significant interest, the publication of *The Order of Things* in 1966 was enthusiastically received, as was *The Archaeology of Knowledge* in 1969. After a brief tenure at the University of Vincennes and a teaching stint in Tunisia, Foucault was appointed professor of the History of Systems of Thought at the prestigious Collège de France in 1970.

Following the tumultuous political climate of 1968, Foucault's interests took a more political turn. Along with other intellectuals, he participated in committees against racism, and for patients' rights and reforms in the field of health. The most prominent of these committees was the *Groupe d'Information sur les Prisons* (GIP), whose aim was to provide a forum for prisoners to address their concerns during a period of prison unrest. Foucault's overall political turn manifested itself in his work in a focus on the institutional representation of power. This theme is explored in some of his major works from this period, such as *Discipline and Punish* and *The History of Sexuality*. In the course of his intellectual career, Foucault also pursued his literary interest through works on writers and artists such as Raymond Roussel, Georges Bataille, Maurice Blanchot, Hölderlin, and René Magritte. Foucault died in 1984.

Before specifically addressing his work, it may be useful to situate Foucault within the political and intellectual climate in France. Intellectuals in post-war France were greatly persuaded by the subject-centered theories of existential phenomenology in understanding the events surrounding the Second World War. As a student at the École, Foucault was particularly familiar with the ideas of Sartre and Merleau-Ponty. During this period, a large number of intellectuals also turned to the Communist Party in their desire to become politically engaged. A number of political events beginning in the mid-1950s, however, led to a reversal of this political trend. O'Farrell (1989) notes that Communist Party support of the center-left government's "pacification" measures in Algeria, the condemnation of the Stalinist regime by the Khrushchev report, and the suppression of the Hungarian Revolution led to disillusionment and depoliticization among intellectuals. It also resulted in a turn away from literature and the humanities toward more "scientific" disciplines, such as epistemology, ethnology, psychoanalysis, linguistics, and the social sciences. This period was also marked by the rise of structuralism.

In their attempt to "decenter" the subject, structuralists wanted to study human activity scientifically by looking for basic elements of people's behavior and the rules or laws by which they are combined. Structuralism owed an intellectual debt to the work of Durkheim (see *Classical Sociological Theory*) and to the linguist Ferdinand de Saussure. Saussure proposed that language must be considered as a self-contained relational structure in which words have linguistic value only in relation to other words, thus shifting the emphasis from the signified to the signifier. Inspired by Saussure, the anthropologist Claude Lévi-Strauss applied structural linguistics to the study of society. In particular, he studied the structural aspects of kinship systems and mythological representations. In his commitment to scientism, Lévi-Strauss shifted the focus away from human subjectivity and epistemology to the formal study of social and cultural life as symbolic systems. For instance, in his analysis of myth in *The Raw and the Cooked*, Lévi-Strauss claimed to reveal the underlying structure of the cultural system in the basic oppositions between the raw, the cooked, and the rotten.

Using a structuralist approach to analyze everyday life, Roland Barthes analyzed ordinary experiences, such as films, advertisements, and propaganda to reveal the semiological structure underlying communications in advanced capitalist societies. Although most structuralists tended to identify themselves as Marxists, it was Louis Althusser (among others, such as Godelier and Sebag) who provided a structuralist reading of Marx. Rejecting the focus on the subject and on historicism in humanist Marxism, structural Marxists sought to redefine dialectical materialism and historical materialism. In doing so, Althusser dismissed empiricism as a form of ideology because it conflated theoretical objects with real objects. In other words, he argued that the "real" world exists only as a product of the ideological representations we make of it. Taking inspiration from the later Marx, Althusser shifted attention instead to a more "scientific" analysis of the structures of society.

Structuralism began to lose favor in France in the 1980s. Post-structuralism arose out of, and in response to, structuralism. Incorporating Nietzschean and psychoanalytic concepts, post-structuralists emphasize the importance of language. For instance, Derrida, whose name has been closely associated with post-structuralism, argues that all claims of originary speech are misleading. Opposing a systemic approach to language, Derrida suggests instead that it is *"différance"* that marks writing. In other words, this term suggest both a differing and deferring of the presence of meaning for language. Like structuralists in general, post-structuralists seek to decenter the subject, but they propose that subjects are created by the discourse in which they are embedded.

Foucault's work has been read in light of this intellectual context in France. He has, for instance, been labeled both a structuralist and a post-structuralist. However, as Dreyfus and Rabinow point out, Foucault constantly sought to move beyond the existing alternatives available for the study of human beings.[3] He avoided the structuralist analysis which eliminates notions of meaning altogether; resisted the phenomenological project of tracing all meaning back to the autonomous, transcendental subject; and finally avoided the hermeneutic unearthing of the deeper meaning that social actors are only dimly aware of. Dreyfus and Rabinow suggest that Foucault managed to "criticize and utilize" the dominant methods available during his time.[4]

Foucault's Work

In his work, Foucault sought to conduct a "genealogy of the modern subject as a historical and cultural reality."[5] His first major work was on madness. In *Madness and Civilization*, Foucault examines the historical conditions of the confinement and exclusion of different groups of people: lepers in the Middle Ages; the mad during the Renaissance; and the poor, the mad, and the homeless during the Classical Age. This story of spatial exclusion is one of the classification of different categories of people as a technology of power. Providing a history of the birth of the asylum at the end of the eighteenth century, Foucault traces the historical conditions of the emergence of modern medical, psychiatric, and human sciences. He unravels the Enlightenment privileging of reason to reveal the connection between power and knowledge. In his next book, *The Birth of the Clinic*, Foucault conducts an archaeology of medicine. He reinterprets the standard explanation provided by the medical profession about its shift in the eighteenth century from superstition to objective truth about the body and disease. In a structuralist mode, Foucault demonstrates how the medical theories of the Classical Age were as much governed by structural "codes of knowledge" as are those of modern medicine. In this book, Foucault traces how the gaze of modern medicine has increasingly come to be directed on the constitution of "man" as an object of knowledge.

Foucault next shifted his attention from an archaeology of institutions to that of discourse. Specifically, he extended his investigation to the human sciences. In *The Order of Things*, Foucault attempts to study the structure of the discourses of various disciplines regarding society, individuals, and language. He identifies the epistemic systems (or relations between the sciences) that underlie three major epochs in Western thought: the Renaissance, the Classical Age, and Modernity. Whereas there was no place for the representation of the activity of human beings in the classical episteme, Modernity is characterized as the Age of Man, in which "man" is the subject and object of his own knowledge. In *The Archaeology of Knowledge*, Foucault presents his method in the analysis of human sciences in greater detail. In the analysis of knowledge, he specifies the difference between his conceptual framework and those of conventional historical accounts in the history of ideas and the history of science. Discounting the standard conceptualization of history in terms of continuity, development and progress, Foucault emphasizes discontinuity, rupture, and transformation in the analysis of discursive formations.

In the 1970s, Foucault's interest shifted from discourse to the problem of power, from archaeology to genealogy. In his later works, *Discipline and Punish* and *The History of Sexuality*, Foucault explores the relations between power, knowledge, and the body in modern society. In *Discipline and Punish*, he conducts a genealogy of modern disciplinary technology. He analyzes the transformation of punishment from torture in medieval times to the representation of crime in the Classical Age to the role of the prison and a normative social science in producing the modern individual. Power is increasingly exercised in the form of surveillance by a large array of apparatuses; through the classification and documentation of individuals; and the turning of subjects into objects of knowledge. Foucault extended his analysis of power relations to the area of sexuality in *The History of Sexuality*. His argument is that, during the eighteenth and nineteenth centuries, sexuality became an object of scientific investigation and social concern. This was the result of a spread of bio-power, which was deployed in the case of sexuality through the practice of the confessional. In his writings on power in general, Foucault makes the case that power is not restricted to political institutions. Rather, it is multidirectional, operating from above and from below.

Foucault's Legacy

Until English translations of Foucault's work began to appear in the 1970s, he was little known in the English-speaking world. By the time of his death in 1984, however, Foucault's influence was so great that his death was reported in newspapers around the world. This influence is also evident in the large body of literature that has been produced on Foucault's work during his life and since. In particular, as O'Farrell notes, many English-speaking critics have expressed an overwhelming interest in classifying Foucault's work.[6] In particular, these commentators have addressed the question of whether Foucault ought to be considered a philosopher or a historian. This elusiveness is probably the reason why some have criticized him for not doing good philosophy and others for not doing good history. Cousins and Hussain suggest that the difference between routine historiography and Foucault's work may lie in his employment of "case-history," which relies more on intelligibility rather than the exhaustiveness of standard historiography.[7] Notwithstanding these criticisms, Foucault's work has inspired a new way of doing history. Among his other intellectual contributions, Foucault has legitimated the study of the body as a subject of inquiry.

Notes

1   Cousins and Hussain (1984: 1).
2   Wuthnow et al. (1984).
3   Dreyfus and Rabinow (1983: xiiiff).
4   Ibid. (xxvii).
5   Cited in Smart (1985: 18).
6   O'Farrell (1989: 20–30).
7   Cousins and Hussain (1984: 3).

Select Bibliography

Cousins, Mark and Athar Hussain. 1984. *Michel Foucault*. New York, NY: St. Martin's Press. (A solid introduction for the general reader.)

Dreyfus, Hubert and Paul Rabinow. 1983. *Beyond Structuralism and Hermeneutics*, 2nd edition. Chicago, IL: University of Chicago Press. (An excellent interpretation of Foucault's work by two of the leading scholars on Foucault.)

Habermas, Jürgen. 1981. "Modernity versus Postmodernity." *New German Critique* 22: 3–14. (An important essay on Foucault's treatment of the Enlightenment by a leading critical theorist.)

Hoy, David (ed.). 1986. *Foucault: A Critical Reader*. Oxford: Basil Blackwell. (A collection of serious essays by leading theorists.)

Lemert, Charles and Garth Gillan. 1982. *Michel Foucault: Social Theory and Transgressions*. New York: Columbia University Press. (A useful source for a sociological discussion of the major themes in Foucault's work.)

Lemert, Charles. 1990. "The Uses of French Structuralisms in Sociology." In George Ritzer (ed.), *Frontiers of Social Theory: The New Syntheses*. New York: Columbia University Press. (A good essay for the intellectual context of Foucault's writings.)

O'Farrell, Clare. 1989. *Foucault: Historian or Philosopher?* New York: St. Martin's Press. (A solid introduction to Foucault's work.)

Poster, Mark. 1975. *Existential Marxism in Postwar France: From Sartre to Althusser*. Princeton, NJ: Princeton University Press. (An excellent intellectual history of post-war France.)

Poster, Mark. 1984. *Foucault, Marxism and History*. Cambridge: Polity. (An analysis of Foucault's work in relation to Marxist theory.)

Rabinow, Paul. 1984. "Introduction." In Paul Rabinow (ed.), *The Foucault Reader*. New York: Pantheon Books. (A good essay on the major themes underlying Foucault's work.)

Sheridan, Alan. 1980. *Michel Foucault: The Will to Truth*. London: Tavistock Publications. (An authoritative commentary on Foucault's work by a leading scholar.)

Shumway, David. 1989. *Michel Foucault*. Boston, MA: Twayne Publishers. (A helpful survey of Foucault's major writings and themes.)

Smart, Barry. 1983. *Foucault, Marxism, and Critique*. London: Routledge & Kegan Paul. (A discussion of Foucault in relation to Marxist theory.)

Smart, Barry. 1985. *Michel Foucault*. London: Tavistock Publications. (A concise summary of Foucault's major works.)

Wuthnow, Robert et al. 1984. *Cultural Analysis: The Work of Peter Berger, Mary Douglas, Michel Foucault, and Jürgen Habermas*. London: Routledge & Kegan Paul. (A discussion of Foucault as a neo-structuralist from a sociological perspective.)

13 The Birth of the Clinic

Michel Foucault

Compared with the medicine of species, the notions of constitution, endemic disease, and epidemic were of only marginal importance in the eighteenth century.

But we must return to Sydenham and to the ambiguity of what he has to teach us: in addition to being the initiator of classificatory thought, he defined what might be a historical and geographical consciousness of disease. Sydenham's 'constitution' is not an autonomous nature, but the complex – a kind of temporary node – of a set of natural events: qualities of soil, climate, seasons, rain, drought, centres of pestilence, famine; and when all these factors do not account for phenomena, there remains no clear species in the garden of disease, but an obscure nucleus, buried in the earth: 'Variae sunt semper annorum constitutiones quae neque calori neque frigori non sicco humidove ortum suum debent, sed ab occulta potius inexplicabili quadam alternatione in ipsis terrae visceribus pendent.'[1] The constitutions hardly have symptoms of their own; they define, by displacements of accent, unexpected groups of signs, phenomena of a more intense or weaker kind: fevers may be violent and dry, catarrhs and serous discharges more frequent; during a long, hot summer, visceral congestion is more common and more tenacious than usual. Of London, between July and September 1661, Sydenham says: 'Aegri paroxysmus atrocior, lingua magis nigra siccaque, extra paroxysmum aporexia obscurio, virium et appetitus prostratio major, major item ad paroxysmum proclinitas, omnia summatim accidentia immaniora, ipseque morbus quam pro more Febrium intermittentium funestior.'[2] The constitution is not related to a specific absolute of which it is the more or less modified manifestation: it is perceived solely in the relativity of differences – by a gaze that is in some sense diacritical.

Not every constitution is an epidemic; but an epidemic is a finer-grained constitution, with more constant, more homogeneous phenomena. There has been, and still is, a great deal of discussion as to whether the doctors of the eighteenth century had grasped its contagious character, and whether they had posed the problem of the agent of their transmission. An idle question, and one that remains alien, or at least derivative, in relation to the fundamental structure: an epidemic is more than a particular form of a disease. In the eighteenth century, it was an autonomous, coherent, and adequate evaluation of disease: 'One calls epidemic diseases all those that attack, at the same time and with unalterable characteristics, a large number of persons.'[3] There is no difference in nature or species, therefore, between an individual disease and an epidemic phenomenon; it is enough that a sporadic malady be reproduced a number of times for it to constitute an epidemic. It is a

Originally translated from the French by A. M. Sheridan Smith.

purely mathematical problem of the threshold: the sporadic disease is merely a submarginal epidemic. The perception involved is no longer essential and ordinal, as in the medicine of species, but quantitative and cardinal.

The basis of this perception is not a specific type, but a nucleus of circumstances. The basis of an epidemic is not pestilence or catarrh: it is Marseilles in 1721, or Bicêtre in 1780; it is Rouen in 1769, where 'there occurred, during the summer, an epidemic among the children of the nature of bilious catarrhal and putrid fevers complicated by miliaria, and ardent bilious fevers during the autumn. This constitution degenerated into putrid biliousness towards the end of that season and during the winter of 1769 and 1770.'[4] The usual pathological forms are mentioned, but as factors in a complex set of intersections in which their role is analogous to that of the symptom in relation to the disease. The essential basis is determined by the time, the place, the 'fresh, sharp, subtle, penetrating' air of Nîmes in winter[5] or the sticky, thick, putrid air of Paris during a long, heavy summer.[6]

The regularity of symptoms does not allow the wisdom of a natural order to show through as in filigree; it treats only the constancy of causes, the obstinacy of a factor whose total, unceasingly repeated pressure determines a preferential form of disease. It may be a cause that survives in time – being responsible, for example, for plica in Poland and scrofula in Spain – in which cases the term endemic will be more readily used; or it may be causes that 'suddenly attack a large number of people in one place, without distinction of age, sex, or temperament. They appear to proceed from a single cause, but as these diseases reign only for a limited period, this cause may be regarded as purely accidental':[7] this is so in the case of smallpox, malign fever, or dysentery, which are epidemics in the true sense. It is hardly surprising that despite the great diversity, in disposition and age, of the people affected, the disease shows the same symptoms in all: this is because dryness or humidity, heat or cold, when prolonged, ensure the domination of one of our constitutive principles: alkalis, salts, phlogiston; 'We are then exposed to the accidents occasioned by this principle, and these accidents must be the same for different subjects.'[8]

The analysis of an epidemic does not involve the recognition of the general form of the disease, by placing it in the abstract space of nosology, but the rediscovery, beneath the general signs, of the particular process, which varies according to circumstances from one epidemic to another, and which weaves from the cause to the morbid form a web common to all the sick, but peculiar to this moment in time and this place in space; in Paris, in 1785, there was an epidemic of quartan fever and putrid synochus, but the essence of the epidemic was that 'the bile had dried up in its passages and turned into melancholy, the blood had become impoverished, thickened, and sticky as it were, the organs of the lower part of the abdomen had swollen and become the causes or centres of obstruction',[9] or a sort of over-all singularity, an individual with many similar heads, whose features are manifested only once in time and space. The specific disease is always more or less repeated, the epidemic is never quite repeated.

In this perceptual structure, the problem of contagion is of little importance. Transmission from one individual to another is never the essence of an epidemic; it may, in the form of 'miasma' or 'leaven', which can be communicated through water, food, contact, the wind, or confined air, constitute one of the causes of the epidemic, either direct or primary (when it is the sole, operant cause), or secondary (when, in a town or hospital, the miasma is the product of an epidemic disease caused by some other factor). But contagion is only one modality of the brute fact of the epidemic. It was readily admitted that malign diseases, like plague, had a transmittable cause; it was more difficult to recognize the same fact in the case of the simple, epidemic diseases (whooping cough, measles, scarlet fever, bilious diarrhoea, intermittent fever).[10]

Whether contagious or not, an epidemic has a sort of historical individuality, hence the need to employ a complex method of observation when dealing with it. Being a collective phenomenon, it requires a multiple gaze; a unique process, it must be described in terms of its special, accidental, unexpected qualities. The event must be described in detail, but it must also be described in accordance with the coherence implied by multi-perception: being an imprecise form of knowledge, insecurely based while ever partial, incapable of acceding of itself to the essential or fundamental, it finds its own range only in the cross-checking of viewpoints, in repeated, corrected information, which finally circumscribes, where gazes meet, the individual, unique nucleus of these collective phenomena. At the end of the eighteenth century, this form of experience was being institutionalized. In each subdelegation a physician and several surgeons were appointed by the *Intendant* (provincial administrator) to study those epidemics that might break out in their canton; they were in constant correspondence with the chief physician of the *généralité* (treasury subdivision of old France) concerning 'both the reigning disease and the medicinal topography of their canton', and when four or five people succumbed to the same disease, the syndic had to notify the subdelegate, who sent the physician to prescribe the treatment to be administered daily by the surgeons; in more serious cases, the physician of the *généralité* visited the scene of the outbreak himself.[11]

But this experience could achieve full significance only if it was supplemented by constant, constricting intervention. A medicine of epidemics could exist only if supplemented by a police: to supervise the location of mines and cemeteries, to get as many corpses as possible cremated instead of buried, to control the sale of bread, wine, and meat,[12] to supervise the running of abattoirs and dye works, and to prohibit unhealthy housing; after a detailed study of the whole country, a set of health regulations would have to be drawn up that would be read 'at service or mass, every Sunday and holy day', and which would explain how one should feed and dress oneself, how to avoid illness, and how to prevent or cure prevailing diseases: 'These precepts would become like prayers that even the most ignorant, even children, would learn to recite.'[13] Lastly, a body of health inspectors would have to be set up that could be 'sent out to the provinces, placing each one in charge of a particular department'; there he would collect information about the various domains related to medicine, as well as about physics, chemistry, natural history, topography, and astronomy, would prescribe the measures to be taken, and would supervise the work of the doctor. 'It is to be hoped that the state would provide for these physicians and spare them the expense that an inclination to make useful discoveries entails.'[14]

A medicine of epidemics is opposed at every point to a medicine of classes, just as the collective perception of a phenomenon that is widespread but unique and unrepeatable may be opposed to the individual perception of the identity of an essence as constantly revealed in the multiplicity of phenomena. The analysis of a series in the one case, the decipherment of a type in the other; the integration of time in the case of epidemics, the determination of hierarchical place in the case of the species; the attribution of a causality – the search for an essential coherence, the subtle perception of a complex historical and geographical space – the demarcation of a homogeneous surface in which analogies can be read. And yet, in the final analysis, when it is a question of these tertiary figures that must distribute the disease, medical experience and the doctor's supervision of social structures, the pathology of epidemics and that of the species are confronted by the same requirements: the definition of a political status for medicine and the constitution, at state level, of a medical consciousness whose constant task would be to provide information, supervision, and constraint, all of which 'relate as much to the police as to the field of medicine proper.'[15]

This was the origin of the Société Royale de Médecine and its insuperable conflict with the Faculté (the university authorities). In 1776, the government decided to set up at Versailles a society for the study of the epidemic and epizootic phenomena that had increased considerably in recent years. The precise occasion was a disease affecting livestock that had broken out in southeastern France, and which had forced the Contrôleur Général des Finances to order the killing off of all suspect animals; this led to a fairly serious disruption of the regional economy. The decree of 29 April 1776 declares in its preamble that epidemics

> are deadly and destructive at the outset only because their character, being little known, leaves the doctor in uncertainty as to the choice of treatment that should be applied; and this uncertainty arises because so little has been done to study the different treatments used, or to describe the symptoms of the different epidemics and the curative methods that have been most successful.

The commission was to have a three-fold role: investigation, by keeping itself informed of the various epidemic movements; elaboration, by comparing facts, recording the treatments used, and organizing experiments; and supervision and prescription, by informing the medical practitioners of the methods that seem to be most suitable to a given situation. It was to be made up of eight doctors: a *directeur*, entrusted with 'the correspondence concerning epidemic and epizootic diseases' (de Lasson), a *commissaire général*, who would co-ordinate the work of the provincial doctors (Vicq d'Azyr), and six doctors of the Faculté, who would devote themselves to work on these same subjects. The Contrôleur des Finances could send them out to the provinces to make inquiries and ask them for reports. Lastly, Vicq d'Azyr was to give a course in human and comparative anatomy to the other members of the commission, the doctors of the Faculté, and 'those students who showed themselves to be worthy of it.'[16] Thus a double check was set up: that of the political authorities over the practice of medicine and that of a privileged medical body over the practitioners as a whole.

The conflict with the Faculté broke out at once. In contemporary eyes, it was a collision of two institutions, one modern and politically supported, the other archaic and inward-looking. A partisan of the Faculté described their opposition thus:

The one ancient, respectable for all manner of reasons and principally in the eyes of the members of the society most of whom have been trained by it; the other, a modern institution whose members have preferred to associate with ministers of the Crown rather than with their own institutions, who have deserted the Assemblies of the Faculté to which the public good and their oaths should have kept them attached for a career of intrigue.[17]

For three months, the Faculté 'went on strike' in protest: it refused to exercise its functions, and its members refused to consult with the members of the society. But the outcome was determined in advance because the Conseil supported the new committee. By 1778, the letters patent confirming its transformation into the Société Royale de Médecine had been registered, and the Faculté had been forbidden 'to employ any kind of defence in this affair'. The Société received an income of 40,000 francs raised from mineral waters, while the Faculté received hardly 2,000 francs.[18] But, above all, its role was constantly being enlarged: as a control body for epidemics, it gradually became a point for the centralization of knowledge, an authority for the registration and judgement of all medical activity. At the beginning of the Revolution, the Finance Committee of the National Assembly was to justify its status thus: 'The object of this society is to link French medicine with foreign medicine by means of a useful correspondence; to gather together isolated observations, to preserve them and to compare them; and, above all, to research into the causes of common diseases, to forecast their occurrence, and to discover the most effective remedies for them.'[19] The Société no longer consisted solely of doctors who devoted themselves to the study of collective pathological phenomena; it had become the official organ of a *collective consciousness* of pathological phenomena, a consciousness that operated at both the level of experience and the level of knowledge, in the international as well as the national space.

Political events had a certain novelty value here, as far as basic structures were concerned. A new type of experience was created whose general lines, formed around the years 1775–80, were to extend far in time and bring with them, during the Revolution and right up to the Consulate, many projects of reform. No doubt very few of these plans were ever implemented. And yet the form of medical perception that they involve is one of the constituent elements of clinical experience.

There was a new style of totalization. The treatises of the eighteenth century, Institutions, Aphorisms, Nosologies, enclosed medical knowledge within a defined space: the table drawn up may not have been complete in every detail, and may have contained gaps here and there owing to ignorance, but in its general form it was exhaustive and closed. It was now replaced by open, infinitely extendable tables. Hautesierck had already provided an example of such a table, when, at Choiseul's request, he proposed a plan of collective work for military physicians and surgeons, comprising four parallel, unlimited series: the study of topographies (location, terrain, water, air, society, the temperaments of the inhabitants), meteorological observations (pressure, temperature, winds), an analysis of epidemics and common diseases, and a description of extraordinary cases.[20] The theme of the encyclopaedia is replaced by that of constant, constantly revised information, where it is a question, rather, of totalizing events and their determination than of enclosing knowledge in a systematic form: 'It is so true that there exists a chain linking, throughout the universe, on earth and in man, all beings, all bodies, all affections; a chain whose subtlety eludes the superficial gaze of the meticulous experimenter and the writer of cold dissertations, but is revealed to the truly observant genius.'[21] At the beginning of the Revolution, Cantin proposed that this work of information should be undertaken in each department by a commission elected from among the doctors;[22] Mathieu Géraud demanded the creation in every large town of a 'government health centre' and in Paris of a 'health court', sitting beside the National Assembly, centralizing information, conveying it from one part of the country to another, discussing questions that still remain obscure, and indicating what research needs to be carried out.[23]

What now constituted the unity of the medical gaze was not the circle of knowledge in which it was achieved but that open, infinite, moving totality, ceaselessly displaced and enriched by time, whose course it began but would never be able to stop – by this time a clinical recording of the infinite, variable series of events. But its support was not the perception of the patient in his singularity, but a collective consciousness, with all the information that intersects in it, growing in a complex, ever-proliferating way until it finally achieves the dimensions of a history, a geography, a state.

In the eighteenth century, the fundamental act of medical knowledge was the drawing up of a 'map' (repérage): a symptom was situated within a disease, a disease in a specific ensemble, and this ensemble in a general plan of the pathological world. In the experience that was being constituted towards the end of the century, it was a question of 'carving up' the field by means of the interplay of series, which, in intersecting one another, made it possible to reconstitute the chain referred to by Menuret. Each day Razoux made meteorological and climatic observations, which he then compared with a nosological analysis of patients under observation and with the evolution, crises, and outcome of the diseases.[24] A system of coincidences then appeared that indicated a causal connexion and also suggested kinships or new links between diseases. 'If anything is able to improve our art,' Sauvages himself wrote to Razoux, 'it is work of this kind carried out over a period of fifty years, by a team of thirty doctors as meticulous and industrious as yourself. . . . I will do all in my power to have one of our doctors carry out the same observations in our Hôtel-Dieu.'[25] What defines the act of medical knowledge in its concrete form is not, therefore, the encounter between doctor and patient, nor is it the confrontation of a body of knowledge and a perception; it is the systematic intersection of two series of information, each homogeneous but alien to each other – two series that embrace an infinite set of separate events, but whose intersection reveals, in its isolable dependence, the individual fact. A sagittal figure of knowledge.

In this movement, medical consciousness is duplicated: it lives at an immediate level, in the order of 'savage' observations; but it is taken up again at a higher level, where it recognizes the constitutions, confronts them, and, turning back upon the spontaneous forms, dogmatically pronounces its judgement and its knowledge. It becomes centralized in structure. At the institutional level this is apparent in the Société Royale de Médecine. And at the beginning of the Revolution there were innumerable projects that schematized this dual and necessary authority (instance) of medical knowledge, with its ceaseless movement between these two levels, at the same time maintaining and traversing the distance between them. Mathieu Géraud proposed the setting up of a Health Court (*Tribunal de Salubrité*) where a prosecutor would denounce 'any person who, without having given proof of his ability, exercises upon another, or upon an animal that does not belong to him, anything pertaining to the direct or indirect application of the art of health';[26] the decisions of this court concerning professional abuses, inadequacies, and imperfections should constitute the jurisprudence of the medical state. In addition to a Judiciary, there should be an Executive that would exercise a policing function over all aspects of health (*la haute et grande police sur toutes les branches de la salubrité*). It would prescribe what books were to be read and what new works were to be written; it would indicate, on the basis of the information received, what treatment was to be administered for prevalent diseases; it would publish whatever was required by an enlightened medical practice, whether the results of inquiries carried out under its own supervision or foreign works. Following an autonomous movement, the medical gaze circulates within an enclosed space in which it is controlled only by itself; in sovereign fashion, it distributes to daily experience the knowledge that it has borrowed from afar and of which it has made itself both the point of concentration and the centre of diffusion.

In that experience, medical space can coincide with social space, or, rather, traverse it and wholly penetrate it. One began to conceive of a generalized presence of doctors whose intersecting gazes form a network and exercise at every point in space, and at every moment in time, a constant, mobile, differentiated supervision. The problem of the settling of doctors in the countryside was raised;[27] there were requests for a statistical supervision of health based on the registration of births and deaths (which would have to mention the disease from which the individual suffered, his mode of life, and the cause of his death, thus constituting a pathological record); there were demands that the reasons for exemption from military service on medical grounds should be given in detail by the recruiting board; in fact, that a medical topography of each department should be drawn up, 'with detailed observations concerning the region, housing, people, principal interests, dress, atmospheric constitution, produce of the ground, time of their perfect maturity and their harvesting, and physical and moral education of the inhabitants of the area'.[28] And since the question of the settling of doctors was not enough, the consciousness of each individual must be alerted; every citizen must be informed of what medical knowledge is necessary and possible. And each practitioner must supplement his supervisory activity with teaching, for the best way of avoiding the propagation of disease is to spread medical knowledge.[29] The locus in which knowledge is formed is no longer the pathological garden where God distributed the species, but a generalized medical consciousness, diffused in space and time, open and mobile, linked to each individual existence, as well as to the collective life of the nation, ever alert to the endless domain in which illness betrays, in its various aspects, its great, solid form.

The years preceding and immediately following the Revolution saw the birth of two great myths with opposing themes and polarities: the myth of a nationalized medical profession, organized like the clergy, and invested, at the level of man's bodily health, with powers similar to those exercised by the clergy over men's souls; and the myth of a total disappearance of disease in an untroubled, dispassionate society restored to its original state of health. But we must not be misled by the manifest contradiction of the two themes: each of these oneiric figures expresses, as if in black and white, the same picture of medical experience. The two dreams are isomorphic: the first expressing in a very positive way the strict, militant, dogmatic medicalization of society, by way of a quasi-religious conversion, and the establishment of a therapeutic clergy; the second expressing the same medicalization, but in a triumphant, negative way, that is to say, the volatilization of disease in a corrected, organized, and ceaselessly supervised environment, in which medicine itself would finally disappear, together with its object and its *raison d'être*.

Sabarot de l'Avernière, a prolific author of projects in the early years of the Revolution, saw priests and doctors as the natural heirs of the Church's two most visible missions – the consolation of souls and the alleviation of pain. So the wealth of the Church, which has been diverted from its original use by the higher clergy, must be confiscated and returned to the nation, which alone knows its own spiritual and material needs. The revenues would be divided equally between the parish clergy and the doctors. Are not doctors the priests of the body? 'The soul cannot be considered separately from animate bodies, and if the ministers of the Altars are venerated, and receive from the state a reasonable living, those who tend your health should also receive a salary sufficient to feed themselves and to succour you. They are the tutelary genii of the integrity of your faculties and sensations.'[30] The doctor would no longer have to demand a fee from his patient; the treatment of the sick would be free and obligatory – a service that the nation would provide as one of its sacred tasks; the doctor would be no more than the instrument of that service.[31] At the end of his studies, the new doctor would occupy not the post of his choice, but the one that was assigned to him according to the needs and vacancies, throughout the country; when he had gained in experience, he could apply for a more responsible, better-paid job. He would have to give an account to his superiors of his activities and would be held responsible for his mistakes. Having become a public, disinterested, supervised activity, medicine could improve indefinitely; in the alleviation of physical misery, it would be close to the old spiritual vocation of the Church, of which it would be a sort of lay carbon copy. To the army of priests watching over the salvation of souls would correspond that of the doctors who concern themselves with the health of bodies.

The other myth proceeds from a historical reflexion carried to its conclusion. Linked as they are with the conditions of existence and with the way of life of individuals, diseases vary from one period and one place to another. In the Middle Ages, at a time of war and famine, the sick were subject to fear and exhaustion (apoplexy, hectic fever); but in the sixteenth and seventeenth centuries, a period of relaxation of the feeling for one's country and of the obligations that such a feeling involves, egotism returned, and lust and gluttony became more widespread (venereal diseases, congestion of the viscera and of the blood); in the eighteenth century, the search for pleasure was carried over into the imagination: one went to the theatre, read novels, and grew excited in vain conversations; one stayed up at night and slept during the day (hysteria, hypochondria, nervous diseases).[32] A nation that lived without war, without violent passions, without idleness would know none of these ills, nor, above all, would a nation that did not know the tyranny of wealth over poverty, nor given to abuses. The rich? 'Living in the midst of ease, surrounded by the pleasures of life, their irascible pride, their bitter spleen, their abuses, and the excesses to which their contempt of all principles leads them makes them prey to infirmities of every kind; soon...their faces are furrowed, their hair turns white, and diseases harvest them before their time.'[33] Meanwhile, the poor, subjected to the despotism of the rich and of their kings, know only taxes that reduce them to penury, scarcity that benefits only the profiteers, and unhealthy housing that forces them 'either to refrain from raising families or to procreate weak, miserable creatures.'[34]

The first task of the doctor is therefore political: the struggle against disease must begin with a war against bad government. Man will be totally and definitively cured only if he is first liberated: 'Who, then, should denounce tyrants to mankind if not the doctors, who make man their sole study, and who, each day, in the homes of poor and rich, among ordinary citizens and among the highest in the land, in cottage and mansion, contemplate the human miseries that have no other origin but tyranny and slavery?'[35] If medicine could be politically more effective, it would no longer be indispensable medically. And in a society that was free at last, in which inequalities were reduced, and in which concord reigned, the doctor would have no more than a temporary role: that of giving legislator and citizen advice as to the regulation of his heart and body. There would no longer be any need for academies and hospitals:

> By training citizens in frugality by means of simple dietary laws, by showing young people above all the pleasures that may be derived from even a hard life, by making them appreciate the strictest discipline in the army and navy, how many ills would be prevented, how much expense avoided, and what new abilities would reveal themselves ...for the greatest, most difficult enterprises.

And gradually, in this young city entirely dedicated to the happiness of possessing health, the face of the doctor would fade, leaving a faint trace in men's memories of a time of kings and wealth, in which they were impoverished, sick slaves.

All this was so much day-dreaming; the dream of a festive city, inhabited by an open-air mankind, in which youth would be naked and age know no winter, the familiar symbol of ancient arcadias, to which has been added the more recent theme of a nature encompassing the earliest forms of truth – all these values were soon to fade.[36]

And yet they played an important role: by linking medicine with the destinies of states, they revealed in it a positive significance. Instead of remaining what it was, 'the dry, sorry analysis of millions of infirmities', the dubious negation of the negative, it was given the splendid task of establishing in men's lives the positive role of health, virtue, and happiness; it fell to medicine to punctuate work with festivals, to exalt calm emotions, to watch over what was read in books and seen in theatres, to see that marriages were made not out of self-interest or because of a passing infatuation, but were based on the only lasting condition of happiness, namely, their benefit to the state.[37]

Medicine must no longer be confined to a body of techniques for curing ills and of the knowledge that they require; it will also embrace a knowledge of *healthy man*, that is, a study of *non-sick man* and a definition of the *model man*. In the ordering of human existence it assumes a normative posture, which authorizes it not only to distribute advice as to healthy life, but also to dictate the standards for physical and moral relations of the individual and of the society in which he lives. It takes its place in that borderline, but for modern man paramount, area where a certain organic, unruffled, sensory happiness communicates by right with the order of a nation, the vigour of its armies, the fertility of its people, and the patient advance of its labours. The dreamer Lanthenas gave medicine a definition that was brief but heavy with history: 'At last, medicine will be what it must be, the knowledge of natural and social man.'[38]

It is important to determine how and in what manner the various forms of medical knowledge pertained to the positive notions of 'health' and 'normality'. Generally speaking, it might be said that up to the end of the eighteenth century medicine related much more to health than to normality; it did not begin by analysing a 'regular' functioning of the organism and go on to seek where it had deviated, what it was disturbed by, and how it could be brought back into normal working order; it referred, rather, to qualities of vigour, suppleness, and fluidity, which were lost in illness and which it was the task of medicine to restore. To this extent, medical practice could accord an important place to regimen and diet, in short, to a whole rule of life and nutrition that the subject imposed upon himself. This privileged relation between medicine and health involved the possibility of being one's own physician. Nineteenth-century medicine, on the other hand, was regulated more in accordance with normality than with health; it formed its concepts and prescribed its interventions in relation to a standard of functioning and organic structure, and physiological knowledge – once marginal and purely theoretical knowledge for the doctor – was to become established (Claude Bernard bears witness to this) at the very centre of all medical reflexion. Furthermore, the prestige of the sciences of life in the nineteenth century, their role as model, especially in the human sciences, is linked originally not with the comprehensive, transferable character of biological concepts, but, rather, with the fact that these concepts were arranged in a space whose profound structure responded to the healthy/morbid opposition. When one spoke of the life of groups and societies, of the life of the race, or even of the 'psychological life', one did not think first of the internal structure of *the organized being*, but of *the medical bipolarity of the normal and the pathological*. Consciousness lives because it can be altered, maimed, diverted from its course, paralysed; societies live because there are sick, declining societies and healthy, expanding ones; the race is a living being that one can see degenerating; and civilizations, whose deaths have so often been remarked on, are also, therefore, living beings. If the science of man appeared as an extension of the science of life, it is because it was *medically*, as well as *biologically*, based: by transference, importation, and, often, metaphor, the science of man no doubt used concepts formed by biologists; but the very subjects that it devoted itself to (man, his behaviour, his individual and social realizations) therefore opened up a field that was divided up according to the principles of the normal and the pathological. Hence the unique character of the science of man, which cannot be detached from the negative aspects in which it first appeared, but which is also linked with the positive role that it implicitly occupies as norm.

Notes

1   Th. Sydenham, 'Observationes medicae', *Opera medica* (Geneva, 1736, I, p. 32).
2   *Ibid.*, p. 27.
3   Le Brun, *Traité historique sur les maladies épidémiques* (Paris, 1776, p. 1).
4   Lepecq de la Clôture, *Collection d'observations sur les maladies et constitutions épidémiques* (Rouen, 1778, p. xiv).
5   Razoux, *Tableau nosologique et météorologique* (Basel, 1787, p. 22).
6   Menuret, *Essai sur l'histoire médico-topographique de Paris* (Paris, 1788, p. 139).
7   Banan and Turben, *Mémoires sur les épidémies du Languedoc* (Paris, 1786, p. 3).
8   Le Brun, *Traité historique sur les maladies épidémiques*, p. 66, n. 1.
9   Menuret, *Essai sur l'histoire médico-topographique de Paris*, p. 139.
10 Le Brun, *Traité historique sur les maladies épidémiques*, pp. 2–3.
11 Anon., *Description des épidémies qui ont régné depuis quelques années sur la généralité de Paris* (Paris, 1783, pp. 35–7).
12 Le Brun, *Traité historique sur les maladies épidémiques*, pp. 127–32.
13 Anon., *Description des épidémies*, pp. 14–17.
14 Le Brun, *Traité historique sur les maladies épidémiques*, p. 124.
15 *Ibid.*, p. 126.
16 Cf. *Précis historique de l'établissement de la Société royale de Médecine* (Undated. The anonymous author is Boussu).
17 Retz, *Exposé succint à l'Assemblée Nationale* (Paris, 1791, pp. 5–6).
18 Cf. Vacher de la Feuterie, *Motif de la réclamation de la Faculté de Médecine de Paris contre l'établissement de la Société royale de Médecine* (Place and date of publication unknown).
19 Quoted in Retz, *Exposé succint à l'Assemblée Nationale*.
20 Hautesierck, *Recueil d'observations de médecine des hôpitaux militaires* (Paris, 1766, vol. I, pp. xxiv–xxvii).
21 Menuret, *Essai sur l'histoire médico-topographique de Paris*, p. 139.
22 Cantin, *Projet de réforme adressé à l'Assemblée Nationale* (Paris, 1790).
23 Mathieu Géraud, *Projet de décret à rendre sur l'organisation civile des médecins* (Paris, 1791, nos. 78–9).
24 Razoux, *Tableau nosologique et météorologique*.
25 Quoted in *ibid.*, p. 14.
26 Géraud, *Projet de décret*, p. 65.
27 Cf. N.-L. Lespagnol, *Projet d'établir trois médecins par district pour le soulagement des gens de la campagne* (Charleville, 1790). Royer, *Bienfaisance médicale et projet financier* (Provins, Year IX).
28 J.-B. Demangeon, *Des moyens de perfectionner la médecine* (Paris, Year VII, pp. 5–9); cf. Audin Rouvière, *Essai sur la topographie physique et médicale de Paris* (Paris, Year II).
29 Bacher, *De la médecine considérée politiquement* (Paris, Year XI, p. 38).
30 Sabarot de L'Avernière, *Vue de Législation médicale adressée aux États généraux* (1789, p. 3).
31 In Menuret, *Essai sur le moyen de former de bons médecins* (Paris, 1791), one finds the idea of financing medicine from church revenues, but only when it is a question of treating the poor.
32 Maret, *Mémoire où on cherche à déterminer quelle influence les moeurs ont sur la santé* (Amiens, 1771).
33 Lanthenas, *De l'influence de la liberté sur la santé* (Paris, 1792, p. 8).

34   *Ibid.*, p. 4.
35   *Ibid.*, p. 8.
36   On 2 June 1793, Lanthenas, who was a Girondist, was put on the proscribed list, then crossed off, Marat having described him as 'weak-headed'. Cf. Mathiez, *La Révolution française* (Paris, 1945, vol II, p. 221).
37   Cf. Ganne, *De l'homme physique et moral, ou recherches sur les moyens de rendre l'homme plus sage* (Strasbourg, 1791).
38   Lanthenas, *De l'influence de la liberté sur la santé*, p. 18.

14 Truth and Power

Michel Foucault

I think one can be confident in saying that you were the first person to pose the question of power regarding discourse, and that at a time when analyses in terms of the concept or object of the 'text', along with the accompanying methodology of semiology, structuralism, etc., were the prevailing fashion. Posing for discourse the question of power means basically to ask whom does discourse serve? . . . Could you briefly situate within your work this question you have posed – if indeed it's true that you have posed it?

I don't think I was the first to pose the question. On the contrary, I'm struck by the difficulty I had in formulating it. When I think back now, I ask myself what else it was that I was talking about, in *Madness and Civilisation* or *The Birth of the Clinic*, but power? Yet I'm perfectly aware that I scarcely ever used the word and never had such a field of analyses at my disposal. I can say that this was an incapacity linked undoubtedly with the political situation we found ourselves in. It is hard to see where, either on the Right or the Left, this problem of power could then have been posed. On the Right, it was posed only in terms of constitution, sovereignty, etc., that is, in juridical terms; on the Marxist side, it was posed only in terms of the State apparatus. The way power was exercised – concretely and in detail – with its specificity, its techniques and tactics, was something that no one attempted to ascertain; they contented themselves with denouncing it in a polemical and global fashion as it existed among the 'others', in the adversary camp. Where Soviet socialist power was in question, its opponents called it totalitarianism; power in Western capitalism was denounced by the Marxists as class domination; but the mechanics of power in themselves were never analysed. This task could only begin after 1968, that is to say on the basis of daily struggles at grass roots level, among those whose fight was located in the fine meshes of the web of power. This was where the concrete nature of power became visible, along with the prospect that these analyses of power would prove fruitful in accounting for all that had hitherto remained outside the field of political analysis. To put it very simply, psychiatric internment, the mental normalisation of individuals, and penal institutions have no doubt a fairly limited importance if one is only looking for their economic significance. On the other hand, they are undoubtedly essential to the general functioning of the wheels of power. So long as the posing of the question of power was kept subordinate to the economic instance and the system of interests which this served, there was a tendency to regard these problems as of small importance.

Originally translated by Colin Gordon, Leo Marshall, John Mepham, and Kate Soper.

Interviewers: Alessandro Fontana and Pasquale Pasquino.

So a certain kind of Marxism and a certain kind of phenomenology constituted an objective obstacle to the formulation of this problematic?

Yes, if you like, to the extent that it's true that, in our student days, people of my generation were brought up on these two forms of analysis, one in terms of the constituent subject, the other in terms of the economic in the last instance, ideology and the play of superstructures and infrastructures.

Still within this methodological context, how would you situate the genealogical approach? As a questioning of the conditions of possibility, modalities and constitution of the 'objects' and domains you have successively analysed, what makes it necessary?

I wanted to see how these problems of constitution could be resolved within a historical framework, instead of referring them back to a constituent object (madness, criminality or whatever). But this historical contextualisation needed to be something more than the simple relativisation of the phenomenological subject. I don't believe the problem can be solved by historicising the subject as posited by the phenomenologists, fabricating a subject that evolves through the course of history. One has to dispense with the constituent subject, to get rid of the subject itself, that's to say, to arrive at an analysis which can account for the constitution of the subject within a historical framework. And this is what I would call genealogy, that is, a form of history which can account for the constitution of knowledges, discourses, domains of objects etc., without having to make reference to a subject which is either transcendental in relation to the field of events or runs in its empty sameness throughout the course of history.

Marxist phenomenology and a certain kind of Marxism have clearly acted as a screen and an obstacle; there are two further concepts which continue today to act as a screen and an obstacle, ideology on the one hand and repression on the other. . . . Could you perhaps use this occasion to specify more explicitly your thoughts on these matters? . . .

The notion of ideology appears to me to be difficult to make use of, for three reasons. The first is that, like it or not, it always stands in virtual opposition to something else which is supposed to count as truth. Now I believe that the problem does not consist in drawing the line between that in a discourse which falls under the category of scientificity or truth, and that which comes under some other category, but in seeing historically how effects of truth are produced within discourses which in themselves are neither true nor false. The second drawback is that the concept of ideology refers, I think necessarily, to something of the order of a subject. Thirdly, ideology stands in a secondary position relative to something which functions as its infrastructure, as its material, economic determinant, etc. For these three reasons, I think that this is a notion that cannot be used without circumspection.

The notion of repression is a more insidious one, or at all events I myself have had much more trouble in freeing myself of it, in so far as it does indeed appear to correspond so well with a whole range of phenomena which belong among the effects of power. When I wrote *Madness and Civilisation*, I made at least an implicit use of this notion of repression. I think indeed that I was positing the existence of a sort of living, voluble and anxious madness which the mechanisms of power and psychiatry were supposed to have come to repress and reduce to silence. But it seems to me now that the notion of repression is quite inadequate for capturing what is precisely the productive aspect of power. In defining the effects of power as repression, one adopts a purely juridical conception of such power, one identifies power with a law which says no, power is taken above all as carrying the force of a prohibition. Now I believe that this is a wholly negative, narrow, skeletal conception of power, one which has been curiously widespread. If power were never anything but repressive, if it never did anything but to say no, do you really think one would be brought to obey it? What makes power hold good, what makes it accepted, is simply the fact that it doesn't only weigh on us as a force that says no, but that it traverses and produces things, it induces pleasure, forms knowledge, produces discourse. It needs to be considered as a productive network which runs through the whole social body, much more than as a negative instance whose function is repression. In *Discipline and Punish* what I wanted to show was how, from the seventeenth and eighteenth centuries onwards, there was a veritable technological take-off in the productivity of power. Not only did the monarchies of the Classical period develop great state apparatuses (the army, the police and fiscal administration), but above all there was established at this period what one might call a new 'economy' of power, that is to say procedures which allowed the effects of power to circulate in a manner at once continuous, uninterrupted, adapted and 'individualised' throughout the entire social body. These new techniques are both much more efficient and much less wasteful (less costly economically, less risky in their results, less open to loopholes and resistances) than the techniques previously employed which were based on a mixture of more or less forced tolerances (from recognised privileges to endemic criminality) and costly ostentation (spectacular and discontinuous interventions of power, the most violent form of which was the 'exemplary', because exceptional, punishment).

> Repression is a concept used above all in relation to sexuality. It was held that bourgeois society represses sexuality, stifles sexual desire, and so forth. And when one considers for example the campaign launched against masturbation in the eighteenth century, or the medical discourse on homosexuality in the second half of the nineteenth century, or discourse on sexuality in general, one does seem to be faced with a discourse of repression. . . .

Certainly. It is customary to say that bourgeois society repressed infantile sexuality to the point where it refused even to speak of it or acknowledge its existence. It was necessary to wait until Freud for the discovery at last to be made that children have a sexuality. Now if you read all the books on pedagogy and child medicine – all the manuals for parents that were published in the eighteenth century – you find that children's sex is spoken of constantly and in every possible context. One might argue that the purpose of these discourses was precisely to prevent children from having a sexuality. But their *effect* was to din it into parents' heads that their children's sex constituted a fundamental problem in terms of their parental educational responsibilities, and to din it into children's heads that their relationship with their own body and their own sex was to be a fundamental problem as far as *they* were concerned;

and this had the consequence of sexually exciting the bodies of children while at the same time fixing the parental gaze and vigilance on the peril of infantile sexuality. The result was a sexualising of the infantile body, a sexualising of the bodily relationship between parent and child, a sexualising of the familial domain. 'Sexuality' is far more of a positive product of power than power was ever repression of sexuality. I believe that it is precisely these positive mechanisms that need to be investigated, and here one must free oneself of the juridical schematism of all previous characterisations of the nature of power. Hence a historical problem arises, namely that of discovering why the West has insisted for so long on seeing the power it exercises as juridical and negative rather than as technical and positive.

> Perhaps this is because it has always been thought that power is mediated through the forms prescribed in the great juridical and philosophical theories, and that there is a fundamental, immutable gulf between those who exercise power and those who undergo it.

I wonder if this isn't bound up with the institution of monarchy. This developed during the Middle Ages against the backdrop of the previously endemic struggles between feudal power agencies. The monarchy presented itself as a referee, a power capable of putting an end to war, violence and pillage and saying no to these struggles and private feuds. It made itself acceptable by allocating itself a juridical and negative function, albeit one whose limits it naturally began at once to overstep. Sovereign, law and prohibition formed a system of representation of power which was extended during the subsequent era by the theories of right: political theory has never ceased to be obsessed with the person of the sovereign. Such theories still continue today to busy themselves with the problem of sovereignty. What we need, however, is a political philosophy that isn't erected around the problem of sovereignty, nor therefore around the problems of law and prohibition. We need to cut off the King's head: in political theory that has still to be done.

> The King's head still hasn't been cut off, yet already people are trying to replace it by discipline, that vast system instituted in the seventeenth century comprising the functions of surveillance, normalisation and control and, a little later, those of punishment, correction, education and so on. One wonders where this system comes from, why it emerges and what its use is. . . .

To pose the problem in terms of the State means to continue posing it in terms of sovereign and sovereignty, that is to say in terms of law. If one describes all these phenomena of power as dependent on the State apparatus, this means grasping them as essentially repressive: the Army as a power of death, police and justice as punitive instances, etc. I don't want to say that the State isn't important; what I want to say is that relations of power, and hence the analysis that must be made of them, necessarily extend beyond the limits of the State. In two senses: first of all because the State, for all the omnipotence of its apparatuses, is far from being able to occupy the whole field of actual power relations, and further because the State can only operate on the basis of other, already existing power relations. The State is superstructural in relation to a whole series of power networks that invest the body, sexuality, the family, kinship, knowledge, technology and so forth. True, these networks stand in a conditioning–conditioned relationship to a kind of 'meta-power' which is structured essentially round a certain number of great prohibition functions; but this meta-power with its prohibitions can only take hold and secure its footing where it is rooted in a whole series of multiple and indefinite power relations that supply the necessary basis for the great negative forms of power. That is just what I was trying to make apparent in my book.

> Doesn't this open up the possibility of overcoming the dualism of political struggles that eternally feed on the opposition between the State on the one hand and Revolution on the other? Doesn't it indicate a wider field of conflicts than that of those where the adversary is the State?

I would say that the State consists in the codification of a whole number of power relations which render its functioning possible, and that Revolution is a different type of codification of the same relations. This implies that there are many different kinds of revolution, roughly speaking as many kinds as there are possible subversive recodifications of power relations, and further that one can perfectly well conceive of revolutions which leave essentially untouched the power relations which form the basis for the functioning of the State.

> You have said about power as an object of research that one has to invert Clausewitz's formula so as to arrive at the idea that politics is the continuation of war by other means. Does the military model seem to you on the basis of your most recent researches to be the best one for describing power; is war here simply a metaphorical model, or is it the literal, regular, everyday mode of operation of power?

This is the problem I now find myself confronting. As soon as one endeavours to detach power with its techniques and procedures from the form of law within which it has been theoretically confined up until now, one is driven to ask this basic question: isn't power simply a form of warlike domination? Shouldn't one therefore conceive all problems of power in terms of relations of war? Isn't power a sort of generalised war which assumes at particular moments the forms of peace and the State? Peace would then be a form of war, and the State a means of waging it.

A whole range of problems emerge here. Who wages war against whom? Is it between two classes, or more? Is it a war of all against all? What is the role of the army and military institutions in this civil society where permanent war is waged? What is the relevance of concepts of tactics and strategy for analysing structures and political processes? What is the essence and mode of transformation of power relations? All these questions need to be explored. In any case it's astonishing to see how easily and self-evidently people talk of war-like relations of power or of class struggle without ever making it clear whether some form of war is meant, and if so what form.

> We have already talked about this disciplinary power whose effects, rules and mode of constitution you describe in *Discipline and Punish*. One might ask here, why surveillance? What is the use of surveillance? . . . Even if you are only perhaps at the beginning

of your researches here, could you say how you see the nature of the relationships (if any) which are engendered between these different bodies: the molar body of the population and the micro-bodies of individuals?

Your question is exactly on target. I find it difficult to reply because I am working on this problem right now. I believe one must keep in view the fact that along with all the fundamental technical inventions and discoveries of the seventeenth and eighteenth centuries, a new technology of the exercise of power also emerged which was probably even more important than the constitutional reforms and new forms of government established at the end of the eighteenth century. In the camp of the Left, one often hears people saying that power is that which abstracts, which negates the body, represses, suppresses, and so forth. I would say instead that what I find most striking about these new technologies of power introduced since the seventeenth and eighteenth centuries is their concrete and precise character, their grasp of a multiple and differentiated reality. In feudal societies power functioned essentially through signs and levies. Signs of loyalty to the feudal lords, rituals, ceremonies and so forth, and levies in the form of taxes, pillage, hunting, war etc. In the seventeenth and eighteenth centuries a form of power comes into being that begins to exercise itself through social production and social service. It becomes a matter of obtaining productive service from individuals in their concrete lives. And in consequence, a real and effective 'incorporation' of power was necessary, in the sense that power had to be able to gain access to the bodies of individuals, to their acts, attitudes and modes of everyday behaviour. Hence the significance of methods like school discipline, which succeeded in making children's bodies the object of highly complex systems of manipulation and conditioning. But at the same time, these new techniques of power needed to grapple with the phenomena of population, in short to undertake the administration, control and direction of the accumulation of men (the economic system that promotes the accumulation of capital and the system of power that ordains the accumulation of men are, from the seventeenth century on, correlated and inseparable phenomena): hence there arise the problems of demography, public health, hygiene, housing conditions, longevity and fertility. And I believe that the political significance of the problem of sex is due to the fact that sex is located at the point of intersection of the discipline of the body and the control of the population.

> Finally, a question you have been asked before: the work you do, these preoccupations of yours, the results you arrive at, what use can one finally make of all this in everyday political struggles? . . . If one isn't an 'organic' intellectual acting as the spokesman for a global organisation, if one doesn't purport to function as the bringer, the master of truth, what position is the intellectual to assume?

The important thing here, I believe, is that truth isn't outside power, or lacking in power: contrary to a myth whose history and functions would repay further study, truth isn't the reward of free spirits, the child of protracted solitude, nor the privilege of those who have succeeded in liberating themselves. Truth is a thing of this world: it is produced only by virtue of multiple forms of constraint. And it induces regular effects of power. Each society has its régime of truth, its 'general politics' of truth:

that is, the types of discourse which it accepts and makes function as true; the mechanisms and instances which enable one to distinguish true and false statements, the means by which each is sanctioned; the techniques and procedures accorded value in the acquisition of truth; the status of those who are charged with saying what counts as true.

In societies like ours, the 'political economy' of truth is characterised by five important traits. 'Truth' is centred on the form of scientific discourse and the institutions which produce it; it is subject to constant economic and political incitement (the demand for truth, as much for economic production as for political power); it is the object, under diverse forms, of immense diffusion and consumption (circulating through apparatuses of education and information whose extent is relatively broad in the social body, not withstanding certain strict limitations); it is produced and transmitted under the control, dominant if not exclusive, of a few great political and economic apparatuses (university, army, writing, media); lastly, it is the issue of a whole political debate and social confrontation ('ideological' struggles).

It seems to me that what must now be taken into account in the intellectual is not the 'bearer of universal values'. Rather, it's the person occupying a specific position – but whose specificity is linked, in a society like ours, to the general functioning of an apparatus of truth. In other words, the intellectual has a three-fold specificity: that of his class position (whether as petty-bourgeois in the service of capitalism or 'organic' intellectual of the proletariat); that of his conditions of life and work, linked to his condition as an intellectual (his field of research, his place in a laboratory, the political and economic demands to which he submits or against which he rebels, in the university, the hospital, etc.); lastly, the specificity of the politics of truth in our societies. And it's with this last factor that his position can take on a general significance and that his local, specific struggle can have effects and implications which are not simply professional or sectoral. The intellectual can operate and struggle at the general level of that régime of truth which is so essential to the structure and functioning of our society. There is a battle 'for truth', or at least 'around truth' – it being understood once again that by truth I do not mean 'the ensemble of truths which are to be discovered and accepted', but rather 'the ensemble of rules according to which the true and the false are separated and specific effects of power attached to the true', it being understood also that it's not a matter of a battle 'on behalf' of the truth, but of a battle about the status of truth and the economic and political role it plays. It is necessary to think of the political problems of intellectuals not in terms of 'science' and 'ideology', but in terms of 'truth' and 'power'. And thus the question of the professionalisation of intellectuals and the division between intellectual and manual labour can be envisaged in a new way.

All this must seem very confused and uncertain. Uncertain indeed, and what I am saying here is above all to be taken as a hypothesis. In order for it to be a little less confused, however, I would like to put forward a few 'propositions' – not firm assertions, but simply suggestions to be further tested and evaluated.

'Truth' is to be understood as a system of ordered procedures for the production, regulation, distribution, circulation and operation of statements.

'Truth' is linked in a circular relation with systems of power which produce and sustain it, and to effects of power which it induces and which extend it. A 'régime' of truth.

This régime is not merely ideological or superstructural; it was a condition of the formation and development of capitalism. And it's this same régime which, subject to certain modifications, operates in the socialist countries (I leave open here the question of China, about which I know little).

The essential political problem for the intellectual is not to criticise the ideological contents supposedly linked to science, or to ensure that his own scientific practice is accompanied by a correct ideology, but that of ascertaining the possibility of constituting a new politics of truth. The problem is not changing people's consciousnesses – or what's in their heads – but the political, economic, institutional régime of the production of truth.

It's not a matter of emancipating truth from every system of power (which would be a chimera, for truth is already power) but of detaching the power of truth from the forms of hegemony, social, economic and cultural, within which it operates at the present time.

The political question, to sum up, is not error, illusion, alienated consciousness or ideology; it is truth itself. Hence the importance of Nietzsche.

15 Discipline and Punish

Michel Foucault

Bentham's *Panopticon* is the architectural figure of this composition. We know the principle on which it was based: at the periphery, an annular building; at the centre, a tower; this tower is pierced with wide windows that open onto the inner side of the ring; the peripheric building is divided into cells, each of which extends the whole width of the building; they have two windows, one on the inside, corresponding to the windows of the tower; the other, on the outside, allows the light to cross the cell from one end to the other. All that is needed, then, is to place a supervisor in a central tower and to shut up in each cell a madman, a patient, a condemned man, a worker or a schoolboy. By the effect of backlighting, one can observe from the tower, standing out precisely against the light, the small captive shadows in the cells of the periphery. They are like so many cages, so many small theatres, in which each actor is alone, perfectly individualized and constantly visible. The panoptic mechanism arranges spatial unities that make it possible to see constantly and to recognize immediately. In short, it reverses the principle of the dungeon; or rather of its three functions – to enclose, to deprive of light and to hide – it preserves only the first and eliminates the other two. Full lighting and the eye of a supervisor capture better than darkness, which ultimately protected. Visibility is a trap.

To begin with, this made it possible – as a negative effect – to avoid those compact, swarming, howling masses that were to be found in places of confinement, those painted by Goya or described by Howard. Each individual, in his place, is securely confined to a cell from which he is seen from the front by the supervisor; but the side walls prevent him from coming into contact with his companions. He is seen, but he does not see; he is the object of information, never a subject in communication. The arrangement of his room, opposite the central tower, imposes on him an axial visibility; but the divisions of the ring, those separated cells, imply a lateral invisibility. And this invisibility is a guarantee of order. If the inmates are convicts, there is no danger of a plot, an attempt at collective escape, the planning of new crimes for the future, bad reciprocal influences; if they are patients, there is no danger of contagion; if they are madmen there is no risk of their committing violence upon one another; if they are school children, there is no copying, no noise, no chatter, no waste of time; if they are workers, there are no disorders, no theft, no coalitions, none of those distractions that slow down the rate of work, make it less perfect or cause accidents. The crowd, a compact mass, a locus of multiple exchanges, individualities merging together, a collective effect, is abolished and replaced by a collection of separated individualities. From the point of view of

Originally translated from the French by Alan Sheridan.

the guardian, it is replaced by a multiplicity that can be numbered and supervised; from the point of view of the inmates, by a sequestered and observed solitude (Bentham, 60–4).

Hence the major effect of the Panopticon: to induce in the inmate a state of conscious and permanent visibility that assures the automatic functioning of power. So to arrange things that the surveillance is permanent in its effects, even if it is discontinuous in its action; that the perfection of power should tend to render its actual exercise unnecessary; that this architectural apparatus should be a machine for creating and sustaining a power relation independent of the person who exercises it; in short, that the inmates should be caught up in a power situation of which they are themselves the bearers. To achieve this, it is at once too much and too little that the prisoner should be constantly observed by an inspector: too little, for what matters is that he knows himself to be observed; too much, because he has no need in fact of being so. In view of this, Bentham laid down the principle that power should be visible and unverifiable. Visible: the inmate will constantly have before his eyes the tall outline of the central tower from which he is spied upon. Unverifiable: the inmate must never know whether he is being looked at at any one moment; but he must be sure that he may always be so. In order to make the presence or absence of the inspector unverifiable, so that the prisoners, in their cells, cannot even see a shadow, Bentham envisaged not only venetian blinds on the windows of the central observation hall, but, on the inside, partitions that intersected the hall at right angles and, in order to pass from one quarter to the other, not doors but zig-zag openings; for the slightest noise, a gleam of light, a brightness in a half-opened door would betray the presence of the guardian. The Panopticon is a machine for dissociating the see/being seen dyad: in the peripheric ring, one is totally seen, without ever seeing; in the central tower, one sees everything without ever being seen.

It is an important mechanism, for it automatizes and disindividualizes power. Power has its principle not so much in a person as in a certain concerted distribution of bodies, surfaces, lights, gazes; in an arrangement whose internal mechanisms produce the relation in which individuals are caught up. The ceremonies, the rituals, the marks by which the sovereign's surplus power was manifested are useless. There is a machinery that assures dissymmetry, disequilibrium, difference. Consequently, it does not matter who exercises power. Any individual, taken almost at random, can operate the machine: in the absence of the director, his family, his friends, his visitors, even his servants (Bentham, 45). Similarly, it does not matter what motive animates him: the curiosity of the indiscreet, the malice of a child, the thirst for knowledge of a philosopher who wishes to visit this museum of human nature, or the perversity of those who take pleasure in spying and punishing. The more numerous those anonymous and temporary observers are, the greater the risk for the inmate of being surprised and the greater his anxious awareness of being observed. The Panopticon is a marvellous machine which, whatever use one may wish to put it to, produces homogeneous effects of power. . . .

'Discipline' may be identified neither with an institution nor with an apparatus; it is a type of power, a modality for its exercise, comprising a whole set of instruments, techniques, procedures, levels of application, targets; it is a 'physics' or an 'anatomy' of power, a technology. And it may be taken over either by 'specialized' institutions (the penitentiaries or 'houses of correction' of the nineteenth century), or by institutions that use it as an essential instrument for a particular end (schools, hospitals), or by pre-existing authorities that find in it a means of reinforcing or reorganizing their internal mechanisms of power (one day we should show how intra-familial relations, essentially in the parents–children cell, have become 'disciplined', absorbing since the classical age external schemata, first educational and military, then medical, psychiatric, psychological, which have made the family the privileged locus of emergence for the disciplinary question of the normal and the abnormal); or by apparatuses that have made discipline their principle of internal functioning (the disciplinarization of the administrative apparatus from the Napoleonic period), or finally by state apparatuses whose major, if not exclusive, function is to assure that discipline reigns over society as a whole (the police).

On the whole, therefore, one can speak of the formation of a disciplinary society in this movement that stretches from the enclosed disciplines, a sort of social 'quarantine', to an indefinitely generalizable mechanism of 'panopticism'. Not because the disciplinary modality of power has replaced all the others; but because it has infiltrated the others, sometimes undermining them, but serving as an inter-mediary between them, linking them together, extending them and above all making it possible to bring the effects of power to the most minute and distant elements. It assures an infinitesimal distribution of the power relations.

A few years after Bentham, Julius gave this society its birth certificate (Julius, 384–6). Speaking of the panoptic principle, he said that there was much more there than architectural ingenuity: it was an event in the 'history of the human mind'. In appearance, it is merely the solution of a technical problem; but, through it, a whole type of society emerges. . . .

The formation of the disciplinary society is connected with a number of broad historical processes – economic, juridico-political and, lastly, scientific – of which it forms part.

1. Generally speaking, it might be said that the disciplines are techniques for assuring the ordering of human multiplicities. It is true that there is nothing excep-tional or even characteristic in this: every system of power is presented with the same problem. But the peculiarity of the disciplines is that they try to define in relation to the multiplicities a tactics of power that fulfils three criteria: firstly, to obtain the exercise of power at the lowest possible cost (economically, by the low expenditure it involves; politically, by its discretion, its low exteriorization, its relative invisibility, the little resistance it arouses); secondly, to bring the effects of this social power to their maximum intensity and to extend them as far as possible, without either failure or interval; thirdly, to link this 'economic' growth of power with the output of the apparatuses (educational, military, industrial or medical) within which it is exer-cised; in short, to increase both the docility and the utility of all the elements of the system. This triple objective of the disciplines corresponds to a well-known histor-ical conjuncture. One aspect of this conjuncture was the large demographic thrust of the eighteenth century; an increase in the floating population (one of the primary objects of discipline is to fix; it is an anti-nomadic technique); a change of quantita-tive scale in the groups to be supervised or manipulated (from the beginning of the seventeenth century to the eve of the French Revolution, the school population had been increasing rapidly, as had no doubt the hospital population; by the end of the eighteenth century, the peace-time army exceeded 200,000 men). The other aspect of

the conjuncture was the growth in the apparatus of production, which was becoming more and more extended and complex; it was also becoming more costly and its profitability had to be increased. The development of the disciplinary methods corresponded to these two processes, or rather, no doubt, to the new need to adjust their correlation. Neither the residual forms of feudal power nor the structures of the administrative monarchy, nor the local mechanisms of supervision, nor the unstable, tangled mass they all formed together could carry out this role: they were hindered from doing so by the irregular and inadequate extension of their network, by their often conflicting functioning, but above all by the 'costly' nature of the power that was exercised in them. It was costly in several senses: because directly it cost a great deal to the Treasury; because the system of corrupt offices and farmed-out taxes weighed indirectly, but very heavily, on the population; because the resistance it encountered forced it into a cycle of perpetual reinforcement; because it proceeded essentially by levying (levying on money or products by royal, seigniorial, ecclesiastical taxation; levying on men or time by *corvées* of press-ganging, by locking up or banishing vagabonds). The development of the disciplines marks the appearance of elementary techniques belonging to a quite different economy: mechanisms of power which, instead of proceeding by deduction, are integrated into the productive efficiency of the apparatuses from within, into the growth of this efficiency and into the use of what it produces. For the old principle of 'levying-violence', which governed the economy of power, the disciplines substitute the principle of 'mildness-production-profit'. These are the techniques that make it possible to adjust the multiplicity of men and the multiplication of the apparatuses of production (and this means not only 'production' in the strict sense, but also the production of knowledge and skills in the school, the production of health in the hospitals, the production of destructive force in the army).

In this task of adjustment, discipline had to solve a number of problems for which the old economy of power was not sufficiently equipped. It could reduce the inefficiency of mass phenomena: reduce what, in a multiplicity, makes it much less manageable than a unity; reduce what is opposed to the use of each of its elements and of their sum; reduce everything that may counter the advantages of number. That is why discipline fixes; it arrests or regulates movements; it clears up confusion; it dissipates compact groupings of individuals wandering about the country in unpredictable ways; it establishes calculated distributions. It must also master all the forces that are formed from the very constitution of an organized multiplicity; it must neutralize the effects of counter-power that spring from them and which form a resistance to the power that wishes to dominate it: agitations, revolts, spontaneous organizations, coalitions – anything that may establish horizontal conjunctions. Hence the fact that the disciplines use procedures of partitioning and verticality, that they introduce, between the different elements at the same level, as solid separations as possible, that they define compact hierarchical networks, in short, that they oppose to the intrinsic, adverse force of multiplicity the technique of the continuous, individualizing pyramid. They must also increase the particular utility of each element of the multiplicity, but by means that are the most rapid and the least costly, that is to say, by using the multiplicity itself as an instrument of this growth. Hence, in order to extract from bodies the maximum time and force, the use of those overall methods known as time-tables, collective training, exercises, total and detailed surveillance. Furthermore, the disciplines must increase the effect of utility proper to the multiplicities, so that each is made more useful than the simple sum of its elements: it is in order to increase the utilizable effects of the multiple that the disciplines define tactics of distribution, reciprocal adjustment of bodies, gestures and rhythms, differentiation of capacities, reciprocal coordination in relation to apparatuses or tasks. Lastly, the disciplines have to bring into play the power relations, not above but inside the very texture of the multiplicity, as discreetly as possible, as well articulated on the other functions of these multiplicities and also in the least expensive way possible: to this correspond anonymous instruments of power, coextensive with the multiplicity that they regiment, such as hierarchical surveillance, continuous registration, perpetual assessment and classification. In short, to substitute for a power that is manifested through the brilliance of those who exercise it, a power that insidiously objectifies those on whom it is applied; to form a body of knowledge about these individuals, rather than to deploy the ostentatious signs of sovereignty. In a word, the disciplines are the ensemble of minute technical inventions that made it possible to increase the useful size of multiplicities by decreasing the inconveniences of the power which, in order to make them useful, must control them. A multiplicity, whether in a workshop or a nation, an army or a school, reaches the threshold of a discipline when the relation of the one to the other becomes favourable.

If the economic take-off of the West began with the techniques that made possible the accumulation of capital, it might perhaps be said that the methods for administering the accumulation of men made possible a political take-off in relation to the traditional, ritual, costly, violent forms of power, which soon fell into disuse and were superseded by a subtle, calculated technology of subjection. In fact, the two processes – the accumulation of men and the accumulation of capital – cannot be separated; it would not have been possible to solve the problem of the accumulation of men without the growth of an apparatus of production capable of both sustaining them and using them; conversely, the techniques that made the cumulative multiplicity of men useful accelerated the accumulation of capital. At a less general level, the technological mutations of the apparatus of production, the division of labour and the elaboration of the disciplinary techniques sustained an ensemble of very close relations (cf. Marx, *Capital*, vol. I, chapter XIII and the very interesting analysis in Guerry and Deleule). Each makes the other possible and necessary; each provides a model for the other. The disciplinary pyramid constituted the small cell of power within which the separation, coordination and supervision of tasks was imposed and made efficient; and analytical partitioning of time, gestures and bodily forces constituted an operational schema that could easily be transferred from the groups to be subjected to the mechanisms of production; the massive projection of military methods onto industrial organization was an example of this modelling of the division of labour following the model laid down by the schemata of power. But, on the other hand, the technical analysis of the process of production, its 'mechanical' breaking-down, were projected onto the labour force whose task it was to implement it: the constitution of those disciplinary machines in which the individual forces that they bring together are composed into a whole and therefore increased is the effect of this projection. Let us say that discipline is the unitary technique by which the body is reduced as a 'political' force at the least cost and maximized as a useful force. The growth of a capitalist economy gave rise to the specific modality of disciplinary power, whose general formulas, techniques of submitting forces and bodies, in short, 'political anatomy', could be operated in the most diverse political régimes, apparatuses or institutions.

2. The panoptic modality of power – at the elementary, technical, merely physical level at which it is situated – is not under the immediate dependence or a direct extension of the great juridico-political structures of a society; it is nonetheless not absolutely independent. Historically, the process by which the bourgeoisie became in the course of the eighteenth century the politically dominant class was masked by the establishment of an explicit, coded and formally egalitarian juridical framework, made possible by the organization of a parliamentary, representative régime. But the development and generalization of disciplinary mechanisms constituted the other, dark side of these processes. The general juridical form that guaranteed a system of rights that were egalitarian in principle was supported by these tiny, everyday, physical mechanisms, by all those systems of micro-power that are essentially non-egalitarian and asymmetrical that we call the disciplines. And although, in a formal way, the representative régime makes it possible, directly or indirectly, with or without relays, for the will of all to form the fundamental authority of sovereignty, the disciplines provide, at the base, a guarantee of the submission of forces and bodies. The real, corporal disciplines constituted the foundation of the formal, juridical liberties. The contract may have been regarded as the ideal foundation of law and political power; panopticism constituted the technique, universally wide-spread, of coercion. It continued to work in depth on the juridical structures of society, in order to make the effective mechanisms of power function in opposition to the formal framework that it had acquired. The 'Enlightenment', which dis-covered the liberties, also invented the disciplines.

In appearance, the disciplines constitute nothing more than an infra-law. They seem to extend the general forms defined by law to the infinitesimal level of individual lives; or they appear as methods of training that enable individuals to become integrated into these general demands. They seem to constitute the same type of law on a different scale, thereby making it more meticulous and more indulgent. The disciplines should be regarded as a sort of counter-law. They have the precise role of introducing insuperable asymmetries and excluding reciprocities. First, because discipline creates between individuals a 'private' link, which is a relation of constraints entirely different from contractual obligation; the acceptance of a discipline may be underwritten by contract; the way in which it is imposed, the mechanisms it brings into play, the non-reversible subordination of one group of people by another, the 'surplus' power that is always fixed on the same side, the inequality of position of the different 'partners' in relation to the common regula-tion, all these distinguish the disciplinary link from the contractual link, and make it possible to distort the contractual link systematically from the moment it has as its content a mechanism of discipline. We know, for example, how many real proced-ures undermine the legal fiction of the work contract: workshop discipline is not the least important. Moreover, whereas the juridical systems define juridical subjects according to universal norms, the disciplines characterize, classify, specialize; they distribute along a scale, around a norm, hierarchize individuals in relation to one another and, if necessary, disqualify and invalidate. In any case, in the space and during the time in which they exercise their control and bring into play the asymmetries of their power, they effect a suspension of the law that is never total, but is never annulled either. Regular and institutional as it may be, the discipline, in its mechanism, is a 'counter-law'. And, although the universal juridicism of modern society seems to fix limits on the exercise of power, its universally widespread panopticism enables it to operate, on the underside of the law, a machinery that is both immense and minute, which supports, reinforces, multiplies the asymmetry of power and undermines the limits that are traced around the law. The minute disciplines, the panopticisms of every day may well be below the level of emergence of the great apparatuses and the great political struggles. But, in the genealogy of modern society, they have been, with the class domination that traverses it, the political counterpart of the juridical norms according to which power was redistributed. Hence, no doubt, the importance that has been given for so long to the small techniques of discipline, to those apparently insignificant tricks that it has invented, and even to those 'sciences' that give it a respectable face; hence the fear of abandoning them if one cannot find any substitute; hence the affirmation that they are at the very foundation of society, and an element in its equilibrium, whereas they are a series of mechanisms for unbalancing power relations definitively and everywhere; hence the persistence in regarding them as the humble, but concrete form of every morality, whereas they are a set of physico-political techniques.

To return to the problem of legal punishments, the prison with all the corrective technology at its disposal is to be resituated at the point where the codified power to punish turns into a disciplinary power to observe; at the point where the universal punishments of the law are applied selectively to certain individuals and always the same ones; at the point where the redefinition of the juridical subject by the penalty becomes a useful training of the criminal; at the point where the law is inverted and passes outside itself, and where the counter-law becomes the effective and institutionalized content of the juridical forms. What generalizes the power to punish, then, is not the universal consciousness of the law in each juridical subject; it is the regular extension, the infinitely minute web of panoptic techniques.

3. Taken one by one, most of these techniques have a long history behind them. But what was new, in the eighteenth century, was that, by being combined and generalized, they attained a level at which the formation of knowledge and the increase of power regularly reinforce one another in a circular process. At this point, the disciplines crossed the 'technological' threshold. First the hospital, then the school, then, later, the workshop were not simply 'reordered' by the disciplines; they became, thanks to them, apparatuses such that any mechanism of objectification could be used in them as an instrument of subjection, and any growth of power could give rise in them to possible branches of knowledge; it was this link, proper to the technological systems, that made possible within the disciplinary element the formation of clinical medicine, psychiatry, child psychology, educational psychology, the rationalization of labour. It is a double process, then: an epistemological 'thaw' through a refinement of power relations; a multiplication of the effects of power through the formation and accumulation of new forms of knowledge.

References

Bentham, J., *Works*, ed. Bowring, IV, 1843.
Guerry, F. and Deleule, D., *Le Corps productif*, 1973.
Julius, N. H., *Leòons sur les prisons*, I, 1831 (Fr. trans.).

Part V

The Sociological Theory of Anthony Giddens

INTRODUCTION TO PART V

Giddens was never a likely candidate to end up as one of the major social theorists of our time. In fact, it was partly his outsider status that made him, as he has put it, so "bloody minded" in his early work. Giddens (b. 1938) grew up in a lower middle-class suburb of London. He did not go to an elite school, and by his own admission did not take his qualifying examinations or his university applications very seriously. He ended up at his university (Hull) and his major (sociology) largely by chance. Even as he began his graduate studies, he intended to become a civil servant rather than an academic. His advisor guided him to a job at the University of Leicester however, where he began to hone his own theoretical views – generally in opposition to the discipline's status quo. His rising prominence was marked in 1970 by a move to Cambridge and visiting positions in North America. He has recently become the director of the London School of Economics. Giddens has also maintained a very active public life beyond the academy. He is the co-founder of Polity Press and has been an active proponent of a "third way" in politics and an occasional advisor to Prime Minister Tony Blair.[1]

Giddens is one of the field's most prolific authors. As writer and editor, he has averaged more than a book a year for the past three decades. In this time, Giddens has pursued some very consistent themes, but there have been three notable stages in his academic work. The readings in this section reflect these stages.

The first stage involved outlining a theoretical and methodological understanding of the field of sociology based on a critical re-reading of the classics. The major works here were *Capitalism and Modern Social Theory* (1971) and *New Rules of Sociological Method* (1976). The selection "Some New Rules of Sociological Method" presents Giddens' vision of what sociology is about and how it should be done. The second stage in his work was devoted to developing the theory of "structuration." It was at this point that Giddens began to be seen as a major theorist in his own right. His key books on this were *Central Problems in Social Theory* (1979) and *The Constitution of Society* (1984). The central elements of structuration theory are presented here in the reading "Agency, Structure." The most recent stage of research concerns modernity and politics. Giddens has examined the impact of modernity on social and personal life (*Consequences of Modernity* [1990], *Modernity and Self-Identity* [1991], *The Transformation of Intimacy* [1992]) and politics (*Beyond Left and Right* [1994], *The Third Way: The Renewal of Social Democracy* [1998]). The reading, "The Consequences of Modernity" develops this argument.

A Vision of Sociology

Anthony Giddens has spent a good deal of time revisiting the question of what the field of sociology is and how it should be done. These of course were contentious questions for the early generations of sociologists – Weber, Simmel, and Durkheim each had different answers. At least in the English-speaking world, the debate was more or less settled in the post-war period by the dominance of Parsons' functionalism. Giddens wanted to rethink these fundamental questions.

What is the topic of sociology? Giddens attempted to wrestle the answer away from the functionalists, and particularly Parsons. Giddens' first book, *Capitalism and Modern Social Theory*, examined the works of Marx, Durkheim, and Weber. Although they had very different approaches, Giddens argued that each was centrally concerned with the connection between capitalism and social life. Giddens' definition of the field of sociology reflects this theme. He argues that the main focus of sociology is "the study of social institutions brought into being by the industrial transformations of the past two or three centuries."[2] By adopting this answer, Giddens effectively did three things. First, he brought the issue of *power* back into the field. It is often pointed out that this book in fact established Marx as one of the "big three" of classical theory. Prior to this, Marx's status was questionable at best, and others – especially Vilfredo Pareto – were considered far more central. Second, he argued that sociology is the study of *modernity*. Third, he emphasized *institutions*. These last two points are discussed at greater length below.

How should sociology be done? Giddens began to assert his own answer to this question in *New Rules of Sociological Method*. The title is a play on Durkheim's famous methodological treatise. The book places two theoretical traditions in dynamic tension. The functionalist approach, from Durkheim to Parsons, treated society as a reality unto itself, not reducible to individuals. Although later functionalists abandoned Durkheim's language of "social facts," they nevertheless focused on "structures" as collective realities to be explained at the social level. The second approach was the interpretive (or "hermeneutic") tradition in sociology and philosophy. This may be traced from Weber's *verstehen* to the work of Schutz, Garfinkel, and others. This tradition focused on understanding agency and motives of individuals.

Giddens firmly rejects the idea that society is a collective reality. However, he does not entirely accept the hermeneutic tradition either; he particularly disagrees with its emphasis on the individual as the central unit of analysis. Rather, Giddens uses the hermeneutic tradition as a basis to argue for the importance of *agency* in sociological theory. Giddens claims that human actors are always to some degree knowledgeable about what they are doing. Social order is therefore a "skilled accomplishment" rather than an automatic response to functional needs. Because actors are knowledgeable, sociology's task is different from that of the natural sciences. Sociologists have to interpret a social world that is already interpreted by the actors that inhabit it. Giddens calls this two-tiered interpretive task the "double hermeneutic." An added difficulty is that this interpretive process leads to a cycle. Once sociological concepts are formed, they often filter back into the everyday world and change the way people think – the concept of "lifestyle" is just one among many examples of this. All of this means that sociological explanations have to be sensitive to the often unstated knowledge of actors in particular times and places.

Structuration

Giddens does not think that people are entirely free to choose their own actions, however. While he begins his major theoretical statements with discussions of action, he does not ignore structure. In fact, the connection between structure and action is the central element in his theory of structuration. Giddens' argument is summed up by his phrase "duality of structure." At a basic level, this means that people make society, but are also constrained by it. Another way to say the same thing is that although action and structure are usually seen as opposing concepts, they are actually two sides of the same coin and cannot be analyzed separately. On the one side, agency is given meaningful form only through the "generative schemes" of structure. On the other side, we can say that structures are maintained and changed through action. The elements of the theory were laid out in *New Rules of Sociological Method*, and developed in later books, especially *Central Problems in Social Theory* and *The Constitution of Society*.

As agents, we are at least partly reflexive – that is, we monitor our actions and orient them to the behavior of others. Giddens suggests that the proper units of analysis for sociologists are not discrete actions but social *practices* – ongoing streams of action. In some cases, we may be able to state relatively conscious motives about our practices. But much of the time we are engaged in routine practices, and we are not guided by conscious, rational motive. In such cases, we are guided by what Giddens calls "practical consciousness." This means that reflexive monitoring of action is a "background" task that we habitually rely upon. It is only when we are doing something non-routine that we are called upon to supply a motive. In either case, Giddens argues, we simply cannot act in any meaningful way without drawing upon collective interpretive schemes.

This brings us to the notion of structure. Many sociologists tend to conflate two meanings when they use the word structure. Giddens distinguishes between "structure" and "system" in order to separate these meanings. By *system*, Giddens means the stable patterns observable in interactions. Systems exist in "time–space," meaning that we can actually observe them in particular locations and times. Giddens defines *structure* as the "rules and resources" that act as common interpretive schemes in a particular social system. Giddens argues that structures are related to practices as language is related to speech – in fact, language is an example of what Giddens means by structure. Structures organize practices, but at the same time, structures are enacted and reproduced by practices. Although we experience structures as forces external to us, they have only a "virtual" existence – they cannot be directly observed except through their effects on practices. Language is a good example. A language is a set of generative rules that organizes our speech. Without such rules, we would not be able to produce interpretable speech, because other people would not be able to decode the sounds that we make. But in turn, a language only exists as it is used and reproduced in speech.

This notion of structure is important because it emphasizes that structures are not just constraining, they are also enabling. Most sociological traditions deal with structural constraints by showing how they limit possible courses of action. Structures do act as constraints, but Giddens points out that as generative rules, they also enable action by providing common frames of meaning. Structures provide the rules that allow new actions to occur. Again, language is a good example. A language has rules of syntax that rule out certain combinations of words. But in so doing, the rules enable us to create new, meaningful sentences. Giddens' argument also suggests that structures are generally quite stable, but they can be changed. One way this occurs is through the unintended consequences of action. This is a subject that Giddens takes up at length in his most recent work.

Modernity and Politics

Giddens' recent work has been concerned with the question of what is characteristic about social institutions in our current historical era. In dealing with this question, Giddens has necessarily entered into the debate over modernity and post-modernity that is also covered in the last section of this reader. Giddens grants that there are very real changes that mark the current era, but he suggests that it should properly be thought of as "radicalized modernity" rather than "post-modernity." That is, it is produced by an extension of the same forces that shaped the "modern" age. Characteristically, Giddens takes a two-sided view of its effects. The current age offers us unparalleled opportunities but also unexpected dangers. This has been his most empirically engaged work by far. Giddens examines three realms in particular: the experience of identity, connections of intimacy, and political institutions.

The current age offers us unparalleled opportunities for individuals because of its high "reflexivity." More than ever before, we have access to information about the world and about each other, and that information allows us to reflect on the causes and consequences of our actions. At the same time, however, we are faced with dangers related to unintended consequences of our actions and by our reliance on the knowledge of experts that we do not know and the working of abstract systems that we do not directly control. In the realm of self-identity, increased reflexivity means we are increasingly free to choose not only what we want to do, but also who we want to be. This can be both liberating and troubling. To exercise choice over your identity involves accepting some anxiety over deciding what might be your "true" identity or your "real" self. It also involves a lot of work to monitor whether your actions and thoughts at any given moment accord with your chosen identity. Both of these points are also obvious in the case of our ties of intimacy. As the family becomes a more flexible institution, we are increasingly free not only to choose our mates, but also to choose how we relate to them. This creates unparalleled opportunities, but it also creates a lot of work, since a relationship becomes a reflexive project that has to be interpreted, maintained and, at times, worried over.

But the consequences of modernity are not confined to the sphere of personal relations. They are also implicated in our relations with abstract systems. Modernity is a double-edged sword here too. The hallmark of modernity is ever-increasing integration and complexity in the impersonal institutions that we deal with. As these systems become more pervasive, we are forced to rely on them. But this also places us at their mercy. Economic systems are just one example. We place our money in banks, and we must trust in the mechanisms they have in place to keep our savings secure. The global integration of economic institutions has led to vast new opportunities for investment and development. But as economic institutions become integrated across the globe, we face large consequences from seemingly far-off events. When the Thai currency nearly collapsed in the "Asian flu" of 1997, Westerners were directly affected. There were a lot of reasons for this, but the most direct was that Thai banks were heavily in debt to Western banks. In other words, as a result of international flows of capital, the finances of everyday people halfway across the world from each other were intricately linked together.

Giddens' most recent work has focused on democratic politics. This work moves the theoretical focus from explanations of how things are to advocacy about how they ought to be. By doing this, Giddens places his work into closer dialogue with that of Habermas (the subject of Part VIII of this reader). Still, Giddens relies on some familiar themes of reflexivity and system integration, which place people into new relations of trust and dependency with each other and with their governments. Giddens argues that the political concepts of "left" and "right," once meaningful labels, are now breaking down. This is a result of a number of factors, most centrally the absence of a clear alternative to capitalism and the eclipse of political oppositions based on class in favor of those based on lifestyle choices. As a result, Giddens advocates a "radical center" in politics – an idea that has been influential in the politics of Tony Blair and Bill Clinton, among others.

Notes

1   On Giddens' biography, see Giddens' own telling in Giddens and Pierson (1998).
2   Giddens (1987).

Select Bibliography

Craib, Ian. 1992. *Anthony Giddens*. New York: Routledge. (A review and critique of Giddens' approach to social theory.)

Kaspersen, Lars Bo. 2000. *Anthony Giddens: An Introduction to a Social Theorist*. Steven Sampson, translator. Malden, MA: Basil Blackwell. (Relatively thorough introduction, but aimed at readers without extensive background in theory. Particularly good source on Giddens' recent work on politics.)

Clark, Jon, Celia Modgil, and Sohan Modgil (eds.) 1990. *Anthony Giddens: Consensus and Controversy*. New York: The Falmer Press. (An introduction to the range of reactions that Giddens' work has sparked, including statements of a number of the key debates.)

Giddens, Anthony. 1987. *Sociology: A Brief But Critical Introduction*. Second edition. San Diego: Harcourt Brace Jovanovich. (A short introduction to the field of sociology. Lays out the rudiments of Giddens' vision of sociology.)

Giddens, Anthony. 1976. *New Rules of Sociological Method: A Positive Critique of Interpretive Sociologies*. New York: Basic Books. (An early statement of Giddens' position.)

Giddens, Anthony. 1979. *Central Problems in Social Theory: Action, Structure and Contradiction in Social Analysis*. Berkeley: University of California Press. (The first major statement on structuration theory. This book is difficult for new readers of Giddens, but it is somewhat easier than later statements on structuration.)

Giddens, Anthony. 1990. *The Consequences of Modernity*. Stanford: Stanford University Press. (Like many of Giddens' works on radicalized modernity, this is written in an accessible style. Giddens here develops many of his earlier arguments into a broad consideration of modernity.)

Giddens, Anthony and Christopher Pierson. 1998. *Anthony Giddens: Making Sense of Modernity*. Stanford, CA: Stanford University Press. (A series of interviews with Giddens. Because of its plain language and directness, this is an important source for interpreting and understanding key issues in Giddens' work.)

16 Some New Rules of Sociological Method

Anthony Giddens

The schools of 'interpretative sociology' have made some essential contributions to the clarification of the logic and method of the social sciences. In summary form, these are the following: the social world, unlike the world of nature, has to be grasped as a skilled accomplishment of active human subjects; the constitution of this world as 'meaningful', 'accountable' or 'intelligible' depends upon language, regarded however not simply as a system of signs or symbols but as a medium of practical activity; the social scientist of necessity draws upon the same sorts of skills as those whose conduct he seeks to analyse in order to describe it; generating descriptions of social conduct depends upon the hermeneutic task of penetrating the frames of meaning which lay actors themselves draw upon in constituting and reconstituting the social world.

These insights derive from schools of thought which stand close to philosophical idealism, however, and manifest the traditional shortcomings of that philosophy when transferred to the field of social analysis: a concern with 'meaning' to the exclusion of the practical involvements of human life in material activity (for while it is true that human beings do not produce the world of nature, they do none the less produce from it, and actively transform the conditions of their own existence by so doing); a tendency to seek to explain all human conduct in terms of motivating ideals at the expense of the causal conditions of action; and a failure to examine social norms in relation to asymmetries of power and divisions of interest in society. These shortcomings cannot be rectified within the traditions of thought in which they originate, but nor can the positive contributions which they go along with be readily accommodated within rival theoretical schemes that have translated human agency into social determinism, and which have retained strong associations with positivism in philosophy. I have claimed essentially that three interlacing orders of problems have to be resolved to be able to transcend the limitations of interpretative sociologies, concerning: the clarification of the concept of action and the correlate notions of intention, reason, and motive; the connecting of the theory of action to the analysis of the properties of institutional structures; and the epistemological difficulties which confront any attempt to elucidate the logic of social-scientific method.

The failure of the Anglo-American philosophy of action to develop a concern with institutional analysis is reflected in an overconcentration upon purposive conduct. Thus many authors have been inclined to assimilate 'action' with 'intended action', and 'meaningful act' with 'intended outcome'; and they have not been much interested in the theoretical analysis of the origins of the purposes that actors endeavour to realize, which are assumed as given, or the unintended consequences that courses of purposive action serve to bring about. Freeing the concept of action as such, and the identification of the meaning of acts, from any necessary connection with intentions distances the hermeneutic tasks of social science from subjectivism, and makes possible a clarification both of the nature of the causal conditions of action and of the double hermeneutic with which the social sciences are inevitably involved.

'Intention', 'reason' and 'motive', I have argued, are all potentially misleading terms, in that they already presuppose a conceptual 'cutting into' the continuity of action, and are aptly treated as expressing an ongoing reflexive monitoring of conduct that 'competent' actors are expected to maintain as a routine part of their day-to-day lives. The reflexive monitoring of conduct only becomes the statement of intentions, or the giving of reasons, when actors either carry out retrospective enquiries into their own conduct or, more usually, when queries about their behaviour are made by others. The rationalization of action is closely bound up with the moral evaluations of 'responsibility' which actors make of each other's conduct, and hence with moral norms and the sanctions to which those who contravene them are subject; thus spheres of 'competence' are defined in law as what every citizen is 'expected to know about' and take account of in the monitoring of his action.

Orthodox functionalism, as represented most prominently by Durkheim and latterly by Parsons, does embody an attempt to draw theoretical connections between intentional action and institutional analysis, via the theorem that the moral values upon which social solidarity rests also appear as motivating elements in personality. This view, I have tried to show, serves only to replace the notion of action with the thesis that the properties of social and personality systems have to be examined in conjunction with one another: the member of society does not figure here as a skilled, creative agent, capable of reflexively monitoring his behaviour (and in principle capable of doing so in the light of anything he may believe he can learn from Parsons' theories!). Moreover, the Parsonian starting-point in the so-called 'Hobbesian problem of order' has the consequence that Parsons' theoretical scheme is no more able adequately to cope with asymmetries of power and divisions of interest in society than are the various traditions of 'interpretative sociology' that I have discussed. I have therefore set out an alternative view, that certainly is capable of more detailed development, but whose outlines should be clear. The production of society is brought about by the active constituting skills of its members, but draws upon resources, and depends upon conditions, of which they are unaware or which they perceive only dimly. Three aspects of the production of interaction can be distinguished: those of the constitution of meaning, morality and relations of power. The means whereby these are brought into being can also be regarded as modalities of the reproduction of structures: the idea of the duality of structure is a central one here, since structures appear both as condition and consequence of the production of interaction. All organizations or collectivities 'consist of' systems of interaction, and can be analysed as structures: but as systems, their existence depends upon modes of *structuration* whereby they are reproduced. The reproduction of structures of domination, one must emphasize, expresses asymmetries in the forms of meaning and morality that are made to 'count' in interaction, thus tying them in to divisions of interest that serve to orient struggles over divergent interpretations of frames of meaning and moral norms.

The production of interaction as 'meaningful', I have proposed, can usefully be analysed as depending upon 'mutual knowledge' which is drawn upon by participants as interpretative schemes to make sense of what each other says and does. Mutual knowledge is not corrigible to the sociological observer, who must draw upon it just as lay actors do in order to generate descriptions of their conduct; in so far as such 'knowledge', however, can be represented as 'commonsense', as a series of factual beliefs, it is in principle open to confirmation or otherwise in the light of social scientific analysis. Recent developments in the philosophy of natural science, I have argued, are relevant to elucidating the logical status of claims to knowledge made in the social sciences. But their relevance is limited by features of the latter which have no immediate parallel in the natural sciences; and in any case such developments themselves have to be subjected to critical scrutiny. Kuhn's use of the term 'paradigm' shares important elements in common with other versions of the notion of what I have called 'frame of meaning', and as Kuhn applies it to analysing the history of science also raises similar difficulties to these other versions. Thus Kuhn exaggerates the internal unity of 'paradigms', as Winch does 'forms of life', and consequently does not acknowledge that the problem of the mediation of different frames of meaning has to be treated as the *starting-point* of analysis. When conjoined to an insistence upon a distinction of sense and reference, this allows us to grasp the significance of the hermeneutic recognition of the authenticity of meaning-frames without slipping into a relativism which forecloses the possibility of any rational evaluation of them. The mediation of paradigms or widely discrepant theoretical schemes in science is a hermeneutic matter like that involved in the contacts between other types of meaning-frames. But sociology, unlike natural science, deals with a pre-interpreted world, where the creation and reproduction of meaning-frames is a very condition of that which it seeks to analyse, namely human social conduct: this is, to repeat, why there is a double hermeneutic in the social sciences that poses as a specific difficulty what Schutz, following Weber, calls the 'postulate of adequacy'. I have suggested that Schutz' formulation of this, based upon the thesis that the technical concepts of social science have to be in some way capable of being reduced to lay notions of everyday action, will not do. It has in fact to be reversed: rather than, in some sense, the concepts of sociology having to be open to rendition in terms of lay concepts, it is the case that the observing social scientist has to be able first to grasp those lay concepts, i.e. penetrate hermeneutically the form of life whose features he wishes to analyse or explain.

The relation between technical vocabularies of social science and lay concepts, however, is a shifting one: just as social scientists adopt everyday terms – 'meaning', 'motive', 'power', etc. – and use them in specialized senses, so lay actors tend to take over the concepts and theories of the social sciences and embody them as constitutive elements in the rationalization of their own conduct. The significance of this is recognized only marginally in orthodox sociology, in the guise of 'self-fulfilling' or 'self-negating' prophecies, which are regarded simply as nuisances that inhibit accurate prediction. But although causal generalizations in the social sciences in some aspects may resemble natural scientific laws, they are in an essential way distinct from the latter because they depend upon reproduced alignments of unintended consequences; in so far as they are announced as generalizations, and are picked up as such by those to whose conduct they apply, their form is altered. This once more reunites us with the theme of reflexivity, central to this study, and leads inevitably to a whole range of further issues, concerning the tasks of social science as critical theory. I shall pursue these issues in another work. But it is important to stress that social science stands in a relation of tension to its 'subject-matter' – as a potential instrument of the expansion of *rational autonomy of action*, but equally as a potential *instrument of domination*.

In conclusion, and in summary form, here are some new 'rules of sociological method'. The latter phrase is only intended ironically. I do not claim that the presuppositions that follow are 'rules' in the sense in which I have suggested that term is most appropriately used in the social sciences. Rather, they are a skeletal statement of some of the themes of the study as a whole, and are merely designed to exemplify its differences from the famous sociological manifesto that Durkheim issued some eighty years ago. This statement does not in and of itself constitute a 'programme' for sociological research, although I regard it as an integral part of such a programme. The sub-classification provided below works roughly as follows. Section A concerns the 'subject-matter of sociology': the production and reproduction of society; Section B, the boundaries of agency, and the modes in which processes of production and reproduction may be examined; Section C, the modes in which social life is 'observed' and characterizations of social activity established; Section D, the formulation of concepts within the meaning-frames of social science as metalanguages.

A

ONE: *Sociology is not concerned with a 'pre-given' universe of objects, but with one which is constituted or produced by the active doings of subjects.* Human beings transform nature socially, and by 'humanizing' it they transform themselves; but they do not, of course, produce the natural world, which is constituted as an object-world independently of their existence. If in transforming that world they create history, and thence live *in* history, they do so because the production and reproduction of society is not 'biologically programmed', as it is among the lower animals. (Theories men develop may, through their technological applications, affect nature, but they cannot come to constitute features *of* the natural world as they do in the case of the social world.)

TWO: *The production and reproduction of society thus has to be treated as a skilled performance on the part of its members*, not as merely a mechanical series of processes. To emphasize this, however, is definitely not to say that actors are wholly aware of what these skills are, or just how they manage to exercise them; or that the forms of social life are adequately understood as the intended outcomes of action.

B

ONE: *The realm of human agency is bounded. Men produce society, but they do so as historically located actors, and not under conditions of their own choosing.* There is an unstable margin, however, between conduct that can be analysed as intentional action, and behaviour that has to be analysed nomologically as a set of 'occurrences'. In respect of sociology, the crucial task of nomological analysis is to be found in the explanation of the properties of structures.

TWO: *Structures must not be conceptualized as simply placing constraints upon human agency, but as enabling.* This is what I call the *duality of structure*. Structures can always in principle be examined in terms of their *structuration* as a series of reproduced practices. To enquire into the structuration of social practices is to seek to explain how it comes about that structures are constituted through action, and reciprocally how action is constituted structurally.

THREE: *Processes of structuration involve an interplay of meanings, norms and power.* These three concepts are analytically equivalent as the 'primitive' terms of social science, and *are logically implicated both in the notion of intentional action and that of structure*: every cognitive and moral order is at the same time a system of power, involving a 'horizon of legitimacy'.

C

ONE: *The sociological observer cannot make social life available as a 'phenomenon' for observation independently of drawing upon his knowledge of it as a resource whereby he constitutes it as a 'topic for investigation'.* In *this* respect, his position is no different from that of any other member of society; 'mutual knowledge' is not a series of corrigible items, but represents the interpretative schemes which both sociologists and laymen use, and must use, to 'make sense' of social activity, i.e. to generate 'recognizable' characterizations of it.

TWO: *Immersion in a form of life is the necessary and only means whereby an observer is able to generate such characterizations.* 'Immersion' here – say, in relation to an alien culture – does not, however, mean 'becoming a full member' of the community, and cannot mean this. To 'get to know' an alien form of life is to know how to find one's way about in it, to *be able* to participate in it as an ensemble of practices. But for the sociological observer this is a mode of generating descriptions which have to be mediated, i.e., transformed into categories of social-scientific discourse.

D

ONE: *Sociological concepts thus obey what I call a double hermeneutic*: (1) Any generalized theoretical scheme in the natural or social sciences is in a certain sense a form of life in itself, the concepts of which have to be mastered as a mode of practical activity generating specific types of descriptions. That this is already a hermeneutic task is clearly demonstrated in the 'newer philosophy of science' of Kuhn and others. (2) Sociology, however, deals with a universe which is already constituted within frames of meaning by social actors themselves, and reinterprets these within its own theoretical schemes, mediating ordinary and technical language. This double hermeneutic is of considerable complexity, since the connection is not merely a one-way one (as Schutz seems to suggest); there is a continual 'slippage' of the concepts constructed in sociology, whereby these are appropriated by those whose conduct they were originally coined to analyse, and hence tend to become integral features *of* that conduct (thereby in fact potentially compromising their original usage within the technical vocabulary of social science).

TWO: *In sum, the primary tasks of sociological analysis are the following: (1) The hermeneutic explication and mediation of divergent forms of life within descriptive metalanguages of social science; (2) Explication of the production and reproduction of society as the accomplished outcome of human agency.*

17 Agency, Structure

Anthony Giddens

The principal issue with which I shall be concerned in this paper is that of connecting a notion of human action with structural explanation in social analysis. The making of such a connection, I shall argue, demands the following: a theory of the human agent, or of the subject; an account of the conditions and consequences of action; and an interpretation of 'structure' as somehow embroiled in both those conditions and consequences.

Time, Agency, Practice

I shall argue here that, in social theory, the notions of action and structure *presuppose one another*, but that recognition of this dependence, which is a dialectical relation, necessitates a reworking both of a series of concepts linked to each of these terms, and of the terms themselves.

In this section I shall consider some issues concerning the theory of action, before attempting to connect agency with a conception of structural analysis. I shall draw upon the analytical philosophy of action, as developed by British and American philosophers over the past two decades. But I shall want to say that, as characteristically formulated by such writers, the philosophy of action has a number of notable *lacunae*. One, which I have already mentioned, is my main concern in what follows: the analytical philosophy of action lacks a theorisation of institutions. Two other considerations, I shall claim, are vital to such a theorisation. The first is the incorporation of *temporality* into the understanding of human agency; the second is the incorporation of *power* as integral to the constitution of social practices. . . .

A. N. Whitehead says somewhere that 'What we perceive as the present is the vivid fringe of memory tinged with anticipation'. Heidegger stresses the link between *Andenken* (memory: literally, 'think-on') and *denken* (think) in holding that the experience of time is not that of a succession of nows, but the interpolation of memory and anticipation in the present-as-Being. Neither time nor the experience of time are aggregates of 'instants'. This emphasis is important for various reasons. One, which bears directly upon the treatment of action by analytical philosophers, concerns the conceptualisation of acts, intentions, purposes, reasons, etc. In ordinary English usage, we speak as if these were distinct unities or elements in some way aggregated or strung together in action. Most British and American philosophers of action have accepted this usage unquestioningly. In so doing they have unwittingly abstracted agency from its location in time, from the temporality of day-to-day conduct. What this literature ignores is the reflexive moment of attention, called into being in discourse, that breaks into the flow of action which constitutes the day-to-day activity of human subjects. Such a moment is involved even in the constitution of 'an' action or of 'an act' from the *durée* of lived-through experience.

'Action' or agency, as I use it, thus does not refer to a series of discrete acts combined together, but to *a continuous flow of conduct*. We may define action, if I may borrow a formulation from a previous work, as involving a 'stream of actual or contemplated causal interventions of corporeal beings in the ongoing process of events-in-the-world'. Certain comments need to be made about this. First, the notion of action has reference to the activities of an agent, and cannot be examined apart from a broader theory of the acting self. It is necessary to insist upon this apparent tautology, because in a substantial part of the philosophical literature the nature of action is discussed primarily in relation to a contrast with 'movements': the characteristics of the actor as a subject remain unexplored or implicit. The concept of agency as I advocate it here, involving 'intervention' in a potentially malleable object-world, relates directly to the more generalised notion of *Praxis*. I shall later treat regularised acts as *situated practices*, and shall regard this concept as expressing a major mode of connection between action theory and structural analysis. Second, it is a necessary feature of action that, at any point in time, the agent 'could have acted otherwise': either positively in terms of attempted intervention in the process of 'events in the world', or negatively in terms of forbearance. The sense of 'could have done otherwise' is obviously a difficult and complex one. It is not important to this paper to attempt to elaborate a detailed justification of it. It is a mistake, however, to suppose that the concept of action can be fully elucidated in this respect outside of the context of *historically located modes of activity*.

Figure 17.1 portrays what could be regarded as a 'stratification model' of action: a model whose implications however cannot be properly worked out separately from the discussion of the properties of structure that I shall provide in a subsequent section. The reflexive monitoring of conduct refers to the intentional or purposive character of human behaviour: it emphasises 'intentionality' *as process*. Such intentionality is a routine feature of human conduct, and does not imply that actors have definite goals consciously held in mind during the course of their activities. That the latter is unusual, in fact, is indicated in ordinary English usage by the distinction between meaning or intending to do something, and doing something 'purposefully', the latter implying an uncommon degree of mental application given to the pursuit of an aim. When lay actors inquire about each other's intentions in respect of particular acts, they abstract from a continuing process of routine monitoring whereby they relate their activity to one another and to the object-world. The distinctive feature about the reflexive monitoring of human actors, as compared to the behaviour of animals, is what Garfinkel calls the accountability of human action. I take 'accountability' to mean that the accounts that actors are able to offer of their

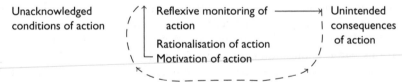

Figure 17.1

conduct draw upon the same stocks of knowledge as are drawn upon in the very production and reproduction of their action. As Harré expresses this, 'the very same social knowledge and skill is involved in the genesis of action and accounts... an individual's ability to do each depends upon his stock of social knowledge'.[1] But we must make an important emendation to the point of view Harré appears to take. The 'giving of accounts' refers to the *discursive* capabilities and inclinations of actors, and does not exhaust the connections between 'stocks of knowledge' and action. The factor missing from Harré's characterisation is *practical consciousness*: tacit knowledge that is skilfully applied in the enactment of courses of conduct, but which the actor is not able to formulate discursively.

The reflexive monitoring of behaviour operates against the background of the rationalisation of action – by which I mean the capabilities of human agents to 'explain' why they act as they do by giving reasons for their conduct – and in the more 'inclusive' context of practical consciousness. Like 'intentions', 'reasons' only form discrete accounts in the context of queries, whether initiated by others, or as elements of a process of self-examination by the actor. It is very important to emphasise that the reflexive monitoring of action includes the monitoring of *the setting of interaction*, and not just the behaviour of the particular actors taken separately. This is shown by Garfinkel to be a basic feature of the ethno-methods involved in the day-to-day constitution of social interaction. The rationalisation of action, as a chronic feature of daily conduct, is a normal characteristic of the behaviour of competent social agents, and is indeed the main basis upon which their 'competence' is adjudged by others. This does not mean that reasons can be linked as directly with norms or conventions as some philosophers have claimed or implied. Reasons do not just include the citing of or the appeal to norms: to suppose that such is the case actually draws the philosophy of action back towards the Parsonian action frame of reference, since conduct then becomes driven by 'internalised' normative imperatives.

The reasons actors supply discursively for their conduct in the course of practical queries, in the context of daily social life, stand in a relation of some tension to the rationalisation of action as actually embodied within the stream of conduct of the agent. The least interesting or consequential aspect of this concerns the possibilities of deliberate dissimulation that exist: where an actor claims to have acted for reasons that he was not in fact guided by. More important are the grey areas of practical consciousness that exist in the relation between the rationalisation of action and actors' stocks of knowledge; and between the rationalisation of action and the unconscious. The stocks of knowledge, in Schutz's terms, or what I call the *mutual knowledge* employed by actors in the production of social encounters, are not usually known to those actors in an explicitly codified form; the practical character of such knowledge conforms to the Wittgensteinian formulation of knowing a rule. The accounts actors are able to provide of their reasons are bounded, or subject to various degrees of possible articulation, in respect of tacitly employed mutual knowledge. The giving of reasons in day-to-day activity, which is closely associated with the moral accountability of action, is inevitably caught up in, and expressive of, the demands and the conflicts entailed within social encounters. But the articulation of accounts as reasons is also influenced by unconscious elements of motivation. This involves possibilities of rationalisation in the Freudian sense, as the dislocating effects of the unconscious upon conscious processes of rational accounting.

Motivational components of action, which I take to refer to the organisation of an actor's wants, straddle conscious and unconscious aspects of cognition and emotion. The whole weight of psychoanalytic theory suggests that motivation has an internal hierarchy of its own. I shall argue in a subsequent paper that a conception of the unconscious is essential to social theory, even if the resultant schema I shall develop departs in some ways from classical Freudian views. But the unconscious, of course, can only be explored in relation to the conscious: to the reflexive monitoring and rationalisation of conduct, grounded in practical consciousness. We have to guard against a reductive theory of institutions in respect of the unconscious: that is, against a theory which, in seeking to connect the forms of social life to unconscious processes, fails to allow sufficient play to autonomous social forces – Freud's own 'sociological' writings leave a lot to be desired in this respect. But we must also avoid a reductive theory of consciousness: that is, one which, in emphasising the role of the unconscious, is able to grasp the reflexive features of action only as a pale cast of unconscious processes which really determine them.

The philosophy of action, as developed by Anglo-Saxon authors, has skirted issues that are indicated at each side of figure 17.1. So far as the unconscious is concerned, this neglect expresses more than just an acceptance of Wittgenstein's suspicions about the logical status of psychoanalysis. Rather it is a consequence of a preoccupation with the relations between reasons and intentional conduct; most authors, if they refer to 'motives' at all, use the term as equivalent to reasons. A theory of motivation is crucial because it supplies the conceptual links between the rationalisation of action and the framework of convention as embodied in institutions (although I shall argue subsequently that large areas of social behaviour can be regarded as not directly motivated). But a theory of motivation also has to relate to the unacknowledged conditions of action: in respect of unconscious motives, operating or 'outside' the range of the self-understanding of the agent. The unconscious comprises only one set of such conditions, which have to be connected to those represented on the other side of the diagram: the unintended consequences of action.

If action philosophy has largely avoided questions of the unconscious, it has also displayed virtually *no interest in the unintended consequences of intentional conduct*. This is certainly responsible in some part for the gulf that has separated the philosophy of action from institutional theories in social science. If functionalist writers have been unable to develop an adequate account of intentional conduct, they have nevertheless been quite rightly concerned with the escape of activity from the scope of the purposes of the actor. The unintended consequences of action are of central importance to social theory in so far as they are systematically incorporated within the process of reproduction of institutions. I shall discuss the implications of this in some detail later. But it is worthwhile pointing out at this juncture that one such implication is that the unintended consequences of conduct relate directly to its unacknowledged conditions as specified by a theory of motivation. For in so far as such unintended consequences are involved in social reproduction, they become conditions of action also. To follow this through further, however, we must turn to the concept of structure.

Time, Structure, System

... The concept of structuration I wish to develop depends upon making distinctions between structure and system (without questioning that these have to be closely connected); but it also involves understanding each of the terms differently from the characteristic usages of both structuralism and functionalism.

I want to suggest that *structure, system* and *structuration*, appropriately conceptualised, are all necessary terms in social theory. To understand why a use can be found for each of these notions, we have to return to the theme of temporality I introduced earlier. In functionalism and structuralism alike, an attempt is made to exclude time (or more accurately, time-space intersections) from social theory, by the application of the synchrony/diachrony distinction. . . .

As I shall employ it, 'structure' refers to 'structural property', or more exactly, to 'structuring property', structuring properties providing the 'binding' of time and space in social systems. I argue that these properties can be understood as rules and resources, recursively implicated in the reproduction of social systems. Structures exist paradigmatically, as an absent set of differences, temporally 'present' only in their instantiation, in the constituting moments of social systems. To regard structure as involving a 'virtual order' of differences, as I have already indicated, does not necessitate accepting Lévi-Strauss's view that structures are simply models posited by the observer. Rather, it implies recognising the existence of: (a) knowledge – as memory traces – of 'how things are to be done' (said, written), on the part of social actors; (b) social practices organised through the recursive mobilisation of that knowledge; (c) capabilities that the production of those practices presupposes.

'Structural analysis' in the social sciences involves examining the structuration of social systems. The connotation of 'visible pattern' which the term 'social structure' ordinarily has, as employed in Anglo-American sociology, is carried in my terminology by the notion of system: with the crucial proviso that social systems are patterned in time as well as space, through continuities of social reproduction. A social system is thus a 'structured totality'. Structures do not exist in time–space, except in the moments of the constitution of social systems. But we can analyse how 'deeply-layered' structures are in terms of the historical duration of the practices they recursively organise, and the spatial 'breadth' of those practices: how widespread they are across a range of interactions. The most deeply-layered practices constitutive of social systems in each of these senses are *institutions*.

It is fundamental to understand that, when I speak of structure as rules and resources, I do not imply that we can profitably study either rules or resources as aggregates of isolated precepts or capabilities. From Saussure to Wittgenstein to Searle the game of chess appears in the philosophical literature as a reference point for illustrating features of linguistic and social rules. But, as I shall suggest below – especially in the way in which they are employed by philosophical authors – such game analogies can be highly misleading. Rules tend to be regarded as isolated formulae, to be related to particular 'moves'. Nowhere in the philosophical literature, to my knowledge, are either the history of chess (which has its origins in warfare), or actual games of chess, made the focus of study. Such study would, however, be much more relevant than the usual analogies for elucidating the standpoint I wish to suggest, which regards rules as media and outcome of the reproduction of social systems. Rules can only be grasped in the context of the historical development of social totalities, as recursively implicated in practices. This point is important in a twofold sense. (a) *There is not a singular relation between 'an activity' and 'a rule'*, as is sometimes suggested or implied by appeal to statements like 'the rule governing the Queen's move' in chess. Activities or practices are brought into being in the context of overlapping and connected sets of rules, given coherence by their involvement in the constitution of social systems in the movement of time. (b) Rules cannot be exhaustively described or analysed in terms of their own content, as prescriptions, prohibitions, etc.: precisely because, apart from those circumstances where a relevant lexicon exists, *rules and practices only exist in conjunction with one another.*

Rules and Resources

The connections between the three concepts in figure 17.2 can be quickly stated at the outset. Social systems involve regularised relations of interdependence between individuals or groups, that typically can be best analysed as *recurrent social practices*. Social systems are systems of social interaction; as such they involve the situated activities of human subjects, and exist syntagmatically in the flow of time. Systems, in this terminology, have structures, or more accurately, have structural properties; they are not structures in themselves. Structures are necessarily (logically) properties of systems or collectivities, and *are characterised by the 'absence of a subject'*. To study the structuration of a social system is to study the ways in which that system, via the application of generative rules and resources, and in the context of unintended outcomes, is produced and reproduced in interaction. . . .

In emphasising the importance of resources as structural properties of social systems, I mean to stress the centrality of the concept of power to social theory. Like 'rule', power is not a description of a state of affairs, but a capability. I think it

STRUCTURE	Rules and resources, organised as properties of social systems. Structure only exists as 'structural properties'.
SYSTEM	Reproduced relations between actors or collectivities, organised as regular social practices.
STRUCTURATION	Conditions governing the continuity or transformation of structures, and therefore the reproduction of systems.

Figure 17.2

true to say that few of the major thinkers or traditions of thought in sociology have accorded power as focal a place in social theory as is warranted. Those who have recognised the essential importance of power, like Nietzsche and Weber, have usually done so only on the basis of a normative irrationalism which I want to repudiate (although I shall not give the grounds for this here). If there is no rational mode of adjudging 'ultimate value' claims, as Weber held, then the only recourse open is that of power or might: the strongest are able to make their values count by crushing others. More common are those standpoints which either treat power as secondary to the meaningful or normative character of social life, or ignore power altogether. Such is the case, for example, with the works of authors in traditions of phenomenology (Schutz) or Wittgensteinian social thought (Winch), just as much as with traditions to which they are opposed in other respects (the functionalism of Durkheim or Parsons). It is even true, in a certain, although a quite different, sense, of Marxism, in so far as Marx connected power directly to class interests, with the possible inference that when class divisions disappear, relations of power do also.

Among the many interpretations of power in social and political theory, two main perspectives appear. One is that power is best conceptualised as the capability of an actor to achieve his or her will, even at the expense of that of others who might resist him – the sort of definition employed by Weber among many other authors. The second is that power should be seen as a property of the collectivity: Parsons's concept of power, for instance, belongs to this latter category. I wish to claim, however, that neither of these modes of conceiving power is appropriate in isolation; and that we should connect them together as features of the duality of structure. I shall treat resources as the 'bases' or 'vehicles' of power, comprising structures of domination, drawn upon by parties to interaction and reproduced through the duality of structure. Power is generated by definite forms of domination in a parallel way to the involvement of rules with social practices: and, indeed, as an integral element or aspect of those practices.

The Theory of Structuration

The concept of structuration involves that of the *duality of structure*, which relates to the *fundamentally recursive character of social life, and expresses the mutual dependence of structure and agency*. By the duality of structure I mean that the structural properties of social systems are both the medium and the outcome of the practices that constitute those systems. The theory of structuration, thus formulated, rejects any differentiation of synchrony and diachrony or statics and dynamics. The identification of structure with constraint is also rejected: structure is both enabling and constraining, and it is one of the specific tasks of social theory to study the conditions in the organisation of social systems that govern the interconnections between the two. According to this conception, the same structural characteristics participate in the subject (the actor) as in the object (society). Structure forms 'personality' and 'society' simultaneously – but in neither case exhaustively: because of the significance of unintended consequences of action, and because of unacknow-ledged conditions of action. Ernst Bloch says, *Homo semper tiro*: man is always a beginner. We may agree, in the sense that every process of action is a production of something new, a fresh act; but at the same time all action exists in continuity with the past, which supplies the means of its initiation. *Structure thus is not to be conceptualised as a barrier to action, but as essentially involved in its production*: even in the most radical processes of social change which, like any others, occur in time. The most disruptive modes of social change, like the most rigidly stable forms, involve structuration. Hence there is no need, nor any room, for a conception of de-structuration such as that suggested by Gurvitch. A notion of de-structuration is only necessary if we retain the idea that structure is simply equivalent to constraint, thereby counterposing structure and freedom (as Gurvitch does, and as Sartre does also)....

According to the notion of the duality of structure, rules and resources are drawn upon by actors in the production of interaction, but are thereby also reconstituted through such interaction. Structure is thus the mode in which the relation between moment and totality expresses itself in social reproduction. This relation is distinct from that involved in the relation of 'parts' and 'wholes' in the co-ordination of actors and groups in social systems as posited in functionalist theory. That is to say, the differences which constitute social systems reflect a dialectic of presences and absences in space and time. But these are only brought into being and reproduced via the virtual order of differences of structures, expressed in the duality of structure. The differences that constitute structures, and are constituted structurally, relate 'part' to 'whole' in the sense in which the utterance of a grammatical sentence presupposes the absent corpus of syntactical rules that constitute the language as a totality. The importance of this relation of moment and totality for social theory cannot be exaggerated, since it involves a dialectic of presence and absence which ties the most minor or trivial forms of social action to structural properties of the overall society (and, logically, to the development of mankind as a whole).

It is an essential emphasis of the ideas developed here that institutions do not just work 'behind the backs' of the social actors who produce and reproduce them. Every competent member of every society knows a great deal about the institutions of that society: such knowledge is not *incidental* to the operation of society, but is necessarily involved in it. A common tendency of many otherwise divergent schools of sociological thought is to adopt the methodological tactic of beginning their analyses by discounting agents' reasons for their action (or what I prefer to call the rationalisation of action), in order to discover the 'real' stimuli to their activity, of which they are ignorant. Such a stance, however, is not only defective from the point of view of social theory, it is one with strongly-defined and potentially offensive political implications. It implies a *derogation of the lay actor*. If actors are regarded as cultural dopes or mere 'bearers of a mode of production', with no worthwhile understanding of their surroundings or the circumstances of their action, the way is immediately laid open for the supposition that their own views can be disregarded in any practical programmes that might be inaugurated. This is not just a question of 'whose side (as social analysts) are we on?' – although there is no doubt that social incompetence is commonly attributed to people in lower socio-economic groupings by those in power-positions, or by their associated 'experts'.

It is not a coincidence that the forms of social theory which have made little or no conceptual space for agents' understanding of themselves, and of their social contexts, have tended greatly to exaggerate the impact of dominant symbol systems or ideologies upon those in subordinate classes: as in Parsons or Althusser. A good case can be made to the effect that only dominant class groups have ever been strongly committed to dominant ideologies. This is not just because of the development of divergent 'sub-cultures' – for example, working-class culture as compared to bourgeois culture in nineteenth-century Britain – but also because *all social actors, no matter how lowly, have some degree of penetration of the social forms which oppress them.* Where partially closed, localised cultures become largely unavailable, as is increasingly the case within advanced capitalism, scepticism about 'official' views of society often is expressed in various forms of 'distancing' – and in humour. Wit is deflationary. Humour is used socially both to attack and to defend against the influence of outside forces that cannot otherwise easily be coped with.

One must not overestimate the degree of conviction with which even those in dominant classes, or other positions of authority, accept ideological symbol-systems. But it is not implausible to suppose that, in some circumstances, and from some aspects, those in subordinate positions in a society might have a greater penetration of the conditions of social reproduction than those who otherwise dominate them. This is related to the *dialectic of control* in social systems that I shall analyse later. Those who in a largely unquestioning way accept certain dominant perspectives may be more imprisoned within them than others are, even though these perspectives help the former to sustain their position of dominance. The point at issue here has a definite similarity to Laing's thesis about schizophrenia: that notwithstanding the distorted nature of schizophrenic language and thought, in some respects the schizophrenic person 'sees through' features of day-to-day existence which the majority accept without demur.

These things having been said, we have to enter major qualifications about what is implied in the proposition that every competent actor has a wide-ranging, yet intimate and subtle, knowledge of the society of which he or she is a member. First, 'knowledge' has to be understood in terms of both practical and discursive consciousness: and even where there is substantial discursive penetration of institutional forms, this is not necessarily, nor normally, expressed in a propositional manner. Schutz in a sense makes this point when he calls typifications 'cookery book knowledge', and contrasts cookery book knowledge to the sort of abstract, theoretical knowledge called for by the relevances of the social scientist. But this does not distinguish satisfactorily between practical consciousness, which is knowledge embodied in what actors 'know how to do', and discourse, that is, what actors are able to 'talk about' and in what manner or guise they are able to talk about it.

Second, every individual actor is only one among others in a society: very many others, obviously, in the case of the contemporary industrialised societies. We have to recognise that what an actor knows as a competent – but historically and spatially located – member of society, 'shades off' in contexts that stretch beyond those of his or her day-to-day activity. Third, the parameters of practical and discursive consciousness are bounded in specifiable ways, that connect with the 'situated' character of actors' activities, but are not reducible to it. These can be identified from figure 17.1: the unconscious conditions of action and the unintended consequences of action. . . .

The Duality of Structure in Interaction

Let us now give more concrete form to the duality of structure in interaction, following on from what has been outlined above.

What I call here the 'modalities' of structuration represent the central dimensions of the duality of structure in the constitution of interaction. The modalities of structuration are drawn upon by actors in the production of interaction, but at the same time are the media of the reproduction of the structural components of systems of interaction. When institutional analysis is bracketed, the modalities are treated as stocks of knowledge and resources employed by actors in the constitution of inter-action as a skilled and knowledgeable accomplishment, within bounded conditions of the rationalisation of action. Where strategic conduct is placed under an *epoché*, the modalities represent rules and resources considered as institutional features of systems of social interaction. The level of modality thus provides the coupling elements whereby the bracketing of strategic or institutional analysis is dissolved in favour of an acknowledgement of their interrelation.

The classification given in figure 17.3 does not represent a typology of interaction or structures, but a portrayal of dimensions that are combined in differing ways in social practices. The communication of meaning in interaction does not take place separately from the operation of relations of power, or outside the context of normative sanctions. All social practices involve these three elements. It is important however to bear in mind what has been said previously in respect of rules: no social practice expresses, or can be explicated in terms of, a single rule or type of resource. Rather, practices are situated within intersecting sets of rules and resources that ultimately express features of the totality. . . .

It is not enough just to stress the need in social theory to relate the constitution and communication of meaning to normative sanctions; each of these has in turn to be linked to power transactions. This is so in the twofold sense indicated by the term duality of structure. Power is expressed in the capabilities of actors to make certain 'accounts count' and to enact or resist sanctioning processes; but these capabilities draw upon modes of domination structured into social systems.

By 'interpretative schemes', I mean standardised elements of stocks of knowledge, applied by actors in the production of interaction. Interpretative schemes form the core of the mutual knowledge whereby an accountable universe of meaning is sustained through and in processes of interaction. Accountability, in Garfinkel's sense, depends upon the mastery of ethno-methods involved in language use, and it is essential to grasp the point, made by Garfinkel and in rather different form by Habermas, that such mastery cannot be adequately understood as 'monological'.

INTERACTION	communication	power	sanction
(MODALITY)	interpretative scheme	facility	norm
STRUCTURE	signification	domination	legitimation

Figure 17.3

This involves more than the proposition (made by Habermas) that a satisfactory approach to semantics cannot be derived from Chomsky's syntactics: it points to features of the relation between language and the 'context of use' that are of essential importance to social theory. In the production of meaning in interaction, context cannot be treated as merely the 'environment' or 'background' of the use of language. *The context of interaction is in some degree shaped and organised as an integral part of that interaction as a communicative encounter.* The reflexive monitoring of conduct in interaction involves the routine drawing upon of physical, social and temporal context in the sustaining of accountability; but the drawing upon of context at the same time recreates these elements as contextual relevances. The 'mutual knowledge' thus employed and reconstituted in social encounters can be regarded as the medium whereby the interweaving of locutionary and illocutionary elements of language is ordered. . . .

Methodological Individualism: A Brief Excursus

In conclusion, it might be useful to comment briefly about the bearing of the ideas advanced in this paper upon the debate over methodological individualism in social theory. There is, of course, no unitary view that can be identified as 'methodological individualism': the phrase has been used to cover a variety of different ideas. One version appears prominently in Weber's works, but I shall briefly consider here the formulation offered by Popper, who has been among the foremost advocates of such a view in modern times. Popper has described his standpoint succinctly as follows: 'all social phenomena, and especially the functioning of all social institutions, should always be understood as resulting from the decisions, actions, attitudes, etc. of human individuals . . . we should never be satisfied by an explanation in terms of so-called "collectives".' There are three key terms in this assertion that need some explanation: *individuals, collectives,* and what is implied in institutions *resulting* from decisions, etc. So far as the first of these is concerned, Popper's statement reflects a characteristic tendency in the literature of methodological individualism (pro and con) to assume that the term 'individual' stands in need of no explication. It might be thought a truism to hold that societies only consist of individuals – one reading that might be made of Popper's claim. But it is only a truism (that is true in a trivial or uninteresting sense) if we understand 'individual' to mean something like 'human organism'. If 'individual', however, means 'agent' in the sense I have employed in this paper, the situation is quite different. The first part of Popper's statement then reflects the inadequacies of action theory that I have analysed above. Institutions do indeed 'result' from human agency: but they are the outcome of action only in so far as they are also involved recursively as the medium of its production. In the sense of 'institution' therefore, the 'collective' is bound to the very phenomenon of action.

The position adopted here can be summarised as follows:

1   Social systems are produced as transactions between agents, and can be analysed as such on the level of strategic conduct. This is 'methodological' in the sense that institutional analysis is bracketed, although structural elements necessarily

enter into the characterisation of action, as modalities drawn upon to produce interaction.

2   Institutional analysis, on the other hand, brackets action, concentrating upon modalities as the media of the reproduction of social systems. But this is also purely a methodological bracketing, which is no more defensible than the first if we neglect the essential importance of the conception of the duality of structure.

Note

1   Peter Marsh, Elisabeth Rosser, and Rom Harré, *The Rules of Disorder*. London: Routledge, 1978, p. 15.

18 The Consequences of Modernity

Anthony Giddens

Abstract Systems and the Transformation of Intimacy

Abstract systems have provided a great deal of security in day-to-day life which was absent in pre-modern orders. A person can board a plane in London and reach Los Angeles some ten hours later and be fairly certain that not only will the journey be made safely, but that the plane will arrive quite close to a predetermined time. The passenger may perhaps only have a vague idea of where Los Angeles is, in terms of a global map. Only minimal preparations need to be made for the journey (obtaining passport, visa, air-ticket, and money) – no knowledge of the actual trajectory is necessary. A large amount of "surrounding" knowledge is required to be able to get on the plane, and this is knowledge which has been filtered back from expert systems to lay discourse and action. One has to know what an airport is, what an air-ticket is, and very many other things besides. But security on the journey itself does not depend upon mastery of the technical paraphernalia which make it possible.

Compare this with the task of an adventurer who undertook the same journey no more than three or four centuries ago. Although he would be the "expert," he might have little idea of where he was traveling *to* – and the very notion of "traveling" sounds oddly inapplicable. The journey would be fraught with dangers, and the risk of disaster or death very considerable. No one could participate in such an expedition who was not physically tough, resilient, and possessed of skills relevant to the conduct of the voyage.

Every time someone gets cash out of the bank or makes a deposit, casually turns on a light or a tap, sends a letter or makes a call on the telephone, she or he implicitly recognises the large areas of secure, coordinated actions and events that make modern social life possible. Of course, all sorts of hitches and breakdowns can also happen, and attitudes of scepticism or antagonism develop which produce the disengagement of individuals from one or more of these systems. But most of the time the taken-for-granted way in which everyday actions are geared into abstract systems bears witness to the effectiveness with which they operate (within the contexts of what is expected from them, because they also produce many kinds of unintended consequences).

Trust in abstract systems is the condition of time-space distanciation and of the large areas of security in day-to-day life which modern institutions offer as compared to the traditional world. The routines which are integrated with abstract systems are central to ontological security in conditions of modernity. Yet this situation also creates novel forms of psychological vulnerability, and trust in abstract systems is not psychologically rewarding in the way in which trust in persons is.

I shall concentrate on the second of these points here, returning to the first later. To begin, I want to advance the following theorems: that there is a direct (although dialectical) connection between the globalising tendencies of modernity and what I shall call the *transformation of intimacy* in contexts of day-to-day life; that the transformation of intimacy can be analysed in terms of the building of trust mechanisms; and that personal trust relations, in such circumstances, are closely bound up with a situation in which the construction of the self becomes a reflexive project. . . .

Trust and Personal Relations

With the development of abstract systems, trust in impersonal principles, as well as in anonymous others, becomes indispensable to social existence. Nonpersonalised trust of this sort is discrepant from basic trust. There is a strong psychological need to find others to trust, but institutionally organised personal connections are lacking, relative to pre-modern social situations. The point here is *not* primarily that many social characteristics which were previously part of everyday life or the "life-world" become drawn off and incorporated into abstract systems. Rather, the tissue and form of day-to-day life become reshaped in conjunction with wider social changes. Routines which are structured by abstract systems have an empty, unmoralised character – this much is valid in the idea that the impersonal increasingly swamps the personal. But this is not simply a diminishment of personal life in favour of impersonally organised systems – it is a genuine transformation of the nature of the personal itself. Personal relations whose main objective is sociability, informed by loyalty and authenticity, become as much a part of the social situations of modernity as the encompassing institutions of time-space distanciation.

It is quite wrong, however, to set off the impersonality of abstract systems against the intimacies of personal life as most existing sociological accounts tend to do. Personal life and the social ties it involves are deeply intertwined with the most far-reaching of abstract systems. It has long been the case, for example, that Western diets reflect global economic interchanges: "every cup of coffee contains within it the whole history of Western imperialism." With the accelerating globalisation of the past fifty years or so, the connections between personal life of the most intimate kind and disembedding mechanisms have intensified. As Ulrich Beck has observed, "The most intimate – say, nursing a child – and the most distant, most general – say a reactor accident in the Ukraine, energy politics – are now suddenly *directly* connected."[1]

What does this mean in terms of personal trust? The answer to this question is fundamental to the transformation of intimacy in the twentieth century. Trust in persons is not focused by personalised connections within the local community and kinship networks. Trust on a personal level becomes a project, to be "worked at" by the parties involved, and demands the *opening out of the individual to the other.* Where it cannot be controlled by fixed normative codes, trust has to be *won*, and the means of doing this is demonstrable warmth and openness. Our peculiar concern with "relationships," in the sense which that word has now taken on, is expressive of this phenomenon. Relationships are ties based upon trust, where trust is not pre-given but worked upon, and where the work involved means *a mutual process of self-disclosure*.

Given the strength of the emotions associated with sexuality, it is scarcely surprising that erotic involvements become a focal point for such self-disclosure. The transition to modern forms of erotic relations is generally thought to be associated with the formation of an ethos of romantic love, or with what Lawrence Stone calls "affective individualism." The ideal of romantic love is aptly described by Stone in the following way:

> the notion that there is only one person in the world with whom one can unite at all levels; the personality of that person is so idealised that the normal faults and follies of human nature disappear from view; love is like a thunderbolt and strikes at first sight; love is the most important thing in the world, to which all other considerations, particularly material ones, should be sacrificed; and lastly, the giving of full rein to personal emotions is admirable, no matter how exaggerated and absurd the resulting conduct might appear to others.[2]

Characterised in this way, romantic love incorporates a cluster of values scarcely ever realisable in their totality. Rather than being an ethos associated in a continuous way with the rise of modern institutions, it seems essentially to have been a transitional phenomenon, bound up with a relatively early phase in the dissolution of the older forms of arranged marriage. Aspects of the "romantic love complex" as described by Stone have proved quite durable, but these have become increasingly meshed with the dynamics of personal trust described above. Erotic relations involve a progressive path of mutual discovery, in which a process of self-realisation on the part of the lover is as much a part of the experience as increasing intimacy with the loved one. Personal trust, therefore, has to be established through the process of self-enquiry: the discovery of oneself becomes a project directly involved with the reflexivity of modernity.

Interpretations of the quest for self-identity tend to divide in much the same way as views of the decline of community, to which they are often linked. Some see a preoccupation with self-development as an offshoot of the fact that the old communal orders have broken down, producing a narcissistic, hedonistic concern with the ego. Others reach much the same conclusion, but trace this end result to forms of social manipulation. Exclusion of the majority from the arenas where the most consequential policies are forged and decisions taken forces a concentration upon the self; this is a result of the powerlessness most people feel. In the words of Christopher Lasch:

> As the world takes on a more and more menacing appearance, life becomes a never-ending search for health and well-being through exercise, dieting, drugs, spiritual regimens of various kinds, psychic self-help, and psychiatry. For those who have withdrawn interest from the outside world except in so far as it remains a source of gratification and frustration, the state of their own health becomes an all-absorbing concern.[3]

Is the search for self-identity a form of somewhat pathetic narcissism, or is it, in some part at least, a subversive force in respect of modern institutions? Most of the debate about the issue has concentrated upon this question, and I shall return to it toward the end of this study. But for the moment we should see that there is something awry in Lasch's statement. A "search for health and well-being" hardly sounds compatible with a "withdrawal of interest in the outside world." The benefits of exercise or dieting are not personal discoveries but came from the lay reception of expert knowledge, as does the appeal of therapy or psychiatry. The spiritual regimens in question may be an eclectic assemblage, but include religions and cults from around the world. The outside world not only enters in here; it is an outside world vastly more extensive in character than anyone would have had contact with in the pre-modern era.

To summarise all this, the transformation of intimacy involves the following:

1   An intrinsic relation between the *globalising tendencies* of modernity and *localised events* in day-to-day life – a complicated, dialectical connection between the "extensional" and the "intensional."
2   The construction of the self as a *reflexive project*, an elemental part of the reflexivity of modernity; an individual must find her or his identity amid the strategies and options provided by abstract systems.
3   A drive towards self-actualisation, founded upon *basic trust*, which in personalised contexts can only be established by an "opening out" of the self to the other.
4   The formation of personal and erotic ties as "relationships," guided by the *mutuality of self-disclosure.*
5   A *concern for self-fulfilment*, which is not just a narcissistic defence against an externally threatening world, over which individuals have little control, but also in part a *positive appropriation* of circumstances in which globalised influences impinge upon everyday life.

Risk and Danger in the Modern World

How should we seek to analyse the "menacing appearance" of the contemporary world of which Lasch speaks? To do so means looking in more detail at the specific risk profile of modernity, which may be outlined in the following way:

1   *Globalisation of risk* in the sense of *intensity*: for example, nuclear war can threaten the survival of humanity.
2   *Globalisation of risk* in the sense of the *expanding number of contingent events* which affect everyone or at least large numbers of people on the planet: for example, changes in the global division of labour.
3   Risk stemming from the *created environment*, or *socialised nature*: the infusion of human knowledge into the material environment.
4   The development of *institutionalised risk environments* affecting the life-chances of millions: for example, investment markets.
5   *Awareness of risk* as *risk*: the "knowledge gaps" in risks cannot be converted into "certainties" by religious or magical knowledge.
6   The *well-distributed awareness of risk*: many of the dangers we face collectively are known to wide publics.

7   *Awareness of the limitations of expertise*: no expert system can be wholly expert in terms of the consequences of the adoption of expert principles.

. . .

In what ways does this array of risks impinge upon lay trust in expert systems and feelings of ontological security? The baseline for analysis has to be the *inevitability* of living with dangers which are *remote* from the control not only of individuals, but also of large organisations, including states; and which are *of high intensity* and *life-threatening* for millions of human beings and potentially for the whole of humanity. The facts that these are not risks anyone *chooses* to run and that there are, in Beck's terms, no "others" who could be held responsible, attacked, or blamed reinforce the sense of foreboding which so many have noted as a characteristic of the current age.[4] Nor is it surprising that some of those who hold to religious beliefs are inclined to see the potential for global disaster as an expression of the wrath of God. For the high consequence global risks which we all now run are key elements of the runaway, juggernaut character of modernity, and no specific individuals or groups are responsible for them or can be constrained to "set things right."

How can we constantly keep in the forefront of our minds dangers which are enormously threatening, yet so remote from individual control? The answer is that most of us cannot. People who worry all day, every day, about the possibility of nuclear war, as was noted earlier, are liable to be thought disturbed. While it would be difficult to deem irrational someone who was constantly and consciously anxious in this way, this outlook would paralyse ordinary day-to-day life. Even a person who raises the topic at a social gathering is prone to be thought hysterical or gauche. In Carolyn See's novel *Golden Days*, which finishes in the aftermath of a nuclear war, the main character relates her fear of a nuclear holocaust to another guest at a dinner party:

> Her eyes were wide. She gazed at me with terrific concentration. "Yes", she said, "I understand what you're saying. I get it. But isn't it true that your fear of nuclear war is a metaphor for all the *other* fears that plague us today?"
>
>   My mind has never been exactly fine. But sometimes it has been good. "No", I said. I may have shouted it through the beautiful, sheltered room. "It's my view that the other fears, all those of which we have spoken, are a metaphor of my fear of nuclear war!"
>
>   She stared at me incredulously, but was spared the difficulty of a response when we were all called to a very pleasant late supper.[5]

The incredulity of the dinner party guest has nothing to do with the argument expressed; it registers disbelief that anyone should become emotional about such an issue in such a setting.

The large majority of people do not spend much of their time, on a conscious level at least, worrying about nuclear war or about the other major hazards for which it may or may not be a metaphor. The need to get on with the more local practicalities of day-to-day life is no doubt one reason, but much more is involved psychologically. In a secular environment, low-probability high-consequence risks tend to conjure up anew a sense of *fortuna* closer to the pre-modern outlook than that cultivated by minor superstitions. A sense of "fate," whether positively or negatively tinged – a vague and generalised sense of trust in distant events over which one has no control – relieves the individual of the burden of engagement with an existential situation which might otherwise be chronically disturbing. Fate, a feeling that things will take their own course anyway, thus reappears at the core of a world which is supposedly taking rational control of its own affairs. Moreover, this surely exacts a price on the level of the unconscious, since it essentially presumes the repression of anxiety. The sense of dread which is the antithesis of basic trust is likely to infuse unconscious sentiments about the uncertainties faced by humanity as a whole.[6]

Low-probability high-consequence risks will not disappear in the modern world, although in an optimal scenario they could be minimised. Thus, were it to be the case that all existing nuclear weapons were done away with, no other weapons of comparable destructive force were invented, and no comparably catastrophic disturbances of socialised nature were to loom, a profile of global danger would still exist. For if it is accepted that the eradication of established technical knowledge could not be achieved, nuclear weaponry could be reconstructed at any point. Moreover, any major technological initiative could thoroughly disturb the overall orientation of global affairs. The juggernaut effect is inherent in modernity, for reasons I shall amplify in the next section of this work.

The heavily counterfactual character of the most consequential risks is closely bound up with the numbness that a listing of them tends to promote. In mediaeval times, the invention of hell and damnation as the fate of the unbeliever in the afterlife was "real." Yet things are different with the most catastrophic dangers which face us today. The greater the danger, measured not in terms of probability of occurrence but in terms of its generalised threat to human life, the more thoroughly counterfactual it is. The risks involved are necessarily "unreal," because we could only have clear demonstration of them if events occurred that are too terrible to contemplate. Relatively small-scale events, such as the dropping of atomic bombs on Hiroshima and Nagasaki or the accidents at Three Mile Island or Chernobyl, give us some sense of what could happen. But these do not in any way bear upon the necessarily counterfactual character of other, more cataclysmic happenings – the main basis of their "unreality" and the narcotising effects produced by the repeated listing of risks. As Susan Sontag remarks, "A permanent modern scenario: apocalypse looms – and it doesn't occur. And still it looms. . . . Apocalypse is now a long-running serial: not 'Apocalypse Now', but 'Apocalypse from now on'".[7]

A Phenomenology of Modernity

Two images of what it feels like to live in the world of modernity have dominated the sociological literature, yet both of them seem less than adequate. One is that of Weber, according to which the bonds of rationality are drawn tighter and tighter, imprisoning us in a featureless cage of bureaucratic routine. Among the three major founders of modern sociology, Weber saw most clearly the significance of expertise in modern social development and used it to outline a phenomenology of modernity. Everyday experience, according to Weber, retains its colour and spontaneity, but only on the perimeter of the "steel-hard" cage of bureaucratic rationality. The image has a great deal of power and has, of course, featured strongly in fictional literature in the twentieth century as well as in more directly sociological discussions. There are many contexts of modern institutions which are marked by bureaucratic fixity. But they are far from all-pervasive, and even in the core settings of its application, namely, large-scale organisations, Weber's characterisation of bureaucracy is inadequate. Rather than tending inevitably towards rigidity, organisations produce areas of autonomy and spontaneity – which are actually often less easy to achieve in smaller groups. We owe this counterinsight to Durkheim, as well as to subsequent empirical study of organisations. The closed climate of opinion within some small groups and the modes of direct sanction available to its members fix the horizons of action much more narrowly and firmly than in larger organisational settings.

The second is the image of Marx – and of many others, whether they regard themselves as Marxist or not. According to this portrayal, modernity is seen as a monster. More limpidly perhaps than any of his contemporaries, Marx perceived how shattering the impact of modernity would be, and how irreversible. At the same time, modernity was for Marx what Habermas has aptly called an "unfinished project." The monster can be tamed, since what human beings have created they can always subject to their own control. Capitalism, simply, is an irrational way to run the modern world, because it substitutes the whims of the market for the controlled fulfilment of human need.

For these images I suggest we should substitute that of the juggernaut* – a runaway engine of enormous power which, collectively as human beings, we can drive to some extent but which also threatens to rush out of our control and which could rend itself asunder. The juggernaut crushes those who resist it, and while it sometimes seems to have a steady path, there are times when it veers away erratically in directions we cannot foresee. The ride is by no means wholly unpleasant or unrewarding; it can often be exhilarating and charged with hopeful anticipation. But, so long as the institutions of modernity endure, we shall never be able to control completely either the path or the pace of the journey. In turn, we shall never be able to feel entirely secure, because the terrain across which it runs is fraught with risks of high consequence. Feelings of ontological security and existential anxiety will coexist in ambivalence.

The juggernaut of modernity is not all of one piece, and here the imagery lapses, as does any talk of a single path which it runs. It is not an engine made up of integrated machinery, but one in which there is a tensionful, contradictory, push-and-pull of different influences. Any attempt to capture the experience of modernity must begin from this view, which derives ultimately from the dialectics of space and time, as expressed in the time-space constitution of modern institutions. I shall sketch a phenomenology of modernity in terms of four dialectically related frameworks of

---

* The term comes from the Hindi *Jagannāth*, "lord of the world," and is a title of Krishna; an idol of this deity was taken each year through the streets on a huge car, which followers are said to have thrown themselves under, to be crushed beneath the wheels.

experience, each of which connects in an integral way with the preceding discussion in this study:

Displacement and reembedding: the intersection of estrangement and familiarity.
Intimacy and impersonality: the intersection of personal trust and impersonal ties.
Expertise and reappropriation: the intersection of abstract systems and day-to-day knowledgeability.
Privatism and engagement: the intersection of pragmatic acceptance and activism.

Modernity "dis-places" in the sense previously analysed – place becomes phantasmagoric. Yet this is a double-layered, or ambivalent, experience rather than simply a loss of community. We can see this clearly only if we keep in mind the contrasts between the pre-modern and the modern described earlier. What happens is not simply that localised influences drain away into the more impersonalised relations of abstract systems. Instead, the very tissue of spatial experience alters, conjoining proximity and distance in ways that have few close parallels in prior ages. There is a complex relation here between familiarity and estrangement. Many aspects of life in local contexts continue to have a familiarity and ease to them, grounded in the day-to-day routines individuals follow. But the sense of the familiar is one often mediated by time-space distanciation. It does not derive from the particularities of localised place. And this experience, so far as it seeps into general awareness, is simultaneously disturbing and rewarding. The reassurance of the familiar, so important to a sense of ontological security, is coupled with the realisation that what is comfortable and nearby is actually an expression of distant events and was "placed into" the local environment rather than forming an organic development within it. The local shopping mall is a milieu in which a sense of ease and security is cultivated by the layout of the buildings and the careful planning of public places. Yet everyone who shops there is aware that most of the shops are chain stores, which one might find in any city, and indeed that innumerable shopping malls of similar design exist elsewhere.

A feature of displacement is our insertion into globalised cultural and information settings, which means that familiarity and place are much less consistently connected than hitherto. This is less a phenomenon of estrangement from the local than one of integration within globalised "communities" of shared experience. The boundaries of concealment and disclosure become altered, since many erstwhile quite distinct activities are juxtaposed in unitary public domains. The newspaper and the sequence of television programmes over the day are the most obvious concrete examples of this phenomenon, but it is generic to the time-space organisation of modernity. We are all familiar with events, with actions, and with the visible appearance of physical settings thousands of miles away from where we happen to live. The coming of electronic media has undoubtedly accentuated these aspects of displacement, since they override presence so instantaneously and at such distance. As Joshua Meyrowitz points out, a person on the telephone to another, perhaps on the opposite side of the world, is more closely bound to that distant other than to another individual in the same room (who may be asking, "Who is it? What's she saying?" and so forth).

The counterpart of displacement is reembedding. The disembedding mechanisms lift social relations and the exchange of information out of specific time-space contexts, but at the same time provide new opportunities for their reinsertion. This is another reason why it is a mistake to see the modern world as one in which large, impersonal systems increasingly swallow up most of personal life. The self-same processes that lead to the destruction of older city neighbourhoods and their replacement by towering office-blocks and skyscrapers often permit the gentrification of other areas and a recreation of locality. Although the picture of tall, impersonal clusters of city-centre buildings is often presented as the epitome of the landscape of modernity, this is a mistake. Equally characteristic is the recreation of places of relative smallness and informality. The very means of transportation which help to dissolve the connection between locality and kinship provide the possibility for reembedding, by making it easy to visit "close" relatives who are far away.

Parallel comments can be made about the intersection of intimacy and impersonality in modern contexts of action. It is simply not true that in conditions of modernity we live increasingly in a "world of strangers." We are not required more and more to exchange intimacy for impersonality in the contacts with others we routinely make in the course of our day-to-day lives. Something much more complex and subtle is involved. Day-to-day contacts with others in pre-modern settings were normally based upon a familiarity stemming in part from the nature of place. Yet contacts with familiar others probably rarely facilitated the level of intimacy we associate with personal and sexual relations today. The "transformation of intimacy" of which I have spoken is contingent upon the very distancing which the disembedding mechanisms bring about, combined with the altered environments of trust which they presuppose. There are some very obvious ways in which intimacy and abstract systems interact. Money, for example, can be spent to purchase the expert services of a psychologist who guides the individual in an exploration of the inner universe of the intimate and the personal.

A person walks the streets of a city and encounters perhaps thousands of people in the course of a day, people she or he has never met before – "strangers" in the modern sense of that term. Or perhaps that individual strolls along less crowded thoroughfares, idly scrutinising passersby and the diversity of products for sale in the shops – Baudelaire's *flâneur*. Who could deny that these experiences are an integral element of modernity? Yet the world "out there" – the world that shades off into indefinite time-space from the familiarity of the home and the local neighbourhood – is not at all a purely impersonal one. On the contrary, intimate relationships can be sustained at distance (regular and sustained contact can be made with other individuals at virtually any point on the earth's surface – as well as some below and above), and personal ties are continually forged with others with whom one was previously unacquainted. We live in a *peopled* world, not merely one of anonymous, blank faces, and the interpolation of abstract systems into our activities is intrinsic to bringing this about.

In relations of intimacy of the modern type, trust is always ambivalent, and the possibility of severance is more or less ever present. Personal ties can be ruptured, and ties of intimacy returned to the sphere of impersonal contacts – in the broken love affair, the intimate suddenly becomes again a stranger. The demand of "opening oneself up" to the other which personal trust relations now presume, the injunction to hide nothing from the other, mix reassurance and deep anxiety. Personal trust demands a level of self-understanding and self-expression which must itself be a source of psychological tension. For mutual self-revelation is combined with the need for reciprocity and support; yet the two are frequently incompatible. Torment and frustration interweave themselves with the need for trust in the other as the provider of care and support.

Deskilling and Reskilling in Everyday Life

Expertise is part of intimacy in conditions of modernity, as is shown not just by the huge variety of forms of psychotherapy and counseling available, but by the plurality of books, articles, and television programmes providing technical information about "relationships." Does this mean that, as Habermas puts it, abstract systems "colonise" a pre-existing "life-world," subordinating personal decisions to technical expertise? It does not. The reasons are twofold. One is that modern institutions do not just implant themselves into a "life-world," the residues of which remain much the same as they always were. Changes in the nature of day-to-day life also affect the disembedding mechanisms, in a dialectical interplay. The second reason is that technical expertise is continuously reappropriated by lay agents as part of their routine dealings with abstract systems. No one can become an expert, in the sense of the possession either of full expert knowledge or of the appropriate formal credentials, in more than a few small sectors of the immensely complicated knowledge systems which now exist. Yet no one can interact with abstract systems without mastering some of the rudiments of the principles upon which they are based.

Sociologists often suppose that, in contrast to the pre-modern era, where many things were mysteries, today we live in a world from which mystery has retreated and where the way "the world works" can (in principle) be exhaustively known. But this is not true for either the lay person or the expert, if we consider their experience as individuals. To all of us living in the modern world things are specifically *opaque*, in a way that was not the case previously. In pre-modern environments the "local knowledge," to adapt a phrase from Clifford Geertz,[8] which individuals possessed was rich, varied, and adapted to the requirements of living in the local milieu. But how many of us today when we switch on the light know much about where the electricity supply comes from or even, in a technical sense, what electricity actually is?

Yet, although "local knowledge" cannot be of the same order as it once was, the sieving off of knowledge and skill from everyday life is not a one-way process. Nor are individuals in modern contexts less knowledgeable about their local milieux than their counterparts in pre-modern cultures. Modern social life is a complex affair, and there are many "filter-back" processes whereby technical knowledge, in one shape or another, is reappropriated by lay persons and routinely applied in the course of their day-to-day activities. As was mentioned earlier, the interaction between expertise and reappropriation is strongly influenced, among other things, by experiences at access points. Economic factors may decide whether a person learns to fix her or his car engine, rewire the electrical system of the house, or fix the roof; but so do the levels of trust that an individual vests in the particular expert systems and known experts involved. Processes of reappropriation relate to all aspects of social life – for example, medical treatment, child-rearing, or sexual pleasure.

For the ordinary individual, all this does not add up to feelings of secure control over day-to-day life circumstances. Modernity expands the arenas of personal fulfilment and of security in respect of large swathes of day-to-day life. But the lay person – and *all* of us are lay persons in respect of the vast majority of expert systems – must ride the juggernaut. The lack of control which many of us feel about some of the circumstances of our lives is real.

It is against this backdrop that we should understand patterns of privatism and engagement. A sense of "survival," in Lasch's use of this term, cannot be absent from our thoughts all of the time in a world in which, for the indefinite future, survival is a real and inescapable issue. On the level of the unconscious – even, and perhaps especially, among those whose attitude is one of pragmatic acceptance towards high-consequence risks – the relation to survival probably exists as existential dread. For basic trust in the continuity of the world must be anchored in the simple conviction that it will continue, and this is something of which we cannot be entirely sure. Saul Bellow remarks in the novel *Herzog*, "The revolution of nuclear terror returns the metaphysical dimension to us. All practical activity has reached this culmination: everything may go now, civilisation, history, nature. Now to recall Mr. Kierkegaard's question..."[9] "Mr. Kierkegaard's question" is, how do we avoid the dread of nonexistence, considered not just as individual death but as an existential void? The possibility of global calamity, whether by nuclear war or other means, prevents us from reassuring ourselves with the assumption that the life of the species inevitably surpasses that of the individual.

How remote that possibility is, literally no one knows. So long as there is deterrence, there must be the chance of war, because the notion of deterrence only makes sense if the parties involved are in principle prepared to use the weaponry they hold. Once again, no one, no matter how "expert" about the logistics of weapons and military organisation or about world politics, can say whether deterrence "works," because the most that can be said is that so far there has been no war. Awareness of these inherent uncertainties does not escape the lay population, however, vague that awareness might be.

Balanced against the deep anxieties which such circumstances must produce in virtually everyone is the psychological prop of the feeling that "there's nothing that I as an individual can do," and that at any rate the risk must be very slight. Business-as-usual, as I have pointed out, is a prime element in the stabilising of trust and ontological security, and this no doubt applies in respect of high-consequence risks just as it does in other areas of trust relations.

Yet obviously even high-consequence risks are not only remote contingencies, which can be ignored in daily life, albeit at some probable psychological cost. Some such risks, and many others which are potentially life-threatening for individuals or otherwise significantly affect them, intrude right into the core of day-to-day activities. This is true, for example, of any pollution damage which affects the health of adults or children, and anything which produces toxic contents in food or affects its nutritional properties. It is also true of a multitude of technological changes that influence life chances, such as reproductive technologies. The mix of risk and opportunity is so complex in many of the circumstances involved that it is extremely difficult for individuals to know how far to vest trust in particular prescriptions or systems, and how far to suspend it. How can one manage to eat "healthily," for example, when all kinds of food are said to have toxic qualities of one sort or another and when what is held to be "good for you" by nutritional experts varies with the shifting state of scientific knowledge?

Trust and risk, opportunity and danger – these polar, paradoxical features of modernity permeate all aspects of day-to-day life, once more reflecting an extraordinary interpolation of the local and the global. Pragmatic acceptance can be sustained towards most of the abstract systems that impinge on individuals' lives, but by its very nature such an attitude cannot be carried on all the while and in respect of all areas of activity. For incoming expert information is often fragmentary or inconsistent,* as is the recycled knowledge which colleagues, friends, and intimates pass on to one another. On a personal level, decisions must be taken and policies forged. Privatism, the avoidance of contestatory engagement – which can be supported by attitudes of basic optimism, pessimism, or pragmatic acceptance – can serve the purposes of day-to-day "survival" in many respects. But it is likely to be interspersed with phases of active engagement, even on the part of those most prone to attitudes of indifference or cynicism. For, to repeat, in respect of the balance of security and danger which modernity introduces into our lives, there are no longer "others" – no one can be completely outside. Conditions of modernity, in many circumstances, provoke activism rather than privatism, because of modernity's inherent reflexivity and because there are many opportunities for collective organisation within the polyarchic systems of modern nation-states.

Objections to Post-Modernity

I have sought to develop an interpretation of the current era which challenges the usual views of the emergence of post-modernity. As ordinarily understood, conceptions of post-modernity – which mostly have their origin in post-structuralist thought – involve a number of distinct strands. I compare this conception of post-modernity (PM) with my alternative position, which I shall call radicalised modernity (RM) in table 18.1.

---

* Consider, as one among an indefinite range of examples, the case of cyclamate, an artificial sweetener, and the U.S. authorities. Cyclamate was widely used in the United States until 1970, and the Food and Drug Administration classified it as "generally recognised as safe." The attitude of the FDA changed when scientific research concluded that rats given large doses of the substance were prone to certain types of cancer. Cyclamate was banned from use in food-stuffs. As more and more people began to drink low-calorie beverages in the 1970s and early 1980s, however, manufacturers exerted pressure on the FDA to change its stance. In 1984, a committee of the FDA decided that cyclamate was not after all a cancer-producing agent. A year later, the National Academy of Sciences intervened, reaching yet a different conclusion. In its report on the subject, the Academy declared that cyclamate is unsafe when used with saccharin, although probably harmless when used on its own as a sweetener. See James Bellini, *High Tech Holocaust* (London: Tarrant, 1986).

Table 18.1   *A comparison of conceptions of "Post-Modernity" (PM) and "Radicalised Modernity" (RM)*

PM	RM
1. Understands current transitions in epistemological terms or as dissolving epistemology altogether.	1. Identifies the institutional developments which create a sense of fragmentation and dispersal.
2. Focuses upon the centrifugal tendencies of current social transformations and their dislocating character.	2. Sees high modernity as a set of circumstances in which dispersal is dialectically connected to profound tendencies towards global integration.
3. Sees the self as dissolved or dismembered by the fragmenting of experience.	3. Sees the self as more than just a site of intersecting forces; active processes of reflexive self-identity are made possible by modernity.
4. Argues for the contextuality of truth claims or sees them as "historical."	4. Argues that the universal features of truth claims force themselves upon us in an irresistible way given the primacy of problems of a global kind. Systematic knowledge about these developments is not precluded by the reflexivity of modernity.
5. Theorises powerlessness which individuals feel in the face of globalising tendencies.	5. Analyses a dialectic of powerlessness and empowerment, in terms of both experience and action.
6. Sees the "emptying" of day-to-day life as a result of the intrusion of abstract systems.	6. Sees day-to-day life as an active complex of reactions to abstract systems, involving appropriation as well as loss.
7. Regards coordinated political engagement as precluded by the primacy of contextuality and dispersal.	7. Regards coordinated political engagement as both possible and necessary, on a global level as well as locally.
8. Defines post-modernity as the end of epistemology/the individual/ethics.	8. Defines post-modernity as possible transformations moving "beyond" the institutions of modernity.

Notes

1 Ulrich Beck, "The Anthropological Shock: Chernobyl and the Contours of the Risk Society," *Berkeley Journal of Sociology* 32 (1987).
2 Lawrence Stone, *The Family, Sex and Marriage in England 1500–1800* (London: Weidenfeld, 1977), p. 282.
3 Christopher Lasch, *Haven in a Heartless World* (New York: Basic, 1977), p. 140. See also his *The Minimal Self* (London: Picador, 1985), in which the formulation of narcissism is sharpened, and the theme of "survivalism" developed further.
4 Cf. W. Warren Wagar, *Terminal Visions* (Bloomington: University of Indiana Press, 1982).
5 Carolyn See, *Golden Days* (London: Arrow, 1989), p. 126.
6 Robert Jay Lifton and Richard Falk, *Indefensible Weapons* (New York: Basic Books, 1982).
7 Susan Sontag: *AIDS and Its Metaphors* (Harmondsworth: Penguin, 1989).
8 Clifford Geertz, *Local Knowledge* (New York: Basic Books, 1983).
9 Saul Bellow, *Herzog* (Harmondsworth: Penguin, 1964), p. 323.

Part VI

The Sociological Theory of Pierre Bourdieu

INTRODUCTION TO PART VI

The most influential and original French sociologist since Durkheim, Pierre Bourdieu (b. 1930) is at once a leading theorist and an empirical researcher of extraordinarily broad interests and distinctive style. In fact, Bourdieu has strongly criticized
what he calls "theoretical theory" – that is, work that is more concerned with
building abstract systems of categories and concepts than with using them to
understand the world. Bourdieu's unique theoretical perspective has been stated
most systematically in *Outline of a Theory of Practice* (1977) and *Logic of Practice*
(1990). But the theory has been developed in an wide array of empirical investigations – among them, studies of labor markets in Algeria (*Algeria 1960* [1979]),
class distinctions in France (*Distinction* [1984]), education (*Homo Academicus*
[1988]), and artistic and literary fields (*The Rules of Art* [1996]). His recent work
has also examined the ways that globalization threatens the achievements of social
struggles and the building of relatively autonomous social fields.

Born in the Béarne region of southwestern France, Bourdieu went on to study at
the Ecole Normale Superieure. He spent time in Algeria, where he did his early field
work, and later began to gain academic notice in France. In 1981, Bourdieu was
awarded a chair at the prestigious Collège de France, a position he held until his
recent retirement. He remains active in a wide variety of research projects, and is the
subject of a feature-length documentary, "La sociologie est un sport de combat"
("Sociology is a Combat Sport").

Structure and Action: False Dichotomies

Bourdieu has described one of his central motivations as a determination to transcend the closely related but misleading dichotomies of objectivism/subjectivism and
of structure/action.[1] Taken together, these dichotomies have marked relatively stable
poles in the social sciences, with structural explanation tending to see social life as
completely external and objective, and action-oriented sociology looking at social
life through subjective experience. Bourdieu suggests that it is crucial not just to see
both sides of the issue, but also to see how they are inseparably related.

In recent French social theory, the structuralist anthropology of Claude Lévi-
Strauss was the dominant representative of objectivist thinking. Structuralism was
in many ways the descendent of Durkheim's work, especially his later examinations
of culture. Bourdieu himself was heavily influenced by structuralism – a good
example is his continued interest in explaining the stable cultural oppositions that
appear in language, physical space, and social space. But structuralism attempted to
understand the meaning of such oppositions by taking up an objective, "scientific"
point of view from outside of the action. It thus tended to explain the structuring of
action only as the result of external forces that either push us in one direction or
constrain us from going in another. Bourdieu, by contrast, has argued for a social
science based on the study of the doings of actors who always have some practical
knowledge about their world, even if they cannot articulate that knowledge. In other

words, social structure is internalized by each of us because we have learned from the experience of previous actions a practical mastery of how to do things that takes objective constraints into account.

Bourdieu's stress on the presence of social structure inside the actor is not only a challenge to objectivism, but also to most forms of subjectivism. In subjectivist accounts, the observer takes the individuals' own motivations as the source of the action. The major representative of this approach in France was Jean-Paul Sartre, but it was also characteristic of the phenomenology of Alfred Schutz and some forms of symbolic interactionism and ethnomethodology. Bourdieu has criticized this way of thinking because it tends to miss the cultural or material constraints that shape people's actions, making each action appear to be "a kind of antecedent-less confrontation between the subject and the world."[2] In other words, they neglect the extent to which people's very abilities to understand and choose and act have been shaped by processes of learning which are themselves objectively structured and socially produced. As a result, subjectivist approaches commonly present social life as much less structured, and much more contingent, than it really is.

In short, objective accounts can help us understand structure, and subjective accounts can help us understand action. But both are one-sided in that they divorce action from structure. Bourdieu's effort has been to develop a "genetic structuralism," that is, a sociology that uses the intellectual resources of structural analysis, but approaches structures in terms of the ways in which they are produced and reproduced in action. Understood in this way, structures are "structuring" in the sense that they guide and constrain action. But they are also "structured" in the sense that they are generated and reproduced by actors. Bourdieu thus insists on a dialectic of structure and action, but he also makes clear that he thinks the crucial first step for social science comes with the discovery of objective structure, and the break with everyday knowledge that this entails. The "objective truth" is not simply the sum total of the facts that happen to exist (as a purely empiricist view might suggest). Rather, what is "objectively" the deepest "reality" in social life is not the surface phenomena that we see all around us, but the underlying structural features that make these surface phenomena possible. The "objectivist" task of sociology is to grasp these underlying structural features. This is hard, because it demands that we call into question our taken-for-granted, preconscious understandings of the world and our place in it.

Habitus and Misrecognition

The way to get an empirical handle on the dynamic relationship between structure and action, Bourdieu contends, is through what he terms a relational analysis of social tastes and practices. By "relational," Bourdieu means that tastes and practices are organized by actors' relative locations in social space. This relational analysis is organized by three central concepts – positions, dispositions ("*habitus*") and position-taking (or "practices").

Actors occupy positions in social space relative to one another. Such positions may be defined by occupation, education, or proximity to power. What matters is not exactly how such positions are measured, but that people stake their claims to social status on them, and therefore use them to understand their place in the world.

Positions are maintained and signaled to others through a process of position-taking (translations sometimes retain the French term *"prises de position"*). For example, certain social positions are signaled by styles of dress, leisure activities, or consumer choices. Bourdieu stresses that there is no direct, mechanical connection between positions in the social structure and the practices that attach to them. In different times and different places, different sets of practices work just as well to signal a given position. In one of the readings included below, Bourdieu uses the example of names that businesses chose for themselves – high-status shops in New York often have French names, while similar ones in Paris often have English names. In other cases, practices can either gain or lose prestige over time.

If there is no direct connection between practices and positions (Bourdieu calls this the "substantialist" position), then what ties the two together? Bourdieu argues that the *habitus* is the site of the interplay between structure and practice. It is on the basis of *habitus* that Bourdieu defines social groups (including social classes), since those who occupy similar positions in the social structure will have the same *habitus*. The problem is that while positions and practices can be observed directly, *habitus* cannot. Because of this, Bourdieu's empirical studies often follow a similar method. First, he outlines the "social space" of positions and the "symbolic space" of practices, and shows how they map onto one another. Then, he uses this correspondence as a guide to reconstruct the *habitus* that links them together. *Habitus* refers to the relatively stable systems of dispositions that are shaped by the experiences of actors in particular positions in the social structure, which "generate and organize practices and representations."[3] The *habitus* is thus the site of our understanding of the world. In order for us to live in the social world, we require the kind of orientation to action and awareness that *habitus* gives.

In this sense, the *habitus* is not only constraining, it is also enabling. It does not operate as a set of strict rules about what to do or not to do, what to like or not to like. Instead, it works as a set of loose guidelines of which actors are not necessarily aware. Because they are loose guidelines, these dispositions are flexible, even though they are deeply rooted. They leave a great deal of room for improvisation and are easily applied to new settings, but in a way shaped by rules and social learning. As the word suggests, *habitus* is acquired through repetition, like a habit; we know it in our bodies, not just our minds. A former rugby player, Bourdieu often uses the metaphor of games to convey his sense of social life. But by "game" he doesn't mean mere diversions or entertainments. Rather, he means the experience of being passionately involved in a kind of activity in which the physical and mental are merged in action. In a game there are formal rules but also a constant need to improvise strategy according to unarticulated but deeply ingrained "sense" of the game. Out of what meets with approval or doesn't, what works or does not, we develop a characteristic way of generating new actions, of improvising the moves of the game of our lives. The resistance we confront in struggling to do well teaches us to accept inequality in our societies. Although it often reflects class or other aspects of social structure, it comes to feel natural. We learn and incorporate into our *habitus* a sense of what we can "reasonably" expect. This shapes how we choose careers, how we decide which people are "right" for us to date or marry, and how we raise our children.

These taken-for-granted dispositions of the *habitus* also imply misrecognitions, partial and distorted understandings. The idea of misrecognition allows Bourdieu a subtle approach to issues commonly addressed through the concept of ideology. Marxist and other analysts have pointed to the ways in which people's beliefs conform to either power structures or the requirements of the social order as a whole. "Ideology" is commonly understood as a set of partial and distorted beliefs that serves some specific set of social interests. Common use of the notion of ideology, however, tends to imply that it is possible to be without ideology, to have an objectively correct or undistorted understanding of the social world. Bourdieu rejects this. One can shake the effects of specific ideologies, but one cannot live without taken-for-granted assumptions that come with *habitus*. Misrecognition is built into the very practical mastery that makes our actions effective.

Because of this, sociology is itself a "combat sport," according to Bourdieu. Sociologists must struggle against the tendency everyone has to accept the products of social history as though they were natural. This means also that we should not accept people's everyday accounts of their action as fully explaining it. We may say, for example, that holiday gifts are given without expectation of return, but in fact where there is no reciprocation we tend to stop giving. More generally, participation in any set of social practices embeds us in characteristic misrecognitions. Bourdieu saw this starkly in his early research in Algeria. The French colonists understood themselves as part of a civilizing mission in which modern France would help traditional Algeria. But they systematically misrecognized the power and exploitation that were basic to the French presence. These sparked the Algerian struggle for independence and became manifest in the bloody French effort to repress it.

Fields and Capital

One of the ways in which Bourdieu uses the metaphor of "games" is to describe the different fields on which distinct games are played. Like a soccer field or a rugby field, a social field is simply the terrain upon which the game is played. Broadly speaking, a field is a domain of social life that has its own rules of organization, generates a set of positions, and supports the practices associated with them. Like players in a game, participants in social fields have different positions. For example, a small town lawyer and a Supreme Court Justice are both participants in the legal field. But their different positions open different sets of opportunities for them, and different sets of strategies that they may take. Bourdieu sees action in a field not simply as a static reflection of established positions, but as the result of many contending projects of position-taking.

The possession of different forms of "capital" provides the basic structure for the organization of fields, and thus the generation of the various *habitus* and practices associated with them. "A capital does not exist and function except in relation to a field," Bourdieu claims.[4] Yet successful lawyers and successful authors both, for example, seek to convert their own successes into improved standards of living and chances for their children. To do so, they must convert the capital specific to their field of endeavor into other forms. In addition to material property (economic capital), families may accumulate networks of connections (social capital) and prestige (cultural capital) by the way in which they raise children and plan their marriages. By conceptualizing capital as taking many different forms, Bourdieu stresses (a) that there are many different kinds of goods that people pursue and resources that they accumulate, (b) that these are inextricably social, because they derive their meaning from the social relationships that constitute different fields (rather than simply from some sort of material things being valuable in and of themselves), and (c) that the struggle to accumulate capital is hardly the whole story; the struggle to reproduce capital is equally basic and often depends on the ways in which it can be converted across fields.

Bourdieu's analysis of the differences in forms of capital and dynamics of conversion between them is one of the most original and important features of his theory (though it builds on Weber's distinction between class and status). There are two senses in which capital is converted from one form to another. One is as part of the intergenerational reproduction of capital. Wealthy people try to make sure that their children go to good colleges. In America at least, this often involves the use of significant economic capital, since good colleges are often expensive colleges. But it also involves cultural capital, for example in knowing which expensive schools are "good" – that is, prestigious – and which are not. The second sense of conversion of capital is more immediate. By attending a prestigious college, and gaining lots of social connections among the people there, a person may then attempt to turn social and cultural capital into economic capital by landing a highly paid job.

In his empirical investigations, Bourdieu generally discusses two ways in which capital orders the social space. The most basic is what he calls "capital volume," which distinguishes between positions with a great deal of capital overall (and the practices associated with them) and those without much capital of any kind. Of course, this contrast between high and low is so obvious to most members of society that not much energy has to go into maintaining the social distance that goes along with it. Much more energy goes into maintaining the second dimension, which might be called the capital mix. This distinguishes between positions that are high on one dimension (for example, cultural capital) and those that are high on another (such as economic capital). Those positions with relatively high capital volume are most invested in maintaining this opposition. This is interesting, because it shifts attention from the opposition between the elites and the masses to the struggle *between* different privileged groups over the control of symbolic goods. As Bourdieu claims, "minimum objective difference in social space can coincide with maximum subjective distance. This is partly because what is 'closest' presents the greatest threat to social identity."[5]

Bourdieu situates his logic of multiple fields and specific forms of capital in relation to a more general notion of power. The field of art, thus, has its own internal struggles for recognition, power, and capital, but it also has a specific relationship to the overall field of power. Even highly rewarded artists generally cannot convert their professional prestige into power in other institutional domains. By contrast, business people and lawyers are more able to do this. The question is not just who is higher or lower in terms of overall capital, but also how different groups relate to each other based on the kind of capital they control. This is true at all levels of the social hierarchy, as for example holders of a "white collar" job may feel superior to "blue collar" workers even if they are paid no more. This is based on a claim to cultural capital and its prestige. It also reflects a general tendency to make social classifications tools of domination. More generally, Bourdieu draws attention to "symbolic violence," the ways in which people may be harmed by the ways they are labeled or categorized socially.

Structure and Practice in Social Life

Bourdieu's key concepts, like *habitus*, symbolic violence, cultural capital, and field are useful in themselves, but derive their greatest theoretical significance from their interrelationships. These are best seen not mechanistically, in the abstract, but at work in sociological analysis. Indeed, Bourdieu is virtually unique among major theorists in the extent to which he has focused on and been influential through empirical research.

Bourdieu's theory is thus often embedded in empirical analyses, but he constantly tries to signal his theoretical positions to his readers. He does this not only in his arguments, but also in his writing style. This can make it difficult to read his work for the first time. Understanding what Bourdieu is doing and why he is doing it can help, however. There are two stylistic elements that are most baffling to new readers. The first is the self-conscious circularity of the sentences. English-language readers who are used to a more linear writing style are often bothered by this, though the style will seem more familiar to those who have some practice reading French social theory. By writing in this manner, Bourdieu hopes to show where his argument might diverge from the reader's assumptions. The second element that causes some confusion is the use of what Bourdieu calls a "hierarchy of text." The main text is broken by passages that are offset or printed in a smaller font. This is meant to break the formal façade of scientific argument with less formal asides and examples that show the development of the ideas. It is also intended to bridge the distance between author and reader by making the text more like a conversation.

The three readings that follow are not meant to cover the entire range of Bourdieu's writing. Instead, they illustrate key points of his theoretical arguments, particularly regarding *habitus*, capital and field. The first selection, "Social Space and Symbolic Space" is an argument for the importance of relational analysis. It is the most plainly written of the three essays, since it was originally presented as a lecture to introduce his work on French society to a Japanese audience. The second reading, "Structures, *Habitus*, Practices," from *The Logic of Practice*, is a more theoretical treatment of the concept of *habitus* and the way it mediates between the social space of positions and the symbolic space of positions-taking. The stress is on the way that the *habitus* is oriented to concrete practices. It is only by studying practices, Bourdieu tells us, that we can see the connection between structure and action. Bourdieu also stresses the social nature of the *habitus*. Even when we are speaking of the *habitus* of an individual rather than a group, we are talking about a set of internalized dispositions that is a result of social interaction. The *habitus* is therefore social in the same way as the concept of "self" in the writing of George Herbert Mead. The last reading, "The Field of Cultural Production, Or: The Economic World Reversed," discusses the way different forms of capital structure a particular field. The case in question is the literary field, which Bourdieu uses as an example of artistic production more generally. Bourdieu shows that while the literary field has its own organizing logic, it is not completely separate from considerations of power. Oppositions between different sets of positions are structured simultaneously by relation to the economic market and by claims to artistic purity. High status in the field demanded not just talent, or vision, but also a commitment to "art for art's sake." This meant producing works specifically designed for the field of art, rather than the market.

Notes

1   See Bourdieu and Wacquant (1992: 7).
2   Bourdieu (1990: 42).
3   Bourdieu (1990: 53).
4   Bourdieu and Wacquant (1992: 101).
5   Bourdieu (1990: 137).

Select Bibliography

Bourdieu, Pierre. 1979. *Algeria 1960*. Translated by Richard Nice. Cambridge: Cambridge University Press. (A collection of early essays from field work in Algeria. More clearly structuralist in orientation than much of his later work.)

Bourdieu, Pierre. 1984. *Distinction: A Social Critique of the Judgment of Taste*. Translated by Richard Nice. Cambridge MA: Harvard University Press. (An analysis of the place of cultural hierarchy in the French class structure: e.g., why do intellectuals like jazz and modernist art, why do elites collect uncomfortable antiques while workers prefer solid, body-friendly furniture?)

Bourdieu, Pierre. 1988. *Homo Academicus*. Translated by Peter Collier. Stanford CA: Stanford University Press. (One of Bourdieu's recent examinations of the field of education.)

Bourdieu, Pierre. 1990. *The Logic of Practice*. Translated by Richard Nice. Stanford CA: Stanford University Press. (Bourdieu's most systematic statement of the core his theory of embodied practice; partially a revision of the more famous *Outline of a Theory of Practice*.)

Bourdieu, Pierre. 1996. *The Rules of Art*. (A study of the origins of the French literary field in the work of Flaubert and Baudelaire which is also Bourdieu's most sustained development of his concept of field and analysis of what "art for art's sake" means and why cultural capital is opposed to economic.)

Bourdieu, Pierre. 1998. *Practical Reason*. Stanford: Stanford University Press. Speeches and essays for relatively general audiences that constitute one of the most accessible introductions to (and clarifications of) Bourdieu's sociological theory.

Bourdieu, Pierre. 2001. *Contre-feux 2*. Paris: Raisons d'Agir. (A collection of Bourdieu's recent political analyses, especially on the threats neoliberal globalization poses to culture and intellectuals and the importance of an alternative form of internationalism. The first *Contre-feux* – literally, counter-fire – was translated into English as *Acts of Resistance: Against the Tyranny of Markets* in 1998 by the New Press; an English translation of the second volume is due out in late 2001.)

Bourdieu, Pierre and Loic Wacquant. 1992. *An Invitation to Reflexive Sociology*. Chicago: University of Chicago Press. (A clarification of various questions about Bourdieu's work, structured as questions from one of his leading students and answers from Bourdieu.)

Calhoun, Craig. 2001. "Pierre Bourdieu," pp. 696–730 in George Ritzer, ed.: *The Blackwell Companion to the Major Social Theorists*. Cambridge, MA: Blackwell. (An introduction to and overview of Bourdieu's sociology.)

Calhoun, Craig, Edward LiPuma, and Moishe Postone (eds.). 1993. *Bourdieu: Critical Perspectives*. Chicago: The University of Chicago Press. (Critical essays on Bourdieu from leading theorists in anthropology, philosophy, linguistics, and sociology.)

Fowler, Bridget 1997. *Pierre Bourdieu and Cultural Theory: Critical Investigations*. London: Sage. (Explicates Bourdieu's theory in relation to Anglo-American cultural studies and sociology of culture.)

Jenkins, Richard. 1992. *Pierre Bourdieu*. London: Routledge. (An introduction, but also one of the more sustained critical accounts.)

Robbins, Derek. 1991. *The Work of Pierre Bourdieu: Recognizing Society*. Boulder: Westview Press. (A somewhat dated introduction to Bourdieu's work, focusing on its larger sociological implications.)

Robbins, Derrick. 2000. *Bourdieu and Culture*. (A very sympathetic but idiosyncratic introduction emphasizing Bourdieu's cultural analyses of the 1980s and 1990s.)

Swartz, David. 1997. *Culture and Power: The Sociology of Pierre Bourdieu*. Chicago: University of Chicago Press. (An accessible introduction to Bourdieu's work and its development; the best one-volume introduction.)

19 Social Space and Symbolic Space

Pierre Bourdieu

I think that if I were Japanese I would dislike most of the things that non-Japanese people write about Japan. Over twenty years ago, at the time when I began to do research on French society, I recognized my irritation at American ethnologies of France in the criticism that Japanese sociologists, notably Hiroshi Miami and Tetsuro Watsuji, had levied against Ruth Benedict's famous book, *The Chrysanthemum and the Sword*. Thus, I shall not talk to you about the "Japanese sensibility," nor about the Japanese "mystery" or "miracle." I shall talk about France, a country I know fairly well, not because I was born there and speak its language, but because I have studied it a great deal. Does this mean that I shall confine myself to the particularity of a single society and shall not talk in any way about Japan? I do not think so. I think, on the contrary, that by presenting the model of social space and symbolic space that I constructed for the particular case of France, I shall still be speaking to you about Japan (just as, in other contexts, I would be speaking about Germany or the United States). For you to understand fully this discourse which concerns you and which might seem to you full of personal allusions when I speak about the French *homo academicus*, I would like to encourage you to go beyond a particularizing reading which, besides being an excellent defense mechanism against analysis, is the precise equivalent, on the reception side, of the curiosity for exotic particularism that has inspired so many works on Japan.

My work, and especially *Distinction*, is particularly exposed to such a reading. Its theoretical model is not embellished with all the marks by which one usually recognizes "grand theory," such as lack of any reference to some empirical reality. The notions of social space, symbolic space, or social class are never studied in and for themselves; rather, they are tested through research in which the theoretical and the empirical are inseparable and which mobilizes numerous methods of observation and measurement – quantitative and qualitative, statistical and ethnographic, macrosociological and microsociological (all of which are meaningless oppositions) – for the purpose of studying an object well defined in space and time, that is, French society in the 1970s. The report of this research does not appear in the language to which certain sociologists, especially Americans, have accustomed us and whose appearance of universality is due only to the imprecision of a vocabulary hardly distinguishable from everyday usage (I shall mention only one example, the notion of "profession"). Thanks to a discursive montage which facilitates the juxtaposition of statistical tables, photographs, excerpts from interviews, facsimiles of documents, and the abstract language of analysis, this report makes the most abstract coexist with the most concrete, a photograph of the president of the Republic playing tennis or an interview with a baker with the most formal analysis of the generative and unifying power of the habitus.

My entire scientific enterprise is indeed based on the belief that the deepest logic of the social world can be grasped only if one plunges into the particularity of an empirical reality, historically located and dated, but with the objective of constructing it as a "special case of what is possible," as Bachelard puts it, that is, as an exemplary case in a finite world of possible configurations. Concretely, this means that an analysis of French social space in the 1970s is comparative history, which takes the present as its object, or comparative anthropology, which focuses on a particular cultural area: in both cases, the aim is to try to grasp the invariant, the structure in each variable observed.

I am convinced that, although it has all the appearance of ethnocentrism, an approach consisting of applying a model constructed according to this logic to another social world is without doubt more respectful of historical realities (and of people) and above all more fruitful in scientific terms than the interest in superficial features of the lover of exoticism who gives priority to picturesque differences (I am thinking, for instance, of what has been said and written, in the case of Japan, about the "culture of pleasure"). The researcher, both more modest and more ambitious than the collector of curiosities, seeks to apprehend the structures and mechanisms that are overlooked – although for different reasons – by the native and the foreigner alike, such as the principles of construction of social space or the mechanisms of reproduction of that space, and that the researcher seeks to represent in a model aspiring to a *universal validity*. In that way it is possible to register the real differences that separate both structures and dispositions (habitus), the principle of which must be sought not in the peculiarities of some national character – or "soul" – but in the particularities of different *collective histories*.

The Real is Relational

In this spirit I will present the model I constructed in *Distinction*, first cautioning against a "substantialist" reading of analyses which intend to be structural or, better, relational (I refer here, without being able to go into detail, to the opposition suggested by Ernst Cassirer between "substantial concepts" and "functional or relational concepts"). The "substantialist" and naively realist reading considers each practice (playing golf, for example) or pattern of consumption (Chinese food, for instance) in and for itself, independently of the universe of substitutable practices, and conceives of the correspondence between social positions (or classes, thought of as substantial sets) and tastes or practices as a mechanical and direct relation. According to this logic, naive readers could consider as a refutation of the model the fact that, to take a perhaps facile example, Japanese or American intellectuals pretend to like French food, whereas French intellectuals like to go to Chinese or Japanese restaurants; or that the fancy shops of Tokyo or Fifth Avenue often have French names, whereas the fancy shops of the Faubourg Saint-Honoré display English names, such as "hairdresser." Another example which is, I believe, even more striking: in Japan, the rate of participation in general elections is highest among the least educated women of rural districts, whereas in France, as I demonstrated in an analysis of nonresponse to opinion polls, the rate of nonresponse – and of indifference to politics – is especially high among women and among the least educated and the most economically and socially dispossessed. This is an example of a false difference that conceals a real one: the apathy associated with dispossession of the means of production of political opinions, which is expressed in France as simple absenteeism, translates, in the case of Japan, as a sort of apolitical participation. We should ask further what historical conditions (and here we should invoke the whole political history of Japan) have resulted in the fact that conservative parties in Japan have been able, through quite particular forms of clientelism, to benefit from the inclination toward unconditional delegation deriving from the conviction of not being in possession of the *statutory* and *technical* competence which is necessary for participation.

The substantialist mode of thought, which characterizes common sense – and racism – and which is inclined to treat the activities and preferences specific to certain individuals or groups in a society at a certain moment as if they were substantial properties, inscribed once and for all in a sort of biological or cultural *essence*, leads to the same kind of error, whether one is comparing different societies or successive periods in the same society. Some would thus consider the fact that, for example, tennis or even golf is not nowadays as exclusively associated with dominant positions as in the past, or that the noble sports, such as riding or fencing (or, in Japan, the martial arts), are no longer specific to nobility as they originally were, as a refutation of the proposed model, which figure 19.1, presenting the correspondence between the space of constructed classes and the space of practices, captures in a visual and synoptic way. An initially aristocratic practice can be given up by the aristocracy – and this occurs quite frequently – when it is adopted by a growing fraction of the bourgeoisie or petit-bourgeoisie, or even the lower classes (this is what happened in France to boxing, which was enthusiastically practiced by aristocrats at the end of the nineteenth century). Conversely, an initially lower-class practice can sometimes be taken up by nobles. In short, one has to avoid turning into necessary and intrinsic properties of some group (nobility, samurai, as well as workers or employees) the properties which belong to this group at a given moment in time because of its position in a determinate social space and in a determinate state of the *supply* of possible goods and practices. Thus, at every moment of each society, one has to deal with a set of social positions which is bound by a relation of homology to a set of activities (the practice of golf or piano) or of goods (a second home or an old master painting) that are themselves characterized relationally.

This formula, which might seem abstract and obscure, states the first conditions for an adequate reading of the analysis of the relation between *social positions* (a relational concept), *dispositions* (or habitus), and *position-takings* (*prises de position*), that is, the "choices" made by the social agents in the most diverse domains of practice, in food or sport, music or politics, and so forth. It is a reminder that comparison is possible only from *system to system*, and that the search for direct equivalences between features grasped in isolation, whether, appearing at first sight different, they prove to be "functionally" or technically equivalent (like Pernod and *shôchû* or saké) or nominally identical (the practice of golf in France and Japan, for instance), risks unduly identifying structurally different properties or wrongly distinguishing structurally identical properties. The very title *Distinction* serves as a reminder that what is commonly called distinction, that is, a certain quality of

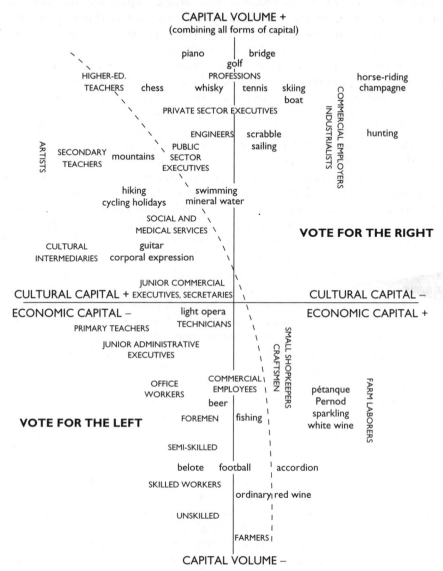

Figure 19.1 *The space of social positions and the space of lifestyles (the dotted line indicates probable orientation toward the right or left)*

bearing and manners, most often considered innate (one speaks of *distinction naturelle*, "natural refinement"), is nothing other than *difference*, a gap, a distinctive feature, in short, a *relational* property existing only in and through its relation with other properties.

This idea of difference, or a gap, is at the basis of the very notion of *space*, that is, a set of distinct and coexisting positions which are exterior to one another and which are defined in relation to one another through their *mutual exteriority* and their relations of proximity, vicinity, or distance, as well as through relations of order, such as above, below, and *between*. Certain properties of members of the petit-bourgeoisie can, for example, be deduced from the fact that they occupy an intermediate position between two extreme positions, without being objectively identifiable and subjectively identified either with one or the other position.

Social space is constructed in such a way that agents or groups are distributed in it according to their position in statistical distributions based on the *two principles of differentiation* which, in the most advanced societies, such as the United States, Japan, or France, are undoubtedly the most efficient: economic capital and cultural capital. It follows that all agents are located in this space in such a way that the closer they are to one another in those two dimensions, the more they have in common; and the more remote they are from one another, the less they have in common. Spatial distances on paper are equivalent to social distances. More precisely, as expressed in the diagram in *Distinction* in which I tried to represent social space (figure 19.1), agents are distributed in the first dimension according to the overall volume of the different kinds of capital they possess, and in the second dimension according to the structure of their capital, that is, according to the relative weight of the different kinds of capital, economic and cultural, in the total volume of their capital.

Thus, in the first dimension, which is undoubtedly the most important, the holders of a great volume of overall capital, such as industrial employers, members of liberal professions, and university professors are opposed, in the mass, to those who are most deprived of economic and cultural capital, such as unskilled workers. But from another point of view, that is, from the point of view of the relative weight of economic capital and cultural capital in their patrimony, professors (relatively wealthier in cultural capital than in economic capital) are strongly opposed to industrial employers (relatively wealthier in economic capital than in cultural capital), and this is no doubt as true in Japan as in France (although it remains to be verified).

The second opposition, like the first, is the source of differences in dispositions and, therefore, in position-takings. This is the case of the opposition between intellectuals and industrial employers or, on a lower level of the social hierarchy, between primary school teachers and small merchants, which, in postwar France and Japan alike, translates, in politics, into an opposition between left and right (as is suggested in the diagram, the probability of leaning politically toward the right or the left depends at least as much on the position in the horizontal dimension as on the position in the vertical dimension, that is, on the relative weight of cultural capital and economic capital in the volume of capital possessed at least as much as on the volume itself).

In a more general sense, the space of social positions is retranslated into a space of position-takings through the mediation of the space of dispositions (or habitus). In other words, the system of differential deviations which defines the different positions in the two major dimensions of social space corresponds to the system of differential deviations in agents' properties (or in the properties of constructed classes of agents), that is, in their practices and in the goods they possess. To each class of positions there corresponds a class of habitus (or *tastes*) produced by the social conditioning associated with the corresponding condition and, through the mediation of the habitus and its generative capability, a systematic set of goods and properties, which are united by an affinity of style.

One of the functions of the notion of habitus is to account for the unity of style, which unites the practices and goods of a single agent or a class of agents (this is what writers such as Balzac or Flaubert have so finely expressed through their descriptions of settings – such as the Pension Vauquer in *Le Père Goriot* or the elegant dishes and drinks consumed in the homes of different protagonists of *L'Éducation sentimentale* – which are at the same time descriptions of the characters who live in them). The habitus is this generative and unifying principle which retranslates the intrinsic and relational characteristics of a position into a unitary lifestyle, that is, a unitary set of choices of persons, goods, practices.

Like the positions of which they are the product, habitus are differentiated, but they are also differentiating. Being distinct and distinguished, they are also distinction operators, implementing different principles of differentiation or using differently the common principles of differentiation.

Habitus are generative principles of distinct and distinctive practices – what the worker eats, and especially the way he eats it, the sport he practices and the way he practices it, his political opinions and the way he expresses them are systematically different from the industrial owner's corresponding activities. But habitus are also classificatory schemes, principles of classification, principles of vision and division, different tastes. They make distinctions between what is good and what is bad, between what is right and what is wrong, between what is distinguished and what is vulgar, and so forth, but the distinctions are not identical. Thus, for instance, the same behavior or even the same good can appear distinguished to one person, pretentious to someone else, and cheap or showy to yet another.

But the essential point is that, when perceived through these social categories of perception, these principles of vision and division, the differences in practices, in the goods possessed, or in the opinions expressed become symbolic differences and constitute a veritable *language*. Differences associated with different positions, that is, goods, practices, and especially *manners*, function, in each society, in the same way as differences which constitute symbolic systems, such as the set of phonemes of a language or the set of distinctive features and of differential "*écarts*" that constitute a mythical system, that is, as *distinctive signs*.

Here I open a parenthesis in order to dispel a frequent, yet disastrous, misunderstanding about the title *Distinction*, which has led some to believe that the entire book was limited to saying that the driving force of all human behavior was the search for distinction. This does not make sense and, moreover, it would not be anything new if one thinks, for example, of Veblen and his notion of conspicuous consumption. In fact, the main idea is that to exist within a social space, to occupy a point or to be an individual within a social space, is to differ, to be different. According to Benveniste's formula regarding language, "to be distinctive, to be significant, is the same thing," significant being opposed to insignificant, or to different meanings. More precisely – Benveniste's formulation is a little too quick...– a difference, a distinctive property, white or black skin, slenderness or stoutness, Volvo or VW Beetle, red wine or champagne, Pernod or scotch, golf or soccer, piano or accordion, bridge or *belote* (I proceed with oppositions, because things tend to operate in this fashion most of the time, although the situation is more complicated than this), only becomes a visible, perceptible, non-indifferent, socially *pertinent* difference if it is perceived by someone who is capable of *making the distinction* – because, being inscribed in the space in question, he or she is not *indifferent* and is endowed with categories of perception, with classificatory schemata, with a certain *taste*, which permits her to make differences, to discern, to distinguish – between a color print and a painting or between Van Gogh and Gauguin. Difference becomes a sign and a sign of distinction (or vulgarity) only if a principle of vision and division is applied to it which, being the product of the incorporation of the structure of objective differences (for example, the structure of the distribution in the social space of the piano or the accordion or those who prefer one or the other), is present among all the agents, piano owners or accordion lovers, and structures the perceptions of owners or lovers of pianos or accordions (there was a need to spell out this analysis of the logic – that of symbolic violence – according to which dominated lifestyles are almost always perceived, even by those who live them, from the destructive and reductive point of view of the dominant aesthetic).

The Logic of Classes

To construct social space, this invisible reality that cannot be shown but which organizes agents' practices and representations, is at the same time to create the possibility of constructing *theoretical classes* that are as homogeneous as possible from the point of view of the two major determinants of practices and of all their attendant properties. The principle of classification thus put into play is genuinely *explanatory*. It is not content with describing the set of classified realities, but rather, like the good taxonomies of the natural sciences, it fixes on determinant properties which, unlike the apparent differences of bad classifications, allow for the prediction of the other properties and which distinguish and bring together agents who are as similar to each other as possible and as different as possible from members of other classes, whether adjacent or remote.

But the very validity of the classification risks encouraging a perception of theoretical classes, which are fictitious regroupings existing only *on paper*, through an intellectual decision by the researcher, as *real* classes, real groups, that are constituted as such in reality. The danger is all the greater as the research makes it appear that the divisions drawn in *Distinction* do indeed correspond to real differences in the most different, and even the most unexpected, domains of practice. Thus, to take the example of a curious property, the distribution of the dog and cat owners is organized according to the model: commercial employers (on the right in figure 19.1) tend to prefer dogs, intellectuals (on the left in figure 19.1) tend to prefer cats.

The model thus defines distances that are *predictive* of encounters, affinities, sympathies, or even desires. Concretely, this means that people located at the top of the space have little chance of marrying people located toward the bottom, first because they have little chance of physically meeting them (except in what are called "bad places," that is, at the cost of a transgression of the social limits which reflect spatial distances); secondly because, if they do accidentally meet them on some occasion, they will not get on together, will not really understand each other, will not appeal to one another. On the other hand, proximity in social space predisposes to closer relations: people who are inscribed in a restricted sector of the space will be both closer (in their properties and in their dispositions, *their tastes*) and more disposed to get closer, as well as being easier to bring together, to mobilize. *But this does not mean that they constitute a class in Marx's sense, that is, a group which is mobilized for common purposes, and especially against another class.*

The theoretical classes that I construct are, more than any other theoretical divisions (more, for example, than divisions according to sex, ethnicity, and so on), predisposed to become classes in the Marxist sense of the term. If I am a political leader and I propose creating one big party bringing together both industrial employers and workers, I have little chance of success, since these groups are very distant in social space; in a certain conjuncture, in a national crisis, on the bases of nationalism or chauvinism, it will be possible for them to draw closer, but this solidarity will still be rather superficial and very provisional. This does not mean that, inversely, proximity in social space automatically engenders unity. It defines an objective potentiality of unity or, to speak like Leibniz, a "claim to exist" as a group, a *probable class*. Marxist theory makes a mistake quite similar to the one Kant denounced in the ontological argument or to the one for which Marx criticized Hegel: it makes a "death-defying leap" from existence in theory to existence in practice, or, as Marx puts it, "from the things of logic to the logic of things."

Marx, who more than any other theoretician exerted the *theory effect* – the properly political effect that consists in making tangible (*theorein*) a "reality" that cannot entirely exist insofar as it remains unknown and unrecognized – paradoxically failed to take this effect into account in his own theory... One moves from class-on-paper to the "real" class only at the price of a political work of mobilization. The "real" class, if it has ever "really" existed, is nothing but the realized class, that is, the mobilized class, a result of the *struggle of classifications*, which is a properly symbolic (and political) struggle to impose a vision of the social world, or, better, a way to construct that world, in perception and in reality, and to construct classes in accordance with which this social world can be divided.

The very existence of classes, as everyone knows from his or her own experience, is a stake in a struggle. And this fact undoubtedly constitutes the major obstacle to a scientific knowledge of the social world and to the resolution (for *there is one*...) of the problem of social classes. Denying the existence of classes, as the conservative tradition has persisted in doing for reasons not all of which are absurd (and all research done in good faith encounters them along the way), means in the final analysis denying the existence of differences and of principles of differentiation. This is just what those who pretend that nowadays the American, Japanese, and French societies are each nothing but an enormous "middle class" do, although in a more paradoxical way, since those who believe this nevertheless preserve the term "class" (according to a survey, 80 percent of the Japanese say they belong to the "middle class"). This position is, of course, unsustainable. All my work shows that in a country said to be on the way to becoming homogenized, democratized, and so on, difference is everywhere. And in the United States, every day some new piece of research appears showing diversity where one *expected to see* homogeneity, conflict where one expected to see consensus, reproduction and conservation where one expected to see mobility. Thus, *difference* (which I express in describing social *space*) exists and persists. But does this mean that we must accept or affirm the existence of classes? No. Social classes do not exist (even if political work, armed with Marx's theory, had in some cases contributed to making them at least exist through instances of mobilization and proxies). What exists is a social space, a space of differences, in which classes exist in some sense in a state of virtuality, not as something given but as *something to be done*.

Nevertheless, if the social world, with its divisions, is something that social agents have to do, to construct, individually and especially *collectively*, in cooperation and conflict, these constructions still do not take place in a social void, as certain ethnomethodologists seem to believe. The position occupied in social space, that is, in the structure of the distribution of different kinds of capital, which are also weapons, commands the representations of this space and the position-takings in the struggles to conserve or transform it.

To summarize the intricate relation between objective structures and subjective constructions, which is located beyond the usual alternatives of objectivism and subjectivism, of structuralism and constructivism, and even of materialism and idealism, I usually quote, with a little distortion, a famous formula of Pascal's: "The world comprehends me and swallows me like a point, but I comprehend it." The social world embraces me like a point. But this point is a *point of view*, the principle of a view adopted from a point located in social space, a *perspective* which is defined, in its form and contents, by the objective position from which it is adopted. The social space is indeed the first and last reality, since it still commands the representations that the social agents can have of it.

I am coming to the end of what has been a kind of introduction to the reading of *Distinction*, in which I have undertaken to state the principles of a relational, structural reading that is capable of developing the full import of the model I propose. A relational but also a *generative* reading. By this I mean that I hope my readers will try to apply the model in this other "particular case of the possible," that is, Japanese society, that they will try to construct the Japanese social space and symbolic space, to define the basic principles of objective differentiation (I think they are the same, but one should verify whether, for instance, they do not have different relative weights – I do not think so, given the exceptional importance which is traditionally attributed to education in Japan) and especially the principles of distinction, the specific distinctive signs in the domains of sport, food, drink, and so on, the relevant features which make significant differences in the different symbolic subspaces. This is, in my opinion, the condition for a *comparativism of the essential* that I called for at the beginning and, at the same time, for the universal knowledge of the invariants and variations that sociology can and must produce.

As for me, I shall undertake in my next lecture to say what the mechanisms are which, in France as in Japan and all other advanced countries, guarantee the reproduction of social space and symbolic space, without ignoring the contradictions and conflicts that can be at the basis of their transformation.

20 Structures, *Habitus*, Practices

Pierre Bourdieu

Objectivism constitutes the social world as a spectacle offered to an observer who takes up a 'point of view' on the action and who, putting into the object the principles of his relation to the object, proceeds as if it were intended solely for knowledge and as if all the interactions within it were purely symbolic exchanges. This viewpoint is the one taken from high positions in the social structure, from which the social world is seen as a representation (as the word is used in idealist philosophy, but also as in painting) or a performance (in the theatrical or musical sense), and practices are seen as no more than the acting-out of roles, the playing of scores or the implementation of plans. The theory of practice as practice insists, contrary to positivist materialism, that the objects of knowledge are constructed, not passively recorded, and, contrary to intellectualist idealism, that the principle of this construction is the system of structured, structuring dispositions, the *habitus*, which is constituted in practice and is always oriented towards practical functions. It is possible to step down from the sovereign viewpoint from which objectivist idealism orders the world, as Marx demands in the *Theses on Feuerbach*, but without having to abandon to it the 'active aspect' of apprehension of the world by reducing knowledge to a mere recording. To do this, one has to situate oneself *within* 'real activity as such', that is, in the practical relation to the world, the preoccupied, active presence in the world through which the world imposes its presence, with its urgencies, its things to be done and said, things made to be said, which directly govern words and deeds without ever unfolding as a spectacle. One has to escape from the realism of the structure, to which objectivism, a necessary stage in breaking with primary experience and constructing the objective relationships, necessarily leads when it hypostatizes these relations by treating them as realities already constituted outside of the history of the group – without falling back into subjectivism, which is quite incapable of giving an account of the necessity of the social world. To do this, one has to return to practice, the site of the dialectic of the *opus operatum* and the *modus operandi*; of the objectified products and the incorporated products of historical practice; of structures and *habitus*.

> The bringing to light of the presuppositions inherent in objectivist construction has paradoxically been delayed by the efforts of all those who, in linguistics as in anthropology, have sought to 'correct' the structuralist model by appealing to 'context' or 'situation' to account for variations, exceptions and accidents (instead of making them simple variants, absorbed into the structure, as the structuralists do). They have thus

Originally translated by Richard Nice.

avoided a radical questioning of the objectivist mode of thought, when, that is, they have not simply fallen back on to the free choice of a rootless, unattached, pure subject. Thus, the method known as 'situational analysis', which consists of 'observing people in a variety of social situations' in order to determine 'the way in which individuals are able to exercise choices within the limits of a specified social structure',[1] remains locked within the framework of the rule and the exception, which Edmund Leach (often invoked by the exponents of this method) spells out explicitly: 'I postulate that structural systems in which all avenues of social action are narrowly institutionalized are impossible. In all viable systems, there must be an area where the individual is free to make choices so as to manipulate the system to his advantage'.[2]

The conditionings associated with a particular class of conditions of existence produce *habitus*, systems of durable, transposable dispositions, structured structures predisposed to function as structuring structures, that is, as principles which generate and organize practices and representations that can be objectively adapted to their outcomes without presupposing a conscious aiming at ends or an express mastery of the operations necessary in order to attain them. Objectively 'regulated' and 'regular' without being in any way the product of obedience to rules, they can be collectively orchestrated without being the product of the organizing action of a conductor.

It is, of course, never ruled out that the responses of the *habitus* may be accompanied by a strategic calculation tending to perform in a conscious mode the operation that the *habitus* performs quite differently, namely an estimation of chances presupposing transformation of the past effect into an expected objective. But these responses are first defined, without any calculation, in relation to objective potentialities, immediately inscribed in the present, things to do or not to do, things to say or not to say, in relation to a probable, 'upcoming' future (*un à venir*), which – in contrast to the future seen as 'absolute possibility' (*absolute Möglichkeit*) in Hegel's (or Sartre's) sense, projected by the pure project of a 'negative freedom' – puts itself forward with an urgency and a claim to existence that excludes all deliberation. Stimuli do not exist for practice in their objective truth, as conditional, conventional triggers, acting only on condition that they encounter agents conditioned to recognize them. The practical world that is constituted in the relationship with the *habitus*, acting as a system of cognitive and motivating structures, is a world of already realized ends – procedures to follow, paths to take – and of objects endowed with a 'permanent teleological character', in Husserl's phrase, tools or institutions. This is because the regularities inherent in an arbitrary condition ('arbitrary' in Saussure's and Mauss's sense) tend to appear as necessary, even natural, since they are the basis of the schemes of perception and appreciation through which they are apprehended.

If a very close correlation is regularly observed between the scientifically constructed objective probabilities (for example, the chances of access to a particular good) and agents' subjective aspirations ('motivations' and 'needs'), this is not because agents consciously adjust their aspirations to an exact evaluation of their chances of success, like a gambler organizing his stakes on the basis of perfect information about his chances of winning. In reality, the dispositions durably inculcated by the possibilities and impossibilities, freedoms and necessities, opportunities and prohibitions inscribed in the objective conditions (which science apprehends through statistical regularities such as the probabilities objectively attached to a group or class) generate dispositions objectively compatible with these conditions and in a sense pre-adapted to their demands. The most improbable practices are therefore excluded, as unthinkable, by a kind of immediate submission to order that inclines agents to make a virtue of necessity, that is, to refuse what is anyway denied and to will the inevitable. The very conditions of production of the *habitus*, a virtue made of necessity, mean that the anticipations it generates tend to ignore the restriction to which the validity of calculation of probabilities is subordinated, namely that the experimental conditions should not have been modified. Unlike scientific estimations, which are corrected after each experiment according to rigorous rules of calculation, the anticipations of the *habitus*, practical hypotheses based on past experience, give disproportionate weight to early experiences. Through the economic and social necessity that they bring to bear on the relatively autonomous world of the domestic economy and family relations, or more precisely, through the specifically familial manifestations of this external necessity (forms of the division of labour between the sexes, household objects, modes of consumption, parent–child relations, etc.), the structures characterizing a determinate class of conditions of existence produce the structures of the *habitus*, which in their turn are the basis of the perception and appreciation of all subsequent experiences.

The *habitus*, a product of history, produces individual and collective practices – more history – in accordance with the schemes generated by history. It ensures the active presence of past experiences, which, deposited in each organism in the form of schemes of perception, thought and action, tend to guarantee the 'correctness' of practices and their constancy over time, more reliably than all formal rules and explicit norms. This system of dispositions – a present past that tends to perpetuate itself into the future by reactivation in similarly structured practices, an internal law through which the law of external necessities, irreducible to immediate constraints, is constantly exerted – is the principle of the continuity and regularity which objectivism sees in social practices without being able to account for it; and also of the regulated transformations that cannot be explained either by the extrinsic, instantaneous determinisms of mechanistic sociologism or by the purely internal but equally instantaneous determination of spontaneist subjectivism. Overriding the spurious opposition between the forces inscribed in an earlier state of the system, outside the body, and the internal forces arising instantaneously as motivations springing from free will, the internal dispositions – the internalization of externality – enable the external forces to exert themselves, but in accordance with the specific logic of the organisms in which they are incorporated, i.e. in a durable, systematic and non-mechanical way. As an acquired system of generative schemes, the *habitus* makes possible the free production of all the thoughts, perceptions and actions inherent in the particular conditions of its production – and only those. Through the *habitus*, the structure of which it is the product governs practice, not along the paths of a mechanical determinism, but within the constraints and limits initially set on its inventions. This infinite yet strictly limited generative capacity is difficult to understand only so long as one remains locked in the usual antinomies – which the concept of the *habitus* aims to transcend – of determinism and freedom, conditioning and creativity, consciousness and the unconscious, or the individual and society. Because the *habitus* is an infinite capacity for generating products – thoughts, perceptions, expressions and actions – whose limits are set by the historically and socially situated conditions of its production, the conditioned and conditional freedom it provides is as remote from creation of unpredictable novelty as it is from simple mechanical reproduction of the original conditioning.

Nothing is more misleading than the illusion created by hindsight in which all the traces of a life, such as the works of an artist or the events at a biography, appear as the realization of an essence that seems to pre-exist them. Just as a mature artistic style is not contained, like a seed, in an original inspiration but is continuously defined and redefined in the dialectic between the objectifying intention and the already objectified intention, so too the unity of meaning which, after the event, may seem to have preceded the acts and works announcing the final significance, retro- spectively transforming the various stages of the temporal series into mere prepara- tory sketches, is constituted through the confrontation between questions that only exist in and for a mind armed with a particular type of schemes and the solutions obtained through application of these same schemes. The genesis of a system of works or practices generated by the same *habitus* (or homologous *habitus*, such as those that underlie the unity of the life-style of a group or a class) cannot be described either as the autonomous development of a unique and always self- identical essence, or as a continuous creation of novelty, because it arises from the necessary yet unpredictable confrontation between the *habitus* and an event that can exercise a pertinent incitement on the *habitus* only if the latter snatches it from the contingency of the accidental and constitutes it as a problem by applying to it the very principles of its solution; and also because the *habitus*, like every 'art of inventing', is what makes it possible to produce an infinite number of practices that are relatively unpredictable (like the corresponding situations) but also limited in their diversity. In short, being the product of a particular class of objective regularities, the *habitus* tends to generate all the 'reasonable', 'common-sense', behaviours (and only these) which are possible within the limits of these regularities, and which are likely to be positively sanctioned because they are objectively adjusted to the logic characteristic of a particular field, whose objective future they anticipate. At the same time, 'without violence, art or argument', it tends to exclude all 'extravagances' ('not for the likes of us'), that is, all the behaviours that would be negatively sanctioned because they are incompatible with the object- ive conditions.

Because they tend to reproduce the regularities immanent in the conditions in which their generative principle was produced while adjusting to the demands inscribed as objective potentialities in the situation as defined by the cognitive and motivating structures that constitute the *habitus*, practices cannot be deduced either from the present conditions which may seem to have provoked them or from the past conditions which have produced the *habitus*, the durable principle of their production. They can therefore only be accounted for by relating the social conditions in which the *habitus* that generated them was constituted, to the social conditions in which it is implemented, that is, through the scientific work of performing the interrelationship of these two states of the social world that the *habitus* performs, while concealing it, in and through practice. The 'uncon- scious', which enables one to dispense with this interrelating, is never anything other than the forgetting of history which history itself produces by realizing the objective structures that it generates in the quasi-natures of *habitus*. As Durkheim[3] puts it:

> In each one of us, in differing degrees, is contained the person we were yesterday, and indeed, in the nature of things it is even true that our past *personae* predominate in us, since the present is necessarily insignificant when compared with the long period of the past because of which we have emerged in the form we have today. It is just that we don't directly feel the influence of these past selves precisely because they are so deeply rooted within us. They constitute the unconscious part of ourselves. Consequently we have a strong tendency not to recognize their existence and to ignore their legitimate demands. By contrast, with the most recent acquisitions of civilization we are vividly aware of them just because they are recent and consequently have not had time to be assimilated into our collective unconscious.

The *habitus* – embodied history, internalized as a second nature and so forgotten as history – is the active presence of the whole past of which it is the product. As such, it is what gives practices their relative autonomy with respect to external determinations of the immediate present. This autonomy is that of the past, enacted and acting, which, functioning as accumulated capital, produces history on the basis of history and so ensures the permanence in change that makes the individual agent a world within the world. The *habitus* is a spontaneity without consciousness or will, opposed as much to the mechanical necessity of things without history in mechanistic theories as it is to the reflexive freedom of subjects 'without inertia' in rationalist theories.

Thus the dualistic vision that recognizes only the self-transparent act of consciousness or the externally determined thing has to give way to the real logic of action, which brings together two objectifications of history, objectification in bodies and objectification in institutions or, which amounts to the same thing, two states of capital, objectified and incorporated, through which a distance is set up from necessity and its urgencies. This logic is seen in paradigmatic form in the dialectic of expressive dispositions and instituted means of expression (morphological, syntactic and lexical instruments, literary genres, etc.) which is observed in the intentionless invention of regulated improvisation. Endlessly overtaken by his own words, with which he maintains a relation of 'carry and be carried', as Nicolai Hartmann put it, the virtuoso finds in his discourse the triggers for his discourse, which goes along like a train laying its own rails.[4] In other words, being produced by a *modus operandi* which is not consciously mastered, the discourse contains an 'objective intention', as the Scholastics put it, which outruns the conscious intentions of its apparent author and constantly offers new pertinent stimuli to the *modus operandi* of which it is the product and which functions as a kind of 'spiritual automaton'. If witticisms strike as much by their unpredictability as by their retrospective necessity, the reason is that the *trouvaille* that brings to light long buried resources presupposes a *habitus* that so perfectly possesses the objectively available means of expression that it is possessed by them, so much so that it asserts its freedom from them by realizing the rarest of the possibilities that they necessarily imply. The dialectic of the meaning of the language and the 'sayings of the tribe' is a particular and particularly significant case of the dialectic between *habitus* and institutions, that is, between two modes of objectification of past history, in which there is constantly created a history that inevitably appears, like witticisms, as both original and inevitable.

This durably installed generative principle of regulated improvisations is a practical sense which reactivates the sense objectified in institutions. Produced by the work of inculcation and appropriation that is needed in order for objective structures, the products of collective history, to be reproduced in the form of the durable, adjusted dispositions that are the condition of their functioning, the *habitus*, which is constituted in the course of an individual history, imposing its particular logic on incorporation, and through which agents partake of the history objectified in institutions, is what makes it possible to inhabit institutions, to appropriate them practically, and so to keep them in activity, continuously pulling them from the state of dead letters, reviving the sense deposited in them, but at the same time imposing the revisions and transformations that reactivation entails. Or rather, the *habitus* is what enables the institution to attain full realization: it is through the capacity for incorporation, which exploits the body's readiness to take seriously the performative magic of the social, that the king, the banker or the priest are hereditary monarchy, financial capitalism or the Church made flesh. Property appropriates its owner, embodying itself in the form of a structure generating practices perfectly conforming with its logic and its demands. If one is justified in saying, with Marx, that 'the lord of an entailed estate, the first-born son, belongs to the land', that 'it inherits him', or that the 'persons' of capitalists are the 'personification' of capital, this is because the purely social and quasimagical process of socialization, which is inaugurated by the act of marking that institutes an individual as an eldest son, an heir, a successor, a Christian, or simply as a man (as opposed to a woman), with all the corresponding privileges and obligations, and which is prolonged, strengthened and confirmed by social treatments that tend to transform instituted difference into natural distinction, produces quite real effects, durably inscribed in the body and in belief. An institution, even an economy, is complete and fully viable only if it is durably objectified not only in things, that is, in the logic, transcending individual agents, of a particular field, but also in bodies, in durable dispositions to recognize and comply with the demands immanent in the field.

In so far – and only in so far – as *habitus* are the incorporation of the same history, or more concretely, of the same history objectified in *habitus* and structures, the practices they generate are mutually intelligible and immediately adjusted to the structures, and also objectively concerted and endowed with an objective meaning that is at once unitary and systematic, transcending subjective intentions and conscious projects, whether individual or collective. One of the fundamental effects of the harmony between practical sense and objectified meaning (*sens*) is the production of a common-sense world, whose immediate self-evidence is accompanied by the objectivity provided by consensus on the meaning of practices and the world, in other words the harmonization of the agents' experiences and the constant reinforcement each of them receives from expression – individual or collective (in festivals, for example), improvised or programmed (commonplaces, sayings) – of similar or identical experiences.

The homogeneity of *habitus* that is observed within the limits of a class of conditions of existence and social conditionings is what causes practices and works to be immediately intelligible and foreseeable, and hence taken for granted. The *habitus* makes questions of intention superfluous, not only in the production but also in the deciphering of practices and works. Automatic and impersonal, significant without a signifying intention, ordinary practices lend themselves to an understanding that is no less automatic and impersonal. The picking up of the objective intention they express requires neither 'reactivation' of the 'lived' intention of their originator, nor the 'intentional transfer into the Other' cherished by the phenomenologists and all advocates of a 'participationist' conception of history or sociology, nor tacit or explicit inquiry ('What do you *mean?*') as to other people's intentions. 'Communication of consciousnesses' presupposes community of 'unconsciouses' (that is, of linguistic and cultural competences). Deciphering the objective intention of practices and works has nothing to do with 'reproduction' (*Nachbildung*, as the early Dilthey puts it) of lived experiences and the unnecessary and uncertain reconstitution of an 'intention' which is not their real origin.

The objective homogenizing of group or class *habitus* that results from homogeneity of conditions of existence is what enables practices to be objectively harmonized without any calculation or conscious reference to a norm and mutually adjusted in the absence of any direct interaction or, *a fortiori*, explicit co-ordination. The interaction itself owes its form to the objective structures that have produced the dispositions of the interacting agents, which continue to assign them their relative positions in the interaction and elsewhere. 'Imagine', Leibniz suggests[5], 'two clocks or watches in perfect agreement as to the time. This may occur in one of three ways. The first consists in mutual influence; the second is to appoint a skilful workman to correct them and synchronize constantly; the third is to construct these two clocks with such art and precision that one can be assured of their subsequent agreement.' So long as one ignores the true principle of the conductorless orchestration which gives regularity, unity and systematicity to practices even in the absence of any spontaneous or imposed organization of individual projects, one is condemned to the naive artificialism that recognizes no other unifying principle than conscious co-ordination. The practices of the members of the same group or, in a differentiated society, the same class, are always more and better harmonized than the agents know or wish, because, as Leibniz again says, 'following only (his) own laws', each 'nonetheless agrees with the other'. The *habitus* is precisely this immanent law, *lex insita*, inscribed in bodies by identical histories, which is the precondition not only for the co-ordination of practices but also for practices of co-ordination. The corrections and adjustments the agents themselves consciously carry out presuppose mastery of a common code; and undertakings of collective mobilization cannot succeed without a minimum of concordance between the *habitus* of the mobilizing agents (prophet, leader, etc.) and the dispositions of those who recognize themselves in their practices or words, and, above all, without the inclination towards grouping that springs from the spontaneous orchestration of dispositions.

It is certain that every effort at mobilization aimed at organizing collective action has to reckon with the dialectic of dispositions and occasions that takes place in every agent, whether he mobilizes or is mobilized (the hysteresis of *habitus* is doubtless one explanation of the structural lag between opportunities and the dispositions to grasp them which is the cause of missed opportunities and, in particular, of the frequently observed incapacity to think historical crises in categories of perception and thought other than those of the past, however revolutionary). It is also certain that it must take account of the objective orchestration established among dispositions that are objectively co-ordinated because they are ordered by more or less identical objective necessities. It is, however, extremely dangerous to conceive collective action by analogy with individual action, ignoring all that the former owes to the relatively autonomous logic of the institutions of mobilization (with their own history, their specific organization, etc.) and to the situations, institutionalized or not, in which it occurs.

Sociology treats as identical all biological individuals who, being the products of the same objective conditions, have the same *habitus*. A social class (in-itself) – a class of identical or similar conditions of existence and conditionings – is at the same time a class of biological individuals having the same *habitus*, understood as a system of dispositions common to all products of the same conditionings. Though it is impossible for all (or even two) members of the same class to have had the same experiences, in the same order, it is certain that each member of the same class is more likely than any member of another class to have been confronted with the situations most frequent for members of that class. Through the always convergent experiences that give a social environment its physiognomy, with its 'closed doors', 'dead ends' and 'limited prospects', the objective structures that sociology apprehends in the form of probabilities of access to goods, services and powers, inculcate the 'art of assessing likelihoods', as Leibniz put it, of anticipating the objective future, in short, the 'sense of reality', or realities, which is perhaps the best-concealed principle of their efficacy.

To define the relationship between class *habitus* and individual *habitus* (which is inseparable from the organic individuality that is immediately given to immediate perception – *intuitus personae* – and socially designated and recognized – name, legal identity, etc.), class (or group) *habitus*, that is, the individual habitus in so far as it expresses or reflects the class (or group), could be regarded as a subjective but non-individual system of internalized structures, common schemes of perception, conception and action, which are the precondition of all objectification and apperception; and the objective co-ordination of practices and the sharing of a world-view could be founded on the perfect impersonality and interchangeability of singular practices and views. But this would amount to regarding all the practices or representations produced in accordance with identical schemes as impersonal and interchangeable, like individual intuitions of space which, according to Kant, reflect none of the particularities of the empirical ego. In fact, the singular *habitus* of members of the same class are united in a relationship of homology, that is, of diversity within homogeneity reflecting the diversity within homogeneity characteristic of their social conditions of production. Each individual system of dispositions is a structural variant of the others, expressing the singularity of its position within the class and its trajectory. 'Personal' style, the particular stamp marking all the products of the same *habitus*, whether practices or works, is never more than a deviation in relation to the style of a period or class, so that it relates back to the common style not only by its conformity – like Phidias, who, for Hegel, had no 'manner' – but also by the difference that makes the 'manner'.

The principle of the differences between individual *habitus* lies in the singularity of their social trajectories, to which there correspond series of chronologically ordered determinations that are mutually irreducible to one another. The *habitus* which, at every moment, structures new experiences in accordance with the structures produced by past experiences, which are modified by the new experiences within the limits defined by their power of selection, brings about a unique integration, dominated by the earliest experiences, of the experiences statistically common to members of the same class. Early experiences have particular weight because the *habitus* tends to ensure its own constancy and its defence against change through the selection it makes within new information by rejecting information capable of calling into question its accumulated information, if exposed to it accidentally or by force, and especially by avoiding exposure to such information. One only has to think, for example, of homogamy, the paradigm of all the 'choices' through which the *habitus* tends to favour experiences likely to reinforce it (or the empirically confirmed fact that people tend to talk about politics with those who have the same opinions). Through the systematic 'choices' it makes among the places, events and people that might be frequented, the *habitus* tends to protect itself from crises and critical challenges by providing itself with a milieu to which it is as pre-adapted as possible, that is, a relatively constant universe of situations tending to reinforce its dispositions by offering the market most favourable to its products. And once again it is the most paradoxical property of the *habitus*, the unchosen principle of all 'choices', that yields the solution to the paradox of the information needed in order to avoid information. The schemes of perception and appreciation of the *habitus* which are the basis of all the avoidance strategies are largely the product of a non-conscious, unwilled avoidance, whether it results automatically from the conditions of existence (for example, spatial segregation) or has been produced by a strategic intention (such as avoidance of 'bad company' or 'unsuitable books') originating from adults themselves formed in the same conditions.

Even when they look like the realization of explicit ends, the strategies produced by the *habitus* and enabling agents to cope with unforeseen and constantly changing situations are only apparently determined by the future. If they seem to be oriented by anticipation of their own consequences, thereby encouraging the finalist illusion, this is because, always tending to reproduce the objective structures that produced them, they are determined by the past conditions of production of their principle of production, that is, by the already realized outcome of identical or interchangeable past practices, which coincides with their own outcome only to the extent that the structures within which they function are identical to or homologous with the objective structures of which they are the product. Thus, for example, in the interaction between two agents or groups of agents endowed with the same *habitus* (say A and B), everything takes place as if the actions of each of them (say a_1 for A) were organized by reference to the reactions which they call forth from any agent possessing the same *habitus* (say b_1 for B). They therefore objectively imply anticipation of the reaction which these reactions in turn call forth (a_2, A's reaction to b_1). But the teleological description, the only one appropriate to a 'rational actor' possessing perfect information as to the preferences and competences of the other actors, in which each action has the purpose of making possible the reaction to the reaction it induces (individual A performs an action a_1, a gift for example, in order to make individual B produce action b₁, so that he can then perform action a₁, a stepped-up gift), is quite as naive as the mechanistic description that presents the action and the riposte as so many steps in a sequence of programmed actions produced by a mechanical apparatus.

To have an idea of the difficulties that would be encountered by a mechanistic theory of practice as mechanical reaction, directly determined by the antecedent conditions and entirely reducible to the mechanical functioning of pre-established devices – which would have to be assumed to exist in infinite number, like the chance configurations of stimuli capable of triggering them from outside – one only has to mention the grandiose, desperate undertaking of the anthropologist, fired with positivist ardour, who recorded 480 elementary units of behaviour in 20 minutes' observation of his wife in the kitchen: 'Here we confront the distressing fact that the sample episode chain under analysis is a fragment of a larger segment of behavior which in the complete record contains some 480 separate episodes. Moreover, it took only twenty minutes for these 480 behavior stream events to occur. If my wife's rate of behavior is roughly representative of that of other actors, we must be prepared to deal with an inventory of episodes produced at the rate of some 20,000 per sixteen-hour day per actor... In a population consisting of several hundred actor-types, the number of different episodes in the total repertory must amount to many millions in the course of an annual cycle'.[6]

The *habitus* contains the solution to the paradoxes of objective meaning without subjective intention. It is the source of these strings of 'moves' which are objectively organized as strategies without being the product of a genuine strategic intention – which would presuppose at least that they be apprehended as one among other possible strategies. If each stage in the sequence of ordered and oriented actions that constitute objective strategies can appear to be determined by anticipation of the future, and in particular, of its own consequences (which is what justifies the use of the concept of strategy), it is because the practices that are generated by the *habitus* and are governed by the past conditions of production of their generative principle are adapted in advance to the objective conditions whenever the conditions in which the *habitus* functions have remained identical, or similar, to the conditions in which it was constituted. Perfectly and immediately successful adjustment to the objective conditions provides the most complete illusion of finality, or – which amounts to the same thing – of self-regulating mechanism.

The presence of the past in this kind of false anticipation of the future performed by the *habitus* is, paradoxically, most clearly seen when the sense of the probable future is belied and when dispositions ill-adjusted to the objective chances because of a hysteresis effect (Marx's favourite example of this was Don Quixote) are nega-tively sanctioned because the environment they actually encounter is too different from the one to which they are objectively adjusted. In fact the persistence of the effects of primary conditioning, in the form of the *habitus*, accounts equally well for cases in which dispositions function out of phase and practices are objectively ill-adapted to the present conditions because they are objectively adjusted to conditions that no longer obtain. The tendency of groups to persist in their ways, due *inter alia* to the fact that they are composed of individuals with durable dispositions that can outlive the economic and social conditions in which they were produced, can be the source of misadaptation as well as adaptation, revolt as well as resignation.

One only has to consider other possible forms of the relationship between dispositions and conditions to see that the pre-adjustment of the *habitus* to the objective conditions is a 'particular case of the possible' and so avoid unconsciously universalizing the model of the near-circular relationship of near-perfect reproduction, which is completely valid only when the conditions of production of the *habitus* and the conditions of its functioning are identical or homothetic. In this particular case, the dispositions durably inculcated by the objective conditions and by a pedagogic action that is tendentially adjusted to these conditions, tend to generate practices objectively compatible with these conditions and expectations pre-adapted to their objective demands (*amor fati*).[7] As a consequence, they tend, without any rational calculation or conscious estimation of the chances of success, to ensure immediate correspondence between the *a priori* or *ex ante* probability conferred on an event (whether or not accompanied by subjective experiences such as hopes, expectation, fears, etc.) and the *a posteriori* or *ex post* probability that can be established on the basis of past experience. They thus make it possible to understand why economic models based on the (tacit) premise of a 'relationship of intelligible causality', as Max Weber[8] calls it, between generic ('typical') chances 'objectively existing as an average' and 'subjective expectations', or, for example, between investment or the propensity to invest and the rate of return expected or really obtained in the past, fairly exactly account for practices which do not arise from knowledge of the objective chances.

By pointing out that rational action, 'judiciously' oriented according to what is 'objectively valid',[9] is what 'would have happened if the actors had had knowledge of all the circumstances and all the participants' intentions'[10], that is, of what is 'valid in the eyes of the scientist', who alone is able to calculate the system of objective chances to which perfectly informed action would have to be adjusted, Weber shows clearly that the pure model of rational action cannot be regarded as an anthropological description of practice. This is not only because real agents only very exceptionally possess the complete information, and the skill to appreciate it, that rational action would presuppose. Apart from rare cases which bring together the economic and cultural conditions for rational action oriented by knowledge of the profits that can be obtained in the different markets, practices depend not on the average chances of profit, an abstract and unreal notion, but on the specific chances that a singular agent or class of agents possesses by virtue of its capital, this being understood, in this respect, as a means of appropriation of the chances theoretically available to all.

Economic theory which acknowledges only the rational 'responses' of an indeterminate, interchangeable agent to 'potential opportunities', or more precisely to average chances (like the 'average rates of profit' offered by the different markets), converts the immanent law of the economy into a universal norm of proper economic behaviour. In so doing, it conceals the fact that the 'rational' *habitus* which is the precondition for appropriate economic behaviour is the product of particular economic condition, the one defined by possession of the economic and cultural capital required in order to seize the 'potential opportunities' theoretically available to all; and also that the same dispositions, by adapting the economically most deprived to the specific condition of which they are the product and thereby helping to make their adaptation to the generic demands of the economic cosmos (as regards calculation, forecasting, etc.) lead them to accept the negative sanctions resulting from this lack of adaptation, that is, their deprivation. In short, the art of estimating and seizing chances, the capacity to anticipate the future by a kind of practical induction or even to take a calculated gamble on the possible against the probable, are dispositions that can only be acquired in certain social conditions, that is, certain social conditions. Like the entrepreneurial spirit or the propensity to invest, economic information is a function of one's power over the economy. This is, on the one hand, because the propensity to acquire it depends on the chances of using it successfully, and the chances of acquiring it depend on the chances of successfully using it; and also because economic competence, like all competence (linguistic, political, etc.), far from being a simple technical capacity acquired in certain conditions, is a power tacitly conferred on those who have power over the economy or (as the very ambiguity of the word 'competence' indicates) an attribute of status.

Only in imaginary experience (in the folk tale, for example), which neutralizes the sense of social realities, does the social world take the form of a universe of possibles equally possible for any possible subject. Agents shape their aspirations according to concrete indices of the accessible and the inaccessible, of what is and is not 'for us', a division as fundamental and as fundamentally recognized as that between the sacred and the profane. The pre-emptive rights on the future that are defined by law and by the monopolistic right to certain possibles that it confers are merely the explicitly guaranteed form of the whole set of appropriated chances through which the power relations of the present project themselves into the future, from where they govern present dispositions, especially those towards the future. In fact, a given agent's practical relation to the future, which governs his present practice, is defined in the relationship between, on the one hand, his *habitus* with its temporal structures and dispositions towards the future, constituted in the course of a particular relationship to a particular universe of probabilities, and on the other hand a certain state of the chances objectively offered to him by the social world. The relation to what is possible is a relation to power; and the sense of the probable future is constituted in the prolonged relationship with a world structured according to the categories of the possible (for us) and the impossible (for us), of what is appropriated in advance by and for others and what one can reasonably expect for oneself. The *habitus* is the principle of a selective perception of the indices tending to confirm and reinforce it rather than transform it, a matrix generating responses adapted in advance to all objective conditions identical to or homologous with the (past) conditions of its production; it adjusts itself to a probable future which it anticipates and helps to bring about because it reads it directly in the present of the presumed world, the only one it can ever know. It is thus the basis of what Marx[11] calls 'effective demand' (as opposed to 'demand without effect', based on need and desire), a realistic relation to what is possible, founded on and therefore limited by power. This disposition, always marked by its (social) conditions of acquisition and realization, tends to adjust to the objective chances of satisfying need or desire, inclining agents to 'cut their coats according to their cloth', and so to become the accomplices of the processes that tend to make the probable a reality.

Notes

1 Gluckman, M. 1961: Ethnographic Data in British social anthropology. *Sociological Review*, 9: 5–17; cf. also Van Velson, J. 1964: *The Politics of Kinship: A Study in Social Manipulation among the Lakeside Tonga*. Manchester: Manchester University Press.

2 Leach, E. 1962: On certain unconsidered aspects of double descent systems. *Man*, 62: 133.

3 Durkheim, E. 1977: *The Evolution of Educational Thought*. London: Routledge & Kegan Paul, p.11.

4 Ruyer, R. 1966: *Paradoxes de la conscience et limites de l'automatisme*. Paris: Albin Michel.

5 Leibniz, G. W. 1866: *Second éclaircissement du système de la communication des substances* (first pub. 1696). In *Œuvres philosophiques*. Ed. P. Janet. Paris: Ladrange.

6 Harris, M. 1964. *The Nature of Cultural Things*. New York: Random House.

7 For some psychologists' attempts at direct verification of this relationship, see Brunswik, E. 1949: Systematic and representative design of psychological experiments. In J. Neyman (ed.), *Proceedings of the Berkeley Symposium on Mathematical Statistics and Probability*. Berkeley, Calif: University of California Press; Preston, M. G. and Baratta, P. 1948: An experimental study of the action-value of an uncertain income. *American Journal of Psychology*, 61: 183–93; Attneave, F. 1953: Psychological probability as a function of experienced frequency. *Journal of Experimental Psychology*, 46: 81–6.

8 Weber, M. 1922: *Gesammelte Aufsätze zur Wissenschaftslehre*. Tübingen: J. C. Mohr.

9 Weber, ibid.

10 Weber, M. 1968: *Economy and Society*, vol. I. New York: Bedminster, p. 6.

11 Marx, K. 1956: *Economic and Philosophic Manuscripts of 1844*. In K. Marx, *Early Writings*, Harmondsworth: Penguin.

21 The Field of Cultural Production, or: The Economic World Reversed

Pierre Bourdieu

Preliminaries

Few areas more clearly demonstrate the heuristic efficacy of *relational* thinking than that of art and literature. Constructing an object such as the literary field[1] requires and enables us to make a radical break with the substantialist mode of thought (as Ernst Cassirer calls it) which tends to foreground the individual, or the visible interactions between individuals, at the expense of the structural relations – invisible, or visible only through their effects – between social positions that are both occupied and manipulated by social agents, which may be isolated individuals, groups or institutions. There are in fact very few other areas in which the glorification of "great men", unique creators irreducible to any condition or conditioning, is more common or uncontroversial – as one can see, for example, in the fact that most analysts uncritically accept the division of the corpus that is imposed on them by the names of authors ("the work of Racine") or the titles of works (*Phèdre* or *Bérénice*).

To take as one's object of study the literary or artistic field of a given period and society (the field of Florentine painting in the Quattrocento or the field of French literature in the Second Empire) is to set the history of art and literature a task which it never completely performs, because it fails to take it on explicitly, even when it does break out of the routine of monographs which, however interminable, are necessarily inadequate (since the essential explanation of each work lies outside each of them, in the objective relations which constitute this field). The task is that of constructing the space of positions and the space of the position-takings (*prises de position*) in which they are expressed. The science of the literary field is a form of *analysis situs* which establishes that each position – e.g. the one which corresponds to a genre such as the novel or, within this, to a sub-category such as the "society novel" (*roman mondain*) or the "popular" novel – is objectively defined by the system of distinctive properties by which it can be situated relative to other positions; that every position, even the dominant one, depends for its very existence, and for the determinations it imposes on its occupants, on the other positions constituting the field; and that the structure of the field, i.e. of the space of positions, is nothing other than the structure of the distribution of the capital of specific properties which governs success in the field and the winning of the external or specific profits (such as literary prestige) which are at stake in the field.

Originally translated from French by Richard Nice.

The *space of literary or artistic position-takings*, i.e. the structured set of the manifestations of the social agents involved in the field – literary or artistic works, of course, but also political acts or pronouncements, manifestoes or polemics, etc. – is inseparable from the *space of literary or artistic positions* defined by possession of a determinate quantity of specific capital (recognition) and, at the same time, by occupation of a determinate position in the structure of the distribution of this specific capital. The literary or artistic field is a *field of forces*, but it is also a *field of struggles* tending to transform or conserve this field of forces. The network of objective relations between positions subtends and orients the strategies which the occupants of the different positions implement in their struggles to defend or improve their positions (i.e. their position-takings), strategies which depend for their force and form on the position each agent occupies in the power relations (*rapports de force*).

Every position-taking is defined in relation to the *space of possibles* which is objectively realized as a *problematic* in the form of the actual or potential position-taking corresponding to the different positions; and it receives its distinctive *value* from its negative relationship with the coexistent position-takings to which it is objectively related and which determine it by delimiting it. It follows from this, for example, that a *prise de position* changes, even when it remains identical, whenever there is change in the universe of options that are simultaneously offered for producers and consumers to choose from. The meaning of a work (artistic, literary, philosophical, etc.) changes automatically with each change in the field within which it is situated for the spectator or reader.

This effect is most immediate in the case of so-called classic works, which change constantly as the universe of coexistent works changes. This is seen clearly when the simple *repetition* of a work from the past in a radically transformed field of compossibles produces an entirely automatic *effect of parody* (in the theatre, for example, this effect requires the performers to signal a slight distance from a text impossible to defend as it stands; it can also arise in the presentation of a work corresponding to one extremity of the field before an audience corresponding structurally to the other extremity – e.g. when an avant-garde play is performed to a bourgeois audience, or the contrary, as more often happens). It is significant that breaks with the most orthodox works of the past, i.e. with the *belief* they impose on the newcomers, often takes the form of *parody* (intentional, this time), which presupposes and confirms *emancipation*. In this case, the newcomers "get beyond" ("*dépassent*") the dominant mode of thought and expression not by explicitly denouncing it but by repeating and reproducing it in a sociologically non-congruent context, which has the effect of rendering it incongruous or even absurd, simply by making it perceptible as the arbitrary convention which it is. This form of heretical break is particularly favoured by ex-believers, who use pastiche or parody as the indispensable means of objectifying, and thereby appropriating, the form of thought and expression by which they were formerly possessed.

This explains why writers' efforts to control the reception of their own works are always partially doomed to failure (one thinks of Marx's "I am not a Marxist"); if only because the very effect of their work may transform the conditions of its reception and because they would not have had to write many things they did write and write them as they did – e.g. resorting to rhetorical strategies intended to "twist the stick in the other direction" – if they had been granted from the outset what they are granted retrospectively.

. . .

When we speak of a *field* of *prises de position*, we are insisting that what can be constituted as a *system* for the sake of analysis is not the product of a coherence-seeking intention or an objective consensus (even if it presupposes unconscious agreement on common principles) but the product and prize of a permanent conflict; or, to put it another way, that the generative, unifying principle of this "system" is the struggle, with all the contradictions it engenders (so that participation in the struggle – which may be indicated objectively by, for example, the attacks that are suffered – can be used as the criterion establishing that a work belongs to the field of *prises de position* and its author to the field of positions).[2]

   In defining the literary and artistic field as, inseparably, a field of positions and a field of *prises de position*, we also escape from the usual dilemma of internal ("tautegorical") reading of the work (taken in isolation or within the system of works to which it belongs) and external (or "allegorical") analysis, i.e. analysis of the social conditions of production of the producers and consumers which is based on the – generally tacit – hypothesis of the spontaneous correspondence or deliberate matching of production to demand or commissions. And by the same token we escape from the correlative dilemma of the charismatic image of artistic activity as pure, disinterested creation by an isolated artist, and the reductionist vision which claims to explain the act of production and its product in terms of their conscious or unconscious external functions, by referring them, for example, to the interests of the dominant class or, more subtly, to the ethical or aesthetic values of one or another of its fractions, from which the patrons or audience are drawn.

The Field of Cultural Production and the Field of Power

In figure 21.1, the literary and artistic field (3) is contained within the field of power (2), while possessing a relative autonomy with respect to it, especially as regards its economic and political principles of hierarchization. It occupies a *dominated position* (at the negative pole) in this field, which is itself situated at the dominant pole of the field of class relations (1). It is thus the site of a double hierarchy: the *heteronomous* principle of hierarchization, which would reign unchallenged if, losing all autonomy, the literary and artistic field were to disappear as such (so that writers and artists became subject to the ordinary law prevailing in the field of power, and more generally in the economic field), is *success*, as measured by indices such as book sales, number of theatrical performances, etc. or honours, appointments, etc. The *autonomous* principle of hierarchization, which would reign unchallenged if the field of production were to achieve total autonomy with respect to the laws of the market, is *degree of specific consecration* (literary or artistic prestige), i.e. the degree of recognition accorded by those who recognize no other criterion of legitimacy than recognition by those whom they recognize. In other words, the

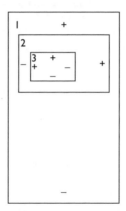

Figure 21.1 *Diagram of the artistic field (3), contained within the field of power (2) which is itself situated within the field of class relations (1). "+" = positive pole, implying a dominant position; "−" = negative pole (dominated)*

specificity of the literary and artistic field is defined by the fact that the more autonomous it is, i.e. the more completely it fulfils its own logic as a field, the more it tends to suspend or reverse the dominant principle of hierarchization; but also that, whatever its degree of independence, it continues to be affected by the laws of the field which encompasses it, those of economic and political profit. The more autonomous the field becomes, the more favourable the symbolic power balance is to the most autonomous producers and the more clearcut is the division between the field of restricted production, in which the producers produce for other producers, and the field of "mass-audience" production (*la grande production*), which is *symbolically* excluded and discredited (this symbolically dominant definition is the one that the historians of art and literature *unconsciously* adopt when they exclude from their object of study, writers and artists who produced for the market and have often fallen into oblivion). Because it is a good measure of the degree of autonomy, and therefore of presumed adherence to the disinterested values which constitute the specific law of the field, the degree of public success is no doubt the main differentiating factor. But lack of success is not in itself a sign and guarantee of election, and "*poètes maudits*", like "successful playwrights", must take account of a secondary differentiating factor whereby some "*poètes maudits*" may also be "failed writers" (even if exclusive reference to the first criterion can help them to avoid realizing it), whilst some box-office successes may be recognized, at least in some sectors of the field, as genuine art.

Thus, at least in the most perfectly autonomous sector of the field of cultural production, where the only audience aimed at is other producers (e.g. Symbolist poetry), the economy of practices is based, as in a generalized game of "loser wins", on a systematic inversion of the fundamental principles of all ordinary economies, that of business (it excludes the pursuit of profit and does not guarantee any sort of correspondence between investments and monetary gains), that of power (it con-demns honours and temporal greatness), and even that of institutionalized cultural authority (the absence of any academic training or consecration may be considered a virtue).

One would have to analyse in these terms the relations between writers or artists and publishers or gallery directors. The latter are equivocal figures, through whom the logic of the economy is brought to the heart of the sub-field of production-for-fellow-producers; they need to possess, simultaneously, economic dispositions which, in some sectors of the fields, are totally alien to the producers and also properties close to those of the producers whose work they valorize and exploit. The logic of the structural homologies between the field of publishers or gallery directors and the field of the corresponding artists or writers does indeed mean that the former present properties close to those of the latter, and this favours the relationship of trust and belief which is the basis of an exploitation presupposing a high degree of misrecognition on each site. These "merchants in the temple" make their living by tricking the artist or writer into taking the consequences of his statutory professions of disinterestedness.

This explains the inability of all forms of economism, which seek to grasp this anti-economy in economic terms, to understand this upside-down economic world. The literary and artistic world is so ordered that those who enter it have an interest in disinterestedness. And indeed, like prophecy, especially the prophecy of misfortune, which according to Weber (1952), demonstrates its authenticity by the fact that it brings in no income, a heretical break with the prevailing artistic traditions proves its claim to authenticity by its disinterestedness. As we shall see, this does not mean that there is not an economic logic to this charismatic economy based on the social miracle of an act devoid of any determination other than the specifically aesthetic intention. There are economic conditions for the indifference to economy which induces a pursuit of the riskiest positions in the intellectual and artistic avant-garde, and also for the capacity to remain there over a long period without any economic compensation.

The struggle for the dominant principle of hierarchization

The literary or artistic field is at all times the site of a struggle between the two principles of hierarchization: the heteronomous principle, favourable to those who dominate the field economically and politically (e.g. "bourgeois art") and the autonomous principle (e.g. "art for art's sake"), which those of its advocates who are least endowed with specific capital tend to identify with degree of independence from the economy, seeing temporal failure as a sign of election and success as a sign of compromise.[3] The state of the power relations in this struggle depends on the overall degree of autonomy possessed by the field, i.e. the extent to which it manages to impose its own norms and sanctions on the whole set of producers, including those who are closest to the dominant pole of the field of power and therefore most responsive to external demands (i.e. the most heteronomous); this degree of autonomy varies considerably from one period and one national tradition to another, and affects the whole structure of the field. Everything seems to indicate that it depends on the value which the specific capital of writers and artists represents for the dominant fractions, on the one hand in the struggle to conserve the established order and, perhaps especially, in the struggle between the fractions aspiring to domination within the field of power (bourgeoisie and aristocracy, old bourgeoisie and new bourgeoisie, etc.), and on the other hand in the production and reproduction of economic capital (with the aid of experts and cadres).[4] All the evidence suggests that, at a given level of overall autonomy, intellectuals are, other things being equal, proportionately more responsive to the seduction of the powers that be, the less well-endowed they are with specific capital.[5]

The struggle in the field of cultural production over the imposition of the legitimate mode of cultural production is inseparable from the struggle within the dominant class (with the opposition between "artists" and "bourgeois") to impose the dominant principle of domination (i.e., ultimately, the definition of human accomplishment). In this struggle, the artists and writers who are richest in specific capital and most concerned for their autonomy are considerably weakened by the fact that some of their competitors identify their interests with the dominant principles of hierarchization and seek to impose them even within the field, with the support of the temporal powers. The most heteronomous cultural producers (i.e. those with least symbolic capital) can offer the least resistance to external demands, of whatever sort. To defend their own position, they have to produce weapons, which the dominant agents (within the field of power) can immediately turn against the cultural producers most attached to their autonomy. In endeavouring to discredit every attempt to impose an autonomous principle of hierarchization, and thus serving their own interests, they serve the interests of the dominant fractions of the dominant class, who obviously have an interest in there being only one hierarchy. In the struggle to impose the legitimate definition of art and literature, the most autonomous producers naturally tend to exclude "bourgeois" writers and artists, whom they see as "enemy agents". This means, incidentally, that sampling problems cannot be resolved by one of those arbitrary decisions of positivist ignorance which are dignified by the term "operational definition": these amount to blindly arbitrating on debates which are inscribed in reality itself, such as the question as to whether such and such a group ("bourgeois" theatre, the "popular" novel, etc.) or such and such an individual claiming the title of writer or artist (or philosopher, or intellectual, etc.) belongs to the population of writers or artists or, more precisely, as to who is legitimately entitled to designate legitimate writers or artists.

The preliminary reflexions on the definition of the object and the boundaries of the population, which studies of writers, artists, and especially intellectuals, often indulge in as to give themselves an air of scientificity, ignore the fact, which is more than scientifically attested, that the definition of the writer (or artist, etc.) is an issue at stake in struggles in every literary (or artistic, etc.) field.[6] In other words, the field of cultural production is the site of struggles in which what is at stake is the power to impose the dominant definition of the writer and therefore to delimit the population of those entitled to take part in the struggle to define the writer. The established definition of the writer may be radically transformed by an enlargement of the set of people who have a legitimate voice in literary matters. It follows from this that every survey aimed at establishing the hierarchy of writers predetermines the hierarchy by determining the population deemed worthy of helping to establish it. In short, the fundamental stake in literary struggles is the monopoly of literary legitimacy, i.e., *inter alia*, the monopoly of the power to say with authority who is authorized to call himself a writer; or, to put it another way, it is the monopoly of the power to consecrate producers or products (we are dealing with a world of belief and the consecrated writer is the one who has the power to consecrate and to win assent when he consecrates an author or a work – with a preface, a favourable review, a prize, etc.). While it is true that every literary field is the site of a struggle over the definition of the writer (a universal proposition), the fact remains if he is not to make the mistake of universalizing the particular case, the scientific analyst needs to know that he will only ever encounter historical definitions of the writer, corresponding to a particular state of the struggle to impose the legitimate definition of the writer. There is no other criterion of membership of a field than the objective fact of producing effects within it. One of the difficulties of orthodox defence against heretical transformation of the field by a redefinition of the tacit or explicit terms of entry is the fact that polemics imply a form of recognition; an adversary whom one would prefer to destroy by ignoring him cannot be combated without consecrating him. The *Théâtre Libre* effectively entered the sub-field of drama once it came under attack from the accredited advocates of bourgeois theatre, who thus helped to produce the recognition they sought to prevent. The *"nouveaux philosophes"* came into existence as active elements in the philosophical field – and no longer just that of journalism – as soon as consecrated philosophers felt called upon to take issue with them.

The *boundary* of the field is a stake of struggles, and the social scientist's task is not to draw a dividing-line between the agents involved in it, by imposing a so-called operational definition, which is most likely to be imposed on him by his own prejudices or presuppositions, but to describe a *state* (long-lasting or temporary) of these struggles and therefore of the frontier delimiting the territory held by the competing agents. One could thus examine the characteristics of this boundary, which may or may not be institutionalized, i.e. protected by conditions of entry that are tacitly and practically required (such as a certain cultural capital) or explicitly codified and legally guaranteed (e.g. all the forms of entrance examination aimed at ensuring a *numerus clausus*). It would be found that one of the most significant properties of the field of cultural production, explaining its extreme dispersion and the conflicts between rival principles of legitimacy, is the extreme permeability of its frontiers and, consequently, the extreme diversity of the "posts" it offers, which defy any unilinear hierarchization. It is clear from comparison that the field of cultural production neither demands as much inherited economic capital as the economic field nor as much educational capital as the university sub-field or even sectors of the field of power such as the top civil service, or even the field of the "liberal professions".[7] However, precisely because it represents one of the *indeterminate sites* in the social structure, which offer ill-defined posts, waiting to be made rather than ready-made, and therefore extremely elastic and undemanding, and career-paths which are themselves full of uncertainty and extremely dispersed (unlike bureaucratic careers, such as those offered by the university system), they attract agents who differ greatly in their properties and dispositions but the most favoured of whom are sufficiently secure to be able to disdain a university career and to take on the risks of an occupation which is not a "job" (since it is almost always combined with a private income or a "bread-and-butter" occupation).

The "profession" of writer or artist is one of the least professionalized there are, despite all the efforts of "writer's associations", "Pen Clubs", etc. This is shown clearly by (*inter alia*) the problems which arise in classifying these agents, who are able to exercise what they regard as their main occupation only on condition that they have a secondary occupation which provides their main income (problems very similar to those encountered in classifying students).

The most disputed frontier of all is the one which separates the field of cultural production and the field of power. It may be more or less clearly marked in different periods, positions occupied in each field may be more or less totally incompatible, moves from one universe to the other more or less frequent, and the overall distance between the corresponding populations more or less great (e.g. in terms of social origin, educational background, etc.).

The effect of the homologies

The field of cultural production produces its most important effects through the play of the *homologies* between the fundamental opposition which gives the field its structure and the oppositions structuring the field of power and the field of class relations. These homologies may give rise to ideological effects which are produced automatically whenever oppositions at different levels are superimposed or merged. They are also the basis of partial alliances: the struggles within the field of power are never entirely independent of the struggle between the dominated classes and the dominant class; and the logic of the homologies between the two spaces means that the struggles going on within the inner field are always overdetermined and always tend to aim at two birds with one stone. The cultural producers, who occupy the economically dominated and symbolically dominant position within the field of cultural production, tend to feel solidarity with the occupants of the economically and culturally dominated positions within the field of class relations. Such alliances, based on homologies of position combined with profound differences in condition, are not exempt from misunderstandings and even bad faith. The structural affinity between the literary avant-garde and the political vanguard is the basis of rapprochements, between intellectual anarchism and the Symbolist movement for example, in which convergences are flaunted (e.g. Mallarmé referring to a book as an *"attentat"* – an act of terrorist violence) but distances prudently maintained. The fact remains that the cultural producers are able to use the power conferred on them, especially in periods of crisis, by their capacity to put forward a critical definition of the social world, to mobilize the potential strength of the dominated classes and subvert the order prevailing in the field of power.

> The effects of homology are not all and always automatically granted. Thus whereas the dominant fractions, in their relationship with the dominant fractions, are on the side of nature, common sense, practice, instinct, the upright and the male, and also order, reason, etc., they can no longer bring certain aspects of this representation into play in their relationship with the dominated classes, to whom they are opposed as culture to nature, reason to instinct. They need to draw on what they are offered by the dominated fractions, in order to justify their class domination, to themselves as well. The cult of art and the artist (rather than of the intellectual) is one of the necessary component of the bourgeois "art of living", to which it brings a *"supplément d'âme"*, its spiritualistic point of honour.

Even in the case of the seemingly most heteronomous forms of cultural production, such as journalism, adjustment to demand is not the product of a conscious arrangement between producers and consumers. It results from the correspondence between the space of the producers, and therefore of the products offered, and the space of the consumers, which is brought about, on the basis of the homology between the two spaces, only through the competition between the producers and through the strategies imposed by the correspondence between the space of possible *prises de position* and the space of positions. In other words, by obeying the logic of the objective competition between mutually exclusive positions within the field, the various categories of producers tend to supply products adjusted to the expectations of the various positions in the field of power, but without any conscious striving for such adjustment.

> If the various positions in the field of cultural production can be so easily characterized in terms of the audience which corresponds to them, this is because the encounter between a work and its audience (which may be an absence of immediate audience) is, strictly speaking, a *coincidence* which is not explained either by conscious, even cynical adjustment (though there are exceptions), or by the constraints of commission and demand. Rather, it results from the homology between positions occupied in the space of production, with the correlative *prises de position*, and positions in the space of consumption, i.e. in this case, in the field of power, with the opposition between the dominant and the dominated fractions, or in the field of class relations, with the opposition between the dominant and the dominated classes. In the case of the relation between the field of cultural production and the field of power, we are dealing with an almost perfect homology between two chiastic structures. Just as, in the dominant class, economic capital increases as one moves from the dominated to the dominant fractions, whereas cultural capital varies in the opposite way, so too in the field of cultural production economic profits increase as one moves from the "autonomous" pole to the "heteronomous" pole, whereas specific profits increase in the opposite direction. Similarly, the secondary opposition which divides the most heteronomous sector into "bourgeois art" and "industrial" art clearly corresponds to the opposition between the dominant and the dominated classes (cf. Bourdieu 1979: 463–541).

. . .

Positions and Dispositions

The meeting of two histories

To understand the practices of writers and artists, and not least their products, entails understanding that they are the result of the meeting of two histories: the history of the positions they occupy and the history of their dispositions. Although position helps to shape dispositions, the latter, insofar as they are the product of independent conditions, have an existence and efficacy of their own and can help to shape positions. In no field is the confrontation between positions and dispositions more continuous or uncertain than in the literary and artistic field. Offering positions that are relatively uninstitutionalized, never legally guaranteed, therefore open to symbolic challenge, and non-hereditary (although there are specific forms of transmission), it is the arena *par excellence* of struggles over job definition. In fact, however great the effect of position – and we have seen many examples of it – it never operates mechanically, and the relationship between positions and *prises de position* is mediated by the dispositions of the agents.

...

The "post" of poet as it presents itself to the young aspirant in the 1880s is the crystallized product of the whole previous history. It is a position in the hierarchy of literary crafts, which, by a sort of effect of *caste*, gives its occupants, subjectively at least, the assurance of an essential superiority over all other writers; the lowest of the poets (Symbolist, at this time) sees himself as superior to the highest of the (Naturalist) novelists. It is a set of "exemplary figures" – Hugo, Gautier, etc. – who have composed the character and assigned roles, such as, for intellectuals (after Zola), that of the intellectual as the champion of great causes. It is a cluster of representations – that of the "pure" artist, for example, indifferent to success and to the verdicts of the market – and mechanisms which, through their sanctions, support them and give them real efficacy, etc. In short, one would need to work out the full social history of the *long, collective* labour which leads to the progressive invention of the crafts of writing, and in particular to *awareness* of the *fundamental law* of the field, i.e. the theory of art for art's sake, which is to the field of cultural production what the axiom "business is business" (and "in business there's no room for feelings") is to the economic field.[8] Nor, of course, must one forget the role of the mechanism which, here as elsewhere, leads people to make a virtue of necessity, in the constitution of the field of cultural production as a space radically independent of the economy and of politics and, as such, amenable to a sort of pure theory. The work of real emancipation, of which the "post" of artist or poet is the culmination, can be performed and pursued only if the post encounters the appropriate dispositions, such as disinterestedness and daring, and the (external) conditions of these virtues, such as a private income. In this sense, the collective invention which results in the post of writer or artist endlessly has to be repeated, even if the objectification of past discoveries and the recognition ever more widely accorded to an activity of cultural production that is an end in itself, and the will to emancipation that it implies, tend constantly to reduce the cost of this permanent reinvention. The more the autonomizing process advances, the more possible it becomes to occupy the position of producer without having the properties – or not all of them, or not to the same degree – that had to be possessed to produce the position; the more, in other words, the newcomers who head for the most "autonomous" positions can dispense with the more or less heroic sacrifices and breaks of the past.

The position of "pure" writer or artist, like that of intellectual, is an institution of freedom, constructed against the "bourgeoisie" (in the artists' sense) and against institutions – in particular against the State bureaucracies, Academies, Salons, etc. – by a series of breaks, partly cumulative, but sometimes followed by regressions, which have often been made possible by diverting the resources of the market – and therefore the "bourgeoisie" – and even the State bureaucracies.[9] Owing to

its objectively contradictory intention, it only exists at the lowest degree of institutionalization, in the form of words ("avant-garde", for example) or models (the
avant-garde writer and his exemplary deeds) which constitute a tradition of freedom
and criticism, and also, but above all, in the form of a field of competition, equipped
with its own institutions (the paradigm of which might be the "*Salon des refusés*" or
the little avant-garde review) and articulated by mechanisms of competition capable
of providing incentives and gratification for emancipatory endeavours. For example,
the acts of prophetic denunciation of which *J'accuse* is the paradigm have become,
since Zola, and perhaps especially since Sartre, so intrinsic to the personage of
the intellectual that anyone who aspires to a position (especially a dominant one)
in the intellectual field has to perform such exemplary acts.[10] This explains why it is
that the producers most freed from external constraints – Mallarmé, Proust, Joyce or
Virginia Woolf – are also those who have taken most advantage of a historical
heritage accumulated through collective labour against external constraints.

Having established, in spite of the illusion of the constancy of the things designated,
which is encouraged by the constancy of the words, artist, writer, bohemian,
academy, etc., what each of the positions is at each moment, one still has to
understand how those who occupy them have been formed and, more precisely,
the shaping of the dispositions which help to lead them to these positions and to
define their way of operating within them and staying in them. The field, as a field of
possible forces, presents itself to each agent as *a space of possibles* which is defined
in the relationship between the structure of average chances of access to the different
positions (measured by the "difficulty" of attaining them and, more precisely, by the
relationship between the number of positions and the number of competitors) and
the dispositions of each agent, the subjective basis of the perception and appreciation of the objective chances. In other words, the objective probabilities (of economic or symbolic profit, for example) inscribed in the field at a given moment only
become operative and active through "vocations", "aspirations" and "expectations",
i.e. insofar as they are perceived and appreciated through the schemes of perception
and appreciation which constitute a habitus. These schemes, which reproduce in
their own logic the fundamental divisions of the field of positions – "pure art"/
"commercial art", "bohemian"/"bourgeois", "left bank"/"right bank", etc. – are one
of the mediations through which dispositions are adjusted to positions. Writers and
artists, particularly newcomers, do not react to an "objective reality" functioning as
a sort of stimulus valid for every possible subject, but to a "problem-raising situation", as Popper puts it; they help to create its intellectual and affective "physiognomy" (horror, seduction, etc.) and therefore even the symbolic force it exerts on
them. A position as it appears to the (more or less adequate) "sense of investment"
which each agent applies to it presents itself either as a sort of necessary locus which
beckons those who are made for it ("vocation") or, by contrast, as an impossible
destination, an unacceptable destiny or one that is acceptable only as temporary
refuge or a secondary, accessory position. This sense of social direction which orients
agents, according to their modesty or daring, their disinterestedness or thirst
for profit, towards the risky, long-term investments of journalism, serials or the
theatre, is the basis of the astonishingly close correspondence that is found between
positions and dispositions, between the social characteristics of "posts" and the

social characteristics of the agents who fill them. The correspondence is such that in all cases of coincidence and concordance in which the position is in a sense materialized in the dispositions of its occupants, it would be equally wrong to impute everything solely to position or solely to dispositions.

> The mechanistic model that is, more or less consciously, put into operation when social origin, or any other variable, is made the principle of a linear series of determinations – e.g. father's occupation, more or less crudely defined, determining position, e.g. occupational position, which in turn determines opinions – totally ignores the effects of the field, in particular those which result from the way in which the influx of newcomers is quantitatively and qualitatively regulated.[11] Thus the absence of statistical relation between the agents' social origin and their *prises de position* may result from an unobserved transformation of the field and of the relationship between social origin and *prise de position*, such that, for two successive generations, the same dispositions will lead to different *prises de position*, or even opposing ones (which will tend to cancel each other out).

There is nothing mechanical about the relationship between the field and the habitus. The space of available positions does indeed help to determine the properties expected and even demanded of possible candidates, and therefore the categories of agents they can attract and above all *retain*; but the perception of the space of possible positions and trajectories and the appreciation of the value each of them derives from its location in the space depend on these dispositions. It follows as a point of method that one cannot give a full account of the relationship obtaining at a given moment between the space of positions and the space of dispositions, and, therefore, of the set of *social trajectories* (or constructed biographies), unless one establishes the configuration, at that moment, and at the various critical turning-points in each career, of the space of available possibilities – in particular, the economic and symbolic hierarchy of the genres, schools, styles, manners, subjects, etc. – the social value attached to each of them, and also the meaning and value they received for the difference agents or classes of agents in terms of the socially constituted categories of perception and appreciation they applied to them.

. . .

The habitus and the possibles

The propensity to move towards the economically most risky positions, and above all the capacity to persist in them (a condition for all avant-garde undertakings which precede the demands of the market), even when they secure no short-term economic profit, seem to depend to a large extent on possession of substantial economic and social capital. This is firstly because economic capital provides the conditions for freedom from economic necessity, a private income (*la rente*) being one of the best substitutes for sales (*la vente*), as Théophile Gautier said to Feydeau: "Flaubert was smarter than us....He had the wit to come into the world with money, something which is indispensable for anyone who wants to get anywhere in art" (quoted by Cassagne 1979: 218).

> Those who do manage to stay in the risky positions long enough to receive the symbolic profit they can bring are indeed mainly drawn from the most privileged categories, who

have also had the advantage of not having to devote time and energy to secondary, "bread-and-butter" activities. Thus, as Ponton shows (1977: 69–70), some of the Parnassians, all from the *petite bourgeoisie*, either had to abandon poetry at some stage and turn to better-paid literary activities, such as the "novel of manners", or, from the outset, devoted part of their time to complementary activities such as plays or novels (e.g. François Coppée, Catulle Mendès, Jean Aicard), whereas the wealthier Parnassians could concentrate almost exclusively on their art (and when they did change to another genre, it was only after a long poetic career). We also find that the least well-off writers resign themselves more readily to "industrial literature", in which writing becomes a job like any other.

It is also because economic capital provides the guarantees (*assurances*) which can be the basis of self-assurance, audacity and indifference to profit – dispositions which, together with the flair associated with possession of a large social capital and the corresponding familiarity with the field, i.e. the art of sensing the new hierarchies and the new structures of the chances of profit, point towards the outposts, the most exposed positions of the avant-garde, and towards the riskiest investments, which are also, however, very often the most profitable symbolically, and in the long run, at least for the earliest investors.

> The sense of investment seems to be one of the dispositions most closely linked to social and geographical origin, and, consequently, through the associated social capital, one of the mediations through which the effects of the opposition between Parisian and provincial origin make themselves felt in the logic of the field.[12] Thus we find that as a rule those richest in economic, cultural and social capital are the first to move into the new positions (and this seems to be true in all fields, economic, scientific, etc.). This is the case with the writers who, around Paul Bourget, abandon Symbolist poetry for a new form of novel which breaks with Naturalism and is better adjusted to the expectations of the cultivated audience. By contrast, a faulty sense of investment, linked to social distance (among writers from the working class or the petite bourgeoisie) or geographical distance (among provincials and foreigners) inclines beginners to aim for the dominant positions at a time when, precisely because of their attractiveness (due, for example, to the economic profits they secure, in the case of the Naturalist novel, or the symbolic profits they promise, in the case of Symbolist poetry) and the intensified competition for them, the profits are tending to decline. It may also make them persist in declining or threatened positions when the best-informed agents are abandoning them. . . .

Finally, we must ask explicitly a question which is bound to be asked: what is the degree of conscious strategy, cynical calculation, in the objective strategies which observation brings to light and which ensure the correspondence between positions and dispositions? One only has to read literary testimonies, correspondence, diaries, and especially perhaps, explicit *prises de position* on the literary world as such (like those collected by Huret) to see that there is no simple answer to these questions and that lucidity is always partial and is, once again, a matter of position and trajectory within the field, so that it varies from one agent and one moment to another. As for awareness of the logic of the game as such, and of the *illusio* on which it is based, I had been inclined to think that it was excluded by membership of the field, which presupposes (and induces) belief in everything which depends on the existence of the field, i.e. literature, the writer, etc., because such lucidity would make the literary or artistic undertaking itself a cynical mystification, a conscious trickery. So I thought, until I came across a text by Mallarmé which provides both the programme and the balance-sheet of a rigorous science of the literary field and the recognized fictions that are engendered within it:

> We know, captives of an absolute formula that, indeed, there is only that which is. Forthwith to dismiss the cheat, however, on a pretext, would indict our inconsequence, denying the pleasure we want to take: for that *beyond* is its agent, and the engine I might say were I not loath to perform, in public, the impious dismantling of the fiction and consequently of the literary mechanism, to display the principal part or nothing. But I venerate how, by a trick, we project to a height forfended – and with thunder! – the conscious lack in us of what shines up there.
>   What is it for?
>   A game. (Mallarmé 1945: 647)

This quasi-Feuerbachian theory reduces beauty, which is sometimes thought of as a Platonic Idea, endowed with an objective, transcendent existence, to no more than the projection into a metaphysical beyond of what is lacking in the here-and-now of literary life. But is that how it is to be taken? Hermeticism, in this case, perfectly fulfils its function: to utter "in public" the true nature of the field, and of its mechanisms, is sacrilege *par excellence*, the unforgivable sin which all the censorships constituting the field seek to repress. These are things that can only be said in such a way that they are not said. If Mallarmé can, without excluding himself from the field, utter the truth about a field which excludes the *publishing* of its own truth, this is because he says it in a language which is designed to be *recognized* within the field because everything, in its very *form*, that of euphemism and *Verneinung*, affirms that he *recognizes* its censorships. Marcel Duchamp was to do exactly the same thing when he made artistic acts out of his bluffs, demystificatory mystifications which denounce fiction as mere fiction, and with it the collective belief which is the basis of this "legitimate" imposture (as Austin would have put it). But Mallarmé's hermeticism, which bespeaks his concern not to destroy the *illusio*, has another basis too: if the Platonic illusion is the "agent" of a pleasure which we take only because "we *want* to take it", if the pleasure of the love of art has its source in unawareness of producing the source of what produces it, then it is understandable that one might, by another willing suspension of disbelief, choose to "venerate" the authorless trickery which places the fragile fetish beyond the reach of critical lucidity.

Notes

1   Or any other kind of field; art and literature being one area among others for application of the method of object-construction designated by the concept of the field.
2   In this (and only this) respect, the theory of the field could be regarded as a generalized Marxism, freed from the realist mechanism implied in the theory of "instances".
3   The status of "social art" is, in this respect, thoroughly ambiguous. Although it relates artistic or literary production to external functions (which is what the advocates of "art for

art's sake" object to about it), it shares with "art for art's sake" a radical rejection of the dominant principle of hierarchy and of the "bourgeois" art which recognizes it.

4   The specific, and therefore autonomous, power which writers and artists possess *qua* writers and artists must be distinguished from the alienated, heteronomous power they wield *qua* experts or cadres – a share in domination, but with the status of dominated mandatories, granted to them by the dominant.

5   Thus, writers and artists who are "second-rank" in terms of the specific criteria may invoke populism and social art to impose their reign on the "leading intellectuals" who, as has happened in China and elsewhere, will protest against the disparity between the revolutionary ideal and the reality, i.e., the reign of functionaries devoted to the Party (see Godman 1967).

6   Throughout this passage, "writer" can be replaced by "artist", "philosopher", "intellectual", etc. The intensity of the struggle, and the degree to which it takes visible, and therefore conscious, forms, no doubt vary according to the genre and according to the rarity of the specific competence each genre requires in different periods, i.e., according to the probability of "unfair competition" or "illegal exercise of the profession". (This no doubt explains why the intellectual field, with the permanent threat of casual essayism, is one of the key areas in which to grasp the logic of the struggles which pervade all fields.)

7   Only just over a third of the writers in the sample studied by Rémy Ponton had had any higher education, whether or not it led to a degree (Ponton 1977: 43). (For the comparison between the literary field and other fields, see Charle 1981.)

8   The painters still had to win their autonomy with respect to the writers, without whom they would perhaps not have succeeded in freeing themselves from the constraints of the bureaucracies and academicism.

9   To those who seek to trace a direct relationship between any producers and the group from which they draw their economic support, it has to be pointed out that the logic of a relatively autonomous field means that one can use the resources provided by a group or institution to produce products deliberately or unconsciously directed against the interests or values of that group or institutions.

10   It goes without saying that freedom with respect to institutions can never be truly institutionalized. This contradiction, which every attempt to institutionalize heresy comes up against (it is the antinomy of the Reformed Church), is seen clearly in the ambivalent image of institutional acts of consecration, and not only those performed by the most heteronomous institutions, such as academies (one thinks of Sartre's refusal of the Nobel Prize).

11   Although I realize that theoretical warnings count for little against the social drives which induce simplistic, apologetic or terroristic use of more-or-less scientific-seeming reference to "father's occupation", it seems useful to condemn the inclination – in which the worst adversaries and acolytes too easily find common ground – to reduce the model that is proposed, to the mechanical and mechanistic mode of thinking in which inherited capital (internalized in habitus, or objectified) determines the position occupied, which in turn directly determines *prises de position*.

12   An example of this is the case of Anatole France, whose father's unusual position (a Paris bookseller) enabled him to acquire a social capital and a familiarity with the world of letters which compensated for his low economic and cultural capital.

References

Bourdieu, P., 1979. *La distinction*. Paris: Ed. de Minuit.

Cassagne, A., 1979. *La théorie de l'art pour l'art en France chez les derniers romantiques et les premiers réalistes*. Geneva: Slatkine Reprints. (Originally published Paris, 1906.)

Charle, C., 1981. *Situation du champ littéraire*. *Littérature* 44: 8–20.

Godman, M., 1967. *Literary Dissent in Communist China*. Cambridge, MA: Harvard University Press.

Mallarmé, Stéphane, 1945. "La musique et les lettres". In: *Oeuvres complètes*. Paris: Gallimard (Pléiade).

Ponton, Rémy, 1977. *Le champ littéraire de 1865 à 1905*. Paris: EHESS.

Weber, Max, 1952. *Ancient Judaism*. Glencoe, IL: Free Press.

Part VII

Race, Gender, and Difference

INTRODUCTION TO PART VII

This section examines work that speaks in various ways to a central issue for contemporary theory: the challenge of difference. Although the question of difference is basic to all social experience, the work included here is focused on race and gender as key dimensions of difference. Race and gender have been important themes in sociology since its inception, and yet the theoretical implications of these classifications were by no means always taken seriously. Particularly in the second half of the twentieth century, sociological theorists have begun to revisit the issue of difference, and to deal with it in increasingly prominent and sophisticated ways.

Many factors were behind the reemergence of questions about identity and difference in contemporary theory. Probably chief among them was the impact of several powerful social movements. Anti-colonial revolutions throughout Africa, civil-rights struggles in America, the continuing development of feminism world-wide, and gay liberation movements all provided a voice to previously marginalized groups. In doing so, they accomplished two things. First, they publicly tied social categories to meaningful identities. Second, the movements made claims for political and cultural recognition based on those identities. The same demands for recognition that motivated these movements also began to emerge in sociological theory, and for many of the same reasons. As these movements emerged, and as the discipline of sociology itself became more diverse, sociological attempts to think seriously about difference also developed.

Theorizing Difference

Recent work has emphasized that gender and race – and other dimensions of difference, such as sexual orientation and nationality – are not simply variables that need to be included in sociological explanations, they are also fundamental categories of experience that themselves need to be analyzed. Theorizing difference has meant at least three things.

First, it has meant simply correcting the false generalizations implicit in much classic thought about social life. Such generalizations did not always go unchallenged, but they were pervasive. For example, in the eighteenth century, almost as soon as Patrick Henry wrote his "Essay on the Rights of Man," Mary Wolstonecraft answered with her "Vindication of the Rights of Women." Wolstonecraft supported Henry's vision of liberty, but not the exclusion of women from it. When Henry wrote of the rights of "Man" he implied that he was writing about people in general, but in fact wrote – and was read – as describing rights that pertained to men only. In this sense, theorizing difference has meant bringing gender, race, and other dimensions of difference back into our thinking about social life, and being clear about the limits of established theory and research.

Second, it has involved questioning whether the categories of gender and race, which we often take for granted, really have objective and stable meanings. This includes inquiry into how the concepts are produced historically, how they are applied in practice, and what ambiguities are ignored to make the distinctions appear natural. It extends into explorations of how gender and race categories are renewed in response to social change. For example, American racial formation has generally – but arbitrarily – categorized the children of Black/White marriages as Black.[1] Recently, however, many such "mixed race" people have demanded distinctive racial categorizations that recognize their "both/and" status – a desire recognized with a new set of census categories in the 2000 enumeration of the US population. This challenges the typically "either/or" way that race has been constructed in the English-speaking world, a construction influenced by the legacy of slavery in the US, European colonialism, and the rise of evolutionary thought in biology.[2] What was new in this was not simply making group distinctions nor even looking down on members of other groups, especially dominated groups. These are both old and nearly universal human habits. The novelty was the production of elaborate systems of alleged (though often pseudoscientific) biological classifications of races. In common with the rest of science, recent sociological theory recognizes that racial distinctions are not simply reflections of biology. Some real biological characteristics may be used in such distinctions, but even the selection of which of these count in identifying racial groups is basically cultural.

A similar point may be made in relation to sex and gender. Obviously biology plays a role in gender distinctions, but here too most sociologists emphasize the role of culture and power relations. It is common to distinguish between "sex," the physical differences relevant to reproduction, and "gender," the social and cultural identifications that we attach to sex. Many sociologists have pointed out the fact that gender is a social construction that varies over time and across cultures. Though this is clarifying, we should also note that there is an intrusion of cultural values into the very linkage of "sex" to reproduction. Historically, this is what has made homosexuality seem a transgression not just of gender roles but also of sexual classification more generally. Such views are changing, in large part because of struggles over gay rights. Increasingly, one can be seen for example as both a lesbian and a woman, without contradiction.

Third, theorizing difference has involved thinking about the role of ideas of gender and race in structuring society itself. This is perhaps especially important in the case of gender – or at least, it applies everywhere in the case of gender and in varying degree in different settings in the case of race. Dealing with this question in part means understanding the social implications of the associations that people apply to categories such as gender. For example, feminist theory has pointed out that the understanding of women as emotional and men as rational has profoundly influenced the distinction between public and private spheres of social life – a distinction which structures the way we conceive of the state, among other things. The issue goes deeper than associations, though, since gender categories are among the most basic used to conceptualize the nature of society itself and of basic social institutions like family. In other words, although building social organization by means of such assumed differences creates certain sorts of problems, it is also basic to some senses of solidarity – as the examples of class and nation show as much as those of race and gender. It is one of the ways social organization is accomplished, for good or ill. Theoretically, this is perhaps the deepest challenge of difference.

Identity and Difference

While critical theoretical attention to race has been increasingly prominent and sophisticated in recent decades, this should not be taken to indicate that the problem of difference has somehow been solved. The issue of difference is still problematic, and one of the major reasons is that people are so deeply invested in social boundaries. There are two sorts of questions that are still very active in the theoretical literature. The first has to do with the nature of identity, and whether categories such as "Black" or "woman" point to something that is essential, or whether such categories are constructed in social life. The second question has to do with whether knowledge is necessarily based on the experiences of actors in particular social positions, or whether objective knowledge is possible.

Gender and race are especially important examples of the more general phenomenon of differentiating people on the basis of "categorical identities." They are often used in ways that suggest that the internal similarities of the members of any such category outweigh their differences from each other, and conversely that all members share the same sort of differences from other people. The issue here is not just sexism or racism. It also arises in the struggles for recognition that seek to oppose such domination. The struggles over such claims for recognition are often termed "identity politics." In many social movements, legitimating claims to identity was a crucial goal as well as a condition of struggle. Thus the slogan "black is beautiful" challenged the tendency of white-dominated culture to treat Black identity as less valuable. The women's movement sought to establish that women were legitimate presences and that women's concerns were legitimately important in public as well as private life. In each case, these claims to identity involved an adoption of the very categories of gender and race that are so theoretically problematic. But this left a crucial theoretical issue unresolved. Did identity exist first, even if it was sometimes hidden or distorted? This was often called the "essentialist" position. Or did the movements together with other dimensions of social action and cultural creativity make the identities, and give them their definition and meaning? This was called the "constructionist" position.

Most sociologists and other social scientists have accepted the constructionist perspective; they regard gender, race, and most other sorts of identities as largely socially and culturally created. At the same time, few argue that such identities are merely matters of choice. First, there may be some aspects of inheritance or biology involved, even if what they mean is shaped by cultural interpretation. Second, culture and social relations are powerful; one cannot throw off the identities one has developed by growing up in a specific social setting simply at will. Moreover, as the American feminist Judith Butler has argued, when people confront shared injustice they may find it strategically valuable to accept the resulting common identities as though they were essential – at least in the context of struggle against injustice.

A closely related issue concerns the ways in which identities and social locations shape the production of knowledge. Since the seventeenth century it has been common to try to achieve a perfectly neutral perspective for the production of scientific knowledge (or for that matter, judicial fairness). This suggested that humans could step outside of their own subjective positions and see the world objectively. Critics argued that this position simply missed the degree to which all social actors – including jurists and sociologists – are bounded, at least to some degree, by their own positions and experiences in society. Following Hegel, Marx, and others, they claimed that knowledge must be shaped by the standpoint of observation. A truly objective position (or, more pejoratively, a "view from no-where") is not possible, they maintain. The question then arises whether some standpoints are better than others. The argument for privileging the standpoint of those in subordinate positions has a rather long history, as it turns out. Hegel, writing about the archetypal characters of "the master" and "the slave," claimed that those in subordinate positions may be able to develop a more complete know-ledge, since they must take account of the conditions of their own knowledge as well as those of the dominant. Simmel, writing about the position of "the stranger," later made the same claim. Marx and his follower Georg Lukacs argued for taking the standpoint of the proletariat, partly on the Hegelian basis and partly because it represented the majority of the members of modern societies and, they thought, the direction of social progress. Later, a number of feminist theorists argued that it was important to create knowledge from the standpoint of women. For some, this meant merely balancing the previous dominance of male standpoints. For others, it suggested a certain superiority, precisely because women's knowledge was clearly privileged with regard to much of social life. While it was relatively straightforward for women to gain access to the dominant forms of male knowledge, it was harder for men to gain access to the kind of knowledge that was based on women's distinctive experience. Somewhat similar arguments have been made concerning race in place of gender.

Relatively few sociologists believe that there is one social standpoint that is clearly superior in all forms of knowledge. They differ on whether they think that it is best to try to overcome the particular standpoints in favor of objectivity, or whether they think that this is an impossible goal and that what is needed instead is (a) an ability to analyze clearly one's own standpoint and its implications, and (b) a theory of knowledge that addresses the ways it is produced. Either way, the ongoing debate shows the connection between issues of gender and racial difference and very basic questions of epistemology and theory.

Race, Gender, and Sociological Theory

The first reading is by Dorothy Smith (b. 1926), excerpted from her book, *The Conceptual Practices of Power: A Feminist Sociology of Knowledge* (1990). Sociological research on gender and race has both contributed to and been shaped by its profoundly interdisciplinary context. Smith, a Canadian researcher, is perhaps the most influential interdisciplinary sociologist in the field of feminist theory. Although she has studied social health and survey methods as well as gender, she is best known as a pioneer in feminist standpoint theory. Her theoretical innovations grow from her reading of existing theory as well as from her own experiences. Smith developed standpoint theory by asking how the social world would look different when seen from the standpoint of women. Among the dimensions this opened up to Smith was a new sense of the everyday world as problematic – a thing to be explained.[3] In exploring this, Smith drew on insights from both ethnomethodology and Marxism, and her work is significant for making important links between "macro" and "micro" dimensions usually left too separate.

Her concern in the reading included here is with the ways that sociological knowledge is produced. She suggests that one major problem is that much of what is touted as "objective" knowledge implicitly has been based on a "male social universe, even when women have participated in its doing." Because of this, she argues, it is not enough for sociology to simply study women. Sociologists must begin to recognize their own position in the social world. Recognizing the standpoint of the researcher, and building into our accounts the standpoint of women, challenges the discipline's claim to scientific objectivity, and Smith thinks this is an important starting point for an alternative vision of what sociology should be.

This challenge to social theory is continued in the reading by Patricia Hill Collins (b. 1948), drawn from her book *Black Feminist Thought: Knowledge, Consciousness, and the Politics of Empowerment*, second edition (2000). She embraces Smith's approach to experience as the basis for knowledge – an epistemology, or theory of knowledge, rooted in practical, everyday life rather than in an attempt at scientific distancing. While she appropriates the general idea of standpoint theory, she also introduces a major critique by suggesting that taking the standpoint of women – implicitly, mainly white women – obscures the more specific standpoint or experience of Black women. Collins draws on diverse sources in sociological research, psychology, literature, and other fields to demonstrate the distinctive perspective afforded Black women (mainly Black American women) by their experience. At the same time, she seeks to show that achieving an understanding of their own experience as a legitimate basis for knowledge is important to Black women's subjectivity.

Collins came to sociology from a prior career as a schoolteacher and remains concerned with the educational dimensions of sociological theory. This refers not only to the extent to which sociology can inform better pedagogical practices, but also to the extent to which good sociological theory grows out of educational activity. She draws on her experience as a teacher, and that of her students, to show how social knowledge develops. She also argues that we should not see theory as being developed only in abstract scientific writings, but as being created as part of narratives that carry their own lessons about how the social world works. Indeed, narrative may be especially important to women, racial minorities, and others seeking to establish and share the legitimacy of views rooted in their own experience, precisely because this experience is obscured or ignored by dominant ways of thinking.

Collins' work broadens standpoint theory, and shows that it can be adapted to more specific perspectives. Collins envisions a three-fold matrix of domination comprised of class, race, and gender. She argues that black women occupy subordinate positions on all three dimensions, and therefore share a particular subjectivity. This of course raises the question of whether race, class, and gender is enough. Collins recognizes this at least implicitly by mentioning sexuality and nationality as other salient dimensions of experience. But how much specificity is enough? Her own theory could be challenged in the same way she challenged Smith's – by pointing to neglected subcategories, such as Black immigrant women. Within this category, one could introduce further distinctions, for example between Somali and Caribbean immigrant women. It remains an open question whether we can decide, either theoretically or empirically, how many dimensions we must consider before we arrive at a social experience unified enough to be treated as an autonomous subjectivity.

Frantz Fanon also engages the question of difference, but from a different perspective. Fanon (1925–61) was born in the French Caribbean colony of Martinique, and trained as a psychiatrist in France. He became one of the most influential Marxist intellectuals of the twentieth century and an advocate of anticolonial revolution. His book, *The Wretched of the Earth* (1963) was among the most widely read accounts of the struggles of the colonized poor. In it, Fanon develops his controversial theory that violence is a necessary (or almost necessary) element of revolutionary struggle not only because it helps to defeat governments and others in power but because it provides an occasion for self-transformation. While many would reject Fanon's argument on moral grounds, there is support for some of the social psychology underpinning it. Fanon draws on psychoanalysis, Marxism, and existentialism to make the case that colonialism involves both external domination and psychological repression. Together, these not only challenge individuals but also make it difficult for the people of a country to forge a national identity that empowers them to make their own future.

The selection here is from his first book, *Black Skin, White Masks* (1967 [1952]), a theoretical reflection on his experiences as a Black professional in the West Indies. More focused on social psychology and less on political struggle, this book emphasizes how the experience of growing up under colonial rule (or other sorts of domination) may produce a kind of psychological internalization of the power of the oppressor. As a French-speaking intellectual, Fanon's theoretical framework was influenced by the existentialist philosophy of Sartre and others. As a result, while Smith and Collins emphasize epistemology, or the theory of knowing, Fanon's emphasis is on ontology, the theory of being. Fanon draws on Hegel's notion of "being for others" to argue that for Black people in a white controlled world, one's self is not framed just by being Black, but by "being black for the white man." Culture plays a crucial role in this. For Fanon, adopting the French language, for example, meant taking on the "whole weight of a civilization," including how that civilization understood the descendents of former slaves in its colonies. Fanon relies on the notion of a potential authentic identity to make clear why the alienation he describes is damaging, but at the same time argues that a strong identity is something people have to achieve, whether as individuals or as collectivities, not something that can be taken for granted on the basis of biology or even culture.

The final reading in this section is by Orlando Patterson (b. 1940). Patterson is also Caribbean, but from the Anglophone West Indies. He attained prominence in Jamaica before continuing his career as a sociology professor at Harvard University. In the 1980s and early 1990s, Patterson published a distinctive series of books on slavery and freedom. In *Slavery and Social Death* (1982), he traced the ways that the institution of slavery reflected a conception of society in which some people could suffer a kind of civic death even while alive and working. Slavery was not merely a matter of domination and oppression, thus, but distinctively an institution that revealed the socially constructed nature of civil rights, citizenship, and indeed freedom. Patterson developed this argument in a larger work on the nature of freedom itself, drawing on ancient Greek as well as more recent American examples to show the extent to which the development of the very specific notion of freedom that is basic to philosophy and much of the discourse of human rights reflected roots in the opposition between slavery and freedom.

These reflections provided a philosophical and historical background for Patterson's analysis of how issues of difference connect with democracy, especially in the United States. The selection included here is from his book, *The Ordeal of Integration: Progress and Resentment in America's "Racial" Crisis* (1997). The central issue is how ideas about difference get incorporated into civil society and the polity. Addressing the legacy of slavery in the US, Patterson focuses attention on its ironic centrality to the history of the idea of freedom so basic to American political culture. In the post-slavery legacy of troubled tolerance and integration, he considers a number of paradoxical legacies that we are left with, including that of having to recognize race in order to overcome its effects, and the danger that this might lead to a kind of reification of the racial divide. Ironically, as Patterson has noted, some Black activists – and theorists – have sought to keep considerations of race within the kind of either/or categorization that was created by racist ideology. Some worry, for example, that the popularity of mixed race identity will dilute the solidarity needed for the struggle against racism. Where Fanon's theory poses the question of whether this might reflect a psychological desire to escape from a stigmatized racial identity, Patterson asks whether there is a way to preserve the struggle for freedom while moving beyond race. Both are possible, but as Patterson's sociology suggests, the answer may be specific to social and historical context.

Notes

1   On the concept of "racial formation" and the ways that racial categories have been applied in American society, see Omi and Winant (1994).
2   For an interesting review of the ways that "race" has been conceptualized within scientific discourse, see Banton (1998).
3   Smith (1987).

Select Bibliography

Banton, Michael. 1998. *Racial Theories*, second edition. Cambridge: Cambridge University Press. (A very interesting review of the history of the concept of "race" in scientific discourse. The book covers both the early biological theories and recent social scientific conceptions.)

Collins, Patricia Hill. 1991. *Black Feminist Thought: Knowledge, Consciousness, and the Politics of Empowerment*. New York: Routledge. (A pioneering synthesis of analyses that try to deal with race and gender together, noteworthy for its integration of literature written by African-American women with sociological theory and for its advocacy of a "matrix" concept of identity – allowing for "both/and" rather than "either/or" constructions.)

Collins, Patricia Hill. 1997. *Fighting Words*. Minneapolis, MN: University of Minnesota Press. (Collins' second major book, which takes up not only the question of hate speech but the relationship of education to sociology and the importance of narrative as an alternative to the conventional abstract presentation of theory.)

Fanon, Frantz. [1963] 1968. *The Wretched of the Earth*. New York: Grove Press. (Fanon's most famous book, one of the major calls to action on behalf of those suffering during and after colonialism and also an influential analysis of the social psychology of domination and resistance.)

Fanon, Frantz. *Black Skins, White Masks*. 1967 (1952). (Fanon's combination of psychological and sociological analysis in examining the ways in which the legacy of colonialism and racial domination can become internalized by those whose lives have been shaped by it, and how they can struggle to overcome this.)

Gilman, Sander L. 1985. *Difference and Pathology: Stereotypes of Sexuality, Race, and Madness*. Ithaca: Cornell University Press. (A brilliant account of the ways in which biology, medicine, and behavioral science joined in developing racialized accounts of pathology, especially in nineteenth-century Europe, and an examination of the question of why race and sexuality have such entangled modern histories.)

Gilroy, Paul. 2000. *Against Race: Imagining Political Culture Beyond the Color Line*. Cambridge, MA: Harvard University Press. (A somewhat unwieldy but important analysis of the difficulties of simultaneously resisting racism and resisting the reification of racial categories or their mobilization in favor of unsavory cultural politics.)

Gilroy, Paul. 1993. *The Black Atlantic*. Cambridge, MA: Harvard University Press. (A pioneering examination of the extent to which the development of post-slavery black identities combine elements from North American, Caribbean, and European experience – an analysis that could be extended to other contexts as well.)

Omi, Michael and Howard Winant. 1994. *Racial Formation in the United States: From the 1960s to the 1990s*. New York: Routledge. (The most important sociological examination of the ways in which "race" is reproduced and mobilized recurrently in the United States.)

Patterson, Orlando. 1982. *Slavery and Social Death: A Comparative Study*. Cambridge, MA: Harvard University Press.

Patterson, Orlando. 1997. *The Ordeal of Integration: Progress and Resentment in America's "Racial" Crisis*. Washington DC: Civitas/Counterpoint. (An engaging work and part of a series on race in America that also includes the recent *Rituals of Blood* [2000].)

Smith, Dorothy 1987: *The Everyday World as Problematic: A Feminist Sociology*. Boston, Northeastern University Press. (Smith's pioneering study in feminist sociology, still the theoretical classic in the field. A remarkable combination of insights from ethnomethodology, feminism, Marxism, and practical research experience to show how the gendered nature of the world of everyday lived experience was obscured by much previous sociology and how research from the standpoint of women can illuminate everyday life.)

Smith, Dorothy E. 1990. *The Conceptual Practices of Power*. Boston: Northeastern University Press. (Smith's examination of the ways in which the making of conceptual schemes both serves as a tool of the powerful and obscures uncomfortable reality from the privileged. Contributes to the sociology of knowledge – and to sociology – drawing on a Marxist–feminist and ethnomethodological heritage; in some ways similar to Foucault, but with much more explicit attention to gender.)

Wallace, Michele. 1976. *Black Macho and the Myth of the Superwoman*. New York: Verso, 2nd edn 1999. (A remarkable early work by a leading Black feminist scholar of literature and culture. Wallace shows both the heritage of slavery and racist institutions and the extent to which certain forms of Black popular identity exacerbate rather than mitigate their effects.)

22 The Conceptual Practices of Power

Dorothy E. Smith

It is not enough to supplement an established sociology by addressing ourselves to what has been left out or overlooked, or by making women's issues into sociological issues. That does not change the standpoint built into existing sociological procedures, but merely makes the sociology of women an addendum to the body of objectified knowledge.

The first difficulty is that how sociology is thought – its methods, conceptual schemes, and theories – has been based on and built up within the male social universe, even when women have participated in its doing. This sociology has taken for granted not only an itemized inventory of issues or subject matters (industrial sociology, political sociology, social stratification, and so forth) but the fundamental social and political structures under which these become relevant and are ordered. There is thus a disjunction between how women experience the world and the concepts and theoretical schemes by which society's self-consciousness is inscribed. . . .

A second difficulty is that the worlds opened up by speaking from the standpoint of women have not been and are not on a basis of equality with the objectified bodies of knowledge that have constituted and expressed the standpoint of men. The worlds of men have had, and still have, an authority over the worlds that are traditionally women's and still are predominantly women's – the worlds of household, children, and neighborhood. And though women do not inhabit only these worlds, for the vast majority of women they are the primary ground of our lives, shaping the course of our lives and our participation in other relations. Furthermore, objectified knowledges are part of the world from which our kind of society is governed. The domestic world stands in a dependent relation to that other, and its whole character is subordinate to it.

The two difficulties are related to each other in a special way. The effect of the second interacting with the first is to compel women to think their world in the concepts and terms in which men think theirs. Hence the established social forms of consciousness alienate women from their own experience.

The profession of sociology has been predicated on a universe grounded in men's experience and relationships and still largely appropriated by men as their "territory." Sociology is part of the practice by which we are all governed; that practice establishes its relevances. Thus the institutions that lock sociology into the structures occupied by men are the same institutions that lock women into the situations in which we have found ourselves oppressed. To unlock the latter leads logically to an unlocking of the former. What follows, then, or rather what then becomes possible – for it is of course by no means inevitable – is less a shift in the subject matter than a different conception of how sociology might become a means of understanding our experience and the conditions of our experience (both women's and men's) in contemporary capitalist society.

Relations of Ruling and Objectified Knowledge

When I speak here of governing or ruling I mean something more general than the notion of government as political organization. I refer rather to that total complex of activities, differentiated into many spheres, by which our kind of society is ruled, managed, and administered. It includes what the business world calls *management*, it includes the professions, it includes government and the activities of those who are selecting, training, and indoctrinating those who will be its governors. The last includes those who provide and elaborate the procedures by which it is governed and develop methods for accounting for how it is done – namely, the business schools, the sociologists, the economists. These are the institutions through which we are ruled and through which we, and I emphasize this *we*, participate in ruling.

Sociology, then, I conceive as much more than a gloss on the enterprise that justifies and rationalizes it, and at the same time as much less than "science." The governing of our kind of society is done in abstract concepts and symbols, and sociology helps create them by transposing the actualities of people's lives and experience into the conceptual currency with which they can be governed.

Thus the relevances of sociology are organized in terms of a perspective on the world, a view from the top that takes for granted the pragmatic procedures of governing as those that frame and identify its subject matter. Issues are formulated because they are administratively relevant, not because they are significant first in the experience of those who live them. The kinds of facts and events that matter to sociologists have already been shaped and given their character and substance by the methods and practice of governing....

Sociologists, when they go to work, enter into the conceptually ordered society they are investigating. They observe, analyze, explain, and examine that world as if there were no problem in how it becomes observable to them. They move among the doings of organizations, governmental processes, and bureaucracies as people who are at home in that medium. The nature of that world itself, how it is known to them, the conditions of its existence, and their relation to it are not called into question. Their methods of observation and inquiry extend into it as procedures that are essentially of the same order as those that bring about the phenomena they are concerned with. Their perspectives and interests may differ, but the substance is the same. They work with facts and information that have been worked up from actualities and appear in the form of documents that are themselves the product of organizational processes, whether their own or those of some other agency. They fit that information back into a framework of entities and organizational processes which they take for granted as known, without asking how it is that they know them or by what social processes the actual events – what people do or utter – are construed as the phenomena known.

Where a traditional gender division of labor prevails, men enter the conceptually organized world of governing without a sense of transition. The male sociologist in these circumstances passes beyond his particular and immediate setting (the office he writes in, the libraries he consults, the streets he travels, the home he returns to) without attending to the shift in consciousness. He works in the very medium he studies.

But, of course, like everyone else, he also exists in the body in the place in which it is. This is also then the place of his sensory organization of immediate experience; the place where his coordinates of here and now, before and after, are organized around himself as center; the place where he confronts people face to face in the physical mode in which he expresses himself to them and they to him as more and other than either can speak. This is the place where things smell, where the irrelevant birds fly away in front of the window, where he has indigestion, where he dies. Into this space must come as actual material events – whether as sounds of speech, scratchings on the surface of paper, which he constitutes as text, or directly – anything he knows of the world. It has to happen here somehow if he is to experience it at all.

Entering the governing mode of our kind of society lifts actors out of the immediate, local, and particular place in which we are in the body. What becomes present to us in the governing mode is a means of passing beyond the local into the conceptual order. This mode of governing creates, at least potentially, a bifurcation of consciousness. It establishes two modes of knowing and experiencing and doing, one located in the body and in the space it occupies and moves in, the other passing beyond it. Sociology is written in and aims at the latter mode of action. Robert Bierstedt writes, "Sociology can liberate the mind from time and space themselves and remove it to a new and transcendental realm where it no longer depends upon these Aristotelian categories." Even observational work aims at description in the categories and hence conceptual forms of the "transcendental realm." Yet the local and particular site of knowing that is the other side of the bifurcated consciousness has not been a site for the development of systematic knowledge.

Women's Exclusion from the Governing Conceptual Mode

The suppression of the local and particular as a site of knowledge has been and remains gender organized. The domestic sites of women's work, traditionally identified with women, are outside and subservient to this structure. Men have functioned as subjects in the mode of governing; women have been anchored in the local and particular phase of the bifurcated world. It has been a condition of a man's being able to enter and become absorbed in the conceptual mode, and to forget the dependence of his being in that mode upon his bodily existence, that he does not have to focus his activities and interests upon his bodily existence. Full participation in the abstract mode of action requires liberation from attending to needs in the concrete and particular. The organization of work in managerial and professional circles depends upon the alienation of subjects from their bodily and local existence. The structure of work and the structure of career take for granted that these matters have been provided for in such a way that they will not interfere with a man's action and participation in that world. Under the traditional gender regime, providing for a man's liberation from Bierstedt's Aristotelian categories is a woman who keeps house for him, bears and cares for his children, washes his clothes, looks after him when he is sick, and generally provides for the logistics of his bodily existence.

Women's work in and around professional and managerial settings performs analogous functions. Women's work mediates between the abstracted and conceptual and the material form in which it must travel to communicate. Women do the clerical work, the word processing, the interviewing for the survey; they take messages, handle the mail, make appointments, and care for patients. At almost every point women mediate for men at work the relationship between the conceptual mode of action and the actual concrete forms in which it is and must be realized, and the actual material conditions upon which it depends.

Marx's concept of alienation is applicable here in a modified form. The simplest formulation of alienation posits a relation between the work individuals do and an external order oppressing them in which their work contributes to the strength of the order that oppresses them. This is the situation of women in this relation. The more successful women are in mediating the world of concrete particulars so that men do not have to become engaged with (and therefore conscious of) that world as a condition to their abstract activities, the more complete men's absorption in it and the more effective its authority. The dichotomy between the two worlds organized on the basis of gender separates the dual forms of consciousness; the governing consciousness dominates the primary world of a locally situated consciousness but cannot cancel it; the latter is a subordinated, suppressed, absent, but absolutely essential ground of the governing consciousness. The gendered organization of subjectivity dichotomizes the two worlds, estranges them, and silences the locally situated consciousness by silencing women.

Knowing a Society from Within: A Woman's Perspective

An alternative sociological approach must somehow transcend this contradiction without reentering Bierstedt's "transcendental realm." Women's standpoint, as I am analyzing it here, discredits sociology's claim to constitute an objective knowledge independent of the sociologist's situation. Sociology's conceptual procedures, methods, and relevances organize its subject matter from a determinate position in society. This critical disclosure is the basis of an alternative way of thinking sociology. If sociology cannot avoid being situated, then it should take that as its beginning and build it into its methodological and theoretical strategies. As it is now, these strategies separate a sociologically constructed world from that of direct experience; it is precisely that separation that must be undone.

I am not proposing an immediate and radical transformation of the subject matter and methods of the discipline nor the junking of everything that has gone before. What I am suggesting is more in the nature of a reorganization of the relationship of sociologists to the object of our knowledge and of our problematic. This reorganization involves first placing sociologists where we are actually situated, namely, at the beginning of those acts by which we know or will come to know, and second, making our direct embodied experience of the everyday world the primary ground of our knowledge.

A sociology worked on in this way would not have as its objective a body of knowledge subsisting in and of itself; inquiry would not be justified by its contribution to the heaping up of such a body. We would reject a sociology aimed primarily at itself. We would not be interested in contributing to a body of knowledge whose uses are articulated to relations of ruling in which women participate only marginally, if at all. The professional sociologist is trained to think in the objectified modes of sociological discourse, to think sociology as it has been and is thought; that training and practice has to be discarded. Rather, as sociologists we would be constrained by the actualities of how things come about in people's direct experience, including our own. A sociology for women would offer a knowledge of the social organization and determinations of the properties and events of our directly experienced world. Its analyses would become part of our ordinary interpretations of the experienced world, just as our experience of the sun's sinking below the horizon is transformed by our knowledge that the world turns away from a sun that seems to sink.

The only way of knowing a socially constructed world is knowing it from within. We can never stand outside it. A relation in which sociological phenomena are objectified and presented as external to and independent of the observer is itself a special social practice also known from within. The relation of observer and object of observation, of sociologist to "subject," is a specialized social relationship. Even to be a stranger is to enter a world constituted from within as strange. The strangeness itself is the mode in which it is experienced.

When Jean Briggs made her ethnographic study of the ways in which an Eskimo people structure and express emotion, what she learned emerged for her in the context of the actual developing relations between her and the family with whom she lived and other members of the group. Her account situates her knowledge in the context of those relationships and in the actual sites in which the work of family subsistence was done. Affections, tensions, and quarrels, in some of which she was implicated, were the living texture in which she learned what she describes. She makes it clear how this context structured her learning and how what she learned and can speak of became observable to her.

Briggs tells us what is normally discarded in the anthropological or sociological telling. Although sociological inquiry is necessarily a social relation, we have learned to dissociate our own part in it. We recover only the object of our knowledge as if it stood all by itself. Sociology does not provide for seeing that there are always two terms to this relation. An alternative sociology must preserve in it the presence, concerns, and experience of the sociologist as knower and discoverer.

To begin from direct experience and to return to it as a constraint or "test" of the adequacy of a systematic knowledge is to begin from where we are located bodily. The actualities of our everyday world are already socially organized. Settings, equipment, environment, schedules, occasions, and so forth, as well as our enterprises and routines, are socially produced and concretely and symbolically organized prior to the moment at which we enter and at which inquiry begins. By taking up a standpoint in our original and immediate knowledge of the world, sociologists can make their discipline's socially organized properties first observable and then problematic.

When I speak of *experience* I do not use the term as a synonym for *perspective*. Nor in proposing a sociology grounded in the sociologist's actual experience am I recommending the self-indulgence of inner exploration or any other enterprise with self as sole focus and object. Such subjectivist interpretations of *experience* are themselves an aspect of that organization of consciousness that suppresses the locally situated side of the bifurcated consciousness and transports us straight into mind country, stashing away the concrete conditions and practices upon which it depends. We can never escape the circles of our own heads if we accept that as our territory. Rather, sociologists' investigation of our directly experienced world as a problem is a mode of discovering or rediscovering the society from within. We begin from our own original but tacit knowledge and from within the acts by which we bring it into our grasp in making it observable and in understanding how it works. We aim not at a reiteration of what we already (tacitly) know, but at an exploration of what passes beyond that knowledge and is deeply implicated in how it is.

Sociology as Structuring Relations between Subject and Object

Our knowledge of the world is given to us in the modes by which we enter into relations with the object of knowledge. But in this case the object of our knowledge is or originates in the co-ordering of activities among "subjects." The constitution of an objective sociology as an authoritative version of how things are is done from a position in and as part of the practices of ruling in our kind of society. Our training as sociologists teaches us to ignore the uneasiness at the junctures where multiple and diverse experiences are transformed into objectified forms. That juncture shows in the ordinary problems respondents have of fitting their experience of the world to the questions in the interview schedule. The sociologist who is a woman finds it hard to preserve this exclusion, for she discovers, if she will, precisely that uneasiness in her relation to her discipline as a whole. The persistence of the privileged sociological version (or versions) relies upon a substructure that has already discredited and deprived of authority to speak the voices of those who know the society differently. The objectivity of a sociological version depends upon a special relationship with others that makes it easy for sociologists to remain outside the others' experience and does not require them to recognize that experience as a valid contention.

Riding a train not long ago in Ontario I saw a family of Indians – woman, man, and three children – standing together on a spur above a river watching the train go by. I realized that I could tell this incident – the train, those five people seen on the other side of the glass – as it was, but that my description was built on my position and my interpretations. I have called them "Indians" and a family; I have said they were watching the train. My understanding has already subsumed theirs. Everything may have been quite different for them. My description is privileged to stand as what actually happened because theirs is not heard in the contexts in which I may speak. If we begin from the world as we actually experience it, it is at least possible to see that we are indeed located and that what we know of the other is conditional upon that location. There are and must be different experiences of the world and different bases of experience. We must not do away with them by taking advantage of our privileged speaking to construct a sociological version that we then impose upon them as their reality. We may not rewrite the other's world or impose upon it a conceptual framework that extracts from it what fits with ours. Their reality, their varieties of experience, must be an unconditional datum. It is the place from which inquiry begins.

A Bifurcation of Consciousness

My experience in the train epitomizes a sociological relation. I am already separated from the world as it is experienced by those I observe. That separation is fundamental to the character of that experience. Once I become aware of how my world is put together as a practical everyday matter and of how my relations are shaped by its concrete conditions (even in so simple a matter as that I am sitting in the train and it travels, but those people standing on the spur do not), I am led into the discovery that I cannot understand the nature of my experienced world by staying within its ordinary boundaries of assumption and knowledge. To account for that moment on the train and for the relation between the two experiences (or more) and the two positions from which those experiences begin I must posit a larger socioeconomic order in back of that moment. The coming together that makes the observation possible as well as how we were separated and drawn apart as well as how I now make use of that here – these properties are determined elsewhere than in that relation itself.

Furthermore, how our knowledge of the world is mediated to us becomes a problem of knowing how that world is organized for us prior to our participation in it. As intellectuals we ordinarily receive it as a media world, a world of texts, images, journals, books, talk, and other symbolic modes. We discard as an essential focus of our practice other ways of knowing. Accounting for that mode of knowing and the social organization that sets it up for us again leads us back into an analysis of the total socioeconomic order of which it is part. Inquiry remaining within the circumscriptions of the directly experienced cannot explore and explicate the relations organizing the everyday matrices of direct experience.

If we address the problem of the conditions as well as the perceived forms and organization of immediate experience, we should include in it the events as they actually happen and the ordinary material world we encounter as a matter of fact: the urban renewal project that uproots four hundred families; how it is to live on welfare as an ordinary daily practice; cities as the actual physical structures in which we move; the organization of academic occasions such as that in which this chapter originated. When we examine them, we find that there are many aspects of how these things come about of which we, as sociologists, have little to say. We have a sense that the events entering our experience originate somewhere in a human intention, but we are unable to track back to find it and to find out how it got from there to here.

Or take this room in which I work or that room in which you are reading and treat that as a problem. If we think about the conditions of our activity here, we can trace how these chairs, this table, the walls, our clothing, our presence come to be here; how these places (yours and mine) are cleaned and maintained; and so forth. There are human activities, intentions, and relations that are not apparent as such in the actual material conditions of our work. The social organization of the setting is not wholly available to us in its appearance. We bypass in the immediacy of the specific practical activity a complex division of labor that is an essential precondition to it. Such preconditions are fundamentally mysterious to us and present us with problems in grasping social relations with which sociology is ill equipped to deal. We experience the world as largely incomprehensible beyond the limits of what we know in a common sense. No amount of observation of face-to-face relations, no amount of commonsense knowledge of everyday life, will take us beyond our essential ignorance of how it is put together. Our direct experience of it makes it (if we will) a problem, but it does not offer any answers. We experience a world of "appearances," the determinations of which lie beyond it.

We might think of the appearances of our direct experience as a multiplicity of surfaces, the properties and relations among which are generated by social organizations not observable in their effects. The relations underlying and generating the characteristics of our own directly experienced world bring us into unseen relations with others. Their experience is necessarily different from ours. If we would begin from our experienced world and attempt to analyze and account for how it is, we must posit others whose experience is not the same as ours.

Women's situation in sociology discloses to us a typical bifurcate structure with the abstracted, conceptual practices on the one hand and the concrete realizations, the maintenance routines, and so forth, on the other. Taking each for granted depends upon being fully situated in one or the other so that the other does not appear in contradiction to it. Women's direct experience places us a step back, where we can recognize the uneasiness that comes from sociology's claim to be about the world we live in, and, at the same time, its failure to account for or even describe the actual features we experience. Yet we cannot find the inner principle of our own activity through exploring what is directly experienced. We do not see how it is put together because it is determined elsewhere. The very organization of the world that has been assigned to us as the primary locus of our being, shaping other projects and desires, is determined by and subordinate to the relations of society founded in a capitalist mode of production. The aim of an alternative sociology would be to explore and unfold the relations beyond our direct experience that shape and determine it. An alternative sociology would be a means to anyone of understanding how the world comes about for us and how it is organized so that it happens to us as it does in our experience. An alternative sociology, from the standpoint of women, makes the everyday world its problematic.

23 Black Feminist Epistemology

Patricia Hill Collins

As critical social theory, U.S. Black feminist thought reflects the interests and standpoint of its creators. Tracing the origin and diffusion of Black feminist thought or any comparable body of specialized knowledge reveals its affinity to the power of the group that created it (Mannheim 1936). Because elite White men control Western structures of knowledge validation, their interests pervade the themes, paradigms, and epistemologies of traditional scholarship. As a result, U.S. Black women's experiences as well as those of women of African descent transnationally have been routinely distorted within or excluded from what counts as knowledge.

U.S. Black feminist thought as specialized thought reflects the distinctive themes of African-American women's experiences. Black feminist thought's core themes of work, family, sexual politics, motherhood, and political activism rely on paradigms that emphasize the importance of intersecting oppressions in shaping the U.S. matrix of domination. But expressing these themes and paradigms has not been easy because Black women have had to struggle against White male interpretations of the world.

In this context, Black feminist thought can best be viewed as subjugated knowledge. Traditionally, the suppression of Black women's ideas within White-male-controlled social institutions led African-American women to use music, literature, daily conversations, and everyday behavior as important locations for constructing a Black feminist consciousness. More recently, higher education and the news media have emerged as increasingly important sites for Black feminist intellectual activity. Within these new social locations, Black feminist thought has often become highly visible, yet curiously, despite this visibility, it has become differently subjugated.

Investigating the subjugated knowledge of subordinate groups – in this case a Black women's standpoint and Black feminist thought – requires more ingenuity than that needed to examine the standpoints and thought of dominant groups. I found my training as a social scientist inadequate to the task of studying the subjugated knowledge of a Black women's standpoint. This is because subordinate groups have long had to use alternative ways to create independent self-definitions and self-valuations and to rearticulate them through our own specialists. Like other subordinate groups, African-American women not only have developed a distinctive Black women's standpoint, but have done so by using alternative ways of producing and validating knowledge.

Epistemology constitutes an overarching theory of knowledge (Harding 1987). It investigates the standards used to assess knowledge or *why* we believe what we believe to be true. Far from being the apolitical study of truth, epistemology points to the ways in which power relations shape who is believed and why. For example, various descendants of Sally Hemmings, a Black woman owned by Thomas Jefferson, claimed repeatedly that Jefferson fathered her children. These accounts forwarded by Jefferson's African-American descendants were ignored in favor of accounts advanced by his White progeny. Hemmings's descendants were routinely disbelieved until their knowledge claims were validated by DNA testing.

Distinguishing among epistemologies, paradigms, and methodologies can prove to be useful in understanding the significance of competing epistemologies (Harding 1987). In contrast to epistemologies, *paradigms* encompass interpretive frameworks such as intersectionality that are used to explain social phenomena. *Methodology* refers to the broad principles of how to conduct research and how interpretive paradigms are to be applied. The level of epistemology is important because it determines which questions merit investigation, which interpretive frameworks will be used to analyze findings, and to what use any ensuing knowledge will be put.

In producing the specialized knowledge of U.S. Black feminist thought, Black women intellectuals often encounter two distinct epistemologies: one representing elite White male interests and the other expressing Black feminist concerns. Whereas many variations of these epistemologies exist, it is possible to distill some of their distinguishing features that transcend differences among the paradigms within them. Epistemological choices about whom to trust, what to believe, and why something is true are not benign academic issues. Instead, these concerns tap the fundamental question of which versions of truth will prevail.

Eurocentric Knowledge Validation Processes and U.S. Power Relations

In the United States, the social institutions that legitimate knowledge as well as the Western or Eurocentric epistemologies that they uphold constitute two interrelated parts of the dominant knowledge validation processes. In general, scholars, publishers, and other experts represent specific interests and credentialing processes, and their knowledge claims must satisfy the political and epistemological criteria of the contexts in which they reside (Kuhn 1962; Mulkay 1979). Because this enterprise is controlled by elite White men, knowledge validation processes reflect this group's interests. Although designed to represent and protect the interests of powerful White men, neither schools, government, the media and other social institutions that house these processes nor the actual epistemologies that they promote need be managed by White men themselves. White women, African-American men and women, and other people of color may be enlisted to enforce these connections between power relations and what counts as truth. Moreover, not all White men accept these power relations that privilege Eurocentrism. Some have revolted and subverted social institutions and the ideas they promote.

Two political criteria influence knowledge validation processes. First, knowledge claims are evaluated by a group of experts whose members bring with them a host of sedimented experiences that reflect their group location in intersecting oppressions. No scholar can avoid cultural ideas and his or her placement in intersecting oppressions of race, gender, class, sexuality, and nation. In the United States, this means that a scholar making a knowledge claim typically must convince a scholarly community controlled by elite White avowedly heterosexual men holding U.S. citizenship that a given claim is justified. Second, each community of experts must maintain its credibility as defined by the larger population in which it is situated and from which it draws its basic, taken-for-granted knowledge. This means that scholarly communities that challenge basic beliefs held in U.S. culture at large will be deemed less credible than those that support popular ideas. For example, if scholarly communities stray too far from widely held beliefs about Black womanhood, they run the risk of being discredited.

When elite White men or any other overly homogeneous group dominates knowledge validation processes, both of these political criteria can work to suppress Black feminist thought. Given that the general U.S. culture shaping the taken-for-granted knowledge of the community of experts is permeated by widespread notions of Black female inferiority, new knowledge claims that seem to violate this fundamental assumption are likely to be viewed as anomalies (Kuhn 1962). Moreover, specialized thought challenging notions of Black female inferiority is unlikely to be generated from within White-male-controlled academic settings because both the kinds of questions asked and the answers to them would necessarily reflect a basic lack of familiarity with Black women's realities. Even those who think they are familiar can reproduce stereotypes. Believing that they are already knowledgeable, many scholars staunchly defend controlling images of U.S. Black women as mammies, matriarchs, and jezebels, and allow these commonsense beliefs to permeate their scholarship.

The experiences of African-American women scholars illustrate how individuals who wish to rearticulate a Black women's standpoint through Black feminist thought can be suppressed by prevailing knowledge validation processes. Exclusion from basic literacy, quality educational experiences, and faculty and administrative positions has limited U.S. Black women's access to influential academic positions. Black women have long produced knowledge claims that contested those advanced by elite White men. But because Black women have been denied positions of authority, they often relied on alternative knowledge validation processes to generate competing knowledge claims. As a consequence, academic disciplines typically rejected such claims. Moreover, any credentials controlled by White male academicians could then be denied to Black women who used alternative standards on the grounds that Black women's work did not constitute credible research.

Black women with academic credentials who seek to exert the authority that our status grants us to propose new knowledge claims about African-American women face pressures to use our authority to help legitimate a system that devalues and excludes the majority of Black women. When an outsider group – in this case, African-American women – recognizes that the insider group – namely, elite White men – requires special privileges from the larger society, those in power must find ways of keeping the outsiders out and at the same time having them acknowledge the legitimacy of this procedure. Accepting a few "safe" outsiders addresses this legitimation problem (Berger and Luckmann 1966). One way of excluding the majority of Black women from the knowledge validation process is to permit a few Black women to acquire positions of authority in institutions that legitimate knowledge, and to encourage us to work within the taken-for-granted assumptions of Black female inferiority shared by the scholarly community and the culture at large. Those Black women who accept these assumptions are likely to be rewarded by their institutions. Those challenging the assumptions can be placed under surveil-lance and run the risk of being ostracized.

African-American women academicians who persist in trying to rearticulate a Black women's standpoint also face potential rejection of our knowledge claims on epistemological grounds. Just as the material realities of powerful and dominated groups produce separate standpoints, these groups may also deploy distinctive epistemologies or theories of knowledge. Black women scholars may know that something is true – at least, by standards widely accepted among African-American women – but be unwilling or unable to legitimate our claims using prevailing scholarly norms. For any discourse, new knowledge claims must be consistent with an existing body of knowledge that the group controlling the interpretive context accepts as true....

Criteria for methodological adequacy associated with positivism illustrate the standards that Black women scholars, especially those in the social sciences, would have to satisfy in legitimating Black feminist thought. Though I describe Western or Eurocentric epistemologies as a single cluster, many interpretive frameworks or paradigms are subsumed under this category. Moreover, my focus on positivism should be interpreted neither to mean that all dimensions of positivism are inher-ently problematic for Black women nor that nonpositivist frameworks are better.

Positivist approaches aim to create scientific descriptions of reality by producing objective generalizations. Because researchers have widely differing values, experi-ences, and emotions, genuine science is thought to be unattainable unless all human characteristics except rationality are eliminated from the research process. By following strict methodological rules, scientists aim to distance themselves from the values, vested interests, and emotions generated by their class, race, sex, or unique situation. By decontextualizing themselves, they allegedly become detached observers and manipulators of nature (Jaggar 1983; Harding 1986).

Several requirements typify positivist methodological approaches. First, research methods generally require a distancing of the researcher from her or his "object" of study by defining the researcher as a "subject" with full human subjectivity and by objectifying the "object" of study (Keller 1985; Asante 1987). A second requirement is the absence of emotions from the research process (Jaggar 1983). Third, ethics and values are deemed inappropriate in the research process, either as the reason for scientific inquiry or as part of the research process itself (Richards 1980). Finally, adversarial debates, whether written or oral, become the preferred method of ascertaining truth: The arguments that can withstand the greatest assault and survive intact become the strongest truths (Moulton 1983).

Such criteria ask African-American women to objectify ourselves, devalue our emotional life, displace our motivations for furthering knowledge about Black women, and confront in an adversarial relationship those with more social, eco-nomic, and professional power. On the one hand, it seems unlikely that Black women would rely exclusively on positivist paradigms in rearticulating a Black women's standpoint. For example, Black women's experiences in sociology illustrate diverse responses to encountering an entrenched positivism. Given Black women's long-standing exclusion from sociology prior to 1970, the sociological knowledge about race and gender produced during their absence, and the symbolic importance of Black women's absence to sociological self-definitions as a science, African-

American women acting as agents of knowledge faced a complex situation. In order to refute the history of Black women's unsuitability for science, they had to invoke the tools of sociology by using positivistic frameworks to demonstrate their capability as scientists. However, they simultaneously needed to challenge the same structure that granted them legitimacy. Their responses to this dilemma reflect the strategic use of the tools of positivism when needed, coupled with overt challenges to positivism when that seemed feasible.

On the other hand, many Black women have had access to another epistemology that encompasses standards for assessing truth that are widely accepted among African-American women. An experiential, material base underlies a Black feminist epistemology, namely, collective experiences and accompanying worldviews that U.S. Black women sustained based on our particular history. The historical conditions of Black women's work, both in Black civil society and in paid employment, fostered a series of experiences that when shared and passed on become the collective wisdom of a Black women's standpoint. Moreover, a set of principles for assessing knowledge claims may be available to those having these shared experiences. These principles pass into a more general Black women's wisdom and, further, into what I call here a Black feminist epistemology.

This alternative epistemology uses different standards that are consistent with Black women's criteria for substantiated knowledge and with our criteria for methodological adequacy. Certainly this alternative Black feminist epistemology has been devalued by dominant knowledge validation processes and may not be claimed by many African-American women. But if such an epistemology exists, what are its contours? Moreover, what are its actual and potential contributions to Black feminist thought?

...

Black Women as Agents of Knowledge

Social movements of the 1950s, 1960s, and 1970s stimulated a greatly changed intellectual and political climate in the United States. Compared to the past, many more U.S. Black women became legitimated agents of knowledge. No longer passive objects of knowledge manipulated within prevailing knowledge validation processes, African-American women aimed to speak for ourselves.

African-American women in the academy and other positions of authority who aim to advance Black feminist thought now encounter the often conflicting epistemological standards of three key groups. First, Black feminist thought must be validated by ordinary African-American women who, in the words of Hannah Nelson, grow to womanhood "in a world where the saner you are, the madder you are made to appear" (Gwaltney 1980, 7). To be credible in the eyes of this group, Black feminist intellectuals must be personal advocates for their material, be accountable for the consequences of their work, have lived or experienced their material in some fashion, and be willing to engage in dialogues about their findings with ordinary, everyday people.

Historically, living life as an African-American woman facilitated this endeavor because knowledge validation processes controlled in part or in full by Black women occurred in particular organizational settings. When Black women were in charge of our own self-definitions, these four dimensions of Black feminist epistemology – lived experience as a criterion of meaning, the use of dialogue, the ethic of personal accountability, and the ethic of caring – came to the forefront. When the core themes and interpretive frameworks of Black women's knowledge were informed by Black feminist epistemology, a rich tradition of Black feminist thought ensued.

Traditionally women engaged in this overarching intellectual and political project were blues singers, poets, autobiographers, storytellers, and orators. They became Black feminist intellectuals both by doing intellectual work and by being validated as such by everyday Black women. Black women in academia could not openly join their ranks without incurring a serious penalty.[. . .]

The community of Black women scholars constitutes a second constituency whose epistemological standards must be met. As the number of Black women academics grows, this heterogeneous collectivity shares a similar social location in higher education, yet finds a new challenge in building group solidarities across differences. African-American women scholars place varying amounts of importance on furthering Black feminist scholarship. However, despite this new-found diversity, since more African-American women earn advanced degrees, the range of Black feminist scholarship has expanded. Historically, African-American women may have brought sensibilities gained from Black feminist epistemology to their scholarship. But gaining legitimacy often came with the cost of rejecting such an epistemology. Studying Black women's lives at all placed many careers at risk. More recently, increasing numbers of African-American women scholars have chosen to study Black women's experiences, and to do so by relying on elements of Black feminist epistemology in framing their work. . . .

A third group whose epistemological standards must be met consists of dominant groups who still control schools, graduate programs, tenure processes, publication outlets, and other mechanisms that legitimate knowledge. African-American women academics who aim to advance Black feminist thought typically must use dominant Eurocentric epistemologies for this group. The difficulties these Black women now face lie less in demonstrating that they could master White male epistemologies than in resisting the hegemonic nature of these patterns of thought in order to see, value, and use existing alternative Black feminist ways of knowing. For Black women who are agents of knowledge within academia, the marginality that accompanies outsider-within status can be the source of both frustration and creativity. In an attempt to minimize the differences between the cultural context of African-American communities and the expectations of mainstream social institutions, some women dichotomize their behavior and become two different people. Over time, the strain of doing this can be enormous. Others reject Black women's accumulated wisdom and work against their own best interests by enforcing the dominant group's specialized thought. Still others manage to inhabit both contexts but do so critically, using perspectives gained from their outsider-within social locations as a source of insights and ideas. But while such women can make substantial contributions as agents of knowledge, they rarely do so without substantial personal cost. "Eventually it comes to you," observes Lorraine Hansberry, "the thing that makes you exceptional, if you are at all, is inevitably that which must also make you lonely" (1969, 148).

Just as migrating between Black and White families raised special issues for Black women domestic workers, moving among different and competing interpretive communities raises similar epistemological concerns for Black feminist thinkers. The dilemma facing Black women scholars, in particular, engaged in creating Black feminist thought illustrates difficulties that can accompany grappling with multiple interpretive communities. A knowledge claim that meets the criteria of adequacy for one group and thus is judged to be acceptable may not be translatable into the terms of a different group....

Once Black women scholars face the notion that on certain dimensions of a Black women's standpoint, it may be fruitless to try to translate into other frameworks truths validated by Black feminist epistemology, then other choices emerge. Rather than trying to uncover universal knowledge claims that can withstand the translation from one epistemology to another (initially, at least), Black women intellectuals might find efforts to rearticulate a Black women's standpoint especially fruitful. Rearticulating a Black women's standpoint refashions the particular and reveals the more universal human dimensions of Black women's everyday lives....

Toward Truth

The existence of Black feminist thought suggests another path to the universal truths that might accompany the "truthful identity of what is." In this volume I place Black women's subjectivity in the center of analysis and examine the interdependence of the everyday, taken-for-granted knowledge shared by African-American women as a group, the more specialized knowledge produced by Black women intellectuals, and the social conditions shaping both types of thought. This approach allows me to describe the creative tension linking how social conditions influenced a Black women's standpoint and how the power of the ideas themselves gave many African-American women the strength to shape those same social conditions. I approach Black feminist thought as situated in a context of domination and not as a system of ideas divorced from political and economic reality. Moreover, I present Black feminist thought as subjugated knowledge in that African-American women have long struggled to find alternative locations and epistemologies for validating our own self-definitions. In brief, I examined the situated, subjugated standpoint of African-American women in order to understand Black feminist thought as a partial perspective on domination.

Because U.S. Black women have access to the experiences that accrue to being both Black and female, an alternative epistemology used to rearticulate a Black women's standpoint should reflect the convergence of both sets of experiences. Race and gender may be analytically distinct, but in Black women's everyday lives, they work together. The search for the distinguishing features of an alternative epistemology used by African-American women reveals that some ideas that Africanist scholars identify as characteristically "Black" often bear remarkable resemblance to similar ideas claimed by feminist scholars as characteristically "female." This similarity suggests that the actual contours of intersecting oppressions can vary dramatically and yet generate some uniformity in the epistemologies used by subordinate groups. Just as U.S. Black women and African women encountered diverse patterns of intersecting oppressions yet generated similar agendas concerning what mattered in their feminisms, a similar process may be at work regarding the epistemologies of oppressed groups. Thus the significance of a Black feminist epistemology may lie in its ability to enrich our understanding of how subordinate groups create knowledge that fosters both their empowerment and social justice.

This approach to Black feminist thought allows African-American women to explore the epistemological implications of transversal politics. Eventually this approach may get us to a point at which, claims Elsa Barkley Brown, "all people can learn to center in another experience, validate it, and judge it by its own standards without need of comparison or need to adopt that framework as their own" (1989, 922). In such politics, "one has no need to 'decenter' anyone in order to center someone else; one has only to constantly, appropriately, 'pivot the center'" (p. 922).

Rather than emphasizing how a Black women's standpoint and its accompanying epistemology differ from those of White women, Black men, and other collectivities, Black women's experiences serve as one specific social location for examining points of connection among multiple epistemologies. Viewing Black feminist epistemology in this way challenges additive analyses of oppression claiming that Black women have a more accurate view of oppression than do other groups. Such approaches suggest that oppression can be quantified and compared and that adding layers of oppression produces a potentially clearer standpoint (Spelman 1988). One implication of some uses of standpoint theory is that the more subordinated the group, the purer the vision available to them. This is an outcome of the origins of standpoint approaches in Marxist social theory, itself reflecting the binary thinking of its Western origins. Ironically, by quantifying and ranking human oppressions, standpoint theorists invoke criteria for methodological adequacy that resemble those of positivism. Although it is tempting to claim that Black women are more oppressed than everyone else and therefore have the best standpoint from which to understand the mechanisms, processes, and effects of oppression, this is not the case.

Instead, those ideas that are validated as true by African-American women, African-American men, Latina lesbians, Asian-American women, Puerto Rican men, and other groups with distinctive standpoints, with each group using the epistemological approaches growing from its unique standpoint, become the most "objective" truths. Each group speaks from its own standpoint and shares its own partial, situated knowledge. But because each group perceives its own truth as partial, its knowledge is unfinished. Each group becomes better able to consider other groups' standpoints without relinquishing the uniqueness of its own standpoint or suppressing other groups' partial perspectives. "What is always needed in the appreciation of art, or life," maintains Alice Walker, "is the larger perspective. Connections made, or at least attempted, where none existed before, the straining to encompass in one's glance at the varied world the common thread, the unifying theme through immense diversity" (1983, 5). Partiality, and not universality, is the condition of being heard; individuals and groups forwarding knowledge claims without owning their position are deemed less credible than those who do.

Alternative knowledge claims in and of themselves are rarely threatening to conventional knowledge. Such claims are routinely ignored, discredited, or simply absorbed and marginalized in existing paradigms. Much more threatening is the challenge that alternative epistemologies offer to the basic process used by the powerful to legitimate knowledge claims that in turn justify their right to rule. If the epistemology used to validate knowledge comes into question, then all prior knowledge claims validated under the dominant model become suspect. Alternative epistemologies challenge all certified knowledge and open up the question of whether what has been taken to be true can stand the test of alternative ways of validating truth. The existence of a self-defined Black women's standpoint using Black feminist epistemology calls into question the content of what currently passes as truth and simultaneously challenges the process of arriving at that truth.

References

Asante, Molefi Kete. 1987. *The Afrocentric Idea*. Philadelphia: Temple University Press.

Berger, Peter L., and Thomas Luckmann. 1966. *The Social Construction of Reality*. New York: Doubleday.

Brown, Elsa Barkley. 1989. "African-American Women's Quilting: A Framework for Conceptualizing and Teaching African-American Women's History." *Signs* 14 (4): 921–29.

Gwaltney, John Langston. 1980. *Drylongso, A Self-Portrait of Black America*. New York: Vintage.

Hansberry, Lorraine. 1969. *To Be Young, Gifted and Black*. New York: Signet.

Harding, Sandra. 1986. *The Science Question in Feminism*. Ithaca, NY: Cornell University Press.

——— 1987. "Introduction: Is There a Feminist Method?" In *Feminism and Methodology* ed. Sandra Harding. 1–14. Bloomington: Indiana University Press.

Jaggar, Alison M. 1983. *Feminist Politics and Human Nature*. Totawa, NJ: Rowman & Allanheld.

Keller, Evelyn Fox. 1985. *Reflections on Gender and Science*. New Haven, CT: Yale University Press.

Kuhn, Thomas. 1962. *The Structure of Scientific Revolution*. 2d ed. Chicago: University of Chicago Press.

Mannheim, Karl. 1936. *Ideology and Utopia*. New York: Harcourt, Brace & World.

Moulton, Janice. 1983. "A Paradigm of Philosophy: The Adversary Method." In *Discovering Reality*, ed. Sandra Harding and Merrill B. Hintikka, 149–64. Boston: D. Reidel.

Mulkay, Michael. 1979. *Science and the Sociology of Knowledge*. Boston: Unwin Hyman.

Richards, Dona. 1980. "European Mythology: The Ideology of 'Progress.'" In *Contemporary Black Thought*, ed. Molefi Kete Asante and Abdulai S. Vandi, 59–79. Beverly Hills, CA: Sage.

Spelman, Elizabeth V. 1988. *Inessential Woman: Problems of Exclusion in Feminist Thought*. Boston: Beacon.

Walker, Alice. 1983. *In Search of Our Mother's Gardens*. New York: Harcourt Brace Jovanovich.

24 Black Skin, White Masks

Frantz Fanon

The Negro and Language

I ascribe a basic importance to the phenomenon of language. That is why I find it necessary to begin with this subject, which should provide us with one of the elements in the colored man's comprehension of the dimension of *the other*. For it is implicit that to speak is to exist absolutely for the other.

The black man has two dimensions. One with his fellows, the other with the white man. A Negro behaves differently with a white man and with another Negro. That this self-division is a direct result of colonialist subjugation is beyond question. ... No one would dream of doubting that its major artery is fed from the heart of those various theories that have tried to prove that the Negro is a stage in the slow evolution of monkey into man. Here is objective evidence that expresses reality.

But when one has taken cognizance of this situation, when one has understood it, one considers the job completed. How can one then be deaf to that voice rolling down the stages of history: "What matters is not to know the world but to change it."

This matters appallingly in our lifetime.

To speak means to be in a position to use a certain syntax, to grasp the morphology of this or that language, but it means above all to assume a culture, to support the weight of a civilization. Since the situation is not one-way only, the statement of it should reflect the fact. Here the reader is asked to concede certain points that, however unaceptable they may seem in the beginning, will find the measure of their validity in the facts.

The problem that we confront in this chapter is this: The Negro of the Antilles will be proportionately whiter – that is, he will come closer to being a real human being – in direct ratio to his mastery of the French language. I am not unaware that this is one of man's attitudes face to face with Being. A man who has a language consequently possesses the world expressed and implied by that language. What we are getting at becomes plain: Mastery of language affords remarkable power. Paul Valéry knew this, for he called language "the god gone astray in the flesh."[1]

In a work now in preparation I propose to investigate this phenomenon.[2] For the moment I want to show why the Negro of the Antilles, whoever he is, has always to face the problem of language. Furthermore, I will broaden the field of this description and through the Negro of the Antilles include every colonized man.

Every colonized people – in other words, every people in whose soul an inferiority complex has been created by the death and burial of its local cultural originality –

Originally translated from the French by Charles Lam Markmann.

finds itself face to face with the language of the civilizing nation; that is, with the culture of the mother country. The colonized is elevated above his jungle status in proportion to his adoption of the mother country's cultural standards. He becomes whiter as he renounces his blackness, his jungle. . . .

The Fact of Blackness

"Dirty nigger!" Or simply, "Look, a Negro!"

I came into the world imbued with the will to find a meaning in things, my spirit filled with the desire to attain to the source of the world, and then I found that I was an object in the midst of other objects.

Sealed into that crushing objecthood, I turned beseechingly to others. Their attention was a liberation, running over my body suddenly abraded into nonbeing, endowing me once more with an agility that I had thought lost, and by taking me out of the world, restoring me to it. But just as I reached the other side, I stumbled, and the movements, the attitudes, the glances of the other fixed me there, in the sense in which a chemical solution is fixed by a dye. I was indignant; I demanded an explanation. Nothing happened. I burst apart. Now the fragments have been put together again by another self.

As long as the black man is among his own, he will have no occasion, except in minor internal conflicts, to experience his being through others. There is of course the moment of "being for others," of which Hegel speaks, but every ontology is made unattainable in a colonized and civilized society. It would seem that this fact has not been given sufficient attention by those who have discussed the question. In the *Weltanschauung* of a colonized people there is an impurity, a flaw that outlaws any ontological explanation. Someone may object that this is the case with every individual, but such an objection merely conceals a basic problem. Ontology – once it is finally admitted as leaving existence by the wayside – does not permit us to understand the being of the black man. For not only must the black man be black; he must be black in relation to the white man. Some critics will take it on themselves to remind us that this proposition has a converse. I say that this is false. The black man has no ontological resistance in the eyes of the white man. Overnight the Negro has been given two frames of reference within which he has had to place himself. His metaphysics, or, less pretentiously, his customs and the sources on which they were based, were wiped out because they were in conflict with a civilization that he did not know and that imposed itself on him.

The black man among his own in the twentieth century does not know at what moment his inferiority comes into being through the other. Of course I have talked about the black problem with friends, or, more rarely, with American Negroes. Together we protested, we asserted the equality of all men in the world. In the Antilles there was also that little gulf that exists among the almost-white, the mulatto, and the nigger. But I was satisfied with an intellectual understanding of these differences. It was not really dramatic. And then. . . .

And then the occasion arose when I had to meet the white man's eyes. An unfamiliar weight burdened me. The real world challenged my claims. In the white world the man of color encounters difficulties in the development of his bodily schema. Consciousness of the body is solely a negating activity. It is a third-person consciousness. The body is surrounded by an atmosphere of certain uncertainty. I know that if I want to smoke, I shall have to reach out my right arm and take the pack of cigarettes lying at the other end of the table. The matches, however, are in the drawer on the left, and I shall have to lean back slightly. And all these movements are made not out of habit but out of implicit knowledge. A slow composition of my *self* as a body in the middle of a spatial and temporal world – such seems to be the schema. It does not impose itself on me; it is, rather, a definitive structuring of the self and of the world – definitive because it creates a real dialectic between my body and the world.

For several years certain laboratories have been trying to produce a serum for "denegrification"; with all the earnestness in the world, laboratories have sterilized their test tubes, checked their scales, and embarked on researches that might make it possible for the miserable Negro to whiten himself and thus to throw off the burden of that corporeal malediction. Below the corporeal schema I had sketched a historico-racial schema. The elements that I used had been provided for me not by "residual sensations and perceptions primarily of a tactile, vestibular, kinesthetic, and visual character,"[3] but by the other, the white man, who had woven me out of a thousand details, anecdotes, stories. I thought that what I had in hand was to construct a physiological self, to balance space, to localize sensations, and here I was called on for more.

"Look, a Negro!" It was an external stimulus that flicked over me as I passed by. I made a tight smile.

"Look, a Negro!" It was true. It amused me.

"Look, a Negro!" The circle was drawing a bit tighter. I made no secret of my amusement.

"Mama, see the Negro! I'm frightened!" Frightened! Frightened! Now they were beginning to be afraid of me. I made up my mind to laugh myself to tears, but laughter had become impossible.

I could no longer laugh, because I already knew that there were legends, stories, history, and above all *historicity*, which I had learned about from Jaspers. Then, assailed at various points, the corporeal schema crumbled, its place taken by a racial epidermal schema. In the train it was no longer a question of being aware of my body in the third person but in a triple person. In the train I was given not one but two, three places. I had already stopped being amused. It was not that I was finding febrile coordinates in the world. I existed triply: I occupied space. I moved toward the other ... and the evanescent other, hostile but not opaque, transparent, not there, disappeared. Nausea....

I was responsible at the same time for my body, for my race, for my ancestors. I subjected myself to an objective examination, I discovered my blackness, my ethnic characteristics; and I was battered down by tom-toms, cannibalism, intellectual deficiency, fetishism, racial defects, slave-ships, and above all else, above all: "Sho' good eatin'."

On that day, completely dislocated, unable to be abroad with the other, the white man, who unmercifully imprisoned me, I took myself far off from my own presence, far indeed, and made myself an object. What else could it be for me but an amputation, an excision, a hemorrhage that spattered my whole body with black blood? But

I did not want this revision, this thematization. All I wanted was to be a man among other men. I wanted to come lithe and young into a world that was ours and to help to build it together.

But I rejected all immunization of the emotions. I wanted to be a man, nothing but a man. Some identified me with ancestors of mine who had been enslaved or lynched: I decided to accept this. It was on the universal level of the intellect that I understood this inner kinship – I was the grandson of slaves in exactly the same way in which President Lebrun was the grandson of tax-paying, hard-working peasants. In the main, the panic soon vanished.

In America, Negroes are segregated. In South America, Negroes are whipped in the streets, and Negro strikers are cut down by machine-guns. In West Africa, the Negro is an animal. And there beside me, my neighbor in the university, who was born in Algeria, told me: "As long as the Arab is treated like a man, no solution is possible."

"Understand, my dear boy, color prejudice is something I find utterly foreign.... But of course, come in, sir, there is no color prejudice among us.... Quite, the Negro is a man like ourselves.... It is not because he is black that he is less intelligent than we are.... I had a Senegalese buddy in the army who was really clever...."

Where am I to be classified? Or, if you prefer, tucked away?

"A Martinican, a native of 'our' old colonies."

Where shall I hide?

"Look at the nigger!... Mama, a Negro!... Hell, he's getting mad.... Take no notice, sir, he does not know that you are as civilized as we...."

My body was given back to me sprawled out, distorted, recolored, clad in mourning in that white winter day. The Negro is an animal, the Negro is bad, the Negro is mean, the Negro is ugly; look, a nigger, it's cold, the nigger is shivering, the nigger is shivering because he is cold, the little boy is trembling because he is afraid of the nigger, the nigger is shivering with cold, that cold that goes through your bones, the handsome little boy is trembling because he thinks that the nigger is quivering with rage, the little white boy throws himself into his mother's arms: Mama, the nigger's going to eat me up.

All round me the white man, above the sky tears at its navel, the earth rasps under my feet, and there is a white song, a white song. All this whiteness that burns me....

I sit down at the fire and I become aware of my uniform. I had not seen it. It is indeed ugly. I stop there, for who can tell me what beauty is?

Where shall I find shelter from now on? I felt an easily identifiable flood mounting out of the countless facets of my being. I was about to be angry. The fire was long since out, and once more the nigger was trembling.

"Look how handsome that Negro is!..."

"Kiss the handsome Negro's ass, madame!"

Shame flooded her face. At last I was set free from my rumination. At the same time I accomplished two things: I identified my enemies and I made a scene. A grand slam. Now one would be able to laugh.

The field of battle having been marked out, I entered the lists.

What? While I was forgetting, forgiving, and wanting only to love, my message was flung back in my face like a slap. The white world, the only honorable one, barred me from all participation. A man was expected to behave like a man. I was expected to behave like a black man – or at least like a nigger. I shouted a greeting to the world and the world slashed away my joy. I was told to stay within bounds, to go back where I belonged.

They would see, then! I had warned them, anyway. Slavery? It was no longer even mentioned, that unpleasant memory. My supposed inferiority? A hoax that it was better to laugh at. I forgot it all, but only on condition that the world not protect itself against me any longer. I had incisors to test. I was sure they were strong. And besides. . . .

What! When it was I who had every reason to hate, to despise, I was rejected? When I should have been begged, implored, I was denied the slightest recognition? I resolved, since it was impossible for me to get away from an *inborn complex*, to assert myself as a BLACK MAN. Since the other hesitated to recognize me, there remained only one solution: to make myself known.

In *Anti-Semite and Jew* (p. 95), Sartre says: "They [the Jews] have allowed themselves to be poisoned by the stereotype that others have of them, and they live in fear that their acts will correspond to this stereotype. . . . We may say that their conduct is perpetually overdetermined from the inside."

All the same, the Jew can be unknown in his Jewishness. He is not wholly what he is. One hopes, one waits. His actions, his behavior are the final determinant. He is a white man, and, apart from some rather debatable characteristics, he can sometimes go unnoticed. He belongs to the race of those who since the beginning of time have never known cannibalism. What an idea, to eat one's father! Simple enough, one has only not to be a nigger. Granted, the Jews are harassed – what am I thinking of? They are hunted down, exterminated, cremated. But these are little family quarrels. The Jew is disliked from the moment he is tracked down. But in my case everything takes on a *new* guise. I am given no chance. I am overdetermined from without. I am the slave not of the "idea" that others have of me but of my own appearance.

I move slowly in the world, accustomed now to seek no longer for upheaval. I progress by crawling. And already I am being dissected under white eyes, the only real eyes. I am *fixed*. Having adjusted their microtomes, they objectively cut away slices of my reality. I am laid bare. I feel, I see in those white faces that it is not a new man who has come in, but a new kind of man, a new genus. Why, it's a Negro! . . .

The Negro and Recognition

Self-consciousness exists in itself and for itself, in that and by the fact that it exists for another self-consciousness; that is to say, it is only by being acknowledged or recognized.

Hegel, *The Phenomenology of Mind*

Man is human only to the extent to which he tries to impose his existence on another man in order to be recognized by him. As long as he has not been effectively recognized by the other, that other will remain the theme of his actions. It is on that other being, on recognition by that other being, that his own human worth and reality depend. It is that other being in whom the meaning of his life is condensed.

There is not an open conflict between white and black. One day the White Master, *without conflict*, recognized the Negro slave.

But the former slave wants to *make himself recognized*.

At the foundation of Hegelian dialectic there is an absolute reciprocity which must be emphasized. It is in the degree to which I go beyond my own immediate being that I apprehend the existence of the other as a natural and more than natural reality. If I close the circuit, if I prevent the accomplishment of movement in two directions, I keep the other within himself. Ultimately, I deprive him even of this being-for-itself.

The only means of breaking this vicious circle that throws me back on myself is to restore to the other, through mediation and recognition, his human reality, which is different from natural reality. The other has to perform the same operation. "Action from one side only would be useless, because what is to happen can only be brought about by means of both. ... "; "*they recognize themselves as mutually recognizing each other.*"[4]

In its immediacy, consciousness of self is simple being-for-itself. In order to win the certainty of oneself, the incorporation of the concept of recognition is essential. Similarly, the other is waiting for recognition by us, in order to burgeon into the universal consciousness of self. Each consciousness of self is in quest of absoluteness. It wants to be recognized as a primal value without reference to life, as a transformation of subjective certainty (*Gewissheit*) into objective truth (*Wahrheit*).

When it encounters resistance from the other, self-consciousness undergoes the experience of *desire* – the first milestone on the road that leads to the dignity of the spirit. Self-consciousness accepts the risk of its life, and consequently it threatens the other in his physical being. "It is solely by risking life that freedom is obtained; only thus is it tried and proved that the essential nature of self-consciousness is not *bare existence*, is not the merely immediate form in which it at first makes its appearance, is not its mere absorption in the expanse of life."[5]

Thus human reality in-itself-for-itself can be achieved only through conflict and through the risk that conflict implies. This risk means that I go beyond life toward a supreme good that is the transformation of subjective certainty of my own worth into a universally valid objective truth.

As soon as I *desire* I am asking to be considered. I am not merely here-and-now, sealed into thingness. I am for somewhere else and for something else. I demand that notice be taken of my negating activity insofar as I pursue something other than life; insofar as I do battle for the creation of a human world – that is, of a world of reciprocal recognitions.

He who is reluctant to recognize me opposes me. In a savage struggle I am willing to accept convulsions of death, invincible dissolution, but also the possibility of the impossible.

The other, however, can recognize me without struggle: "The individual, who has not staked his life, may, no doubt, be recognized as a *person*, but he has not attained the truth of this recognition as an independent self-consciousness."[6]

Historically, the Negro steeped in the inessentiality of servitude was set free by his master. He did not fight for his freedom.

Out of slavery the Negro burst into the lists where his masters stood. Like those servants who are allowed once every year to dance in the drawing room, the Negro is looking for a prop. The Negro has not become a master. When there are no longer slaves, there are no longer masters.

The Negro is a slave who has been allowed to assume the attitude of a master.

The white man is a master who has allowed his slaves to eat at his table.

One day a good white master who had influence said to his friends, "Let's be nice to the niggers...."

The other masters argued, for after all it was not an easy thing, but then they decided to promote the machine-animal-men to the supreme rank of *men*.

Slavery shall no longer exist on French soil.

The upheaval reached the Negroes from without. The black man was acted upon. Values that had not been created by his actions, values that had not been born of the systolic tide of his blood, danced in a hued whirl round him. The upheaval did not make a difference in the Negro. He went from one way of life to another, but not from one life to another. Just as when one tells a much improved patient that in a few days he will be discharged from the hospital, he thereupon suffers a relapse, so the announcement of the liberation of the black slaves produced psychoses and sudden deaths.

It is not an announcement that one hears twice in a lifetime. The black man contented himself with thanking the white man, and the most forceful proof of the fact is the impressive number of statues erected all over France and the colonies to show white France stroking the kinky hair of this nice Negro whose chains had just been broken.

"Say thank you to the nice man," the mother tells her little boy ... but we know that often the little boy is dying to scream some other, more resounding expression....

The white man, in the capacity of master,[7] said to the Negro, "From now on you are free."

But the Negro knows nothing of the cost of freedom, for he has not fought for it. From time to time he has fought for Liberty and Justice, but these were always white liberty and white justice; that is, values secreted by his masters. The former slave, who can find in his memory no trace of the struggle for liberty or of that anguish of liberty of which Kierkegaard speaks, sits unmoved before the young white man singing and dancing on the tightrope of existence.

When it does happen that the Negro looks fiercely at the white man, the white man tells him: "Brother, there is no difference between us." And yet the Negro *knows* that there is a difference. He *wants* it. He wants the white man to turn on him and shout: "Damn nigger." Then he would have that unique chance – to "show them...."

But most often there is nothing – nothing but indifference, or a paternalistic curiosity.

The former slave needs a challenge to his humanity, he wants a conflict, a riot. But it is too late: The French Negro is doomed to bite himself and just to bite. I say "the French Negro," for the American Negro is cast in a different play. In the United States, the Negro battles and is battled. There are laws that, little by little, are invalidated under the Constitution. There are other laws that forbid certain forms of discrimination. And we can be sure that nothing is going to be given free.

There is war, there are defeats, truces, victories.

"The twelve million black voices" howled against the curtain of the sky. Torn from end to end, marked with the gashes of teeth biting into the belly of interdiction, the curtain fell like a burst balloon.

On the field of battle, its four corners marked by the scores of Negroes hanged by their testicles, a monument is slowly being built that promises to be majestic.

And, at the top of this monument, I can already see a white man and a black man *hand in hand.*

For the French Negro the situation is unbearable. Unable ever to be sure whether the white man considers him consciousness in-itself-for-itself, he must forever absorb himself in uncovering resistance, opposition, challenge.

This is what emerges from some of the passages of the book that Mounier has devoted to Africa.[8] The young Negroes whom he knew there sought to maintain their alterity. Alterity of rupture, of conflict, of battle.

The self takes its place by opposing itself, Fichte said. Yes and no.

I said in my introduction that man is a *yes.* I will never stop reiterating that.

Yes to life. *Yes* to love. *Yes* to generosity.

But man is also a *no. No* to scorn of man. *No* to degradation of man. *No* to exploitation of man. *No* to the butchery of what is most human in man: freedom.

Man's behavior is not only reactional. And there is always resentment in a *reaction.* Nietzsche had already pointed that out in *The Will to Power.*

To educate man to be *actional,* preserving in all his relations his respect for the basic values that constitute a human world, is the prime task of him who, having taken thought, prepares to act.

Notes

1 *Charmes* (Paris, Gallimard, 1952).
2 *Le langage et l'agressivité.*
3 Jean Lhermitte, *L'Image de notre corps* (Paris, Nouvelle Revue critique, 1939), p. 17.
4 G. W. F. Hegel, *The Phenomenology of Mind*, trans. by J. B. Baillie, 2nd rev. ed. (London, Allen & Unwin, 1949), pp. 230, 231.
5 Ibid., p. 233.
6 Hegel, *Phenomenology of Mind*, p. 233.
7 I hope I have shown that here the master differs basically from the master described by Hegel. For Hegel there is reciprocity; here the master laughs at the consciousness of the slave. What he wants from the slave is not recognition but work.

   In the same way, the slave here is in no way identifiable with the slave who loses himself in the object and finds in his work the source of his liberation.

   The Negro wants to be like the master.

   Therefore he is less independent than the Hegelian slave.

   In Hegel the slave turns away from the master and turns toward the object.

   Here the slave turns toward the master and abandons the object.
8 Emmanuel Mounier, *L'éveil de l'Afrique noire* (Paris, Éditions du Seuil, 1948).

25 The Paradoxes of Integration

Orlando Patterson

After two and a half centuries of slavery, followed by a century of rural semiserfdom and violently imposed segregation, wanton economic discrimination, and outright exclusion of Afro-Americans from the middle and upper echelons of the nation's economy, it was inevitable that when the nation finally committed itself to the goal of ethnic justice and integration the transition would be painful, if not traumatic. The prejudices of centuries die hard, and even when they wane, the institutional frameworks that sustained them are bound to linger.

What is more, Afro-Americans, like once-oppressed peoples and classes everywhere, were bound to develop strategies of survival and patterns of adaptation to their centuries of discrimination and exclusion that were to become dysfunctional under newer, less constrained circumstances. Only supermen remain unimpaired by sustained systemic and personal assault. Centuries of public dishonor and ritualized humiliation by Euro-Americans were also certain to engender deep distrust, not only of those who actively humiliated and exploited them, but of all those who passively benefited from their oppression, which is to say, all persons of European ancestry.

In light of all this, the achievements of the American people over the past half century in reducing racial prejudice and discrimination and in improving the socioeconomic and political condition of Afro-Americans are nothing short of astonishing. Viewed from the perspective of comparative history and sociology, it can be said, unconditionally, that the changes that have taken place in the United States over the past fifty years are unparalleled in the history of minority-majority relations. With the possible exception of the Netherlands – which is really too small to be meaningfully compared to America – there does not exist a single case in modern or earlier history that comes anywhere near the record of America in changing majority attitudes, in guaranteeing legal and political rights, and in expanding socioeconomic opportunities for its disadvantaged minorities. . . .

In what follows I attempt to make sense of the sociological knot of "race" in America, fraught with paradox at almost every turn. I argue that the present condition of Afro-Americans is itself paradoxical, and the perceptions of this condition and the attempts to understand it are further riddled with paradoxes and contradictions. Observing this is like watching the foreplay of two octopuses through the distorting window of a glass-bottom boat. They appear to be consuming each other when, in fact, they are really trying to connect. . . .

The experiential and perceptual mismatch I have just described is exacerbated further by yet another paradox of changing ethnic relations, what I call the outrage of liberation. A formerly oppressed group's sense of outrage at what has been done to them increases the more equal they become with their former oppressors.

This is, in part, simply a case of relative deprivation. It is also partly a result of having a greater voice – more literate and vocal leadership, more access to the media, and so on.

But it also reflects the formerly deprived group's increased sense of dignity and, ironically, its embrace of the formerly oppressive Other within its moral universe. The slave, the sharecropping serf, the Afro-American person living under Jim Crow laws administered by vicious Euro-American policemen and prejudiced judges – all were obliged, for reasons of sheer survival, to accommodate somehow to the system. One form of accommodation was to expect and demand less from the discriminating group. To do so was in no way to diminish one's contempt, even hatred and loathing, for the racist oppressors. Indeed, one's lowered expectations may even have been a sign of contempt.

In the discourse on racism, it has often been observed that one of its worst consequences is the denial of the Afro-American person's humanity. What often goes unnoticed is the other side of this twisted coin: that racism left most Afro-Americans persuaded that Euro-Americans were less than human. Technically clever, yes; powerful, well armed, and prolific, to be sure; but without an ounce of basic human decency. No one whose community of memory was etched with the vision of lynched, barbecued ancestors, no Afro-American person who has seen the flash of greedy, obsessive hatred in the fish-blue stare of a cracker's cocked eyes could help but question his inherent humanness. Most Afro-Americans, whatever their outward style of interaction with Euro-Americans, genuinely believed, as did the mother of Henry Louis Gates, that most Euro-Americans were inherently filthy and evil, or that, as the poet Sterling Brown once wrote, there was no place in heaven for "Whuffolks . . . being so onery," that indeed, for most of them "hell would be good enough – if big enough."

Integration, however partially, began to change all that. By disalienating the Other, the members of each group came, however reluctantly, to accept each other's humanness. But that acceptance comes at a price: for Euro-Americans, it is the growing sense of disbelief at what the nightly news brings in relentless detail from the inner cities. For Afro-Americans, it is the sense of outrage that someone truly human could have done what the evidence of over three and a half centuries makes painfully clear. Like a woman chased and held down in a pitch dark night who discovers, first to her relief, then to her disbelief, that the stranger recoiling from her in the horror of recognition had been her own brother, the moral embrace of integration is a liberation with a doubletake of outrage verging on incomprehension.

The Paradoxes of Ideology and Interpretation

The paradox of antiracist racism

A good part of the present turmoil in American ethnic relations – both the problem itself and the attempt to explain it – springs from the failure of Afro-American leaders to recognize the limits of one important, but risky and necessarily transitional, strategy in the struggle for ethnic equality. That strategy is itself a paradox, first described by Jean Paul Sartre with the gripping phrase "anti-racist racism."

What Sartre was getting at is the fact that any group that has experienced centuries of racial hatred and oppression has, of necessity, to go through a period of self-liberation in which it draws attention to, and even celebrates, the very thing that was used against it. Afro-Americans had no choice but to emphasize their Afro-Americanness in mobilizing against the iniquities of a system that discriminated against them because they were Afro-American. And after centuries of being brain-washed by every symbol and medium of the dominant culture into a sense of their own inferiority and unattractiveness, it was inevitable that Afro-Americans go through a process of psychological liberation that entailed not just the denial of their worthlessness but some emphasis on the positive worth of being Afro-American.

What was true on the psychological level held equally on the economic and political fronts. Some recognition of "race" had to inform policies aimed at alleviating centuries of racial injuries. It is disingenuous in the extreme to argue – as Euro-American and Afro-American conservatives do – that because the ideal of the civil rights movement, and of all persons of ethnic good will, is a color-blind world, any policy that takes account of African ancestry betrays this ideal.

Fire, as the old saying goes, can sometimes only be fought with fire. The Afro-American identity movements and some form of affirmative action were the inevitable social fires that had to be ignited in the fight against the centuries-long holocaust of Euro-American racism.

We are approaching the limits of the antiracist strategy in politics, but, tragically, Afro-American leaders now seem trapped by the fire they started. The results are disastrous for the mass of Afro-American people. Afro-American identity rhetoric and race-conscious politics not only have negative educational consequences but play straight into the hands of the most reactionary political forces in society....

The paradox of the "one-drop" rule

Commitment to the risky strategy of antiracist racism partly explains another ethnic paradox, although sheer cultural and political inertia and elite self-interest may be as important in understanding it. This is the persistence of what once went by the name of the "one-drop" rule. America is unusual among Western Hemisphere societies in its traditional commitment to a binary conception of race. Despite the fact that the vast majority of non-Euro-American persons of African ancestry are mixed, all persons with the proverbial "one drop" of African ancestry are classified as "black."

This unusual mode of racial classification has a vicious ideological history rooted in the notion of "racial" purity and in the racist horror of miscegenation. Traditionally, it was used as a major ideological bulwark of legalized segregation, and was at the heart of the "white" supremacist opposition to any form of integration. There is no gainsaying the fact that this conception of "race" historically rationalized the most pernicious legal, social, and political injustices against Afro-Americans.

An important aspect of contemporary ethnic change is the fact that this binary conception of "race" is under siege, for reasons I will mention shortly. The paradox is that the two groups of Americans now most committed to its survival are "white" supremacists and most Afro-American intellectual and political leaders!

First, we should note the social factors undermining the one-drop rule. One was the integrationist ideal of the early phase of the civil rights movement. By definition, this struggle called into question the one-drop "purist" rule. Integrating schools meant accepting the prospect of mixed dating, the ultimate anathema of "white" supremacists. The direct assault on antimiscegenation laws, culminating in their prohibition by the Supreme Court, implicitly attacked the one-drop rule.

Of even greater importance, however, have been the demographic and cultural changes resulting from the current wave of immigration with the inflow of mainly brown-skinned Latin Americans and Asians. Previous immigrants played by the binary rule as soon as they landed on these shores: those who were visibly brown, such as West Indians, were assimilated into the Afro-American population whether they wished to be or not (and most did not, coming from societies in which minute, socially meaningful distinctions of color were the norm). Those who were visibly or vaguely "white" eagerly sought membership within the Caucasian chalk circle and were usually welcomed as long as they could prove no trace of African "blood." Indeed, "whiteness," or rather non-"blackness," became a powerful unifying force in the integration of immigrants who previously never imagined that they had anything so important in common. Swarthy Sicilians and Arabs now found themselves one with blond Northern Europeans, Irish Catholics with English Protestants, formerly persecuted Jews with Gentiles, refugees from Communist Eastern Europe and Cuba with Western Europeans – all were united in the great "white republic" of America by virtue simply of not being tainted by one drop of the despised Afro-American blood. The demonization of blackness in the one-drop rule not only served the interests of "white" supremacists but was a major unifying force in the rise of this great democracy of the non-blacks.

This pernicious system of racial ideology worked only as long as there were no ambiguous third "races" to muddy the binary construction. Native Americans were not only too small in numbers but also, cut off on reservations, out of sight and out of mind. All this was to change with the massive inflow of brown people. The sheer strength of their numbers was enough to bring the binary conception of "race" into question. In addition, the new wave of immigrants refused to play by the binary game. Unlike previous Latin immigrants, recently arrived Latinos insist that they are neither "white" nor "black." And Asians not only look different but are usually sufficiently proud of their distinctive somatic type not to want to play the binary game either. East Indians are the main exceptions.

In recent years, there has also been a significant increase in children of mixed Afro-American and Euro-American parentage. Although still small proportionately, their absolute numbers have been growing phenomenally. The census found 1.5 million mixed marriages in 1990, with 2 million children claiming mixed ancestry. They are also disproportionately middle and upper class and are concentrated in the major metropolitan centers. They have recently broken ranks with the established Afro-American leadership in insisting on being classified for what they are: mixed. In July 1996 they held a Multiracial Solidarity March in Washington to register their demand for a census category recognizing their mixed heritage.

All these developments have had a profound impact on the nation's traditional conception of ethnic norms and ideals. The traditionally staid Census Bureau has now become what one report calls a "political hotbed" as numerous groups challenge the five official racial and ethnic categories in use since 1977. The most cursory review of recent media images and of intermarriage rates clearly indicates that the nation's traditional Western European somatic norm is being replaced by a mixed or "morphed" type that is a blend of darker-skinned and lighter-skinned peoples. Shadowing this development has been a similar change in the physical-beauty ideal from its traditional Nordic image to one that reflects a mix. Euro-Americans increasingly risk skin cancer and the plastic surgeon's knife to acquire darker skin and larger, more trans-Saharan lips. And whatever Afrocentrists or multiculturalists may say, the huge proportion of their incomes that Afro-Americans devote to processing and lengthening their hair indicates an appearance ideal that is neither European nor African but something in-between, more like Tiger Woods, the ultimate hybrid prodigy in whom America sees its somatic future.

In the face of all this, it is odd that the orthodox line among Afro-American leaders is now a firm commitment to the one-drop rule. The extent to which Afro-American leaders will go to defend what was once a cardinal principle of "white" supremacy is best illustrated by the position of the National Association of Black Social Workers on "transracial" adoption. Not only is the group adamantly opposed to such adoption on the grounds that it constitutes what the social workers claim to be a form of "genocide," but many of their spokespeople imply that it is better for an Afro-American child to suffer the hardship and impoverishment of multiple foster families and state wardship than to be subjected to adoption by Euro-American middle-class parents. Astonishingly, both the Congressional Black Caucus and a number of liberal Euro-American politicians have been intimidated into accepting this blatantly racist and cruel dogma. It is one of the many ironies and paradoxes of modern American ethnic politics that it took a Republican-controlled Congress to legislate against it.

Afro-Americans offer two main reasons in defense of the one-drop rule. One is the Afrocentrist position that it is good to preserve the Africanness of the Afro-American population. "Blackness" is to be celebrated as a virtue in itself. While Afrocentrists are at least honest enough to openly acknowledge this, many more established Afro-Americans are uncomfortable with the idea for the simple reason that it is merely the Afro-American version of the Euro-American purist position.

More commonly heard is the political defense of the one-drop rule: the fact that a recognition of the mixed segment of the Afro-American population will dilute the demographic and political base of Afro-Americans. There is something amiss, even circular, in this argument. If mixed persons choose to identify with other non-Euro-Americans politically – as many of them insist they do – there is nothing to fear, since they will continue to join forces with all such non-Euro-Americans. But if their insistence on a separate identification entails separate political interests, it is un-democratic and possibly illegal to force them to continue doing so. I strongly suspect that most ordinary Afro-Americans would just as soon say "good riddance" to any group of light-skinned non-Euro-Americans wishing to dissociate themselves from an "Afro-American" identity, a point made with some emphasis in Spike Lee's *School Daze*.

Ironically, a study conducted by the Census Bureau in 1995 on this subject indicated that, should the "multiracial" category be included, Afro-American leadership has nothing to fear concerning the dilution of their political base. While 1.5

percent of the surveyed population identified themselves as "multiracial," the proportion identifying themselves as Afro-American was not affected by the introduction of the multiracial option in the list of "racial" categories.

The paradox of liberal racialization in academic and public discourse

A strange contradiction has emerged in liberal discourse and studies of "race" in
America. It is somewhat related to the one-drop paradox, but is more insidious and
pervades all scholarship and popular writings on intergroup relations. Having
demolished and condemned as racist the idea that observed group differences have
any objective, biological foundation, the liberal intellectual community has revived
the "race" concept as an essential category of human experience with as much
ontological validity as the discarded racist notion of biologically distinct groups.

The paradox lies hidden in the seemingly innocent distinction between "race" and
ethnicity. Almost all social scientists, social commentators, and journalists, not to
mention ordinary Americans, now routinely use the terms *race* and *ethnicity* as if
they referred to different, if related, social things. My question is, why do we need
the term *race* at all? What explains its nonredundancy in the phrase "race and ethnic
relations"? Trying to understand why social scientists, in particular, insist on making
this distinction leads us into a Pandora's box of liberal contradictions and unwitting
racism.

The standard liberal explanation is that "race," while not meaningful biologically,
is nonetheless important because people believe it to be important, and this has
severe consequences in "multiracial" societies such as our own. The problem with
this explanation is that the same holds true for "ethnic" differences and prejudices.
Why then distinguish between the terms *racial* and *ethnic?* The conventional response is that ethnic distinctions and prejudices, while admittedly similar in their
believed-in and self-fulfilling nature, nonetheless differ from "racial" distinctions
and beliefs because they refer not to observed and believed-in "physical" differences,
but to observed and believed-in cultural ones. The object of a false belief, then, is
what justifies the distinction even among speakers who recognize and reject its
falseness. "Racial" beliefs, the argument goes, are based on observed differences
that, while not biologically salient, are outwardly real and somehow immutable, and
this differentiates interactions and beliefs pertaining to racial differences from those
pertaining to ethnic differences. Afro-Americans, we often hear, cannot hide or
conceal their "blackness," whereas in Irish-WASP or Jewish-Gentile relations such
visible markers are absent. Furthermore, "racial" relations are also held to be more
intense, conflict ridden, and horrible in their consequences for the believed-to-be
inferior "race."

Is any of this true? On the one hand, as the psychoanalyst Michael Vannoy Adams
recently noted, "People differ much more culturally than they do naturally. And
there is no necessary connection between psychical differences and physical differences. The reason that natural categories like color are so useless (except to racists,
for whom they are all too useful) is that they convey very little, if any, information
about significant psychical differences. . . .

The simple truth of the matter is that however similar people may look to
outsiders, those who believe that there are differences tend to have very little

difficulty identifying the believed-in different group and to see gross physical differences that outsiders find it hard to identify. Indeed, the comparative data on intergroup relations strongly suggest that wherever people believe that there are important differences between them, they tend to interpret these differences as biologically grounded....

Not only do people find it easy to make "racial" or believed-in socially meaningful physical distinctions where none seem to exist (to outsiders), but they have an equally powerful capacity not to make these distinctions, even when they seem strikingly obvious to outsiders. The classic case in point here is one we have discussed already: America's one-drop rule. The Afro-American population is somatically extremely varied. Nonetheless, we categorize and perceive of them as a single type in our binary system of racial beliefs. If Afro-Americans and Euro-Americans find it so easy not to see differences where outward differences are so manifestly present, there is no reason to believe that they lack the capacity to see no differences between the groups categorized as "Afro-American" and "white." That they recognize differences is clearly a matter of cultural and political beliefs and of an identity that is, like all others, part chosen and part imposed.

What, then, is the basis of the distinction between the "racial" and the "ethnic"? We must conclude that making this distinction is itself a belief, a distinctively American belief, an essential part of American racist ideology. The distinction, we now see, plays a crucial role in maintaining the binary conception of "race" that prevails in America, and remains the foundation of racist and purist dividing lines between Americans. This is its only linguistic function. It conceptually bedevils the meaning of integration.

So the question we must now ask is this: If the history of relations between peoples has been, as the distinguished American anthropologist Virginia Dominguez correctly puts it, "the continuous historical pattern of determining race by man-made law rather than by processes of nature," why on earth are American social scientists (presumably the most liberal group in the nation) actively promoting a purist conception of "race"?

Could it be that these emperors of liberalism really have no clothes? Do these mainly Euro-American social scientists find the "racial" identity of "whiteness" so deeply gratifying, so essential a part of their understanding of themselves as true-blue Americans, that they unwittingly promote a distinction that is implicitly racist? Why is it not enough to be simply Jewish-American, Anglo-American, Irish-American, or, if one so chooses, just plain American? Why the added need for "white-Jewish American," "white-Anglo-American" ... unless there remains the age-old American desire to define being truly American as not being that essential contradistinctive definition of oneself as "white": namely, "black." And have Afro-American social scientists and intellectuals so rejected the ideal of integration and so mistakenly committed themselves to a racialized identity that they are prepared to reinforce this racist distinction? Why is it not enough to be simply, and gloriously, Afro-American or, if one so chooses, just plain American, which anyway is already a good deal Afro-American?

We must resolve this paradox if we are serious about achieving the ideal of integration, and we can do so simply by dropping the distinction and all that it implies. All this requires is a little clear thinking. The distinction between "race" and ethnicity is only meaningful if we wish to reinforce the racist belief that Euro-Americans and Afro-Americans are, indeed, biologically and immutably different. The distinction invigorates the salience of "race" in our private and public life. And by legitimizing the binary conception of "race," the distinction perpetuates, to the detriment of Afro-Americans (the self-serving disagreements of their political leadership notwithstanding), the nastiest dogma from our painful ethnic past.

Part VIII

The Sociological Theory of Jürgen Habermas

INTRODUCTION TO PART VIII

The importance of Jürgen Habermas for contemporary social theory is in part due to renewed interest in the Frankfurt School in the 1960s and '70s (see *Classical Sociological Theory*). Indeed, Habermas directly engaged many of the criticisms that radical intellectuals of the period leveled against domination and inequality in modern society. This resurgence of critical theory and the ensuing debates had a number of intellectual consequences. One was that a new field of cultural studies inspired by a linguistic turn emerged that critically analyzed the mass media and the way that the field of cultural representations was shaped by prevailing relations of power. In this new field figures associated with the Frankfurt School's critical theory proved influential, especially Theodor Adorno and Walter Benjamin. Cultural studies in turn provided a terrain for the development of a new philosophical movement known as postmodernism (see Part IX). In his critical dialogue with these developments, Habermas has become one of the most important theorists of communication in society and of the role of public discourse in shaping political life.

A Critical Dialogue with Modernity

Later, in the 1970s and '80s, a new group of postmodern thinkers were critical of what they saw as Englightenment-inspired philosophical obsessions with reason, universalism and totality that suppressed social and cultural differences alongside more spontaneous emotional and cultural expression. For them, modern thought had privileged a distinct category of elite actors possessed of the tools of scientific analysis and the techniques of rationalization. This domination was justified, in large part, by linking it to narratives of the triumph of reason and the scientific improvement of society. Figures such as Jean-François Lyotard and Michel Foucault suggested that in a contemporary world that was increasingly socially and culturally fragmented and in which the manifest irrationality of unchecked scientific reason was plainly evident, modernity's "metanarratives" – the shared stories through which modern institutions are legitimated – were being exhausted.

The crisis of the modern metanarratives of progress, universal prosperity, and the objectivity of science meant that the old Enlightenment ideals had to be rethought or abandoned. Postmodernism further posed a direct challenge to Western Marxism by rejecting the notion of an objective standpoint of knowledge, that reason was embedded in history, or that social liberation was anything more than a set of discourses. In response to these critiques, in a series of philosophical and political writings Habermas warned of the pessimism, misdirected radicalism and exaggerations of much postmodern thought. While Habermas was ready to concede that Enlightenment was an "unfinished project," he saw the best hope for human emancipation in a correction and completion of Enlightenment rather than in its repudiation. Throughout his career, Habermas would turn again and again to the perspectives of the Frankfurt School while countering its pessimism. He developed a theoretical system devoted to revealing the *possibility* of reason, emancipation and rational-critical communication embedded in modern liberal institutions and in the human capacities to communicate, deliberate, and pursue rational interests.

Life and Work

Jürgen Habermas (b. 1929) is closely associated with the second generation of the Frankfurt School. After completing his dissertation, he moved to the Institute for Social Research at the University of Frankfurt in 1956. There he worked with Theodor, Adorno, under whom he hoped to write his *Habilitation*, or second dissertation, that is required for the position of professor in the German university system. In spite of his evident intellectual gifts, however, both Adorno and Max Horkheimer considered Habermas's work too politically engaged and insufficiently critical for them to support it. Habermas, too, apparently had serious intellectual differences with these leading lights of the Frankfurt School, who in his view had become paralyzed with political skepticism and, particularly in their anti-rationalist critiques, by disdain for modern culture and institutions. This estrangement occurred in spite of the fact that Habermas considered *The Dialectic of Enlightenment* to be one of the most influential books in his philosophical development.

Habermas's thought is firmly rooted in the German philosophical tradition, drawing not only on the Frankfurt School and Western Marxism, but also on the thought of Max Weber, Wilhelm Dilthey and the neo-Kantians, as well as systems theorists such as Talcott Parsons and Niklas Luhmann. Although Habermas rejects the dogmatism of much Marxist thought, as well as its confidence in a scientific theory of history, he saw in Marx's work an enormous contribution to the idea and method of critique. In critical analysis, theories are subjected to tests of their internal validity and by their capacity to be realized in the material world. Moving away from what he saw as the critical *dis*engagement of Adorno and Horkheimer, Habermas embarked on the lifelong project of reshaping critical theory along the lines of its original intentions as a "theory of society conceived with a practical intention." Accordingly, since the 1960s Habermas's work has developed in two principal directions. The first has been to develop a more comprehensive theory of reason, intersubjective communication and practical understanding. The second has been Habermas's efforts to elaborate and defend a conception of the rational or emancipated society guided by principles of deliberation and autonomy.

For Habermas, all knowledge has to be understood in terms of the human interests of practical actors. His sociology of knowledge considers the historical context in which thought is formed, the knowledge-forming interests behind it, and epistemological foundation of the claim to knowledge it embodies or employs. In *Knowledge and Human Interests* (1973) Habermas is critical of how ideology distorts communication and undercuts the validity of knowledge. Unlike Marx, however, Habermas maintains that a purely objective, unmediated "purely scientific" knowledge is impossible. Rather than seeing utopian transformation linked to inevitable triumph of the proper theory, Habermas does not think reason will necessarily defeat distortion and false consciousness but he does try to reveal how knowledge may simultaneously advance reason and serve human interests. In posing this alternative, Habermas identifies three cognitive areas where interests generate knowledge. These may be *instrumental* knowledge linked to science and oriented towards reliability, prediction and causal analysis, *practical* knowledge linked to communication, understanding and interpretation, and *emancipatory* knowledge linked to criticism, self-reflection, liberation, and utopian visions. In devising this analysis, Habermas tries to move to a more sophisticated understanding of how knowledge is generated and the ends to which it is put.

In "Theory and Practice," provided in this section, we can see how, in line with his conception of knowledge-forming interests, Habermas contends that philosophy plays a vital role in the social sciences. Philosophy furnishes the capacity to construct ethical claims and to introduce normative considerations into the practice of science that make it appropriate to the study of human affairs. In this way, philosophy can help to connect the particular aims of specialized research with broader universal aims and interests. Habermas means to challenge not only the positivist conception of science, but also the traditional understanding of philosophy. In Frankfurt School thought, philosophy disengages itself from metaphysics in favor of an analysis of what can be empirically known and verified. Through social science, philosophy abandons its remove from society and becomes an applied discipline. Habermas maintains that philosophy has a hermeneutical function in understanding the life-world of experience and practical knowledge alongside the abstract, rational knowledge that is the domain of science. The task of a critical theorist is to move between the empirical facts of the social world and the normative and philosophical motives that inspire social inquiry.

Social change in contemporary industrial societies has also been an area of concern for Habermas. In his magnum opus the *Theory of Communicative Action* (2 volumes, 1984), Habermas criticized the one-side process of modernization led by forces of economic and administrative rationalization. Habermas traced the growing intervention of formal systems in the everyday lives of people that penetrated areas of life centered on social reproduction, cultural transmission, and socialization. In "The Tasks of a Critical Theory of Society," Habermas contends that the increasing regulation and reorganization of private life, the family and intimate relations is traced to the parallel development of the administrative functions of the welfare state, on the one hand, and, on the other, to the expanding power and influence of corporate capitalism and a culture of mass consumption. These powerful, reinforcing systems rationalize widening areas of social life and submit them to a generalizing logic of efficiency and control. As routinized political parties and interest groups substitute for participatory democracy, society is increasingly administered at a level remote from the input of citizens. As a result of these developments, the boundaries between public and private, the individual and society, the system and the lifeworld begin to collapse. Habermas saw the student revolt of the 1960s, feminism and civil rights, and ecology and the New Social Movements of the 1980s as attempts by citizens to resist the penetration of the system into everyday life. Against the rule of expert administrators and executives, these were efforts by citizens to exert an influence over society, to steer government in a more humane direction, and to empower the disenfranchised through efforts to change public opinion.

Much of Habermas's work is concerned with politics and achieving a rational society. Humans are endowed with the capacity for language and the basic normative consensus that is implied by the structure of language and in speech rules. Reconstructing this competence has allowed Habermas to escape the trap of relativism, in which there are an endless number of possible standpoints and competing truth claims. He points out that there is an underlying presumption of validity invested in the act of intersubjective communication itself in which actors take turns and observe practical rules of conversation. Habermas points out that in everyday situations actors routinely seek to convince others who do not share their standpoint and that these others are sometimes persuaded. This suggests that actors in communication do recognize that there is a truth that is not reducible to the identity of the speaker. In their efforts to make their interests and identities known and recognized, actors thus make the commonplace assumption that communication with others is possible. This basic fact of social life implies that rational collective action and self-determination is possible, even across lines of cultural and social difference, because communication and persuasion are possible.

As Habermas observes in "Civil Society and the Political Public Sphere," democratic political life only thrives where institutions enable citizens to debate matters of public importance. What is necessary is to craft norms and institutions in such a way that a realm of public life can be created that supports free communication. In order to move beyond practice to construct an ethical foundation for communication, Habermas evokes the counterfactual "ideal speech situation" in which actors are equally endowed with the capacities of discourse, recognize each other's basic social equality, and in which their speech is completely undistorted by ideology or misrecognition. In evoking this ideal situation Habermas is not claiming that it ever fully obtains in practice, nor that it necessarily can be achieved, but rather that it provides a heuristic tool that empowers critical analysis of actual social communication and provides a utopian ideal after which people can strive.

In an important early work, *The Structural Transformation of the Public Sphere* (1991), Habermas explored the origins, radical potential, and ultimate degeneration of the bourgeois public sphere of the eighteenth century. It was this public sphere of rational debate on matters of political importance that helped to make parliamentary democracy possible and which promoted Enlightenment ideals of equality, human rights, and justice. Habermas described this sphere in terms of both the actual infrastructure that supported it and the norms and practices that helped critical political discourse flourish. Habermas saw this public sphere as having been made possible by the development of a bourgeois culture centered around coffeehouses, intellectual and literary salons, and the print media. In this nascent public sphere communication was guided by a norm of rational argumentation and critical discussion in which the strength of argument was more important than the identity of the speaker. Although Habermas tracked the decay of the public sphere as an institution with industrialization and the rise of the mass popular media, it nevertheless provided him with a historical example of a public culture guided by the exercise of reason.

In recent work such as *Between Facts and Norms* (1996), Habermas moves away from the critique of liberalism shared by Marxists and a host of contemporary radical critics to defend Kant's ethical vision of the liberal state as a "community of free citizens." Habermas sees the law as an instrument with which principles of universalism and individual rights are – if not always happily – practically reconciled. In modern liberal societies in which tightly knit communal relations and religious unity fray, law becomes the principal medium through which stability and social control are exercised. But alongside this regulatory function, the law also provides a set of discourses and practices designed to ensure individual rights and the limits of governmental authority. Although universal adherence to like worldviews and norms is impossible in a disenchanted world, if citizens become convinced of the legitimacy and effectiveness of the law as a framework for society, then law provides a new foundation for society by contending between competing claims to validity and promoting the practical resolution of conflicts. Given rational deliberation and protection of individual rights, a society of free subjects can be achieved so long as individuals defer to the rules of legal contention. Habermas believes that law – strictly bound by constitutional norms – can thus help to overcome the old dualism between individual autonomy and the maintenance of community.

Habermas's Continuing Influence

Habermas sees hope for the future in new era of political community that transcends the national state based on ethnic and cultural likeness for one based on the equal rights and obligations of legally vested citizens. This "discursive" theory of democracy requires more than just a "constitutional patriotism" whereby citizens pledge to honor the political community on the basis of their joint normative and practical investment of the law. It also requires that the political community can collectively define its political will and implement it as policy at the level of the legislative system. Essential to this is an activist public sphere where matters of common interest can be discussed, political issues deliberated, and the force of public opinion brought to bear on the political system.

Habermas has been criticized for inadequate exploration of the problem of difference in social theory. His critics claim that his efforts to resolve the problem of reason through communication ethics remain idealistic and unconvincing. The ideal speech situation that Habermas imagines is one in which actors "bracket" their social differences and cultural identities in favor of impersonal reason. They counter this by arguing that to do so would mean renouncing much of what is meaningful about communication and do nothing to address the persistent inequalities among actors that constrain their actual exercise of voice. Others maintain that Habermas's ideal of citizenship privileges a certain type of deliberative and critical discourse over other forms of expression, thereby narrowing the range, content, and creativity of the public sphere. Against these criticisms Habermas contends that the ideal speech situation is not a reality but a useful counterfactual against which distortion can be measured. Intersubjective communication is the best way to ensure that ideas stand or fall of their merits alone making the identity of the speaker irrelevant if truthful discourse is the desired aim. Similarly, Habermas contends that the logic of self-discovery is not identical to the logic of critical discourse. The creation of identities, while always in dialogue with society, is primarily a private and intimate process of the lifeworld. Nevertheless, Habermas has conceded that the "politics of recognition" have become a chief concern of public culture and provide some opportunity for the discussion of matters of universal concern.

Currently, Habermas is regarded as the most important contemporary figure in the Frankfurt School tradition of critical theory. His ideas are used not only to explore philosophical and theoretical issues, but also in analytical studies of communications and media, the sociology of law, and political sociology. Habermas is a much-read essayist and public critic, particularly in his native Germany. With the rise of the Internet and discussion of "virtual" communities and cyber democracy, Habermas's work takes on special importance as we debate the meaning and ethics of new forms of communication and new indirect social relationships. In his passionate engagement in public culture, Habermas is still clinging to German idealism's conception of reason being manifest in history.

For Habermas, this means the challenge of rescuing Enlightenment from its decay into the oppressive forces of rationalization that Adorno and Horkheimer, and Weber before them, decried (see Parts III and V of *Classical Sociological Theory*). His project entails a recovery and vindication of reason's original promise of self-understanding, autonomy and emancipation. He contends that reason needs to be recovered not only from the forces of rationalization and disenchantment, conformity and order, but also from the reaction against it that takes flight in relativism, nihilism, political romanticism, and hedonism. In Habermas's view the implications of these philosophical debates are of dire importance. His work reminds us that though the potential for reason and rational deliberation still exists, it is by no means assured that it will prevail. Accordingly, Habermas has been heavily involved in public issues and debates on questions relating to politics, social reform, European integration, and an honest confrontation with the crimes of Germany's past. In a sense, this is the hallmark of critical theory properly understood: the thinker interpreting the world while at the same time in and of it.

Select Bibliography

Benhabib, Seyla (ed.). 1997. *Habermas and the Unfinished Project of Modernity*. Cambridge, MA: MIT Press. (This edited volume contains Habermas's address of the same title along with essays on the theme by a number of sympathetic critics.)

Berstein, Richard J. (ed.). 1985. *Habermas and Modernity*. Cambridge, MA: MIT Press. (A valuable collection of essays on the social and political thought of Habermas.)

Calhoun, Craig (ed.). 1992. *Habermas and the Public Sphere*. Cambridge, MA: MIT Press. (An excellent introduction to Habermas's theory of the public sphere, including critical commentary from a number of important authors. Valuable also for Habermas's thoughtful response to his critics in the conclusion of the volume.)

Dews, Peter (ed.) 1999. *Habermas: A Critical Reader*. Oxford: Basil Blackwell. (Introductory essay provides a useful summary of Habermas's philosophical contribution along with essays on wide variety of topics by some of the most important critics.)

Habermas, Jürgen. 1972. *Knowledge and Human Interests*. Boston: Beacon Press. (Habermas's key statement on epistemology and the sociology of knowledge.)

Habermas, Jürgen. 1984. *The Theory of Communicative Action* (2 volumes). Boston: Beacon Press. (In this two volume work, Habermas examines reason and the rationalization of society and the lifeworld as a site of practical knowledge, experience and resistance.)

Habermas, Jürgen. 1987. *The Philosophical Discourse of Modernity*. Cambridge, MA: MIT Press. (In these twelve essays, Habermas criticizes postmodernism and an array of critics of modern society ranging from Horkheimer and Adorno to Michel Foucault.)

Habermas, Jürgen. 1991. *The Structural Transformation of the Public Sphere*. Cambridge, MA: MIT Press. (Habermas's most historical work, tracing the rise and fall of a democratic, bourgeois public culture in the Age of Enlightenment.)

Habermas, Jürgen. 1996. *Between Facts and Norms*. Cambridge, MA: MIT Press. (In a fascinating and wide-ranging study, Habermas develops his discursive theory of law and democracy and points to constitutional patriotism, pluralism and the institution of law as foundations for a rational society.)

McCarthy, Thomas A. 1978. *The Critical Theory of Jürgen Habermas*. Cambridge, MA: MIT Press. (One of the best single-volume introductions to the philosophy of Habermas by one of the most prominent scholars and translators of his work.)

26 Civil Society and the Political Public Sphere

Jürgen Habermas

Civil Society, Public Opinion, and Communicative Power

Up to now, I have generally dealt with the public sphere as a communication structure rooted in the lifeworld through the associational network of civil society. I have described the political public sphere as a sounding board for problems that must be processed by the political system because they cannot be solved elsewhere. To this extent, the public sphere is a warning system with sensors that, though unspecialized, are sensitive throughout society. From the perspective of democratic theory, the public sphere must, in addition, amplify the pressure of problems, that is, not only detect and identify problems but also convincingly and *influentially* thematize them, furnish them with possible solutions, and dramatize them in such a way that they are taken up and dealt with by parliamentary complexes. Besides the "signal" function, there must be an effective problematization. The capacity of the public sphere to solve problems *on its own* is limited. But this capacity must be utilized to oversee the further treatment of problems that takes place inside the political system. I can provide only a broad estimate of the extent to which this is possible. I start by clarifying the contested concepts of the public sphere and civil society. This allows me to sketch some barriers and power structures inside the public sphere. These barriers, however, can be overcome in critical situations by escalating movements. I then summarize those elements the legal system must take into consideration when it forms its picture of a complex society like ours.

I

The public sphere is a social phenomenon just as elementary as action, actor, association, or collectivity, but it eludes the conventional sociological concepts of "social order." The public sphere cannot be conceived as an institution and certainly not as an organization. It is not even a framework of norms with differentiated competences and roles, membership regulations, and so on. Just as little does it represent a system; although it permits one to draw internal boundaries, outwardly it is characterized by open, permeable, and shifting horizons. The public sphere can best be described as a network for communicating information and points of view (i.e., opinions expressing affirmative or negative attitudes); the streams of communication are, in the process, filtered and synthesized in such a way that they coalesce into bundles of topically specified *public* opinions. Like the lifeworld as a whole, so, too, the public sphere is reproduced through communicative action, for which mastery of a natural language suffices; it is tailored to the *general comprehensibility* of everyday communicative practice. We have become acquainted with the "life-world" as a reservoir for simple interactions; specialized systems of action and knowledge that are differentiated within the lifeworld remain tied to these inter-actions. These systems fall into one of two categories. Systems like religion, educa-tion, and the family become associated with general reproductive functions of the lifeworld (that is, with cultural reproduction, social integration, or socialization). Systems like science, morality, and art take up different validity aspects of everyday communicative action (truth, rightness, or veracity). The public sphere, however, is specialized in neither of these two ways; to the extent that it extends to politically relevant questions, it leaves their specialized treatment to the political system. Rather, the public sphere distinguishes itself through a *communication structure* that is related to a third feature of communicative action: it refers neither to the *functions* nor to the *contents* of everyday communication but to the *social space* generated in communicative action.

Unlike success-oriented actors who mutually observe each other as one observes something in the objective world, persons acting communicatively encounter each other in a *situation* they at the same time constitute with their cooperatively negotiated interpretations. The intersubjectively shared space of a speech situation is disclosed when the participants enter into interpersonal relationships by taking positions on mutual speech-act offers and assuming illocutionary obligations. Every encounter in which actors do not just observe each other but take a second-person attitude, reciprocally attributing communicative freedom to each other, unfolds in a linguistically constituted public space. This space stands open, in principle, for potential dialogue partners who are present as bystanders or could come on the scene and join those present. That is, special measures would be required to prevent a third party from entering such a linguistically constituted space. Founded in communicative action, this spatial structure of simple and episodic encounters can be expanded and rendered more permanent in an abstract form for a larger public of present persons. For the public infrastructure of such *assemblies*, performances, presentations, and so on, architectural metaphors of structured spaces recommend themselves: we speak of forums, stages, arenas, and the like. These public spheres still cling to the concrete locales where an audience is physically gathered. The more they detach themselves from the public's physical presence and extend to the virtual presence of scattered readers, listeners, or viewers linked by public media, the clearer becomes the abstraction that enters when the spatial structure of simple interactions is expanded into a public sphere.

When generalized in this way, communication structures contract to informational content and points of view that are uncoupled from the thick contexts of simple interactions, from specific persons, and from practical obligations. At the same time, context generalization, inclusion, and growing anonymity demand a higher degree of explication that must dispense with technical vocabularies and special codes. Whereas the *orientation to laypersons* implies a certain loss in differentiation, uncoupling communicated opinions from concrete practical obligations tends to have an *intellectualizing* effect. Processes of opinion-formation, especially when they have to do with political questions, certainly cannot be separated from the transformation of the participants' preferences and attitudes, but they can be separ-ated from putting these dispositions into action. To this extent, the communication structures of the public sphere *relieve* the public *of the burden of decision making*; the postponed decisions are reserved for the institutionalized political process. In the public sphere, utterances are sorted according to issue and contribution, whereas the contributions are weighted by the affirmative versus negative responses they receive. Information and arguments are thus worked into focused opinions. What makes such "bundled" opinions into *public opinion* is both the controversial way it comes about and the amount of approval that "carries" it. Public opinion is not representative in the statistical sense. It is not an aggregate of individually gathered, privately expressed opinions held by isolated persons. Hence it must not be confused with survey results. Political opinion polls provide a certain reflection of "public opinion" only if they have been preceded by a focused public debate and a corresponding opinion-formation in a mobilized public sphere.

The diffusion of information and points of view via effective broadcasting media is not the only thing that matters in public processes of communication, nor is it the most important. True, only the broad circulation of comprehensible, attention-grabbing messages arouses a sufficiently inclusive participation. But the rules of a *shared* practice of communication are of greater significance for structuring public opinion. Agreement on issues and contributions *develops* only as the result of more or less exhaustive controversy in which proposals, information, and reasons can be more or less rationally dealt with. In general terms, the *discursive level* of opinion-formation and the "quality" of the outcome vary with this "more or less" in the "rational" processing of "exhaustive" proposals, information, and reasons. Thus the success of public communication is not intrinsically measured by the requirement of inclusion either but by the formal criteria governing how a qualified public opinion comes about. The structures of a power-ridden, oppressed public sphere exclude fruitful and clarifying discussions. The "quality" of public opinion, insofar as it is measured by the procedural properties of its process of generation, is an empirical variable. From a normative perspective, this provides a basis for measuring the legitimacy of the influence that public opinion has on the political system. Of course, actual influence coincides with legitimate influence just as little as the belief in legitimacy coincides with legitimacy. But conceiving things this way at least opens a perspective from which the relation between actual influence and the procedurally grounded quality of public opinion can be empirically investigated.

Parsons introduced "influence" as a symbolically generalized form of communication that facilitates interactions in virtue of conviction or persuasion. For example, persons or institutions can enjoy a reputation that allows their utterences to have an influence on others' beliefs without having to demonstrate authority or to give explanations in the situation. "Influence" feeds on the resource of mutual understanding, but it is based on advancing trust in beliefs that are not currently tested. In this sense, public opinion represents political potentials that can be used for influencing the voting behavior of citizens or the will-formation in parliamentary bodies, administrative agencies, and courts. Naturally, political *influence* supported by public opinion is converted into political *power* – into a potential for rendering binding decisions – only when it affects the beliefs and decisions of *authorized* members of the political system and determines the behavior of voters, legislators, officials, and so forth. Just like social power, political influence based on public opinion can be transformed into political power only through institutionalized procedures.

Influence develops in the public sphere and becomes the object of struggle there. This struggle involves not only the political influence that has already been acquired (such as that enjoyed by experienced political leaders and officeholders, established parties, and well-known groups like Greenpeace and Amnesty International). The reputation of groups of persons and experts who have acquired their influence in special public spheres also comes into play (for example, the authority of religious leaders, the public visibility of literary figures and artists, the reputation of scientists, and the popularity of sports figures and movie stars). For as soon as the public space has expanded beyond the context of simple interactions, a differentiation sets in among organizers, speakers, and hearers; arenas and galleries; stage and viewing space. The *actors' roles* that increasingly professionalize and multiply with organizational complexity and range of media are, of course, furnished with unequal opportunities for exerting influence. But the political influence that the actors gain through public communication must *ultimately* rest on the resonance and indeed the approval of a lay public whose composition is egalitarian. The public of citizens must be *convinced* by comprehensible and broadly interesting contributions to issues it finds relevant. The public audience possesses final authority, because it is *constitutive* for the internal structure and reproduction of the public sphere, the *only* place where actors can appear. There can be no public sphere without a public.

To be sure, we must distinguish the actors who, so to speak, emerge from the public and take part in the reproduction of the public sphere itself from actors who occupy an already constituted public domain in order to use it. This is true, for example, of the large and well-organized interest groups that are anchored in various social subsystems and affect the political system *through* the public sphere. They cannot make any manifest use in the public sphere of the sanctions and rewards they rely on in bargaining or in nonpublic attempts at pressure. They can capitalize on their social power and convert it into political power only insofar as they can advertise their interests in a language that can mobilize convincing reasons and shared value orientations – as, for example, when parties to wage negotiations inform the public about demands, strategies, or outcomes. The contributions of interest groups are, in any case, vulnerable to a kind of criticism to which contributions from other sources are not exposed. Public opinions that can acquire visibility only because of an undeclared infusion of money or organizational power lose their credibility as soon as these sources of social power are made public. Public opinion can be manipulated but neither publicly bought nor publicly blackmailed. This is due to the fact that a public sphere cannot be "manufactured" as one pleases. Before it can be captured by actors with strategic intent, the public sphere together with its public must have developed as a structure that stands on its own and reproduces itself *out of itself*. This lawlike regularity governing the formation of a public sphere remains latent in the constituted public sphere – and takes effect again only in moments when the public sphere is mobilized.

The political public sphere can fulfill its function of perceiving and thematizing encompassing social problems only insofar as it develops out of the communication taking place among *those who are potentially affected*. It is carried by a public recruited from the entire citizenry. But in the diverse voices of this public, one hears the echo of private experiences that are caused throughout society by the externalities (and internal disturbances) of various functional systems – and even by the very state apparatus on whose regulatory activities the complex and poorly coordinated subsystems depend. Systemic deficiencies are experienced in the context of individual life histories; such burdens accumulate in the lifeworld. The latter has the appropriate antennae, for in its horizon are intermeshed the private life histories of the "clients" of functional systems that might be failing in their delivery of services. It is only for those who are immediately affected that such services are paid in the currency of "use values." Besides religion, art, and literature, only the spheres of "private" life have an existential language at their disposal, in which such socially generated problems can be *assessed in terms of one's own life history*. Problems voiced in the public sphere first become visible when they are mirrored in personal life experiences. To the extent that these experiences find their concise expression in the languages of religion, art, and literature, the "literary" public sphere in the broader sense, which is specialized for the articulation of values and world disclosure, is intertwined with the political public sphere.

As both bearers of the political public sphere and as *members of society*, citizens occupy two positions at once. As members of society, they occupy the roles of employees and consumers, insured persons and patients, taxpayers and clients of bureaucracies, as well as the roles of students, tourists, commuters, and the like; in such complementary roles, they are especially exposed to the specific requirements and failures of the corresponding service systems. Such experiences are first assimilated "privately," that is, are interpreted within the horizon of a life history intermeshed with other life histories in the contexts of shared lifeworlds. The communication channels of the public sphere are linked to private spheres – to the thick networks of interaction found in families and circles of friends as well as to the looser contacts with neighbors, work colleagues, acquaintances, and so on – and indeed they are linked in such a way that the spatial structures of simple interactions are expanded and abstracted but not destroyed. Thus the orientation to reaching understanding that is predominant in everyday practice is also preserved for a *communication among strangers* that is conducted over great distances in public spheres whose branches are quite complex. The threshold separating the private sphere from the public is not marked by a fixed set of issues or relationships but by *different conditions of communication*. Certainly these conditions lead to differences in the accessibility of the two spheres, safeguarding the intimacy of the one sphere and the publicity of the other. However, they do not seal off the private from the public but only channel the flow of topics from the one sphere into the other. For the public sphere draws its impulses from the private handling of social problems that resonate in life histories. It is symptomatic of this close connection, incidentally, that a modern bourgeois public sphere developed in the European societies of the seventeenth and eighteenth centuries as the "sphere of private persons come together as a public." Viewed historically, the connection between the public and the private spheres is manifested in the clubs and organizational forms of a reading public composed of bourgeois private persons and crystallizing around newspapers and journals.

2

This sphere of civil society has been rediscovered today in wholly new historical constellations. The expression "civil society" has in the meantime taken on a meaning different from that of the "bourgeois society" of the liberal tradition, which Hegel conceptualized as a "system of needs," that is, as a market system involving social labor and commodity exchange. What is meant by "civil society" today, in contrast to its usage in the Marxist tradition, no longer includes the economy as constituted by private law and steered through markets in labor, capital, and commodities. Rather, its institutional core comprises those nongovernmental and non-economic connections and voluntary associations that anchor the communication structures of the public sphere in the society component of the lifeworld. Civil society is composed of those more or less spontaneously emergent associations, organizations, and movements that, attuned to how societal problems resonate in the private life spheres, distill and transmit such reactions in amplified form to the public sphere. The core of civil society comprises a network of associations that institutionalizes problem-solving discourses on questions of general interest inside the framework of organized public spheres. These "discursive designs" have an egalitarian, open form of organization that mirrors essential features of the kind of communication around which they crystallize and to which they lend continuity and permanence.

Such associations certainly do not represent the most conspicuous element of a public sphere dominated by mass media and large agencies, observed by market and opinion research, and inundated by the public relations work, propaganda, and advertising of political parties and groups. All the same, they do form the organizational substratum of the general public of citizens. More or less emerging from the private sphere, this public is made of citizens who seek acceptable interpretations for their social interests and experiences and who want to have an influence on institutionalized opinion- and will-formation.

One searches the literature in vain for clear definitions of civil society that would go beyond such descriptive characterizations. S. N. Eisenstadt's usage reveals a certain continuity with the older theory of pluralism when he describes civil society as follows:

> Civil society embraces a multiplicity of ostensibly "private" yet potentially autonomous public arenas distinct from the state. The activities of such actors are regulated by various associations existing within them, preventing the society from degenerating into a shapeless mass. In a civil society, these sectors are not embedded in closed, ascriptive or corporate settings; they are open-ended and overlapping. Each has autonomous access to the central political arena, and a certain degree of commitment to that setting.

Jean Cohen and Andrew Arato, who have presented the most comprehensive study on this topic, provide a catalog of features characterizing the civil society that is demarcated from the state, the economy, and other functional systems but coupled with the core private spheres of the lifeworld:

> (1) *Plurality*: families, informal groups, and voluntary associations whose plurality and autonomy allow for a variety of forms of life; (2) *Publicity*: institutions of culture and communication; (3) *Privacy*: a domain of individual self-development and moral choice; (4) *Legality*: structures of general laws and basic rights needed to demarcate plurality, privacy, and publicity from at least the state and, tendentially, the economy. Together, these structures secure the institutional existence of a modern differentiated civil society.

The *constitution of this sphere through basic rights* provides some indicators for its social structure. Freedom of assembly and freedom of association, when linked with freedom of speech, define the scope for various types of associations and societies: for voluntary associations that intervene in the formation of public opinion, push topics of general interest, and act as advocates for neglected issues and underrepresented groups; for groups that are difficult to organize or that pursue cultural, religious, or humanitarian aims; and for ethical communities, religious denominations, and so on. Freedom of the press, radio, and television, as well as the right to engage in these areas, safeguards the media infrastructure of public communication; such liberties are thereby supposed to preserve an openness for competing opinions and a representative diversity of voices. The political system, which must remain sensitive to the influence of public opinion, is intertwined with the public sphere and civil society through the activity of political parties and general elections. This intermeshing is guaranteed by the right of parties to "collaborate" in the political will-formation of the people, as well as by the citizens' active and passive voting rights and other participatory rights. Finally, the network of associations can assert its autonomy and preserve its spontaneity only insofar as it can draw support from a mature pluralism of forms of life, subcultures, and worldviews. The constitutional protection of "privacy" promotes the integrity of private life spheres: rights of personality, freedom of belief and of conscience, freedom of movement, the privacy of letters, mail, and telecommunications, the inviolability of one's residence, and the protection of families circumscribe an untouchable zone of personal integrity and independent judgment.

The tight connection between an autonomous civil society and an integral private sphere stands out even more clearly when contrasted with totalitarian societies of bureaucratic socialism. Here a panoptic state not only directly controls the bureaucratically desiccated public sphere, it also undermines the private basis of this public sphere. Administrative intrusions and constant supervision corrode the communicative structure of everyday contacts in families and schools, neighborhoods and local municipalities. The destruction of solidary living conditions and the paralysis of initiative and independent engagement in overregulated yet legally uncertain sectors go hand in hand with the crushing of social groups, associations, and networks; with indoctrination and the dissolution of cultural identities; with the suffocation of spontaneous public communication. Communicative rationality is thus destroyed *simultaneously* in both public and private contexts of communication. The more the bonding force of communicative action wanes in private life spheres and the embers of communicative freedom die out, the easier it is for someone who monopolizes the public sphere to align the mutually estranged and isolated actors into a mass that can be directed and mobilized in a plebiscitarian manner.

Basic constitutional guarantees alone, of course, cannot preserve the public sphere and civil society from deformations. The communication structures of the public sphere must rather be kept intact by an energetic civil society. That the political public sphere must in a certain sense reproduce and stabilize itself from its own resources is shown by the odd *self-referential character of the practice of communication in civil society.* Those actors who are the carriers of the public sphere put forward "texts" that always reveal the same subtext, which refers to the critical function of the public sphere in general. Whatever the manifest content of their public utterances, the performative meaning of such public discourse at the same time actualizes the function of an undistorted political public sphere as such. Thus, the institutions and legal guarantees of free and open opinion-formation rest on the unsteady ground of the political communication of actors who, in making use of them, at the same time interpret, defend, and radicalize their normative content. Actors who know they are involved in the *common* enterprise of reconstituting and maintaining structures of the public sphere as they contest opinions and strive for influence differ from actors who merely use forums that already exist. More specifically, actors who support the public sphere are distinguished by the *dual orientation* of their political engagement: with their programs, they directly influence the political system, but at the same time they are also reflexively concerned with revitalizing and enlarging civil society and the public sphere as well as with confirming their own identities and capacities to act.

Cohen and Arato see this kind of "dual politics" especially in the "new" social movements that simultaneously pursue offensive and defensive goals. "Offensively," these movements attempt to bring up issues relevant to the entire society, to define ways of approaching problems, to propose possible solutions, to supply new information, to interpret values differently, to mobilize good reasons and criticize bad ones. Such initiatives are intended to produce a broad shift in public opinion, to alter the parameters of organized political will-formation, and to exert pressure on parliaments, courts, and administrations in favor of specific policies. "Defensively," they attempt to maintain existing structures of association and public influence, to generate subcultural counterpublics and counterinstitutions, to consolidate new collective identities, and to win new terrain in the form of expanded rights and reformed institutions:

> On this account, the "defensive" aspect of the movements involves preserving *and developing* the communicative infrastructure of the lifeworld. This formulation captures the dual aspect of movements discussed by Touraine as well as Habermas's insight that movements can be the carriers of the potentials of cultural modernity. This is the sine qua non for successful efforts to redefine identities, to reinterpret norms, and to develop egalitarian, democratic associational forms. The expressive, normative and communicative modes of collective action ... [also involve] efforts to secure *institutional* changes within civil society that correspond to the new meanings, identities, and norms that are created.

In the self-referential mode of reproducing the public sphere, as well as in the Janus-faced politics aimed at the political system and the self-stabilization of public sphere and civil society, the space is provided for the extension and radicalization of existing rights: "The combination of associations, publics, and rights, when supported by a political culture in which independent initiatives and movements represent an ever-renewable, legitimate, political option, represents, in our opinion, an effective set of bulwarks around civil society within whose limits much of the program of radical democracy can be reformulated."

In fact, the *interplay* of a public sphere based in civil society with the opinion- and will-formation institutionalized in parliamentary bodies and courts offers a good starting point for translating the concept of deliberative politics into sociological terms. However, we must not look on civil society as a focal point where the lines of societal self-organization as a whole would converge. Cohen and Arato rightly emphasize the *limited scope for action* that civil society and the public sphere afford to noninstitutionalized political movements and forms of political expression. They speak of a structurally necessary "self-limitation" of radical-democratic practice:

First, a robust civil society can develop only in the context of a liberal political culture and the corresponding patterns of socialization, and on the basis of an integral private sphere; it can blossom only in an already rationalized lifeworld. Otherwise, populist movements arise that blindly defend the frozen traditions of a lifeworld endangered by capitalist modernization. In their forms of mobilization, these fundamentalist movements are as modern as they are antidemocratic.

Second, within the boundaries of the public sphere, or at least of a liberal public sphere, actors can acquire only influence, not political power. The influence of a public opinion generated more or less discursively in open controversies is certainly an empirical variable that can make a difference. But public influence is transformed into communicative power only after it passes through the filters of the institutionalized *procedures* of democratic opinion- and will-formation and enters through parliamentary debates into legitimate lawmaking. The informal flow of public opinion issues in beliefs that have been *tested* from the standpoint of the generalizability of interests. Not influence per se, but influence transformed into communicative power legitimates political decisions. The popular sovereignty set communicatively aflow cannot make itself felt *solely* in the influence of informal public discourses – not even when these discourses arise from autonomous public spheres. To generate political power, their influence must have an effect on the democratically regulated deliberations of democratically elected assemblies and assume an authorized form in formal decisions. This also holds, mutatis mutandis, for courts that decide politically relevant cases.

Third, and finally, the instruments that politics has available in law and administrative power have a limited effectiveness in functionally differentiated societies. Politics indeed continues to be the addressee for all unmanaged integration problems. But political steering can often take only an indirect approach and must, as we have seen, leave intact the modes of operation internal to functional systems and other highly organized spheres of action. As a result, democratic movements emerging from civil society must give up holistic aspirations to a self-organizing society, aspirations that also undergirded Marxist ideas of social revolution. Civil society can directly transform only itself, and it can have at most an indirect effect on the self-transformation of the political system; generally, it has an influence only on the personnel and programming of this system. But in no way does it occupy *the position* of a macrosubject supposed to bring society as a whole under control and simultaneously act for it. Besides these limitations, one must bear in mind that the administrative power deployed for purposes of social planning and supervision is not a suitable medium for fostering emancipated forms of life. These can *develop* in the wake of democratization processes but they cannot be *brought about* through intervention.

The self-limitation of civil society should not be understood as incapacitation. The knowledge required for political supervision or steering, a knowledge that in complex societies represents a resource as scarce as it is desirable, can certainly become the source of a new systems paternalism. But because the administration does not, for the most part, itself produce the relevant knowledge but draws it from the knowledge system or other intermediaries, it does not enjoy a natural monopoly on such knowledge. In spite of asymmetrical access to expertise and limited problem-solving capacities, civil society also has the opportunity of mobilizing counter-knowledge and drawing on the pertinent forms of expertise to make *its own* translations. Even though the public consists of laypersons and communicates with ordinary language, this does not necessarily imply an inability to differentiate the essential questions and reasons for decisions. This can serve as a pretext for a technocratic incapacitation of the public sphere only as long as the political initiatives of civil society fail to provide sufficient expert knowledge along with appropriate and, if necessary, multilevel translations in regard to the managerial aspects of public issues.

3

The concepts of the political public sphere and civil society introduced above are not mere normative postulates but have empirical relevance. However, additional assumptions must be introduced if we are to use these concepts to translate the discourse-theoretic reading of radical democracy into sociological terms and reformulate it in an empirically falsifiable manner. I would like to defend the claim that *under certain circumstances* civil society can acquire influence in the public sphere, have an effect on the parliamentary complex (and the courts) through its own public opinions, and compel the political system to switch over to the official circulation of power. Naturally, the sociology of mass communication conveys a skeptical impression of the power-ridden, mass-media-dominated public spheres of Western democracies. Social movements, citizen initiatives and forums, political and other associations, in short, the groupings of civil society, are indeed sensitive to problems, but the signals they send out and the impulses they give are generally too weak to initiate learning processes or redirect decision making in the political system in the short run.

In complex societies, the public sphere consists of an intermediary structure between the political system, on the one hand, and the private sectors of the lifeworld and functional systems, on the other. It represents a highly complex network that branches out into a multitude of overlapping international, national, regional, local, and subcultural arenas. Functional specifications, thematic foci, policy fields, and so forth, provide the points of reference for a substantive differentiation of public spheres that are, however, still accessible to laypersons (for example, popular science and literary publics, religious and artistic publics, feminist and "alternative" publics, publics concerned with health-care issues, social welfare, or environmental policy). Moreover, the public sphere is differentiated into levels according to the density of communication, organizational complexity, and range – from the *episodic* publics found in taverns, coffee houses, or on the streets; through the *occasional* or "arranged" publics of particular presentations and events, such as theater performances, rock concerts, party assemblies, or church congresses; up to the *abstract* public sphere of isolated readers, listeners, and viewers scattered across large geographic areas, or even around the globe, and brought together only through the mass media. Despite these manifold differentiations, however, all the partial publics constituted by ordinary language remain porous to one another. The one text of "the" public sphere, a text continually extrapolated and extending radially in all directions, is divided by internal boundaries into arbitrarily small texts for which everything else is context; yet one can always build hermeneutical bridges from one text to the next. Segmented public spheres are constituted with the help of exclusion mechanisms; however, because publics cannot harden into organizations or systems, there is no exclusion rule without a proviso for its abolishment.

In other words, boundaries inside the universal public sphere as defined by its reference to the political system remain permeable in principle. The rights to unrestricted inclusion and equality built into liberal public spheres prevent exclusion mechanisms of the Foucauldian type and ground a *potential for self-transformation*. In the course of the nineteenth and twentieth centuries, the universalist discourses of the bourgeois public sphere could no longer immunize themselves against a critique from within. The labor movement and feminism, for example, were able to join these discourses in order to shatter the structures that had initially constituted them as "the other" of a bourgeois public sphere.

The more the audience is widened through mass communications, the more inclusive and the more abstract in form it becomes. Correspondingly, the *roles of the actors* appearing in the arenas are, to an increasing degree, sharply separated from the roles of the spectators in the galleries. Although the "success of the actors in the arena is ultimately decided in the galleries," the question arises of how autonomous the public is when it takes a position on an issue, whether its affirmative or negative stand reflects a process of becoming informed or in fact only a more or less concealed game of power. Despite the wealth of empirical investigations, we still do not have a well-established answer to this cardinal question. But one can at least pose the question more precisely by assuming that public processes of communication can take place with less distortion the more they are left to the internal dynamic of a civil society that emerges from the lifeworld.

One can distinguish, at least tentatively, the more loosely organized actors who "emerge from" the public, as it were, from other actors merely "appearing before" the public. The latter have organizational power, resources, and sanctions available *from the start*. Naturally, the actors who are more firmly anchored in civil society and participate in the reproduction of the public sphere also depend on the support of "sponsors" who supply the necessary resources of money, organization, knowledge, and social capital. But patrons or "like-minded" sponsors do not necessarily reduce the authenticity of the public actors they support. By contrast, the collective actors who merely enter the public sphere from, and utilize it for, a specific organization or functional system have *their own* basis of support. Among these political and social actors who do not have to obtain their resources from other spheres, I primarily include the large interest groups that enjoy social power, as well as the established parties that have largely become arms of the political system. They draw on market studies and opinion surveys and conduct their own professional public-relations campaigns.

In and of themselves, organizational complexity, resources, professionalization, and so on, are admittedly insufficient indicators for the difference between "indigenous" actors and mere users. Nor can an actor's pedigree be read directly from the interests actually represented. Other indicators are more reliable. Thus actors differ in how they can be identified. Some actors one can easily identify from their functional background; that is, they represent political parties or pressure groups; unions or professional associations; consumer-protection groups or rent-control organizations, and so on. Other actors, by contrast, must first *produce* identifying features. This is especially evident with social movements that initially go through a phase of self-identification and self-legitimation; even after that, they still pursue a self-referential "identity politics" parallel to their goal-directed politics – they must continually reassure themselves of their identity. Whether actors merely use an already constituted public sphere or whether they are involved in reproducing its structures is, moreover, evident in the above-mentioned sensitivity to threats to communication rights. It is also shown in the actors' willingness to go beyond an interest in self-defense and take a universalist stand against the open or concealed exclusion of minorities or marginal groups. The very existence of social movements, one might add, depends on whether they find organizational forms that produce solidarities and publics, forms that allow them to fully utilize and radicalize existing communication rights and structures as they pursue special goals.

A third group of actors are the journalists, publicity agents, and members of the press (i.e., in the broad sense of *Publizisten*) who collect information, make decisions about the selection and presentation of "programs," and to a certain extent control the entry of topics, contributions, and authors into the mass-media-dominated public sphere. As the mass media become more complex and more expensive, the effective channels of communication become more centralized. To the degree this occurs, the mass media face an increasing pressure of selection, on both the supply side and the demand side. These selection processes become the source of a new sort of power. This *power of the media* is not sufficiently reined in by professional standards, but today, by fits and starts, the "fourth branch of government" is being subjected to constitutional regulation. In the Federal Republic, for example, it is both the legal form and the institutional structure of television networks that determine whether they depend more on the influence of political parties and public interest groups or more on private firms with large advertising outlays. In general, one can say that the image of politics presented on television is predominantly made up of issues and contributions that are professionally produced as media input and then fed in via press conferences, news agencies, public-relations campaigns, and the like. These official producers of information are all the more successful the more they can rely on trained personnel, on financial and technical resources, and in general on a professional infrastructure. Collective actors operating outside the political system or outside large organizations normally have fewer opportunities to influence the content and views presented by the media. This is especially true for messages that do not fall inside the "balanced," that is, the centrist and rather narrowly defined, spectrum of "established opinions" dominating the programs of the electronic media.

Moreover, before messages selected in this way are broadcast, they are subject to *information-processing strategies* within the media. These are oriented by reception conditions as perceived by media experts, program directors, and the press. Because the public's receptiveness, cognitive capacity, and attention represent unusually scarce resources for which the programs of numerous "stations" compete, the presentation of news and commentaries for the most part follows market strategies. Reporting facts as human-interest stories, mixing information with entertainment, arranging material episodically, and breaking down complex relationships into smaller fragments – all of this comes together to form a syndrome that works to depoliticize public communication. This is the kernel of truth in the theory of the culture industry. The research literature provides fairly reliable information on the institutional framework and structure of the media, as well as on the way they work, organize programs, and are utilized. But, even a generation after Paul Lazarsfeld, propositions concerning the *effects of the media* remain controversial. The research on effect and reception has at least done away with the image of passive consumers as "cultural dopes" who are manipulated by the programs offered to them. It directs our attention to the *strategies of interpretation* employed by viewers, who communicate with one another, and who in fact can be provoked to criticize or reject what programs offer or to synthesize it with judgments of their own.

Even if we know something about the internal operation and impact of the mass media, as well as about the distribution of roles among the public and various actors, and even if we can make some reasonable conjectures about who has privileged access to the media and who has a share in media power, it is by no means clear how the mass media intervene in the diffuse circuits of communication in the political public sphere. The *normative reactions* to the relatively new phenomenon of the mass media's powerful position in the competition for public influence are clearer. Michael Gurevitch and Jay G. Blumler have summarized the tasks that the media *ought* to fulfill in democratic political systems:

1   surveillance of the sociopolitical environment, reporting developments likely to impinge, positively or negatively, on the welfare of citizens;
2   meaningful agenda-setting, identifying the key issues of the day, including the forces that have formed and may resolve them;
3   platforms for an intelligible and illuminating advocacy by politicians and spokespersons of other causes and interest groups;
4   dialogue across a diverse range of views, as well as between power-holders (actual and prospective) and mass publics;
5   mechanisms for holding officials to account for how they have exercised power;
6   incentives for citizens to learn, choose, and become involved, rather than merely to follow and kibitz over the political process;
7   a principled resistance to the efforts of forces outside the media to subvert their independence, integrity and ability to serve the audience;
8   a sense of respect for the audience member, as potentially concerned and able to make sense of his or her political environment.

Such principles orient the professional code of journalism and the profession's ethical self-understanding, on the one hand, and the formal organization of a free press by laws governing mass communication, on the other. In agreement with the concept of deliberative politics, these principles express a simple idea: the mass media ought to understand themselves as the mandatary of an enlightened public whose willingness to learn and capacity for criticism they at once presuppose, demand, and reinforce; like the judiciary, they ought to preserve their independence from political and social pressure; they ought to be receptive to the public's concerns and proposals, take up these issues and contributions impartially, augment criticisms, and confront the political process with articulate demands for legitimation. The power of the media should thus be neutralized and the tacit conversion of administrative or social power into political influence blocked. According to this idea, political and social actors would be allowed to "use" the public sphere only insofar as they make convincing contributions to the solution of problems that have been perceived by the public or have been put on the public agenda with the public's consent. In a similar vein, political parties would have to participate in the opinion- and will-formation from the public's own perspective, rather than patronizing the public and extracting mass loyalty from the public sphere for the purposes of maintaining their own power.

The sociology of mass communication depicts the public sphere as infiltrated by administrative and social power and dominated by the mass media. If one places this image, diffuse though it might be, alongside the above normative expectations, then one will be rather cautious in estimating the chances of civil society having an influence on the political system. To be sure, this estimate pertains only to a *public sphere at rest*. In periods of mobilization, the structures that actually support the authority of a critically engaged public begin to vibrate. The balance of power between civil society and the political system then shifts.

4

With this I return to the central question of who can place issues on the agenda and determine what direction the lines of communication take. Roger Cobb, Jennie-Keith Ross, and Marc Howard Ross have constructed models that depict how new and compelling issues develop, from the first initiative up to formal proceedings in bodies that have the power to decide. If one suitably modifies the proposed models – inside access model, mobilization model, outside initiative model – from the viewpoint of democratic theory, they present basic alternatives in how the public sphere and the political system influence each other. In the first case, the initiative comes from officeholders or political leaders, and the issue continues to circulate inside the political system all the way to its formal treatment, while the broader public is either excluded from the process or does not have any influence on it. In the second case, the initiative again starts inside the political system, but the proponents of the issue must mobilize the public sphere, because they need the support of certain groups, either to obtain formal consideration or to implement an adopted program successfully. Only in the third case does the initiative lie with forces at the periphery, outside the purview of the political system. With the help of the mobilized public sphere, that is, the pressure of public opinion, such forces compel formal consideration of the issue:

> The outside initiative model applies to the situation in which a group outside the government structure 1) articulates a grievance, 2) tries to expand interest in the issue to enough other groups in the population to gain a place on the public agenda, in order to 3) create sufficient pressure on decision makers to force the issue onto the formal

agenda for their serious consideration. This model of agenda building is likely to predominate in more egalitarian societies. Formal agenda status, ... however, does not necessarily mean that the final decisions of the authorities or the actual policy implementation will be what the grievance group originally sought.

In the normal case, issues and proposals have a history whose course corresponds more to the first or second model than to the third. As long as the informal circulation of power dominates the political system, the initiative and power to put problems on the agenda and bring them to a decision lies more with the Government leaders and administration than with the parliamentary complex. As long as in the public sphere the mass media prefer, contrary to their normative self-understanding, to draw their material from powerful, well-organized information producers and as long as they prefer media strategies that lower rather than raise the discursive level of public communication, issues will tend to start in, and be managed from, the center, rather than follow a spontaneous course originating in the periphery. At least, the skeptical findings on problem articulation in public arenas accord with this view. In the present context, of course, there can be no question of a conclusive empirical evaluation of the mutual influence that politics and public have on each other. For our purposes, it suffices to make it plausible that in a perceived crisis situation, the *actors in civil society* thus far neglected in our scenario *can* assume a surprisingly active and momentous role. In spite of a lesser organizational complexity and a weaker capacity for action, and despite the structural disadvantages mentioned earlier, at the critical moments of an accelerated history, these actors get the chance to *reverse* the normal circuits of communication in the political system and the public sphere. In this way they can shift the entire system's mode of problem solving.

The communication structures of the public sphere are linked with the private life spheres in a way that gives the civil-social periphery, in contrast to the political center, the advantage of greater sensitivity in detecting and identifying new problem situations. The great issues of the last decades give evidence for this. Consider, for example, the spiraling nuclear-arms race; consider the risks involved in the peaceful use of atomic energy or in other large-scale technological projects and scientific experimentation, such as genetic engineering; consider the ecological threats involved in an overstrained natural environment (acid rain, water pollution, species extinction, etc.); consider the dramatically progressing impoverishment of the Third World and problems of the world economic order; or consider such issues as feminism, increasing immigration, and the associated problems of multiculturalism. Hardly any of these topics were *initially* brought up by exponents of the state apparatus, large organizations, or functional systems. Instead, they were broached by intellectuals, concerned citizens, radical professionals, self-proclaimed "advocates," and the like. Moving in from this outermost periphery, such issues force their way into newspapers and interested associations, clubs, professional organizations, academies, and universities. They find forums, citizen initiatives, and other platforms before they catalyze the growth of social movements and new subcultures. The latter can in turn dramatize contributions, presenting them so effectively that the mass media take up the matter. Only through their controversial presentation in the media do such topics reach the larger public and subsequently gain a place on the "public agenda." Sometimes the support of sensational actions, mass protests, and incessant campaigning is required before an issue can make its way via the surprising election of marginal candidates or radical parties, expanded platforms of "established" parties, important court decisions, and so on, into the core of the political system and there receive formal consideration.

Naturally, there are other ways in which issues develop, other paths from the periphery to the center, and other patterns involving complex branchings and feedback loops. But, in general, one can say that even in more or less power-ridden public spheres, the power relations shift as soon as the perception of relevant social problems evokes a *crisis consciousness* at the periphery. If actors from civil society then join together, formulate the relevant issue, and promote it in the public sphere, their efforts can be successful, because the endogenous mobilization of the public sphere activates an otherwise latent dependency built into the internal structure of every public sphere, a dependency also present in the normative self-understanding of the mass media: the players in the arena owe their influence to the approval of those in the gallery. At the very least, one can say that insofar as a rationalized lifeworld supports the development of a liberal public sphere by furnishing it with a solid foundation in civil society, the authority of a position-taking public is strengthened in the course of escalating public controversies. Under the conditions of a *liberal* public sphere, informal public communication accomplishes two things in cases in which mobilization depends on crisis. On the one hand, it prevents the accumulation of indoctrinated masses that are seduced by populist leaders. On the other hand, it pulls together the scattered critical potentials of a public that was only abstractly held together through the public media, and it helps this public have a political influence on institutionalized opinion- and will-formation. Only in *liberal* public spheres, of course, do subinstitutional political movements – which abandon the conventional paths of interest politics in order to boost the constitutionally regulated circulation of power in the political system – take this direction. By contrast, an authoritarian, distorted public sphere that is brought into alignment merely provides a forum for plebiscitary legitimation.

This sense of a reinforced demand for legitimation becomes especially clear when subinstitutional protest movements reach a high point by escalating their protests. The last means for obtaining more of a hearing and greater media influence for oppositional arguments are acts of civil disobedience. These acts of nonviolent, symbolic rule violation are meant as expressions of protest against binding decisions that, their legality notwithstanding, the actors consider illegitimate in the light of valid constitutional principles. Acts of civil disobedience are directed simultaneously to two addressees. On the one hand, they appeal to officeholders and parliamentary representatives to reopen formally concluded political deliberations so that their decisions may possibly be revised in view of the continuing public criticism. On the other hand, they appeal "to the sense of justice of the majority of the community," as Rawls puts it, and thus to the critical judgment of a public of citizens that is to be mobilized with exceptional means. Independently of the current object of controversy, civil disobedience is also always an implicit appeal to connect organized political will-formation with the communicative processes of the public sphere. The message of this subtext is aimed at a political system that, as constitutionally organized, may not detach itself from civil society and make itself independent vis-à-vis the periphery. Civil disobedience thereby refers to its own origins in a civil society that in crisis situations actualizes the normative contents of constitutional democracy in the medium of public opinion and summons it against the systemic inertia of institutional politics.

This *self-referential character* is emphasized in the definition that Cohen and Arato have proposed, drawing on considerations raised by Rawls, Dworkin, and me:

> Civil disobedience involves illegal acts, usually on the part of collective actors, that are public, principled, and symbolic in character, involve primarily nonviolent means of protest, and appeal to the capacity for reason and the sense of justice of the populace. The aim of civil disobedience is to persuade public opinion in civil and political society... that a particular law or policy is illegitimate and a change is warranted. Collective actors involved in civil disobedience invoke the utopian principles of constitutional democracies, appealing to the ideas of fundamental rights or democratic legitimacy. Civil disobedience is thus a means for reasserting the link between civil and political society..., when legal attempts at exerting the influence of the former on the latter have failed and other avenues have been exhausted.

This interpretation of civil disobedience manifests the self-consciousness of a civil society confident that at least in a crisis it can increase the pressure of a mobilized public on the political system to the point where the latter switches into the conflict mode and neutralizes the unofficial countercirculation of power.

Beyond this, the justification of civil disobedience relies on a *dynamic understanding* of the constitution as an unfinished project. From this long-term perspective, the constitutional state does not represent a finished structure but a delicate and sensitive – above all fallible and revisable – enterprise, whose purpose is to realize the system of rights *anew* in changing circumstances, that is, to interpret the system of rights better, to institutionalize it more appropriately, and to draw out its contents more radically. This is the perspective of citizens who are actively engaged in realizing the system of rights. Aware of, and referring to, changed contexts, such citizens want to overcome in practice the tension between social facticity and validity. Although legal theory cannot adopt this participant perspective as its own, it can reconstruct the paradigmatic *understanding* of law and democracy that guides citizens whenever they form an idea of the structural constraints on the self-organization of the legal community in their society.

5

From a reconstructive standpoint, we have seen that constitutional rights and principles merely explicate the performative character of the self-constitution of a society of free and equal citizens. The organizational forms of the constitutional state make this practice permanent. Every historical example of a democratic constitution has a double temporal reference: as a historic document, it recalls the foundational act that it interprets – it marks a beginning in time. At the same time, its normative character means that the task of interpreting and elaborating the system of rights poses itself *anew* for each generation; as the project of a just society, a constitution articulates the horizon of expectation opening on an ever-present future. From this perspective, as an *ongoing* process of constitution making set up for the long haul, the democratic procedure of legitimate lawmaking acquires a privileged status. This leads to the pressing question of whether such a demanding procedure can be implemented in complex societies like our own and, if it can, how this can be done effectively, so that a constitutionally regulated circulation of power actually prevails in the political system. The answers to this question in turn inform our own paradigmatic understanding of law. I note the following four points for elucidating such a historically situated understanding of the constitution.

(a) The constitutionally organized political system is, on the one hand, specialized for generating collectively binding decisions. To this extent, it represents only one of several subsystems. On the other hand, in virtue of its internal relation to law, politics is responsible for problems that concern society as a whole. It must be possible to interpret collectively binding decisions as a realization of rights such that the structures of recognition built into communicative action are transferred, via the medium of law, from the level of simple interactions to the abstract and anonymous relationships among strangers. In pursuing what in each case are particular collective goals and in regulating specific conflicts, politics simultaneously deals with general problems of integration. Because it is constituted in a legal form, a politics whose mode of operation is functionally specified still refers to society-wide problems: it carries on the tasks of social integration at a reflexive level when other action systems are no longer up to the job.

(b) This asymmetrical position explains the fact that the political system is subject to constraints on two sides and that corresponding standards govern its achievements and decisions. As a functionally specified action system, it is limited by other functional systems that obey their own logic and, to this extent, bar direct political interventions. On this side, the political system encounters limits on the effectiveness of administrative power (including legal and fiscal instruments). On the other side, as a constitutionally regulated action system, politics is connected with the public sphere and depends on lifeworld sources of communicative power. Here the political system is not subject to the external constraints of a social environment but rather experiences its internal dependence on enabling conditions. This is because the conditions that make the production of legitimate law possible are ultimately not at the disposition of politics.

(c) The political system is vulnerable on both sides to disturbances that can reduce the *effectiveness* of its achievements and the *legitimacy* of its decisions, respectively. The regulatory competence of the political system fails if the implemented legal programs remain ineffective or if regulatory activity gives rise to disintegrating effects in the action systems that require regulation. Failure also occurs if the instruments deployed overtax the legal medium itself and strain the normative composition of the political system. As steering problems become more complex, irrelevance, misguided regulations, and self-destruction can accumulate to the point where a "regulatory trilemma" results. On the other side, the political system fails as a guardian of social integration if its decisions, even though effective, can no longer be traced back to legitimate law. The constitutionally regulated circulation of power is nullified if the administrative system becomes independent of communicatively generated power, if the social power of functional systems and large organizations (including the mass media) is converted into illegitimate power, or if the lifeworld resources for spontaneous public communication no longer suffice to guarantee an uncoerced articulation of social interests. The independence of illegitimate power, together with the weakness of civil society and the public sphere, can deteriorate into a "legitimation dilemma," which in certain circumstances can combine with the steering trilemma and develop into a vicious circle. Then the political system is pulled into the whirlpool of legitimation deficits and steering deficits that reinforce one another.

(d) Such crises can at most be explained historically. They are not built into the structures of functionally differentiated societies in such a way that they would intrinsically compromise the project of self-empowerment undertaken by a society of free and equal subjects who bind themselves by law. However, they are symptomatic of the peculiar position of political systems as asymmetrically embedded in highly complex circulation processes. Actors must form an idea of this context whenever, adopting the performative attitude, they want to engage successfully as citizens, representatives, judges, or officials, in realizing the system of rights. Because these rights must be interpreted in various ways under changing social circumstances, the light they throw on this context is refracted into a spectrum of changing legal paradigms. Historical constitutions can be seen as so many ways of construing one and the *same* practice – the practice of self-determination on the part of free and equal citizens – but like every practice this, too, is situated in history. Those involved must start with their *own current* practice if they want to achieve clarity about what such a practice means *in general*.

27 The Tasks of a Critical Theory of Society

Jürgen Habermas

My purpose in discussing the thesis of internal colonization in connection with recent tendencies toward juridification in the Federal Republic of Germany was, among other things, to show by example how processes of real abstraction, to which Marx directed his attention, can be analyzed without our having any equivalent for his theory of value. This brings us back to the central question of whether, in the present state of the social sciences, it is necessary and possible to replace the theory of value, at least insofar as it enables us to connect theoretical statements about lifeworld and system to each other. As we have seen, Marx conceived the systemic context of capital self-realization as a fetishistic totality; from this there followed the methodological requirement that we decipher anything that might correctly be brought under a systems theoretical description simultaneously as a process of reification of living labor. This far-reaching claim has to be dropped, however, if we see in the capitalist economic system not only a new formation of class relationships but an advanced level of system differentiation in its own right. Under these premises, the *semantic question* of how something can be translated from one language into the other can be converted into the *empirical question* of when the growth of the monetary-bureau-cratic complex affects domains of action that cannot be transferred to system-integrative mechanisms without pathological side effects. The analysis of Parsonian media theory led me to the assumption that this boundary is overstepped when systemic imperatives force their way into domains of cultural reproduction, social integration, and socialization. This assumption needs to be tested empirically in connection with "real abstractions" detected in the core zones of the lifeworld. The semantic problem of connecting systems-theoretic and action-theoretic descriptions requires a solution that does not prejudge substantive questions.

I introduced the system concept of society by way of a *methodological objectification* of the lifeworld and justified the shift in perspective connected with this objectification – a shift from the perspective of a participant to that of an observer – in action-theoretic terms. Like the theory of value, this justification has the form of a conceptual explication. It is supposed to explain what it means for the symbolic reproduction of the lifeworld when communicative action is replaced by media-steered interaction, when language, in its function of coordinating action, is replaced by media such as money and power. Unlike the transformation of concrete into abstract labor, this does not *eo ipso* give rise to reifying effects. The conversion to another mechanism of action coordination, and thereby to another principle of sociation, results in reification – that is, in a pathological de-formation of the communicative infrastructure of the lifeworld – only when the lifeworld cannot be withdrawn from the functions in question, when these functions cannot be painlessly transferred to media-steered systems of action, as those of material reproduction sometimes can. In this way phenomena of reification lose the dubious status of facts that can be inferred from economic statements about value relations by means of semantic transformations alone. "Real abstractions" now make up instead an object domain for empirical inquiry. They become the object of a research program that no longer has need of value theory or any similar translation tool.

In other respects a theory of capitalist modernization developed by means of a theory of communicative action does follow the Marxian model. It is *critical* both of contemporary social sciences and of the social reality they are supposed to grasp. It is critical of the reality of developed societies inasmuch as they do not make full use of the learning potential culturally available to them, but deliver themselves over to an uncontrolled growth of complexity. As we have seen, this increasing system complexity encroaches upon nonrenewable supplies like a quasinatural force; not only does it outflank traditional forms of life, it attacks the communicative infrastructure of largely rationalized lifeworlds. But the theory is also critical of social-scientific approaches that are incapable of deciphering the paradoxes of societal rationalization because they make complex social systems their object only from one or another abstract point of view, without accounting for the historical constitution of their object domain (in the sense of a reflexive sociology). Critical social theory does not relate to established lines of research as a competitor; starting from its concept of the rise of modern societies, it attempts to explain the specific limitations and the relative rights of those approaches.

If we leave to one side the insufficiently complex approach of behaviorism, there are today three main lines of inquiry occupied with the phenomenon of modern societies. We cannot even say that they are in competition, for they scarcely have anything to say to one another. Efforts at theory comparison do not issue in reciprocal critique; fruitful critique that might foster a common undertaking can hardly be developed across these distances, but at most within one or another camp. There is a good reason for this mutual incomprehension: the object domains of the competing approaches do not come into contact, for they are the result of one-sided abstractions that unconsciously cut the ties between system and lifeworld constitutive for modern societies.

Taking as its point of departure the work of Max Weber, and also in part Marxist historiography, an approach – sometimes referred to as the history of society [*Gesellschaftsgeschichte*] – has been developed that is comparative in outlook, typological in procedure, and, above all, well informed about social history. The dynamics of class struggle are given greater or lesser weight according to the positions of such different authors as Reinhard Bendix, R. Lepsius, C. Wright Mills, Barrington Moore, and Hans-Ulrich Wehler; however, the theoretical core is always formed by assumptions about the structural differentiation of society in functionally specified systems of action. Close contact with historical research prevents the *theory of structural differentiation* from issuing in a more strongly theoretical program, for instance, in some form of systems functionalism. Rather, analysis proceeds in such a way that modernization processes are referred to the level of institutional differentiation. The functionalist mode of investigation is not so widely separated from the structuralist mode that the potential competition between the two conceptual strategies could develop. The modernization of society is, to be sure, analyzed in its various ramifications, but a one-dimensional idea of the whole process of structural differentiation predominates. It is not conceived as a second-order differentiation process, as an uncoupling of system and lifeworld that, when sufficiently advanced, makes it possible for media-steered subsystems to react back on structurally differentiated lifeworlds. As a result, the pathologies of modernity do not come into view as such from this research perspective; it lacks the conceptual tools to distinguish adequately between (a) the structural differentiation of the lifeworld, particularly of its societal components, (b) the growing autonomy of action systems that are differentiated out via steering media, as well as the internal differentiation of these subsystems, and finally (c) those differentiation processes that simultaneously dedifferentiate socially integrated domains of action in the sense of colonizing the life world.

Taking as its point of departure neoclassical economic theory, on the one hand, and social-scientific functionalism, on the other, a *systems-theoretical approach* has established itself above all in economics and in the sciences of administration. These systems sciences have, so to speak, grown up in the wake of the two media-steered subsystems. As long as they were occupied chiefly with the internal complexity of the economic and administrative systems, they could rest content with sharply idealized models. To the extent that they had to bring the restrictions of the relevant social environments into their analyses, however, there arose a need for an integrated theory that would also cover the interaction between the two functionally inter-meshed subsystems of state and economy.

It is only with the next step in abstraction, which brought society as a whole under systems-theoretical concepts, that the system sciences overdrew their account. The systems theory of society first developed by Parsons and consistently carried further by Luhmann views the rise and development of modern society solely in the func-tionalist perspective of growing system complexity. Once systems functionalism is cleansed of the dross of the sociological tradition, it becomes insensitive to social pathologies that can be discerned chiefly in the structural features of socially integrated domains of action. It hoists the vicissitudes of communicatively struc-tured lifeworlds up to the level of media dynamics; by assimilating them, from the observer perspective, to disequilibria in intersystemic exchange relations. It robs them of the significance of identity-threatening deformations, which is how they are experienced from the participant perspective.

Finally, from phenomenology, hermeneutics, and symbolic interactionism there has developed an *action-theoretical approach*. To the extent that the different lines of *interpretive sociology* proceed in a generalizing manner at all, they share an interest in illuminating structures of worldviews and forms of life. The essential part is a theory of everyday life, which can also be linked up with historical research, as it is in the work of E. P. Thompson. To the extent that this is done, modernization processes can be presented from the viewpoint of the lifeworlds specific to different strata and groups; the everyday life of the subcultures dragged into these processes are disclosed with the tools of anthropological research. Occasionally these studies condense to fragments of history written from the point of view of its victims. Then modernization appears as the sufferings of those who had to pay for the establish-ment of the new mode of production and the new system of states in the coin of disintegrating traditions and forms of life. Research of this type sharpens our perception of historical asynchronicities; they provide a stimulus to critical recollection in Benjamin's sense. But it has as little place for the internal systemic dynamics of economic development, of nation and state building, as it does for the structural logics of rationalized lifeworlds. As a result, the subcultural mirrorings in which the sociopathologies of modernity are refracted and reflected retain the subjective and accidental character of *uncomprehended* events.

Whereas the theory of structural differentiation does not sufficiently separate systemic and lifeworld aspects, systems theory and action theory, each isolates and overgeneralizes one of the two aspects. The methodological abstractions have the same result in all three cases. The theories of modernity made possible by these approaches remain insensitive to what Marx called "real abstractions"; the latter can be gotten at through an analysis that at once traces the rationalization of lifeworlds *and* the growth in complexity of media-steered susbystems, and that keeps the paradoxical nature of their interference in sight. As we have seen, it is possible to speak in a nonmetaphorical sense of paradoxical conditions of life if the structural differentiation of lifeworlds is described as rationalization. Social pathologies are not to be measured against "biological" goal states but in relation to the contradictions in which communicatively intermeshed interaction can get caught because deception and self-deception can gain objective power in an everyday practice reliant on the facticity of validity claims.

By "real abstractions" Marx was referring not only to paradoxes experienced by those involved as deformations of their lifeworld, but above all to paradoxes that could be gotten at only through an analysis of reification (or of rationalization). It is in this latter sense that we call "paradoxical" those situations in which systemic relief mechanisms made possible by the rationalization of the lifeworld turn around and overburden the communicative infrastructure of the lifeworld. After attempting to render a fourth approach to inquiry – the *genetic structuralism* of developmental psychology – fruitful for appropriating Weber's sociology of religion, Mead's theory of communication, and Durkheim's theory of social integration, I proposed that we read the Weberian rationalization thesis in that way. The basic conceptual framework I developed by these means was, naturally, not meant to be an end in itself; rather, it has to prove itself against the task of explaining those pathologies of modernity that other approaches pass right by for methodological reasons.

It is just this that critical theory took as its task before it increasingly distanced itself from social research in the early 1940s. In what follows I will (A) recall the complex of themes that originally occupied critical theory, and (B) show how some of these intentions can be taken up without the philosophy of history to which they were tied. In the process, I shall (C) go into one topic at somewhat greater length: the altered significance of the critique of positivism in a postpositivist age.

A.—The work of the Institute for Social Research was essentially dominated by six themes until the early 1940s when the circle of collaborators that had gathered in New York began to break up. These research interests are reflected in the lead theoretical articles that appeared in the main part of the *Zeltschrift für Sozialforschung*. They have to do with (a) the forms of integration in postliberal societies, (b) family socialization and ego development, (c) mass media and mass culture, (d) the social psychology behind the cessation of protest, (e) the theory of art, and (f) the critique of positivism and science. This spectrum of themes reflects Horkheimer's conception of an interdisciplinary social science. In this phase the central line of inquiry, which I characterized with the catchphrase "rationalization as reification," was to be worked out with the differentiated means of various disciplines. Before the "critique of instrumental reason" contracted the process of reification into a topic for the philosophy of history again, Horkheimer and his circle had made "real abstractions" the object of empirical inquiry. From this theoretical standpoint it is not difficult to see the unity in the multiplicity of themes enumerated above.

(a) To begin with, after the far-reaching changes in liberal capitalism the concept of reification needed to be specified. National Socialism, above all, provided an incentive to examine the altered relationship between the economy and the state, to tackle the question of whether a new principle of social organization had arisen with the transition from the Weimar Republic to the authoritiarian state, of whether fascism evinced stronger similarities to the capitalist societies of the West or, given the totalitarian features of its political system, had more in common with Stalinism. Pollock and Horkheimer were inclined to the view that the Nazi regime was like the Soviet regime, in that a state-capitalist order had been established in which private ownership of the means of production retained only a formal character, while the steering of general economic processes passed from the market to planning bureaucracies; in the process the management of large concerns seemed to merge with party and administrative elites. In this view, corresponding to the authoritarian state we have a totally administered society. The form of societal integration is determined by a purposive rational – at least in intention – exercise of centrally steered, administrative domination.

Neumann and Kirchheimer opposed to this theory the thesis that the authoritarian state represented only the totalitarian husk of a monopoly capitalism that remained intact, in that the market mechanism functioned the same as before. On this view, even a developed fascism did not displace the primacy of economic imperatives in relation to the state. The compromises among the elites of economy, party, and administration came about *on the basis* of an economic system of private capitalism. From this standpoint, the structural analogies between developed capitalist societies – whether in the political form of a totalitarian regime or a mass democracy – stood out clearly. Since the totalitarian state was not seen as the center of power, societal integration did not take place exclusively in the forms of technocratically generalized, administrative rationality.

(b and c) The relation between the economic and administrative systems of action determined how society was integrated, which forms of rationality the life-contexts of individuals were subjected to. However, the subsumption of sociated individuals under the dominant pattern of social control, the process of reification itself, had to be studied elsewhere: in the family, which, as the agency of socialization, prepared coming generations for the imperatives of the occupational system; and in the political-cultural public sphere, where, via the mass media, mass culture produced compliance in relation to political institutions. The theory of state capitalism could only explain the *type* of societal integration. The analytical social psychology that Fromm, in the tradition of left Freudianism, linked with questions from Marxist social theory was supposed, on the other hand, to explain the *processes* through which individual consciousness was adjusted to the functional requirements of the system, in which a monopolistic economy and an authoritarian state had coalesced.

Institute co-workers investigated the structural change of the bourgeois nuclear family, which had led to a loss of function and a weakening of the authoritarian position of the father, and which had at the same time mediatized the familial haven and left coming generations more and more in the socializing grip of extrafamilial forces. They also investigated the development of a culture industry that desublimated culture, robbed it of its rational content, and functionalized it for purposes of the manipulative control of consciousness. Meanwhile, reification remained, as it was in Lukacs, a category of the philosophy of consciousness; it was discerned in the attitudes and modes of behavior of individuals. The phenomena of reified consciousness were to be explained empirically, with the help of psychoanalytic personality theory. The authoritarian, easily manipulable character with a weak ego appeared in forms typical of the times; the corresponding superego formations were traced back to a complicated interplay of social structure and instinctual vicissitudes.

Again there were two lines of interpretation. Horkheimer, Adorno, and Marcuse held on to Freudian instinct theory and invoked the dynamics of an inner nature that, while it did react to societal pressure, nevertheless remained in its core resistant to the violence of socialization. Fromm, on the other hand, took up ideas from ego psychology and shifted the process of ego development into the medium of social interaction, which permeated and structured the natural substratum of instinctual impulses. Another front formed around the question of the ideological character of mass culture, with Adorno on one side and Benjamin on the other. Whereas Adorno (along with Löwenthal and Marcuse) implacably opposed the experiential content of authentic art to consumerized culture, Benjamin steadfastly placed his hopes in the secular illuminations that were to come from a mass art stripped of its aura.

(d) Thus in the course of the 1930s the narrower circle of members of the institute developed a consistent position in regard to all these themes. A monolithic picture of a totally administered society emerged corresponding to it was a repressive mode of socialization that shut out inner nature and an omnipresent social control exercised through the channels of mass communication. Over against this, the positions of Neumann and Kirchheimer, Fromm and Benjamin are not easily reduced to a common denominator. They share a more differentiated assessment of the complex and contradictory character both of forms of integration in postliberal societies and of family socialization and mass culture. These competing approaches might have provided starting points for an analysis of potentials still resistant to the reification of consciousness. But the experiences of the German émigrés in the contemporary horizon of the 1930s motivated them rather to investigate the mechanism that might explain the suspension of protest potentials. This was also the direction of their studies of the political consciousness of workers and employees, and especially of the studies of anti-Semitism begun by the institute in Germany and continued in America up to the late 1940s.

(e and f) Processes of the reification of consciousness could be made the object of a wide-ranging program of empirical research only after the theory of value had lost its foundational role. With this, of course, also went the normative content of rational natural law theory that was preserved in value theory. As we have seen, its place was then occupied by the theory of societal rationalization stemming from

Lukacs. The normative content of the concept of reification now had to be gotten from the rational potential of modern culture. For this reason, in its classical period critical theory maintained an emphatically affirmative relation to the art and philosophy of the bourgeois era. The arts – for Lowenthal and Marcuse, classical German literature above all; for Benjamin and Adorno, the literary and musical avant-garde – were the preferred object of an ideology critique aimed at separating the transcendent contents of authentic art – whether utopian or critical – from the affirmative, ideologically worn-out components of bourgeois ideals. As a result, philosophy retained central importance as the keeper of those bourgeois ideals. "Reason," Marcuse wrote in the essay that complemented Horkheimer's programmatic demarcation of critical theory from traditional theory, "is the fundamental category of philosophical thought, the only one by means of which it has bound itself to human destiny." And further on: "Reason, mind, morality, knowledge, and happiness are not only categories of bourgeois philosophy, but concerns of mankind. As such they must be preserved, if not derived anew. When critical theory examines the philosophical doctrines in which it was still possible to speak of man, it deals first with the camouflage and misintepretation that characterized the discussion of man in the bourgeois period."

This confrontation with the tradition through the critique of ideology could aim at the truth content of philosophical concepts and problems, at appropriating their systematic content, only because critique was guided by theoretical assumptions. At that time critical theory was still based on the Marxist philosophy of history, that is, on the conviction that the forces of production were developing an objectively explosive power. Only on this presupposition could critique be restricted to "bringing to consciousness potentialities that have emerged within the maturing historical situation itself." Without a *theory* of history there could be no immanent critique that applied to the manifestations of objective spirit and distinguished what things and human beings could be from what they actually were. Critique would be delivered up to the reigning standards in any given historical epoch. The research program of the 1930s stood and fell with its historical–philosophical trust in the rational potential of bourgeois culture – a potential that would be released in social movements under the pressure of developed forces of production. Ironically, however, the critiques of ideology carried out by Horkheimer, Marcuse, and Adorno confirmed them in the belief that culture was losing its autonomy in postliberal societies and was being incorporated into the machinery of the economic-administrative system. The development of productive forces, and even critical thought itself, was moving more and more into a perspective of bleak assimilation to their opposites. In the totally administered society only instrumental reason, expanded into a totality, found embodiment; everything that existed was transformed into a real abstraction. In that case, however, what was taken hold of and deformed by these abstractions escaped the grasp of empirical inquiry.

The fragility of the Marxist philosophy of history that implicity serves as the foundation of this attempt to develop critical theory in interdisciplinary form makes it clear why it had to fail and why Horkheimer and Adorno scaled down this program to the speculative observations of the *Dialectic of Enlightenment*. Historical-materialist assumptions regarding the dialectical relation between productive forces and productive relations had been transformed into pseudonormative propositions concerning an objective teleology in history. This was the motor force behind the realization of a reason that had been given ambiguous expression in bourgeois ideals. Critical theory could secure its normative foundations only in a philosophy of history. But this foundation was not able to support an empirical research program.

This was also evident in the lack of a clearly demarcated object domain like the communicative practice of the everyday lifeworld in which rationality structures are embodied and processes of reification can be traced. The basic concepts of critical theory placed the consciousness of individuals directly vis-à-vis economic and administrative mechanisms of integration, which were only extended inward, intrapsychically. In contrast to this, the theory of communicative action can ascertain for itself the rational content of anthropologically deep-seated structures by means of an analysis that, *to begin with*, proceeds reconstructively, that is, unhistorically. It describes structures of action and structures of mutual understanding that are found in the intuitive knowledge of competent members of modern societies. There is no way back from them to a theory of history that does not distinguish between problems of developmental logic and problems of developmental dynamics.

In this way I have attempted to free historical materialism from its philosophical ballast. Two abstractions are required for this: (i) abstracting the development of cognitive structures from the historical dynamic of events, and (ii) abstracting the evolution of society from the historical concretion of forms of life. Both help in getting beyond the confusion of basic categories to which the philosophy of history owes its existence.

A theory developed in this way can no longer start by examining concrete ideals immanent in traditional forms of life. It must orient itself to the range of learning processes that is opened up at a given time by a historically attained level of learning. It must refrain from critically evaluating and normatively ordering totalities, forms of life and cultures, and life-contexts and epochs *as a whole*. And yet it can take up some of the intentions for which the interdisciplinary research program of earlier critical theory remains instructive.

B.—Coming at the end of a complicated study of the main features of a theory of communicative action, this suggestion cannot count even as a "promissory note." It is less a promise than a conjecture. So as not to leave it entirely ungrounded, in what follows I will comment briefly on the theses mentioned above, and in the same order. With these illustrative remarks I also intend to emphasize the fully open character and the flexibility of an approach to social theory whose fruitfulness can be confirmed only in the ramifications of social and philosophical research. As to what social theory can accomplish in and of itself – it resembles the focusing power of a magnifying glass. Only when the social sciences no longer sparked a single thought would the time for social theory be past.

(a) On the forms of integration in postliberal societies. Occidental rationalism arose within the framework of bourgeois capitalist societies. For this reason, following Marx and Weber I have examined the initial conditions of modernization in connection with societies of this type and have traced the capitalist path of development. In postliberal societies there is a fork in this path: modernization pushes forward in one direction through endogenously produced problems of economic

accumulation, in the other through problems arising from the state's efforts at rationalization. Along the developmental path of organized capitalism, a political order of welfare-state mass democracy took shape. In some places, however, under the pressure of economic crises, the mode of production, threatened by social disintegration, could be maintained for a time only in the political form of authoritarian or fascist orders. Along the developmental path of bureaucratic socialism a political order of dictatorship by state parties took shape. In recent years Stalinist domination by force has given way to more moderate, post-Stalinist regimes; the beginnings of a democratic workers' movement and of democratic decision-making processes within the Party are for the time visible only in Poland. Both the fascist and the democratic deviations from the two dominant patterns depend rather strongly, it seems, on national peculiarities, particularly on the political culture of the countries in question. At any rate, these branchings make historical specifications necessary even at the most general level of types of societal integration and of corresponding social pathologies. If we permit ourselves to simplify in an ideal-typical manner and limit ourselves to the two dominant variants of postliberal societies, and if we start from the assumption that alienation phenomena arise as systemically induced deformations of the lifeworld, then we can take a few steps toward a comparative analysis of principles of societal organizations, kinds of crisis tendencies, and forms of social pathology.

On our assumption, a considerably rationalized lifeworld is one of the initial conditions for modernization processes. It must be possible to anchor money and power in the lifeworld as media, that is, to institutionalize them by means of positive law. If these conditions are met, economic and administrative systems can be differentiated out, systems that have a complementary relation to one another and enter into interchanges with their environments via steering media. At this level of system differentiation modern societies arise, first capitalist societies, and later – setting themselves off from those – bureaucratic-socialist societies. A capitalist path of modernization opens up as soon as the economic system develops its own intrinsic dynamic of growth and, with its endogenously produced problems, takes the lead, that is, the evolutionary primacy, for society as a whole. The path of modernization runs in another direction when, on the basis of state ownership of most of the means of production and an institutionalized one-party rule, the administrative action system gains a like autonomy in relation to the economic system.

To the extent that these organizational principles are established, there arise interchange relations between the two functionally interlocked subsystems and the societal components of the lifeworld in locked subsystems and the societal components of the lifeworld in which the media are anchored. The lifeworld, more or less relieved of tasks of material reproduction, can in turn become more differentiated in its symbolic structures and can set free the inner logic of development of cultural modernity. At the same time, the private and public spheres are now set off as the environments of the system. According to whether the economic system or the state apparatus attains evolutionary primacy, either private households or politically relevant memberships are the points of entry for crises that are shifted from the subsystems to the lifeworld. In modernized societies disturbances in the material reproduction of the lifeworld take the form of stubborn systemic disequilibria; the latter either take effect directly as *crises* or they call forth *pathologies* in the lifeworld.

Steering crises were first studied in connection with the business cycle of market economies. In bureaucratic socialism, crisis tendencies spring from self-blocking mechanisms in planning administrations, as they do on the other side from endogenous interruptions of accumulation processes. Like the paradoxes of exchange rationality the paradoxes of planning rationality can be explained by the fact that rational action orientations come into contradiction with themselves through unintended systemic effects. These crisis tendencies are worked through not only in the subsystem in which they arise, but also in the complementary action system into which they can be shifted. Just as the capitalist economy relies on organizational performances of the state, the socialist planning bureaucracy has to rely on self-steering performances of the economy. Developed capitalism swings between the contrary policies of "the market's self-healing powers" and state interventionism. The structural dilemma is even clearer on the other side, where policy oscillates hopelessly between increased central planning and decentralization, between orienting economic programs toward investment and toward consumption.

These *systemic disequilibria* become *crises* only when the performances of economy and state remain manifestly below an established level of aspiration and harm the symbolic reproduction of the lifeworld by calling forth conflicts and reactions of resistance there. It is the societal components of the lifeworld that are directly affected by this. Before such conflicts threaten core domains of social integration, they are pushed to the periphery – before anomic conditions arise there are appearances of withdrawal of legitimation or motivation. But when steering crises – that is, perceived disturbances of material reproduction – are successfully intercepted by having recourse to lifeworld resources, pathologies arise in the lifeworld. These resources appear as contributions to cultural reproduction, social integration, and socialization. For the continued existence of the economy and the state, it is the resources listed in the middle column as contributing to the maintenance of society that are relevant, for it is here, in the institutional orders of the lifeworld, that subsystems are anchored.

We can represent the replacement of steering crises with lifeworld pathologies as follows: anomic conditions are avoided, and legitimations and motivations important for maintaining institutional orders are secured, at the expense of, and through the ruthless exploitation of, other resources. Culture and personality come under attack for the sake of warding off crises and stabilizing society. The consequences of this substitution can be seen instead of manifestations of anomic (and instead of the withdrawal of legitimation and motivation in place of anomic), phenomena of alienation and the unsettling of collective identity emerge. I have traced such phenomena back to a colonization of the lifeworld and characterized them as a reification of the communicative practice of everyday life.

However, deformations of the lifeworld take the form of a reification of communicative relations only in capitalist societies, that is, only where the private household is the point of incursion for the displacement of crises into the lifeworld. This is not a question of the overextension of a single medium but of the monetarization and bureaucratization of the spheres of action of employees and of consumers, of citizens and of clients of state bureaucracies. Deformations of the lifeworld take a different form in societies in which the points of incursion for the penetration of crises into the lifeworld are politically relevant memberships. There too, in bureaucratic-socialist societies, domains of action that are dependent on social integration are switched over to mechanisms of system integration. But instead of the reification of communicative relations we find the shamming of communicative relations in bureaucratically desicated, forcibly "humanized" domains of pseudopolitical intercourse in an overextended and administered public sphere. This pseudopoliticization is symmetrical to reifying privatization in certain respects. The lifeworld is not directly assimilated to the system, that is, to legally regulated, formally organized domains of action; rather, systemically self-sufficient organizations are fictively put back into a simulated horizon of the lifeworld. While the system is draped out as the lifeworld, the lifeworld is absorbed by the system.

(b) Family socialization and ego development. The diagnosis of an uncoupling of system and lifeworld also offers a different perspective for judging the structural change in family, education, and personality development. For a psychoanalysis viewed from a Marxist standpoint, the theory of the Oedipus complex, interpreted sociologically, was pivotal for explaining how the functional imperatives of the economic system could establish themselves in the superego structures of the dominant social character. Thus, for example, Löwenthal's studies of drama and fiction in the nineteenth century served to show in detail that the constraints of the economic system – concentrated in status hierarchies, occupational roles, and gender stereotypes – penetrated into the innermost aspects of life history via intrafamilial dependencies and patterns of socialization. The intimacy of highly personalized relations merely concealed the blind force of economic interdependencies that had become autonomous in relation to the private sphere – a force that was experienced as "fate."

Thus the family was viewed as the agency through which systemic imperatives influenced our instinctual vicissitudes; its communicative internal structure was not taken seriously. Because the family was always viewed only from functionalist standpoints and was never given its own weight from structuralist points of view, the epochal changes in the bourgeois family could be misunderstood; in particular, the results of the leveling out of paternal authority could be interpreted wrongly. It seemed as if systemic imperatives now had the chance – by way of a mediatized family – to take hold directly of intrapsychic events, a process that the soft medium of mass culture could at most slow down. If, by contrast, we *also* recognize in the structural transformation of the bourgeois family the inherent rationalization of the lifeworld; if we see that, in egalitarian patterns of relationship, in individuated forms of intercourse, and in liberalized child-rearing practices, some of the potential for rationality ingrained in communicative action is *also* released; then the changed conditions of socialization in the middle-class nuclear family appear in a different light.

Empirical indicators suggest the growing autonomy of a nuclear family in which socialization processes take place through the medium of largely deinstitutionalized communicative action. Communicative infrastructures are developing that have freed themselves from latent entanglements in systemic dependencies. The contrast between the *homme* who is educated to freedom and humanity in the intimate sphere and the *citoyen* who obeys functional necessities in the sphere of social labor was always an ideology. But it has now taken on a different meaning. Familial lifeworlds see the imperatives of the economic and administrative systems coming at them from outside, instead of being mediatized by them from behind. In the families and their environments we can observe a polarization between communicatively structured and formally organized domains of action; this places socialization processes under different conditions and exposes them to a different type of danger. This view is supported by two rough sociopsychological clues: the diminishing significance of the Oedipal problematic and the growing significance of adolescent crises.

For some time now, psychoanalytically trained physicians have observed a symptomatic change in the typical mainfestations of illness. Classical hysterias have almost died out; the number of compulsion neuroses is drastically reduced; on the other hand, narcissistic disturbances are on the increase. Christopher Lasch has taken this symptomatic change as the occasion for a diagnosis of the times that goes beyond the clinical domain. It confirms the fact that the significant changes in the present escape sociopsychological explanations that start from the Oedipal problematic, from an internalization of societal repression which is simply masked by parental authority. The better explanations start from the premise that the communication structures that have been set free in the family provide conditions for socialization that are as demanding as they are vulnerable. The potential for irritability grows, and with it the probability that instabilities in parental behavior will have a comparatively strong effect – a subtle neglect.

The other phenomenon, a sharpening of the adolescence problematic, also speaks for the socializatory significance of the uncoupling of system and lifeworld. Systemic imperatives do not so much insinuate themselves into the family, establish themselves in systematically distorted communication, and inconspicuously intervene in the formation of the self as, rather, openly come at the family from outside. As a result, there is a tendency toward disparities between competences, attitudes, and motives, on the one hand, and the functional requirements of adult roles on the other. The problem of detaching oneself from the family and forming one's own identity have in any case turned adolescent development (which is scarcely safeguarded by institutions anymore) into a critical test for the ability of the coming generation to connect up with the preceding one. When the conditions of socialization in the family are no longer functionality in tune with the organizational membership conditions that the growing child will one day have to meet, the problems that young people have to solve in their adolescence become insoluble for more and more of them. One indication of this is the social and even political significance that youth protest and withdrawal cultures have gained since the end of the 1960s.

This new problem situation cannot be handled with the old theoretical means. If we connect the epochal changes in family socialization with the rationalization of the lifeworld, socializatory interaction becomes the point of reference for the analysis of ego development, and systematically distorted communication – the reification of interpersonal relations – the point of reference for investigating pathogenesis. The theory of communicative action provides a framework within which the structural model of ego, id, and superego can be recast. Instead of an instinct theory that represents the relation of ego to inner nature in terms of a philosophy of consciousness – on the model of relations between subject and object – we have a theory of socialization that connects Freud with Mead, gives structures of intersubjectivity their due, and replaces hypotheses about instinctual vicissitudes with assumptions about identity formation. This approach can (i) appropriate more recent developments in psychoanalytic research, particularly the theory of object relations and ego psychology, (ii) take up the theory of defense mechanisms in such a way that the interconnections between intrapsychic communication barriers and communication disturbances at the interpersonal level become comprehensible, and (iii) use the assumptions about mechanisms of conscious and unconscious mastery to establish a connection between orthogenesis and pathogenesis. The cognitive and sociomoral development studied in the Piagetian tradition takes place in accord with structural patterns that provide a reliable foil for intuitively recorded clinical deviations.

(c) Mass media and mass culture. With its distinction between system and lifeworld, the theory of communicative action brings out the independent logic of socializatory interaction; the corresponding distinction between two contrary types of communication media makes us sensitive to the ambivalent potential of mass communications. The theory makes us skeptical of the thesis that the essence of the public sphere has been liquidated in postliberal societies. According to Horkheimer and Adorno, the communication flows steered via mass media *take the place of* those communication structures that had once made possible public discussion and self-understanding by citizens and private individuals. With the shift from writing to images and sounds, the electronic media – first film and radio, later television – present themselves as an apparatus that completely permeates and dominates the language of everyday communication. On the one hand, it transforms the authentic content of modern culture into the sterilized and ideologically effective stereotypes of a mass culture that merely replicates what exists; on the other hand, it uses up a culture cleansed of all subversive and transcending elements for an encompassing system of social controls, which is spread over individuals, in part reinforcing their weakened internal behavioral controls, in part replacing them. The mode of functioning of the culture industry is said to be a mirror image of the psychic apparatus, which, as long as the internalization of paternal authority was still functioning, had subjected instinctual nature to the control of the superego in the way that technology had subjected outer nature to its domination.

Against this theory we can raise the empirical objections that can always be brought against stylizing oversimplifications – that it proceeds ahistorically and does not take into consideration the structural change in the bourgeois public sphere; that it is not complex enough to take account of the marked national difference – from differences between private, public-legal, and state-controlled organizational structures of broadcasting agencies, to differences in programming, viewing practices, political culture, and so forth. But there is an even more serious objection, an objection in principle, that can be derived from the dualism of media discussed above.

I distinguished two sorts of media that can ease the burden of the (risky and demanding) coordinating mechanism of reaching understanding: on the one hand, steering media, via which subsystems are differentiated out of the lifeworld; on the other hand, generalized forms of communication, which do not replace reaching agreement in language but merely condense it, and thus remain tied to lifeworld contexts. Steering media uncouple the coordination of action from building consensus in language altogether and neutralize it in regard to the alternative of coming to an agreement or failing to do so. In the other case we are dealing with a specialization of linguistic processes of consensus formation that remains dependent on recourse to the resources of the lifeworld background. The mass media belong to these generalized forms of communication. They free communication processes from the provinciality of spatiotemporally restricted contexts and permit public spheres to emerge, through establishing the abstract simultaneity of a virtually present network of communication contents far removed in space and time and through keeping messages available for manifold contexts.

These media publics hierarchize and at the same time remove restrictions on the horizon of possible communication. The one aspect cannot be separated from the other – and therein lies their ambivalent potential. Insofar as mass media one-sidedly channel communication flows in a centralized network – from the center to the periphery or from above to below – they considerably strengthen the efficacy of social controls. But tapping this authoritarian potential is always precarious because there is a counterweight of emancipatory potential built into communication structures themselves. Mass media can simultaneously contextualize and concentrate processes of reaching understanding, but it is only in the first instance that they relieve interaction from yes/no responses to criticizable validity claims. Abstracted and clustered though they are, these communications cannot be reliably shielded from the possibility of opposition by responsible actors.

When communications research is not abridged in an empiricist manner and allows for dimensions of reification in communicative everyday practice it confirms this ambivalence. Again and again reception research and program analysis have provided illustrations of the theses in culture criticism that Adorno, above all, developed with a certain overstatement. In the meantime, the same energy has been put into working out the contradications resulting from the facts that

- the broadcasting networks are exposed to competing interests; they are not able to smoothly integrate economic, political and ideological, professional and aesthetic viewpoints;
- normally the mass media cannot, without generating conflict, avoid the obligations that accrue to them from their journalistic mission and the professional code of journalism;
- the programs do not only, or even for the most part, reflect the standards of mass culture; even when they take the trivial forms of popular entertainment, they may contain critical messages – "popular culture as popular revenge";
- ideological messages miss their audience because the intended meaning is turned into its opposite under conditions of being received against a certain subcultural background;
- the inner logic of everyday communicative practice sets up defenses against the direct manipulative intervention of the mass media; and
- the technical development of electronic media does not necessarily move in the direction of centralizing networks, even though "video pluralism" and "television democracy" are at the moment not much more than anarchist visions.

(d) *Potentials for protest* My thesis concerning the colonization of the lifeworld, for which Weber's theory of societal rationalization served as a point of departure, is based on a critique of functionalist reason, which agrees with the critique of instrumental reason only in its intention and in its ironic use of the word 'reason'. One major difference is that the theory of communicative action conceives of the lifeworld as a sphere in which processes of reification do not appear as mere reflexes – as manifestations of a repressive integration emanating from an oligopolistic economy and an authoritarian state. In this respect, the earlier critical theory merely repeated the errors of Marxist functionalism. My references to the socializatory relevance of the uncoupling of system and lifeworld and my remarks on the ambivalent potentials of mass media and mass culture show the private and public spheres in the light of a rationalized life-world in which system imperatives *clash with* independent communication structures. The transposition of communicative action to media-steered interactions and the deformation of the structures of a damaged intersubjectivity are by no means predecided processes that might be distilled from a few global concepts. The analysis of life-world pathologies calls for an (unbiased) investigation of tendencies *and* contradictions. The fact that in welfare-state mass democracies class conflict has been institutionalized and thereby pacified does not mean that protest potential has been altogether laid to rest. But the potentials for protest emerge now along different lines of conflict – just where we would expect them to emerge if the thesis of the colonization of the lifeworld were correct.

In the past decade or two, conflicts have developed in advanced Western societies that deviate in various ways from the welfare-state pattern of institutionalized conflict over distribution. They no longer flare up in domains of material reproduction; they are no longer channeled through parties and associations; and they can no longer be allayed by compensations. Rather, these new conflicts arise in domains of cultural reproduction, social integration, and socialization; they are carried out in subinstitutional – or at least extraparliamentary – forms of protest; and the underlying deficits reflect a reification of communicatively structured domains of action that will not respond to the media of money and power. The issue is not primarily one of compensations that the welfare state can provide, but of defending and restoring endangered ways of life. In short, the new conflicts are not ignited by distribution problems but by questions having to do with the grammar of forms of life.

This new type of conflict is an expression of the "silent revolution" in values and attitudes that R. Inglehart has observed in entire populations. Studies by Hildebrandt and Dalton, and by Barnes and Kaase, confirm the change in themes from the "old politics" (which turns on questions of economic and social security, internal and military security) to a "new politics." The new problems have to do with quality of life, equal rights, individual self-realization, participation, and human rights. In terms of social statistics, the "old politics" is more strongly supported by employers, workers, and middle-class tradesmen, whereas the new politics finds stronger support in the new middle classes, among the younger generation, and in groups with more formal education. These phenomena tally with my thesis regarding internal colonization.

If we take the view that the growth of the economic-administrative complex sets off processes of erosion in the lifeworld, then we would expect old conflicts to be overlaid with new ones. A line of conflict forms between, on the one hand, a center composed of strata *directly* involved in the production process and interested in maintaining capitalist growth as the basis of the welfare-state compromise, and, on the other hand, a periphery composed of a variegated array of groups that are lumped together. Among the latter are those groups that are further removed from the "productivist core of performance" in late capitalist societies, that have been more strongly sensitized to the self-destructive consequences of the growth in complexity or have been more strongly affected by them. The bond that unites these heterogeneous groups is the critique of growth. Neither the bourgeois emancipation movements nor the struggles of the organized labor movement can serve as a model for this protest. Historical parallels are more likely to be found in the social-romantic movements of the early industrial period, which were supported by craftsmen, plebians, and workers, in the defensive movements of the populist middle class, in the escapist movements (nourished by bourgeois critiques of civilization) undertaken by reformers, the *Wandervögel*, and the like.

The current potentials for protest are very difficult to classify, because scenes, groupings, and topics change very rapidly. To the extent that organizational nuclei are formed at the level of parties or associations, members are recruited from the same diffuse reservoir. The following catchphrases serve at the moment to identify the various currents in the Federal Republic of Germany: the antinuclear and environmental movements; the peace movement (including the theme of north-south conflict); single-issue and local movements; the alternative movement (which encompasses the urban "scene," with its squatters and alternative projects, as well as the rural communes); the minorities (the elderly, gays, handicapped, and so forth); the psychoscene, with support groups and youth sects; religious fundamentalism; the tax-protest movement, school protest by parents' associations, resistance to "modernist" reforms; and, finally, the women's movement. Of international significance are the autonomy movements struggling for regional, linguistic, cultural, and also religious independence.

In this spectrum I will differentiate emancipatory potentials from potentials for resistance and withdrawal. After the American civil rights movement – which has since issued in a particularistic self-affirmation of black subcultures – only the feminist movement stands in the tradition of bourgeois-socialist liberation movements. The struggle against patriarchal oppression and for the redemption of a promise that has long been anchored in the acknowledged universalistic foundations of morality and law gives feminism the impetus of an offensive movement, whereas the other movements have a more defensive character. The resistance and withdrawal movements aim at stemming formally organized domains of action for the sake of communicatively structured domains, and not at conquering new territory. There is an element of particularism that connects feminism with these movements; the emancipation of women means not only establishing formal equality and eliminating male privilege, but overturning concrete forms of life marked by male monopolies. Furthermore, the historical legacy of the sexual division of labor to which women were subjected in the bourgeois nuclear family has given them access to contrasting virtues, to a register of values complementary to those of the male world and opposed to a one-sidedly rationalized everyday practice.

Within resistance movements we can distinguish further between the defense of traditional and social-rank (based on property) and a defense that already operates on the basis of a rationalized lifeworld and tries out new ways of cooperating and living together. This criterion makes it possible to demarcate the protest of the traditional middle classes against threats to neighborhoods by large technical projects, the protest of parents against comprehensive schools, the protest against taxes (patterned after the movement in support of Proposition 13 in California), and most of the movements for autonomy, on the one side, from the core of a new conflict potential, on the other; youth and alternative movements for which a critique of growth sparked by themes of ecology and peace is the common focus. It is possible to conceive of these conflicts in terms of resistance to tendencies toward a colonization of the lifeworld, as I hope now to indicate, at least in a cursory way. The objectives, attitudes, and ways of acting prevalent in youth protest groups can be understood, to begin with, as reactions to certain problem situations that are perceived with great sensitivity.

"Green" problems. The intervention of large-scale industry into ecological balances, the growing scarcity of nonrenewable natural resources, as well as demographic developments present industrially developed societies with major problems; but these challenges are abstract at first and call for technical and economic solutions, which must in turn be globally planned and implemented by administrative means. What sets off the protest is rather the tangible destruction of the urban environment; the despoliation of the countryside through housing developments, industrialization, and pollution; the impairment of health through the ravages of civilization, pharmaceutical side effects, and the like – that is, developments that noticeably affect the organic foundations of the lifeworld and make us drastically aware of standards of livability, of inflexible limits to the deprivation of sensual-aesthetic background needs.

Problems of excessive complexity. There are certainly good reasons to fear military potentials for destruction, nuclear power plants, atomic waste, genetic engineering, the storage and central utilization of private data, and the like. These real anxieties are combined, however, with the terror of a new category of risks that are literally invisible and are comprehensible only from the perspective of the system. These risks invade the lifeworld and at the same time burst its dimensions. The anxieties function as catalysts for a feeling of being overwhelmed in view of the possible consequences of processes for which we are morally accountable – since we do set them in motion technically and politically – and yet for which we can no longer take moral responsibility – since their scale has put them beyond our control. Here resistance is directed against abstractions that are forced upon the lifeworld, although they go beyond the spatial, temporal, and social limits of complexity of even highly differentiated lifeworlds, centered as these are around the senses.

Overburdening the communicative infrastructure. Something that is expressed rather blatantly in the manifestations of the psychomovement and renewed religious fundamentalism is also a motivating force behind most alternative projects and many citizens' action groups – the painful manifestations of deprivation in a culturally impoverished and one-sidedly rationalized practice of everyday life. For this reason, ascriptive characteristics such as gender, age, skin color, neighborhood or locality, and religious affiliation serve to build up and separate off communities, to establish subculturally protected communities supportive of the search for personal and collective identity. The revaluation of the particular, the natural, the provincial, of social spaces that are small enough to be familiar, of decentralized forms of commerce and despecialized activities, of segmented pubs, simple interactions and dedifferentiated public spheres – all this is meant to foster the revitalization of possibilities for expression and communication that have been buried alive. Resistance to reformist interventions that turn into their opposite, because the means by which they are implemented run counter to the declared aims of social integration, also belongs in this context.

The new conflicts arise along the seams between system and life-world. Earlier I described how the interchange between the private and public spheres, on the one hand, and the economic and administrative action systems, on the other, takes place via the media of money and power, and how it is institutionalized in the roles of employees and consumers, citizens and clients of the state. It is just these roles that are the targets of protest. Alternative practice is directed against the profit-dependent instrumentalization of work in one's vocation, the market-dependent mobilization of labor power, against the extension of pressures of competition and performance all the way down into elementary school. It also takes aim at the monetarization of services, relationships, and time, at the consumerist redefinition of private spheres of life and personal life-styles. Furthermore, the relation of clients to public service agencies is to be opened up and reorganized in a participatory mode, along the lines of self-help organizations. It is above all in the domains of social policy and health policy (e.g., in connection with psychiatric care) that models of reform point in this direction. Finally, certain forms of protest negate the definitions of the role of citizen and the routines for pursuing interests in a purposive-rational manner – forms ranging from the undirected explosion of disturbances by youth ("Zurich is burning!"), through calculated or surrealistic violations of rules (after the pattern of the American civil rights movement and student protests), to violent provocation and intimidation.

According to the programmatic conceptions of some theoreticians, a partial disintegration of the social roles of employees and consumers, of clients and citizens of the state, is supposed to clear the way for counterinstitutions that develop from within the lifeworld in order to set limits to the inner dynamics of the economic and political-administrative action systems. These institutions are supposed, on the one hand, to divert out of the economic system a second, informal sector that is no longer oriented to profit and, on the other hand, to oppose to the party system new forms of a "politics in the first person," a politics that is expressive and at the same time has a democratic base. Such institutions would reverse just those abstractions and neutralizations by which in modern societies labor and political will-formation have been tied to media-steered interaction. The capitalist enterprise and the mass party (as an "ideology-neutral organization for acquiring power") generalize their points of social entry via labor markets and manufactured public spheres; they treat their employees and voters as abstract labor power and voting subjects; and they keep at a distance – as environments of the system – those spheres in which personal and collective identities can alone take shape. By contrast, the counterinstitutions are intended to dedifferentiate some parts of the formally organized domains of action, remove them from the clutches of the steering media, and return these "liberated areas" to the action-coordinating mechanism of reaching understanding.

However unrealistic these ideas may be, they are important for the polemical significance of the new resistance and withdrawal movements reacting to the colonization of the lifeworld. This significance is obscured, both in the self-understanding of those involved and in the ideological imputations of their opponents, if the

communicative rationality of cultural modernity is rashly equated with the functionalist rationality of self-maintaining economic and administrative action systems –
that is, whenever the rationalization of the lifeworld is not carefully distinguished
from the increasing complexity of the social system. This confusion explains the
fronts – which are out of place and obscure the real political oppositions – between
the antimodernism of the Young Conservatives and the neoconservative defense of
postmodernity that robs a modernity at variance with itself of its rational content
and its perspectives on the future.

C—In this work I have tried to introduce a theory of communicative action that
clarifies the normative foundations of a critical theory of society. The theory of
communicative action is meant to provide an alternative to the philosophy of history
on which earlier critical theory still relied, but which is no longer tenable. It is
intended as a framework within which interdisciplinary research on the selective
pattern of capitalist modernization can be taken up once again. The illustrative
observations (a) through (d) were meant to make this claim plausible. The two
additional themes (e) and (f) are a reminder that the investigation of what Marx
called "real abstraction" has to do with the social-scientific tasks of a theory of
modernity, not the philosophical. Social theory need no longer ascertain the normative contents of bourgeois culture, of art and of philosophical thought, in an indirect
way, that is, by way of a critique of ideology. With the concept of a communicative
reason ingrained in the use of language oriented to reaching understanding, it again
expects from philosophy that it take on systematic tasks. The social sciences can
enter into a cooperative relation with a philosophy that has taken up the task of
working on a theory of rationality.
    It is no different with modern culture as a whole than it was with the physics of
Newton and his heirs: modern culture is as little in need of a philosophical
grounding as science. As we have seen, in the modern period culture gave rise of
itself to those structures of rationality that Weber then discovered and described as
value spheres. With modern science, with positive law and principled secular ethics,
with autonomous art and institutionalized art criticism, three moments of reason
crystalized without help from philosophy. Even without the guidance of the critiques
of pure and practical reason, the sons and daughters of modernity learned how to
divide up and develop further the cultural tradition under these different aspects of
rationality – as questions of truth, justice, or taste. More and more the sciences
dropped the elements of worldviews and do without an interpretation of nature and
history as a whole. Cognitive ethics separates off problems of the good life and
concentrates on strictly deontological, universalizable aspects, so that what remains
from the Good is only the Just. And an art that has become autonomous pushes
toward an ever purer expression of the basic aesthetic experiences of a subjectivity
that is decentered and removed from the spatiotemporal structures of everyday life.
Subjectivity frees itself here from the conventions of daily perception and of purposive activity, from the imperatives of work and of what is merely useful.
    These magnificient "one-sidednesses," which are the signature of modernity, need
no foundation and no justification in the sense of a transcendental grounding, but
they do call for a self-understanding regarding the character of this knowledge. Two
questions must be answered: (i) whether a reason that has objectively split up into its

moments can still preserve its unity, and (ii) how expert cultures can be mediated with everyday practice. The reflections offered earlier are intended as a provisional account of how formal pragmatics can deal with these questions. With that as a basis, the theory of science, the theory of law and morality, and aesthetics, in cooperation with the corresponding historical disciplines, can then reconstruct both the emergence and the internal history of those modern complexes of knowledge that have been differentiated out, each under a different single aspect of validity – truth, normative rightness, or authenticity.

The mediation of the moments of reason is no less a problem than the separation of the aspects of rationality under which questions of truth, justice, and taste were differentiated from one another. The only protection against an empiricist abridgement of the rationality problematic is a steadfast pursuit of the tortuous routes along which science, morality, and art communicate with one another. In each of these spheres, differentiation processes are accompanied by countermovements that, under the primacy of one dominant aspect of validity, bring back in again the two aspects that were at first excluded. Thus nonobjectivist approaches to research within the human sciences bring viewpoints of moral and aesthetic critique to bear – without threatening the primacy of questions of truth; only in this way is critical social theory made possible. Within universalistic ethics the discussion of the ethics of responsibility and the stronger consideration given to hedonistic motives bring the calculation of consequences and the interpretation of needs into play – and they lie in the domains of the cognitive and the expressive; in this way materialist ideas can come in without threatening the autonomy of the moral. Finally, post-avant-garde art is characterized by the coexistence of tendencies toward realism and engagement with those authentic continuations of classical modern art that distilled out the independent logic of the aesthetic; in realist art and *l'art engagé*, moments of the cognitive and of the moral-practical come into play again in art itself, and at the level of the wealth of forms that the avant-garde set free. It seems as if the radically differentiated moments of reason want in such countermovements to point toward a unity – not a unity that could be had at the level of worldviews, but one that might be established *this side* of expert cultures, in a nonreified communicative everyday practice.

How does this sort of affirmative role for philosophy square with the reserve that critical theory always maintained in regard to both the established scientific enterprise and the systematic pretensions of philosophy? Is not such a theory of rationality open to the same objections that pragmatism and hermeneutics have brought against every kind of foundationalism? Do not investigations that employ the concept of communicative reason without blushing bespeak universalistic justificatory claims that will have to fall to those – only too well grounded – metaphilosophical doubts about theories of absolute origins and ultimate grounds? Have not both the historicist enlightenment and materialism forced philosophy into a self-modesty for which the tasks of a theory of rationality must already appear extravagant? The theory of communicative action aims at the moment of unconditionality that, with criticizable validity claims, is built into the conditions of processes of consensus formation. *As claims* they transcend all limitations of space and time, all the provincial limitations of the given context. Rather than answer these questions here with arguments already set out, I shall close by adding two methodological arguments that speak against the suspicion that the theory of communicative action is guilty of foundationalist claims.

First we must see how philosophy changes its role when it enters into cooperation with the sciences. As the "feeder" [*Zubringer*] for a theory of rationality, it finds itself in a division of labor with reconstructive sciences; these sciences take up the pretheoretical knowledge of compentently judging, acting, and speaking subjects, as well as the collective knowledge of traditions, in order to get at the most general features of the rationality of experience and judgment, action and mutual understanding in language. In this context, reconstructions undertaken with philosophical means also retain a hypothetical character; precisely because of their strong universalistic claims, they are open to further, indirect testing. This can take place in such a way that the reconstructions of universal and necessary presuppositions of communicative action, of argumentative speech, of experience and of objectivating thought, of moral judgments and of aesthetic critique, enter into empirical theories that are supposed to explain *other* phenomena – for example, the ontogenesis of language and of communicative abilities, of moral judgment and social competence; the structural transformation of religious-metaphysical worldviews; the development of legal systems or of forms of social integration generally.

From the perspective of the history of theory, I have taken up the work of Mead, Weber, and Durkheim and tried to show how in their approaches, which are simultaneously empirical and reconstructive, the operations of empirical science and of philosophical conceptual analysis intermesh. The best example of this cooperative division of labor is Piaget's genetic theory of knowledge.

A philosophy that opens its results to indirect testing in this way is guided by the fallibilistic consciousness that the theory of rationality it once wanted to develop on its own can now be sought only in the felicitous coherence of different theoretical fragments. Coherence is the sole criterion of considered choice at the level on which mutually fitting theories stand to one another in relations of supplementing and reciprocally presupposing, for it is only the individual propositions derivable from theories that are true or false. Once we have dropped foundationalist claims, we can no longer expect a hierarchy of sciences; theories – whether social scientific or philosophical in origin – have to fit with one another, unless one puts the other in a problematic light and we have to see whether it suffices to revise the one or the other.

The test case for a theory of rationality with which the modern understanding of the world is to ascertain its own universality would certainly include throwing light on the opaque figures of mythical thought, clarifying the bizarre expressions of alien cultures, and indeed in such a way that we not only comprehend the learning processes that separate "us" from "them," but also become aware of what we have *unlearned* in the course of this learning. A theory of society that does not close itself off a priori to this possibility of unlearning has to be critical also in relation to the preunderstanding that accrues to it from its own social setting, that is, it has to be open to self-criticism. Processes of unlearning can be gotten at through a critique of deformations that are rooted in the selective exploitation of a potential for rationality and mutual understanding that was once available but is now buried over.

There is also another reason why the theory of society based on the theory of communicative action cannot stray into foundationalist byways. Insofar as it refers to structures of the lifeworld, it has to explicate a background knowledge over which no one can dispose at will. The lifeworld is at first "given" to the theoretician (as it is to the layperson) as his or her own, and in a paradoxical manner. The mode of preunderstanding or of intuitive knowledge of the lifeworld from within which we live together, act and speak with one another, stands in peculiar contrast, as we have seen, to the explicit knowledge of something. The horizontal knowledge that communicative everyday practice *tacitly* carries with it is paradigmatic for the *certainty* with which the lifeworld background is present; yet it does not satisfy the criterion of knowledge that stands in internal relation to validity claims and can therefore be criticized. That which stands beyond all doubt seems as if it could never become problematic; as what is simply unproblematic, a lifeworld can at most fall apart. It is only under the pressure of approaching problems that relevant components of such background knowledge are torn out of their unquestioned familiarity and brought to consciousness as something in need of being ascertained. It takes an earthquake to make us aware that we had regarded the ground on which we stand everyday as unshakable. Even in situations of this sort, only a small segment of our background knowledge becomes uncertain and is set loose after having been enclosed in complex traditions, in solidaric relations, in competences. If the objective occasion arises for us to arrive at some understanding about a situation that has become problematic, background knowledge is transformed into explicit knowledge only in a piecemeal manner.

This has an important methodological implication for sciences that have to do with cultural tradition, social integration, and the socialization of individuals – an implication that became clear to pragmatism and to hermeneutic philosophy, each in its own way, as they came to doubt the possibility of Cartesian doubt. Alfred Schutz, who so convincingly depicted the lifeworld's mode of unquestioned familiarity, nevertheless missed just this problem: whether a lifeworld, in its opaque take-for-grantedness, eludes the phenomenologist's inquiring gaze or is opened up to it does not depend on just *choosing* to adopt a theoretical attitude. The totality of the background knowledge constitutive for the construction of the lifeworld is no more at his disposition than at that of any social scientist – unless an objective challenge arises, in the face of which the lifeworld as a whole becomes problematic. Thus a theory that wants to ascertain the general structures of the lifeworld cannot adopt a transcendental approach; it can only hope to be equal to the *ratio essendi* of its object when there are grounds for assuming that the objective context of life in which the theoretician finds himself is opening up to him its *ratio cognoscendi*.

This implication accords with the point behind Horkheimer's critique of science in his programmatic essay "Traditional and Critical Theory": "The traditional idea of theory is abstracted from scientific activity as it is carried on within the division of labor at a particular stage in the latter's development. It corresponds to the activity of the scholar which takes place alongside all the other activities of a society, but in no immediately clear connection with them. In this view of theory, therefore, the real social function of science is not made manifest; it conveys not what theory means in human life, but only what it means in the isolated sphere in which, for historical reasons, it comes into existence." As opposed to this, critical social theory is to become conscious of the self-referentiality of its calling; it knows that in and through the very act of knowing it belongs to the objective context of life that it strives to grasp. The context of its emergence does not remain external to the theory; rather, the theory takes this reflectively up into itself: "In this intellectual activity the needs and goals, the experiences and skills, the customs and tendencies of the contemporary form of human existence have all played their part." The same holds true for the context of application: "As the influence of the subject matter on the theory, so also the application of the theory to the subject matter is not only an intrascientific process but a social one as well."

In his famous methodological introduction to his critique of political economy of 1857, Marx applied the type of reflection called for by Horkheimer to one of his central concepts. He explained there why the basic assumptions of political economy rest on a seemingly simple abstraction, which is in fact quite difficult:

> It was an immense step forward for Adam Smith to throw out every limiting specification of wealth-creating activity – not only manufacturing, or commercial, or agricultural labor, but one as well as the others, labor in general. With the abstract universality of wealth-creating activity we now have the universality of the object defined as wealth, the product as such or again labor as such, but labor as past objectified labor. How difficult and great this transition was may be seen from how Adam Smith himself from time to time still falls back into the Physiocratic system. Now it might seem that all that had been achieved thereby was to discover the abstract expression for the simplest and most ancient relation in which human beings – in whatever form of society – play the role of producers. This is correct in one respect. Not in another... Indifference toward specific labors corresponds to a form of society in which individuals can with ease transfer from one labor to another, and where the specific kind is a matter of chance for them, hence of indifference. Not only the category 'labor', but labor in reality has here become the means of creating wealth in general, and has ceased to be organically linked with particular individuals in any specific form. Such a state of affairs is at its most developed in the modern form of existence of bourgeois society – in the United States. Here, then, for the first time, the point of departure of modern economics, namely the abstraction of the category 'labor', 'labor as such', labor pure and simple, becomes true in practice.

Smith was able to lay the foundations of modern economics only after a mode of production arose that, like the capitalist mode with its differentiation of an economic system steered via exchange value, forced a transformation of concrete activities into abstract performances, intruded into the world of work with this real abstraction, and thereby created a problem for the workers themselves: "Thus the simplest abstraction which modern economics places at the head of its discussions and which expresses an immeasurably ancient relation valid in all forms of society, nevertheless achieves practical truth as an abstraction only as a category of the most modern society."

A theory of society that claims universality for its basic concepts, without being allowed simply to bring them to bear upon their object in a conventional manner, remains caught up in the self-referentiality that Marx demonstrated in connection with the concept of abstract labor. As I have argued above, when labor is rendered abstract and indifferent, we have a special case of the transference of communicatively structured domains of action over to media-steered interaction. This interpretation decodes the deformations of the lifeworld with the help of another category, namely, "communicative action." What Marx showed to be the case in regard to the category of labor holds true for this as well: "how even the most abstract categories, despite their validity – precisely because of their abstractness – for all epochs, are nevertheless, in the specific character of this abstraction, themselves likewise a product of historical relations, and possess their full validity only for and within these relations." The theory of communicative action can explain why this is so: the development of society must *itself* give rise to the problem situations that *objectively* afford contemporaries a privileged access to the general structures of the lifeworld.

The theory of modernity that I have here sketched in broad strokes permits us to recognize the following: In modern societies there is such an expansion of the scope of contingency for interaction loosed from normative contexts that the inner logic of communicative action "becomes practically true" in the deinstitutionalized forms of intercourse of the familial private sphere as well as in a public sphere stamped by the mass media. At the same time, the systemic imperatives of autonomous subsystems penetrate into the lifeworld and, through monetarization and bureaucratization, force an assimilation of communicative action to formally organized domains of action – even in areas where the action-coordinating mechanism of reaching understanding is functionally necessary. It may be that this provocative threat, this challenge that places the symbolic structures of the lifeworld as a whole in question, can account for why they have become accessible to us.

28 Theory and Practice

Jürgen Habermas

Knowledge and Interest

In the social philosophical essays on Theory and Praxis I have not treated epistemological questions systematically. Nor is that the context within which the history of these problems is treated in my book *Knowledge and Human Interests* or in my inaugural lecture of the same title, if one were to apply rigid standards. Still, I have carried my historical investigations and exploratory considerations sufficiently far, that the program for a theory of science becomes clearly discernible, a theory which is intended to be capable of grasping systematically the constitutive conditions of science and those of its application. I have let myself be guided by the problem posed by the system of primitive terms (or the "transcendental framework") within which we organize our experience *a priori* and prior to all science, and do so in such a manner that, of course, the formation of the scientific object domains is also prejudiced by this. In the functional sphere of instrumental action we encounter objects of the type of moving bodies; here we experience things, events, and conditions which are, in principle, capable of being manipulated. In interactions (or at the level of possible intersubjective communication) we encounter objects of the type of speaking and acting subjects; here we experience persons, utterances, and conditions which in principle are structured and to be understood symbolically. The object domains of the empirical-analytic and of the hermeneutic sciences are based on these objectifications of reality, which we undertake daily always from the viewpoint either of technical control or intersubjective communication. This is revealed by a methodological comparison of the fundamental theoretical concepts, the logical construction of the theorems, the relationship of theory to the object domain, the criteria of verification, the testing procedures, and so forth. Striking above all is the difference in the pragmatic function which the information produced by the different sciences can have. Empirical analytic knowledge can assume the form of causal explanations or conditional predictions, which also refer to the observed phenomena; hermeneutic knowledge as a rule has the form of interpretations of traditional complexes of meaning. There is a systematic relationship between the logical structure of a science and the pragmatic structure of the possible applications of the information generated within its framework.

This differentiated relevance to action of the two categories of science just mentioned, I have traced back to the condition that in the constitution of scientific object domains we merely extend the everyday procedure of objectifying reality under the

Originally translated by John Vierte.

viewpoints either of technical control or of intersubjective communication. These two viewpoints express anthropologically deep-seated interests, which direct our knowledge and which have a quasi-transcendental status. These interests of knowledge are of significance neither for the psychology nor for the sociology of knowledge, nor for the critique of ideology in any narrower sense; for they are invariant. Nor, on the other hand, can they be traced back to the biological heritage of a concrete motivational potential; for they are abstract. Rather, they result from the imperatives of a sociocultural life-form dependent on labor and language. Therefore the technical and practical interests of knowledge are not regulators of cognition which have to be eliminated for the sake of the objectivity of knowledge; instead, they themselves determine the aspect under which reality is objectified, and can thus be made accessible to experience to begin with. They are the conditions which are necessary in order that subjects capable of speech and action may have experience which can lay a claim to objectivity. Of course, the expression "interest" is intended to indicate the unity of the life context in which cognition is embedded: expressions capable of truth have reference to a reality which is objectified (i.e. simultaneously disclosed and constituted) as such in two different contexts of action and experience. The underlying "interest" establishes the unity between this constitutive context in which knowledge is rooted and the structure of the possible application which this knowledge can have.

The sciences do not incorporate into their methodological understanding of themselves this basis of interest which serves as the *a priori* link between the origins and the applications of their theories. However, the critiques which Marx developed as a theory of society and Freud as metapsychology are distinguished precisely by incorporating in their consciousness an interest which directs knowledge, an interest in emancipation going beyond the technical and the practical interest of knowledge. By treating psychoanalysis as an analysis of language aiming at reflection about oneself, I have sought to show how the relations of power embodied in systematically distorted communication can be attacked directly by the process of critique, so that in the self-reflection, which the analytic method has made possible and provoked, in the end insight can coincide with emancipation from unrecognized dependencies – that is, knowledge coincides with the fulfillment of the interest in liberation through knowledge. Therefore the relation of theory to therapy is just as constitutive for Freudian theory as the relation of theory to praxis is for Marxist theory. This can be shown in detail in the logical form of general interpretations and in the pragmatic achievements of explanatory understanding (in comparison to causal explanation and hermeneutic understanding).

Methodological Problems

From the circumstance that theories of the critical type themselves reflect on their (structural) constitutive context and their (potential) context of application, results a changed relation to empirical practice, as a kind of methodological inner view of the relation of theory to practice. In the investigations which were collected in the anthology *On the Logic of the Social Sciences* (Frankfurt 1970) and also in the essay "Universalitätsanspruch der Hermeneutik" ["The Claim to Universality of Hermeneutics"] as well as in my discussions with Luhmann, I have sought to trace the most important methodological questions, to be sure, in a rather problematic and not sufficiently explicit form: the questions which arise from the program and the conceptual strategy of a theory of society which has practical aims. If we begin with the distinctive position of the cognitive subject with respect to an object domain which is constructed of the generative performance of subjects capable of speech and action, and which at the same time has gained objective power over these subjects, we can delimit our perspective in terms of four competing approaches:

(1) Confronted with the objectivism of strictly behavioral sciences, critical sociology guards itself against a reduction of intentional action to behavior. When the object domain consists of symbolically structured formations which are generated according to underlying rule systems, then the categorial framework cannot remain indifferent toward that which is specific to ordinary language communication. Access to the data via understanding of meanings must be permitted. From this results the problem of measurement which is typical for the social sciences. In place of controlled observation, which guarantees the anonymity (exchangeability) of the observing subject and thus of the reproducibility of the observation, there arises a participatory relation of the understanding subject to the subject confronting him [*Gegenueber*] (alter ego). The paradigm is no longer the observation but the dialogue – thus, a communication in which the understanding subject must invest a part of his subjectivity, no matter in what manner this may be controllable, in order to be able to meet confronting subjects at all on the intersubjective level which makes understanding possible. To be sure (as the example of the ground rules for the psychoanalytic dialogue shows) this makes disciplinary constraints more necessary than ever. The fashionable demand for a type of "action research," that is to combine political enlightenment with research, overlooks that the uncontrolled modification of the field is incompatible with the simultaneous gathering of data in that field, a condition which is also valid for the social sciences. All operations which can be traced back to the language game of physical measurement (even those with instruments which can only be constructed with the aid of complicated theories) can be coordinated with sense perceptions ("observations") and a thing-event language in which the observations can be expressed descriptively. On the other hand, there is no corresponding system of basic measuring operations with which we can coordinate, in an analogous manner, the understanding of meanings based on the observation of signs, as well as a language expressive of a person, that is, in which the understood utterances could be expressed descriptively. There we resort to interpretation based on hermeneutic disciplines, that is, we employ hermeneutics instead of a measurement procedure, which hermeneutics is not. It can be assumed that a theory of ordinary language communication would first be required which does not perfect communicative competence but rather explains it, in order to permit a controlled translation of communicative experience into data (just as logic provides a normative basis for the construction of measurement procedures in certain investigations into the psychology of cognitive development, or transformational grammar in the investigation of the psycholinguistics of children's language acquisition).

(2) Confronted with the idealism of the hermeneutics developed for the sciences of the mind, critical sociology guards itself against reducing the meaning complexes objectified within social systems to the contents of cultural tradition. Critical of

ideology, it asks what lies behind the consensus, presented as a fact, that supports the dominant tradition of the time, and does so with a view to the relations of power surreptitiously incorporated in the symbolic structures of the systems of speech and action. The immunizing power of ideologies, which stifle the demands for justification raised by discursive examination, goes back to blockages in communication, independently of the changing semantic contents. These blocks have their origin within the structures of communication themselves, which for certain contents limit the options between verbal and nonverbal forms of expression, between the communicative and the cognitive uses of language, and finally between communicative action and discourse, or even exclude such options entirely; they thus require explanation within the framework of a theory of systematically distorted communication. And if such a theory, in conjunction with a universal pragmatics, could be developed in a satisfactory manner and could be linked convincingly with the precisely rendered fundamental assumptions of historical materialism, then a systematic comprehension of cultural tradition would not be excluded. Perhaps verifiable assumptions about the logic of the development of moral systems, of structures of the world images and corresponding cult practices, could result from a theory of social evolution; this would reveal whether, as it seems, the contingent manifold of traditional meanings, which are organized within the framework of world images, vary systematically according to features understandable in terms of universal pragmatics.

(3) Confronted with the universalism of a comprehensively designed systems theory, critical sociology guards itself against the reduction of all social conflicts to unsolved problems in the regulation of self-governing systems. It is certainly meaningful to conceive social systems as entities which solve objectively posed problems by means of supra-subjective learning processes; however, the reference system of machine cybernetics proves useful only insofar as a solution of problems of control is involved. Among other things, social systems are distinguished from machines (with learning capacity) and from organisms by the fact that subjective learning processes take place and are organized within the framework of ordinary language communication. A systems concept which is more appropriate to the social sciences (and which is not designed solely for the production of strategies and organizations, that is, for the extension of control capabilities) can therefore not be taken over from general systems theory; it must be developed in relation with a theory of ordinary language communication, which also takes into consideration the relationship of intersubjectivity and the relation between ego and group identity. Ultra-stability – or in Luhmann's formulation, the reduction of the world's complexity by means of increasing system complexity [*Eigenkomplexitaet*] – represents a designation of goals which results unavoidably from a functionalistic conceptual strategy, although especially on the sociocultural level of evolution the problem of continued existence [*Bestandsproblem*] becomes diffuse, and the talk of "survival" metaphorical.

(4) Finally, confronted with the dogmatic heritage of the philosophy of history, critical sociology must guard against overburdening the concepts of the philosophy of reflection [German Idealism]. From the conceptual strategy of transcendental philosophy there results (already in the followers of Kant, and today also among those who wish to develop a Marxist theory of society in conjunction with Husserl's

analyses of the "life-world") a peculiar compulsion to conceive the social world as a continuum in the same way as the world of the objects of possible experience. Thus to the objective structures within which socialized individuals encounter each other and act communicatively, large-scale subjects are assigned. The projective generation of higher-order subjects has a long tradition. Marx too did not always make clear that the attributes ascribed to social classes (such as class consciousness, class interest, class action) did not represent a simple transference from the level of individual consciousness to that of a collective. These are rather designations for something that can only be arrived at intersubjectively, in the consultation or the cooperation of individuals living together.

Objections

In this extremely selective and oversimplified retrospective summary I have emphasized three lines of argumentation along which I have pursued the relation of theory and praxis beyond those historical investigations which are collected in this volume. These arguments are certainly unsatisfactory as far as their degree of explication and completeness is concerned; I have always been aware of the fragmentary and provisional character of these considerations. But only a clearly stated position makes discursive attack and defense possible – that is, substantive argument. Yet certainly inaccuracies have crept in, and to a greater degree than I would have liked. Though I have exposed myself to criticism on this level, I will not deal with this here. However, the objections with respect to my construction itself are on another level. At the moment I can see three objections which must be taken seriously (other opponents of my views have not been able to convince me that their arguments carry weight; naturally I cannot exclude the possibility that psychological reasons are responsible for this; I can only hope that this is not the case). Here too I must confine myself to an outline:

(1) The first objection refers to the inadequately clarified status of the interests that direct knowledge. The formula "quasi-transcendental" is a product of an embarrassment which points to more problems than it solves. On the one hand, I have relinquished taking the position of transcendental logic in the strict sense in my attempt to clarify the systematic relations between the logic of scientific investigation and the logic of the contexts in which the corresponding sciences are constituted and applied. I do not assume the synthetic achievements of an intelligible ego nor in general a productive subjectivity. But I do presuppose, as does Peirce, the real interrelationship of communicating (and cooperating) investigators, where each of these subsystems is part of the surrounding social systems, which in turn are the result of the sociocultural evolution of the human race. On the other hand, the logical-methodological complexes cannot simply be reduced to empirical ones; at least not without paying the price of a naturalism which would claim to explain the technical as well as the practical interest of knowledge in the manner of natural history and thus, ultimately, as biological, or at the cost of a historicism which would, at the very least, tie the emancipatory interest of knowledge to fortuitous historical constellations and would thus relativistically deprive self-reflection of the possibility of a justificatory basis for its claim to validity. In neither of these two cases could it be made plausible how theories could have any truth at all – including one's own theories.

(2) The second objection is directed against the assertion that in the insights produced by self-reflection, knowledge and the emancipatory interest of knowledge are "one." Even if one admits that inherent within reason is also partisanship in favor of reason, still the claim to universality, which reflection as knowledge must make, is not to be reconciled with the particularity which must adhere to every interest, even that which aims at self-liberation. Is not a specific content already claimed for reason, when linked to emancipatory interest, namely that of a substantive rationality – while reason itself, as a consequence of its own idea, must exclude any specification in terms of particular goals? Is the element of decision and commitment, on which every praxis of subjects instructed by critique depends, especially a revolutionary praxis, not suppressed in a dogmatically asserted interest of reason, and thereby at the same time immunized? In the end the normative basis for a critical sociology is smuggled in surreptitiously, when one considers that in the interest of the liberation from the objectified self-deception of dogmatic power, two things are inevitably mingled: on the one hand, the interest in enlightenment, in the sense of a relentless discursive validation of claims to validity (and the discursive dissolution of opinions and norms the validity of which is based on unjustified claims, no matter to what extent it is actually accepted); on the other hand, the interest in enlightenment, in the sense of practical change of established conditions (and the realization of goals which demand the risks of taking sides, and thus, precisely, the relinquishment of the neutral role of a participant in discourse).

(3) The third objection is directed against the irresponsibility of discussions about the relationship of theory and praxis which fail to deal with questions of the organization of enlightenment and of enlightened praxis. Oskar Negt has formulated this objection most clearly on the political level. As I do not pose the question of organization, and thus do not draw the consequences of knowledge directed toward liberation, I remain confined to a *prepolitical* concept of objective partisanship. Instead, an organizational praxis adequate for the requirements of enlightenment on a mass scale would have to be discussed; Negt himself had in mind the decentralized activities which were widespread in the student movement of his time; hence the examples of spontaneous self-organization "for which enlightenment and revolutionary overthrow were no longer posed as alternatives."

An analogous objection is directed, on the theoretical level, against the possibility of carrying the model of psychoanalysis over into social theory. For I actually did investigate the critically motivated process of self-reflection in terms of the example of the psychoanalytic dialogue, in order to clarify in terms of this the logic underlying the translation of critique into self-liberation. Now however, therapy is bound by the rules of the art and by inhibiting institutional conditions, to which the political struggle, and especially the revolutionary struggle, is not subject. Therefore from the conservative side the misgivings readily arise that a transferring of the doctor-patient model to political praxis of large groups would encourage the uncontrolled exercise of force on the part of self-appointed elites, who close themselves off against potential opponents with dogmatic claims of privileged access to true insight. On the other side the misgiving arises that the same model leads to a rationalistic denial of the militant element in the confrontation with political opponents, because the pacifist illusion arises that the critical insight will by itself destroy the dominating dogmatism of existing institutions.

Objectivity of Knowledge and Interest

I would like to treat the *first two objections* jointly. In the light of the newly introduced system of relations between action and discourse, the following points, which, of course, I can only discuss in terms of a few strategic indications, present themselves to me in a different light than previously.

(1) In the investigations up to this point I have brought out the interrelation between knowledge and interest, without making clear the critical threshold between communication (which remains embedded within the context of action) and discourses (which transcend the compulsions of action). To be sure, the constitution of scientific object domains can be conceived as a continuation of the objectivations which we undertake in the world of social life prior to all science. But the genuine claim to objectivity which is raised with the instauration of science is based on a virtualization of the pressure of experience and decision, and it is only this which permits a discursive testing of *hypothetical* claims to validity and thus the generation of *rationally grounded* knowledge. Against the sciences' objectivistic understanding of themselves, which naïvely relates itself to the facts, an indirect relationship to action can be shown for theoretical knowledge, but not anything like a direct derivation from the imperatives posed by the praxis of life (nor have I ever asserted that there is such a derivation). The opinions which form the input of discourse – and thus the raw material which is subjected to argumentation with the aim of substantiation – do indeed have their origin in the diverse interrelations of experience and action. The logic of these experiential relations is manifested even in discourse itself by the fact that opinions can only be specified, and their derivation made clear, in languages of a specific form and can only be tested by methods of a specific kind (on a high level of generalization): by "observation" and "interviewing" [*Befragung*]. Therefore the discursively substantiated theoretical statements (which survive argumentation) can in turn be relevant only to specific contexts of application: statements about the phenomenal domain of things and events (or the deep structures which manifest themselves in terms of things and events) can only be translated back into orientations for goal-directed rational action (in technologies and strategies); statements about the phenomenal domain of persons and utterances (or about the deep structures of social systems) can only be translated back into orientations for communicative action (in practical knowledge). The interests which direct knowledge preserve the unity of the relevant system of action and experience vis-à-vis discourse; they retain the latent reference of theoretical knowledge to action by way of the transformation of opinions into theoretical statements and their retransformation into knowledge oriented toward action. But by no means do they remove or resolve (sublate) the difference between opinions about objects based on experience related to action, on the one hand, and statements about facts, founded on discourse that is free of experience and unencumbered by action, on the other; just as little do they affect the difference between those claims to validity which are simply recognized as factual and those which have a reasoned justification.

The status of the two "lower" interests, the technical and the practical interest of knowledge, can, to begin with, be clarified aporetically by the fact that they can neither be comprehended like empirical inclinations or attitudes nor be proposed or justified like variable values in relation to norms of action. Instead we "encounter" these deep-seated anthropological interests in the attempt to clarify the "constitution" of the facts about which theoretical statements are possible (that is, the systems of primitive terms which categorize the objects of possible experience, on the one hand, and, on the other, the methods by which action-related primary experiences are selected, extracted from their own system, and utilized for the purpose of the discursive examination of claims to validity, and thus transformed into "data"). The interests of knowledge can be conceived as generalized motives for systems of action, which are guided by means of the communication of statements which can be true. Actions are channeled by the recognition of claims to validity that can be resolved discursively. That is why, on the higher levels of sociocultural development, the fundamental regulators no longer take the form of particular stimuli (or instincts) but precisely that of general cognitive strategies of the action-related organization of experience. As long as these interests of knowledge are identified and analyzed by way of reflection on the logic of inquiry that structures the natural and the humane sciences, they can claim a "transcendental" status; however, as soon as they are understood in terms of an anthropology of knowledge, as results of natural history, they have an "empirical" status. I place "empirical" within quotation marks, because a theory of evolution which is expected to explain emergent properties characteristic of the sociocultural life-form – in other words, to explain the constituents of social systems as part of natural history – cannot, for its part, be developed within the transcendental framework of objectifying sciences. If the theory of evolution is to assume these tasks, it cannot wholly divest itself of the form of a reflection on the prehistory of culture that is dependent on a prior understanding of the sociocultural life-form. For the time being these are speculations, which can only be confirmed by a scientific clarification of the status enjoyed by the contemporary theory of evolution and research in ethology. Till then, at most, they designate a perspective for the formulation of the problems.

(2) As far as the third, the emancipatory, interest of knowledge is concerned, a more distinct delimitation appears, in my view, to offer itself. This interest can only develop to the degree to which repressive force, in the form of the normative exercise of power, presents itself permanently in structures of distorted communication – that is, to the extent that domination is institutionalized. This interest aims at reflection on oneself. As soon as we seek to clarify the structure of this reflection within the reference system of action-discourse, its difference from scientific argumentation becomes clear: the psychoanalytic dialogue is not a discourse, and reflection on oneself does not provide reasoned justification. What is reasoned justification within the context of acts of reflection on oneself bases itself on theoretical knowledge which has been gained independently of the reflection on oneself, namely, the rational reconstruction of rule systems which we have to master if we wish to process experience cognitively or participate in systems of action or carry on discourse. Till now I have not adequately distinguished posterior reconstruction [*Nachkonstruktion*] from reflection on oneself.

Self-reflection brings to consciousness those determinants of a self-formative process of cultivation and spiritual formation [*Bildung*] which ideologically determine a contemporary praxis of action and the conception of the world. Analytic memory thus embraces the particulars, the specific course of self-formation of an individual subject (or of a collective held together by group identity). Rational reconstructions, in contrast, deal with anonymous rule systems, which any subjects whatsoever can comply with, insofar as they have acquired the corresponding competence with respect to these rules. Reconstructions thus do not encompass subjectivity, within the horizon of which alone the experience of reflection is possible. In the philosophical tradition these two legitimate forms of self-knowledge have generally remained undifferentiated and have both been included under the term of reflection. However, a reliable criterion of distinction is available. Self-reflection leads to insight due to the fact that what has previously been unconscious is made conscious in a manner rich in practical consequences: analytic insights intervene in life, if I may borrow this dramatic phrase from Wittgenstein. A successful reconstruction also arises an "unconsciously" functioning rule system to consciousness in a certain manner; it renders explicit the intuitive knowledge that is given with competence with respect to the rules in the form of "know how." But this theoretical knowledge has no practical consequences. By learning logic or linguistics I acquire theoretical knowledge, but in general I do not thereby change my previous practice of reasoning or speaking.

This circumstance finds its explanation in the fact that self-reflection, as can be shown in the model of the psychoanalytic dialogue between doctor and patient, is not a discourse, but effects, at the same time, both more and less than a discourse. The therapeutic "discourse" effects less, as the patient by no means takes up a symmetrical posture vis-à-vis the doctor from the very beginning; the conditions for a participant in discourse are precisely what is not fulfilled by the patient. It is only the successful therapeutic discourse which brings, as its result that which in ordinary discourse must be required from the very outset; the effective equality of opportunities in perceiving the roles within the dialogue, and in general, in the choice and exercise of speech acts, must first be established between partners in a dialogue who are so unequally equipped. On the other hand, the therapeutic discourse effects more than the ordinary one. Because it remains contained in a peculiar way within the system of action and experience, which has as its theme exclusively questions of validity and must import all contents and information from the outside, successful self-reflection results in insight which satisfies not only the conditions of the discursive realization of a claim to truth (or correctness) but in addition satisfies the condition of the realization of a claim to authenticity [*Wahrhaftigkeit*], which normally is not to be attained discursively at all. In the patient's acceptance of the "worked out" interpretations which the doctor suggests to him and his confirming that these are applicable, he at the same time sees through a self-deception. The true interpretation at the same time makes possible the authentic intention of the subject with respect to those utterances, with which he has till then deceived himself (and possibly others). Claims to authenticity as a rule can only be tested within the context of action. That distinctive communication in which the distortions of the communicative structure themselves can be overcome is the only one in which claims to truth can be tested "discursively" together and simultaneously with a claim to authenticity, or be rejected as unjustified.

Reconstructions are, on the other hand, the object of ordinary discourse. To be sure, compared to other discursive objects they are distinguished by being first generated within a reflexive attitude. Cognitive components of the praxis of life, the claims to validity of which have been rendered problematic, are not what is dealt with in reconstructed rule systems; nor is it those scientific theorems, which cumulate in the rational grounds of such claims to validity; rather the reconstruction of rule systems requires an impulse which originates in the discourses themselves. It is precisely that reflection about presuppositions on which we always already rely naïvely in rational speech. Accordingly, this type of knowledge has always claimed the status of a special, of a "pure" knowledge; in logic, mathematics, epistemology, and linguistics today it forms the core of the philosophic disciplines. This type of knowledge is not constitutive for the objectivating sciences; accordingly, it remains untouched by the technical as well as the practical interest. For sciences of the critical type, which, like psychoanalysis, make self-reflection into a method of procedure, reconstruction, of course, appears to have a constitutive significance on the horizontal as well as the vertical level. It is only reliance upon reconstruction which permits the theoretical development of self-reflection. In this way reconstructions therefore attain an indirect relation to the emancipatory interest of knowledge, which enters directly only into the capacity for self-reflection.

Part IX

Modernity and Postmodernity

INTRODUCTION TO PART IX

In recent years, there has been a rather sterile debate between self-proclaimed "modernists" and "postmodernists." Theorists in both camps generally agree that something has fundamentally changed in the patterns of social relations, economic flows, and moral regulation in modern societies. The question at the center of the debate has been whether these changes should best be considered part and parcel of the same ever-transforming "modern" era that the founding figures of sociology spent their lives studying, or whether it is best to conceive of this as a new "postmodern" era. It has been a heated exchange to be sure, but it has not produced many fruitful outcomes.

Rather than attempting to reproduce this debate, this section is designed to move beyond it by taking postmodernist claims seriously but avoiding problematic historicist assumptions. This introduction will outline the different trends in "postmodern" social theory, but it will also emphasize how its style and substance were immediately linked to its historical and social context. The goal is to suggest that the concepts of modernity and postmodernity are deeply linked. On the one hand, "postmodernity is undoubtedly part of the modern" as Jean-François Lyotard has claimed[1]. On the other hand, postmodernism has actually been beneficial in helping us reinterpret our understanding of the modern.[2]

Postmodernism as an intellectual and cultural movement gained momentum in the late twentieth century. Any attempt to date the exact emergence of this movement is elusive as it spans a large number of academic and cultural domains. Following Lemert,[3] however, it may be safe to say that, for social theorists, the 1979 publication of Jean François Lyotard's *The Postmodern Condition* and Richard Rorty's *Philosophy and the Mirror of Nature*, marks its inauguration as a subject of academic inquiry. Because it is not a coherent intellectual movement, postmodernism does not lend itself to easy description. Instead, it draws its inspiration from different social and cultural contexts.

Postmodernism and the Social Landscape

Postmodernism perhaps finds its clearest expression as an aesthetic movement in the cultural sphere. It arose as a rejection of modernism, especially "high modernism," a movement in the late nineteenth and early twentieth century that sought to redefine literature, music, architecture, and the visual arts. While modernism rejects formal aesthetic theories in favor of the functional, postmodernism questions the adequacy of the functional as an inspiration of artistic expression. According to Charles Jencks, a proponent of postmodern architecture, this shift from modernism to postmodernism in architecture, for instance, occurred symbolically with the demolition of the modernist low-income Pruitt-Igoe housing project in 1972. This act is considered to be a statement of the failure of the modernist faith in the redemptive ability to improve human life through the construction of the best "machine for modern life." Signification and intertextuality replace the functional as the aesthetic principles of postmodernism. One of the distinguishing features of postmodern architecture, for instance, has been the juxtaposition of symbols and forms from different historical and design periods. In general, it may be said that where modernists tend to think in terms of totality, genre, or system, postmodernists think in terms of fragmentation, ephemerality, and discontinuity. While it is the case that this emphasis on fragmentation and discontinuity in postmodernist thought is carried over from modernism, the distinction between the two has more to do with attitude. While modernism laments the fragmentary and the chaotic, postmodernism accepts, and even valorizes it.

Theoretically, postmodernism has its roots in, although it is not coterminous with, post-structuralism, an intellectual movement that emerged in France following the political and social events of May 1968. Central figures associated with this movement are Foucault, Lacan, Barthes, and Kristeva, among others. Following structuralists, post-structuralists seek to decenter the subject. This theoretical position poses a challenge to the modernist belief in subject-centered reason. In other words, it questions the assumption that the rational mind (*any* rational mind) is capable of understanding and depicting the "real" world around us. In general, the postmodernist position is critical of truth claims and monological texts or readings. An important component of this critique is to question the very status of knowledge in modern discourse. Modernism privileges science, above all, as the source of objective knowledge and truth. Post-structuralism (and postmodernism) makes the claim instead that language is central to the production of knowledge, including scientific knowledge, which is also a form of discourse. This linguistic turn is central to the work of postmodern theorists. Jacques Derrida, whose name is associated with deconstruction, suggests that it is "*différance*" that marks writing, a differing and deferring of the linguistic presence of meaning. Texts must be treated as linguistic products, independent of authors with specific intentions. Thus, it may be said that postmodernism is suspicious of the modernist faith in the straightforward relationship between the signifier and the signified.

Postmodern thought critiques the kind of grand narratives that it associates with modernism, in particular humanism and the Enlightenment. As Jean-François Lyotard,[4] one of the leading theorists of postmodernism, puts it, postmodernism may be characterized as "incredulity toward meta-narratives." These meta-narratives refer to grand theories about, for instance, the Spirit, Man, the rational subject, the proletariat, etc. Such grand theories, like those associated with Marx and Freud, are taken to have at their center a category (or a set of categories) that is assumed to be universal, thereby masking any internal differentiation. Instead, postmodernism favors more small-scale, local narratives that take into account the contingent, provisional, and unstable nature of the social world. An example of such an approach is Foucault's conceptualization of power. Moving away from the idea that power is most importantly vested in the state, Foucault traces the micro-politics of power in multiple locations and social contexts. In a similar vein, Lyotard argues that, in a postmodern world, people live at the intersection of numerous "language games." In fact, he proposes that the social bond is ultimately linguistic, following different discursive rules in different situations.

Modernism and Postmodernism

Having noted some of the main characteristics associated with postmodernism, the question remains whether these theoretical and cultural approaches arose in response to radical changes in our social world. Is postmodernism a theory of postmodernity? In considering these changes, postmodern theory assimilated other theories from the 1970s and 1980s that engaged the same question. Earlier versions of such theories were Daniel Bell's and Alain Touraine's accounts of a postindustrial society. They base their analysis of postindustrial society on the increasing dominance of information and knowledge in the economic sphere. Theorists of postmodernity continue to pursue this interest in the implications of new communication technologies and media, making more radical pronouncements than those made by scholars like Bell and Touraine. For instance, Jean Baudrillard, reflecting on the power of mass communication media, questions the notion of reality in postmodern societies. The power of mediated images, he argues, has led to the production of the "hyperreal" in which it becomes impossible to differentiate between the imaginary and the real. The world becomes a world of simulation, of images without an original. Since the postmodern world has come to be characterized largely by consumption and seduction, Baudrillard suggests that relations of production have now given way to relations of signs.

Admittedly, our social world has experienced some significant structural changes in the past few decades. The economy, for instance, has witnessed deindustrialization and the increasing dominance of post-Fordist practices in which capital has become more flexible and disorganized. In other words, capital accumulation increasingly occurs through flexible work practices that have resulted in significant spatial de-concentration of work and labor. Consumption dominates this "new" economy. Global information and communication technologies have come to assume a powerful role in our world. Manuel Castells, in his influential book *The Rise of the Network Society*, examines the economic and technological changes that have occurred in our "informational society." He argues that capitalism has evolved in its organizational logic due to the speed and scope with which information is transmitted in this global network society. In a society in which business projects are embedded in global networks, the space of flows supercedes (to some extent) the space of places, with important implications for social relations. Communication networks allow organizations to disperse spatially. In other words, while high-level executives live in "world cities," they manage to remain "connected," and thus control, the actual management of their operations anywhere in the world. In addition to the transformations noted by Castells, other globalizing impulses, for instance migrations, have imbricated us in new social networks that bring to fore the play of difference in contemporary life.

Having made a note of these changes, it is worth considering, however, whether these changes amount to an epochal shift that renders redundant the categories (especially Marxist) of industrial, capitalist societies. David Harvey[5] argues that, while there have indeed been recent changes in political economic practices, the underlying logic of capitalism remains the same. An acknowledgment of these changes does not lead Harvey to conclude the end of modernity. Rather, he sees them as internal shifts in the organization of capitalism. Calhoun[6] makes the case that, despite obvious changes, there is no evidence that capital accumulation does not continue to be basic to economic activity today. In fact, he argues that the cultural orientation of society still remains primarily productivist. These accounts, then, advance the view that postmodernity is merely another phase of modernity. Giddens[7] argues that what we are witnessing is the radicalization of modernity rather than the emergence of postmodernity.

Also acknowledging that postmodernity is a part of modernity, Lyotard sees it as a vantage point for the rewriting of modernity. In a similar vein, Zygmunt Bauman argues that postmodernity has not replaced modernity. Rather, it is the stage that may be characterized as the culmination of modernity. It is a position from which we can reflect upon modernity. For instance, in his 1989 book *Modernity and the Holocaust*, Bauman explores the limits of modernity witnessed in the Holocaust. The Holocaust, according to him, was a product of the modernist faith in progress embodied in the bureaucracy and technocracy. It was the desire to remake the world that motivated the Nazi project. While generally believing that postmodernity does not replace modernity, Bauman suggests that it is a new phase. Like Baudrillard, he is of the opinion that capitalism has evolved from a system based on production to one based on consumption. In such a society, freedom has come to be associated with the freedom to consume. In light of some of these transformations, Bauman proposes the coining of a "new vocabulary" that would enable a sociology of postmodernity.

While there is perhaps more agreement on the beginnings of modernity in the eighteenth century, there is less agreement on those of postmodernity. An example of an historical examination of the emergence of modernity as a social and political form is Norbert Elias's *The Civilizing Process*. It is a rigorous social history of the process of civilization. Elias examines the modern social habitus, or personality, which has increasingly come to be dominated by manners, or self-restraint and self-approbation. Through the formation of gradually more effective monopolies of force, the threat which one person represents for another is subjected to control. He also shows how the emergence of this "civilized" behavior is closely interrelated to the sociogenesis of the state. The exercise of force, which was earlier the privilege of rival warriors, becomes increasingly more centralized in the organization of modern states. Similar accounts of the beginnings of postmodernity are harder to find. Calhoun[8] attributes this difficulty to the fact that postmodernism is more "pseudohistory" than a historically and culturally specific account of postmodernity. It is even more difficult to establish the link between postmodernism and postmodernity. Some, like Jameson,[9] argue that postmodernism arose as an aesthetic movement in response to economic and social changes. He proposes that postmodern cultural formations are associated with the stage of late capitalism, which he characterizes as multinational or consumer capitalism. Others point out, however, that postmodernism is merely an extension of modernism rather than a theory associated with some real empirical changes. As a critique of modernism, it comprises less a stylistic shift than a carry-over from counter-movements within modernity itself represented by, for instance, Dadaism, Surrealism, the Bauhaus movement, or Russian formalism. In this sense, it bears a "family resemblance" with antimodernism, the critique of modernity within modernity. Habermas makes a stronger claim. Following in the tradition of other Frankfurt school critical theorists like Horkheimer and Adorno, Habermas is critical of Enlightenment rationality. However, he believes that this is a tradition that can be traced back to modern thinkers like Schiller, Fichte, the Young Hegelians, and Nietzsche. Rather than abandoning the modern project, Habermas proposes "communicative reason" in place of "subject-centered reason." Communicative reason refers to the idea that consensual agreement can be dialogically arrived at through the articulation of validity claims. While modernity has always found hope in the redemptive potential of the future, Niklas Luhmann draws attention to the uncertainty and contingency associated with the future. This "loss of uncertainty" is manifested as ignorance about the future of contemporary societies, especially with reference to the calculation of risks.

In the final analysis, the debate about whether we live in a modern or postmodern world is largely an empty one, and we have seen the difficulty of defining definitively what a "postmodern" society looks like. What can be said, however, is that, as Kumar states, postmodernism provides a valuable corrective to the standard accounts of modernity[10]. Perhaps most importantly, it has brought into the scholarly and popular discourse, for instance, the "problem" of difference.

Notes

1   Lyotard (1984: 79).
2   See Calhoun (1995).
3   Lemert (1997: 103).
4   Lyotard (1984: xxiv).
5   Harvey (1989).
6   Calhoun (1995).
7   Giddens (1990).
8   Calhoun (1995).
9   Jameson (1992).
10   Kumar (1995: 178–9).

Select Bibliography

Beck, Ulrich, Anthony Giddens, and Scott Lash (eds.). 1994. *Reflexive Modernization, Politics, Tradition and Aesthetics in the Modern Social Order*. Cambridge: Polity Press. (A useful collection of essays on "late" modernity.)

Baudrillard, Jean. 1988. *Selected Writings*. Edited by Mark Poster. Cambridge: Polity Press. (An important voice that has come to be associated with postmodernism.)

Calhoun, Craig. 1995. *Critical Social Theory*. Cambridge, MA: Blackwell. (Includes a critique of postmodernism's historical claims.)

Derrida, Jacques. 1978. *Writing and Difference*. Chicago: University of Chicago Press. (A key text by the leading proponent of deconstruction.)

Giddens, Anthony. 1990. *Modernity and its Discontents*. Palo Alto, CA: Stanford University Press. (A notable contribution to thinking on the transformation of modernity.)

Habermas, Jürgen. 1987. *The Philosophical Discourse of Modernity: Twelve Lectures*. Translated by Frederick Lawrence. Cambridge, MA: MIT Press. (An important contribution to the discussions on modernity and postmodernity.)

Harvey, David. 1989. *The Condition of Postmodernity: An Inquiry into the Origins of Cultural Change*. Oxford: Basil Blackwell. (An engaging book on the postmodern condition in the social, cultural, and political realm.)

Jameson, Frederic. 1992. *Postmodernism, or, The Cultural Logic of Late Capitalism*. London: Verso. (A Marxist account that figures prominently in discussions of postmodernism.)

Kilminster, Richard (ed.). 1996. *Culture, Modernity and Revolution: Essays in Honor of Zygmunt Bauman*. London: Routledge. (One of the most comprehensive collections of essays on Bauman.)

Kumar, Krishan. 1995. *From Post-Industrial to Post-Modern Society: New Theories of the Contemporary World*. Cambridge, MA: Blackwell. (A sophisticated account of modernity and postmodernity that is based in historical and theoretical explorations.)

Lemert, Charles. 1997. *Postmodernism Is Not What You Think*. Cambridge, MA: Blackwell. (An insightful account of postmodernism and its implications for the practice of sociology.)

Lyotard, Jean-François. 1984. *The Postmodern Condition: A Report on Knowledge*. Translated by G. Bennington and B. Massumi. Minneapolis: University of Minnesota Press. (One of the most influential works on postmodernism.)

Seidman, Steven and David Wagner (eds.). 1992. *Postmodernism and Social Theory: The Debate over General Theory*. Cambridge, MA: Blackwell. (A collection of essays on the practice of sociology from a modernist, postmodernist, and a "between-modernist-and-postmodernist" position.)

29 The Social Constraint towards Self-Constraint

Norbert Elias

What has the organization of society in the form of "states", what have the monop-olization and centralization of taxes and physical force over a large area, to do with "civilization"?

The observer of the civilizing process finds himself confronted by a whole tangle of problems. To mention a few of the most important at the outset, there is, first of all, the most general question. We have seen that the civilizing process is a change of human conduct and sentiment in a quite specific direction. But, obviously, individual people did not at some past time intend this change, this "civilization", and grad-ually realize it by conscious, "rational", purposive measures. Clearly, "civilization" is not, any more than rationalization, a product of human "ratio" or the result of calculated long-term planning. How would it be conceivable that gradual "rational-ization" could be founded on pre-existing "rational" behaviour and planning over centuries? Could one really imagine that the civilizing process had been set in motion by people with that long-term perspective, that specific mastery of all short-term affects, considering that this type of long-term perspective and self-mastery already presuppose a long civilizing process?

In fact, nothing in history indicates that this change was brought about "ration-ally", through any purposive education of individual people or groups. It happened by and large unplanned; but it did not happen, nevertheless, without a specific type of order. It has been shown in detail above how constraints through others from a variety of angles are converted into self-restraints, how the more animalic human activities are progressively thrust behind the scenes of men's communal social life and invested with feelings of shame, how the regulation of the whole instinctual and affective life by steady self-control becomes more and more stable, more even and more all-embracing. All this certainly does not spring from a rational idea conceived centuries ago by individual people and then implanted in one generation after another as the purpose of action and the desired state, until it was fully realized in the "centuries of progress". And yet, though not planned and intended, this transformation is not merely a sequence of unstructured and chaotic changes.

What poses itself here with regard to the civilizing process is nothing other than the general problem of historical change. Taken as a whole this change is not "rationally" planned; but neither is it a random coming and going of orderless patterns. How is this possible? How does it happen at all that formations arise in the human world that no single human being has intended, and which yet are anything but cloud formations without stability or structure?

Originally translated by Edmund Jephcott.

It is simple enough: plans and actions, the emotional and rational impulses of individual people, constantly interweave in a friendly or hostile way. *This basic tissue resulting from many single plans and actions of men can give rise to changes and patterns that no individual person has planned or created. From this interdependence of people arises an order sui generis, an order more compelling and stronger than the will and reason of the individual people composing it.* It is this order of interweaving human impulses and strivings, this social order, which determines the course of historical change; it underlies the civilizing process.

This order is neither "rational" – if by "rational" we mean that it has resulted intentionally from the purposive deliberation of individual people; nor "irrational" – if by "irrational" we mean that it has arisen in an incomprehensible way. It has occasionally been identified with the order of "Nature"; it was interpreted by Hegel and some others as a kind of supra-individual "Spirit", and his concept of a "cunning of reason" shows how much he too was preoccupied by the fact that all the planning and actions of people give rise to many things that no one actually intended. But the mental habits which tend to bind us to opposites such as "rational" and "irrational", or "spirit" and "nature", prove inadequate here. In this respect, too, reality is not constructed quite as the conceptual apparatus of a particular standard would have us believe, whatever valuable services it may have performed in its time as a compass to guide us through an unknown world. *The immanent regularities of social figurations are identical neither with regularities of the "mind", of individual reasoning, nor with regularities of what we call "nature", even though functionally all these different dimensions of reality are indissolubly linked to each other.* . . . Civilization is not "reasonable"; not "rational", any more than it is "irrational". It is set in motion blindly, and kept in motion by the autonomous dynamics of a web of relationships, by specific changes in the way people are bound to live together. But it is by no means impossible that we can make out of it something more "reasonable", something that functions better in terms of our needs and purposes. For it is precisely in conjunction with the civilizing process that the blind dynamics of men intertwining in their deeds and aims gradually leads towards greater scope for planned intervention into both the social and individual structures – intervention based on a growing knowledge of the unplanned dynamics of these structures.

But which specific changes in the way people are bonded to each other mould their personality in a "civilizing" manner? The most general answer to this question too, an answer based on what was said earlier about the changes in Western society, is very simple. From the earliest period of the history of the Occident to the present, social functions have become more and more differentiated under the pressure of competition. The more differentiated they become, the larger grows the number of functions and thus of people on whom the individual constantly depends in all his actions, from the simplest and most commonplace to the more complex and uncommon. As more and more people must attune their conduct to that of others, the web of actions must be organized more and more strictly and accurately, if each individual action is to fulfil its social function. The individual is compelled to regulate his conduct in an increasingly differentiated, more even and more stable manner. That this involves not only a conscious regulation has already been stressed. Precisely this is characteristic of the psychological changes in the course of civilization: the more complex and stable control of conduct is increasingly instilled in the individual from his earliest years as an automatism, a self-compulsion that he cannot resist even if he consciously wishes to. The web of actions grows so complex and extensive, the effort required to behave "correctly" within it becomes so great, that beside the individual's conscious self-control an automatic, blindly functioning apparatus of self-control is firmly established. This seeks to prevent offences to socially acceptable behaviour by a wall of deep-rooted fears, but, just because it operates blindly and by habit, it frequently indirectly produces such collisions with social reality. But whether consciously or unconsciously, the direction of this transformation of conduct in the form of an increasingly differentiated regulation of impulses is determined by the direction of the process of social differentiation, by the progressive division of functions and the growth of the interdependency chains into which, directly or indirectly, every impulse, every move of an individual becomes integrated. . . .

The pattern of self-constraints, the template by which drives are moulded, certainly varies widely according to the function and position of the individual within this network, and there are even today in different sectors of the Western world variations of intensity and stability in the apparatus of self-constraint that seem at face value very large. At this point a multitude of particular questions are raised, and the sociogenetic method may give access to their answers. But when compared to the psychological make-up of people in less complex societies, these differences and degrees within more complex societies become less significant, and the main line of transformation, which is the primary concern of this study, emerges very clearly: as the social fabric grows more intricate, the sociogenic apparatus of individual self-control also becomes more differentiated, more all-round and more stable.

But the advancing differentiation of social functions is only the first, most general of the social transformations which we observe in enquiring into the change in psychological make-up known as "civilization". Hand in hand with this advancing division of functions goes a total reorganization of the social fabric. It was shown in detail earlier why, when the division of functions is low, the central organs of societies of a certain size are relatively unstable and liable to disintegration. It has been shown how, through specific figurational pressures, centrifugal tendencies, the mechanisms of feudalization, are slowly neutralized and how, step by step, a more stable central organization, a firmer monopolization of physical force, are established. The peculiar stability of the apparatus of mental self-restraint which emerges as a decisive trait built into the habits of every "civilized" human being, stands in the closest relationship to the monopolization of physical force and the growing stability of the central organs of society. Only with the formation of this kind of relatively stable monopolies do societies acquire those characteristics as a result of which the individuals forming them get attuned, from infancy, to a highly regulated and differentiated pattern of self-restraint; only in conjunction with these monopolies does this kind of self-restraint require a higher degree of automaticity, does it become, as it were, "second nature".

When a monopoly of force is formed, pacified social spaces are created which are normally free from acts of violence. The pressures acting on individual people within them are of a different kind than previously. Forms of non-physical violence that always existed, but hitherto had always been mingled or fused with physical force, are now separated from the latter; they persist in a changed form internally within the more pacified societies. They are most visible so far as the standard thinking of our time is concerned as types of economic violence. In reality, however, there is a whole set of means whose monopolization can enable men as groups or as individuals to enforce their will upon others. The monopolization of the means of production, of "economic" means, is only one of those which stand out in fuller relief when the means of physical violence become monopolized, when, in other words, in a more pacified state society the free use of physical force by those who are physically stronger is no longer possible.

In general, the direction in which the behaviour and the affective make-up of people change when the structure of human relationships is transformed in the manner described, is as follows: societies without a stable monopoly of force are always societies in which the division of functions is relatively slight and the chains of action binding individuals together are comparatively short. Conversely, societies with more stable monopolies of force, always first embodied in a large princely or royal court, are societies in which the division of functions is more or less advanced, in which the chains of action binding individuals together are longer and the functional dependencies between people greater. Here the individual is largely protected from sudden attack, the irruption of physical violence into his life. But at the same time he is himself forced to suppress in himself any passionate impulse urging him to attack another physically. And the other forms of compulsion which now prevail in the pacified social spaces pattern the individual's conduct and affective impulses in the same direction. The closer the web of interdependence becomes in which the individual is enmeshed with the advancing division of functions, the larger the social spaces over which this network extends and which become integrated into functional or institutional units – the more threatened is the social existence of the individual who gives way to spontaneous impulses and emotions, the greater is the social advantage of those able to moderate their affects, and the more strongly is each individual constrained from an early age to take account of the effects of his own or other people's actions on a whole series of links in the social chain. The moderation of spontaneous emotions, the tempering of affects, the extension of mental space beyond the moment into the past and future, the habit of connecting events in terms of chains of cause and effect – all these are different aspects of the same transformation of conduct which necessarily takes place with the monopolization of physical violence, and the lengthening of the chains of social action and interdependence. It is a "civilizing" change of behaviour. . . .

As the structure of human relations changes, as monopoly organizations of physical force develop and the individual is held no longer in the sway of constant feuds and wars but rather in the more permanent compulsions of peaceful functions based on the acquisition of money or prestige, affect-expressions too slowly gravitate towards a middle line. The fluctuations in behaviour and affects do not disappear, but are moderated. The peaks and abysses are smaller, the changes less abrupt.

We can see what is changing more clearly from its obverse. Through the formation of monopolies of force, the threat which one man represents for another is subject to stricter control and becomes more calculable. Everyday life is freer of sudden reversals of fortune. Physical violence is confined to barracks; and from this store-house it breaks out only in extreme cases, in times of war or social upheaval, into individual life. As the monopoly of certain specialist groups it is normally excluded from the life of others; and these specialists, the whole monopoly organization of force, now stand guard only in the margin of social life as a control on individual conduct.

Even in this form as a control organization, however, physical violence and the threat emanating from it have a determining influence on individuals in society, whether they know it or not. It is, however, no longer a perpetual insecurity that it brings into the life of the individual, but a peculiar form of security. It no longer throws him, in the swaying fortunes of battle, as the physical victor or vanquished, between mighty outbursts of pleasure and terror; a continuous, uniform pressure is exerted on individual life by the physical violence stored behind the scenes of everyday life, a pressure totally familiar and hardly perceived, conduct and drive economy having been adjusted from earliest youth to this social structure. It is in fact the whole social mould, the code of conduct which changes; and accordingly with it changes, as has been said before, not only this or that specific form of conduct but its whole pattern, the whole structure of the way individuals steer themselves. The monopoly organization of physical violence does not usually constrain the individual by a direct threat. A strongly predictable compulsion or pressure mediated in a variety of ways is constantly exerted on the individual. This operates to a considerable extent through the medium of his own reflection. It is normally only potentially present in society, as an agency of control; the actual compulsion is one that the individual exerts on himself either as a result of his knowledge of the possible consequences of his moves in the game in intertwining activities, or as a result of corresponding gestures of adults which have helped to pattern his own behaviour as a child. The monopolization of physical violence, the concentration of arms and armed men under one authority, makes the use of violence more or less calculable, and forces unarmed men in the pacified social spaces to restrain their own violence through foresight or reflection; in other words it imposes on people a greater or lesser degree of self-control.

This is not to say that every form of self-control was entirely lacking in medieval warrior society or in other societies without a complex and stable monopoly of physical violence. The agency of individual self-control, the super-ego, the conscience or whatever we call it, is instilled, imposed and maintained in such warrior societies only in direct relation to acts of physical violence; its form matches this life in its greater contrasts and more abrupt transitions. Compared to the self-control agency in more pacified societies, it is diffuse, unstable, only a slight barrier to violent emotional outbursts. The fears securing socially "correct" conduct are not yet banished to remotely the same extent from the individual's consciousness into his so-called "inner life". As the decisive danger does not come from failure or relaxation of self-control, but from direct external physical threat, habitual fear predominantly takes the form of fear of external powers. And as this fear is less stable, the control apparatus too is less encompassing, more one-sided or partial. In such a society extreme self-control in enduring pain may be instilled; but this is complemented by what, measured by a different standard, appears as an extreme form of freewheeling of affects in torturing others. Similarly, in certain sectors of medieval society we find extreme forms of asceticism, self-restraint and renunciation, contrasting to a no less extreme indulgence of pleasure in others, and frequently enough we encounter sudden switches from one attitude to the other in the life of an individual person. The restraint the individual here imposes on himself, the struggle against his own flesh, is no less intense and one-sided, no less radical and passionate than its counterpart, the fight against others and the maximum enjoyment of pleasures.

What is established with the monopolization of physical violence in the pacified social spaces is a different type of self-control or self-constraint. It is a more dispassionate self-control. The controlling agency forming itself as part of the individual's personality structure corresponds to the controlling agency forming itself in society at large. The one like the other tends to impose a highly differentiated regulation upon all passionate impulses, upon men's conduct all around. Both – each to a large extent mediated by the other – exert a constant, even pressure to inhibit affective outbursts. They damp down extreme fluctuations in behaviour and emotions. As the monopolization of physical force reduces the fear and terror one man must have for another, but at the same time reduces the possibility of causing others terror, fear or torment, and therefore certain possibilities of pleasurable emotional release, the constant self-control to which the individual is now increasingly accustomed seeks to reduce the contrasts and sudden switches in conduct, and the affective charge of all self-expression. The pressures operating upon the individual now tend to produce a transformation of the whole drive and affect economy in the direction of a more continuous, stable and even regulation of drives and affects in all areas of conduct, in all sectors of his life.

And it is in exactly the same direction that the unarmed compulsions operate, the constraints without direct physical violence to which the individual is now exposed in the pacified spaces, and of which economic restraints are an instance. They too are less affect-charged, more moderate, stable and less erratic than the constraints exerted by one person on another in a monopoly-free warrior society. And they, too, embodied in the entire spectrum of functions open to the individual in society, induce incessant hindsight and foresight transcending the moment and corresponding to the longer and more complex chains in which each act is now automatically enmeshed. They require the individual incessantly to overcome his momentary affective impulses in keeping with the longer-term effects of his behaviour. Relative to the other standard, they instil a more even self-control encompassing his whole conduct like a tight ring, and a more steady regulation of his drives according to the social norms. Moreover, as always, it is not only the adult functions themselves which immediately produce this tempering of drives and affects; partly automatically, partly quite consciously through their own conduct and habits, adults induce corresponding behaviour-patterns in children. From earliest youth the individual is trained in the constant restraint and foresight that he needs for adult functions. This self-restraint is ingrained so deeply from an early age that, like a kind of relay-station of social standards, an automatic self-supervision of his drives, a more differentiated and more stable "super-ego" develops in him, and a part of the forgotten drive impulses and affect inclinations is no longer directly within reach of the level of consciousness at all.

Earlier, in warrior society, the individual could use physical violence if he was strong and powerful enough; he could openly indulge his inclinations in many directions that have subsequently been closed by social prohibitions. But he paid for this greater opportunity of direct pleasure with a greater chance of direct and open fear. Medieval conceptions of hell give us an idea of how strong this fear between man and man was. Both joy and pain were discharged more openly and freely. But the individual was their prisoner; he was hurled back and forth by his own feelings as by forces of nature. He had less control of his passions; he was more controlled by them.

Later, as the conveyor belts running through his existence grow longer and more complex, the individual learns to control himself more steadily; he is now less a prisoner of his passions than before. But as he is now more tightly bound by his functional dependence on the activities of an ever-larger number of people, he is much more restricted in his conduct, in his chances of directly satisfying his drives and passions. Life becomes in a sense less dangerous, but also less emotional or pleasurable, at least as far as the direct release of pleasure is concerned. And for what is lacking in everyday life a substitute is created in dreams, in books and pictures. So, on their way to becoming courtiers, the nobility read novels of chivalry; the bourgeois contemplate violence and erotic passion in films. Physical clashes, wars and feuds diminish, and anything recalling them, even the cutting up of dead animals and the use of the knife at table, is banished from view or at least subjected to more and more precise social rules. But at the same time the battlefield is, in a sense, moved within. Part of the tensions and passions that were earlier directly released in the struggle of man and man, must now be worked out within the human being. The more peaceful constraints exerted on him by his relations to others are mirrored within him; an individualized pattern of near-automatic habits is established and consolidated within him, a specific "super-ego", which endeavours to control, transform or suppress his affects in keeping with the social structure. But the drives, the passionate affects, that can no longer directly manifest themselves in the relationships *between* people, often struggle no less violently *within* the individual against this supervising part of himself. And this semi-automatic struggle of the person with himself does not always find a happy resolution; not always does the self-transformation required by life in this society lead to a new balance between drive-satisfaction and drive-control. Often enough it is subject to major or minor disturbances, revolts of one part of the person against the other, or a permanent atrophy, which makes the performance of social functions even more difficult, or impossible. The vertical oscillations, if we may so describe them, the leaps from fear to joy, pleasure to remorse are reduced, while the horizontal fissure running right through the whole person, the tension between "super-ego" and "unconscious" – the wishes and desires that cannot be remembered – increases.

Here too the basic characteristics of these patterns of intertwining, if one pursues not merely their static structures but their sociogenesis, prove to be relatively simple. Through the interdependence of larger groups of people and the exclusion of physical violence from them, a social apparatus is established in which the constraints between people are lastingly transformed into self-constraints. These self-constraints, a function of the perpetual hindsight and foresight instilled in the individual from childhood in accordance with his integration in extensive chains of action, have partly the form of conscious self-control and partly that of automatic habit. They tend towards a more even moderation, a more continuous restraint, a more exact control of drives and affects in accordance with the more differentiated pattern of social interweaving. But depending on the inner pressure, on the condition of society and the position of the individual within it, these constraints also produce peculiar tensions and disturbances in the conduct and drive economy of the individual. In some cases they lead to perpetual restlessness and dissatisfaction, precisely because the person affected can only gratify a part of his inclinations and impulses in modified form, for example in fantasy, in looking-on and overhearing, in daydreams or dreams. And sometimes the habituation to affect-inhibition goes so far – constant feelings of boredom or solitude are examples of this – that the individual is no longer capable of any form of fearless expression of the modified affects, or of direct gratification of the repressed drives. Particular branches of drives are as it were anaesthetized in such cases by the specific structure of the social framework in which the child grows up. Under the pressure of the dangers that their expression incurs in the child's social space, they become surrounded with automatic fears to such an extent that they can remain deaf and unresponsive throughout a whole lifetime. In other cases certain branches of drives may be so diverted by the heavy conflicts which the rough-hewn, affective and passionate nature of the small human being unavoidably encounters on its way to being moulded into a "civilized" being, that their energies can find only an unwanted release through bypasses, in compulsive actions and other symptoms of disturbance. In other cases again, these energies are so transformed that they flow into uncontrollable and eccentric attachments and repulsions, in predilections for this or that peculiar hobby-horse. And in all these cases a permanent, apparently groundless inner unrest shows how many drive energies are dammed up in a form that permits no real satisfaction.

Until now the individual civilizing process, like the social, runs its course by and large blindly. Under the cover of what adults think and plan, the relationship that forms between them and the young has functions and effects in the latter's personalities which they do not intend and of which they scarcely know. Unplanned in that sense are those results of social patterning of individuals to which one habitually refers as "abnormal"; psychological abnormalities which do not result from social patterning but are caused by unalterable hereditary traits need not be considered here. But the psychological make-up which keeps within the social norm and is subjectively more satisfying comes about in an equally unplanned way. It is the same social mould from which emerge both more favourably and more unfavourably structured human beings, the "well-adjusted" as well as the "mal-adjusted", within a very broad spectrum of varieties. The automatically reproduced anxieties which, in the course of each individual civilizing process and in connection with the conflicts that form an integral part of this process, attach themselves to specific drives and affect impulses sometimes lead to a permanent and total paralysis of these impulses, and sometimes only to a moderate regulation with enough scope for their full satisfaction. Under present conditions it is from the point of view of the individuals concerned more a question of their good or bad fortune than that of anybody's planning whether it is the one or the other. In either case it is the web of social relations in which the individual lives during his most impressionable phase, during childhood and youth, which imprints itself upon his unfolding personality where it has its counterpart in the relationship between his controlling agencies, super-ego and ego, and his libidinal impulses. The resulting balance between controlling agencies and drives on a variety of levels determines how an individual person steers himself in his relations with others; it determines that which we call, according to taste, habits, complexes or personality structure. However, there is no end to the intertwining, for although the self-steering of a person, malleable during early childhood, solidifies and hardens as he grows up, it never ceases entirely to be affected by his changing relations with others throughout his life. The learning of self-controls, call them "reason" or "conscience", "ego" or "super-ego", and the consequent curbing of more animalic impulses and affects, in short the civilizing of the human young, is never a process entirely without pain; it always leaves scars. If the person is lucky – and as no one, no parent, no doctor, and no counsellor, is at present able to steer this process in a child according to a clear knowledge of what is best for its future, it is still largely a question of luck – the wounds of the civilizing conflicts incurred during childhood heal; the scars left by them are not too deep. But in less favourable cases the conflicts inherent in the civilizing of young humans – conflicts with others and conflicts within themselves – remain unsolved, or, more precisely, though perhaps buried for a while, open up once more in situations reminiscent of those of childhood; the suffering, transformed into an adult form, repeats itself again and again, and the unsolved conflicts of a person's childhood never cease to disturb his adult relationships. In that way, the interpersonal conflicts of early youth which have patterned the personality structure continue to perturb or even destroy the interpersonal relationships of the grown-up. The resulting tensions may take the form either of contradictions between different self-control automa- tisms, sunk-in memory traces of former dependencies and needs, or of recurrent struggles between the controlling agencies and the libidinal impulses. In the more fortunate cases, on the other hand, the contradictions between different sections and layers of the controlling agencies, especially of the super-ego structure, are slowly reconciled; the most disruptive conflicts between that structure and the libidinal impulses are slowly contained. They not only disappear from waking consciousness, but are so thoroughly assimilated that, without too heavy a cost in subjective satisfaction, they no longer intrude unintentionally in later interpersonal relation- ships. In one case the conscious and unconscious self-control always remains diffuse in places and open to the breakthrough of socially unproductive forms of drive energy; in the other this self-control, which even today in juvenile phases is often more like a confusion of overlapping ice-floes than a smooth and firm sheet of ice, slowly becomes more unified and stable in positive correspondence to the structure of society. But as this structure, precisely in our times, is highly mutable, it demands a flexibility of habits and conduct which in most cases has to be paid for by a loss of stability.

Theoretically, therefore, it is not difficult to say in what lies the difference between an individual civilizing process that is considered successful and one that is con- sidered unsuccessful. In the former, after all the pains and conflicts of this process, patterns of conduct well adapted to the framework of adult social functions are finally formed, an adequately functioning set of habits and at the same time – which does not necessarily go hand-in-hand with it – a positive pleasure balance. In the other, either the socially necessary self-control is repeatedly purchased, at a heavy cost in personal satisfaction, by a major effort to overcome opposed libidinal ener- gies, or the control of these energies, renunciation of their satisfaction is not achieved at all; and often enough no positive pleasure balance of any kind is finally possible, because the social commands and prohibitions are represented not only by other people but also by the stricken self, since one part of it forbids and punishes what the other desires.

In reality the result of the individual civilizing process is clearly unfavourable or favourable only in relatively few cases at each end of the scale. The majority of civilized people live midway between these two extremes. Socially positive and negative features, personally gratifying and frustrating tendencies, mingle in them in varying proportions.

The social moulding of individuals in accordance with the structure of the civilizing process of what we now call the West is particularly difficult. In order to be reasonably successful it requires with the structure of Western society, a particularly high differentiation, an especially intensive and stable regulation of drives and affects, of all the more elementary human impulses. It therefore generally takes up more time, particularly in the middle and upper classes, than the social moulding of individuals in less complex societies. Resistance to adaptation to the prevailing standards of civilization, the effort which this adaptation, this profound transformation of the whole personality costs the individual, is always very considerable. And later, therefore, than in less complex societies the individual in the Western world attains with his adult social function the psychological make-up of an adult, the emergence of which by and large marks the conclusion of the individual civilizing process.

But even if in the more differentiated societies of the West the modelling of the individual self-steering apparatus is particularly extensive and intense, processes tending in the same direction, social and individual civilizing processes, most certainly do not occur only there. They are to be found wherever, under competitive pressures, the division of functions makes large numbers of people dependent on one another, wherever a monopolization of physical force permits and imposes a co-operation less charged with emotion, wherever functions are established that demand constant hindsight and foresight in interpreting the actions and intentions of others. What determines the nature and degree of such civilizing spurts is always the extent of interdependencies, the level of the division of functions, and within it, the structure of these functions themselves.

30 A Sociological Theory of Postmodernity

Zygmunt Bauman

I propose that:

1 The term *postmodernity* renders accurately the defining traits of the social condition that emerged throughout the affluent countries of Europe and of European descent in the course of the twentieth century, and took its present shape in the second half of that century. The term is accurate as it draws attention to the continuity and discontinuity as two faces of the intricate relationship between the present social condition and the formation that preceded and gestated it. It brings into relief the intimate, genetic bond that ties the new, postmodern social condition to *modernity* – the social formation that emerged in the same part of the world in the course of the seventeenth century, and took its final shape, later to be sedimented in the sociological models of modern society (or models of society created by modern sociology), during the nineteenth century; while at the same time indicating the passing of certain crucial characteristics in whose absence one can no longer adequately describe the social condition as modern in the sense given to the concept by orthodox (modern) social theory.

2 Postmodernity may be interpreted as fully developed modernity taking a full measure of the anticipated consequences of its historical work; as modernity that acknowledged the effects it was producing throughout its history, yet producing inadvertently, rarely conscious of its own responsibility, by default rather than design, as by-products often perceived as waste. Postmodernity may be conceived of as modernity conscious of its true nature – *modernity for itself*. The most conspicuous features of the postmodern condition: institutionalized pluralism, variety, contingency and ambivalence – have been all turned out by modern society in ever increasing volumes; yet they were seen as signs of failure rather than success, as evidence of the unsufficiency of efforts so far, at a time when the institutions of modernity, faithfully replicated by the modern mentality, struggled for *universality, homogeneity, monotony* and *clarity*. The postmodern condition can be therefore described, on the one hand, as modernity emancipated from false consciousness; on the other, as a new type of social condition marked by the overt institutionalization of the characteristics which modernity – in its designs and managerial practices – set about to eliminate and, failing that, tried to conceal.

3 The twin differences that set the postmodern condition apart from modern society are profound and seminal enough to justify (indeed, to call for) a separate sociological theory of postmodernity that would break decisively with the concepts and metaphors of the models of modernity and lift itself out of the mental frame in which they had been conceived. This need arises from the fact that (their notorious

disagreements notwithstanding), the extant models of modernity articulated a shared vision of modern history as a *movement with a direction* – and differed solely in the selection of the ultimate destination or the organizing principle of the process, be it universalization, rationalization or systemization. None of those principles can be upheld (at least not in the radical form typical of the orthodox social theory) in the light of postmodern experience. Neither can the very master-metaphor that underlies them be sustained: that of the process with a pointer.

4 Postmodernity is not a transitory departure from the 'normal state' of modernity; neither is it a diseased state of modernity, an ailment likely to be rectified, a case of 'modernity in crisis'. It is, instead, a self-reproducing, pragmatically self-sustainable and logically self-contained social condition defined by *distinctive features of its own*. A theory of postmodernity therefore cannot be a modified theory of modernity, a theory of modernity with a set of negative markers. An adequate theory of postmodernity may be only constructed in a cognitive space organized by a different set of assumptions; it needs its own vocabulary. The degree of emancipation from the concepts and issues spawned by the discourse of modernity ought to serve as a measure of the adequacy of such a theory.

Conditions of Theoretical Emancipation

What the theory of postmodernity must discard in the first place is the assumption of an *'organismic'*, equilibrated social totality it purports to model in Parsons-like style: the vision of a 'principally co-ordinated' and enclosed totality (a) with a degree of cohesiveness, (b) equilibrated or marked by an overwhelming tendency to equilibration, (c) unified by an internally coherent value syndrome and a core authority able to promote and enforce it and (d) defining its elements in terms of the function they perform in that process of equilibration or the reproduction of the equilibrated state. The sought theory must assume instead that the social condition it intends to model is essentially and perpetually *unequilibrated*: composed of elements with a degree of autonomy large enough to justify the view of totality as a kaleidoscopic – momentary and contingent – outcome of interaction. The orderly, structured nature of totality cannot be taken for granted; nor can its pseudo-representational construction be seen as the purpose of theoretical activity. The randomness of the global outcome of uncoordinated activities cannot be treated as a departure from the pattern which the totality strives to maintain; any pattern that may temporarily emerge out of the random movements of autonomous agents is as haphazard and unmotivated as the one that could emerge in its place or the one bound to replace it, if also for a time only. All order that can be found is a local, emergent and transitory phenomenon; its nature can be best grasped by a metaphor of a whirlpool appearing in the flow of a river, retaining its shape only for a relatively brief period and only at the expense of incessant metabolism and constant renewal of content.

The theory of postmodernity must be free of the metaphor of progress that informed all competing theories of modern society. With the totality dissipated into a series of randomly emerging, shifting and evanescent islands of order, its temporal record cannot be linearly represented. Perpetual local transformations do not add up so as to prompt (much less to assure) in effect an increased homogeneity, rationality or organic systemness of the whole. The postmodern condition is a site of constant mobility and change, but no clear direction of development. The image of Brownian movement offers an apt metaphor for this aspect of postmodernity: each momentary state is neither a necessary effect of the preceding state nor the sufficient cause of the next one. The postmodern condition is both *undetermined* and *undetermining*. It 'unbinds' time; weakens the constraining impact of the past and effectively prevents colonization of the future.

Similarly, the theory of postmodernity would do well if it disposed of concepts like *system* in its orthodox, organismic sense (or, for that matter, *society*), suggestive of a sovereign totality logically prior to its parts, a totality bestowing meaning on its parts, a totality whose welfare or perpetuation all smaller (and, by definition, subordinate) units serve; in short, a totality assumed to define, and be practically capable of defining, the meanings of individual actions and agencies that compose it. A sociology geared to the conditions of postmodernity ought to replace the category of *society* with that of *sociality*; a category that tries to convey the processual modality of social reality, the dialectical play of randomness and pattern (or, from the agent's point of view, of freedom and dependence); and a category that refuses to take the structured character of the process for granted – which treats instead all found structures as emergent accomplishments.

With their field of vision organized around the focal point of system-like, re-sourceful and meaning-bestowing totality, sociological theories of modernity (which conceived of themselves as sociological theories *tout court*) concentrated on the vehicles of homogenization and conflict-resolution in a relentless search for a solution to the 'Hobbesian problem'. This cognitive perspective (shared with the one realistic referent of the concept of 'society' – the national state, the only totality in history able seriously to entertain the ambition of contrived, artificially sustained and managed monotony and homogeneity) a priori disqualified any 'uncertified' agency; unpatterned and unregulated spontaneity of the autonomous agent was pre-defined as a destabilizing and, indeed, anti-social factor marked for taming and extinction in the continuous struggle for societal survival. By the same token, prime importance was assigned to the mechanisms and weapons of order-promotion and pattern-maintenance: the state and the legitimation of its authority, power, social-ization, culture, ideology, etc. – all selected for the role they played in the promotion of pattern, monotony, predictability and thus also manageability of conduct.

A sociological theory of postmodernity is bound to reverse the structure of the cognitive field. The focus must be now on agency; more correctly, on the *habitat* in which agency operates and which it produces in the course of operation. As it offers the agency the sum total of resources for all possible action as well as the field inside which the action-orienting and action-oriented relevancies may be plotted, the habitat is the territory inside which both freedom and dependency of the agency are consti-tuted (and, indeed, perceived as such). Unlike the system-like totalities of modern social theory, habitat neither determines the conduct of the agents nor defines its meaning; it is no more (but no less either) than the setting in which both action and meaning-assignment are *possible*. Its own identity is as under-determined and motile, as emergent and transitory, as those of the actions and their meanings that form it.

There is one crucial area, though, in which the habitat performs a determining (systematizing, patterning) role: it sets the agenda for the 'business of life' through supplying the inventory of ends and the pool of means. The way in which the ends and means are supplied also determines the meaning of the 'business of life': the nature of the tasks all agencies confront and have to take up in one form or another. In so far as the ends are offered as potentially alluring rather than obligatory, and rely for their choice on their own seductiveness rather than the supporting power of coercion, the 'business of life' splits into a series of choices. The series is not pre-structured, or is pre-structured only feebly and above all inconclusively. For this reason the choices through which the life of the agent is construed and sustained is best seen (as it tends to be seen by the agents themselves) as adding up to the process of *self-constitution*. To underline the graduated and ultimately inconclusive nature of the process, self-constitution is best viewed as *self-assembly*.

I propose that sociality, habitat, self-constitution and self-assembly should occupy in the sociological theory of postmodernity the central place that the orthodoxy of modern social theory had reserved for the categories of society, normative group (like class or community), socialization and control.

Main Tenets of the Theory of Postmodernity

1 Under the postmodern condition, habitat is a *complex system*. According to contemporary mathematics, complex systems differ from mechanical systems (those assumed by the orthodox, modern theory of society) in two crucial respects. First, they are unpredictable; second, they are not controlled by statistically significant factors (the circumstance demonstrated by the mathematical proof of the famous 'butterfly effect'). The consequences of these two distinctive features of complex systems are truly revolutionary in relation to the received wisdom of sociology. The 'systemness' of the postmodern habitat no longer lends itself to the organismic metaphor, which means that agencies active within the habitat cannot be assessed in terms of functionality or dysfunctionality. The successive states of the habitat appear to be unmotivated and free from constraints of deterministic logic. And the most formidable research strategy modern sociology had developed – statistical analysis – is of no use in exploring the dynamics of social phenomena and evaluating the probabilities of their future development. Significance and numbers have parted ways. Statistically insignificant phenomena may prove to be decisive, and their decisive role cannot be grasped in advance.

2 The postmodern habitat is a complex (non-mechanical) system for two closely related reasons. First, there is no 'goal setting' agency with overall managing and co-ordinating capacities or ambitions – one whose presence would provide a vantage point from which the aggregate of effective agents appears as a 'totality' with a determined structure of relevances; a totality which one can think as of an *organization*. Second, the habitat is populated by a great number of agencies, most of them single-purpose, some of them small, some big, but none large enough to subsume or otherwise determine the behaviour of the others. Focusing on a single purpose considerably enhances the effectiveness of each agency in the field of its own operation, but prevents each area of the habitat from being controlled from a single source, as the field of operation of any agency never exhausts the whole area the action is affecting. Operating in different fields yet zeroing in on shared areas,

agencies are *partly* dependent on each other, but the lines of dependence cannot be fixed and thus their actions (and consequences) remain staunchly under-determined, that is autonomous.

3 Autonomy means that agents are only partly, if at all, constrained in their pursuit of whatever they have institutionalized as their purpose. To a large extent, they are free to pursue the purpose to the best of their mastery over resources and managerial capacity. They are free (and tend) to view the rest of the habitat shared with other agents as a collection of opportunities and 'problems' to be resolved or removed. Opportunity is what increases output in the pursuit of purpose, problems are what threatens the decrease or a halt of production. In ideal circumstances (maximization of opportunities and minimization of problems) each agent would tend to go in the pursuit of their purpose as far as resources would allow; the availability of resources is the only reason for action they need and thus the sufficient guarantee of the action's reasonability. The possible impact on other agents' opportunities is not automatically re-forged into the limitation of the agent's own output. The many products of purpose-pursuing activities of numerous partly interdependent but relatively autonomous agents must yet find, *ex post facto*, their relevance, utility and demand-securing attractiveness. The products are bound to be created in volumes exceeding the pre-existing demand motivated by already articulated problems. They are still to seek their place and meaning as well as the problems that they may claim to be able to resolve.

4 For every agency, the habitat in which its action is inscribed appears therefore strikingly different from the confined space of its own autonomic, purpose-subordinated pursuits. It appears as a space of chaos and chronic *indeterminacy*, a territory subjected to rival and contradictory meaning-bestowing claims and hence perpetually *ambivalent*. All states the habitat may assume appear equally *contingent* (that is, they have no overwhelming reasons for being what they are, and they could be different if any of the participating agencies behaved differently). The heuristics of pragmatically useful 'next moves' displaces, therefore, the search for algorithmic, certain knowledge of deterministic chains. The succession of states assumed by the relevant areas of the habitat no agency can interpret without including its own actions in the explanation; agencies cannot meaningfully scan the situation 'objectively', that is in such ways as allow them to eliminate, or bracket away, their own activity.

5 The existential modality of the agents is therefore one of insufficient determination, inconclusiveness, motility and rootlessness. The identity of the agent is neither given nor authoritatively confirmed. It has to be construed, yet no design for the construction can be taken as prescribed or foolproof. The construction of identity consists of successive trials and errors. It lacks a benchmark against which its progress could be measured, and so it cannot be meaningfully described as 'progressing'. It is now the incessant (and non-linear) *activity* of self-constitution that makes the identity of the agent. In other words, the self-organization of the agents in terms of a *life-project* (a concept that assumes a long-term stability; a lasting identity of the habitat, in its duration transcending, or at least commensurate with, the longevity of human life) is displaced by the *process of self-constitution*. Unlike the life-project self-constitution has no destination point in reference to which it could be evaluated and monitored. It has no visible end; not even a stable direction.

It is conducted inside a shifting (and, as we have seen before, unpredictable) constellation of mutually autonomous points of reference, and thus purposes guiding the self-constitution at one stage may soon lose their current authoritatively confirmed validity. Hence the self-assembly of the agency is not a cumulative process; self-constitution entails disassembling alongside the assembling, adoption of new elements as much as shedding of others, learning together with forgetting. The identity of the agency, much as it remains in a state of permanent change, cannot be therefore described as 'developing'. In the self-constitution of agencies, the 'Brownian movement'-type spatial nature of the habitat is projected onto the time axis.

6 The only visible aspect of continuity and of the cumulative effects of self-constitutive efforts is offered by the human body – seen as the sole constant factor among the protean and fickle identities: the material, tangible substratum, container, carrier and executor of all past, present and future identities. The self-constitutive efforts focus on keeping alive (and preferably enhancing) the *capacity* of the body for absorbing the input of sensuous impressions and producing a constant supply of publicly legible self-definitions. Hence the centrality of *body-cultivation* among the self-assembly concerns, and the acute attention devoted to everything 'taken internally' (food, air, drugs, etc.) and to everything coming in touch with the skin – that interface between the agent and the rest of the habitat and the hotly contested frontier of the autonomously managed identity. In the postmodern habitat, DIY operations (jogging, dieting, slimming, etc.) replace and to a large extent displace the panoptical drill of modern factory, school or the barracks; unlike their predecessors, however, they are not perceived as externally imposed, cumbersome and resented necessities, but as manifestos of the agent's freedom. Their heteronomy, once blatant through coercion, now hides behind seduction.

7 As the process of self-constitution is not guided or monitored by a sovereign life-project designed in advance (such a life-project can only be imputed in retrospect, reconstructed out of a series of emergent episodes), it generates an acute demand for a substitute: a constant supply of orientation points that may guide successive moves. It is the other agencies (real or imagined) of the habitat who serve as such orientation points. Their impact on the process of self-constitution differs from that exercised by normative groups in that they neither monitor nor knowingly administer the acts of allegiance and the actions that follow it. From the vantage point of self-constituting agents, other agents can be metaphorically visualized as a randomly scattered set of free-standing and unguarded totemic poles which one can approach or abandon without applying for permission to enter or leave. The self-proclaimed allegiance to the selected agent (the act of selection itself) is accomplished through the adoption of *symbolic tokens* of belonging, and freedom of choice is limited solely by the availability and accessibility of such tokens.

8 *Availability* of tokens for potential self-assembly depends on their *visibility*, much as it does on their material presence. Visibility in its turn depends on the perceived *utility* of symbolic tokens for the satisfactory outcome of self-construction; that is, on their ability to reassure the agent that the current results of self-assembly are indeed satisfactory. This reassurance is the substitute for the absent certainty, much as the orientation points with the attached symbolic tokens are collectively a substitute for pre-determined patterns for life-projects. The reassuring capacity of symbolic tokens rests on borrowed (ceded) authority; of *expertise*, or of *mass*

following. Symbolic tokens are actively sought and adopted if their relevance is vouched for by the trusted authority of the expert, or by their previous or concurrent appropriation by a great number of other agents. These two variants of authority are in their turn fed by the insatiable thirst of the self-constituting agents for reassurance. Thus *freedom* of choice and *dependence* on external agents reinforce each other, and arise and grow together as products of the same process of self-assembly and of the constant demand for reliable orientation points which it cannot but generate.

9   *Accessibility* of tokens for self-assembly varies from agent to agent, depending mostly on the resources that a given agent commands. Increasingly, the most strategic role among the resources is played by knowledge; the growth of individually appropriated knowledge widens the range of assembly patterns which can be realistically chosen. Freedom of the agent, measured by the range of realistic choices, turns under the postmodern condition into the main dimension of inequality and thus becomes the main stake of the *re-distributional* type of conflict that tends to arise from the dichotomy of privilege and deprivation; by the same token, access to knowledge – being the key to an extended freedom – turns into the major index of social standing. This circumstance increases the attractiveness of *information* among the symbolic tokens sought after for their reassuring potential. It also further enhances the authority of experts, trusted to be the repositories and sources of valid knowledge. Information becomes a major resource, and experts the crucial brokers of all self-assembly.

Postmodern Politics

Modern social theory could afford to separate theory from policy. Indeed, it made a virtue out of that historically circumscribed plausibility, and actively fought for the separation under the banner of value-free science. Keeping the separation watertight has turned into a most distinctive mark of modern theory of society. A theory of postmodernity cannot follow that pattern. Once the essential contingency and the absence of supra- or pre-agentic foundations of sociality and of the structured forms it sediments has been acknowledged, it becomes clear that the politics of agents lies at the core of the habitat's existence; indeed, it can be said to be its existential modality. All description of the postmodern habitat must include politics from the beginning. Politics cannot be kept outside the basic theoretical model as an epiphenomenon, a superstructural reflection or belatedly formed, intellectually processed derivative.

It could be argued (though the argument cannot be spelled out here) that the separation of theory and policy in modern *theory* could be sustained as long as there was, unchallenged or effectively immunized against challenge, a *practical* division between theoretical and political practice. The latter separation had its foundation in the activity of the modern national state, arguably the only social formation in history with pretensions to and ambitions of administering a global order, and of maintaining a total monopoly over rule-setting and rule-execution. Equally policy was to be the state's monopoly, and the procedure for its formulation had to be made separate and independent from the procedure legitimizing an acceptable theory and, more generally, intellectual work modelled after the latter procedure. The gradual, yet relentless erosion of the national state's monopoly (undermined simultaneously from above and from below, by transnational and subnational agencies, and weakened by the fissures in the historical marriage between nationalism and the state, none needing the other very strongly in their mature form) ended the plausibility of theoretical segregation.

With state resourcefulness and ambitions shrinking, responsibility (real or just claimed) for policy shifts away from the state or is actively shed on the state's own initiative. It is not taken over by another agent, though. It dissipates; it splits into a plethora of localized or partial policies pursued by localized or partial (mostly one issue) agencies. With that, vanishes the modern state's tendency to condensate and draw upon itself almost all social protest arising from unsatisfied redistributional demands and expectations – a quality that further enhanced the inclusive role of the state among societal agencies, at the same time rendering it vulnerable and exposed to frequent political crises (as conflicts fast turned into political protests). Under the postmodern condition grievances which in the past would cumulate into a collective political process and address themselves to the state, stay diffuse and translate into self-reflexivity of the agents, stimulating further dissipation of policies and autonomy of postmodern agencies (if they do cumulate for a time in the form of a one-issue pressure group, they bring together agents too heterogeneous in other respects to prevent the dissolution of the formation once the desired progress on the issue in question has been achieved; and even before that final outcome, the formation is unable to override the diversity of its supporters' interests and thus claim and secure their *total* allegiance and identification). One can speak, allegorically, of the 'functionality of dissatisfaction' in a postmodern habitat.

Not all politics in postmodernity is unambiguously postmodern. Throughout the modern era, politics of *inequality* and hence of *redistribution* was by far the most dominant type of political conflict and conflict-management. With the advent of postmodernity it has been displaced from its dominant role, but remains (and in all probability will remain) a constant feature of the postmodern habitat. Indeed, there are no signs that the postmodern condition promises to alleviate the inequalities (and hence the redistributional conflicts) proliferating in modern society. Even such an eminently modern type of politics acquires in many cases a postmodern tinge, though. Redistributional vindications of our time are focused more often than not on the winning of *human rights* (a code name for the agent's autonomy, for that freedom of choice that constitutes the agency in the postmodern habitat) by categories of population heretofore denied them (this is the case of the emancipatory movements of oppressed ethnic minorities, of the black movement, of one important aspect of the feminist movement, much as of the recent rebellion against the 'dictatorship over needs' practiced by the communist regimes), rather than at the express redistribution of wealth, income and other consumable values by society at large. The most conspicuous social division under postmodern conditions is one between *seduction* and *repression*: between the choice and the lack of choice, between the capacity for self-constitution and the denial of such capacity, between autonomously conceived self-definitions and imposed categorizations experienced as constraining and incapacitating. The redistributional aims (or, more precisely, consequences) of the resulting struggle are mediated by the resistance against repression of human agency. One may as well reverse the above statement and propose that in its postmodern rendition conflicts bared their true nature, that of the drive toward freeing of human agency, which in modern times tended to be hidden behind ostensibly redistributional battles.

Alongside the survivals of the modern form of politics, however, specifically postmodern forms appear and gradually colonize the centre-field of the postmodern political process. Some of them are new; some others owe their new, distinctly postmodern quality to their recent expansion and greatly increased impact. The following are the most prominent among them (the named forms are not necessarily mutually exclusive; and some act at cross-purposes):

1 *Tribal politics.* This is a generic name for practices aimed at collectivization (supra-agentic confirmation) of the agents' self-constructing efforts. Tribal politics entails the creation of tribes as *imagined communities*. Unlike the premodern communities the modern powers set about uprooting, postmodern tribes exist in no other form but the symbolically manifested commitment of their members. They can rely on neither executive powers able to coerce their constituency into submission to the tribal rules (seldom do they have clearly codified rules to which submission could be demanded), nor on the strength of neighbourly bonds or intensity of reciprocal exchange (most tribes are de-territorialized, and communication between their members is hardly at any time more intense than the intercourse between members and non-members of the tribe). Postmodern tribes, are, therefore, constantly in *statu nascendi* rather than *essendi*, brought over again into being by repetitive symbolic rituals of the members but persisting no longer than these rituals' power of attraction (in which sense they are akin to Kant's *aesthetic communities* or Schmalenbach's *communions*). Allegiance is composed of the ritually manifested support for positive tribal tokens or equally symbolically demonstrated animosity to negative (anti-tribal) tokens. As the persistence of tribes relies solely on the deployment of the affective allegiance, one would expect an unprecedented condensation and intensity of emotive behaviour and a tendency to render the rituals as spectacular as possible – mainly through inflating their power to shock. Tribal rituals, as it were, compete for the scarce resource of public attention as the major (perhaps sole) resource of survival.

2 *Politics of desire.* This entails actions aimed at establishing the relevance of certain types of conduct (tribal tokens) for the self-constitution of the agents. If the relevance is established, the promoted conduct grows in attractiveness, its declared purposes acquire *seductive* power, and the probability of their choice and active pursuit increases: promoted purposes turn into agents' needs. In the field of the politics of desire, agencies vie with each other for the scarce resource of individual and collective dreams of the good life. The overall effect of the politics of desire is heteronomy of choice supported by, and in its turn sustaining, the autonomy of the choosing agents.

3 *Politics of fear.* This is, in a sense, a supplement (simultaneously a complement and a counterweight) of the politics of desire, aimed at drawing boundaries to heteronomy and staving off its potentially harmful effects. If the typical modern fears were related to the threat of totalitarianism perpetually ensconced in the project of rationalized and state-managed society (Orwell's 'boot eternally trampling a human face', Weber's 'cog in the machine' and 'iron cage', etc.), postmodern fears

arise from uncertainty as to the soundness and reliability of advice offered through the politics of desire. More often than not, diffuse fears crystallize in the form of a suspicion that the agencies promoting desire are (for the sake of self-interest) oblivious or negligent of the damaging effects of their proposals. In view of the centrality of body-cultivation in the activity of self-constitution, the damage most feared is one that can result in poisoning or maiming the body through penetration or contact with the skin (the most massive panics have focused recently on incidents like mad cow disease, listeria in eggs, shrimps fed on poisonous algae, dumping of toxic waste – with the intensity of fear correlated to the importance of the body among the self-constituting concerns, rather than to the statistical significance of the event and extent of the damage).

The politics of fear strengthens the position of experts in the processes of self-constitution, while ostensibly questioning their competence. Each successive instance of the suspension of trust articulates a new area of the habitat as problematic and thus leads to a call for more experts and more expertise.

4 *Politics of certainty.* This entails the vehement search for social confirmation of choice, in the face of the irredeemable pluralism of the patterns on offer and acute awareness that each formula of self-constitution, however carefully selected and tightly embraced, is ultimately one of the many, and always 'until further notice'. Production and distribution of certainty is the defining function and the source of power of the experts. As the pronouncements of the experts can be seldom put to the test by the recipients of their services, for most agents certainty about the soundness of their choices can be plausibly entertained only in the form of *trust*. The politics of certainty consists therefore mainly in the production and manipulation of trust; conversely, 'lying', 'letting down', 'going back on one's words', 'covering up' the unseemly deeds or just withholding information, betrayal of trust, abuse of privileged access to the facts of the case – all emerge as major threats to the already precarious and vulnerable self-identity of postmodern agents. Trustworthiness, credibility and perceived sincerity become major criteria by which merchants of certainty – experts, politicians, sellers of self-assembly identity kits – are judged, approved or rejected.

On all four stages on which the postmodern political game is played, the agent's initiative meets socially produced and sustained offers. Offers potentially available exceed as a rule the absorbing capacity of the agent. On the other hand, the reassuring potential of such offers as are in the end chosen rests almost fully on the perceived superiority of such offers over their competitors. This is, emphatically, a *perceived* superiority. Its attractiveness relies on a greater volume of allocated trust. What is perceived as superiority (in the case of marketed utilities, life-styles or political teams alike) is the visible amount of *public attention* the offer in question seems to enjoy. Postmodern politics is mostly about the reallocation of attention. Public attention is the most important – coveted and struggled for – among the scarce commodities in the focus of political struggle.

Postmodern Ethics

Like politics, ethics is an indispensable part of a sociological theory of postmodernity pretending to any degree of completeness. The description of modern society could leave ethical problems aside or ascribe to them but a marginal place, in view of the fact that the moral regulation of conduct was to a large extent subsumed under the legislative and law-enforcing activity of global societal institutions, while whatever remained unregulated in such a way was 'privatized' or perceived (and treated) as residual and marked for extinction in the course of full modernization. This condition does not hold anymore; ethical discourse is not institutionally pre-empted and hence its conduct and resolution (or irresolution) must be an organic part of any theoretical model of postmodernity.

Again, not all ethical issues found in a postmodern habitat are new. Most importantly, the possibly extemporal issues of the orthodox ethics – the rules binding short-distance, face-to-face intercourse between moral agents under conditions of physical and moral proximity – remain presently as much alive and poignant as ever before. In no way are they postmodern; as a matter of fact, they are not modern either. (On the whole, modernity contributed little, if anything, to the enrichment of moral problematics. Its role boiled down to the substitution of legal for moral regulation and the exemption of a wide and growing sector of human actions from moral evaluation.)

The distinctly postmodern ethical problematic arises primarily from two crucial features of the postmodern condition: *pluralism* of authority, and the centrality of *choice* in the self-constitution of postmodern agents.

1 Pluralism of authority, or rather the absence of an authority with globalizing ambitions, has a twofold effect. First, it rules out the setting of binding norms each agency must (or could be reasonably expected to) obey. Agencies may be guided by their own purposes, paying in principle as little attention to other factors (also to the interests of other agencies) as they can afford, given their resources and degree of independence. 'Non-contractual bases of contract', devoid of institutional power support, are thereby considerably weakened. If unmotivated by the limits of the agency's own resources, any constraint upon the agency's action has to be negotiated afresh. Rules emerge mostly as reactions to strife and consequences of ensuing negotiations; still, the already negotiated rules remain by and large precarious and under-determined, while the needs of new rules – to regulate previously unanticipated contentious issues – keep proliferating. This is why the *problem* of rules stays in the focus of public agenda and is unlikely to be conclusively resolved. In the absence of 'principal coordination' the negotiation of rules assumes a distinctly *ethical* character: at stake are the principles of non-utilitarian self-constraint of autonomous agencies – and both non-utility and autonomy define *moral* action as distinct from either self-interested or legally prescribed conduct. Second, pluralism of authorities is conducive to the resumption by the agents of moral responsibility that tended to be neutralized, rescinded or ceded away as long as the agencies remained subordinated to a unified, quasi-monopolistic legislating authority. On the one hand, the agents face now point-blank the consequences of their actions. On the other, they face the evident ambiguity and controversiality of the purposes which actions were to serve, and thus the need to justify argumentatively the values that inform their activity. Purposes can no longer be substantiated *monologically*; having become perforce subjects of a *dialogue*, they must now refer to principles wide enough to command authority of the sort that belongs solely to ethical values.

2 The enhanced autonomy of the agent has similarly a twofold ethical consequence. First – in as far as the centre of gravity shifts decisively from heteronomous
control to self-determination, and autonomy turns into the defining trait of postmodern agents – self-monitoring, self-reflection and self-evaluation become principal activities of the agents, indeed the mechanisms synonymical with their self-
constitution. In the absence of a universal model for self-improvement, or of a
clear-cut hierarchy of models, the most excruciating choices agents face are between
life-purposes and values, not between the means serving the already set, uncontroversial ends. Supra-individual criteria of propriety in the form of technical precepts
of instrumental rationality do not suffice. This circumstance, again, is potentially
propitious to the sharpening up of moral self-awareness: only ethical principles may
offer such criteria of value-assessment and value-choice as are at the same time
supra-individual (carry an authority admittedly superior to that of individual self-
preservation), and fit to be used without surrendering the agent's autonomy. Hence
the typically postmodern heightened interest in ethical debate and increased attractiveness of the agencies claiming expertise in moral values (e.g., the revival of
religious and quasi-religious movements). Second, with the autonomy of all and
any agents accepted as a principle and institutionalized in the life-process composed
of an unending series of choices, the limits of the agent whose autonomy is to be
observed and preserved turn into a most closely guarded and hotly contested
frontier. Along this borderline new issues arise which can be settled only through
an ethical debate. Is the flow and the outcome of self-constitution to be tested before
the agent's right to autonomy is confirmed? If so, what are the standards by which
success or failure are to be judged (what about the autonomy of young and still
younger children, of the indigent, of parents raising their children in unusual ways,
of people choosing bizarre lifestyles, of people indulging in abnormal means of
intoxication, people engaging in idiosyncratic sexual activities, individuals pro-
nounced mentally handicapped)? And, how far are the autonomous powers of the
agent to extend and at what point is their limit to be drawn (remember the
notoriously inconclusive contest between 'life' and 'choice' principles of the abortion
debate)?

All in all, in the postmodern context agents are constantly faced with moral issues
and obliged to choose between equally well founded (or equally unfounded) ethical
precepts. The choice always means the assumption of responsibility, and for this
reason bears the character of a moral act. Under the postmodern condition, the
agent is perforce not just an actor and decision-maker, but a *moral subject*. The
performance of life-functions demands also that the agent be a morally *competent*
subject.

31 Describing the Future

Niklas Luhmann

One way to understanding the current situation is to compare it with older forms of descriptions of the future. It is certainly not true that the future is an invention of modern times, although in earlier times one spoke mostly of things to come – "de futuris" – in the plural as opposed to the singular. But the degree of variability has increased along with the complexity of the social system, and this determines the semantic forms that must be considered for a description of the future.

Until far into the present age, social life was experienced within a cosmos of essences that guaranteed the constancy of forms of being and the elements and thereby also the order of scale. This cosmos could be described as nature or as the creation of God (and in each case only religious powers held sway over essences and substances). Nature saw the future as the final form of movements, as the perfection of nature, and any uncertainty was related to possible corruptions, to chance events, or to a natural variability that was itself not necessarily related to nature, not to substances but to accidental properties. With all the constancy of forms of being, what was important was a variation on the level of events. An early death was a daily occurrence that did not, however, affect the existence of humankind. Whatever was tried in this world could go wrong. People were delivered up to good luck or bad luck. Life was experienced as endangered life. History was to be reckoned with not in a substantial but in an accidental way. In light of constant forms of being and good purposes, one could learn from history and withdraw to concepts of virtue (especially in the early modern period) that recommended steadiness, robustness, and ataraxia in holding on to what was right. The uncertainties of the future stayed within the framework of a fundamental regulation of the world as the entirety of invisible and visible things. The "harmonia mundi" was beyond question.

This model could no longer be maintained in modern times in view of an increasing complexity of society and its knowledge. Signs of corrosion and criticism have been observable since the eighteenth century. As Arthur Lovejoy demonstrated in a famous monograph, the hierarchical order of beings is turned on its side and temporalized. For essentially logical reasons, the world can only have come into being as a historical-length sequence to which even God, the creator, had to submit, and so it is by no means finished. In this way perfection was followed by perfectibility, although with much less certainty as to whether perfection could ever be achieved. Rousseau's *Emile*, the grand efforts of education in only one case, offered one perspective.

At the same time there appeared a newly conceived trust in the future. Human action was conceptualized as a parallel construction to creation with the same

Originally translated by William Whobrey.

archetypes but with better results. The rigid framework of creation was set into motion through the idea of progress and the criterion of utility. In the time between John Locke and Jeremy Bentham, the principle of utility itself was secularized and thereby rewritten to historically variable preferences. History was finally reconstructed as evolution, with the result that the substantial could be explained through the accidental, through the employment of coincidences. The wisdom of common law is seen in a long history of the determination of individual cases – from Coke to Hale to Hume – and not in principles or determined forms of essence. Concepts of substance are replaced by concepts of function (a process that can itself be explained as an exchange of functions). The concept of humankind as a species of nature was replaced by a double concept that in both variations allowed more latitude for individuals: through the concept of the subject that acquires the world for itself according to its own methods and through the concept of a population that improves itself by selection on an individual level with the result that only the strongest, prettiest, most well adjusted have a chance in the future.

Given this background, it must be understood that modern society was able to bet on the future from the beginning of its self-awareness. It was no longer the caste society of tradition, but it was also not yet that which awaited it in the future. It found itself balanced between no longer and not yet. Romanticism formulated this as poetry. Political theory directed corresponding hopes toward constitutional theory and the liberation of freedom. Economic theory believed that it could determine circumstances of growing prosperity. All in all we have the impression that around 1800 the impossibility of describing the new structures of modern society would be compensated for with projections of the future. Until well into our own century, there is talk of the unfinished project of the Modern and demands for more democracy, more emancipation, more opportunities for self-realization, but also more and better technology – in short, more of everything that was promised to be the future. Both in the technological and in the humanistic, society described itself in the projections of its future.

But is this Modern, is Habermas's Modern, still our Modern? Is the society that employs the embarrassment of its self-description as a projection of a future still our society? Can we – and it could certainly be asked: must we – hold such a view of the future because we could not otherwise know who we are and where we stand?

After well over two hundred years of self-inspection, modern society has at its command better, more realistic means for self-description. It can in any case perceive more and more structural effects. These can be self-induced because they are inseparably linked with the institutions on which the continuation of social reproduction on the achieved level depends. It began with the observation of the consequences of the Industrial Revolution: more wealth and more poverty than ever before, remarks Hegel in his lectures on the philosophy of law. And already before the French Revolution, Minister Necker, experienced in practical matters, thought that, in light of the situation, the traditionally stable ideas of virtue and harmony had failed justice. The new fanatization of the absolute as a party platform and the corresponding dissolution of any unifying semantics in ideologies following the French Revolution are also consequences recognized early on, along with the legitimization of unselfish crimes. These aspects drove Friedrich Schlegel back into the arms of religion, the only thing that can bring true happiness (or at least rest). But in the meantime there have been more such irritating insights. Consider the burden placed on the economy and law by the well-intentioned, politically nearly mandatory welfare state or the overarching ecological consequences of technology.

Today we find ourselves in a completely different situation from that at the time of the Enlightenment, the French Revolution, or Prussian New Humanism. We can better describe contemporary society in its consequences, even if we do not yet have access to an appropriate social theory, and therefore we are concerned when we look to the future. This does not necessarily concern the individual in everyday life, retirement demands, or, to the contrary, the deep sense of hopelessness that most people must deal with. But we ask ourselves, and public opinion asks, What will become of humankind, of society? What living conditions will "future generations" face – provided that a comparable humanity even exists and not some gene-manipulated, normed humanoids who are differentiated according to programs?

As never before, the continuity from past to future is broken in our time. Novalis already described the present as "the differential of the function of future and past", and the poetry of the romantic period appropriately dealt with metaphors and settings that could safely be assumed to be disbelieved by all. The present actuality, especially of the early romantic, might be explained by this. But these settings, pointing to the transcendental, are no longer useful. This is most certainly true of poetry, that is to say, of trusting in words, in language, in a fixed meaning. We can only be certain that we cannot be certain whether or not anything that we remember as being past will in the future remain as it was.

But that is not all. We also know that much of what will be true in future presents depends on decisions we must make now. The two are related: the dependence of future circumstances on decision making and the break of the continuity of being between past and future. Decision making is possible only if and insofar as what will happen is uncertain.

This deterministic relationship, which keeps us undetermined, can be made clearer with a quick glance back to antiquity. The contrast is evident. Aristotle also admitted, in a famous text (*Peri hermeneias* 9), that he could not know whether a future sea battle would take place or not. This was the point of departure for a long-winded medieval discussion "de futuris contingentibus." But Aristotle saw no difficulty for decisions, since he had related the problem not at all to the dependence on decision making but rather simply to the possibility of characterizing statements as true or false. His recommendation was not, therefore, not to risk a sea battle, but instead to forgo judgment, as if it were already determined that the sea battle would or would not take place, although one could not know which. Our problem would be: should we risk a sea battle or not?

If for our description of the future we look to what is at present intellectually à la mode and what appears to be acceptable or unacceptable, we must distinguish a possible strategy, a factual, a social, and a timely dimension of meaning. In respect to the factual, it seems that the reference of all sign usage, all use of language, all information processing has become a problem. This begins with the replacement at the end of the eighteenth century of the old theory of ideas with language theory; it can be seen in romanticism's realistic settings, in Saussure's linguistics, in the critique of logical empiricism by Quine, in the play with a referenceless semiotics, as with Roland Barthes, but also in the theory of operatively closed yet cognitive systems, as in the biological epistemology of Humberto Maturana. Reality is in no way denied, and no supporter of this trend would think of making the old mistakes of solipsism. But the guaranty now lies exclusively in systems operations, and these must adhere to what they succeed at – as long as all goes well. Internally one can distinguish between self-reference and external reference, but only internally, only in a kind of prime difference of internal operations and consequently in a different way in each different system. Every teleological perspective of the future, the natural as well as the mental, is radically abandoned with the apt concept of autopoiesis. Intention and purpose are only the self-simplifications of the systems. And the discrepancy from reality shows itself in unexpected side effects, for which the costs cannot be planned. All is well, as long as all goes well. This is the message. And the technical advice aims at a change of preferences.

In the social dimension something similar exists in the form of a loss of authority. Here, authority is defined as the ability to represent the world in the world and to convince others of the same representation. Authority can be founded on knowledge or power or on the knowledge of the future or on the ability to create it according to desire, in any case on the future. This becomes apparent only when the security that extends beyond the present is removed. As long as authority still holds, it works, to use a formulation from Carl Joachim Friedrich, as an insinuated "capacity for reasoned elaboration." Only the resonating argumentation remains. This argumentation may even become more esteemed, at least in certain circles. But authority lay in the fact that, on the basis of knowledge or power, this argumentation was superfluous.

Something seems to have taken the place of authority that could be termed the politics of understanding. Understandings are negotiated provisos that can be relied upon for a given time. They do not imply consensus, nor do they represent reasonable or even correct solutions to problems. They fix the reference points that are removed from the argument for further controversies, in which coalitions and oppositions can form anew. Understandings have one big advantage over the claims of authority: they cannot be discredited but must be constantly renegotiated. Their value does not increase but instead decreases with age. And this, too, makes it likely that the real problem of modernity lies in the time dimension.

In the dimension of time, the present refers to a future that only exists as what is probable or improbable. Said another way, the form of the future is the form of probability that directs a two-sided observation as something more or less probable or more or less improbable, with a distribution of these modalities across everything that is possible. Modernity has invented probability calculations just in time to maintain a fictionally created, dual reality. The present can calculate a future that can always turn out otherwise. The present can in this way assure itself that it calculated correctly, even if things turn out differently. This assumes that we can distinguish between the future (or the future horizon), the present as the realm of the probable and improbable, and the future presents that will always be exactly what they will be and never otherwise. This break between the present future and the future presents does not necessarily rule out prognoses. But their only value lies in the quickness with which they can be corrected and in knowing what is important in this regard. There exists, therefore, only a "provisional" foresight, and its value lies not in the certainty that it provides but in the quick and specific adjustment to a reality that comes to be other than what was expected.

Currently, decisions can only be made with a view to the probable and improbable even with the knowledge that whatever happens will happen as it happens and not otherwise. To translate back to the social dimension: what can always be assumed, in all attempts to be understood, is the uncertainty of the other side. If someone denies this, it can be proven. Negotiations can then be defined as an attempt to increase uncertainty to the point that the only option that remains is understanding one another. This corresponds to the modern type of the expert, that is, someone who, when asked questions he cannot answer, can be led back toward a mode of uncertainty. This also corresponds to the modern figure of catastrophe, that is, the occurrence that no one wants and for which neither probability calculations nor risk assessments nor expert opinions are acceptable. This threshold of catastrophe is always defined in social terms, and the catastrophe of one is not necessarily the catastrophe of all.

All of these considerations can be summed up in a final *risk* formula. Modern society experiences its future in the form of the risk of deciding. For such a formulation, we must appropriately define the concept of risk with a precision that is seldom achieved in the far-reaching field of present-day risk research.

What must be emphasized above all is the association with decisions and thereby with the present. A risk is an aspect of decisions, and decisions can only be made in the present. We can naturally speak of past decisions and also of future decisions. But then we refer to past or future presents and not the present past or future that is no longer or not yet actualized. Risk is therefore a form for present descriptions of the future under the viewpoint that one can decide, with regard to risks, on the one or other alternative.

Risks concern possible but not yet determined, or improbable, losses that result from a decision. These losses can be effected by a particular decision and would not result from any other decision. We speak of risks only when and insofar as consequences result from decisions. This has led to the idea that risk is avoidable and that we can play it safe if we decide differently, for example, if we decide not to install nuclear power plants. This is, however, a fallacy. Every decision can cause unwelcome results. Advantages and disadvantages as well as probabilities and improbabilities are distributed differently according to what decision is made.

Insofar as situations can even be thematized under the viewpoint of decisions and risks, there is no escape. The logic of situational definition transfers itself to all alternatives. We are concerned with a universal principle of the thematization of time and future that only allows variations in regard to the extent of loss and probability, that is, the usual risk calculations.

To the extent that society imputes decisions and a corresponding mobility, there are no longer any dangers that are strictly externally attributable. People are affected by natural catastrophes, but they could have moved away from the endangered area or taken out insurance. To be exposed to danger is a risk. We do not have to fly, although there is much to argue in its favor; we are, after all, mammals who can live without flying.

Additionally, the concept of risk considers a time difference, namely the difference between a judgment before and a judgment after the occurrence of loss. And it aims directly at this difference. Risky decisions are only those that would be regretted in the case of loss. In management science this is called postdecisional regret. This does not include only those cost increases that do not lead to decisional regret. Rather, the concept aims exactly at the paradox of the contradictory judgment before and after the event. In the language of romanticism, one could already formulate this anticipation of a subsequent revaluation. "He set his illuminating presence deeply in a future, shadowy past," is said of Albano in Jean Paul's *Titan*. For romanticism this was an impetus for reflection, for a reflection of mood, even for sadness. Our contemporaries take photographs. However one sees this paradox of the simultaneity of opposed views of time, the paradox is itself, as logicians say, unfolded by time itself, that is, solved by the time differential, with the result that at every point in time there exists only *one* plausible judgment. The concept of risk annuls this way of life, this sequence of different judgments. It unifies contradictions in the present, lets the paradox reappear and solves it another way, namely through rational risk management. If the improbable happens, one can defend oneself with the argument that one decided correctly, namely in a risk-rational manner.

We see that we have defined, in the concept of risk, a multidimensional, complex problem with regard to logic that cannot be adequately dealt with in terms of the relatively simple classical two-valued logic. As demonstrated by Elena Esposito, this problem requires a structurally richer logic. The practical consequence is that risks can be observed in very different ways, according to how distinctions are weighted. The problem therefore returns to the social dimension, to society, and finally to politics. And unlike the cosmos of Einstein's flying observers, a mathematics of recalculating one perspective to another is unavailable.

There are numerous indications that modern society is actually precipitating its future in the form of a present risk. We need only think of the possibility of *insuring* ourselves against many different kinds of accident. Insurances do not create any certainty that an accident will not happen. They only guarantee that an accident will not alter the financial status of the victim. The economy offers the opportunity to insure ourselves. But we still must make a decision. All *dangers* against which we could insure ourselves are thereby transformed into *risks*. The risk lies in the decision to insure or not to insure.

Other kinds of risk problems result from a general participation in the economy. Between income and expenses there exist, as there do not in direct barter, distances in time, because we can give out money only after having obtained it, or because we invest money in the hope of earning more. In modern society a part of these risks is taken by banks, but even in everyday life an economic risk is present, hidden only by the fact that to a large extent it remains undetermined what needs and wishes should be fulfilled with moneys received.

A final example can be taken from politics. In older societies the difference between rulers and ruled was thought to be a *natural* order, and it was assumed that nature would not allow something arbitrary; that pure chance was impossible. Or it was believed that the ruler was emplaced by God and could then, in difficult cases, lift his eyes in prayer to heaven. Today, in contrast, the occupation of all offices, including the highest, is a matter of decision making. And this turns the danger of the misuse of power or of making politically wrong decisions into a risk.

The adaptation of dangers into risks is, as these examples show, the counter-intuitive, unwanted purpose of many institutions of modern society that were conceived for completely different reasons.

The thematization of risk bridges very different situations. In its logical complexity and the paradoxical unity of risk is mirrored, it could be surmised, the complexity of modern society that can only describe, or then again not describe, its future in the present. Do the semantics of risk take the place of earlier societies' calculations with God?

We are prevented from drawing this final conclusion by an insight that also concerns the limits of risk semantics. In ecological contexts we find ourselves faced with a complexity that defies an attribution of decisions. We know, or at least can presume, that important ecological conditions for life can be changed by the employment of technology and its products, with the prospect of grave harm. But we can hardly ascribe this problem to individual decisions, because the extremely complex mesh of causes of numerous factors and the longevity of these trends do not allow such an attribution. The fascination with technology, decision making, and the risk syndrome goes to the point that we even try to capture it in our semantics. We incessantly search for decisions, be they political decisions with which we counter this problem, or evade it, or in any case try to neutralize or delay it. We define as a risk not doing something that could possibly help. It would be inconceivable, even irresponsible, to not try what is possible, even if only to redistribute the risk. Nothing speaks against it and everything for it.

Nevertheless we recognize the inappropriateness of all attempts to solve problems of this nature with preference shifts in the sphere of decision making. Social evolution will decide on future presents, and presumably it is the prospect of an unavailable fate that feeds the nagging worry that we can only satisfy on the surface in risk taking and risk communication. We no longer belong to the family of tragic heroes who subsequently found out that they had prepared their own fates. We now know it beforehand.

Index